Temiar Religion, 1964–2012

Enchantment, Disenchantment and
Re-enchantment in Malaysia's Uplands

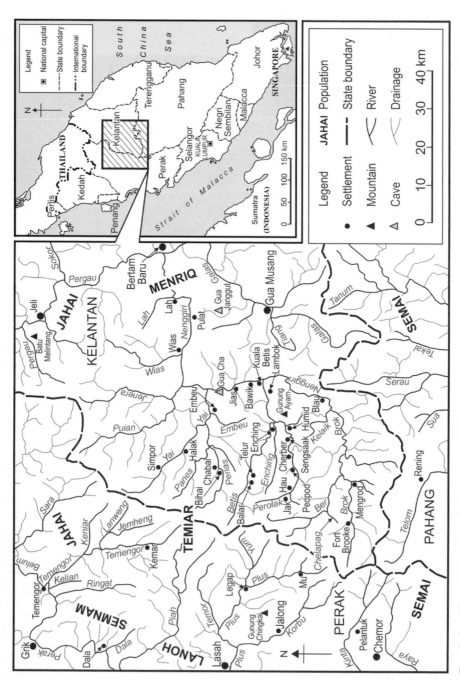

Frontispiece Places, rivers and populations mentioned in the text.
The names are given in their Malay versions. To accord with Temiar practice, the Yai and Perias river-names are reversed here and throughout the text. Lake Temengor, constructed after 1967, is not shown. (Drawn by Lee Li Kheng)

Temiar Religion, 1964–2012

Enchantment, Disenchantment and Re-enchantment in Malaysia's Uplands

Geoffrey Benjamin

NUS PRESS
SINGAPORE

© 2014 Geoffrey Benjamin

Published by:
NUS Press
National University of Singapore
AS3-01-02, 3 Arts Link
Singapore 117569
Fax: (65) 6774-0652
E-mail: nusbooks@nus.edu.sg
Website: http://www.nus.edu.sg/nuspress

ISBN: 978-9971-69-706-8 (Paper)

National Library Board, Singapore Cataloguing-in-Publication Data

Benjamin, Geoffrey
    Temiar religion, 1964–2012: enchantment, disenchantment and re-enchantment in Malaysia's uplands / Geoffrey Benjamin. -- Singapore: NUS Press, 2014.
    pages cm.
    ISBN: 978-9971-69-706-8 (paperback)

    1. Senoi (Southeast Asian people)--Malaysia--Religion. 2. Ethnology--Malaysia.
    3. Conversion I. Title.

DS595.2.S3
299.59 -- dc23   OCN877855258

Designed by: Nelani Jinadasa
Printed by: Markono Print Media Pte Ltd

Contents

List of Tables and Figures		vi
Foreword		ix
Preface		xiii
Orthography and Pronunciation		xviii
1.	The Historical and Intellectual Background	1
2.	The Temiars and their Religion [3–8. '*Temiar Religion* (PhD thesis)']	20
3.	*Temiar Religion (1967)*—Preface and Introduction	41
4.	*Temiar Religion (1967)*—The Cosmos	55
5.	*Temiar Religion (1967)*—Species	76
6.	*Temiar Religion (1967)*—Souls	106
7.	*Temiar Religion (1967)*—Spirit-mediumship	155
8.	*Temiar Religion (1967)*—Theology	188
9.	Field-report Correspondence with Edmund Leach	212
10.	Temiar Mediumship in Context	239
11.	Indigenous Religious Systems of the Malay Peninsula	260
12.	Danger and Dialectic in Temiar Childhood	279
13.	Rationalisation and Re-enchantment: Temiar Religion, 1964–94	301
14.	Temiar Religions, 1994–2012: Islam, Christianity, ʔalɨj Səlamad	339
Afterword		384
Appendices 1–4		385
Bibliography		417
Index		438

List of Tables

Table 2.1   The Temiar animistic framework   35
Table 4.1   *Misik* species   69
Table 4.2   Demoniac (*mɛrgəəh*) trees   71
Table 4.3   Wild seasonal fruit trees (*bərək*)   74
Table 5.1   *Sabat*-causing species (in Rening, Pahang)   83
Table 5.2   *Gɛnhaaʔ* animals   90
Table 6.1   *Kənoruk*-possessing species   122
Table 7.1   Mediumship types   180
Table 10.1   The great mediums (*halaaʔ rayaaʔ*) of the southern
             Temiar valleys (1965)   255
Table 11.1   The Malay animistic framework   263
Table 11.2   The Temiar animistic framework   264
Table 13.1   Distribution of the Orang Asli population by religion   309

List of Figures

Frontispiece Places, rivers and populations mentioned in the text   ii
Figure 2.1   The location of Temiar country   21
Figure 2.2   Temiar houses, Humid (1964)   22
Figure 2.3   Letter from Edmund Leach to G. William Domhoff   25
Figure 2.4   H. D. Noone and Kilton Stewart at Jalong (1938)   28
Figure 2.5   A *halaaʔ* singer and chorus at a *gənabag* (1964)   36
Figure 2.6   The same singer (Salɛh) in 2006   38
Figure 2.7   Chorus of children and young women at a Səlumbaŋ
              séance (1965)   38
Figure 2.8   Mediumistic treatment at a séance (1979)   39
Figure 3.1   Aerial photo of Humid village (1964)   42
Figure 3.2   Vertical aerial view of Humid village (1964)   46
Figure 4.1   Wakil ʔaŋah ʔabaaɲ and his wife ʔawããs (1964)   56
Figure 4.2   Sketch by Edmund Leach (1967)   57
Figure 4.3   Gunung Chingkai (Cɛŋkey) seen from Jalong village (2006)   63
Figure 4.4   Sɛŋsaak village (1964)   67
Figure 4.5   The author next to a hastily constructed *diŋ-rəb* hut in
              deep forest, Kelantan–Perak border (April 1968)   72
Figure 6.1   Discarded cans at Jias (2010), deliberately punctured
              to prevent *təracɔɔg*   107

Figure 6.2	Young girls with *wɔɔj* tufts at the back of their tonsures (1964)	112
Figure 6.3	A burial (from the documentary film *Timeless Temiar*, 1956)	132
Figure 6.4	Penghulu Dalam and his wife ʔahəəd with their foster-daughter (1964)	150
Figure 7.1	Penghulu Hitam Tamboh (1964)	156
Figure 7.2	*Kəwaar* whisk and floral *tənamuuʔ*	162
Figure 7.3	*Tɛnhool*, Lambok (1970)	165
Figure 7.4	Women dancing in *caciiʔ* style (1970)	171
Figure 7.5	Batu Janggut, Kelantan (2008)	179
Figure 8.1	Galɛɛŋ (Gunung Ayam) (2006)	201
Figure 9.1	Diagram to explain the *mənəəy* relation	224
Figure 9.2	Leach's structural analysis of 'The Story of Karey', stage 1	227
Figure 9.3	Leach's structural analysis of 'The Story of Karey', stage 2	228
Figure 9.4	Leach's structural analysis of 'The Story of Karey', stage 3	229
Figure 9.5	Leach's structural analysis of 'The Origin of Rats'	237
Figure 10.1	Aerial view along the Humid valley (1964)	243
Figure 10.2	Detail of old-style Temiar house (2006)	244
Figure 10.3	Séance at Lambok (1979), showing the extensive use of plant materials	244
Figure 10.4	Abilem and his fellow villagers at the University of Malaya (1995)	246
Figure 10.5	*Tənamuuʔ*, University of Malaya (1995)	246
Figure 10.6	Close-up view of *Tənamuuʔ* (2006)	247
Figure 10.7	*Tənamuuʔ*, near Fort Brooke (2006)	247
Figure 10.8	ʔalus (ʔampɔɔh) retrieving a fish-trap (1964)	257
Figure 10.9	Singapore's Deputy Prime Minister with Malaysia's Finance Minister II wearing *tɛmpɔɔʔ* crowns	258
Figure 11.1	Orang Asli woodcarvings, early 1960s	272
Figure 12.1	The dialectical soul-economy of Temiar parenthood	280
Figure 12.2	Temiar allo-decoration (early 1960s?)	284
Figure 13.1	Calligraphic design on the *pəlɛk*	318
Figure 13.2	Front cover of a Baha'i book in Temiar	320
Figure 13.3	Ancient Buddhist votive tablets found in Temiar country (1992)	329
Figure 13.4	Prehistoric cave drawings, Gua Chawas, Kelantan (1994)	331
Figure 13.5	Ading Kerah at his shrine, Lambok (1994)	332
Figure 13.6	Abilem Lum performs at the University of Malaya (1995)	334
Figure 13.7	Ading Kerah holds up a ritual object (1994)	336
Figure 14.1	The house of a Temiar supporter of Partai Islam, Kuala Betis, Kelantan (2008)	340
Figure 14.2	Vertical aerial view of the former Humid village (2010)	341
Figure 14.3	A street of modern Temiar houses (2006)	343
Figure 14.4	Traditional Temiar houses (2006) next to inter-state route C185	344

Figure 14.5   Chinese shrine (*tokong*) at the former site of Humid
               village (2006)   346
Figure 14.6   Modern housing at Galaaŋ (2006)   349
Figure 14.7   Surau at Mengrod, Kelantan (2006)   353
Figure 14.8   Certificates of attendance at Islamic training courses (2006)   358
Figure 14.9   The uncompleted new church at Pariʔ (2010)   363
Figure 14.10   Temiar church near Bihaay (2012)   367
Figure 14.11   The Lord's Prayer in Temiar and Malay (2012)   368
Figure 14.12   Jidaʔ and his father ʔayaaw (1964)   371
Figure 14.13   The Dewan Səndindul at Lambok (2008)   373
Figure 14.14   Preparing the *calun*-leaf hanging at head-level (2008)   374
Figure 14.15   The ʔalɨj celebrants, wearing distinctive crowns and holding
               ritual posies (2008)   374
Figure 14.16   A Temiar follower of ʔalɨj Səlamad wearing a
               distinctive crown (*tɛmpɔɔʔ*) in town (2008)   377
Figure A.1   The 'great white recording van' of the Malaya
               Broadcasting Corporation at Grik, 8 December 1941   392

Foreword

James C. Scott, Yale University

Geoffrey Benjamin's *Temiar Religion* is a scholarly achievement I both admire and, to be frank, envy. It is an impressive tribute to the enormous insights that await a talented scientist capable of sustained, scrupulous, long-term observation and analysis of any phenomenon. I envy Benjamin in the same way I envy the understanding of the social insects arising from E. O. Wilson's lifetime of close observation of ant colonies or the insights from Erving Goffman's meticulous social dissection of the seemingly banal greeting rituals of everyday social life. In the same fashion, the analytical dividends of Benjamin's lifetime of field work among the Temiar evident in the oeuvre that follows are sufficiently impressive to make magpie scholars like myself, chasing a succession of shiny objects to the horizon, wonder whether they have made a fundamentally wrong turn.

This volume is confined to the cosmological, animist, life world of the Temiars up to and including their recent engagements with Baha'i, Islam, Christianity and their own syncretic 'modern' religion, ʔalʉj Səlamad. Readers should know however, if they don't already, that Benjamin has in his other work, radically recast the entire field of Aslian Studies generally. He has reformulated Aslian ethnogenesis, migration patterns, Malay–Aslian history, linguistic history, and processes of cultural identity. He has reformulated much of what was and still is considered 'common knowledge' about the Orang Asli: who they are, where they came from, their history and the distinctions among them. Were his persuasive new insights installed in the heads and historical consciousness of Malaysian authorities, they would revolutionise policy toward upland peoples. See, for example, his co-edited book with Cynthia Chou, *Tribal Communities in the Malay World* (2002). Much of what Benjamin has to say about Orang Asli may be applied, *mutatis mutandis*, to upland peoples elsewhere in Southeast Asia. His concept of dissimilation, to describe the more-or-less deliberate selection of a practice or habit by which a group will then culturally mark itself off from another group is, I believe, a powerful analytical tool that can be applied to a large range of historically invented identities.

Temiar Religion is a unique book for many reasons, not least of which is its pedagogical value as a window into the growing understanding of a scholar constantly re-evaluating his field notes, revisiting his field-sites, shifting his conceptual lenses, and enlarging his understanding. Benjamin need not have apologised at all for the 'lack of tidiness' of this collection because, as he hoped, it is 'compensated for by its unusually extended first-hand reportage and analysis.' 'Few single-author studies have followed the religious trajectory of the same tribal and then post-tribal society for a half-century as I have attempted …' (p. 384). Far from being a distraction, *Temiar Religion* provides the reader—and the student—with an unparalleled view of the stochastic odyssey of a gifted anthropologist 'at work' over five decades. The revisions, reformulations, reconsiderations are something of an intellectual history of anthropology over the past half century but also a salutary reminder that all social analyses are 'works-in-progress'. We get to see Benjamin's long-run effort to make sense of the ordering principles behind the cosmology of the Temiars refracted in the work of Durkheim, Fortes, Radcliffe-Brown, Evans-Pritchard, Geertz and, above all, Lévi-Strauss. The *pièce de résistance* of this lesson in pedagogy is Chapter 9, which consists of lengthy extracts of Benjamin's exchange of letters with Edmund Leach. The moment was extraordinary inasmuch as Leach was in the middle of a deep engagement with the structuralist work of Lévi-Strauss and the exchange involved a series of binary-structuralist diagrams traded back and forth between Leach and Benjamin attempting to schematise the logic of Temiar cosmology. It's exceptionally rare that we get to see the process itself by which successive approximations are devised and revised instead of the codified results that leaves out all the mystery and hesitations. It's more than exceptionally rare that we get to see this process at work in intellects as sharp as Leach and Benjamin. Leach's deep engagement with Benjamin's Temiar material sets a very high standard for what intellectual mentorship ought to mean.

Benjamin is determined, with the persistence of a pit-bull, to wrestle Temiar cosmology to the ground in terms of the structural binaries he has adapted from Lévi-Strauss. In my view he triumphantly succeeds. The systematic binaries of above ground/on the ground; upper-body/lower-body; head/heart; hair/blood that order the world of nature and the world of man provide a well-nigh comprehensive, ordered view for Temiar reasoning. Always, Benjamin's aim is to extract the 'underlying calculus' (p. 188) of Temiar ideas about disease, rites of passage, mortuary rituals, and, above all, their way of classifying plants and animals from which they reason about the wider world. Their classificatory principles are, of course, different from our own, let alone Linnaean classification, but, within their own assumptions they are clear and logical. Animals, for example are divided into (a) species that eat humans, (b) species that humans eat, and (c) species that humans feed (e.g., domesticates) and whom they may on no account eat. Benjamin's convincing and detailed accounts of Temiar classification of the natural world—our term, not theirs; for them their animist world is filled with objects and living things possessing spirit/soul and having agency—are elaborate and utterly convincing and deserve to be read alongside such other classics as Lévi-Strauss's own *La Pensée Sauvage* and the tome from which Lévi-Strauss drew much inspiration: Harold Conklin's *Hanunó'o Agriculture* (1957).

The stakes of this structuralist exercise are not trivial. It allows Benjamin to address what at least for most Westerners is the central paradox of acephalous, swiddener societies which emphasise the autonomy of the individual. How is it that such societies maintain any order at all in the absence of sanctions, how is it that they do not dissolve, as Thomas Hobbes supposed, into the short, nasty, and brutish war of all against all? Here, Benjamin answers that the conceptual oppositions with which the Temiars reason provide an orderly map of culture and nature on the one hand and a corresponding map of good and evil on the other. These concepts regulate the social action of the Temiars despite their inability to impose their wishes on others or the absence of any formal authority. Benjamin also examines this issue in an article, 'Egalitarianism and Ranking in the Malay World', in Kenneth Sillander and Thomas Gibson, eds., *Anarchic Solidarity: Autonomy, Equality and Fellowship in Southeast Asia* (2011) but here in *Temiar Religion* it is given the kind of documented intellectual foundation that makes the case in irrefutable terms.

From an external perspective the world in which the Temiars move seems exceptionally dense, complex, and quite dangerous despite the ordering principles that help them make sense of it. The sheer number of dos and don'ts, of avoidances and appeasements, seem to require constant work of ritual repair. I get the same impression from *Temiar Religion* that I got a long while back from reading Georges Condominas's account of the Mnong, *Nous Avons Mangé la Forêt* (1954), which is filled with feasts and rituals triggered by some inauspicious sign or misstep; though in Condominas's case the constant ritual repair seemed always to be happily and copiously lubricated with alcohol. 'Karey' the Temiar god of thunder and the font of most evil, unlike his younger brother, seems very active and malevolent and the Temiars must work very hard to keep the world in order and not run afoul of him. Serious ritual transgressions often require the residents of a settlement to burn their huts and flee to a more auspicious place. A comprehensive animism, it would seem, conjures up many potential dangers and, by the same token, the rich, dense ritual life that aim to keep those dangers at bay.

Benjamin insists, like the inductive but system-building ethnographer he is, on working out Temiar religion from its practices and activities and what those imply, rather than from articulated principles, let alone doctrine. He is scrupulous about extracting Temiar subjectivity from behaviour and 'enactments'. Thanks to his exceptionally long engagement with Temiar practice he offers us an unmatched account of Temiar spirit-mediumship, of how the Temiar organise and evaluate their world of plants, animals, and deity/spirits, and the sophisticated ways in which they reason about the human and non-human world about them. If you would like to make sense of the Temiar world and, at the same time, wonder at an example of ethnographic analysis at its very best, you can do no better than to start here.

Preface

This collection of essays began in response to a request to publish my PhD thesis ('Temiar Religion', 1967) as an 'historical' reprint. The thesis long ago became truly historical in both content and approach. It therefore seemed more appropriate to publish it, warts and all, together with the other studies on Temiar religion that I have written during the decades following the thesis. Two of these later papers have appeared elsewhere in slightly abridged versions, and they are presented here (Chapters 11 and 12) as revised reprints. Chapters 9, 10, 13 and 14 are essentially new studies. Chapter 10 has been expanded from the notes of lectures I have given over the years. Chapter 13 appeared previously only in the form of a working paper (albeit with an ISBN number). The preliminary version of Chapter 14, based on fieldwork between 1994 and 2010, was first drafted more recently as a conference paper. To all of these I have added additional ethnographic material gathered at various times between 1964 and 2010 along with some more recent third-party information, incorporated into the main text or footnotes. This has added to the book's length and complexity, but it is the obvious place to present important ethnographic and historical data that would otherwise be lost, and which demonstrate just how variable Temiar culture is from place to place and from generation to generation.

As described in Chapter 1, the original doctoral study was made under very different conditions than would be the case today. First, let me acknowledge the extensive support, both institutional and individual, that I received in the United Kingdom and Malaysia during that period of research. The following note is taken verbatim from the published paper (Benjamin 1966) that I submitted along with the thesis. (Most of the people mentioned have since died.)

> Fieldwork in Malaya from February 1964 to August 1965 was made possible by the award of a Horniman Scholarship of the Royal Anthropological Institute, and latterly by a Studentship

of the Ministry of Education and Science [United Kingdom]. Supplementary grants were received from the Esperanza Trust [Royal Anthropological Institute] and the Henry Ling Roth Fund of the University of Cambridge. I hereby express my deep gratitude to the administrators of these funds for the help they extended to me.

In Malaya my path was made smooth at every turn by so many people that it may seem invidious to single out some of them by name; those I mention represent others too numerous to name. Without the unstinting help of the Department of Orang Asli Affairs nothing would have been possible. My thanks go to the Commissioner, Dr Iskandar Carey, the Deputy Commissioner, Inche' Baharon Raffie'i Azhar, and the Protector in charge of Administration, Mr R. Cabatit, not only for ensuring my freedom from the immense practical problems that would otherwise have beset me, but for their informal advice and discussion on many different aspects of Aboriginal life; my present ideas owe much to them. Special thanks go to the Medical Officer, Dr Malcolm Bolton, who throughout many months was my only lifeline to the outside world; his detailed knowledge of Aborigines was always of the greatest help.

My closest contact with members of the Orang Asli Department was in Kelantan, where I spent the longest period. To the Protector of Aborigines, Mr Howard F. Biles, and his staff I extend my warmest gratitude for their co-operation and friendship. For the shorter periods I spent in Pahang and Perak I thank for their co-operation the Protectors in those states, Inche' Badrillah bin Abdullah Karim and Inche' Mohamed Noor bin Osman, respectively.

Outside the Orang Asli Department I must mention the support and valuable discussion I had from the Director of Museums, Inche' Shahrum bin Yub, and with Dr Ivan Polunin of the University of Singapore. In England, Professor Meyer Fortes has shown active interest in my work throughout. Dr Edmund Leach has at all stages aided, advised and encouraged me to a degree far greater than his formal status of teacher and supervisor would suggest; to him must go the credit for turning my first vague plans into reality.

My greatest debt of all, however, must be to the Temiars themselves for having unself consciously made me one of them; fortunately, one does not thank kinsmen, for I could find no satisfactory way of doing so. In each village, I found informants who were wonderfully eager to ensure not only that I recorded much information, but that I understood it. They were all busy people, and for their undertaking such a trying and apparently thankless task, I have nothing but the warmest gratitude. Though many individual Temiars helped me in different aspects of my work, it is only right that I should mention here those upon whom my understanding of Temiar religion chiefly depends. In Humid, the headman Panglima Dalam [Figure 6.2], his deputy Wakil Angah (Ɂaŋah) [Figure 4.1], and the guardian of the landing zone, Malam, took the greatest of pains. Further upstream, in the village of Jak, the headman Hitam Tamboh (Tambɔɔh) [Figure 7.1] gave me much information not available to the lowlanders. In Mengrod (Mɛnrɔɔd), the headman Kechik (KɔciɁ) was a useful debunker of untrustworthy information.[1] My especial friend there, Josh (Jɔs), saw to it that other informants clearly understood what I wanted from them, while adding much information about the practices in his native Perak. In Fort Brooke a wise and well travelled old man, Pacat, gave of his extensive knowledge. An equally well-travelled man is Jamah, who patiently told me of what goes on at the peripheries of Temiar territory. He also told wonderful stories.

My later work on Temiar religion, especially as incorporated into Chapters 10–14, has also incurred debts of gratitude. Earlier versions of Chapter 11, 'Indigenous religious systems of the Malay Peninsula', were presented in the 1970s at seminars in the Anthropology Department, London School of Economics; the Sociology Department, University of Singapore; the Faculty of Social Sciences, University of Penang; the Anthropology Department, Research School of Pacific Studies, Australian National University; and the Anthropology Department,

---

1. A photograph of Kechik as a boy appeared in an extended anonymous article in the *Sunday Times* (Singapore) newspaper, 24 May 1936 (pp. 12–13) entitled 'With the Temiar in Kelantan's jungle: honest, virtuous, peaceable people in danger of what is called progress' (http://newspapers.nl.sg/ Digitised/Article/straitstimes19360524-1.2.83.aspx).

Monash University. I would like to thank the participants for their helpful comments. I thank Kirk Endicott, Robert McKinley and Vivienne Wee for their discussion of many of the problems raised in the paper. I would also like to express my gratitude to the late Professor Derek Freeman and the Research School of Pacific Studies, Australian National University, for their award of a Visiting Fellowship at the Anthropology Department, October–November 1973, which gave me the opportunity to prepare this paper.

Chapter 12, 'Danger and dialectic in Temiar childhood', was written on the basis of my own field materials, but owes much to Marina Roseman's comments on an earlier draft and to her own Temiar studies, especially her book *Healing Sounds From the Malaysian Rain Forest* (1993). Gérard Diffloth's compendious knowledge of the Mon-Khmer languages saved me from some linguistic errors at a late stage in the writing.

Chapter 13, 'Rationalisation and re-enchantment: Temiar religion, 1964–94', was originally written in response to an invitation from the late Gehan Wijeyewardene to attend a conference on religion at the Australian National University in 1996. It provided just the right opportunity to prepare a paper I had been meaning to write for several years. I received valuable comments there from James J. Fox, Grant Evans, Anthony Reid and Gehan Wijeyewardene. In Singapore, Michael Hill, Syed Farid Alatas, Leong Wai Teng and Kwok Kian Woon took time to comment on the text or provide me with further information. I would also like to thank Marina Roseman and Mohd Anis Md Nor for arranging my involvement in the Temiar Music and Dance Workshop at the University of Malaya in July 1995, reported on in the last part of Chapter 13.

G. William Domhoff kindly supplied me with unpublished materials on the work of H. D. Noone and Kilton Stewart in the 1930s, including a draft 'autobiography' ostensibly by Stewart himself. Eduardo Hazera supplied further recent information on Christianity among the Kelantan Temiars, which I have incorporated into Chapter 14.

As always, I am indebted to many Malaysian friends, Temiar and non-Temiar, who have aided my researches over the years. I hope that they or their family members will not be offended at anything said here, for no offence was meant. In addition to the Temiars mentioned above, I would especially like to mention Ading Kerah (ʔadiŋ Kərah) and the late Abilem Lum (ʔabiləm Lum). Jabbar Bin Salleh, better known as Abur (ʔabur, the son of Salleh in Figures 2.5 and 2.6, who also helped greatly), has continued to aid me in countless ways since his childhood in the 1960s (figure 2.2) right up to his current status as grandfather. Bah Tony Williams-Hunt (also known as Amani Williams Hunt Abdullah) introduced me to Temiars in Perak whom I would otherwise have had less chance to talk to. Juli Edo and Colin Nicholas, along with Bah Tony, have also shared their deep knowledge of Orang Asli matters with me over the years.

The present text has benefitted from careful comments by Robert Dentan and Kirk Endicott, but they are not responsible for the defects that remain.

I am grateful to James Scott for his approving Foreword. I am also grateful to Charles Wheeler for copyediting the manuscript; Christine Chong, Nelani Jinadasa and Lena Qua at NUS Press for successfully taming my typographically unruly text; and to the Centre for Liberal Arts and Social Sciences (CLASS) at Nanyang Technological University, headed by K. K. Luke, for defraying some of the production costs.

Orthography and Pronunciation

In this volume, words in Temiar and related Aslian languages are transcribed in a slightly simplified version of the orthography currently used by most Mon-Khmer linguistic specialists. The symbols employed are pronounced approximately as shown below. Ordinary Temiar and Malay words are printed italicised, but the proper-noun names of persons, places and ritual genres are not italicised, even when written phonemically.

Personal names have been treated as follows. The names of individual Temiars who have appeared in the published literature (primarily by Sue Jennings and Marina Roseman) are spelled throughout in the conventionalised non-phonemic form by which they are already known, except on the first appearance of their name, when a phonemic version is also provided in parentheses, thus: 'Ading Kerah (ʔadiŋ Kərah)'. This will facilitate cross-reference between the various publications. Names that have not been published outside of my own studies are usually given only in phonemic form, including the frequent (upper-case) initial glottal stop, thus: 'Taaʔ ʔamaaw'. Where the conventional spelling is the same as the phonemic version, only a single version is given, thus: 'Dalam'.

A similar procedure is followed with the names of major rivers and mountains, where the Temiar and regular Malay versions differ, thus: 'Perolak (Pɛrlɔɔb)' on first appearance, thereafter just 'Perolak'. (In a few other places it has proved necessary to employ the Temiar version.) In many cases, however, the mountains and smaller streams are referred to solely by their Temiar names, as the context requires or where no alternatives exist.

Vowels

i   As in Malay *tapis*: *ʔapil* 'mat'.

e   As in Malay *leher*: *teh* 'above'.

ɛ   As the *e* in (British) English *get*: *lɛh* 'wife'.

ʉ   As the *u* in Scottish *hus* ('house') or the *ü* in German *Hütte*: *kəbʉs* 'dead'.

ə   The 'neutral' schwa (*pĕpĕt*) vowel, like the *e* in Malay *betul* or *sumber*: *ləg* 'dart quiver'. In pre-final syllables it is non-phonemic and its pronunciation varies between a short *ə*, *i*, or *u* (as in *rəwaay* (*rᵘwaay*) 'headsoul'). This non-phonemic vowel is often omitted in formal linguistic publications, but is retained in this volume as a reading aid.

a   As in Malay *belah*: *cah* 'to slash undergrowth'.

u   As the first *u* in Malay *pucuk*: *lug* 'laugh'.

o   As the *o* in Malay *gol* ('goal' in football): *doo*ˀ 'father'.

ɔ   As the *o* in British English *cot*: *sɔh* 'to untie'.

Phonemically long vowels are written doubled: *tɛɛ*ˀ 'earlier today' (cf. *tɛ*ˀ 'earth'). Phonemically nasal vowels are written with a superscript tilde: *wɛdwɛ̃ɛ̃d* 'giddy' (cf. *ˀawɛɛd* 'barkcloth'). Word-stress always falls on the final syllable.

Consonants

These are mostly written and pronounced as in the modern romanised spelling used for Bahasa Malaysia, but the following symbols require further explanation:

c   Pronounced like the *c* in Malay *cuci*; unlike Malay, this consonant also occurs word-finally: *bəcuuc* 'sour'.

j   Pronounced like the *j* in Malay *janji*; this too can occur in positions unknown in Malay: *bɛjbɔɔj* 'lick'.

ɲ   Pronounced like the *ny* in Malay *nyanyi*. The upper case form is *N*. This can also appear word-finally: *mɔɲ* 'tooth'.

ŋ   Pronounced like the *ng* in Malay *nganga* or English *singer* (not as in *finger*). The upper case form is *Ŋ*.

ˀ   The glottal stop (*hamzah*), a consonantal phoneme, sounding like the *k* in Peninsular Malay pronunciations of *duduk* or *rakyat*. The upper case form is *Ɂ*.

k   Always pronounced as a velar, like the *k* in Malay *makan*, and not as a glottal stop, even word-finally: *cɔɔk* 'to set birdlime'.

Chapter 1 | The Historical and Intellectual Background

S ince this is in part an avowedly 'historical' publication, let me try to place the various studies—the doctoral thesis (Chapters 3–8) especially—into their temporal and intellectual contexts.[1] The circumstances of my initial fieldwork in Temiar country from April 1964 to August 1965 were very different from what researchers now encounter when working in Orang Asli communities. The anti-Communist 'Emergency' had not yet ceased in the forests of the northern interior, and the Temiar area was still officially labelled 'black'. Movements were tightly controlled by the security services, and permission had to be sought almost every time I visited another valley. Moreover, Indonesia's *Konfrontasi* against newly-formed Malaysia was active, generating much suspicion. For example, my Temiar companions and I were once arrested for a few hours at Fort Legap in Perak after walking across the uninhabited watershed from Kelantan, although we had received radioed permission to proceed. Even the Temiars living there ran away from us. Later, shopkeepers in Taiping misidentified our Temiar speech as an Indonesian language, and threatened to call the police.

Temiar country was remote and accessible only on foot or by helicopter, except for a few downstream settlements that could be reached by boat. (This remoteness is well captured in the earlier accounts of the area by Baker (1933) and Noone (1936: 14–20).) My initial installation into the field was by helicopter on April Fools' Day 1964, but most of my later travels were on foot or by raft. The aerial photographs in this volume (figures 3.1, 3.2 and 10.1) were taken with the help of a passing British military helicopter whose pilot, out of curiosity, had dropped in at my home village of Kuala Humid (Bɔɔk Həmij).[2] Every month, my supplies were delivered by parachute as part of the airdrops to security forces stationed several hours' march downriver at Fort Betis (Bətʉs). (For this invaluable service I owe a great debt of thanks to the

---

1. Several important studies of Orang Asli religion appeared after my thesis was written. These include: Endicott (1979) and Lye (1994) on the Bateks; Karim (1981) on the population variously known as the Mah Meri, Besisi, Betisék or Betsisi'; Howell (1984) on the Cewong (also known as Ceq Wong, Che' Wong or Siwang); Couillard (1980) on the Jah Hut (also known as Jah Hĕt); Roseman (1991) and Jennings (1995) on the Temiars; Dentan (2000, 2002a, 2002b, 2008) and Kroes (2002) on the Semais; Hood (1978) on the Semelais; and two books, Amran (1991) and Nobuta (2009), on religious change among the Orang Asli generally.
2. Except where otherwise stated, the photographs in this book were taken by the author.

Royal Malaysian Air Force and to the JHEOA—the Department of Orang Asli Affairs.[3]) The packages were then portered on foot to Kuala Humid by some of the people who lived there.

Gua Musang, the nearest town, was just a railhead settlement not yet connected by road to the rest of Malaysia, and two or three days' walk away for my initially untrained physique. The Malay village of Bertam Bahru, the site of the nearest JHEOA office, was at least three days downstream by raft. My communications with the outside world were mostly through letters carried by the flying doctor, Malcolm Bolton, on his monthly visits by helicopter to the landing zone (Temiar: *lesek*, from 'LZ') at Kuala Humid.[4] It took up to a month to receive replies to written messages between me and Kuala Lumpur, and up to two months for the more detailed correspondence with my research supervisor, Edmund Leach, in Cambridge, significant portions of which are presented in Chapter 9.[5]

These details may help explain the functionalism and structuralism that some commentators have claimed to see in my earlier accounts of Temiar life. I have never been a Radcliffe-Brownian functionalist, and my 'structuralism' has been more a matter of presentation than of explanatory theory—though this is certainly evident in the doctoral thesis. But the Temiar communities I was working in at that time were indeed like worlds-to-themselves. Non-Temiars were rarely seen, and the arrival even of Temiars from other villages was unusual. At the time, my solution to this was to travel as widely as I could within and beyond Temiar country in order to discover just how much variation there was in 'Temiar culture'. Some of the discoveries I made were reported in the doctoral thesis (see especially Chapter 7). On later visits (supported in part by a small grant from the Wenner-Gren Foundation), I extended these investigations to encompass the Orang Asli and Malay societal patterns adjacent to Temiar country. My paper on 'Indigenous religious systems' (reproduced here as Chapter 11) was the first formal result of this comparative work, and should dispel any impression of a closed-system approach. The later chapters set the scene in a much broader historical, intellectual and sociological context than was possible in the 1960s, being based on shorter visits made at various times between 1979 and 2010.

These later visits led to a shift in the way I made sense of the data. What initially seemed cut-and-dried, and written up as such in the PhD thesis, now appeared more as a snapshot from a variable and changing reality. It also emerged that individual Temiars often ascribed different interpretations to the

---

3. JHEOA stands for Jabatan Hal Ehwal Orang Asli (Department of Orang Asli Affairs). This government agency operates only in the states of Peninsular Malaysia; there is no equivalent agency for the so-called 'native' peoples—the majority—of Sabah and Sarawak. Since 2011, this agency has been known as the Jabatan Kemajuan Orang Asli (JAKOA), the Department of Orang Asli Development. I refer to it variously as the JHEOA or JAKOA, as appropriate to the immediate context.
4. For an obituary of Dr Bolton, see Cranbrook (2006).
5. Edmund Leach's role as supervisor of my doctoral research is discussed in some detail by Tambiah (2001: 64–67, 79–81).

words they all used and the practices most of them followed. In Chapters 3–9 and 11, I have signalled these areal, temporal and individual variations in the many additional notes marked '[Added 2014]' while keeping the main text mostly unaltered. This extra information is theoretically and historically important. To have omitted it would have made for an easier read but it would have presented a far too simple picture of the ethnographic reality. Moreover, as both Andaya (2008) and Scott (2009) have demonstrated, an understanding of the long-ignored upland tribal populations of Southeast Asia, such as the Temiars, generates insights into the region's history and politics that cannot be gained solely through studying the dominant societies. The details matter, and I have accordingly tried to avoid anonymising and over-generalising the ethnographic reportage.

Since this book is based on a series of studies that were not originally intended as parts of a larger monograph, it might be useful if I say something of the background to each of them.

The doctoral thesis (Chapters 3–8)

The most obviously 'historical' and hitherto least readily available part of this volume consists of my doctoral thesis in social anthropology (Cambridge University, 1967). The thesis appears here unrevised in content and approach, even to the extent of retaining certain forms of expression that I would not employ today. These include 'Negritos' used non-biologically,[6] 'Aborigines' (instead of 'Orang Asli'), 'jungle' (instead of 'forest'), 'system', 'tribe' (as opposed to the adjective 'tribal', which I do find useful), '*the* Temiars' (instead of '[some] Temiars'), 'nature/culture', 'theological' instead of 'religious', 'informant' instead of 'respondent', and imperial measures ('3½ feet') instead of metric. I have also retained the traditional spellings of the river names Plus and Brok. However, I have replaced 'shamanism' with 'mediumship' throughout, and 'Temiar' in the plural has been replaced by 'Temiars', and similarly for the other ethnonyms when euphony allows.[7] In places (Chapter 8 especially) I have modified the style to make the text easier to read. Several hundred semicolons have been replaced by full stops, and unnecessary adjectives and adverbs have been removed. Many clichés have been expunged and convoluted sentences untangled. The Temiar orthography has been upgraded to a version of the phonemic one I currently use. Where possible, the idiom has been de-gendered. Certain passages have been removed or revised to avoid unnecessary repetition of material that appears elsewhere in the volume. The original endnotes have mostly been inserted

---

6. An unavoidable exception is Benjamin (2013), a study expressly concerned with biological aspects of the 'Negrito' hypothesis.
7. See Benjamin (2002: 7–8, 58–59) for a justification of this change, which is still resisted by many anthropologists. For the sake of historical accuracy, however, I have not made this change in Chapter 9, which contains verbatim quotations from the letters that passed between Edmund Leach and myself while I was in the field.

into the main text, but many new footnotes have been supplied, marked as '[Added 2014]'. References to unpublished studies (including my own) in the original text have been updated if they were subsequently published. This explains the occasional appearance of dates later than 1967.

The other major change has been the addition of photographs, which were absent from the original text. Many of these were taken during the initial period of fieldwork, and will therefore serve to increase the historical value of this volume. I took the photography seriously, employing a Rolleiflex twin-lens camera, stocked with good-quality Ilford black-and-white film (in the now defunct FP3 and HP3 stock in the equally defunct 127 size), which was sent out for fine-grain development at Robinson's department store in Kuala Lumpur. I also employed a poorer-quality 35mm camera as a back-up, occasionally using it to take colour photographs on Agfacolor stock; these (figure 4.5, for example) have faded badly. Usually, several months elapsed before I could monitor the quality of my photography. I also made many tape-recordings of Temiar music and spoken statements.[8] Temiars have now overcome the unease, amounting to a taboo, that they once felt against looking at photographs or hearing recordings of deceased relatives. For that reason I have not held back from presenting such photographs in this volume. The positive value of photography as an aid to the public presentation of Temiar history has come to outweigh the earlier negative considerations.[9] Besides, Temiars themselves now keep albums of family photographs and have become used to seeing the images and in some cases hearing the recorded voices of their deceased relatives.

Despite these cosmetic changes, the thesis still differs considerably from the way in which I would choose to write it today. Let me therefore say more about the intellectual context in which it was written, and about the various defects that now strike me most strongly—and why, given those defects, I have decided nevertheless to publish it. For the latter decision, there are

---

8. The recordings were made on open-reel tapes, using a barely portable, wooden-cased, German-made Butoba MT5 machine, powered by eight large, expensive and highly polluting Mallory mercury cells. This was paid for by Edmund Leach from his own research funds. See www.butoba.net/homepage/ mt5.html (retrieved 31 May 2013) for a description of this model of tape recorder, apparently one of the first to be used for 'such varying tasks as recording native peoples chants in far corners of the world'. The recordings were monophonic and on relatively bulky five-inch reels; but the Butoba's large speaker allowed me to play the results back to the performers the next day. Fifty years later, those early recordings (digitised and distributed on compact disc, along with reprints of my black & white photographs) have been giving pleasure to a new generation of Temiars. Currently, of course, I take digital cameras and a laptop computer into the field, allowing instant appraisal of hundreds of photographs, which can be displayed enlarged and in colour to the people themselves. I make stereophonic field recordings digitally in very high fidelity on an almost weightless device that literally fits into my pocket; but I can no longer play these back so satisfactorily to the performers themselves.
9. The same motivation underlies my decision to name many of the Temiars who shared their knowledge with me. To have kept them anonymous—as required by certain widely followed ethical principles— would have written these key individuals out of history and presented an irresponsibly homogenous picture of Temiar society. Jennings and Roseman have also regularly named their individual Temiar sources, and I see every need to continue doing so (except where there is a specific reason not to). In my recent fieldwork, I explicitly asked my respondents whether I might publish their names; none of them refused. (For a closely argued critique of anonymity in indigenous (tribal) studies more generally, with which I agree, see Svalastog & Eriksson (2010).)

three main reasons. First, the fieldwork I undertook in 1964–65 was only the second piece of intensive modern ethnographic research work on any Orang Asli population, an approach that had been pioneered just two years earlier by Robert Dentan, working on the neighbouring Semais (Dentan 1965, 1968a). Second, the thesis contains solid ethnographic material that is not otherwise available; much of it will no longer be recoverable in the field. It therefore supplies historical documentation for an important population that even now is too rarely incorporated into Malaysian studies. Third, the thesis has been referred to by other authors, most extensively by Marina Roseman (1991) and Sue Jennings (1995), who studied related aspects of Temiar culture in later years. Those who have enjoyed their books will find it useful to have access to the same source that they employed. The present volume—especially the later chapters on the religious changes the Temiars have undergone in the last three decades—adds a distinctively sociological understanding to the materials dealt with by all three of us. Readers will therefore derive more benefit from it if they also consult the contributions of Jennings and Roseman.

More generally, the thesis was probably the first for many years in British anthropology to employ the word 'religion' in its title. The decision was intentional. Social anthropologists were ignoring religion in favour of a narrowly empiricist concern with 'ritual', an approach that I regarded as a device to avoid dealing with anything that could not be directly observed. Nevertheless, I organised the thesis largely within the structuralist framework originated by Lévi-Strauss, which was brand-new at the time, but which had little concern with religion (as opposed to ritual or myth). Something of this structuralist background can been seen in Edmund Leach's published comments (1967: xiii–xiv) on my field reports, which appeared in print before the thesis was completed. (I myself published a short essay (Benjamin 1967b) on Lévi-Strauss's ideas shortly after completing the thesis.)

In relation to the theoretical discussion presented in the opening pages of the thesis (Chapter 3 below), I should explain that my undergraduate training in social anthropology had been based largely on the works of Durkheim and Radcliffe-Brown. There were no textbooks of the subject as understood today, since American materials were mostly ignored, although we were certainly expected to read whole books, ethnographic monographs especially. Extraordinary as it must now seem, the *first* book I was given to study and write an essay on was Durkheim's *The Division of Labour in Society*, followed soon after by Radcliffe-Brown's *Structure and Function in Primitive Society*. These were treated in effect as contemporary textbooks rather than as 'classics' of the subject. In the thesis, my remarks make it clear that I did not gain as much help as I needed from that body of literature when confronted with the ethnographic reality. Nevertheless, in what would today be cordoned off as a 'literature survey', I still attempted to rescue as much as I could of that approach before presenting the ethnographic findings in the succeeding chapters of the thesis. However, by the time I returned from the field in late 1965, the major intellectual problem in British anthropology had shifted from structure to values and morality. I attempted this task, awkwardly, in the final chapter of the thesis, reprinted here as Chapter 8. Today, this would hardly be considered worth discussing, and I would not now bother to devote space to the issue. It is retained here simply to accord with the part-historical aim of the book. In any case, my shift from Lévi-Straussian concerns to the broader issues posed by other scholars is apparent in the later studies reprinted here, especially Chapters 10, 13 and 14.

How then would I organise the thesis if I were writing it today?

First, the thesis lacks any serious sociology of Temiar religion—a fault woefully apparent in the short concluding section of Chapter 8, titled 'Religion and society'. My sociological views developed later, through a broadened study of Weber and through Ernest Gellner's liberating development of Weber's work (see especially Gellner 1988). I have also been influenced in this by the several university courses on religion that I have taught over the years, in which the underlying question has been 'What kinds of religion are there in the world, and why do they differ?' The later chapters of this book expound some of the answers I would give to this question, with specific reference to Temiar religion.

The distinction between 'society' and 'culture' deriving from the work of Clifford Geertz that runs through much of the thesis no longer seems the best way to deal with the apparent independence of the two domains. Geertz, basing his ideas in turn on those of Sorokin (1957: 7–19), regularly contrasted the 'mechanical-functional' integration of society with the 'logico-meaningful' integration of culture. While this dialectic certainly provides a fruitful approach at the descriptive level, it fails to take account of the deeper understandings of cultural process that have come out of more sceptical traditions of analysis. The 'society'/'culture' approach pays insufficient attention to the fact that 'culture' does not simply *happen*, but is actively *cultivated*. Moreover, it too easily ignores the *interests* that lie behind the propagation of cultural ideology and institutions. In retrospect, my adoption of the 'society'/'culture' divide now seems like a device to avoid engaging in deeper sociological analysis of my findings.

Second, and more specifically, I failed in the thesis to achieve a serious understanding of animism, which I now see as the ascription of communicable-with subjectivity (consciousness, mind) to an open-ended range of entities in the people's surroundings. Several influences that deserve mention here reached me after the thesis was completed. The first of these was Kirk Endicott's ground-breaking study (1970) of Malay animism, originally written as a BLitt thesis before he set foot in Malaysia. This represented a thorough working out of ideas proposed by those British anthropologists, such as Mary Douglas, who had been striving to find room for values and emotion within the broadly structuralist framework of the time. My initial response to this approach appeared in the essay reprinted here as Chapter 11; later, more extensive, discussions appear as Chapters 10 and 12.

Also important was Dan Sperber's view of symbolism as a constitutive activity of the human mind, rather than as the label for a class of cultural objects (Sperber 1975). I was introduced to Sperber's work by my then student, Ananda Rajah. (Sadly, Ananda died suddenly in 2007.) The ideas of Michael Polanyi, initially brought to my attention by the linguist William A. Foley when we were both teaching at the Australian National University in the late 1970s, complemented Sperber's views. Polanyi's analysis of the way in which people 'pour themselves' into their cultural products as a means of fully subjectivising them, enabled me to make a richer sense of animism. (See especially Polanyi & Prosch 1975.) The views of Jan van Baal (1971), recommended to me by Robert McKinley, made it possible to link these approaches more directly to specifically religious forms of action. Van Baal's underlying suggestion was that the existential loneliness of the human subject leads people to communicate the contents of their subjectivity to non-empirical beings in an I–you manner that leaves them feeling less existentially 'lonely'.[10]

Third, in the thesis I made several references to what I saw as a distinctive figuration in Temiar thought, but which I could not fully characterise. I later discovered that the figuration in question is rather widely exhibited in tribal societies, and in some non-tribal circumstances too. It corresponds to what I now usually refer to as the 'dialectical mode of orientation', which (along with the 'immanent', 'transcendental' and 'Zen' modes) forms one of the components of a theory of cultural regimes that I have been employing with varying degrees of explicitness in the past three decades. Overt awareness of this dialecticism came largely in response to Robert Bellah's essay on 'Religious evolution' (1964)—perhaps the most thoughtful general study of religion by a sociologist since Weber. Bellah implied that the varying degrees of socio-cultural differentiation form a continuum between the two poles that theologians and Weber have labelled 'immanence' and 'transcendence'; Bellah's terms were 'compact' and 'differentiated'. It occurred to me instead that the apparently middle sector of that supposed continuum, which I had taken as displaying both immanence and transcendence, really constituted a distinct type of orientation (the dialectical). This led to two conclusions. First, that the differences did not fall on a continuum, but constituted a set of distinct modes that allowed only of discontinuous movements (flip-flops,

---

10. I have previously identified Jan van Baal (1971) as the source of this phraseology, but an Internet search shows that the expression 'the existential loneliness of the human subject' does not occur in his work. It must therefore have been my own creation. Nevertheless, the phrase well summarises a core theme in van Baal's approach to the anthropology of religion. (This has not prevented some other authors from also attributing the phrase to van Baal!)

so to speak) between them. Second, that these modes were not simply self-constituting cultural 'systems', but the consequences of politically imposed cultural *regimes*.

Although several instances of this distinctively dialectical mode of thought were mentioned in the thesis, I made little further sense of it. Consequently, the thesis suffers from a lack of broader contextualisation. (In the ethnographically focused 'intensive fieldwork' approach of the 1960s, this would not have been deemed a shortcoming.) In the succeeding comparative study of Peninsular religious patterns reprinted here as Chapter 11, I did explicitly recognise the distinctively 'dialectical' character of Temiar religion, without however incorporating that approach into a broader theory of orientations. That was to come in subsequent studies I made of other areas: social organisation (Benjamin 1985, 2011a) and language (Benjamin 1993a, 2011b, 2014). It was only in the three later studies printed here as Chapters 12–14 that I applied this approach more explicitly to Temiar religion.

However, these changes of direction were not motivated solely, or even primarily, by academic issues. The major influence came through witnessing the great shifts that took place during the late 1970s in the lives of the same Temiar individuals and communities on which I had written the doctoral thesis. In particular, the voluntary conversion of many Temiars to the Baha'i religion, which had taken place in my absence in the mid-1970s, delivered a salutary shock to the way I had been thinking about Temiar culture and society. (It also led me to develop the new ideas about social theory more generally that I am still working on.) This is retold in detail in Chapters 13 and 14, which (with Chapter 10) are the most recent of the studies in this volume.

Let me now say something of the backgrounds to the remaining six chapters.

Chapter 9. Field-report correspondence with Edmund Leach

This chapter was first drafted as an appendix to the present volume, but it grew so large and so closely linked with the material on which the thesis had been based, that I decided to reorganise it as a full chapter. In addition to throwing further light on Temiar mythology and 'theology', the chapter provides detailed examples of Edmund Leach's close involvement as supervisor of my initial fieldwork, previously commented on by Tambiah (2001: 64–67, 79–81). Those interested in the history of social anthropology will also find much of significance here in the informal and hitherto unpublished material in which Leach works out his own distinctive responses to Lévi-Strauss's work on myth (1964), which had just been published while I was in the field. Leach's copious notes, mailed back to me in the field, include extended analyses in words and hand-drawn diagrams of the materials I had been sending him, on daily-life rituals and myth in particular.

Chapter 10. Temiar mediumship in context

This relatively short chapter derives mainly from two presentations that I gave at a conference on *Shamans and Spirit Mediums* at Singapore's Asian Civilisations Museum in 2007. Bringing them together in this volume has enabled a closer look at issues that had been disguised in the thesis, where they were originally treated as 'shamanism' rather than 'mediumship'. For example, the experiential domain—the generating of a sense of authenticity for both the medium and the community—was almost completely ignored in the thesis but is discussed here. Some of the ideas also derive from having observed Chinese spirit-mediumship as practised in Singapore and Kuala Lumpur. The chapter presents insights gained from explicitly recognising the 'dialectical' mode of orientation, which was only hinted at in the thesis. It also incorporates important additional ethnographic data on Temiar mediumship gathered during my doctoral field research and later visits.

Chapter 11. Indigenous religious systems of the Malay Peninsula

In this chapter I examine more closely some of the findings concerning areal variations in religious patterns that were first reported in the thesis. These variations were arrayed along an east–west axis, both among the Temiars themselves and between them and the neighbouring Orang Asli groups. During my initial fieldwork, I had managed to spend a little time in Menriq, Jahai and Semai settlements. But it was not until I joined the (former) University of Singapore in 1967 that I was able to follow this up more systematically. In a series of fieldwork visits in 1968, 1970 and 1972, I investigated the relevant religious and social-organisational features among Bateks, Menriqs, Jahais (in both Kelantan and Perak), Lanohs, Kintaqs and Kensiws. I also investigated the related issues among Malays by interview and from the literature, for I had by then come to regard *all* the endogenous Peninsular traditions as part of the same field of analysis.[11] Without recognising it explicitly at the time, I was clearly influenced in this approach by the work of Edmund Leach (1954) in northern Burma, which I had read under his direction as an undergraduate (and which, privately, he regarded as his best book). Leach had argued, *inter alia*, that each socio-cultural formation is best understood as part of a wider regional array, in which the alternative ways of life mutually set the scene for each other.[12]

---

11. Especially useful in this regard were the discussions I had with Ahmad Ezanee bin Mansor, who was carrying out his Honours fieldwork for Universiti Sains Malaysia in the same Kensiw settlement near Baling that I was briefly working in myself (Ahmad 1972).

12. Strangely, De Josselin de Jong's review (1981: 486) of the 'Indigenous religious systems' paper objected to my use of this procedure, on the grounds that Orang Asli and Malays constituted distinct 'fields of anthropological study', presumably on account of their different linguistic affiliations. But this view would have us exclude, for example, the non-Indo-European-speaking Finns, Hungarians and Basques from consideration within the same European field of study despite their massively shared cultural background. The high density of communication between the various Peninsular populations makes such separation unfeasible, regardless of the obvious socio-political inequalities that have resulted from it.

Some of the social-organisational material that I gathered during these visits has appeared elsewhere (see especially Benjamin 1985, 2011a, 2013), but most of what I learnt about the religious components still has to be published in its own terms. However, the findings that bore directly on my picture of Temiar religion were incorporated into the 'Indigenous religious systems' paper, which, as already noted, also derived much of its shape from the more comprehensive approach to animism that had been developed by Kirk Endicott (1970). (Because of problems in the mail, the version that was eventually published as Benjamin (1979) was a non-final draft. The intended final revision of the text is the basis for the one used here.)

Bellah (1964) had suggested that religious institutions and orientations varied with the degree of societal complexity and cultural differentiation. While I accepted this view in general terms, it seemed to me that differences of this kind did not simply *happen*, for they are also reflective of and imposed by political process. The desire of power-holders to orientate people's attention towards or away from the political centre or in some other direction motivates much of the cultural engineering that lies behind religions as we know them. (At least, that is certainly how it now seems to me in hindsight.) This may be less apparent in segmentary tribal circumstances than in more centralised ones, but it is nevertheless present.

In the 'Indigenous religious systems' paper, I brought politics into the picture by comparing the socio-political circumstances of the Temiars and Semang with the rather different circumstances of the Jah Hut (Jah Hĕt), Mah Meri (Besisis) and Malays. I argued that these populations had carved their religious frameworks out of the same shared animistic outlook, but that the different shapings had resulted from their different experience of power. For the Temiars and Semang, power was endogenous, coming from within their own communities, while for the other populations it was felt as exogenous, coming from 'outside'. Thus, politics impressed itself on culture through its effects on the 'cline of person'—a phrase of Alton ('Pete') Becker's that I have since found valuable in other contexts too.[13]

While I still hold to most of the claims made in this paper, there are at least three features that I would treat differently today. First, as already remarked, my view of the nature of animism has changed. As discussed in Chapters 2 and 10, I now regard animism as a label for any religious orientation that sees the world as populated with entities possessing communicable-with

---

13. Becker's own statement reads as follows:
    A central thread—perhaps the central thread in the semantic structure of all languages is the cline of person, an ordering of linguistic forms according to their distance from the speaker. Between the subjective, pointed, specific pronominal 'I' and the objective, generic common noun, between these poles the words of all languages—words for people, animals, food, time space, indeed words for everything—are ordered and categorized according to their distance—spatial, temporal, social, biological, and metaphorical—from the first person, the speaker. The cline of person also underlies most linguistic systems as well as words, systems of deixis, number, definiteness, tense, and nominal classification among others. (Becker & Oka 1974: 229.)

subjectivities. This puts the emphasis more on the communicative actions involved in religious life than on the cognitive approach emphasised in most writings on animism, in which the existence of souls is said to 'explain' such phenomena as life, fertility and dreaming. I do not regard 'explanation' as the primary source of religion's attraction.

Second, my discussion of Semang religion is no longer reliable. When I first wrote the paper, the only significant material on Semang religion was the much older work of Schebesta, dating from the 1920s. Rich studies, primarily Endicott (1979a) and Lye (1994), have become available since. However, apart from adding newer references to some of Endicott's information, I have decided not to overload the present volume by discussing that material in detail—except to say that, where Semang religion is concerned, matters are more complicated and variable than my account suggested.

Third, much religious change has taken place since the paper was published. A high proportion of the Orang Asli are now variously adherents of several imported religions (Islam, Baha'i, Christianity), at least nominally, as well as of several endogenously developed cults. However, since these changes are given detailed discussion in the two final chapters, I have not thought it necessary to modify the text, apart from adding a few explanatory footnotes.

Chapter 12. Danger and dialectic in Temiar childhood

This essay was originally stimulated by investigating certain linguistic features of the Temiar lexicon, in particular the key concepts *hup*, *rəwaay*, *sabat*, *pocuk* and *gɛnhaaʔ*, which had all been discussed in the doctoral thesis. In this, I was greatly helped by the detailed studies into Mon-Khmer historical linguistics that Gérard Diffloth had been pursuing since the 1960s. On several occasions over the years, Diffloth and I have devoted many days to uncovering what we could of the semantic history of the more 'culturally loaded' Temiar words. (Many of his etymological suggestions also appear in the newer footnotes added to the earlier chapters.)

While I was working on this material, Josiane Massard, who had done extensive fieldwork on Pahang Malay society (Massard 1983), invited me to contribute to a volume she was editing on childhood in Southeast Asia, eventually published as Massard & Koubi (1994). Since many of the words I had been examining related to the dangers that Temiars see as attending childbirth and infancy, I decided to see what light the linguistic evidence could throw on these issues. As the paper progressed, however, the linguistic argument receded into the background while the text came to be increasingly concerned with ethnographic issues. After no fewer than seven revisions, occasioned partly by reviewers' comments, the paper achieved publishable shape. The linguistic material was by now confined to a few footnotes; it had in any case been reduced at the editors' request. The version printed here as Chapter 12 has restored some of the removed linguistic material, which has been further updated after discussion with Gérard Diffloth on the Mon-Khmer issues and with John Wolff on the Austronesian ones.

Two main themes are treated explicitly in this chapter. First, the Temiars' dialectical frame of thought is examined in detail, especially as regards their 'soul' beliefs. Second, the attempt made in the thesis to link together 'structure' and values (Chapter 8) is revisited, but through a non-cognitive approach that takes physiology as a more appropriate starting point for dealing with 'feelings'.

Chapter 13. Rationalisation and re-enchantment: Temiar religion, 1964–1994

As already noted, the original version of this chapter was written in response to a request from Gehan Wijeyewardene to contribute to a small conference on *Enchantment and Re-enchantment: Religion in Modern Southeast Asia* at the Australian National University in 1996. The conference title made obvious reference to the ideas of Max Weber, and my paper made explicit use of those ideas. I had already admired Weber's work, but closer acquaintance came as a result of sharing the teaching in a course on classical social theory organised by Kwok Kian Woon at the National University of Singapore in the mid-1990s. To most sociologists, 'Weber' still means just *The Protestant Ethic and the 'Spirit' of Capitalism*. But there is much more to his ideas than that relatively brief and all-too-frequently misunderstood work—which I deliberately avoided mentioning in this chapter. Throughout his writings, Weber's tracing of the connection between the different forms of rationality, life-circumstances and patterns of authority is especially valuable, though not often made explicit. I was also interested to see how far Weber's approach would apply to the non-urban set of circumstances of Temiar life. Could formal rationality and disenchantment also come to characterise religious life in remote rural conditions?

I employed Weber's ideas and Gellner's elaborations of them to help understand the motivations lying behind three different kinds of religious orientation displayed by Temiars as their lives changed in the 1970s and 1980s. These were (1) sticking to the old ways, (2) adopting the highly 'rationalised' Baha'i religion, or (3) developing new synthetic cults. Weber's typological differentiation of religious innovators into 'exemplary' and 'emissary' prophets helped inject some order into the data. His discussion of the political correlates of the distinction enabled connections to be drawn with the broader Malaysian context, showing that the various choices made were a complicated vector result of the government's urgings to adopt a 'religion' (*agama*) and some younger Temiars' own religious search.

Although the Baha'i moment and the new cults reported on in this chapter have barely endured, they were important components of Temiar religious history that would have gone unrecorded if I had not chanced upon them. I have therefore recorded my ethnographic findings in some detail, to highlight the Temiars' varied responses to the changing situation as well as the responses of those who were asserting authority over them.

Chapter 14. Temiar religions, 1994–2012: Islam, Christianity, ʔaluj Səlamad

The initial version of this chapter was presented at the *International Conference on Religion in Southeast Asian Politics: Resistance, Negotiation and Transcendence* at the Institute of Southeast Asian Studies, Singapore, in December 2008. The revised version presented here has added materials on Temiar Christianity and further updates to other sections, gathered during a fieldtrip in 2010. Further material on Christianity kindly supplied by Eduardo Hazera has brought the account up to 2012. As indicated by the title's shift from singular to plural ('religions'), this final chapter examines the religious dimensions of the differentiation that has overtaken Temiar society in recent decades. The localistic and animistic Temiar Religion described in Chapters 2–12 is still practised, but it is now followed, sometimes syncretically, alongside Islam, Protestant Christianity and the remnants of Baha'i. There has also emerged an endogenous new religion known as ʔaluj Səlamad, which has spread widely throughout the Temiar population.

With few exceptions, Temiar conversions to Islam have resulted from state-generated pressures, as discussed in Chapter 13. So far, this has been a matter of identity, not religious practice; but pressures on practice will probably increase in future. Conversion to Christianity, a very recent development, is the result of missionising by non-Temiars (unlike what happened with Baha'i). The monotheism of ʔaluj Səlamad, on the other hand, has been developed by Temiars themselves, out of resources already present in Temiar Religion but with obvious echoes of Baha'i, Islam and Christianity. These various innovations are largely explicable as reactions to the radical loss of autonomy that the Temiars, along with other Orang Asli, are now experiencing as the most put-upon sector of Malaysia's population. But that is not the sole factor, for specifically religious motives are also involved.

Chapter 14 contains the first (admittedly incomplete) published accounts of the new ʔaluj Səlamad religion and of Temiar Christianity, while the new information on Islam extends the account presented in Chapter 13. The data on all three religions come from Perak as well as Kelantan, further illustrating the considerable socio-economic, political and religious differentiation that the Temiars are currently experiencing. At the time of writing, it is hard to see where these changes are leading, but the materials presented in this chapter provide an historical snapshot of Temiar society at a time of considerable flux.

The appendices

The four appendices present material that does not fit easily into the main text, but which throws further light on topics discussed there. Appendix 1 presents further evidence of H. D. Noone's Temiar work from first-hand witnesses, including Noone himself. Appendix 2 turns to a more internal view of Temiar religious history, by recounting their own views of the various named cults that have arisen, and sometimes fallen away, within their mediumistic practices. Appendix 3 presents further ethnographic details on Temiar practices surrounding death and burial, including a fuller account of one of the burials outlined in Chapter 6. Finally, because of its relevance to the work of Kilton Stewart in the 1930s, referred to at several points in the main text, Appendix 4 presents all of the children's recalled dreams that I recorded in 1964.

Theoretical issues: Religion, animism, belief and dialecticism

As already mentioned, the ideas of several scholars have affected my approach to religion in the years since my doctoral research. Although the newer views have more direct relevance to the later chapters of this volume than to the doctoral thesis, it will be appropriate to present them here, as it will help signpost the book's course and avoid unnecessary repetition in the remainder of the text.

For analytical purposes, religious manifestations can be separated into 'core' and 'peripheral' phenomena, which nevertheless constitute each other's context.[14] The peripheral phenomena relate to the socially maintained orientational frameworks that affect people's religious practices. The core phenomena are those that relate to individuals' predispositions to engage in religious activities in the first place. As I argue below, religion is primarily a matter of things *done*; any explicitly stated 'beliefs' are secondarily attendant on those actions.

The core phenomena of religion is a direct outcome of the emergence of self-consciousness in our species, through which we have each become a subject reflexively aware of ourself as both an agent and a patient. This subjectivity is the particular property of human consciousness that permits reflective thought, constructed of articulated concepts. But we also retain the basic mammalian way of personally and non-reflectively knowing the world through condensed notions and feelings—through *symbols*, in the full sense of the word. As Michael Polanyi (1959, 1964) argued, it is through this condensed personal knowledge rather than articulated conceptual thought that most of our daily actions are constructed. We quite simply *know* what we are

---

14. The following paragraphs derive partly from a long working paper (Benjamin 1987b) that has yet to be fully published.

doing; but if we stop to think—to shift from unfocused-on notions to focused-on concepts—our ability to act on that knowledge becomes greatly reduced, or even blocked.[15]

It is the emergence of language—deriving perhaps from the action-schemata involved in tool-using—that added articulated thought to our mental repertoire. This may be why our brains usually exhibit hemispheric lateralisation of function, with the left cerebral cortex engaging primarily in analytic-sequential-conceptual *thinking* and the right cerebral cortex in symbolic-simultaneous-notional *knowing* (cf. Galin 1977). The production of articulate speech requires us to carry out at least two mental operations: first, to focus analytically on our notions so as to map them onto concepts, and then to externalise those concepts in turn by encoding them onto a linearly organised flow of speech.

Language, then, is a phenomenal threat. Speaking forces us out of the undisturbed pre-reflective state in which we each just *know* the world through our own personal authentic symbolism, into a state where we have to work hard at reflectively modelling that knowledge onto unyielding articulated concepts. Moreover, the act of speaking forces us into the realisation that, for everything we succeed in saying, most of our personal knowledge must remain unsaid and hence unshared. This has led to what I earlier characterised as the essential loneliness of the human subject. As individuals, we are aware of our personal knowledge but cannot easily say more than a little of just what it is that we know, and hence cannot fully communicate it to other human beings.

This places each of us in a condition of potential or actual existential anxiety as to the authenticity of the mental representations that we live by. Unless these representations can be shared, how are we to know whether they might not be unique flights of fancy? Yet the attempt to share them with other human beings traps us in the need to *articulate* our knowledge, thereby reshaping it into a form other than that which serves as the functioning basis for our personal knowledge of the world. The attempt at sharing also necessarily leaves us with the impression that we have left too much unsaid. Only a direct intersubjective communication with another, second-person, subjectivity can serve, unmediated by any translation into the articulated forms of ordinary language. Such a pouring-out of our otherwise quite private subjectivity in the pre-reflective form it takes within our own consciousness can hardly be achieved except by communication with a non-empirical 'thou'. 'Non-empirical' does not mean 'unreal' or 'non-existing':[16] it means

---

15. The view of symbolism taken here also relates to Sperber's argument (1975) that symbolism is a particular mode of mental operation rather than a response to supposedly pre-formed 'symbols'. The contrast drawn between notional and conceptual knowledge derives from the innovative phenomenological approach adopted by Mimica (1981) in his study of Ikwaye religion in highland Papua New Guinea, the cosmogony-linked dialecticism of which closely echoes that of the Temiars despite the very different form in which it is manifested.

16. Cf. Blagden (1900: viii) in his Preface to Skeat's *Malay Magic*: 'A belief which is actually held, even a mere fancy that is entertained in the mind, has a real existence, and is a fact just as much as any

only that the communicated-with entity is so constituted that it cannot be the object of sensory perception. It cannot be smelled, seen, touched, weighed or heard. It can, however, be the object of mental awareness, and as such it can certainly generate or correspond to empirically sensed physiological activity in the brain and other parts of the body. It is this direct, unmediated, non-articulated communication with a non-empirical Thou—a second-person called into existence by that very communicative act—that forms the core of religion as a human phenomenon.[17]

The physiological and psychological satisfactions achieved in such communicative acts lead people to wish for a world that is communicable-with, personal and intentional, yet not forcing them into articulating their tacit knowledge. Consequently, except where their consciousness has been severely subverted by other modes—as, for example, when most of the monotheistic traditions accord a central role to written texts—they will prefer to treat the world as relatively undifferentiated and as possessing subjectivity. In its basic manifestation, this preference constitutes classical *animism*. By animism is meant acting as if the subjectivity and attendant animacy thereby glimpsed in other objects and people (as well as in oneself) consists in some essence or vital principle conceptually distinct from, though usually situated in, material substance. Analytically, we talk of such incorporated essence as 'soul(s)', and of free unbounded essence as 'spirit(s)' (Endicott 1970: 47–95). But these familiar English words can be misleading when applied uncritically to other religious frameworks. The basic animistic stance—that it is in the nature of all salient things to be constituted of a complex interpenetration of essence and matter—is not in itself *a* religion. Nevertheless, animism forms the underlying substance of all the world's religions *as practised*. (For further discussion, see Chapters 10–12.)

What, then, is going on when people enter into direct, symbolically condensed, communicative relations with non-empirical second-persons ('thou', 'you')? What is the phenomenal nature of these communications? What is the epistemological status of the overt 'beliefs' that people make appeal to in justifying or rationalising them? Most people are content to leave their religious experience untalked-about. Indeed, they will normally *resist* talking about it, fearing that any such articulation will destroy the symbolical wholeness that they wish to enjoy. But if an interlocutor—a pesky friend, a

---

other. As a piece of psychology it must always have a certain interest, and it may on occasions become of enormous practical importance.'

17. Music, poetry, art, dance and other expressive activities (including, perhaps, talking to oneself) may serve much the same purpose, for these too involve a condensed symbolic mode of communication and a constantly present (if often only virtual) audience. On the other hand, the frequent use of language as the medium of religious communication might suggest that such communication is, after all, articulated in character. But religious language is always characterised by special properties that ensure a high degree of non-articulatedness, since it employs an essentially mythic, allusive, poetic and symbolic mode of discourse. As the leading biologist J. B. S. Haldane (2001 [1927]: 232–233) once put it, 'religious experience is a reality.... It cannot be communicated directly, but those who experience it can induce it in others by myth and ritual.'

visiting ethnographer, a fellow religionist, or even a formal tribunal—forces discussion of those experiences, only then will the performer try to articulate and rationalise what he or she underwent. We must therefore distinguish between explicit 'beliefs' as talked about before or after the event and the communicant's state of mind when actually involved *in* the event. In this sense, we should be concerned not with 'belief' or 'beliefs' but with *believing*, as an action that people engage themselves in. On this view, explicit 'beliefs' are statements produced later in the attempt to rationalise or justify to *others* the experiences undergone when embedded in those actions. It is on this point, it seems to me, that recent widely read criticisms of religion (such as Dawkins 2006, Hitchens 2007 and Onfray 2007) have misconstrued their target, by focusing on the misdeeds of religious institutions and the absurdity of religious 'beliefs' when appraised literally (as these authors mostly do), instead of attending to religion as primarily a form of communicative *action*. (Dawkins especially, as a biologist, might have been expected to pay more attention to this.)

In other words, religious 'beliefs' are not simply there for the gathering. As with 'values' (a favoured topic of sociologists), beliefs can be teased out of what people say only by also observing what they *do*. In such cases, people's stated 'beliefs' will not truly represent their belief *as they experience it*. At best, the stated or assented-to 'beliefs' will merely *allude* to those experiences. Consequently, whenever people say what they believe, they do so from a position outside of their actual state of believing. This does little harm if the interlocutor gets the point, by building up a parallel subjective imagery of whatever it is they are alluding to. C. S. Lewis (1962: 39–40) characterised this manner of understanding as 'magistral'. If, on the other hand, the interlocutor fails to move beyond the uttered words and takes them literally (that is, referentially), the stated 'beliefs' will assuredly not be a reliable guide to the actual beliefs.[18] This mode of understanding, which bleaches metaphor of its allusive content, was termed 'pupillary' by C. S. Lewis.

When talking *about* their activities, religious practitioners will know that their gods and spirits are not empirical, even though they have treated them as such in practice; but they will not usually explicitly admit as much. Phenomenally, they can only communicate with entities to which they ascribe a subjectivity essentially the same as their own. The entity is effectively a *person* at that moment—otherwise, they might literally find themselves talking to a wall. This is the source of the regular iconographic anthropomorphisation of religious objects.[19] However, this can also work in reverse, as when the

---

18. There is a third possibility: if people seem too ready with an answer, they are probably relaying formulated dogma rather than struggling to give an honest account of what they privately 'believe'. This is typical of situations that are under political constraint.
19. This remains so even if people talk of these entities as if they were quite other than human. Sometimes, this occurs when the dogmatics of the particular tradition demand such a resistance to

expectation is projected reciprocally onto *other* species, thought of as subjects. This, surely, is why shamans, mediums, masked dancers and other such practitioners so frequently dress up or act as animals or plants. As recounted in Chapter 10, for example, Temiars wishing to invite an animal or plant spirit to their ceremonies should meet the spirit half-way by becoming more animal or plant-like in their deportment or dress.

How can such a flip-flop be maintained—knowing that the gods and spirits are non-empirical yet acting towards them as if they were empirical, and for the moment 'personally' *knowing* that they are empirical? As remarked earlier, the brain's cortical lateralisation may be involved here, with the right hemisphere undergoing the experience and the left hemisphere remodelling or *articulating* that experience so that it can be talked about. This could have resulted only from a very long period during which human beings have *had* to flip-flop between the two modes of mental representation, commencing most probably with the emergence of language and its requirement for articulation (cf. Eccles 1977: 172–175).

It might be thought that 'bad faith' must necessarily accompany this difference between the way in which people talk *to* the gods and the way they talk *of* them.[20] But this is not necessarily so, for people everywhere are probably aware, just as visiting researchers are aware, that the efficacy of their ritual procedures really *is* symbolic, not instrumental. They must know, deep down, that their religious actions are symbolic actions, while normally insisting that they are instrumental. To admit otherwise would be to reduce the symbolic efficacy of what they are doing. This, surely, is why a Catholic priest is required to insist to his congregants that they must believe that the wafer and wine in the Eucharist truly become flesh and blood. Both priest and congregants will nevertheless expect to taste wafer and wine, not flesh and blood, on their tongues. If the offering should indeed have turned into flesh and blood, the communicants would surely spit it out in shock. Thus, if people openly articulated the real basis of their religious actions, they would destroy the efficacy of those actions, the essential nature of which is that they *are* symbolic—non-articulated, condensed configurations of meaning and reference. By talking of their gods or spirits as empirical, they are shielding the truth that the felt efficacy of their beliefs derives from action that they know to be symbolic. 'Faith

---

anthropomorphisation. In some religious traditions, on the other hand, such as that of China, the gods are explicitly regarded as promoted human beings, who may under certain circumstances be demoted.
20. I use the term 'bad faith' here slightly adapted from Peter Berger's discussion (1966: 164): 'To put it very simply, "bad faith" is to pretend something is necessary that in fact is voluntary'. For Berger's 'necessary', here read 'ontologically and empirically existent'; for 'voluntary', read 'willed into phenomenal but non-empirical existence'. Berger's application of the notion of bad faith to sociological issues is derived in turn from Jean-Paul Sartre's philosophical writings. I return to this question in Chapter 13.

is believing in something you know ain't true' (Mark Twain 1898).[21]

Up to this point, I have been discussing the core phenomena of religion. But these never occur in isolation: their manner of performance is always affected by 'peripheral' factors emanating from the social context. The context, as already intimated, exerts varying degrees of constraint relating to whatever mode-of-orientation is operating at the moment in question. These modes of orientation—the transcendental, the immanent and the dialectical—are built out of the institutionalised differential focusing of our attention as between SELF and OTHER (so written to indicate that these are not formulated concepts but pre-reflective and directly felt *notions*). The Temiar cultural regime, as already mentioned, has typically followed the dialectical mode—at least until the changes discussed in the final two chapters allowed alternatives to appear. I shall not elaborate on Temiar dialecticism at this stage, as it is discussed at several places later in the text.[22] Suffice it to say that it appears to have been established as part of the dissimilatory social processes through which the Temiars, early in the period of their ethnogenesis, came to maintain a complementary relation with neighbouring Peninsular populations.[23]

---

21. A more difficult problem is posed by those who readily *admit* that their religious actions are symbolic, not instrumental, and that the entities they are in communication with are indeed non-empirical. Those proclaiming such a view probably intend to make matters harder for themselves in order to increase their sense of personal 'victory' over unbelief. They also make matters harder for the sociologist of religion: see the final section of Bellah (1964) for a discussion of 'modern' religion as self-avowedly symbolic in its mode of discourse and practice.

22. For further theoretical discussion, including detailed characterisations of all three modes of orientation, see Benjamin (1993a: 348–349).

23. I shall have more to say about this in the companion volume, *Temiar Society* (NUS Press, forthcoming (b)). For the wider evidence, see Benjamin (1985, 2002a, 2005, 2011a, 2013).

<table>
<tr><td>Chapter</td><td></td></tr>
<tr><td>2</td><td></td></tr>
</table>

Chapter 2 — The Temiars and their Religion

The Temiar people

The Mon-Khmer-speaking Temiars inhabit the upland parts of Kelantan, Perak and northern Pahang (figure 2.1). They constitute the third largest group among the Orang Asli populations of Peninsular Malaysia, but culturally and linguistically they effectively form the largest uniform group. The Temiars are broadly similar to the other Mon-Khmer-speaking hill peoples of mainland Southeast Asia. They have followed their own unexportable, localised religion in an area where the main religions of civilisation were formerly Mahayana Buddhism or Shivaite Hinduism, now replaced by Islam. They have lived, probably for millennia, by swidden farming supplemented by hunting and fishing, while the rural plains-dwellers have lived variously by swiddening, trading, coastal fishing and, latterly, wet-rice cultivation.

In a country where indigenous records extend to the fourteenth century, the Temiars have no recorded history or writing of their own. But this does not mean that they have remained outside of history, for their circumstances have witnessed several changes of direction, in step with changes elsewhere in the Peninsula and beyond.[1] Consider only the following examples:

- Large numbers of millennium-old Buddhist votive tablets have recently been found in parts of Temiar country.[2] (See figure 13.3 for examples.)
- There are Indic and pre-Malay Austronesian loan words in the Temiar language.

---

1. For discussions of the Orang Asli in relation to Peninsular linguistics, archaeology and history, see Benjamin (1987a, 1997, 2002b, 2011a, 2013, forthcoming (a)). Historical data relating to the ethnonym 'Temiar' are presented in Benjamin (2012a). For summaries of the wider long-term perspectives, see Bauer (1992), Bellwood (1993, 2004), Fix (1995, 2011), Bulbeck (2004, 2011) and Burenhult, Kruspe & Dunn (2011). Leary (1995) was the first extended piece of document-based historical writing on the Orang Asli. This has now been followed by the work of Manickam (2010) and Baer (2012), whose researches are continuing. For a comprehensive bibliography of writings about the Orang Asli, now unavoidably somewhat out of date, see Lye (2001).
2. These sites and their contents were unknown to me and apparently also to the Temiars during the time of my initial research. They came to notice as a result of the forest clearing that preceded the planting of commercial estates in the area. The caves include prehistoric cave drawings of ritual performances, and were researched archaeologically by Adi Haji Taha, former Director of the National Museum, Kuala Lumpur (Adi 2004, 2007: 197–241). I say more about the drawings and votive tablets in Chapter 13.

Figure 2.1 The location of Temiar country

- The considerable dialectal uniformity and morphological regularity of the Temiar language suggest that, although the Temiars constitute a segmentary and politically non-centralised population, they have somehow managed to produce a degree of language standardisation.
- Temiar isolation—especially from neighbouring Malay communities—was greater immediately after the Second World War than it was before. On the other hand, their contact with British, Australian and Malaysian security forces, and with Communist insurgents, was sometimes intense during the succeeding Emergency.

As of 1988, the Temiars numbered more than 12,000, and now (2014) probably number around 28,000. When I began my fieldwork in 1964, however, there were reported to be fewer than 9,000 Temiars, with an overall population density of about two persons per square kilometre, despite some locally higher densities. Until the 1970s, they were living in small or very small villages lying some kilometres from each other. The village populations ranged from one dozen (figure 4.4) to about 150, with a modal size between 30 and 45. In such circumstances, and with kinship and relative age as the main principles of social categorisation, relations were necessarily mostly of the 'face-to-face' type. This was moderated by the inclusive and classificatory kinship system that also allowed them to maintain wider social relations (including marriage) beyond the village and even with non-Temiars, sometimes at great distances. Temiar society has usually been highly solidary at the village level[3]—though this is now changing, in step with the massive changes that have taken place more broadly in Malaysian society over the past 30 years.

Temiar livelihood was based on the swidden farming of cassava (*Manihot esculenta*) and hill-rice (*Oryza sativa*, var *japonica*) or millet (*Setaria italica*), supplemented by hunting, fishing and the trading of forest products. They therefore had to move their settlements every few years to new sites. These were situated within territories defined by the presence of still-productive fruit trees growing in former village sites. Rights in the trees were lodged in the cognatic descent group (ramage) that constituted the core-group in each village. The senior member of the descent group usually served as the village leader—a post with little authority. He often acted also as the headman, appointed by state agencies to organise the villagers' relations with wider Malayan society.[4]

Figure 2.2 Temiar houses, Humid (1964)
Note the wɔɔj tuft at the front of the boy's tonsure. The man in the middle is crafting a sheath for his bushknife.

3. I make this claim not out of any respect for functionalist social theory, but solely because that is how matters seemed *in this instance*. I do not hold solidarity to be a general—or even, necessarily, a desirable—feature of social relations as such.
4. For the author's ethnographic accounts of Temiar social organisation, see Benjamin (1966, 1967c, 1968a, 1968b, 1999, 2002a). These studies will be brought together in revised form in *Temiar Society* (Benjamin, forthcoming (b)).

Temiar settlements contained one or more communal houses, raised off the ground on pillars and built of an open construction (figure 2.2). This allowed air, sounds and smells to circulate freely. Internally, the central floor space was surrounded, sometimes on all sides, by the separate conjugal-family compartments. Privacy was not easily achieved, for these compartments were usually separated from the more public space by low partitions or permanent openings in the wall. This may explain why Temiar villages alternated every few years between a single 'longhouse' containing the whole community and separate houses each containing one to three closely related households.

Village life was highly communal. For example, although there was no requirement to share swidden crops beyond the household, larger catches of meat were obligatorily shared throughout the village community, and sometimes beyond. The heavier swidden labour was shared by the settlement as a whole, and the boundaries between farms were merely nominal. There was little occupational specialisation, although Temiars did sometimes express generalised ideas about the different roles of men and women (Roseman 1991: 118–128). Most activities, including farming, fishing, cooking and child-minding, were carried out by men, women or children indiscriminately. Tree-felling, shooting game animals and raising roof-beams, on the other hand, were treated as uniquely adult male activities, while pandanus plaiting was thought of as typically female. But women and children also caught animals, and men wove baskets. Children were not normally prevented from undertaking adult activities if they wished, even when the activities were dangerous.

Viewed on its own terms, Temiar social organisation was segmentary and non-hierarchical; each village community ran its own affairs. There were no formal rules of organisation apart from the kinship and descent structures. More important than formal rules, however, were two dialectically conjoined values that pervaded Temiar social life: non-interference in other individuals' wishes, and a profound concern for communality. This dialectic was not always easy to maintain; it was kept embedded in daily life by a variety of cultural mechanisms seated in language, kinship and religion.

Although I have employed the past tense in the last few paragraphs, some Temiars (especially at higher altitudes) still live in the manner just described. In most places, though, much government-directed resettlement has taken place in both Orang Asli and rural Malay communities, partly in response to the security-related relocation programmes of the 1970s. More recently, further changes have resulted from education, road-building, the inflow of cash, an increasing density of governmental administration, and the commercial logging and opening of oil-palm estates by non-Temiars on Temiar land. Consequently, many Temiars have shifted from tribal autonomy to a more peasant-like or proletarian status; a few have even become entrepreneurial businessmen. Following a generation of primary education, most Temiar youngsters are now literate in Malay, the national language. Nevertheless, most Temiars were still living in relative isolation until paved roads (figures 14.1 and 14.3), now including an interstate highway (figure 14.4), were built through their territory. Previously—and in most places still—there were tracks accessible only to four-wheel-drive vehicles. This, among other factors, greatly restricted the Temiars' access to secondary and tertiary education—especially as compared to other less isolated large Orang Asli populations, who now count several university graduates among their numbers. As I write, however, this is changing. An increasing number of younger Temiars are attending secondary school and even tertiary institutions. This has resulted in an emerging consciousness of their politically disadvantaged position, resulting from the combined effects of the severely restrictive *Aboriginal Peoples Act 1954*, revised 1974, and the lack of land rights in their own territory (Rusaslina 2010, 2011). This has led to a growth in overt political action, including the blockading of logging tracks, the mounting of legal action over land and other rights, and the linking up with pan-Malaysian and international 'indigenous peoples' movements. Temiars have also begun to take voting seriously in state and federal elections, although they do not all vote for the same party.

In Chapters 13 and 14, I trace the connection between these recent social changes and the shifting religious life of the Temiars, especially as manifested in the south-western corner of Kelantan state, but also in other places.

Temiar religion: previous studies

Desultory reports on the 'Northern Sakai', as the Temiars were then usually known, survive from the nineteenth and early twentieth centuries. These include Clifford's accounts from the late nineteenth century, thinly disguised as short stories (or 'tales and sketches' as Clifford himself described them). Most of his stories concern the population known today as Semais, but at least one of them, 'The flight of the jungle folk', dating from 1899 and republished as Clifford (1927: 244–271), displays a surprisingly close knowledge of the Temiars of the Plus valley in Perak before the turn of the twentieth century. The first descriptions of the people under the ethnonym 'Temiar' or 'Temer' in those spellings are in the few chapters by Schebesta in the second volume of his Malayan studies (1928: 49–97), and by Baker (1933).[5] Intensive ethnographic research began only in 1931, with the work of Herbert Deane ('Pat') Noone, the staff ethnographer at the Perak Museum in Taiping, who had completed an anthropology degree at Cambridge University shortly before going out to Malaya. The preliminary and sole instalment of his unfinished account (Noone 1936) concentrated on

---

5. In the nineteenth century, Stevens (1892: 81) also reported on a population he labelled variously as 'Tummior', 'Temia', 'Tembeh (Temia)' or even 'Tembeh (Temia or Tummiyor)', but according to Schebesta (1926: 272) these were people who would today be called Semai, not Temiar.

three main issues: the environment, both natural and social; Temiar social organisation at the village level; and his own proposals for the setting up of Temiar reserves in Perak state and for the enacting of protective legislation. The latter were eventually incorporated into the code of operation of the

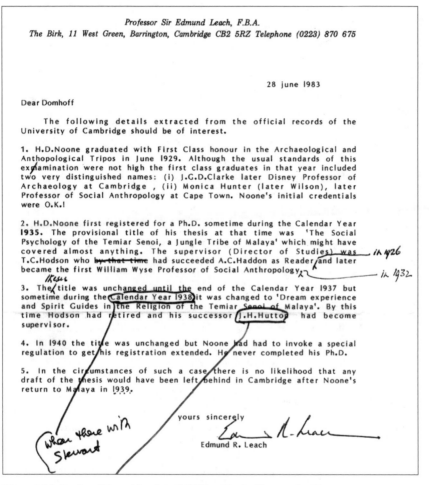

Figure 2.3 Letter from Edmund Leach to G. William Domhoff concerning Noone
Reproduced by courtesy of G. William Domhoff, whose annotations are included along with Leach's own corrections.

Department of Orang Asli Affairs (JHEOA), which was first set up in the late 1950s. Since then, the JHEOA (now JAKOA) has been the single most important factor in the shaping of Orang Asli society.

Of more direct relevance to the study of Temiar religion is Noone's emphasis on the highly communal, violence-avoiding, character of Temiar society. In an extended radio talk broadcast from Singapore (Noone 1937), he described them as 'a people so communistic or rather, co-operative'. Although he never published a detailed analysis, Noone presented some lectures on the topic in England in the late 1930s, with the intention of developing his ideas into a doctoral thesis. (Appendix 1.3 reproduces a report on one of those lectures.) The thesis was probably never written, and it has generally been reported that Noone never registered as a candidate.[6] Edmund Leach, however, in a letter to G. William Domhoff (figure 2.3), did eventually unearth a record of Noone's registration at Cambridge University, and also of a later change of topic.

Temiar religion and 'Senoi dreamwork'

Noone's association in 1934 and 1938 with Kilton Stewart, a freelance psychotherapist, was to lead three decades later (long after Noone's presumed murder some time between 1943 and 1945)[7] to the wide dissemination of the view that the Temiars held the secret to the maintenance of world peace through their supposed discovery of a technique of controlled dream-maturation. Noone's role in the 1938 fieldwork that provided the background to these claims was substantial, but there is no evidence that he (or Stewart at that stage) regarded the Temiars as able to *control* their dreams. I have come across only one possible exception to this, namely Holman's third- or fourth-party account (1962) of what Noone supposedly said to Robert Chrystal when they met up behind enemy lines in a Temiar village—probably Rening (Rɛŋnɛɛŋ)—during the Japanese occupation:

> [Noone] believed the Temiar were the world's greatest psychiatrists and that they had invented a secret method of bringing up their children to make them perfectly adjusted adults. The secret lay in their method of manipulating dreams. The Temiar didn't just dream. They were taught to dream along certain positive lines. In their dreams they were often violent—they fought, murdered, raped, committed incest. And in this

---

6. Strangely, Stewart Wavell (6 May 1983), in an unpublished letter to Peggy Robertson, claimed to have once possessed a copy of Noone's thesis before losing it when moving house (http://www.dspace. cam.ac.uk/handle/1810/230169). I suspect that Wavell was actually referring to the long paper that Noone published in 1936. This impression is reinforced by Wavell's statement that 'My recollection of Pat's thesis is that he did not attempt to include much on Temiar dreams. He was more concerned with an anthropological study of their co-operative way of life.'

7. Following the investigation reported by Holman (1958), Noone's death—said to be a murder committed by one or two Temiars—has usually been thought to have occurred in late 1943. A military source (http://www.specialforcesroh.com/roll-4095.html) states that Noone was last seen alive on 3 November 1943—a surprisingly specific date. However, an article in the 6 January 1946 issue of *The Straits Times* (Singapore) states that he was reliably seen alive just six months before the Japanese surrender in September 1945—that is, in March of 1945, some sixteen months later than Holman's date. *The Straits Times* later (28 July 1962, p.7) published an extensive extract from Holman's book (1962) on the wartime experiences of the rubber planter Robert Chrystal, who claimed to be the first to obtain the truth about Noone's murder, directly from one of the Temiars who had been sworn to secrecy about it. That account is essentially the same as the one presented in Holman's earlier book. Although Noone's body was never found, his name is inscribed on column 389 of the Commonwealth War Memorial in Singapore, as a Lieutenant in the First (Perak) Battalion of the Federated Malay States Volunteer Force; but no date is given there. I therefore regard the date and manner of Noone's death as still something of the 'mystery' that it was described as in the 1940s.

way the dream became a safety valve through which they worked off all their sexual and emotional repressions. In Noone's opinion, a Temiar was psychologically incapable of committing murder. What a fatal mistake that was to prove. (*The Straits Times*, 28 July 1962, p.7, extracted from Holman (1962).)

If authentic, this passage would show signs of Noone's interaction with Stewart. More likely, however, the quoted passage is less than authentic, since it probably derives from Holman's later acquaintance with Stewart's ideas. In either case, it raises questions. Was this Noone's own view in 1943, some years before Stewart wrote his PhD thesis (which makes no mention of dream control)? Or, more likely, was it Holman's view 20 years later, based on reading Stewart's published articles? Unfortunately, the true source and chronology of the report is unclear. In any case, 'being taught' to dream in a certain way is not evidence of effective dream *control*. And, as Quadens (1990: 81) points out, such *teaching* would be at odds with the Temiars' concern for individual autonomy, including that of their young children (as discussed in Chapter 12).

Noone made no mention of dream control in his radio talk (Noone 1937), even though he asserted in it that 'all inspiration, invention and novelty in Temiar life is the result of dreaming'. Claudia Parsons (1941: 179–180), who worked briefly with Noone and Stewart as their typist at the 'convenient and not too remote' Temiar settlement of Jalong in Perak (figure 2.4), reported that 'Noone's treatise showed the relationship between dreams, dance and philosophy in Sakai [Temiar] communities'.[8] It seems likely, then, that during the few weeks of their working together in the field,[9] Stewart fused some of Noone's ideas with his own psychotherapeutic approach deriving from the work of Otto Rank, which he had encountered in Paris after his first Malayan trip. Noone and Stewart must have cooperated closely, for the latter could speak neither Malay nor Temiar, and would therefore have been entirely dependent on Noone when communicating with Temiars.[10]

Stewart's analysis first appeared in the form of a doctoral thesis in anthropology (1947) at the London School of Economics (LSE), supervised

8. For an obituary of Claudia Parsons, who died aged 98 in 1998, see *The Independent*, 27 June 1998 (http://www.independent.co.uk/arts-entertainment/obituary-claudia-parsons-1167736.html).
9. Stewart's claim (1947: 10) of ten months' field experience among the Temiars has been shown by Domhoff (2003) to be an overestimate. On the testimony of Parsons (1941: 179), Stewart spent just seven weeks there in 1938. Domhoff has calculated from Stewart's own unpublished records (Ms) that his earlier stay in 1934 also lasted just a few weeks. (Lindskoog (1981: 181) and several other writers wrongly state that this was in 1935.) Parsons's mention of Noone's 'treatise' suggests that he was working on the text of his planned PhD thesis, of which no trace has been discovered.
10. One other direct reminiscence of the relationship between Stewart and Noone is Eric Robertson's statement, in a letter (17 May 1983) to John Wren-Lewis (http://www.dspace.cam.ac.uk/handle/1810/230159), that 'Pat used to refer to him as "Stonk!" I had the impression that Noone thought him somewhat eccentric.'

The anthropologist and the psycho-analyst

Figure 2.4 H. D. Noone (left) and Kilton Stewart at Jalong (1938) *(Parsons 1942: plate IX)*

by the distinguished anthropologists S. F. Nadel and Raymond Firth.[11] My initial acquaintance with Stewart's work came through Edmund Leach's collection of his papers.[12] I also made notes from the 200 pages devoted to the Temiars (whom he called 'Senoi') in Stewart's thesis, lodged in the LSE library. Maurice Freedman helped me gain access, but unfortunately he could not arrange permission to have the text photocopied, probably because it was

---

11. Raymond Firth chaired the interview at the Royal Anthropological Institute in 1963 that led to the award of an Emslie Horniman Scholarship to fund my doctoral research in Malaysia. At the interview, Firth (who had twice carried out fieldwork in Kelantan) attempted to converse with me in Malay, a language that I had only just begun to study. The failure was mine, not his.

12. Leach had worked with Stewart briefly in 1936–37—as a statistician, according to Stewart (1947: 2)—carrying out ethnographic fieldwork among the small Yami population on Botel Tobago island, off the southern tip of Taiwan. For Leach's own self-dismissive account of this two-month fieldtrip, see Kuper (1986: 376). Stewart later incorporated the Yami findings into his PhD thesis (1947: 339–434). In a letter to me dated 10 May 1965 in response to my initial field report on Temiar dreaming, Leach wrote 'I am delighted to hear that my old friend Kilton Stewart, rogue though he was (and is) didn't really "make it all up".' Stewart died that year, before I could communicate with him directly.

embargoed. I did not regain access to the thesis until 2012, when I was finally able to download a copy from the Ethos collection of the British Library.

The comments on Stewart's work in my own thesis were non-committal, in that I took his claims at face value—all the more so since his psychologistic approach was very different from the framework that I was operating within. Given that Stewart's views were later to become the source of much controversy, my remarks in Chapters 6 and 7 should therefore not be taken as confirming his later ideas. In particular, those of his ideas that depended on the claim that the Temiars could *control* their dreams found no support in my own fieldwork[13] or in that of Jennings (1995: 99–103) and Faraday & Wren-Lewis (1984), who deliberately searched for it. More to the point, Stewart himself made no such claim in his thesis, nor did he state there that Temiars ever said they could control their dreams. The lack of any mention of 'dream control' in Stewart's thesis must be the reason why it had long been inaccessible, as 'dream control' is generally thought to be the underlying rationale of the Senoi Dreamwork psychotherapeutic movement. Lindskoog (1981) blames Stewart's widow, Clara Stewart Flagg, for placing an embargo on the thesis. This is confirmed by Domhoff's 2003 report (http://www2. ucsc.edu/dreams/Library/senoi3.html) that she threatened to sue him if he should ever obtain a copy of the thesis! It is therefore unsurprising that no specific references to Stewart's thesis appear either in his own or others' publications dealing with Senoi Dreamwork. The few dreams that I did collect, almost entirely from children (Appendix 4), certainly fitted into the patterns that Stewart, with his 312 dreams (1947: 452–496), recorded much more extensively than I. In my opinion, though, there is nothing out of the ordinary about these, apart from some evidence of growing 'maturity' in the dreams of older people (this is hardly surprising[14]) and, as he said, events involving the dreamer's dying in the dream.

However, as already suggested, the dreams must have been collected by Noone rather than Stewart. Indeed, in the Acknowledgments to his thesis, Stewart thanked 'the late Mr. H. D. Noone whose years of intensive work with the Senoi and thorough knowledge of their language and culture made the present study possible'. The dreams were gathered from named individuals in six different settlements in Perak, Kelantan and Pahang, all of which I too have visited at various times. Stewart himself worked mainly at Jalong in Perak (where the photograph of him and Noone, figure 2.4, was taken), but he did briefly visit some of the other sites. The sites from which the dreams were collected are known to have been visited by Noone, for they

---

13. Alex Randall (2010) therefore assumes too much in claiming that my fieldwork data supported Stewart's dream-control idea. I merely refrained from questioning it in my thesis, which Randall doesn't cite.

14. Domhoff (2005–06), citing some important empirical evidence, states 'If we can trust laboratory studies, and I think we can, dreaming is not adult-like until ages 9–10 and not comparable to adult dreams in frequency, length, content, or emotions until ages 11–13.'

are all described in his 1936 account. In one of these settlements, Rening in Pahang, I talked to people in 1965 who remembered Noone well, and who could even imitate the diphthongising English accent with which he had spoken Temiar 25 years earlier.

The need for third-party translation between Temiar and English was not the only obstacle to Stewart's access to the dreams *as dreamt*. Domhoff (2003: Chapter 3), who has researched Stewart's life-history very closely, is critical of the manner in which the dreams were collected and of Stewart's failure to confront the methodological issues in his thesis:

> The Senoi dreams were collected in different ways from different age groups. Children's dreams were collected by asking parents what their children had dreamed about, which is in fact a totally worthless method. The dreams of teenagers and young adults were collected by asking them to report recent dreams. In the case of the older men, still another procedure was used. They were asked to recall all those dreams that they believed to be significant in bringing them to the status of adept or shaman. This is an invitation to storytelling and fabrication.

Stewart's dream reports are the main basis for the comments on his work in my own thesis (Chapter 6, below). In an early and unpublished autobiographical account of his travels, Stewart (Ms) states that he sometimes employed hypnosis to put research subjects into a light trance—a skill that even Edmund Leach vouched for (Domhoff 2003: Chapter 3). Stewart reports that when he did this with some Temiar spirit-mediums they immediately called up their spirit-guides (Stewart: 506–508). I suspect, therefore, that some of the Temiar dreams he collected in Jalong might have been gathered from hypnotised subjects and then dictated to Parsons for typing.[15] To the extent that Stewart employed hypnosis, two points would be significant. First, on Leach's evidence, Stewart was able to carry out hypnosis even through a chain of interpreters. Second, recounting a 'dream' that one is supposedly experiencing while in hypnotic trance is probably functionally equivalent and physiologically identical to the lucid-dream or waking-dream states. (A lucid dream is regarded as one in which the dreamer is consciously aware that it is a dream (LaBerge 1985).) This might seem to lend greater plausibility to Stewart's later idea of dream control, except that it would certainly not be 'dreaming'

---

15. On stylistic grounds, it must be assumed that the well balanced, concise sentences reporting the Temiar dreams in Stewart's thesis were also due to Parsons's editing as she typed, for she was an accomplished writer. The style differs considerably from the sometimes rambling character of the rest of the text, itself typed out from dictation by Clara Marcus, who later became Stewart's wife. Domhoff (2003: Chapter 3) states explicitly that Parsons not only typed the dream accounts but kept the carbon copies that ensured their survival. I suspect that the dark object on the left of figure 2.4 is the typewriter she was using. There is no mention of Parsons in Stewart's thesis, however.

as commonly understood. It would also not correspond to the views of some sleep physiologists, one of whom (Quadens 1990: 81–92) recorded the brain activity of Temiars while they slept, both in their home settlement and again at a hospital in Kuala Lumpur.

Stewart's claim that Temiar dream 'maturation' was under their deliberate control first appeared in his 1951 article, 'Dream theory in Malaya'. The Senoi Dreamwork therapeutic movement did not get under way, however, until the reprinting in the 1960s of this and other somewhat messianic papers (Stewart 1953, 1954, 1962). These included the obscurely published papers that Leach had lent me, and which Stewart himself had sent him. (None of Stewart's papers appeared in scholarly journals, peer-reviewed or otherwise, with the very marginal exception of the two he published in *Mental Hygiene*.) As Domhoff (2003: Chapter 3) points out, the distinctive character ascribed to Temiar dreams by Stewart in these publications differs considerably from what he reported in his thesis. Nevertheless, this material led to a flowering of Senoi Dreamwork groups in the United States and elsewhere. By then, the Temiars of popular imagination outside Malaysia had become mythologised, while researchers working directly with the Temiars in Malaysia found themselves dealing with a quite different reality.[16] Spurred mainly by Robert Dentan's widely read and very different account (1968a/1979) of how the Semais (the Temiars' southern neighbours) maintain their non-violent approach to communal life, the supposed 'Senoi' psychotherapy, now long out of the hands of Stewart himself, was brought into direct confrontation with actual Senoi (that is, Temiar and Semai) ethnography. Unfortunately, its proponents continue to ignore the first-hand material that now exists on the real 'Senoi' people, whom they still characterise (wrongly, in all three of the following regards) as a previously uncontacted, hunter-gatherer population, whose culture was changed beyond recognition by the Second World War.

The best known advocacy for 'Senoi Dreamwork' is contained in Garfield (1995, first edition 1974). An accessible brief account in 'coffee-table book' format can be found on page 11 of Coxhead & Hiller (1976). There are many other articles on the topic in a variety of magazines and specialist newsletters, but they add nothing useful to our understanding of the Temiar situation in the 1930s or since. The main research-based critical sources are Lindskoog (1981, 1993: 203–205), Dentan (1983), Faraday & Wren-Lewis (1984), Domhoff (1985, 2003), Quadens (1990: 71–94), and Hickson & Jennings (2014). (I have a file of correspondence from several of these critics, but I refer here only to their published contributions.) Dentan presents a detailed analysis of what, in his view, is really going on when Temiars and Semais

---

16. Evans-Pritchard's comment (1965: 67) on the avoidable errors of the *Année Sociologique* school would also apply to the Senoi Dreamwork movement: 'One sometimes sighs—if only Tylor, Marett, Durkheim, and all the rest of them could have spent a few weeks among the peoples about whom they so freely wrote!'

pay attention to their dreams.[17] Domhoff presents a sociological analysis and psychological critique of the rise of 'Senoi Dreamwork' in the United States.[18] Faraday & Wren-Lewis recount their failure to find evidence for dream control despite several months of interviewing Temiars, including some of Stewart's surviving 'subjects'. Quadens, in addition to her professional interest in dreaming and brain function, emphasises the historical, environmental and social factors in explaining the varying degrees of Temiar peaceability, which she regards as having been overstated. Similarly, Hickson & Jennings report on their failure to find supporting evidence for dream control during their extended period of Temiar-speaking residence in the community, and are critical of the use that has been made of the idea. Two German studies, Strunz (1985) and Bräunlein (2000), discuss the issues from wider theoretical (including sociological) perspectives.

An informative part-documentary, part-fantasy video on the topic (Halonen & Wellman 1998) incorporates materials filmed among the Temiars in the late 1990s (as well as a cameo appearance by me). It includes shots of Temiars performing mediumistic ceremonies and talking (mostly in Temiar, subtitled) about their religion. It also has shots of an English-speaking Temiar—ʔawis, the reputed founder of the ʔalɥj Sǝlamad religion that emerged later (see Chapter 14)—replying to a direct question by agreeing that Temiars can indeed 'control' their dreams. In my view, this involved a semantic confusion, calqued perhaps on the Malay word *kawal* 'to guard, police, watch over'. In other words, I suspect that he meant that dreams are *monitored* rather than actively controlled.

These persistent misrepresentations would be avoided, therefore, if the Dreamwork movement simply ceased to employ the epithet 'Senoi', thereby releasing the Temiars from the false image that has been attached to them for so long.

Post-War studies of Temiar religion

Post-War field research on Temiar culture began with Iskandar Carey, an anthropologist and former student of Edmund Leach, who headed the JHEOA in the 1960s. His accounts of the Temiars (Carey 1961 and parts of Carey 1976) concentrated on their social organisation and language, but also incorporated a few details on Temiar religion. I first entered the field in 1964–65, in pursuit of my doctoral research, working initially in the same area that Carey had studied, and with Carey himself as my local

---

17. For Dentan's own views of Semai religion presented without reference to 'Senoi dreamwork', see Dentan (2002).

18. Domhoff's own detailed studies of dreaming as a research psychologist can be accessed from his *Dream Research Library* at http://www2.ucsc.edu/dreams/Library/index.html. These make no further reference to 'Senoi Dreamwork' (except for his book-length treatment of the topic, which is also available there), but they provide valuable background reading for those who might wish to assess its claims.

field supervisor. My published accounts of Temiar social organisation, ethnohistory, religion and language (listed in the Bibliography) are based on that intensive fieldwork and on follow-up visits in the late 1960s and the 1970s. These were supplemented after a long gap by a brief visit in 1994, and by several further visits from 2006 onwards.

Succeeding my own earlier Temiar work are the important studies of Sue Jennings (1995) and Marina Roseman (1991), based on their doctoral research in the 1970s and 1980s, in the same part of Temiar country that Carey and I had worked in, and where they continue to carry out fieldwork. Their intensive but independent research into Temiar life approached the materials from perspectives not considered in the earlier studies. Jennings paid close attention to the ways in which Temiar cultural conceptions are literally embodied in their physical movements and other bodily preoccupations. Roseman covered similar ethnographic ground, especially with regard to religious matters, but with an emphasis on how the Temiars express their view of the world in music and in their aural responses to the sounds around them. Both studies present rich material on Temiar mediumship and related matters, and I refer to them frequently in the following chapters.

We thus now possess substantial information on Temiar religion. The time has come to subject it to some sociological analysis.

Temiar Religion as it was

The relation between Western 'Senoi Dreamwork' and the practices of the Malaysian Orang Asli has turned out to be spurious, but this revelation has left undisclosed the reasons for the high regard in which dreams and trance states are held by the Senoi peoples themselves. To the extent that the Temiars' propensity for dream-based activities has anything to do with their reasonably good mental health, it results not from any formalised psychotherapeutic counselling techniques that they are reputed to have developed, but from the way in which their trancing and lucid 'dreaming' puts them in direct touch with what their cosmological notions lead them to think of as the fundamental basis of existence.[19]

Like everybody else, Temiars are forced to map less graspable notions onto a more familiar surrogate (cf. Harris 1980: 44–78). The Temiar mode of surrogation represents the cosmos, and the religious and social relations that occur within it, not in terms of things ('reocentrically') or words ('logocentrically'), but 'psychocentrically' in terms of the direct experience that individual human beings have of their own subjectivity. This

---

19. Mental illness does nevertheless occur among the Temiars, and there is no reason to think that it is a new phenomenon. See Dentan (1968b) for a discussion of how the neighbouring Semais regard mental illness.

psychocentrism is founded, moreover, on a dialectical orientation of attention as between SELF and OTHER. (Small caps are employed here to indicate that these are felt notions, not explicit concepts.) Unlike more familiar modes of orientation, in which either SELF or OTHER is suppressed as the explicit focus of attention, the dialectical mode takes as its starting point the very mutuality of SELF and OTHER. In Temiar culture, this dialectic serves as the tacit, pre-reflective notion out of which coherence is constructed: the Temiar self can be focused on and talked about not as an autonomous entity, but only in ways that also implicate other, and *vice versa*.

This construction derives its plausibility from individual Temiars' experience of their own subjectivity as being simultaneously a controlling actor and an undergoing patient. The closest they come to verbally articulating this central unspoken mystery is when talking of the various souls—communicable-with subjectivities—that are thought of as animating the people, animals, plants and other salient things that inhabit their world.

In human beings these souls are the *hup* 'heart(-soul)' and the *rəwaay* 'head-soul', the corporeal seats of doing (or willing) and of experiencing (or undergoing) respectively.[20] The same animistic imagery extends throughout the rest of creation: any entity that appears capable of attracting to itself the attention of a human being is thought of as being able to do so by virtue of the simultaneously *hup-* and *rəwaay*-like subjectivity that constitutes its essential core. The same holds, in reverse, for the supposed ability of non-human entities to become aware of and to act upon the subjectivity of individual human beings.[21]

This dialectical relation of actor and patient, subject and object, colours all domains of the Temiar worldview. Ordinary social relations exhibit a complicated balance between extreme communalism and extreme individual autonomy, sustained by their dialectical mode of orientation. The cosmos itself is thought of as a subjectivity, linked somehow with thunder, the deity Karey. It is simultaneously both the creator and the world it creates, constantly employing the bootstrap cosmogonic power of its own thought and imagination to maintain the differentiated character of the physical world as the Temiars know it. If the actions of human beings or any other

20. The association of *hup* specifically with the anatomical heart is not as clear-cut as implied here; see Chapter 6 for a more detailed discussion. Both *hup* and *rəwaay* have impeccable Mon-Khmer etymologies that demonstrate their long-established religious roots in Mainland Southeast Asia. For the details as worked out by Gérard Diffloth see Benjamin (2012b: 209–212). Roseman's suggestion (2007: S62) that *rəwaay* is derived from Hebrew *ruaḥ* and its Arabic cognate *roḥ,* via Malay, is interesting semantically but linguistically unsustainable. Notwithstanding this correction, Temiar has indeed borrowed the Arabo-Malay word *roh*, but not as *rəwaay*. It occurs, with further morphological derivation, as *rəwah ~ ʔewɔh* 'to hold a feast [to entertain the spirits]', ultimately from the (Arabic) plural form *arwah* 'spirits'.
21. This animism-based approach to Temiar and other Malayan religions is explored in more detail in Chapters 10–12. The ethnographic details on which it is based are presented in Chapter 5, but in rather different terms. However, the emphasis placed here on 'soul' as a representation of communicable-with subjectivity was not fully worked out in that early account. The independent accounts by Jennings and Roseman present essentially the same picture, albeit with some differences of detail and emphasis.

Table 2.1 The Temiar animistic framework (Corrected from Benjamin 1979: 13)

	Upper-body	**Lower-body**
Humans, animals	*rəwaay* Mon-Khmer: 'soul', 'sing', 'tiger'	*hup* Temiar: 'heart', 'liver' (Mon-Khmer 'breath')
Plants	*kahyɛk* Temiar: 'mystical watery substance'	*kənoruk* Malay: *kurung* 'enclosed space'
Mountains	*pətərii²*, *poterii²* Malay: *puteri* 'princess'	*sarak* Malay: *sarang* 'nest', 'lair'
Spirit-guides	*cənɔɔy, gunig*	*gunig* Malay: *gundik* 'concubine', 'spirit-guide'
Appears as:	Young man, young woman	Tiger (or occasionally as *daŋgaa²* 'dragon')

agency should distract the cosmos's subjectivity away from this task, then it is thought likely that the world will de-differentiate, through the agency of thunder (Karey's voice) and flood, into a muddy undifferentiated chaos. If that should happen, all things would lose their identity, and disappear through the cosmic merging of subjectivity and objectivity. (See the discussions of *misik* in later sections.)

Plants and animals are thought to partake in this interplay just as fully as human beings. It is the temporarily disembodied upper- and lower-body souls of various mountains, animals and plants (seasonal fruit trees, especially) that become the personal spirit-guides to which Temiars direct their religious action. These spirits—disembodied souls—are called by various special names (table 2.1), but they are uniformly reported to take the same shape when they appear in dreams or trances: upper-body souls become young men or women, and lower-body souls become tigers.

Individuals enter into initial communication with their spirit-guides through dreams. They may then, if they choose, make their spirit-guide's power-for-good available to the rest of the community by serving as a *sɛn²ɔɔy bə-halaa²*—a person adept at spirit-mediumship, more usually referred to simply as a *halaa²*. In the strictest sense, however, *halaa²* refers to the spirit-guide rather than the medium, and *sɛn²ɔɔy bə-halaa²* therefore means 'person with a spirit-guide.'[22] Mediumship centres on night-time trance-dancing ceremonies involving one or more *halaa²*-mediums performing to the accompaniment of contrapuntally sung music (figures 2.5 and 2.7). Each song is passed on by its supposed composer (the spirit-guide) to its initial performer (the *halaa²*) in revelations that occur while the latter was in a lucid

---

22. See footnote 7 in Chapter 7 for further discussion of the semantics and etymology of *halaa²*.

Figure 2.5 A *halaaˀ* singer and chorus at a *gənabag*, Humid (Həmij), Kelantan (1964)
The singer is Salleh (Saleh), accompanied by his wife and wife's sister [now all deceased]. At the time, Salleh was referred to by some as 'the P. Ramlee of the Perolak valley'. Although he had not been very active as a medium, the high quality of his singing had always been appreciated. Note the baby slung on the back of the woman at the right: this is a typical example of how Temiars just grow into their religion, without need for special introductions or explanations.

or waking dream, most typically around dawn. The *halaaˀ* will often be called upon to perform healing rituals on the sick during the ceremonies, but also in non-ceremonial circumstances during the daytime. (See Chapters 7 and 10 for detailed accounts of Temiar mediumship.)

Trancing and lucid dreaming are forms of subjectively meaningful role-playing—sometimes regarded as 'altered states of consciousness'—in which one becomes simultaneously one's own subject and object, since one is then *undergoing* whatever one is *doing*. In Temiar terms, these are activities in which one's *rəwaay* is experiencing what one's *hup* is simultaneously willing into existence. Trance, for example, is talked of as 'forgetting one's *hup*'; but the trancer still retains his or her own *rəwaay*, or there would be no means of *experiencing* the trance. Lucid dreaming, on the other hand, requires one to retain one's *hup*, as the locus of one's active participation in whatever is going on in the dream, which is thought of in turn as being located in one's *rəwaay*'s experience. Thus, the *rəwaay* ~ *hup* dialectic is founded on the trance- and lucid-dream-experience of being simultaneously the undergoing object and the agentive subject of one's own imagination, thought of as autonomous real-world entities. By giving themselves over to trance and lucid-dreaming, Temiars are thus able to experience directly the self-same subjective processes that the cosmos itself is thought to employ in keeping itself going. (See the accounts of Temiar cosmogony in Chapter 4.) But that experience is ineffable in character, being formed of notions, not concepts. It involves the dreamer or trancer in a symbolic condensation that fuses mind, body, social relations and the world onto a dialectically self-transforming, indescribable (and hence unspoken) unity. Relatively few Temiars become specialists in these activities, but virtually all seek to enter into trance and lucid dreaming on occasion. They thus disguise the surrogational character of their psychocentrically constructed cosmos by fusing it with what for them is the 'really real', namely the direct experience of seeming to control and being controlled by the creatures of their own imagination. In this way, they provide themselves with an authentically unmediated experience of the very state-of-mind that supposedly holds everything together on both the cosmic and mundane levels.

The ceremonial centrepiece of Temiar religious life consists of public spirit-mediumship performances performed at night within the house and involving choral singing, dance and trance, as described in detail in Chapters 7 and 10. (These performances continue today even in households that have adopted the other religions discussed in Chapters 13 and 14.) However, trance is not always present. Performances are put on when there is a demand for mediumistic healing rituals, or when someone's spirit-guide has indicated in a dream that it wishes to be entertained, or simply for amusement. (See figures 2.5 and 2.7: the first photograph was taken at an amusement session without mediumship, the second at a mediumistic session.) The sessions are known as *gənabag* 'singsongs'. Most of the community is involved, with the women and children repeating the lead verses sung by one or more mediums, usually in overlapping canon. (See Roseman (1984, 2002) for accounts of this musical structure, and Jennings (1985, 1995) for the associated dance techniques.) The song lyrics are thought of as the spirit-guide's own, sung *through*—not by—the medium. A much rarer kind of performance involves tiger-mediumship, performed by a medium squatting within a special palm-leaf hut set up inside the house. This is performed only by a so-called 'big' *halaaʔ*, without dancing, with the fires extinguished, and with distinctively minor-key melodies. (An example of such a song can be heard on track 17 of Roseman (1995).)

Figure 2.6 The same singer (Salɛh) in 2006
*Salleh died in 2010, by which time he had become a more important
medium and a great-grandfather.*

Figure 2.7 Chorus of children and young women at a Səlumbaŋ séance, Jak, Kelantan (1965)
*This photograph was taken in Jak village, high in the headwaters of the Perolak valley. This was the home of
Penghulu Hitam Tamboh (Tambɔɔh) (figure 7.1), mentioned several times in this volume. The young woman
in the middle was his daughter.*

Other rituals are performed more casually and on a small scale, and
are typically 'magical' in character. These include the pouring of warmed
('enculturated') water over a newly delivered woman or into the post-
holes of a new house, and the special treatment accorded to some specially
selected rice grains at the beginning of the planting season. There are also
what might called anti-rituals—an open-ended collection of rather oddly
characterised acts (*misik*, *joluŋ*, etc.) that must be avoided if the thunder
deity is not to strike.

Figure 2.8 Mediumistic treatment at a séance, Lambok, Kelantan (1979)
This was a mourning-cessation séance. The ceremony was also held to celebrate the cure of a child who had suffered rɛywaay 'head-soul-loss'.

Temiar ideas about disease also reflect their broader cosmic and animistic conceptions. For example, disease is often ascribed to the improper interpenetration of domains or spiritual agencies that should remain separate. This can occur between spatial domains or through soul-loss and spirit-invasion. The attendant symptoms do not always fit tidily into a biomedical framework of analysis, though they are certainly often real enough. (See Chapters 6 and 11.) Treatment includes herbal and mineral remedies ingested or rubbed on the body, shaded segregation within the house, casual laying on of hands by anyone with *halaa'* powers, or full ceremonial mediumship performed in trance by several *halaa'* acting together. (See Chapter 7.) The spiritual treatment offered by the *halaa'* (figure 2.8) must be judged as often successful in psychiatric terms: certainly, Temiars express themselves uneasy at the thought of falling ill with no *halaa'* to help them. Jennings's and Roseman's studies have gone a long way toward explaining the therapeutic efficacy of Temiar mediumship, a topic I take up again briefly in Chapter 10.

The séance shown in figure 2.8 occurred during the cessation-of-mourning (*tərɛnpʉk tɛnmɔɔh*) celebrations some weeks after the death of a villager at Lambok (Lamug). The medium at the right is transferring (*pɛrlʉb*) the essence (*kahyɛk*) of his spirit-guide (*gunig*) to another man, a member of the deceased's family. Note that the medium's hands are placed on the mourner's head and chest—respectively the sites of the latter's head-soul (*rəwaay*) and heart-soul (*hup*). The leafy wreaths hanging from the rafters serve as the places of welcome (*tənamuu'*) for the visiting spirit-guides. Note also the generally vegetal character of the ceremonial dress. As discussed further in Chapter 10, I take this to be an unspoken acknowledgement by the Temiars that, while *they* see their spirits in essentially human terms, they nevertheless expect their mostly plant-derived spirits to see *them* in essentially plant-like terms. Thus, their dialecticism requires them, in effect, to look like trees when they welcome the spirit-guides into the human domain.

Such then, in broad outline, is the content of indigenous Temiar Religion, which continues to be practised alongside the various new forms of religion discussed later. But in the new circumstances of Temiar life, this seemingly complicated way of approaching the world poses a problem. Unlike the easily expressible ideas of the various monotheistic religions, the traditional Temiar conception is far too complicated to be put into words and talked about explicitly. Its worldview is therefore hard to share with others and far from easy to maintain in one's own mind. Many Temiars, especially the younger ones who have been to school, have responded to this situation by taking up more easily catechised and apparently 'rational' religions: Baha'i (Chapter 13), Islam, Christianity, and—not quite so 'rational', because unwritten—the new Temiar religion called ʔalʉj Səlamad (Chapter 14).

Most of these issues are taken up again in the following chapters, though not always within the framework just presented. As already explained, my doctoral thesis (Chapters 3–8) in particular was written long before I had come to these newer understandings. But the ethnographic details it contains still constitute an historically and ethnographically relevant account of Temiar life.

| Chapter | *Temiar Religion (1967)—* |
| 3 | Preface and Introduction |

The material contained in this dissertation was gathered in Malaya between April 1964 and August 1965. The visit was made possible financially by substantial awards from the Horniman Anthropological Scholarship Fund and the Esperanza Trust of the Royal Anthropological Institute. The work was continued with the help of a Studentship and further funds from the Ministry of Education and Science, London.

The number of people to whom I owe a debt of gratitude is high. A full acknowledgment will be found in my paper 'Temiar social groupings' (Benjamin 1966: 2–3). But I would like to repeat here my special thanks to my Supervisor, Dr Edmund Leach, who from the beginning has encouraged me in all possible ways. He spared no effort to smoothen practical difficulties (and there were many), and his detailed discussion of my work as it slowly took shape has been of the highest value.

Since returning from Malaya, I have been in contact with colleagues in Cambridge who have been carrying out similar work elsewhere. The weekly research seminars for social anthropologists held under the guidance of Professor Meyer Fortes have provided opportunities for the exchange of ideas, without which it would have proved impossible to proceed with my work on the Temiars. I apologise in advance if the ideas of any of my colleagues should appear here in distorted form; the responsibility and blame are entirely mine.

The field research itself is in no way complete. The present account of a selected aspect of Temiar culture suffers from at least two unavoidable defects. It was possible to visit only about one sixth of the Temiar population and most of the work was done in the three most southeasterly valleys in which they live: the Telom (Tələp) in Pahang state, and the Brok (Bərɔk) and Perolak (Pɛrlɔɔb) valleys in Kelantan state. My longest stay was in the village of Humid (Həmij), at the bottom end of the Perolak (see figures 3.1 and 3.2). This village became in many ways my home, where I was accepted into the kinship system and expected to behave accordingly. However, since Temiar villages are so small (Humid contained no more than 35 people of all ages), it proved necessary to travel around as far as possible in an attempt to encompass the quite large variations in Temiar culture. In this way, I spent extended periods in the villages of Mengrod (Mɛnrɔɔd) on the Brok river,

41

Figure 3.1 Aerial photo of Humid village, Kelantan, looking north-west (1964)
This settlement and the surrounding forest no longer exist, having been replaced by an extensive oil-palm estate (as shown in figure 14.2). The white patch was the helicopter landing zone for the flying doctor service. The lighter-coloured patches of vegetation are the then-current and recent swiddens. The mountains in the distance are the Titiwangsa range between Kelantan and Perak. No other village is visible in this photograph.

Kuala Blatop (Bəlatəp, 'Fort Brooke'), and Kuala Rening (Rɛŋnɛɛŋ, Rəŋnɛɛŋ) in the Semai-surrounded Telom valley.

Much in Temiar culture depends on personal revelation, so the more detailed parts of this study derive from a relatively limited area and number of sources, most of which are identified. Nevertheless, I discussed matters with many other people, from children to old men and women. In addition, living right in the centre of things, I was able to observe most of what went on: much of what follows is based on questioning carried out on the spot immediately after observing something that I had not seen before. In extenuation, then, I can at least claim that the course of my research followed closely on the promptings of the Temiars themselves, rather than on any preconceived notions. My aim has been to present what the Temiars themselves find important in life.

Certain conventions have been followed in the writing. The basic problem is that of language. The major part of the fieldwork depended on a thorough speaking and listening knowledge of the Temiar language, which I spent the first few months in obtaining. Unfortunately, many of the key words are untranslatable in any satisfactory manner, and it has been necessary to use more Temiar words than the reader may comfortably absorb, especially as the phonemic script used here may be unfamiliar. I have tried to keep Temiar words to a minimum, but I apologise for those occasions where it has proved impossible to avoid them. The second problem is also a linguistic one. The content of Temiar religion is rich in natural species, and to get on well with the people it is necessary to know the names of many plants and animals. Now, although the flora and fauna of Malaya are probably the richest in the world, there is an astonishing lack of published field identification guides. Consequently, nearly all identifications made here are to be treated sceptically. I was able to identify few plants, but I fared rather better with animals. Of the greatest value was a visit I managed to make to the museums at Taiping and Kuala Lumpur, taking with me three Temiar experts to identify animals from mounted specimens. Nevertheless, the standard caution still holds: in the absence of any detailed ethnoscientific investigation into Temiar biological taxonomy, any identification made here must be treated as no more than a label or gloss indicating merely a part of what the Temiar name indicates to a native speaker. The English vernacular names used in the text have been taken mainly from Corner (1940),[1] Glenister (1959), Harrison (1955), and Tweedie & Harrison (1954).

Some topics have been broached barely or not at all. Augury, for example, is a field that might well have been written up here, for it does in part relate to much else in Temiar religion. Mythology, too, might well have received fuller treatment. But I doubt whether the strain on space would have added anything to the overall understanding of Temiar religion that is the aim of this study to present. It is hoped that further fieldwork may serve to fill these and other gaps before a full account is prepared for publication.

Finally, although other writers have published work on Malayan Aboriginal religion (notably Schebesta and Evans), the data on which this dissertation is based and the way in which it is analysed are the result of work carried out solely by myself, except where otherwise indicated in the text. Even when the ideas and data of other workers have been used, the responsibility for the overall interpretation remains my own.

---

1. [Added 2014] Professor E. J. H. Corner, formerly Assistant Director of the Botanic Gardens in Singapore, had been a much appreciated lecturer when I was a biology student at Cambridge before switching to social anthropology. He gave me valuable practical advice before I sailed to Malaysia in early 1964, including the warning never to pass anything to anyone with my left hand once I had travelled east of Suez! On the basis of Corner's lectures, the Malayan forest turned out to be exactly as I had imagined it, apart from the incessant insect noise.

Introduction

The present study rises directly out of the difficulties that beset me in trying to understand Temiar ritual life. Explanations of religion that had been current in British social anthropology simply proved inadequate for the task. Failing to discern any meaningful relationship between my field data on Temiar religion and what I knew of their social structure, I was left floundering in incomprehension for the first year of my stay in the field. This went so far that in letters to my supervisor I began seriously to doubt whether the Temiars 'had' a religion, in any useful sense of the word.[2] A new approach had to be found if I was not to retire with a mass of completely undigested information. That new approach *was* found, I believe, in the writings of those who had obviously had to puzzle out problems similar to my own. The following pages bear witness to the success or failure of the results. But at the outset, readers are warned that they will find here little that is strictly sociological: this is a study of a *culture* rather than a society. The final pages contain no dramatic dénouement of a close one-to-one relationship between social structure and ritual, and this warning is aimed at relieving any disappointment on that account before it arises.[3]

The people

Although conventional enumerations (such as Holman (1958), frontispiece) rank the Temiars as the third largest group among the Malayan Aborigines, it is probable that they form in fact the largest self-avowedly uniform group, both culturally and linguistically. The other large groups, the Semais and the Jakuns, are much more heterogeneous and do not seem to maintain as much awareness of common culture. Furthermore, the Temiars occupy a central position among the groups to which they are most closely related, the Negrito (Semang) populations to the north and east, and the Semais to the south. The close similarity between the Temiars and these other groups has interesting consequences, some of which I examine later. Here, let me note that a great deal of what I say about the Temiars applies also to the Negritos and the Semais, as anyone who cares to refer to the published accounts may verify (Evans 1923; Schebesta 1954, 1957; Dentan 1964). The cultural interrelationships of the Temiars with the Lanoh, Jahai and Menriq Negritos are particularly close, so that there is a sense in which they may be said to 'have the same religion'. Traditional ethnological classifications have tended to disguise the essential unity of Malayan Aboriginal culture (I talk of the Senoi and Negrito groups, not the Aboriginal Malays). It is to be hoped that the evidence presented here will lend credence to Evans's remark (1923: 198) that 'several years' experience of the Malay Peninsula has served rather to

---

2. [Added 2014] The relevant parts of this letter are presented in Chapter 9.
3. [Added 2014] As noted earlier, the lack of a sociological understanding was repaired in the later essays reprinted as Chapters 11, 13 and 14 of this volume.

impress upon my mind the similarities in belief and custom which prevail among the pagan tribes, than to accentuate differences'.

I have described elsewhere the larger features of Temiar social organisation (Benjamin 1966),[4] but to set the scene it will be useful to give a short description of where and how the Temiars live. In many ways, the Temiars are typical of the Austroasiatic-speaking hill peoples of Southeast Asia, though preliminary glottochronological calculations suggest that the Senoi and Negritos have been separated from groups outside Malaya for at least 4,000 years.[5] They are pagans in an area where the religion of civilisation is Islam; they live by swidden agriculture, hunting and fishing, while the plains-dwellers live by wet rice cultivation; and they have no recorded history or writing, in a country where literary records extend back to the fourteenth century.

The Temiars, who numbered 9,722 souls at the census of 1965, inhabit an area of about 2,000 square miles.[6] This low population density means that they live in small (sometimes very small) villages, lying at some distance from each other (figures 3.1, 3.2 and 4.4). The average number of villagers is about 45, with a range from one dozen to about 150. In such a society, where kinship and relative age are used as the organising principles, relationships are bound to be of a classically 'face-to-face' type. Some of the consequences of this I have discussed in detail elsewhere (Benjamin 1967c, 1968a); the major point that emerged is that Temiar society is highly solidary (see especially Benjamin 1968a: 130–131). Although traditional ethnological classifications would make them out to be 'cultivators', the intensely communal ethos of Temiar society makes them far more reminiscent of the typical 'hunting' society organised in tight bands. Several writers have commented on the importance of a thorough-going system of social morality in such societies—see, for example, Linton (1936: 216–225) and Service (1966: 64–77). The local groups are so small that, without what Linton aptly refers to as 'esprit de corps', such interpersonal tensions might arise that they would fall open at the seams. In larger-scale societies, it is possible to avoid conflict simply by removing oneself from the scene. In Temiar society there is no room to hide, and one just has to learn the difficult task of preventing conflicts from arising in the first place.

---

4. [Added 2014] Further studies of Temiar social organisation include Benjamin (1967c, 1968a, 1968b). Of these, the first two, then in unpublished typescript, were also referred to in the doctoral thesis. References here are to their later published versions. All four studies will be reprinted, slightly revised, in my book *Temiar Society* (NUS Press, forthcoming).
5. [Added 2014] I can no longer recover the basis on which this statement was made. Nevertheless, it turns out to be reasonably close to current estimates that place the distinctive emergence of the Aslian sub-family of Austroasiatic languages at between 3,500 and 4,500 years ago (Benjamin 2013: 455, 458; Dunn, Kruspe & Burenhult 2013: 384).
6. [Added 2014] There has been a considerable population increase since the 1960s. Precise figures are hard to come by, and all published demographic data are therefore estimates. In 1999, there were estimated to be 17,706 Temiars. By 2008 the figure had risen to 24,908, according to a poster in the Orang Asli Museum at Ulu Gombak. At least some of this apparent increase must be due to inadequacies in the earlier counts, but there is no doubt that the Temiars have increased in number over the years.

This is not made any easier by the absence of formal mechanisms of social control. Charismatic leaders may proffer advice, but they have no means of enforcing their wishes on others.

Nor is much help to be gained from clearly stated principles of social organisation, for there are none strong enough to lead to the formation of all-embracing corporate groups. Corporate groups do exist—the cognatic 'ramages' discussed in my other papers (Benjamin 1966, 1967c, 1968b)—but these have conceptual rather than practical importance. The ramage estate is little more than symbolic, consisting of a few old seasonal fruit trees. Ramage membership is in any case overlapping. The function of ramage ideology for the Temiars is not so much to provide guidance in everyday life as to provide a definition for the 'village' in a society that shifts its

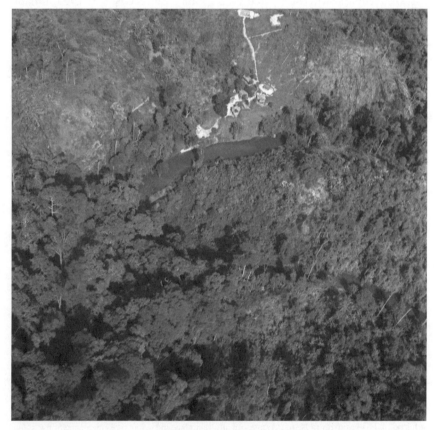

Figure 3.2 Vertical aerial view of Humid village (1964), south-west at top
The rectangular white area at the top is the helicopter landing zone, situated on a small rise. The main village lies below. To its right is the medical hut, containing basic supplies for treating wounds, diarrhoea and malaria. The river forming a horizontal U-bend across the middle of the frame is the Perolak; the Humid river flows into it from the top left of the frame. Newly felled swiddens can be seen towards the top of the frame, left and right. Compare this with figure 14.2, the same location greatly altered, as photographed by satellite in 2010.

habitations every two or three years. It is true that there is a lower-level group much more corporate in character than the ramage. But this group, the 'household' (Benjamin 1967c: 20–24), until recently had little material property to demonstrate as its own corporate property. The Temiars have been too poor in material goods for the question to arise. Even the crops that belong nominally to distinct households are in the final outcome distributed throughout the village and beyond, according to the rules of generalised exchange described in Chapter 8.

The problem that poses itself is this: what is the source and nature of the moral sentiments that bind the Temiars into a society? It would be false to claim that ecological and sociological factors play no part in the generation of Temiar social morality, but that part is limited. The physical facts of the environment dictate that in most areas, where soil fertility is low, villages shall be small and well spaced. The land simply will not support more when subsistence is based on swidden agriculture. Now, although physical facts in themselves do not constitute a moral system, we may safely assume that the Temiars are to some extent rationally aware of the need for cooperation in life and labour. Jungle cultivation is just too much for one person to handle unaided. Certain parts of the cycle, such as burning-off and harvesting, will fail without such cooperation, and other jobs too are made bearable by joint working.[7] In any case, given that communities are usually small, cooperation is essential to the task of simply living together, as we have just seen. Part of the moral order may result, then, from a rational decision that they must live for each other. But no social system can survive for long on the sole basis of so bald a social contract. Besides, much else is involved.

People can continue to live together socially only to the extent that they have a reasonable expectation of what the people around them will do in any given circumstance. Such expectations presuppose a common set of understandings—'culture'—in terms of which people may share in each other's activities. I shall shortly develop this argument into a more general statement, but here let me note that a straightforward way of indicating social expectations is by instituting some sort of readily assimilable model of social structure. Such a simple model of social structure is indeed to be found within Temiar culture, and I have described (Benjamin 1967c, 1968a) how this model is embedded within the kinship nomenclatural and personal naming systems in the form of tightly structured cultural paradigms (to borrow a phrase from Geertz & Geertz 1964).[8] However, even paradigms of this sort, built out of the fabric of everyday life, are in the final analysis no better than pictures, means of making experience more meaningful. They do not in themselves constitute instructions for how to behave. They serve only to reduce the mortifying

---

7. [Added 2014] For an account of Temiar swiddening as practised in Kelantan shortly before the time of my fieldwork, see Cole (1959).
8. [Added 2014] On the kinship terminology, see also Benjamin (1999).

influence on behaviour of the state of not-knowing, when the world appears too randomly constituted for the mind to grasp.

Ultimately, a social system functions because the individuals that make it up are somehow provided with instructions as to how they should behave. We have just seen that in Temiar society the 'structure' that resides in the restraints of ecology and in the two major paradigmatic statements of social structure falls far short of performing this task, providing only the barest minimum of guidance for individual social behaviour. We are forced to look further for the source of these guiding moral sentiments. It is my contention that this will be found deeply embedded in what I have chosen to call 'Temiar religion'. Accordingly, the major part of this study is devoted to a detailed examination of the ideas and practices that constitute Temiar religion, along with an attempt to show how they come to provide a highly efficient guide to social action. First, my theoretical standpoint must be made explicit.[9]

Religion and morality

It has been customary among social anthropologists to look upon 'morals' as the constraints to behaviour exerted upon individuals by the social system that envelops them. For British scholars especially, this approach is associated with the tradition that has grown up around Radcliffe-Brown's interpretation of the writings of Émile Durkheim. The unstated premise seems to be that unless they are so constrained, people would somehow go on 'behaving' in an unordered, completely random way that would preclude the formation or continued existence of society. This approach has proved to be fruitful, and many penetrating studies of exotic religious systems have been published under its influence (not least Radcliffe-Brown's own study of Andamanese religion). Yet, a glance through anthropological journals of the past few years will show that the whole question of religion has come up for searching re-examination, and with it the question of the nature of morality. It would be out of place to review this literature here (see, for example, Horton (1960), Goody (1961), Geertz (1966), Spiro (1966)). Its preoccupation with the *definition* of religion is, in any case, not centrally relevant to my argument. Nevertheless, it is worth noting that this busy re-examination of an old problem signals some dissatisfaction with accepted approaches. One of the points over which dissatisfaction has been expressed *is* directly relevant to my argument.

Recent work on human evolution has led some social anthropologists to think more carefully about the nature of 'culture'. (See, for example, Hallowell (1960).) What transpires is that culture is necessary not only for the

---

9. [Added 2014] As already noted in Chapter 2, this is not the theoretical stance I currently hold to in all respects. It is solely the attempt at theory that was presented in the thesis, reprinted here for 'historical' reasons. I no longer regard 'culture' as telling people how to behave. Rather, I see culture as requiring that individuals choose how to act in each particular circumstance. (Note the Weberian shift from 'behave' to 'act', as also indicated in the ideas of Dorothy Lee, discussed in the next section.)

emergence of society, but also for the emergence of human behaviour at all. Authors commonly posit the vegetable-like existence that would be the lot of a human being removed early from the influence of a cultural tradition, left to fend for itself like some feral animal. No one doubts that a feral animal would fare better. Assuming that it could survive physically, too great a mental leap is required for us to imagine what would be the life of a feral human baby left to its own devices. The reason is not hard to find: the baby's innate behaviour patterns would allow it to do little more than eat, sleep, excrete, and perhaps find shelter and food. It is obvious that relying entirely on its own internal resources the baby would never survive into adulthood. Clearly, for behaviour that is recognisably human to emerge at all, human beings must be presented with some sort of extrinsic instructions—they must be taught how to behave. Learning presupposes replicability of behaviour. Replicability, in turn, presupposes that the instructions are not totally random—which is another way of saying that any 'instructions' will be useless unless they are the expression of some deeper-lying structure. Recasting the argument into more conventional anthropological language, we are led to the proposition that human behaviour (and hence social behaviour) requires the presence of a structured cultural system.[10]

Note that having turned attention to the 'emergence' of behaviour, I am no longer talking of 'constraints' on behaviour. If at such a basic level of investigation we are concerned with the positive rather than negative forces (as yet undefined) that lead to individual behaviour, then how much more might we learn by examining in the same light the forces that lead to the less basic behaviour that we call 'social'. In other words, it might prove enlightening to regard morals not as negative constraining forces, but as positive forces that somehow draw social behaviour out of individuals. Of course, I am not suggesting that there are two kinds of morals, merely that a change of analytical perspective may lead us to a new understanding of how human society works. It is precisely this positive perspective that lies behind some of the more interesting of the recent discussions on religion and morality.

Dorothy Lee (1963) has argued eloquently that anthropologists may have been misusing the notion of 'constraint'. For her (as also in my present argument) constraint is a result of the absence of rules, if only we would see the problem from the actor's viewpoint. 'Freedom', on the other hand (and her paper appears significantly in a volume entitled *The Concept of Freedom in Anthropology*), consists in the availability of guiding rules for behaviour.

---

10. [Added 2014] I have let this section and equivalent ones elsewhere stand as in the original text, even though I no longer accept that 'cultures' or 'societies' are structured into 'systems'. I now see 'cultures' as essentially shapeless: any 'structure' they may seem to display would then be evidence of deliberate régime-like shaping rather than something that just emerges spontaneously. I have presented this revised approach explicitly elsewhere (Benjamin 1993: 349–350; 2005: 262–264; 2011a: 176).

In Lee's own words, 'the clarity of the structure in which I find myself—that is, the "social constraint"—not only frees me from the interference of others, but actually makes it possible for me to act; that is, it furnishes me with the conditions of freedom'.

It is but a short step from here to the much-used sociological term 'motivations'. Geertz has stated clearly that for him religion is ultimately concerned with motivations (1966)—with the generation of a 'motivational ambience' within which individuals may get on with the task of social living. This it achieves by synthesising a people's ethos and worldview in such a way as to make it all seem intellectually reasonable. The means employed are those of religious symbolism, and Geertz takes Langer's view that a symbol is 'any object, act, event, quality, or relation which serves as a vehicle for a conception; the conception is the symbol's "meaning"' (Geertz 1966: 5). This leads to Geertz's working definition that

> *a* religion is a system of symbols which acts to establish powerful, pervasive, and long-lasting moods and motivations in men by formulating conceptions of a general order of existence and clothing these conceptions with such an aura of factuality that the moods and motivations seen uniquely realistic.

This is the approach to religion that will be followed in the succeeding pages of this thesis. As a definition, it may fail to satisfy those who would wish to see the field of religion delimited in terms of some specific sort of content.[11] But to attempt a delimitation of the Temiar religious field in that way would be both irrelevant to the problem I have set out to discuss and well nigh impossible to carry out. What is important is that there is a field of activity within Temiar culture that, though hardly separable from the rest of the culture, does seem to hold together sufficiently to provide a valid subject for investigation, while corresponding well with what any unbiased observer would intuitively regard as 'religion'. I shall, it is true, be discussing such classically 'religious' concepts as deities, souls, mediumship, and so on. But I also examine ways of behaving that at first sight have nothing of the 'religious' about them, which are nevertheless so closely interrelated with the more explicitly religious activities that to ignore them would be both arbitrary and stultifying. Geertz's approach, it seems to me, allows us to proceed fruitfully within the framework of a formalised definition, even though that definition gives no guidance as to what we should expect to find. This lack of specific

---

11. [Added 2014] In an important paper written many years later, the sociologists Wallis & Bruce (1995) reaffirmed a preference for a 'substantive' content-based approach to religion, concentrating on supernaturalism as the defining feature. However, I still feel that the 'functional' (not functional*ist*!), 'what-it-*does*', approach that Wallis & Bruce reject is a better starting-point for the kind of exploratory research that anthropologists are likely to be engaged in, especially as the substantive approach leads to the problems concerning 'belief' that were discussed in the previous chapter.

direction is more of an advantage than otherwise, for it draws our attention not to the rather boring problem of what religion is, but to the much more vital and challenging question of what it *does*—and how it does it. As Geertz himself says (1966: 4), 'the notion that religion tunes human actions to an envisaged cosmic order and projects images of cosmic order onto the plane of human experience is hardly novel. But it is hardly investigated either, so that we have very little idea of how, in empirical terms, this particular miracle is accomplished.' The present study aims to show how, in one closely examined case, the miracle is achieved.

The reader should not assume that any iconoclasm was intended in the earlier remarks about Durkheim and Radcliffe-Brown, for the approach outlined here is not really so novel: it was implied long ago in the works of those very writers. Both Durkheim and Radcliffe-Brown showed a curious indecision as to whether their studies on religion should concentrate on what people do or on what they believe. Durkheim's magnum opus on the subject (1912) treats ostensibly of religious behaviour, but, as Worsley (1956) has shown, it is infused with a not very clearly stated concern for the epistemological aspects of the societies he discusses. Radcliffe-Brown was largely responsible for introducing Durkheim's ideas into British anthropology, but he presented a rather one-sided account of the latter's views. His famous paper on religion (Radcliffe-Brown 1945) bluntly states his opinion that religions consist primarily of ritual acts, through the performing of which the members of the society come to be imbued with a deep sense of solidarity. Yet, neither Durkheim nor Radcliffe-Brown stuck consistently to such a view of religion. In writings still not as well known (in Britain) as they deserve to be, both authors showed great concern for the role of ideology in society. The differences in approach exhibited by Radcliffe-Brown's two papers on the problem of totemism (1929, 1951) are at first sight very striking. The early paper has been caricaturised as a view of totems as 'good to eat', the latter as the view that they are 'good to think'. Durkheim's earlier papers put forward very clearly the view that society is in essence a system of shared ideas (especially Durkheim 1953 [1898]).

In view of the approach that was outlined a few pages ago, none of this apparent inconsistency should now worry us. 'Morals' and 'epistemology' are to a great extent the two sides of the same coin. Durkheim and Radcliffe-Brown were not really inconsistent: they failed merely to make their thoughts completely explicit.

Earlier, I warned against assuming that one can best explain religion as a reflection of social structure, although this has been the accepted view of most social anthropologists. It is surprising that many of those who hold such views do so in the name of Durkheim. But once we accept that human beings behave in the first place in response to ideas, these views become less tenable, and it was Durkheim himself who pointed this out most forcibly. Discussing the nature of collective representations as a system of ideas, he says

> once a basic number of representations has been thus created, they become ... partially autonomous realities with their own way of life. They have the power to attract and repel each other and to form among themselves various syntheses, which are determined by their natural affinities and not by the condition of their matrix. As a consequence, the new representations born of these syntheses have the same nature; they are immediately caused by other collective representations and not by this or that characteristic of the social structure. (Durkheim 1953: 31)

This is very different from the conventional accounts of what Durkheim said. I have quoted the passage because it states an important corollary of the approach to religion that I am following here. If what we are seeking as the prime exponent of religion is a certain type of structured idea system, then we must be prepared to recognise that religion will often show a considerable degree of autonomy from the rest of the culture. 'Structure' means that the constituent elements of the system are arranged in some determinate relation to each other. That they may also be arranged in a way that reflects the structuring of some other system (say, 'social structure') is a secondary and contingent circumstance.

If, then, we accord to a religion the status of an autonomous structured set of ideas, we are in effect saying that we cannot fully understand it until we have first grasped hold of it as a theology. The way is then clear for us to ask what functions, sociological or otherwise, are fulfilled by that theology; but our first duty is to understand the theology in terms of itself. It is surely significant that, among British anthropologists, these views have been put forward most forcibly by Evans-Pritchard, the only leading practitioner of the discipline to have published a truly sympathetic account (Evans-Pritchard 1965: 51–67) of what Durkheim was trying to say (though not necessarily in agreement with his views). Our present task accordingly is, first, to discover the nature of Temiar theology as an autonomous system and, second, to lay bare the miracle by which it becomes what Geertz calls a 'model for' action (1966: 7).

Temiar religion outlined

Having made explicit the sources of the ideas to be employed later in describing and explaining Temiar religion, it will help the reader to have a brief summary of what I have just said, arranged so that it also forms a preview of what is to follow.[12]

---

12. Ideas have also been taken, usually without further reference, from the following sources: Burridge

It is in people's nature that, because of their need to live in society and because as individuals their innate behavioural responses are extremely generalised (amounting to little more than a plastic potentiality for behaviour), they can take only the most elementary of actions unless they are provided with an extrinsic 'model for' action. Temiar society has a 'loose', informal structure with no strongly marked overall structural principles (such as lineage or alliance) that could serve as detailed guides to action. The local groups are very small and usually rather distant from neighbouring groups. Such a society can persist only if the tensions arising out of social interaction are contained by a strong moral ideology.

This moral ideology must, in the absence of a literate tradition and with only minimal contact with a Great Tradition, develop out of the fabric of everyday life. For the Temiars, every aspect of repeated everyday behaviour has an associated value deriving from its categorisation within the totemo-ritual-cosmological system. The detailed description of this system forms the body of this study. It takes the form of a pervasive conceptual calculus, a long chain of mutually implying category oppositions that in the final analysis (or 'interpretation') adds up to the opposition between good and evil.[13] In this study, without specific acknowledgement, I make use of the recent ideas of Claude Lévi-Strauss (1958, 1962a, 1962b), who has shown wherein lies the structure that pervades every human culture. This overall totemic system— 'totemic' in the sense of Lévi-Strauss (1962a)—is open-ended, and fed with new elements deriving from individual inspiration in dreams, sanctioned by mediumistic authority. In this way, virtually every 'species' in the environment may be drawn into the symbolic system—whether they be natural species, diseases, souls, outboard motors, and so on. Change in the environment can thus be contained and coped with in a constructive manner

The theology implicit (and occasionally explicit) in the system is that, if society is not to fall back from the state of culture into that of nature (in the Rousseau-an sense, as revitalised by Lévi-Strauss), it is up to its members individually and collectively to ensure through their behaviour that the correct balance is maintained between the principles of good and evil that coexist in all things. (For a rather different formulation, see Chapter 8.)

Everyday behaviour thus generates the necessary motivational ambience for the society to function in a situation where otherwise only a few vague

(1967); Douglas (1966, 1967); Fortes (1966); Leach (1954, 1964, 1967); Worsley (1967). These ideas have become so homogenised in the writing of this dissertation that I now find it hard to point unambiguously to the source of each one. [Added 2014] This outdated section is included solely for 'historical reprint' purposes and to provide continuity with the following few chapters. My very different current views were outlined in Chapter 2, and are taken up again from Chapter 10 onwards.
13. [Added 2014] Howell (1984: 218), in what amounts to a partial review of this study, asserted that this claim is inadmissible. Since the present volume is largely an 'historical' reprint, I shall not attempt here to justify this conceptualisation, which was originally made privately by Edmund Leach (as shown in Chapter 9) and also, in my view, reasonably well supported ethnographically in Chapter 8, the concluding chapter of the thesis. In any case, as the later chapters of this volume make clear, I nowadays deal with these materials in a different way.

social-structural principles would guide social action. The 'model of' the society that I have described elsewhere (Benjamin 1966, 1967c, 1968a) arises, by a dialectical process, out of the social behaviour that the aforementioned motivational ambience allows to emerge.

The problem that faces us is the difficult one of trying to explain non-linear ('feedback') processes through the written word, the medium that is archetypically linear (McLuhan 1964). Indeed, natural language in any form is, unaided, inherently incapable of fully achieving this end. If I had the necessary skills, I would much prefer to recast this whole study into the sort of mathematical form favoured by experts in the study of cybernetics.[14] But the Temiars also have the same problem of reducing a complex system into a readily managed, pocket-sized, 'instant' form—and they have to do it without the (sometimes doubtful) advantages of writing. It was his appreciation of this problem that sent Lévi-Strauss off into his now epic search for *la pensée sauvage*, the coding of a vast amount of complex information into a form sufficiently concrete for individuals to carry around for themselves. Professor Meyer Fortes, after reading some of my earlier ethnographic notes, decided that the Temiars had a 'knapsack culture' that they can take with them in its totality at a moment's notice. We are about to peer into the darker corners of this knapsack and bring out into the light some of the valuables and some of the crumbs that lie within.

---

14. [Added 2014] At his *viva voce* examination of the thesis, Rodney Needham quite properly took exception to this misplaced and pretentious assertion. The only 'mathematical' analysis of any aspect of Temiar culture that I have ever produced, or would now wish to produce, is that of the kinship terminology (Benjamin 1999: 16–24), which took many years to check and re-check! I suspect that the current vogue for 'Complexity Theory' may be falling into the same trap. My view today is that the social sciences are dealing with open-ended history, not self-sustaining 'systems'—which is essentially what Max Weber was saying.

Temiar Religion (1967)—
The Cosmos

I commence this account of Temiar religion by examining the way in which the Temiars categorise the world around them. These categorisations are at two levels. In the first place, they idealise their world by describing it in terms of mythology and what might be called theological 'dogma'. In the second place, they talk about it in ordinary language while dealing with the problems of day-to-day existence. The two levels of description have, of course, much in common, and the one may safely be regarded as a projection of the other. I deal first with Temiar cosmological ideas.

Cosmology

I collected a number of separate accounts of Temiar cosmological ideas from individual informants. Each informant gave a rather different account, but since these questions are largely a matter of individual revelation (as we shall see later) this is hardly surprising. Although the stories are not mutually consistent in detail, the ideas that they express do fall in with the overall structure of Temiar religious beliefs.

Heaven and earth

The following account of the constitution of heaven and earth was given to me by Wakil ('Deputy Headman') Paɲah Pabaaɲ of Humid village (figure 4.1), referred to from here on simply as 'Wakil'.

The universe consists of the heavens or upper (*baliik*) world and the earth (*tɛʔ*) or lower world. Each is delimited by its own named firmament (*cɛntud*) of flat rock, said to be 'like a mat'. The upper world is limited by the layer known as Tɛrlaar (or Taŋlar), and the lower world rests on the layer Gənacəb. These two firmaments are connected by a continuous pillar of rock, the Batuuʔ Gərɛm, by which the upper world is supported on the lower.[1] (This is the

---

1. [Added 2014:] The prototypes for Batuuʔ Gərɛm are to be found in the limestone tors that abound in the northern parts of the Peninsula. Gua Janggut (figure 7.5) is one such, and is known to be an important ritual site for some of the Orang Asli populations of Kelantan, as described later. However, in 1970, Penghulu Cawan, a senior chief living far downstream from Humid, said that he thought Batuuʔ Gərɛm was in the Pergau valley, which would place it in Jahai and Menriq country; but he knew no more about it than that. If there is any truth in his statement, it would lend support to the view (which

Figure 4.1 Wakil ʔaŋah ʔabaaŋ and his wife ʔawããs (1964)

same as the *Batu H'rem* that Evans reports (1936: 185f) as being so highly developed a concept among the Negritos.) The rest of the universe is formed of a system of layers, lying between the two firmaments, and parallel to them (figure 4.2).

Immediately below Tɛrlaar in the upper world lies the layer Səwiik (or Raŋgɔw), the part of the skies where the light comes from; when dark at night it is known as Kɛgraag Bəlak (*bəlak* = 'dark'). Beneath Səwiik are two successive layers, Bɛrnɔɔŋ and Sɛrgaaʔ, which, together with Səwiik, form

I have long suspected) that the primary prototype for Batuuʔ Gərɛm is the spectacular limestone tower known as Gunung Reng at Batu Melintang in Jeli district. The Aslian word *gərɛm* and the Malay *reng* might possibly be related, though clearly not in any phonologically regular manner. (See also Chapter 7 and the descriptions of the Mojiiʔ and Bəlajur cults in Appendix 2.2.)

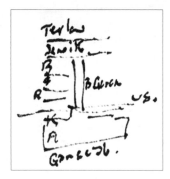

Figure 4.2   Sketch by Edmund
Leach in the margin of the earliest
draft of this section (1967)

the site of the sun, moon and stars. Below this is Rahuu?, the atmosphere, in
which are found the clouds and animate life.

The lower world is similarly structured. Immediately above its
firmament lies the layer ?ampal (or Buhmin). This is the continuous rock
that underlies the inhabited world, occasionally obtruding into it as outcrops
and mountains. Overlying Buhmin is the layer Kɛrlɛɛk, the soil proper, upon
which human life runs its course and within which the various underworld
demons live. The inhabited world—?ɛɛ?, 'we (inclusive)'—is regarded
as lying in between (*gagid*), abutting on both Rahuu? above and Kɛrlɛɛk
below. Few of these terms appear to be pure Mon-Khmer words. Buhmin is
obviously a loan from the Malay (ultimately Sanskrit) *bumi*, 'world, soil'.
Sɛrgaa? is the Hindu Swarga, the heaven of the gods; and Rahuu? is related
to the Hindu eclipse demon Rahu. Further investigation would probably
show a similar origin for the other non-Aslian terms. In view of the complex
history of the Malay Peninsula, with its long period of Indian influence, this
line of investigation should prove extremely interesting.

Temiars agree that these matters are understood much better by the
Negritos who live around them to the west, north and east. That they
believe this to be so is in itself structurally significant. The Menriq and
Batek Negritos to the east have an intimate knowledge of the nature
of the underworld, while the Kensiw and Jahai Negritos to the west
and north are more concerned with the upper world. The in-between
Temiars correspondingly have reduced knowledge of either. This
distinction is reflected especially in the forms of mediumship typical
of the various Aboriginal groups. (See Chapter 7 for a more detailed
discussion of this question.)

Outside the context of straight recitations of 'dogma' (such as the one
just recounted), I encountered few references to the notion that the cosmos
is divided into layers of heaven and earth. The improvised spirit-guide songs
sung at ceremonial séances do, however, contain references of this sort. These

songs are generally supposed to state poetically the thoughts and deeds of the spirit-guide as it makes its way to the welcome prepared for it. The words are the spirit-guide's own, expressed through the voice of its 'father', the medium (see Chapter 7).

Batuuʔ Gərɛm, the pillar that supports the heavens, appears in the songs of the Piah (Pəyaʔ) and Temengor (Tumŋɔɔʔ) valleys of Perak, where Negrito (Lanoh and Jahai) influence is strong. Səwiik, the second highest layer of the heavens, used to appear in the songs of Taaʔ ʔamaaw, once the great spirit-medium of the Perolak valley. He used the name when singing of his mountain-peak spirit-guides:

> *ʔim-lɔy kərum-Səwiik*   I shall arrive below Səwiik
> *Sɛŋwiik ba-leluuʔ*   passing beyond Səwiik

Bɛrnɔɔŋ, the next layer down, is sung by the medium ʔindan of Blau (Bəlaaw) village, Kelantan, also when calling down spirit-guides of the mountain peak type:

> *Bə-dampaʔ bəleɲɔw kərum-Bɛrnɔɔŋ*   Peering and catching sight of it
>   from below Bɛrnɔɔŋ
> *Tabeʔ jəleŋaay riɲcoŋ Galɛɛŋ*   I salute with bent neck the summit of
>   Gunong Ayam.

Penghulu Tuis (Təwis) of Lambok village, Kelantan, sings of ʔampal, the last layer of the lower world, when singing songs of the Səlumbaŋ type, which refer to an originally Malay earth-spirit:

> *ʔampal gɛlwal Jaŋrad*   From ʔampal to the whirls of the
>   Jaŋrad river
> *ʔim-lumpad təbaleʔ Lawɛɛd*   I shall jump to the eddies of the
>   Lawɛɛd.

The remaining layers were not known by my informants to be sung about in spirit-guide songs, but Tɛrlaar was mentioned as the layer along which the sun travels on its daily traverse. At sunset, it falls through a door and follows a night-time course 'on the other side'. The moon follows an opposite course, its course being reckoned as the locus of its successive appearances at sunset.

It is clear that these cosmological ideas are only vaguely held, for several alternative versions are to be found in the one village. The uncle of the man who gave the version quoted above recounted several inconsistent versions of the cosmic layers. In one of his accounts, for example, Səwiik was the layer where the clouds are and where the thunder deity, Karey, dwells. Above lies Bɛrnɔɔŋ, the 'blue' of the sky and the limit of human vision. The next layer is Sɛrgaaʔ, 'where our eyes do not reach', followed by a layer, Lamir, 'the far region about which we can say nothing', not mentioned by the younger informant. Finally, he regarded the outermost layer as ʔampar, presumably a transposition of ʔampal from the lower to the upper world.

Sun, moon and stars

Apart from close observation of the moon's phases for keeping account of the lunar calendar, the Temiars have no astronomical interest in the night sky. No stars are named nor are constellations recognised. Unlike some other forest peoples in the region (cf. Freeman 1955: 40, on the Ibans), the Temiars do not reckon the year as a celestial phenomenon. The lunar cycle, though, is of high importance to them and a matter of concern in everyday life. The details are too complex to describe here since they depend to an extent on where the investigator happens to be, but the effect of the lunar cycle is worth outlining.

The month is divided into periods when any form of work may be carried out and tabooed (*tɛnlaaʔ*) periods when it is forbidden to do any housebuilding or farming. In a normal month (starting from the new moon), the first day is tabooed. Then after a free period of about one week, there follows another tabooed period of (usually) six days. After a further free week, there is finally a tabooed period of about five days. During the tabooed periods, one is expected to go hunting or fishing. Working on the house or swidden at that time is thought likely to lead to scorpion- and snake-bites, or to crop failure.

The relationship between the sun, moon and stars is the subject of a myth that has also been recorded by other writers (for example, Schebesta 1957: 62–63).[2] This myth is quoted by Temiars as the rationale behind the lunar calendrical cycle.

> The Moon gave birth to her children, thousands and thousands of stars. She said to the Sun, 'How many children have you got?', and the sun gave birth to many. But the people on earth could not support the heat of the Sun's many children, and the trees all withered and dried up.
>
> Then the Moon pondered, and she decided to conceal her children. So the Sun asked her, 'Where are your children?'
>
> 'I swallowed them,' came the reply.
>
> At this, the Sun asked, 'Well, what shall I do with my children?'
>
> 'Swallow them just like I did.'
>
> And so the Sun swallowed up all her children. The Moon released her own children, saying, 'Oh, I played a trick on you—I didn't swallow them at all! I deceived you because your many children were too hot, and I pretended to swallow mine because I am a cold being.'

---

2. [Added 2014] Schebesta's account presents a Kintaq version of the myth, fully transcribed in the original language. A Semai version is briefly reported by Evans (1923: 207).

So she set free her children, the stars, all over the skies. The stars in turn gave birth to snakes, millipedes large and small, caterpillars, flies, ants stinging and biting, centipedes, scorpions, and so on. The Moon sent them all down to the earth below.

When finally all her children had been born, she ordered us humans to keep taboo periods: 'When you see me large, round and smooth you will know that I am pregnant and am to be called *jɛnlap* ['waning'] then you keep the taboo period *jɛnlap*. Next, I give birth and let my offspring down to earth, the taboo is over and you may work again. After four days'[3] work I conceive once more, and when you see from my shape that I am about to give birth you start again on another taboo period. Two days later, I give birth, and the taboo is over. Then I descend, getting steadily nearer to the horizon each dawn; I am then to be called *sɛnreh* ['descent']. For seven days I set below the horizon before morning, and I am called *kɛɲcɔb* ['staying below']. Eventually it stays completely dark at night for a period—*hɔj mənaso*ʔ ['having gone in']. At last I come out again at night, and you will call me *hɛnwal* ['emerging'], until finally I am right over the roof of your house and you will call me *wɛrnar* ['waxing']. And so I give birth all over again.'

Then she returned to giving birth once more.

The elements

The other natural phenomena find a place in the scheme of things, expressed in the form of various deities. Chief among them is thunder, which the Temiars conceive of quite explicitly as a deity existing in four different aspects.[4] In its neutral sky-dwelling form, thunder is the god Ɂɛŋkuuʔ (or, in some places, Ɂɛŋkããy). But thunder plays a major part in Temiar religion as the embodiment of evil, and this aspect of the deity is known as Karey. More positively, the deity is known as Hiwəəw when he thunders and as Hilɔk when he makes lightning. One informant described the relationship between these four deities by an analogy: 'It's just like with dogs—they each have their own name, but in the end they are all just as much "dog".'

None of the Temiars that I knew could give any description of the thunder-deity's appearance. They claimed that people living in other valleys had more knowledge of such things, and there is good reason for believing

---

3. The figures given in the story are conventional, and do not correspond exactly with my own field records of the practical operation of the lunar calendar. Numbers have little importance for the Temiars.
4. [Added 2014] See also Carey (1961:177) and Baharon (1966). As Endicott (1979) has pointed out with respect to the celestial ideas of the Bateks, it is often difficult to determine how far these are being spoken of as deities or just as natural phenomena, as Schebesta (1957: 11) also noted with respect to the Jahais and Lanohs. In Chapter 13, I discuss Gellner's view that such apparently undifferentiated modes of expression are typical of 'many-stranded' social situations. Dentan (2002a, 2002b) discusses the relation between Thunder and other high gods among the Orang Asli and elsewhere in Asia. He pays special attention to the use of Ɂɛŋkuuʔ and its relatives (which also occur as Malay titles of nobility) as one of Thunder's names, and suggests that these ideas form part of a widespread and ancient religious complex.

this to be so. In the Perolak valley, for example, where the present data were collected, Karey, though feared, was something the Temiars felt they could discuss freely. In the neighbouring valley to the south (the Brok), on the other hand, even the name was quite ineffable. The various physical features of that area had some legendary connection with the deity and were specifically linked with him in a series of local myths. To talk about him on his home territory would be to incur the danger of violent thunderstorms directly overhead. (The name Hilɔk, however, appears occasionally as a swear-word, as when an almost impassable path, for example, is referred to annoyedly as a 'Hilɔk path'.[5])

Later, I discuss the precise circumstances in which Karey is believed to take violent action against people on earth below, but this is a convenient point at which to discuss the manner in which he does so. Despite their ignorance of his resting state, this is something that the Perolak Temiars claim to know about. Lightning is the blinking (*kənalɲɛb*) of Karey's eyes; thunder is his voice. In accord with the violence of the sound, various degrees of thunder are recognised. Normal thunder is called onomatopoeically *gəəw*: 'his real speaking voice—he speaks to his dependents, siblings and children, the seasonal fruits'. *Gədar* marks his louder voice: 'his tree-splitting voice when he is angry and wicked.' The final stages of his anger, when he thunders right overhead, are called *pər laaw*. Ordinary people see of Karey only his lightning, but mediums can see also that he acts by sending down snake-like cords. These either come straight down or make a deviation under the house and come up through the floor. In the former case they are brought by Karey's familiar, Papaat, a creature that has no terrestrial equivalent but which was described as a 'shadow' of the bee fraternity. The directly arriving cords may be intercepted by a medium and cut apart. The second kind are more dangerous, however, since they avoid interception. In both cases, the cords coil around and pull the unfortunate victim onto the fire.

Karey's cords are also present in forked lightning, where they form the feeding tube through which he sucks sustenance from the sap of the *cah*, *tɛɲreek* and *lalɔʔ* trees. (*Lalɔʔ* is said to be an hallucinatory tree that gives off an intoxicating vapour when cut.) Karey causes the rains to arrive, and then thunders as he trances the seasonal fruit trees into flower. According to this version, then, Karey (as *ʔɛɲkuuʔ*) is responsible for much of the annual cycle, and this serves to associate him with one of the most highly valued aspects of the Temiar world.

The wind deity, like Karey, appears under various aspects, though there seems to be no formal relationship between the two. The neutral strong-wind

---

5. [Added 2014] Strangely, Means (1998: 41) gives 'deik Hilok', i.e. *deek Hilɔk* 'Hilɔk's house' (or perhaps 'a Hilɔk house'), as the Temiar for 'place of worship'. Given that Mrs Means was a Lutheran missionary, it would be interesting to know what was in her Temiar consultant's mind in suggesting this translation. Perhaps it was proposed as a disapproving generic term for any non-Christian temple or shrine.

aspect is known as Payɔɔw and dwells in the Sɔwiik layer of heaven. Payɔɔw stands as the overall name of the wind-deity. The violent, and possibly fatal, gale aspect is known as Paŋhũũd, and this, like Payɔɔw, is a name that may not be uttered without serious consequences (at least in the Perolak valley). The wind's familiar is fire, and to utter its name in the house is believed to lead to the speaker being submerged in a sudden flurry of blinding smoke. Utterance of the name Paŋhũũd leads to the speaker suffering the fatal wasting disease known as sɔrɛhlɔh.

The wind has three less violent deity-aspects whose names may be uttered with impunity. Ordinary light wind is known as Pɛypooy (from *pooy* 'to blow gently'). The heavier breeze that causes the boughs to sway is called Hɛnhũl (from *hũl*, 'to blow (wind)'). Less violent than Payɔɔw is Parɔk, responsible for the winds that blow trees down. Parɔk is called upon when a good swidden burn is desired; once again, some connection is postulated between wind and fire.[6]

Fire itself possesses three ranked aspects-cum-deities. Regarded neutrally, fire is ʔoos, the ordinary Temiar word (*ʔoos*) for the element, and utterable quite without restriction. The more severe aspects are respectively Jamput, and Tɛŋgɔlɔɔŋ, names that may not be uttered within the house. They may, however, be called upon outside the village by just one man at a time when their aid is required in swidden-burning. The fire-deities, unlike the others, live in the ground.

The overall rain-deity is Lojɛɛw, whose name may be freely uttered. The more and less violent aspects, Lalooʔ and Tɛhtɔɔh (*tɔɔh*, 'to rain') respectively, are regarded as the elder and younger siblings of Lojɛɛw. The rain-deities live in the heavens.

The 'real' world

Temiar cosmic ideas are somewhat vague, but since their concern is primarily with *this* world, this need hardly surprise us. It is in fact the 'real' world that they categorise much more surely.

The creation

Several creation stories are current in part or whole, but they suggest an essentially uniform way of viewing the land on which the Temiars and the other Aboriginal peoples live. Below, in outline, is the version that I was given in the most detail. It resulted from a sort of seminar held over a period of days in the longhouse at Humid, with several informants helping so that nothing essential should be missed out. Certain details are given even in this outline, especially of the natural species involved, as they will prove to be important later.

---

6. [Added 2014] In 1968, I discovered that *parɔk* is a normal Lanoh word for 'wind'.

Figure 4.3 Gunung Chingkai (Cɛŋkey) seen, in the distance, from Jalong village, Perak (2006)

The world commenced when two mountain peaks rose out of the primordial floodwaters (Limbaŋ). These were the female Cɛŋkey (Gunong Chingkai in Ulu Korbu (Kɛrbuʔ), Perak; figure 4.3) and the male Merooy[7] (said to lie near Chingkai, but farther upstream). The floodwater cast two fruits up, a *maŋɔy* (a wild brinjal, *Solanum verbascifolium*) and a *ladaaʔ* (cultivated chilli pepper, *Capsicum frutescens* and *C. annuus*).[8] These took root and flourished on Cɛŋkey and Merooy respectively. Cɛŋkey in her role of mother/ancestress-cum-medium then dreamt the two fruits into a human sibling pair: Wild Brinjal was the younger sister and Cultivated Pepper the elder brother.

To assuage their hunger, Cɛŋkey sent her spirit-guide ʔalʉj Beraay (Last-born Magpie Robin) to create the fundamental food crops—millet, maize, sweet potato,[9] cassava, yam, six varieties of sugarcane, caladium, squash, and banana, in that order. The brother and sister grew up, and on reaching maturity Cɛŋkey ordered them to sleep together and become husband and wife—not without much persuasion, as their fear of incest

7. [Added 2014] The name Merooy is obviously related to the Mount (Maha) Meru of Southeast Asian mythology.
8. [Added 2014] It is puzzling that the chilli pepper should appear in this myth. The plant originated in the Americas, and probably did not reach Asia until introduced by European colonial activities. The same is true of cassava a little later in the story, which has been the Temiars' staple crop for at least 150 years. The brinjal, however, was probably first cultivated in South Asia.
9. [Added 2014] The inclusion of sweet potato in this list is puzzling, given its known South American origin. However, it has been available in Southeast Asia for many centuries, and possibly since before the advent of European colonialism.

was very great. But eventually they did marry, producing nine children, alternately male and female.[10]

These children in turn married each other to form four ancestral couples, leaving the last-born Ɂaluj unmarried. Each couple then had ten children, five males and five females, until the mountain top was crowded and there was no room left. But the flood began to subside, exposing a large expanse of sand.

Cɛŋkey ordered the original man to go and spy out the newly formed land. He went first to the direction of the sunrise, where he found that the land was scored by rivulets. The next day he found that the same had happened in the direction of the sunset. When he had reported this to Cɛŋkey, she called up her motley collection of animal familiars to emerge from the rocks. Each was to turn into a human being and carry an appointed task in the process of creation.

And so they set out to complete their tasks. The Short-tailed Porcupine (*kuus*) fixed the soil in place. The Pangolin (*wɛjwooj*) planted up the *təlayaak* tree. The Monitor Lizard [*Varanus nebulosus*] (*tərakɔ̃l*) planted up the *cah* tree. Another Monitor [*V. dumerili*] (*kabug*) planted the *cantɔɔy* tree. The Ringed Monitor (*gɛryɛk*) planted the *haɁoog* tree. The Ocellated Water-lizard (*harɛŋ*) planted the *laŋgoɁ* tree. The Horned Toad (*kɛŋkak*) tranced the rivers into being. A *bakɔh* bird tranced the mountains. The Scrub Bulbul (*ɁɛsɁããs*) drilled fire into existence with its beak. And, finally, the Bronzed Black Drongo (*tɛrhɛɛh*) tranced the year and the seasonal fruit trees into being.

When all was finished, Cɛŋkey ordered Ɂaluj (the last-born man) to check that everything was well. This he did, whereupon he was ordered to distribute the human beings over the face of the earth. His next task was to divide the waters into the main rivers[11] of the Aboriginal world and place each of the human groups into their appointed places along them: the Perak (Perag), the Kelantan and Upper Nenggiri (Bərɔk), the Pahang (Pahak), and the Kinta (GɛntaaɁ). Next, he cut out the tributaries of the main rivers: the Perak, for example, was split into the Belum (Bəluum), Ringat (Rəŋaaj), Temor (Təmuur), Temengor (TumŋɔɔɁ), Lanweng (Lɛŋwɛɛk), Piah (PəyaɁ), Plus (Pəlus) and Korbu (KɛrbuɁ) rivers. Then, in turn, Ɂaluj went round to teach people the various place-names (essentially those of mountains and rivers), the Aboriginal ethnic groupings—Temiar (Təmɛɛr), Lanoh (Lanɔh), Kensiw (Kɛnsiiw), Semnam (Sɛmnaam), Menriq (MɛnriɁ), Jahai (Jəhaay), and Semai (Səmaay)[12]—and their respective degrees of mediumship (see Chapter 7).

10. [Added 2014] Cf. Benjamin (1968a: 106), where the set of birth-order names also amounts to nine.
11. These are the so-called *hum-booɁ* rivers. See Chapter 8 for a discussion of *hum-booɁ*.
12. [Added 2014] Most of these ethnonyms are not very old. For a discussion of Aslian ethnonymy, centred on the etymology of 'Temiar', see Benjamin (2012a).

After he had dealt with the Aborigines he turned to the world's other races and civilisations, allocating to each its characteristic features. To each group were then distributed its characteristic domestic animals, typical foods and methods of cooking, edible wild animals, and dietary taboos—the Temiars first, the other peoples afterwards.

Cɛŋkey's last world-creating acts were to set free all the remaining natural species; to trance the deity Karey into existence so that he might thunder from over the mountain tops; and to transform her familiars into normal specimens of the animal species they represented.

There is much in this myth that reflects the way in which the Temiars categorise their environment. Various points are to be noted as the story progresses. First, we find that mountains are regarded as distinctive features of the landscape. An immediate opposition is set up between wild and cultivated species of food plants. Later, the food crops are set apart as possessing a distinctive status in relation to humans. Topographically the world's main axis is stated to be that following the sun's daily path. The familiars of Cɛŋkey are structurable into 'natural' earth-associated species, and 'cultural' upper-world species. Mountains are further set apart along with the rivers as in some way opposed to the land simple. Ordinary trees are regarded as quite separate from seasonal fruit trees. Lastly, we find a distinction between the cluster of Aboriginal peoples and the other, non-Aboriginal, populations. In what follows, I demonstrate the significance of all these points as recurrent themes in Temiar thought. For the moment though, it will suffice to return to Temiar topographical ideas.

Rivers

Basically, the inhabited world consists of a substratum of land, differentiated by named mountain peaks and cut into by named rivers. In practice, the Aboriginal world is split into four distinct river systems: the Kinta, Perak, Kelantan and Pahang valleys. These four rivers, however, provide little more than a theoretical skeleton for the Aboriginal world. What really counts in everyday affairs are their major tributaries, such as the Korbu, Plus and Piah in the creation story (see the frontispiece map). The Temiars express their division into recognisable sub-cultural areas in terms of these rivers (Benjamin 1966: 13f), and they orientate themselves by reference to these same rivers. Moreover, these rivers are patterned in a manner so striking as to be apparent not only to the map-reader but to the Temiars themselves. Rising on opposite sides of the central north-south watershed, the major tributaries lie like the fingers of two hands apposed at their tips—a gesture the Temiars often make when discussing topographical matters. (There is a Temiar verb, *cɛdcuud*, meaning 'to rise opposite to', said of a river when attempting to describe its location.) Implicit is the directional element associated with knowing both the sources and debouchments of the rivers, the former since they lie within Aboriginal territory and the latter as part of traditional knowledge that all eventually flows into the sea (*lawud*). (Some Temiars, especially in Kelantan, have actually followed their rivers almost to the coast, in search of trade or adventure.) In effect, then, the known world is that which lies between the rivers' risings and their debouchments. In song-texts one occasionally hears the phrase *num-tərosaad ma-mɛŋkah* 'from source to estuary', in reference to the vast distances covered by spirit-guides in their travels. Consequently, the Temiars see themselves and the other Aboriginal populations as an island of 'upland' population surrounded by lowland civilised peoples, whom they often refer to as 'sea people'.

The ability of the Temiars, though illiterate, to accurately read the one-inch-to-the-mile maps of the Malayan jungle reflects the importance they ascribe to rivers. If the map is of an area they have visited, they will without further prompting carefully trace the shapes of the various rivers and streams that it contains until the whole takes on meaningful familiarity for them. Then, if the map is sufficiently accurate, they will proceed to name in turn all the rivers that are marked on it. At a more practical level, when lost in the forest their response is to follow the nearest stream until it leads them to a familiar point. Rivers are also accorded linguistic significance. The Temiar language possesses several locative particles, among them *teh* 'above', *rɛh* 'below', and *tuuy* 'at the other side'. Normally and without further qualification these words mean respectively 'upstream', 'downstream', and 'on the other bank' or 'in another valley'.[13]

As I have described elsewhere (Benjamin 1966: 13–15), the primacy of the major tributary valleys in Temiar social organisation may be explained as the result of purely topographical restraints—each valley is separated from its parallel neighbour along most of its length by a range of mountains passable only with some difficulty. That this should be reflected in the conceptual system, both as in the foregoing exposition and in much else besides, is hardly surprising. The siting of village areas further strengthens the dependence on rivers, as they are mostly situated at the mouths of secondary tributaries and take their names from them.

The forest

The Temiars inhabit tropical evergreen rain forest, and this above all others is the environmental factor showing the most intimate relationship with their way of life. Their attitudes towards the forest therefore deserve some attention before I proceed further.

In Temiar, the forest is referred to as *bɛɛk*, the basic meaning of which is 'outside'. This semantic association suggests a great deal about their

---

13. [Added 2014] For a detailed analysis of river-based semantics in a neighbouring Aslian language, see Burenhult (2008) on Jahai.

attitude towards the forest. As we might expect, the Temiars do not regard themselves as truly living *in* the forest; they merely hold that the forest somehow contains whatever it is they do live in. It is in this sense that they often refer to themselves as 'forest people' (*sɛnˀɔɔy bɛɛk*) or 'we of the forest' (*ˀɛɛˀ bɛɛk*), in contradistinction to the non-Aboriginal peoples (*gɔb*, meaning Malays especially) who live in areas where the forest is kept permanently at bay. The villages of both Aborigines and Malays are built in clearings, and this is of crucial importance. The Temiar ideal is that their houses should be surrounded by as large a treeless area as possible, as sudden tree-fall in the wind is one of their constant fears (cf. Needham 1964: 145). But the rationale goes beyond simply physical preventive measures. The essence of a village area is that it should be 'clear land' (*tɛˀ lalah*), an expression frequently used metaphorically to designate excellence. Physically, of course, the contrast

Figure 4.4 Sɛŋsaak village (May 1964)
This village, situated on the Perolak river a few hours' walk upstream from Humid, consisted of a single house with just 12 residents. The cleared area was planted with cassava, maize, bananas and fruit trees. The tethered raft was used for bathing, washing clothes, fetching water and butchering game. The trees nearer the house were secondary forest; those in the distance were primary forest.

between the dark, damp and relatively cool forest and the light, dry and hot clearings is marked (as, for example, in figure 4.4). Temiars do not 'enter' (*mɔɔj*) a clearing; they 'emerge' (*həwal*) into it, employing the word used of issuing from a constricted place. Normally, the full expression is *həwal ma-deek* 'emerge out to the house'—'house' (*deek*) being used metonymically for both 'village' and 'clearing'. As we shall see later, the true antithesis of 'forest' is 'house, village'. Everything that the village is, the forest is not.

The forest is the domain of the men. Women and children never go far from the village unless they are accompanied by men, who always lead the way. Indeed, few men are brave enough to travel unaccompanied. All sorts of dangers are believed to reside in the forest, subsumed usually under the rubric of 'tiger' (*mamuug*). Other beasts are also greatly feared, notably the elephant and the *seladang* wild cattle (gaur). But the stress on the tiger—one of the arch-symbols of malevolence in Temiar thought—suggests that the rather infrequent real dangers have little to do with the unease that the forest evokes in most Temiars. Their attitude is an ambivalent one, for although they are ostensibly primarily swidden farmers (their subsistence depends on cultivating and some fishing), they place great value on an activity—hunting—that requires them to penetrate deeply into the forest. This is an exclusively male occupation, which women accompany only to undertake some gathering of jungle products while the men are around.[14]

Ethnologists usually draw a distinction between hunters and cultivators. The Temiars are both, but they too draw a formalised distinction between the two activities, by reference to the lunar cycle, as I showed earlier. During normal non-taboo periods, the expected activities are work on the house or the swidden, which takes place not in the forest but in the cleared areas. During the three taboo periods in each month, on the other hand, housebuilding and farming are tabooed activities. At this time, hunting becomes the preferred occupation, or as one man put it, 'we go *hun-tɛʔ* (disorderedly over the land) and hunt.' The notion of *hun-tɛʔ* is a crucial element of Temiar thought and will be discussed later (Chapter 8). What is important here is its association with the forest-based activity of hunting, which in this way becomes the antithesis of the essentially *ordered* activities of housebuilding and cultivating. (In a sense, it could be claimed that the Temiars are themselves aware of a Lévi-Straussian 'passage from nature to culture'.) Housebuilding and cultivation are precisely the activities that differentiate Temiar culture from that of the neighbouring Negritos, who for the Temiars represent the archetypal 'natural' forest way of life that they are at such pains to avoid.

Behaviour towards natural phenomena and species is for the Temiars not to be left to chance. There are hardly any species that do not have attached

---

14. [Added 2014] This should not be thought of as a general feature of Orang Asli society. Endicott & Endicott (2008), for example, have shown that the Bateks, further east in Kelantan, exhibit a negligible degree of gender differentiation in subsistence activities, hunting included.

to them some positive value expressed in an unambiguously prescribed behaviour. Later, I say much more about the rationale underlying this system of prescribed behaviour. What is important here is that many of these observances are relevant effectively only for those individuals who find themselves in the depths of the forest; or they may be ritual practices concerned with expressing the distinction between forest and village. There is a whole series of arboreal or aerial animals, birds and others (table 4.1), that variously—for fear of committing *misik* (discussed later)—must not be blowpiped, or whose call must not be imitated, or which may not be pointed at, imitated or mocked, or during whose call one dare not speak. To ignore these prohibitions leads, it is claimed, to supernatural retribution in the form of violent local thunderstorms

Table 4.1 *Misik* species

Key to characteristics
R—reputed in Rening village to cause thunder when mocked
a—reputed in Humid village to cause thunder when mocked
b—reputed in Humid village to cause thunder when blowpiped
c—reputed in Humid village to cause thunder when imitated
d—reputed in Humid village to cause thunder when its call is interrupted
e—reputed in Humid village to cause welling floods when mocked

Temiar name	Standardised English name	Characteristics
ʔamaŋ	gibbon (siamang)	R a b e
ʔambood	fish owl, eagle owl, Malayan wood owl	c d
ʔenrɛl	cicadas	R
bakaaŋ	bear civet	R
bəroduk	black babbling thrush	R
boyaaʔ	crocodile	a e
capɔɔg	polydesmoid millipedes	a
cɛhcah	bird sp.	a b c d
cɛhcẽh	bird sp.	a b c
cəlɔɔŋ	tree-frog sp.	a b c d e
cəralaah	crested jay	R
dɔk	pig-tailed macaque	R
gertəwaʔ	stinging wasp sp.	a
gintʉs	scarab beetles	a
hɔɔŋ	rail babbler	a b c d
huldɔk	chestnut-backed scimitar-babbler	R a b c d
jerʔaar	spiny land-tortoise	e
jəlẽẽw	long-tailed macaque	R
kabɛd	ants	R a
kaŋkooŋ	common toad	a b c d e

Table 4.1 (cont'd)

kɛrʔɛk	long red juloid millipede sp.	a
kɛrpəək	palm weevil	a
kəmɛlwak	large racquet-tailed drongo	a b c d
kəmɔɔr	caterpillars and maggots	a
maŋaay	large scorpion	a
maŋkeek	white-throated bulbul	c
payɛh	ferruginous babbler	R
rəway	true flies	R
saŋʔẽd	chestnut-winged flycatcher	a b c d
sããy bayas	velvet-fronted nuthatch	a b c d
sɛnloor	snake sp.	a
sɛŋlɔk	orange-bellied leaf-bird	R
səmɛrluŋ	white-winged black jay	R a c d
sorah	white-headed babbler	R
soyaaw	water skaters	R a
tabəl	biting wasp spp.	a
talãy	black juloid millipedes	a
talək	carpenter bees	R a
tampẽl	slow loris	a c e
tanɔŋ	dragonflies	R a
tarook	lizard sp.	a
tawaag	butterflies	Ra
tawiik	spiders	a
tawɔɔh	white-handed gibbon	a e
tɛŋtɔɔk	lesser racquet-tailed drongo	a d
wɛdwaad	paradise flycatcher, pied fantail flycatcher	R a b c d
wɔt	young of prawn	a
yaaʔ cɛrwes[15]	small longhorn beetle	a
yaaʔ haʔoog	longhorn beetle sp.	a
yaaʔ kəbɔk	water-fleas	a

---

15. [Added 2014] The term *yaaʔ* 'grandmother' is used to name animals and (in some cases) plants that regularly accompany other species (such as *yaaʔ hagaab*, a bird that regularly sits on a rhinoceros's [*hagaab*] neck) or are believed to have transformed (*sid*) from whatever is their original source: *yaaʔ haʔoog* 'grandma *haʔoog*', for example, is a beetle that supposedly transformed from the *haʔoog* tree. Many species of beetle are named in this way, and there is usually a traditional story accounting for each such transformation. In a dialectical switch typical of Temiar ideas, the 'grandmother' transform is said to address its source as *booʔ*, which means both 'trunk' and 'mother' (Chapter 12).

Table 4.2 Demoniac (*mɛrgəəh*) trees
*Informants were unable to supply the Malay names of most of
these trees, and they remain unidentified.*

bədɔk (jelutong)	*mɛmsup*
bɛrbɔw (merbau)	*pəlatŭw*
cəlẽẽl	*rɛŋkɔh*
cərah	*rəguul*
gərəəh	*rəŋeej*
kɛrmal (buah rambut?)	*sərooj* (keledang)
kə'uuk	*sɔc* (perah)
kəmaluŋ	*tajaar*
lalɔ'	*tampuy* (tampoi)
lɛjkəwaj	*tɛŋreek*

sent by the thunder-deity Karey. Similarly, there are about a dozen 'demoniac' (*mɛrgəəh*) tree species (table 4.2) occurring in primary forest that the Temiars hold in fear. To utter curses at the living tree or to have too much contact with decaying trunks of the same species is thought liable to cause an attack by one or more serious ground-borne diseases.

Yet enter the forest they must, frequently. Swiddens are often situated so far from the village that they require up to half an hour's walk through unfelled areas. Travel between villages usually involves several hours' march through forest and not infrequently an overnight stop far from any cleared area. Then, it becomes necessary to construct a shelter or hut to keep the travellers dry and to give them security at night. Huts of this sort (*diŋ-rəb*, 'hastily built house', figure 4.5) differ greatly from full-scale village houses (*deek baliik*, 'raised house', figures 2.2 and 4.4), in one particular feature especially: unlike village houses, they are not raised off the ground. Overnight shelters vary considerably in elaboration, from a simple beehive structure of palm fronds stuck radially in the ground, to long-lasting huts with thatched roofing and plaited walling. But in all cases, the forest floor forms the floor of the shelter, although the individual may be separated from it by a layer of wild banana leaves or a low narrow slit-bamboo platform (figure 4.5). The raising of village houses off the ground (by between 4 and 15 feet) is an expression of their status as part of culture, whereas to build a house right on the ground is in the Temiar system a clear statement that one is in the realm of nature.

This earth symbolism is a recurrent theme throughout Temiar culture, not restricted to contrasts in dwelling types. There is, for example, a class of diseases known collectively as *təracɔɔg* (Chapter 6) that relate to the contamination of things belonging properly above the earth with the earth itself in the form of soil. It is only in the forest that the danger of human contact with these contaminations becomes serious. There, one must be careful not to

Figure 4.5 The author next to a hastily constructed *diŋ-rɔb* hut in deep
forest, Kelantan–Perak border (April 1968)
Photograph by Penghulu Hitam Tamboh.

sit on contaminated trunks, kick over contaminating ant-hills, leave traces of
food on the forest floor, and so on. Added to the other prohibitions concerning
natural species, these restrictions make going into the forest a somewhat
restrained activity, considerably less free than when one is within the village
area. Of course, this is not to suggest that the Temiars are necessarily afraid of
the forest—some are, and some are not. What we do find is that it is marked
off unambiguously as a distinct domain where one can no longer rely on the
certainties and warmth that one expects while in the village.

The village
Certain other ritual observances clearly involve a 'passage from nature to
culture'. With food, it is not always a simple matter of bringing it straight
back from the forest into the village. Most large and many small meat-
yielding animals (to be specified later) must be brought into the first house
passed on entering the village, and then in no way allowed down again to
the ground. Even the uneaten remains must be completely destroyed off
the ground, in the fire. In other words, once having been brought into the
domain of culture the species may not be allowed to devolve again into
nature. This particular prohibition is regarded very seriously, and death is
the supposed result of its non-observance in the case of many species. The
general class of observances to which this belongs (*gɛnhaaʔ*) is concerned
with a cluster of ideas that mark off the house as a domain quite distinct
from all others. Later (Chapter 5), I look at this in more detail and in relation
to other classes of observance.

There are other restrictions that apply even to species not required to be
treated in the way just mentioned. Meat is generally butchered not within
the village, but at the forest edge or even within the forest. The preliminary

singeing and all that follows is exclusively the work of the men. Even the cooking and distributing inside the house is work that women do not share in. Sexual division of labour among the Temiars is not on the whole strongly marked, but there is one exception: work in the forest is primarily that of the adult men. Other types of cooking are shared equally between the sexes, but when nature enters culture in the form of meat brought into the house then it is the job of the men to carry out the necessary tasks. Furthermore, once the animal becomes meat it must be referred to by an avoidance name different from those used to refer to it while still alive in the forest (cf. Benjamin 1968a: footnote 5).

Seasonal fruits

In principle, human ownership may not be extended to things in nature. The forest and land, then, are free goods that no one may lay claim to against anyone else.[16] Only the products of human endeavour are ownable—artefacts and crops. Consequently, swiddens constitute a sort of intermediate category, being non-owned pieces of land in forest cleared by human effort, both male *and* female, and bearing for a while individually owned crops. If, however, any of these crops should persist for a much longer period than usual, then the originally clear land reverts to unowned forest containing some trees in which individual rights are still maintained. These trees are for the most part seasonal fruit trees (durian, jackfruit, citrus, rambutan, mangosteen, etc.) which, as we saw in the creation myth, constitute a special category. The importance of these trees as an element in Temiar social organisation has been commented on elsewhere (Benjamin 1966: 18). The groves that remain when the forest regenerates mark the sites of former habitation, and provide virtually the only material indication of the continuity of the ramage descent groups that underlie Temiar society. Most of the seasonal fruit trees in the forest were not planted by human hands, however. They were, as Temiars say, planted by squirrels and rats, or, more picturesquely, 'planted by the World'. Nevertheless, these trees share one property with the cultivated species: they may be owned by individual persons, even though in many cases they grow in deep forest far from human habitations. Seasonal fruit trees, then—and at least 50 natural species are recognised (table 4.3 lists some of them)—constitute islands of ownable culture in a sea of unownable nature. That this

16. [Added 2014] I should make it clear that this was the Temiars' understanding with respect to any Orang Asli (or local Malay?) who wished to make temporary use of a piece of land lying within Temiar country. But it does not apply to the inroads of non-Aborigines who nowadays permanently alienate the land by cutting timber or opening up commercial oil-palm estates on it—as they have done at many places, including the former site of Humid village (figure 14.2). This objection has been made clear by the many Temiars in Kelantan who, under circumstances very different from those described here, are currently (2014) engaged in legal and other actions to defend themselves against such alienation. Temiar land is definitely not a free good under these latter circumstances. Nevertheless, in a profound misrepresentation of the reality, the Temiars are regarded as 'tenants at will' under Malaysian law, which (under the Torrens title system) treats unregistered land as belonging to the state, effectively defining them as squatters on their own land.

special role should be played by seasonal fruit trees accords fully with the role of such trees in other sectors of Temiar thought.

Seasonal fruit trees provide the Aborigines of northern Malaya with their clearest evidence of the otherwise too subtly marked annual cycle. At the low latitude of 4°N, the seasonal changes are so slight that they are well known in their entirety by the forest people, who use them to order the annual cycle of subsistence activities. The creation story makes a direct association between these 'seasonal fruits' (*bɜrɜk*) and the 'year' (*pɜnaaʔ, guur, tahut, tawun*); in everyday speech, seasonal fruits are often referred to casually as *tahut* 'year'. Chief of these trees is the perah (*Elateriospermum tapos*), the leaf-fall of which around January marks the arrival of the proper time for felling the millet swiddens. Rice, on the other hand, is planted once the perah buds have opened (July or August). The first seasonal change to be noticed is the fall of the soft-stalked leaves of the merbau tree (*Intsia bakeri*) which occurs during November, followed by the fall of its wiry-stalked leaves a month later. As indicators of the annual cycle, these changes are related to the dry season

Table 4.3 Wild seasonal fruit trees (*bɜrɜk*)
The following species are ownable (unless otherwise indicated: u), and their fruits may not be cooked. The Malay names were given by informants, but many of these do not correspond with published lists.

ʔagooʔ (kemalong)	*pɜrɔɔh* (buah selat)
bajaaw (?)	*rambey* (rambai)
bɜraak (macang hutan)	*raɲiik* (?) u
bɛŋbɔɔk (?)	*raŋkẽẽs* (type of pulasan)
caɲeh (pulasan)	*rarɔh* (tabang, kesan)
cɜpuuʔ (manggis asam, manggis hutan)	*reŋmaaŋ* (tampoi kunyit)
cɛrmɛɛr (?)	*rɜlɔg* (?)
gayɛɛk (buah lada)	*rɜyɛl* (buah selat)
gɛrcɜyɛs (a type of langsat)	*sɛmpaaʔ* (durian)
gɜrɜɜh (?) (eaten by game animals)	*sɜpɜp* (a type of macang)
hakɔɔr (?)	*setaar* (buah setong)
huuh (habok mas)	*sɜtool* (type of rambutan asam)
kabaak (rambutan asam)	*sɜwɛɛd* (buah kapur)
koriiʔ (tengka bewa [biawak?])	*tampuy* (tampoi)
kɛlwɛɛk (buah tajam)	*tɛgtag* (ulat galas) u
kɛrmal (buah rambut)	*tɛrlɯɯy* (type of bitter manggis)
kɜnɛŋrɛɛk (?)	*tɜbaar* (manggis hutan)
lɜgɔs (rambutan)	*taŋɔʔ* (?)
lɜyɛg (buah mas)	*tihooʔ* (?)
pɛryɛs (a type of rambai)	*wɯd* (a type of pulasan)
pɜlɔɔl (mountain pulasan)	

that lasts roughly from late January to early April. But it is the fruiting of the trees between June and September that most excites the people. During this period, they visit the trees in nearby groves daily, sometimes in large numbers, while one of them climbs up precariously to cut down the fruit for those waiting below. It is then shared throughout the community in much the same way as meat.

It must be noted, though, that individual ownership of seasonal fruit obtains only for as long as it is still on the tree. Once it has fallen freely to the ground, it becomes available to whoever takes the trouble to gather it. This is of course a further example of the recurrent earth symbolism used by Temiar culture: what is humanly ownable when naturally off the ground becomes unownable once it has made contact with the earth.

Food crops

Swidden crops are differentiated with respect to their relationship to the house. Sugarcane and banana may be picked from any swidden without notifying the owner. They constitute the category of 'heat food' (*canaa? bɨd*), so called because they are eaten as refreshment outdoors when one's mood (*hup*) is 'hot' (*bɨd*). In contrast is a group of root crops that may not be collected without the owner's permission: cassava, yam and caladium. These constitute 'food requiring to be prepared within the house' or 'food eaten to satisfy our hunger'. In other words, the below-ground- and root-crops require to be brought into the house and cooked before consumption, while the above-ground crops may be consumed raw when one is away from the village area. The swidden, which bears in close proximity crops that divide into a natural and a cultural series (but only in this context), is hereby again stressed as an intermediate category.

The basic dimensions of the Temiar conceptual system have now been presented. What follows describes the richness of the religious system that is built up by filling out these dimensions with an expressive content.

Temiar Religion (1967)— Species

I come now to what is perhaps the most complex part of the ethnographic data upon which this study is based. Temiar behaviour towards natural species of plants and animals is not easily understood at first approach. At the present stage of the argument, it is possible to demonstrate only some of the underlying systematic relationships in the data. The presentation is based on conventional, and therefore more easily grasped, categories. Even so, it will not be possible to discuss all of the categories in terms of natural species alone. Some of the categories also include items of behaviour that have nothing to do with plants or animals, and a full understanding of their meaning requires that we take full note of all the relevant facets.

Dietary rules

Food is an ever-present concern of the Temiars, as for people everywhere. But, unlike many other peoples, obtaining and preparing food is the major activity of each individual Temiar alike; it is not something that can be left regularly in the hands of others. Rules restricting dietary behaviour will therefore become embedded deep in the fabric of everyday life and any cultural meaning they contain will thereby be the more firmly anchored to actual social behaviour. Indeed, the most efficient cultural systems of meaning—the 'cultural paradigms' of Geertz & Geertz (1964: 104)—are those constructed out of elements deriving from necessarily recurrent items of everyday behaviour: personal hygiene, genealogical relationship, and especially food. A great deal of what the individual does day after day thereby comes to carry implications reaching out into wider domains of the culture as a whole.

The Temiars regard few foods as *simply* eatable. Almost all foods are associated either with a rule of edibility or with rules prescribing the behaviour to be followed while eating. Some rules divide the population into distinct groupings. Others are individually self-imposed on the basis of personal preferences or revelations. Yet other rules apply to all members of the community equally. These last must be considered in the context of the overall ritual representations of Temiar culture. Here, attention will be confined to those species that the Temiars regard as at least potentially edible by humans, even though many of them may not be considered as permissible food for the Temiars in particular.

'Animals to be feared'

In the first place are species of animals that no Temiars regard as food even though they are aware that other peoples may eat them. These fall into two broad categories. Among wild animals are several that in life are regarded as altogether too fear-generating to provide fit meat when dead. These are sometimes informally referred to as 'animals to be feared', and include elephant, wild cattle (seladang, gaur), rhinoceros and (primarily) tiger. Each of these animals possesses several names. Most of these are used as avoidance terms when travelling in the forest so as not to attract the animal's attention by uttering its highly charged 'true name' (cf. Benjamin 1968a: footnote 5). For example, the elephant has *talam* as its 'true name', but to call it this while one is in the forest is to court danger. Instead, one employs the avoidance names *gajah* (Malay: 'elephant'), *gadik* (Malay: *gading* 'tusk'), or others. But the tiger possesses associations going far beyond mere physical danger. As we shall see later in more detail, this animal appears as one of the prime symbols of malevolence in Temiar ideology. Certain individual tigers are regarded as the transmogrified heart-soul of a deceased medium, or as the metamorphosed form of the principle of evil that inhabits many plant species and topographical features.

The Temiars have no qualms, however, about killing these dangerous animals should it prove necessary for the safety of people or crops; but they never eat the flesh.[1] It may be that according to the logic of the idea-system, these animals are opposed to all others precisely in that they are the ones capable of consuming or killing humans rather than of being consumed by them. Indeed, it was several times suggested by informants that a special fate awaits people killed by one of these animals, especially the tiger. Their spilled blood becomes transformed into a small headless tiger-like were-creature (*kəpej*), which haunts the area thereafter in much the same way as a deceased medium's heart-soul tiger. But this, along with a whole cluster of further beliefs about blood, is a topic on which I failed to obtain much clear information.[2]

Domestic animals

Domestic animals constitute the second broad category of those that no Temiar will eat, and this includes both those species that are characteristically domesticated and those individual animals that have been taken from the wild and then tamed. The typical domestic animal of the Temiars is the

---

1. [Added 2014] I was later told that some Temiars ate elephant meat in the past, and there are occasional references in the literature to the eating of seladang. Noone (1936: 16, 49, 64) reported that Temiars in parts of Perak regularly served as skilled elephant-drivers, sometimes helping travellers to cross the watershed over to Kelantan and Pahang; but these were, of course, tame elephants.
2. [Added 2014] This deficit is repaired at several places later in this volume.

dog, which seems to have been associated with the Aborigines of Malaya for a very long time. As Harrison tells us (Tweedie & Harrison 1954: 10), 'the aborigines have a distinctive breed of dog about half the size of a wild dog but this is almost certainly derived not from the Serigala but from the Asiatic Jackal'. Dogs live closely in the family circle within the house, and may possess individual 'personal' names on the pattern of the human autonym (Benjamin 1968a: 102). Healthy dogs may be trained to take part in hunting (which is then known as *pəjul*, 'to cause to bark'), but although the mangy flea-ridden majority will be kicked about—not without occasional remorse—it would be unthinkable ever to kill a dog, let alone eat it. The same is true of the recently imported cats, now well-integrated into all Temiar communities.

Few people would be surprised to learn that the Temiars do not eat their dogs or cats—although one author (Stacey 1953: 101) plainly thought it possible, when he referred to 'the little wild jungle dogs they keep (I suppose to eat)'. What surprises some observers is that the Temiars resolutely refuse to eat animals they have raised themselves that in the rest of Malaya are regarded as eminently edible: goats, ducks, geese, and occasionally sheep and cows. Their explanation for this abstention is simple: 'having fed them, we feel pity (*kalɔɔn*)'. These animals were given to them initially by outside authorities to increase the supply of dietary protein. The Temiars are well aware of this intention, but they insist on treating livestock as no more than playful or decorative pets that by their scavenging activities also help make the villages cleaner and more pleasant to live in. Fortunately for those concerned for Aboriginal economic progress (both outside and within the community), it does not seem to trouble the Temiars overmuch to sell the animals to non-Aborigines who, they know, will slaughter them to eat. They prefer not to be too strongly reminded of this, however. This I realised after joining some Malay schoolteachers in consuming a goat that had been bought the day before from the Temiar village in which I was then living. The villagers' disgust showed that I yet had much to learn about comporting myself as a Temiar.

These same strictures apply to wild animals that have been tamed to keep as pets. The various species that may be tamed (table 5.2) include many that are normally regarded as good to eat—pigs, porcupines and macaque monkeys in particular. But as pets, these animals are so well-integrated into the community as honorary members that to eat them would be unthinkable. They have the run of the house, often possess rooms of their own, bear names of the autonymic and birth-order types (Benjamin 1968a: footnote 5), and may even be suckled by their human 'mothers'. When they die, domesticated or tamed village animals receive a burial that parallels in essential details the burial given to human members of the community[3]—a sure sign of their

---

3. [Added 2014] See Appendix 3.2 for an example.

incorporation from the world of nature into that of culture (see Chapter 6), from edibility into inedibility.

There is one striking exception to this pattern: the domestic fowl. A certain ambivalence attaches to this species, allowing it both to be kept as a pet and to be eaten. The fowl (*Gallus gallus gallus*) is an endemic species in the Malayan jungle, and the domestic variety was originally developed from it by selection. The Temiars themselves are well aware of the fact, and recognise that the jungle fowl is essentially the same as the domestic fowl. Furthermore, they know that village fowls still frequently interbreed with their jungle cousins to produce fertile offspring. When villagers do eventually slaughter their fowls (which is not often, and usually only for feasts or to welcome visitors), they do so in a ritualised manner away from the house. Several times they told me of their feelings of guilty sorrow at killing a fowl that had been raised carefully within the house or in special boxes under the house and which had borne nicknames of the sort I have elsewhere (1968a) referred to as 'designations'. The contrast between extending autonyms and birth-order (fratronymic) names to cats, dogs and tamed pets and employing designations with domestic fowls is, in terms of the Temiar naming system, a way of saying that the former category of animals are more closely bound into Temiar human society than are the latter. (For the rationale behind this argument, see Benjamin (1968a).)

An obvious interpretation of these attitudes towards domesticated and tamed animals would be that they clearly express an opposition between society and nature. The associated linguistic usages bear this out. The word *bɛrcaaʔ* 'to feed' used to describe how the animals are tended is also used to describe the relationship of fostering towards a motherless Temiar child: *ki-bɛrcaaʔ ʔə-lah*, 'we fed (i.e., fostered) her'. To tame an animal is *bɛrcɔɔʔ*, the causative verbal derivative of *cɔɔʔ*, semantically one of the richest words in the language.[4] In this context *cɔɔʔ* means much the same as the English word 'pet', but its wider meaning seems to be 'one, by naming, brought into relationship with the namer'. Thus, *bɛrcɔɔʔ* also means 'to name' (in the context of setting up a relationship). More interestingly, *cɔɔʔ* is used in an entirely human 'societal' context to refer to the quasi-kinship relation obtaining between a medium and his cured patient, or between a midwife and the person whose birth she aided. Its reciprocal is the term *tohaat*, 'healer'.[5] In other words, the relationship between a pet and its protector is conceptualised on the model of relationships holding squarely within the sphere of human society. This is not the case for truly wild animals, which do not enter as individuals into 'personal' relationships with human beings. Relationships with wild animals are of an entirely different order, as we are

---

4. [Added 2014] Details of the polysemy of *cɔɔʔ* can be found in Benjamin (1999: 15).
5. [Added 2014] For more information on the *cɔɔʔ–tohaat* relation, see Roseman (1991: 124–125) and Jennings (1995: 142–143).

about to see. The partial exception is of course the fowl; but since this is both a wild and a domesticated animal, it is no disruption of the ideational order that it should be both edible and become the 'pet' of an individual human owner. It is ambivalent precisely *because* of the distinction between nature and society, and not in spite of it.

Species-bound misfortunes

I turn now to a group of categories that identify the various ways in which Temiar behaviour is closely linked to natural species. Each category names the unhappy state that results when the rules of correct behaviour are transgressed. Some are diseases, some lead to an eruption of violent natural phenomena, and others are simply a state of withdrawal from positively good influences. In many ways, these categories hang together as logically overlapping sets, the detailed consequences of which I examine later. However, a brief summary of what is to follow will aid the reader in grasping material that is unavoidably complex.

Two categories, *sabat* and *pocuk*, label illnesses that result from eating species forbidden to people either as individuals or as members of a social grouping ('child', 'female', etc.). *Sabat* is a sort of allergic reaction to the forbidden species in general, whereas *pocuk* is a more limited reaction to the blood of a few special species, especially before they have been brought into the village.[6] In contrast to *pocuk* are two categories, *gɛnhaa*' and *joruu*', that are concerned with the integrity of the village (more strictly, the house) as a clear-cut domain. Both accordingly involve behaviour that takes place after the food has entered the village. *Gɛnhaa*' and *joruu*' are themselves contrasted in the most noticeable (but not the only) of their associated rituals. The former is concerned with the careful retention of the meat within the house so that none is returned to the ground, while the latter is concerned with ensuring the return of seasonal-fruit leftovers to the ground after consumption. Lastly, I discuss two categories of behaviour towards natural species, not as food, but as living creatures. The two, *misik* and *joluŋ*, have as their primary characteristics respectively the incurring of thunderstorms by the mockery of animals and other conspicuous acts, and the scaring away of the protective spirit-guide swarm through committing similarly conspicuous acts. *Misik* and *joluŋ* are the names given to the potentially dangerous state that the perpetrators find themselves in.

These six categories will now be discussed in turn, and through a detailed examination of their content I shall attempt to discern the meanings that underlie them and which relate them to the rest of Temiar culture.

---

6. [Added 2014] The categories *sabat* and *pocuk* are discussed in more detail in Chapter 12 (along with *tɛnruu*' mentioned later), and also by Roseman (1991: 136–142) and Jennings (1995: 44–48).

Sabat

The Temiars equate *sabat* with the Malay term *sawan*, which the dictionaries define as 'convulsions'.[7] A further gloss given by a Temiar informant (in Malay) was *penyakit makan-hati*. Idiomatically, this expression should mean something like 'brooding, resentful sickness'. But I think that here a more literal meaning was intended, perhaps 'the sickness that wears away the feelings'. Normally, however, the Temiars regard *sabat* as an 'illness' (*jani⁷*), the main symptom of which is vomiting. (As described in Chapters 6 and 12, there is a more acute form of *sabat* known as *tɔruu⁷* or *tɛnruu⁷*.)

It is important to note that there are no inherently *sabat*-causing species of food. Foods are classed as *sabat* only in relation to defined persons. Those for whom the food is not *sabat* may eat it without incurring any of the dangers that attend those for whom it is *sabat*. Without further qualification, *sabat* refers primarily to those foods forbidden to children, women of child-bearing age, the fathers of young children, and to both spouses during the wife's pregnancy. The list of species believed to cause *sabat* in these persons varies somewhat from valley to valley, but the differences are few and generally known.[8] The hundred or so Temiars who live in Pahang state, however, regard fewer species as *sabat*-causing than do their fellows, the vast majority, to the north in Kelantan and Perak. The result is that pork and fowl, among others, may be freely eaten by all members of the Pahang community. For most Temiars, on the other hand, women, children and many men are deprived of what would otherwise provide the major sources of meat. In Humid, the village in Kelantan where I did the major part of my work, at feasts where pork or fowl was the main item the women and children were regularly provided with fish so that they too could join in the meal. If available, permissible species of monkey meat were also provided.

There is a belief that *sabat*-causing species of the kind just discussed attain that status because they are the protagonists in one or more of the many animal and plant stories (myths) that the Temiars possess. Now, it is certainly true that the repertoire of stories varies considerably from valley to valley. It seems possible, therefore, that the local variations in the list of *sabat* species may indeed be correlatable with the stories recounted by the people there. It is more likely, though, that the attempt to relate *sabat* species to some ideally existing but often unknown story is itself somewhat of a myth. We shall see shortly that species may alternatively be declared in a rather different manner to be *sabat*-causing. Table 5.1 sets out some of the species regarded as *sabat*-causing to women, children and actual or expectant fathers in the Temiar village of Rening, Pahang. My information for Humid is less detailed, but I

---

7. [Added 2014] I present a more extended discussion of the puzzling etymology of *sabat* in Chapter 12.
8. [Added 2014] A very comprehensive list of such taboos as followed in nine different Temiar settlements is provided by Bolton (1972: 794–795), whose data were gathered at approximately the same time as the material in this chapter.

was told that at least the following are considered *sabat* there: chicken, goat, pig, hornbills, macaques, leaf-monkeys and mousedeers. I leave undiscussed here, as in the remainder of the present stage of the exposition, the question of how certain species and not others enter into the overall categorisation. My immediate focus is the categories themselves.

Although parents of a young child would neither dare to contravene the rules forbidding the eating of *sabat* foods nor allow the child to do so, the time eventually comes when the child is old enough for the rules to be relaxed somewhat. The mother, if still of childbearing age, resolutely keeps her diet restricted; but her husband and child are free to experiment with the hitherto forbidden foods—and experimentation is indeed necessary. In the first place, the taboo associated with *sabat* foods generally evokes repugnance in the person for whom the food is regarded as dangerous. Jida', a lad of about eight years,[9] was asked by his uncle to pass him a piece of dropped pig flesh while he was watching the butchering. He responded by flicking it delicately with the back of his hand, and with a look of horror he said, 'I feel revolted.' Responses of this sort are quite usual for adults also. (I should report, though, the expressions of jealousy, rather than horror, by women seated at a safe distance watching a pork feast in which they could not join.)

Second, experiment is involved in the trial eating of the hitherto forbidden food by the father. Only if no untoward repercussions ensue—vomiting merely, let alone a full attack of *sabat* convulsions—will he reinstate the food as a permissible part of his child's diet. The same applies to the child, but it is now no longer enough that the father suffers no illness. Whereas children generally rationalise their adherence to *sabat* prohibitions as obeying father's orders, the position is reversed when the time comes to throw off the prohibitions. The young child must independently feel sufficiently 'brave', *galag* (which also means 'greedy'), to wish to try the new food, and this generally comes about as an integral part of his dream-life maturation, a subject discussed in detail by Stewart (1947: 155–157); see also Chapter 6 below.[10] To eat the food, the child must somehow first overcome in dreams any feelings of repugnance and horror. To actually eat the food in waking life then serves as the public sign of the child's increasing maturity and self-control. But, as autonomy of the individual is a cardinal principle of Temiar society, the father must wait for his son or daughter to have favourable dreams before allowing them the new food.

So far, I have discussed *sabat* observances that take as their reference the child-centred nuclear family, which in Temiar society is coterminous with the household. Yet within this group the dietary observances effect a

---

9. [Added 2014] We meet Jida' again in Chapter 14, as an adult and a leader in the new ʔaluj Salamad religion.

10. [Added 2014] This reference to Kilton Stewart's PhD thesis predates the controversy that broke out later over the 'Senoi Dream Therapy' movement that had been developed out of his ideas, as discussed in Chapter 2. The brief mentions of Stewart's work in my doctoral thesis were uncritical, and should not be taken as confirming his account.

Table 5.1 *Sabat*-causing species (in Rening, Pahang)
The list is partial. The English-language names are based on identifications of stuffed animals at the Perak State Museum in Taiping by Temiars in 1965, but they should not be taken as definitive.

Forbidden to young children, their mothers and midwives

ʔamaŋ	gibbon	kuus	short-tailed porcupine
ʔamboj	pig	kənɔg	serrated large land tortoise
ʔampak	large red flying squirrel	lɛllɛed	white-whiskered palm civet
ʔarɔŋ, jɛed	barking deer	lɛnlut	palm civet sp.
ʔiŋgɛel	linsang	rɛgraag	flat-headed cat
bəsik	leaf-monkey	rusaaʔ	sambur deer
cɔɔs	mongoose	səl	large land tortoise
dɔk	pig-tailed macaque	tabɛeg	bullfrog
kalak	marbled cat	tood	brush-tailed porcupine
kayiiʔ	flying lemur	wɛjwooj	pangolin
kɔɔh	yellow-striped box tortoise		

Permitted only to adult men and women

jilɛw	long-tailed macaque	tampɛl	slow loris
kəbɔk	smooth otter	tawɔɔh	white-handed gibbon
kəbəəl	otter		

Permitted only to adult men

bərogaaʔ	jungle fowl	labiiʔ	river turtle
dəkuug	hornbill sp.	moor	goat antelope
gɛryɛk	ringed monitor	məwaaʔ	peafowl
hagaab	rhinoceros	pəgər	fireback pheasant
harɛŋ	ocellated monitor	raab	? green iora
jerʔaar	spiny land tortoise	səruntɛeŋ	partridge sp
kajɛeʔ	flat-backed land tortoise	tajuuʔ	snakes
kakeh	hornbill sp.	tərakɔl	large monitor
kəwɔɔk	argus pheasant	tərək	hornbill sp.

Permitted to old men only

barɛew	tapir	sənaan	palm civet sp.
bəcɔk	mousedeer		

further differentiation, as between young children on the one hand and the domestically active women and the older males on the other. This corresponds in principle with the distinction between those who mostly stay in the village and those who regularly go out into the forest. And it is here perhaps that the belief becomes relevant that *sabat*-causing species have traditional stories associated with them. Temiars regard the telling of these stories as incompatible with the explicitly house-bound activity of ritual song performances. To carry on both activities during the same night within the same village is forbidden: 'it would be *gɛnhaaʔ*—it is a taboo and we would die'. *Gɛnhaaʔ*, as we shall shortly see, is a class of ritual observances setting the house off as unambiguously within the domain of Culture. So it seems that, in some contexts at least, story-telling and, by association, *sabat*-causing foods are to be placed in the realm of Nature. The underlying relational logic may be expressed in paradigmatic form:

Gɛnhaaʔ	:	*Sabat*
Ritual singing	:	Story-telling
Women & children	:	Adult men
Culture	:	Nature

One interpretation, then, of *sabat* observances of the sort I have been discussing is that they serve as everyday behavioural tropes of household structure and sexual division of labour. At a less sociological level of argument, they serve also as tropes of the overall nature/culture opposition that lies behind Temiar theology. I return to this in Chapter 8.

There are food observances, also falling under the rubric of *sabat*, that imply a rather different classification of social groupings. This is especially clear for the data I collected in Pahang. Table 5.1 shows that many animal species may be eaten only by the elders of the community—males and, in most cases, females too. Any full sociological account of the Temiars would have to take cognisance of the importance of relative age in the ordering of social relations, but since my intentions in the present study are only minimally sociological, I discuss the matter no further here. (I have touched on the point in separate brief accounts of Temiar sociology: Benjamin (1966, 1967c), cf. Needham (1966).) The present treatment leaves several apparent irregularities unexplained, as for example the reckoning of certain species as edible for old men only, or adult males only, or males (not females) only. But the answers to these problems seem to be intimately connected with the historical accidents of local mythology, which is too complicated a topic to be pursued here, even if the requisite data were available. However, my informants did give me many hints as to the course a future field investigation might profitably take.

Not all *sabat* observances are to be understood in terms of socially relevant groupings. The label also covers certain self-imposed food taboos observed by particular individuals without reference to any social category that they might belong to. For the most part, these taboos arise by a reversal of the process by which young children come to throw off their childhood *sabat* taboos: they learn in a dream that henceforth they should not eat the food in question. This may often form part of the agreement between themselves and their *gunig* (spirit-guide) by which the relationship is set up in the first place. However, many *sabat* taboos arise in dreams that have no spirit-guide content: the dreamer has an unpleasant experience in relation to some animal species, which in waking life they then transform into a food taboo. Sometimes dreaming plays no part whatever in the generation of an individual *sabat* taboo, and most Temiars would place in this class their refusal to eat edible snakes. They are repulsed by the living animal and treat it formally as *ɲam sabat yeh*, 'my *sabat*-causing animal', in other words 'my own individual food taboo'.

It may seem as if *sabat* covers semantically a rather wide range of food-prohibitions, and in fact the category is capable of some open-ended extension. Nowadays, more foods are available to the Temiars than they formerly had knowledge of, and most are simply not subsumable under any of the familiar plant or animal categories. Until these foods become familiar by gradual experimentation, they are generally treated as *sabat*-causing. An interesting case occurred when one small boy of Humid village had to stop accepting gifts of foil-wrapped cheese from me: his father had declared it *sabat*. At the same time it was perfectly permissible for the boy to eat cheese in its—to them—more familiar canned form. Most Temiar women refuse to eat beef when they have the opportunity 'because we are not yet accustomed' and hence would suffer an attack of *sabat*.[11]

It is difficult to give a systematic explanation of these individual *sabat* observances. It does seem possible that, in principle at least, each individual in the community has a unique constellation of food taboos, and my Temiar informants agreed that this well might be so. Unfortunately, I have insufficient data upon which to decide the issue. But if this is indeed the case, there would be a correlation between such 'totemic' individuation and the autonomy of the individual so highly stressed in Temiar culture.

Pocuk

Even though *sabat* covers a wide field of dietary observances relating to social groupings or to specified individuals, some such observances are covered by another Temiar term, *pocuk*.[12] This too is essentially the name of the bodily

---

11. [Added 2014] The range of *sabat* prohibitions is open-ended, with new items added to the list from time to time. Sharifah, Nilan & Germov (2012: 247), for example, mention several food prohibitions, such as against cabbage and plastic-wrapped foods, that would not have been available during my initial fieldwork. They also report that their respondents explained many of the prohibitions in terms of sympathetic magic: items with no obvious opening (such as cans), and especially if they are globular like the women's womb (such as cabbages and coconuts), were rejected as endangering the foetus's exit through the birth canal.

12. [Added 2014] The word *pocuk* has no transparent meaning in Temiar, but on phonological grounds it could well be related etymologically either to the Malay word *moncong* 'snout, beak' or, perhaps more appropriately, to *pocong* 'shroud, winding sheet'. If the former, it would refer to the presumed animalian origin of the affliction. If the latter, it would be connected with the infamous Malay *hantu bungkus* (wrapped ghost), alternatively known as *hantu pocong*, which is thought of as an undead corpse wrapped in a white burial shroud. In Malay ideas, when a person is buried, the shroud (*pocong*) should be loosened; but if it remains tied at the top, the body is supposed to become a *pocong* ghost, feeding on the blood of babies. On both phonological and semantic grounds, either derivation seems possible, but *pocong* is normally found as an independent entry only in Indonesian-Malay or Javanese dictionaries.

affliction believed to attack those who fail to observe the relevant rules of behaviour. *Pocuk* results in an overall failure of bodily motor control, with giddiness, unstable vision, and staggering fits. It is particularly likely to affect women and children. (Nevertheless, some Temiars insisted that *pocuk* is not an 'illness' (*jani?*), unlike *sabat*.)

The immediate cause of *pocuk* is over-close contact with the *cə?aay*, or evil emanation, given off by certain animals when being slaughtered: sambar deer, barking deer, mousedeer, domestic fowl, jungle fowl, fireback pheasant, and an unidentified ground-dwelling game bird (*jarɛgpaag*). *Cə?aay* was explained as 'the odour of the blood', and was equated with the Malay concept of *badi*. This, Skeat (1900: 427f) discusses as the mischievous principle inherent in many natural objects and species. One special case of the Malay belief is that 'all kinds of evil influences and principles' may enter into a man 'who has unguardedly touched a dead animal or bird from which the *badi* has not yet been expelled'. However, the Malay term *badi* covers a much wider range of phenomena than the Temiar term *cə?aay*, and the Temiars do not seem to have any developed rituals such as are described for the Malays to rid the carcase of the offending principle. As far as I can judge, the only precautions taken are that the animals should be slaughtered and butchered away from any house or path and that they should not be eaten by women and children. It is these requirements that suggest a possible interpretation of *pocuk* beliefs. Viewed sociologically, *pocuk* avoidances, like much of the behaviour subsumed under *sabat*-avoidances, serve to distinguish the domestic grouping of women and children from the forest-going grouping constituted by their menfolk. Furthermore, the requirement that care be taken not to contaminate houses or paths with *cə?aay* again implies the important distinction between *deek*, house or village, and *bɛɛk*, the 'outer' forest, that I commented on in Chapter 4. (The significance of the relationship of *pocuk* with blood is an important point, discussed in Chapter 6.)

Gɛnhaa?

I mentioned earlier a category of behaviour that in some ways forms the other side of the coin from *pocuk*. *Gɛnhaa?* labels what at first sight seems a rather heterogeneous collection of behaviour concerned with delimiting the house as a distinct and crucial domain. But whereas *pocuk* beliefs do this by reference primarily to what occurs before the domestic domain is entered—and indeed serve to prevent contamination of the domestic domain—*gɛnhaa?* beliefs are concerned explicitly with maintaining the integrity of the domestic domain by reference to what goes on within it. Now, although *gɛnhaa?* beliefs receive their strongest regular expression in the form of behaviour concerning certain species of food, we must also examine the other behavioural contexts in which the term appears. This is even more necessary in the absence of any obvious etymology for the word. Linguistically, it should be the nominalised form of a root *gəhaa?*, but my informants recognise no such word, nor could they give any gloss for the actually occurring form *gɛnhaa?*.[13] Its 'meaning' had to be worked out by attempting to abstract the common elements from the confusingly wide range of behaviours that it identifies.

One of the first things that visitors to a Temiar house notice is that they will not be allowed to leave until they have partaken of some refreshment within—sugarcane, cassava, etc.[14] If they arrive during the harvesting of the grain crop and wish not to cause offence then they should either eat some of the freshly-cooked rice or millet, or, if that is not possible, they should take a few handfuls of the new grain with them when they leave. In both cases they will hear some muttered phrases such as 'let them eat, for it will be our *gɛnhaa?*'; or they may be asked to take with them some '*gɛnhaa?* padi'. For their part, the visitors should not leave the house and descend to the ground before making at least a token acceptance of the proffered food. One informant regarded the *gɛnhaa?* of padi with such equivocation as to claim, 'in our grandfathers' time they were afraid of the padi and they used not to plant it'. They felt it perfectly safe, however, to eat rice in the villages (Temiar or Malay) further downstream, where they would no longer incur the dangers of failing to share it out in their own house.

Gɛnhaa?, then, is dangerous and feared. It is conceptualised as a disease-causing propensity somehow inherent in the object of the prohibited behaviour. If that object is a natural species, as it usually is, the *gɛnhaa?* attack is regarded as a direct intervention by its *rəwaay*, the vital principle corresponding to the head-soul of animal species and man. This is thought to cause, at least, fits of ague (*jani? lɛghuug*) and, at most, immediate death. But it is the offended person—the one who failed to receive a share—who suffers the attack. Some informants claimed even that *gɛnhaa?* is the name of the *rəwaay* of dead plant and animal species in its malevolent aspect. The *gɛnhaa?*-causing activities discussed so far would lead only to the milder attacks of illness, although the fear shown by the old-time highland Temiars for the *gɛnhaa?* inherent in padi suggests that dire consequences were then in store for the one who took insufficient care in its treatment. This echoes the concern shown also by the Malays—from whom the Temiars first obtained the grain—for the *semangat padi* (rice-soul), which Temiars explicitly identify with their *rəwaay* concept.[15]

---

13. [Added 2014] The word *gɛnhaa?* might just be cognate with the Proto-Mon-Khmer form **bha?* 'to frighten' (Shorto 2006: 126). Alternatively, it may be related to Semai *tnhã?* 'very sinful' and/or to Khmer *grhəə* [krɔhɔː] 'rude, nasty, impolite, indecent' (Gérard Diffloth, personal communication). But Semai also has words, such as *gɲhãã?* and *ŋnhãã?*, closer in form and meaning to Temiar *gɛnhaa?*.
14. This is different from another superficially similar institution, known as *səlantab*, according to which someone who is eating must offer food to whoever possesses none. In this case, however, it is the potential recipient who suffers supernatural retributive harm, through leaving his desires unsated when the donor possesses the means to satisfy them. The recipient may therefore decline to eat the food, without harm to anyone. This is just one of several diffuse supernatural sanctions intimately tied in with the flux of Temiar social relations, and which I examine more systematically in Chapter 8.
15. [Added 2014] In 1968, I was told by a Temiar from Pahang that *gɛnhaa? padii?* 'rice *gɛnhaa?*' results from strangers frightening away the *rəwaay padii?* 'rice soul', leading to a form of *joluŋ* in which the reaper suffers the disease, caused by the rice-soul itself.

Certain other acts are regarded as somewhat fate-tempting and likely to lead to a mild *gɛnhaaʔ* attack. The removal from a house of a domestic object that has been there for a long time, and sometimes even the cannibalising of an old house for constructional materials, may be seen in this light. An example occurred in Humid before I understood what the term *gɛnhaaʔ* implied. As I was carrying some mats from the longhouse to my own house, several people rather worriedly cried '*gɛnhaaʔ!*'. When, puzzled, I asked why, they replied that since I was carrying the mats rolled into a long cylinder over my shoulder it was just like the carrying away of a dead person for burial—the act that entails the most complete removal possible from a house of something that has long been part of it.

Gɛnhaaʔ animals

I have already presented one example of an activity believed to give rise to a serious, even fatal, attack of *gɛnhaaʔ*: the mixing of story-telling and communal singing on the same night in the same house (or village). However, serious concern for the dangers of *gɛnhaaʔ* is most apparent in relation to a class of ritual observances associated with the eating of many species of animals, and it is these food taboos that the Temiars feel most typically to represent the idea of *gɛnhaaʔ*. The basic idea is that once the meat of any *ɲam gɛnhaaʔ*, '*gɛnhaaʔ* animal', has been brought into the domestic domain it must remain there until it has been entirely consumed. But the behaviour associated with the *gɛnhaaʔ* animals shows considerable variation and gradation in expressing this basic idea. One species alone fully exemplifies the 'ideal type' of a *gɛnhaaʔ* animal: the scaly anteater or pangolin.

The pangolin is the only species placed in the grade of greatest *gɛnhaaʔ* severity, the grade known as *gɛnhaaʔ rayaaʔ*, 'great *gɛnhaaʔ*'. In relation to all the other *gɛnhaaʔ* animals it is in this respect the *təwaaʔ səkaliiʔ*, 'chiefest headman'. If a pangolin is killed, it must be brought into the village circumspectly so that the carcase is not carried nearer to any other house than to the house where it will finally be cooked. Once cooked, a portion of the meat must be distributed to anyone who is accustomed to eat it (essentially, those for whom it is not *sabat*-causing) and who saw the carcase being brought home by the hunters. Eating the flesh is fraught with danger. In the words of an informant, 'we must not drop the bones down to the ground, but eat carefully by incinerating them in the fire; and then we must burn up the bamboo sections we ate from'. The sanction for contravening any of these rules is believed to be rapid death of the miscreant. *Gɛnhaaʔ* also attaches to the pangolin while it is still alive: it is one of the species classed as *cəwaliiʔ*, 'non-tameable' (cf. Malay *cuali*, 'independent'), and to attempt to tame it as a village pet is believed to cause death by *gɛnhaaʔ*. In myth too, the pangolin (*wɛjwooj*) seems to bear a special relationship to the human domain. In the creation story (Chapter 5), Wɛjwooj is responsible for planting the *təlayaak* tree, which ever since has been used as the best source of fertile wood ash in which to plant tobacco.

Thus, the 'ideal type' features of the *genhaa?* animal, displayed at least in part by the other members of the class, are the following: the obligatory retention of the carcase or meat within the house whose domain it first enters; the avoidance of subsequent contact of any part of the animal with the ground; the statutory sharing-out of the meat; the taboo against taming the living animal; and the appearance of the species as a protagonist in myth. The Temiars use these features to set up a rough and ready division of *genhaa?* animals into three grades of severity. The pangolin, as we have seen, is the only species regarded as entailing 'great *genhaa?*': the result of ignoring any of the rules is believed to be immediate death. (I speak with certainty only of the Perolak valley.) Most *genhaa?* species, however, fall into the *genhaa? ?ɛn-gagid* 'intermediately *genhaa?*' division, the constantly recurring features of which are: that the meat should not be shared outside the house in which it is cooked; if there is more than one house in the village, the other villagers must congregate in the first house; the bones and the cooking bamboo must be burnt in the fire and not allowed to fall to the ground beneath; and the sanction for wrong behaviour is sure but delayed death. It is also true of most, but not all, intermediately *genhaa?* animals that they may not be tamed. Many of them appear in creation myths, but if the remainder also do so, my informants seemed ignorant of the fact. Lastly, the residual *genhaa?* species are classed as *genhaa? ?amɛs*, 'small *genhaa?*'. The only constant feature of this group is that the meat must be shared around the village. Nevertheless, the meat may be carried from house to house and the bones may be thrown to the ground beneath like any normal waste. The result of refusing to share it out properly is an attack of non-fatal ague (*lɛghuug*). There seems to be no specific prohibition on taming the animals classed as small *genhaa?*, nor did my informants report that these animals generally appear in myths. However, most of them, along with the majority of *genhaa?* animals, are believed to have metamorphosed from other natural species. The complex constellation of these various characteristics is displayed in table 5.2.

Temiars view the correct observance of the various *genhaa?* requirements with great concern. Early on, I was taught to be scrupulously careful when eating any of the species. Although the Temiars generally inducted me into their behaviour patterns (correct kinship appellations, singing in chorus, cultivation techniques, etc.) with a fair degree of amusement, this particular task was one they undertook in complete seriousness. And it was not solely a matter of my personally taking care: whenever they had caught a *genhaa?* animal, they would bring it into the village, not along the cleared path passing right by my house, but by breaking off about 50 yards before and taking the hard way through the undergrowth. This was to prevent my gaze being the first to fall on it, and my house from being the first it was brought close to.

Table 5.2 *Gɛnhaaʔ* animals
Characteristics are indicated thus: (1) great gɛnhaaʔ, *(2) medium* gɛnhaaʔ, *(3) small* gɛnhaaʔ, *(u) untameable,*
(m) undergoes metamorphosis (with the initial species shown in parentheses).

Temiar name	English name	Characteristics	Initial metamorphic species or role in creation myths
ʔamaŋ	siamang gibbon	2	
bagɛɛt, tərakɔl, payãã̃d	monitor lizard (*Varanus nebulosus*)	2, u, m	*bəyɛʔ* (paradise tree snake); planted the *cah* tree, used for boatbuilding
bakaaɲ, ʔapəəp	bear civet	2, u, m	*yaaʔ ləwaak*, a dangerous animal (?); a pet of *ʔɛŋkuuʔ*, who sends it to bite people in the neck
bɛrkɔg	larger thick-billed green pigeon	2	
bɛrwẽl	smaller thick-billed green pigeon	3	
bəcɔk	small mousedeer	2, m	gemmae of the *bal* leaf
bəyɔɔg	squirrel sp.	3	
gɛryɛk, gɛryuy	ringed monitor lizard	2, u, m	*rəlaay*, python; planted the *haʔoog* tree (*Artocarpus*, used for barkcloth)
haleew	frog sp. (Malay: *katak ringkok*)	3, m	*tajuuʔ haleew*, a small water snake
harɛŋ	ocellated water lizard	2, u, m	*baroh*, a snake sp.; planted the *laŋoʔ* tree (used for firewood)
hohẽẽw	crested green wood partridge	2	
jajɔɔʔ	tiger civet	2, u	
jɛrʔaar	spiny land tortoise	2, m	leaves fallen into mud
jəyɛs	monitor lizard (*Varanus nebulosus*)	2, m	a small jungle snake
kabug	monitor lizard (*Varanus dumerili*)	2, u, m	*pɛhrɔɔh*, hamadryad snake; planted the *cantɔɔy* tree (used for firewood)
kariih	box tortoise	2, m	an unidentified leaf
kayiiʔ	flying lemur	2, u, m	*kəmɔɔr geep*, a poisonous spiny caterpillar
kɛŋkak	horned toad	2, m	leaf of the *sərik* tree, *keledang*
kəbɔk	smooth otter	2	

Table 5.2 (cont'd)

kəbuuk	cat snake (? *Boiga trapezii*)	2, m	*diŋʔaay mənuuʔ*, large banded bamboo rat
kənɔg	serrated large land tortoise	2, m	*cəlakoh*, banded wolf snake
kəwɔɔk	argus pheasant	2, u, m	*rɛgraag*, flat-headed cat, leopard cat
məwaaʔ	peafowl	2	
pahɔɔŋ	black wood partridge	2, u	
pəgər	fireback pheasant	2, u	
popooy	Vieillot's fireback pheasant	2	
rosaaʔ	sambur deer	3	
sɛgnug barpɛɛl	frog sp.	3, m	*bɛrbɔw*, leaf of the *merbau* tree
sɛgnug mənuuʔ	toad sp. (*Bufo melanostictus*)	2, m	an unidentified large leaf
sɛgyɛɛg	freshwater turtle	2, m	unknown origin
sɛŋsɛk	masked civet cat	2, u	
suryɛn	hornless small frog sp.	3, m	*kacuuh* leaves, betel leaves
tampẽl	slow loris	2, u	
tawɔɔh	white-handed gibbon	2	
wɛjwooj	pangolin	1, u	planted the *təlayaak* tree

Otherwise, it would have been necessary for the whole village to assemble in my small cooking room in order to eat the meat according to the rules. Again, on several occasions I wished to photograph the animals they had brought back. But I was usually too late as the carcases had already been taken up into the house, where it was too dark to photograph and from where it was not permissible to remove the object out into a better light. I did manage, however, to take one such photograph—a sad picture of a villager coyly holding up a beautiful, but dead, argus pheasant in the shadow of the longhouse doorway. He was afraid to bring it out past the threshold.

The convenient tripartite division of *gɛnhaaʔ* species into hierarchical grades of severity should not lead one to suppose either that the system is fixed or that within each division there is no further gradation. The Temiars readily admit that things are changing. They know that their present practice differs somewhat from that of their grandparents. For example, the crested green wood partridge is conventionally regarded as an intermediately *gɛnhaaʔ*, animal. Although in the old days it was forbidden to take its meat from house to house, nowadays it is becoming permissible to do so. It may well be that this species is on its way to becoming a 'small *gɛnhaaʔ*' one, with a much milder sanction against refusing to share out its meat than applies at present. Furthermore, it is a species that may be tamed, and perhaps there is some underlying logical implication that leads to the feeling that any such animal is anomalous with regard to the 'intermediately *gɛnhaaʔ*' division.

Within any grade of *gɛnhaaʔ* severity the various species are to some extent ranked in relation to each other. Among the 'intermediately *gɛnhaaʔ*' species, my informants felt that the various monitor lizards deserved far more careful treatment than the ground-dwelling game birds that the grade also contains. Some of the mammals and tortoises are believed to be *gɛnhaaʔ*-causing to an extent reflecting their intermediate ranking between the most and the least dangerous of the 'intermediately *gɛnhaaʔ*' animals. This hierarchy is partly reflected in the roles played by some of the species in the mythology, as we shall shortly see.

What meaning lies behind these ideas and observances? The question is best answered by examining the structural implications of the full ideal-type constellation of features. In the first place, the stipulations that the meat of a *gɛnhaaʔ* animal be retained within the house even to the extent that its remains be burned up in the fire, and that it be shared out completely within the community, suggests an irreversible transfer from the domain of nature into that of culture. As we have seen, the term *gɛnhaaʔ* carries the implication in all its various contexts that whatever it labels is in some way concerned with the symbolisation of the house as the primary realm of culture. In so doing, it makes an identification of culture with human society. It is in this light that we should interpret the insistence that the meat be shared throughout the community. Conceptually there is a clear identification of house (*deek*) with village (also *deek*), even in cases (the majority) where the village contains more than one house. (Temiar villages may always be viewed as virtual, if not actual, longhouses.)

If it is true of the dead animal that once transferred into the domain of culture it must irreversibly remain there, it is likely (by logical reversal) that the opposite holds true for the animal while it is still alive. This surely is the meaning of the frequent prohibition on taming *gɛnhaaʔ* animals: they must on no account enter the domain of culture and human society while still alive. Referring back to a topic discussed earlier, we may say that the typical *gɛnhaaʔ* animal is an unownable part of nature when alive but an ownable part of culture when dead (by the hand of man). That is not all: recalling the Temiar creation myth, it is interesting to examine precisely what parts are played by those *gɛnhaaʔ* animals that make their appearance in the story. The pangolin (*wɛjwooj*) planted the *təlayaak* tree, in the ashes of which the Temiars now plant their tobacco. The monitor lizard *Varanus nebulosus* (*tərakɔ̃l*) planted the *cah* tree (*Shorea* sp.), which is now used for building dugout boats. The monitor *V. dumerili* (*kabug*) planted the *cantɔɔy* tree, one of the best sources of firewood for the domestic hearth. This is also true of the *laŋgoʔ* tree planted by the common water monitor, *V. rudicollis* (*harɛŋ*). A fourth monitor, the ringed variety (*gɛryɛk*), planted the *ha²oog* tree (*Artocarpus sp.*), the source of the barkcloth the Temiars formerly used to clothe themselves. The horned toad (*kɛŋkak*), which unlike the others is a 'small *gɛnhaa²*' species, tranced the rivers into being, the particular rivers on which present-day Temiar life depends. All these species, then, are *gɛnhaa²* animals that play a markedly 'cultural' part in the mythology and which in real life may not be tamed. Furthermore, they are all 'ground-dwelling animals'.

Yet there are many species of this grade of *gɛnhaa²* that do not appear in the creation myth. On the other hand, there are species appearing in the myth that are not, according to my records, *gɛnhaa²*-causing. Of these latter, only the short-tailed porcupine (*kuus*) is edible in any case. All that my informants would say of this species is that Cɛŋkey, the mountain-creator-ancestress, ordained in the beginning that the porcupine should be both tameable and edible. Of the *gɛnhaa²* species that do not appear in the creation myth, it is hard to detect any regular patterning, although there may well be other creation myths in which they do appear, along with other species. Three of the most highly *gɛnhaa²* animals are regarded as siblings: siamang, gibbon and flying lemur, from oldest to youngest respectively. Collectively these species are known as the *ɲam jɛgjɛɛg*, 'brachiating animals', and are regarded in a recurrent Temiar tradition as the bringers of death in some of the forms it is believed to assume (Chapter 6). All these species are classed as 'animals living off the ground' (*ɲam baliik*), in contrast to those *gɛnhaa²* animals that appear in the creation myth. Furthermore, as if to complete the pattern, two of the brachiators are regarded as tameable: the siamang and the gibbon. But there the patterning ends: the third brachiator, the flying lemur, is untameable, like the majority of *gɛnhaa²* animals.

There is, then, an incipient patterning involving the variables of culture, *gɛnhaa²*, myth, and tameability. But it holds only for a few species and is either contrary to the facts in the case of one or two species, or simply irrelevant to the majority that do not have important roles to play in the mythology. However, the whole question of the interrelationship between everyday ritual observances towards natural species and their appearance in myth is a topic on which I do not have sufficient data from which to generalise. What I have said of a few species may prove on further examination to be true for many more, if not all. Or it may be that the major part of the *gɛnhaa²* classification results more from the vagaries of individual revelation (such as holds for many *sabat* observances and, as we shall see, for many other Temiar ritual categories) than from some overall tribal mythology.

Whatever may be the more remote implications of *gɛnhaa²* beliefs, there is one structural element of general significance throughout all areas of Temiar culture: the earth symbolism I mentioned earlier (Chapter 4). With the exception of the few 'small *gɛnhaa²*' species, the stipulations about eating any of these animals insist that the whole process, even the final disposal of the waste, should take place off the ground.[16] This element is so crucial in its own right that it is stressed even when the whole process takes place in deep jungle away from any house. Indeed, it is only because the Temiar house is in itself an expression of the basic earth symbolism that it becomes so involved in the performance of *genhaaʔ*-type ritual observances. If a *genhaaʔ* animal is caught and eaten while travelling in the forest, care will be taken to ensure that the meat is placed on broad leaves of wild banana to prevent any direct contact with the ground, even though they have to sit on the ground to partake of the meal. All uneaten portions of meat, the bones, and the bamboo pieces used in the cooking, must be completely burnt off in the fire before the journey is continued. I had to observe these rules closely myself on several occasions while travelling from village to village. It seems, then, that the act of incorporation into culture in its elementary form (as it must be, in the absence of a house or even a clearing) consists in the irreversible separation of the incorporated object from the earth. This act of separation is elaborated to the degree permitted by the available means, allowing the 'restricted code' employed in jungle surroundings to develop into the full 'elaborated code' employed within the house. Again, the fact that some few 'small *genhaaʔ*' species may have their bones safely thrown to the ground suggests that what I have said applies to some ideal type of behaviour that is diverged from for a minority of species for reasons that have yet to be discovered. The overall symbolic system remains quite clear in its structure, however.[17]

The structure remains clear because it is repeated over and over in other sectors of the Temiar religious system. But it is not a matter of simple repetition of individual elements. The validity of what I have claimed to be the essential

16. [Added 2014] In 1968, from patients at the Orang Asli hospital in Ulu Gombak, I gathered information on some rather different ideas about *genhaaʔ* then current in the Telom valley of Pahang. The connection with the ground was apparent there too. Indeed, *genhaaʔ* was described as the earth itself, or more strictly the heat retained by the earth after dark. Mediums could see it as a spirit in the shape of a Malay. Very few animals were regarded in the Telom valley as *genhaaʔ*-causing—mainly the pangolin, the *kəbuuk* snake, the masked civet cat and perhaps the flying lemur. However, they agreed that *genhaaʔ* could be caused by the telling of stories on the same occasion as a song-session (a prohibition found elsewhere, as noted earlier, along with the view sometimes expressed that bamboo flutes and zithers should not be played at night). The *genhaaʔ* spirit would arise and stab everyone present, skewering their bodies stiffly from the crown of the head to the base of the spine so that movements of the trunk are impossible. On the other hand, they did not regard *genhaaʔ* as something that could be caused by the improper bringing of food between houses, nor did they observe any special eating rules when in the forest, being unconcerned about throwing the leftovers onto the ground. In 1970, Hitam Tamboh, from the Perolak valley, added the following to the list of actions that cause *genhaaʔ*: failing to fill one's bag while harvesting food; missing a game animal when shooting with a blowpipe; or hitting the animal but failing to find where it fell. He said that these were all signs that some close relative (*sakey*) had died elsewhere without our knowing about it from any other source. It was also *genhaaʔ* to step over food while it was being prepared; but this simply meant that there would be less food to eat, not that a relative had died.

17. [Added 2014] In 1979, I gathered more information about the complicated cooking rules that apply to *genhaaʔ* animals, at least in the Perolak–Betis areas. Some of them may not be stewed in a metal vessel; they must be cooked instead in the traditional way, in a stoppered bamboo tube. These include leaf monkeys, monitor lizards, argus pheasant, and certain civets. However, some *genhaaʔ* animals, such as the pangolin can be cooked in a metal pot. Penghulu Dalam, who told me about these rules, was unable to provide any reason for them, beyond saying that this is what was done in the old days.

symbolic structure of the *gɛnhaaʔ* complex is borne out by the existence of a related ritual complex in which the same structure is expressed through a point-by-point reversal of its component elements. This ritual complex is known as *joruuʔ*.

Joruuʔ

Essentially, *joruuʔ* is the fate-tempting act of throwing new seasonal fruits (the *bərək* of the creation myth) onto the fire. (See table 4.3 for a fairly complete listing of these fruits.) This is regarded not so much as dangerous, as likely to lead to misfortune. It is believed that the burgeoning of the new season's fruits coincides with the annual release from the afterworld of the head-souls of dead human beings. Some say that the seasonal fruits are the returning human souls; others merely say that the souls return in order to suck on the sappy essence of the fruits.[18] The special relationship believed to hold between people and seasonal fruits is discussed more fully later, when examining Temiar concepts of the soul. What needs to be stressed at this point is the inherently 'cultural' status of seasonal fruit trees, finding expression in a special relationship with human beings. *Joruuʔ* is regarded as an unfortunate act because it is believed to frighten away the human head-souls that are still disporting themselves on the fruits.[19] For a variety of reasons, the Temiars feel that the presence of the human souls is greatly beneficial and highly desirable. For the moment, though, I shall ignore the wider ramifications of beliefs about seasonal fruits and concentrate instead on the structure of the behavioural complex involved in eating and tending them, for which *joruuʔ* serves as an inadequate label. The argument will become clearer through a point-by-point comparison of *joruuʔ* (and other features of behaviour towards seasonal fruits) with the various elements of the *gɛnhaaʔ* complex, rather than through an account of *joruuʔ* alone.

The correct way to eat new seasonal fruits is to let the waste fall onto the ground beneath the house. At all costs, it must not be thrown on the fire. These stipulations are relaxed somewhat as the season progresses, but

18. [Added 2014] In 1978, I was told that *bərək*, translated here as 'seasonal fruits', are the souls of deceased people. See also the note on Talɛŋ in Appendix 2.2. However, in 1968, I was told that what I have here reported as *joruuʔ* should more strictly be called *rəwaay bərək* 'seasonal-fruit soul(-loss)', the main result of which is to cause a failure of that fruit the next year. The same respondent said that *joruuʔ* means 'to turn up while people are talking'. This was later clarified by Hitam Tamboh, who said that *joruuʔ* refers to interrupting a séance while it is in progress, which leads to the arrival of unspecified *mɛrgəəh* terrors. Jennings too (1995: 47) 'found it difficult to pin the Temiars down' on what exactly was so foolhardy about committing *joruuʔ*.

19. It may also lead to *kərabɔɔʔ* (or *lag*), which is said to result in a purulent inflammation of the eyelid that prevents clear vision. This is not uncommon among the Temiars, and I treated cases of it successfully with antibiotic ointment. A severe *misik*-like thunderstorm may also result, especially if certain lianas, such as *tɛɛk manɔw (Calamus ornatus),* are thrown on the fire too soon after being cut. [Added 2014] *Kərabɔɔʔ* is a more significant category than indicated here. In 1979, I gathered detailed information on this and related ideas (including *təracɔɔg* and *gɛnhaaʔ*) from among the Semnam group of Lanohs at Tawai, near Gerik, in Perak. They were familiar with Temiar practices too and could speak contrastively and at length about the two traditions, but there is no space here to incorporate what I learnt. I hope to publish the information elsewhere.

it is regarded as safer to observe the rules throughout the year. That this is a direct reversal of the rules pertaining to *gɛnhaaʔ* animals is immediately striking. It also fits with what we already know of Temiar religious beliefs. Just as the essentially 'natural' *gɛnhaaʔ* animals are incorporated into culture by irreversible removal from contact with the ground by burning, the essentially 'cultural' seasonal fruits are ejected into nature by the avoidance of burning, thereby leading to contact with the ground. The significant point is that these rituals are concerned with the proper ends of animals and plants that are dead or dying, which suggests that we are looking at actions that closely parallel the mortuary rituals for people and their domestic animals. And there is indeed a striking parallel between the two series of rituals.

Human corpses may be disposed of in either of two directly opposed manners. Most are disposed of by ritual burial in the ground, and this is the normal way (for domestic animals also), but there are two classes of corpses that are disposed of by exposure instead of burial. Stillborn babies are suspended in a bag from a tree in a part of the forest that will never again be wittingly revisited. Traditionally, 'great' mediums were, at their own expressed wish, left exposed on a platform in their dwelling house within the village, which was then deserted by the remaining inhabitants. Exposure is thus the means of disposing of the remains of 'abnormal' human beings—the baby because it never had any soul, and the medium because he possessed souls more powerfully developed than usual (cf. Benjamin 1968a: 120). Moreover, it is just this distinction that applies to *gɛnhaaʔ* animals and seasonal fruits: at death the former are 'exposed' while the latter are 'buried'. *Gɛnhaaʔ* animals are somehow 'abnormal' in relation to the 'normal' cultural status of seasonal fruits—a redundant ritual statement of their essentially 'natural' status.

We can now more easily understand the belief that *gɛnhaaʔ* animals metamorphose from other natural species. For the most part the species that metamorphose in this way are dangerous snakes, obnoxious insects, tigers, or plants that sometimes metamorphose into tigers (see table 5.2): *gɛnhaaʔ* animals, in other words, arise primordially in nature. We have seen that many Temiars believe that the opposite holds for seasonal fruits, in that these represent the end of a metamorphic series beginning with humans, the cultural beings par excellence. A substantial number of Temiar myths recount the frequent transformations of people into seasonal fruits and vice versa. We have also seen how the typical *gɛnhaaʔ* animal must not be tamed (there are few exceptions), and this accords with the general unownability of objects in the domain of nature, commented on the previous chapter. The Temiar (Malay) term for this is *cəwaliiʔ*, 'independent'—independent, that is, from humankind. We saw also (Chapter 4) that the concept of human ownership in the forest extends only to seasonal fruit-trees and a few other ownable plants. The operative word here is *cəwak*, 'to claim, by taking responsibility for'. An object that a person may *cəwak* is not so much 'owned' outright as brought into a state of dependence upon a human protector. (*Cəwak* also applies to a person's pre-emptive sexual rights over someone in the *mənəəy* 'opposite-sex sibling-in-law' category (Benjamin 1967c: 11).) The alternative way of expressing this form of tree ownership is *gagə*' 'to protect'. In summary, the typical *gɛnhaa*' animal is believed to metamorphose from nature and to be correspondingly unownable, whereas the typical seasonal fruit is believed to metamorphose from culture and to be correspondingly ownable.

There is a further contrast between the two. Seasonal fruits are shared throughout the community just as is the meat of *gɛnhaa*' animals. But, whereas in the latter case those who desire a share must come into the house where the meat is cooked, fruits are taken from house to house by those who gathered them. They are dumped in the central floor spaces for all to take their share.

A formalisation of the structural oppositions between the ritual complexes of *gɛnhaa*' and *joruu*' may be expressed as follows. (This discussion is taken up again in Chapters 9 and 12.)

Gɛnhaa'	:	*Joruu*'
Off-the-ground	:	Ground
Exposure	:	Burial
Unownable	:	Ownable
Metamorphosis from nature	:	Metamorphosis from culture
Shared within the house	:	Shared between houses

Ownership of seasonal fruits lasts only for as long as they remain on the tree. Once the fruits have fallen to the ground, they become the property of whoever undertakes the task of gathering them. The trees themselves remain ownable only to the extent that the owner bothers to clear away the undergrowth from around them shortly before the season commences. A tree not marked in this way may be considered as unclaimed and open to general exploitation.[20] The two facts accord well with points stressed earlier: the pervading presence of earth symbolism in Temiar religious conceptions; and the striking parallel between the clearing of forest to build human habitations and the clearing of the growth around a seasonal fruit tree to make clear its status as intimately associated with human society.

---

20. [Added 2014] Noone (1937) also mentions this stipulation, in regard to perah trees. The usufruct right, however, does not extend to chopping the tree down, especially by outsiders wishing to permanently alienate the land for other purposes—a point that should be borne in mind with regard to present-day disputes and litigation over land rights in Temiar country.

As in the case of the *genhaaʔ* animals, the list of seasonal fruit trees (table 4.3) in which the Temiars take interest contains some exceptions to the rules I have just discussed. In the first place are a few species that, contrary to the rule, *must* be cooked before being eaten, But this seems to be not so much a ritual as a purely practical matter: these fruits would be physically inedible if left raw. Second, there are species that may not be claimed as the prerogative of one person against another: some Temiars refer to these species by the English loan-word *pariih* 'free'. On the present list there are only two such unownable species, and one of these, *tegtag*, is not strictly a tree but a bramble growing sufficiently close to the ground for the previous stipulations not to apply. In any case, some others of the listed species are not regarded as edible for humans. Instead, they are laid claim to because they provide valuable feeding for the arboreal animals such as squirrels, which the Temiars hunt with their blowpipes.

Misik

So far, I have discussed the beliefs and observances associated primarily with the plants and animals that provide the Temiars with their food. In doing so, it has proved necessary to comment also on the relationship of certain elements in food rituals to elements appearing in other areas of Temiar culture. I turn now to one of those other areas: ritual behaviour towards natural species that for the most part do not provide food, but which are nevertheless of considerable importance in everyday life.

In the preceding chapter, notice was taken of actions that are prohibited in relation to wild animals, and which if performed are believed to lead to the direct intervention of the thunder-deity Karey. Any act thought likely to attract Karey's insatiably curious attention in this way is known as *misik*.[21] Or, more strictly, *misik* is the state of ritual danger that people find themselves in as a result of such actions. The key 'ideal type' of a *misik* action is to draw undue attention by mocking animals regarded as the 'familiars' of Karey, whether by direct contact or by pointing. There are many other actions, not involving animals, that are also believed to lead to *misik*.[22] Altogether, actions of this sort, including mockery of animals, are known as *terlaac*, which Schebesta (1957: 95) regarded as meaning 'to

---

21. [Added 2014] On phonological and semantic grounds, I long suspected that *misik* was etymologically a Temiarised version of the Malay *bising* 'disturbing noise'. But the Temiars I questioned always denied the connection—until 1979, when one man not only acknowledged it but wondered how anyone could have failed to see such an obvious linkage. The alternative suggestion of derivation from Malay *bisik* 'to whisper' is phonologically unsustainable, as that becomes *bisig* when borrowed into Temiar; the meaning too would hardly apply to thunder.

22. [Added 2014] According to Wakil ʔabaaɲ in 1968, there are two basic categories of *misik* actions. The first are those, such as the mocking of animals, that cause thunder, lightning and flood; the second are those involving blood-related actions, that attract tigers and their ilk. The latter is also known as *misik lɔɔt* 'blood *misik*', more properly called *belʔak,* or in tiger language (sic!), *maniiʔ*. In ordinary speech it is sometimes referred to simply as *ɲɔɔy* 'odour'. Wakil said that there was now a new word, *labur,* to label all forms of *misik*.

sin'.[23] Karey's intervention varies according to the gravity of the offence. If just one person commits an act of *misik*, then Karey does no more than cause a local thunderstorm. If several people misbehave, then he reacts by sending down his cords to throw the offenders about, perhaps to their death, in the manner described in Chapter 4. In an extreme case, Karey will also order the various subterranean devils with which he is associated to cause landslides and the welling-up of all-destroying floodwaters, on the pattern of the original Limbaŋ flood in the creation myth. This is also believed to be the normal reaction to mockery of those species classified as *jɛrʔaar* ('welling-up', of flood waters) in table 4.1. Most *misik* species are classed simply as *dɛŋdək* ('to thunder').

My informants in Humid claimed that such a flood had actually happened two generations ago in a village further upstream, where most of the inhabitants had mocked ants of the type known in Temiar as *tagaɲ*. The earth overturned and there was a great flood, both of which were caused by the subterranean devil-dragon Daŋgaaʔ (the Temiar version of the Southeast Asian *naga*) pulling on its widely extended cords on the orders of Karey.[24] Everyone was buried but for the one man who had not joined in the impious laughter; he escaped by fleeing to the nearest high ridge. The Temiars did not regard this tale as a 'legendary myth' (*cənal*) but as a 'recounting' (*kərɛnwəəh*) of an event that really took place during the lifetime of the present headman's father—which is to say that *misik* beliefs refer not to a remote possibility but to something that could affect every one of them at the slightest provocation. When thunder occurs, they undertake various rituals aimed to turn away the anger of Karey. I examine these later (Chapter 6), in another context. For the present, the task is simply to discuss the nature of *misik*-causing acts.

Essentially, it is *misik* to point at, laugh at, tease, or even refer to by name too frequently, any of the species listed in table 4.1. These species are believed to be particularly close to Karey as his *cɔɔʔ*, 'pets, familiars', or his *cɛʔ*, 'lice'. Many of them are further associated variously with prohibitions on blowpiping them, mimicking their calls, or speaking during their calls. As table 4.1 shows, there is a close but not quite complete correlation between these various features. The logic (if such there be) behind these further prohibitions seems to lie not in

---

23. [Added 2014] *Tɛrlaac* is the causative form of a root with many Mon-Khmer cognates, with such meanings as 'collapse, be destroyed, disappear, be lost, devastate, melt down'. See Shorto (2006) under **[r]laac* (p. 255) and **ləɲ* (p. 271) for the relevant forms. An obvious cognate is Khmer *plaaɲ* 'destroy, liquidate, abolish, kill, annihilate' (Gérard Diffloth, personal communication). Aslian examples include the *talaidn* and *lawaidn* of Schebesta (1927: 222–223), where the notated *ai* diphthong indicates that the final consonant was actually palatal (*ɲ, c* or *j*), not dental. All of these meanings, unlike Schebesta's guessed-at 'sin', are appropriate to the Thunder deity's reputed destructive power.
24. [Added 2014] This probably relates to the 'great flood' of 1926, which is regarded as the source of the dragon-based Səlumbaŋ cult, referred to several times in this volume. (See especially Appendix 2.2, and on the great flood, Winstedt (1927).)

any structural relationships between the various prohibited acts, but in the different opportunities, so to speak, provided by the various species for drawing unwanted attention towards themselves. They are all *misik* species in the usual way. But in addition they have distinctive calls that are easy to mimic, or calls that can be frequently heard while walking through the forest, or they are conspicuous fleshy tree-dwelling animals ideally suited to capture by blowpiping. The other *misik* species are not considered edible and make either no sound or sounds difficult to mimic. They compensate for this, though, by being so conspicuous as to make their presence noticed by any normally observant person. Many of them, such as butterflies, dragonflies or ants, are very common, to the extent that one would need to take positive action *not* to notice them. Whatever may be the 'message' carried by *misik* observances, it is firmly impressed on each individual Temiar in everyday contexts. The *misik* animals serve as potent tropes of what might otherwise be a much more obscure symbolic category.

This interpretation is strengthened by an examination of the other acts that are prohibited as *misik*. First comes a group of acts that may not be performed outdoors or within an abandoned house until it has been reoccupied for at least three days: plaiting, basketry, cane (rattan) scraping, tobacco shredding, and the weaving of fishing nets. In addition, during the daytime either outdoors or in an abandoned house, one may not spread out a dyed mat, boil food or water in metal vessels, use a mirror, or search one's body for lice. Also, one may not whittle blowpipe darts, go to sleep (*sic!*), or heat a blowpipe over the fire. (The latter is part of the normal maintenance procedure for blowpipes, and it *is* permissible to do it during the daytime within an abandoned house.) Finally, wherever one finds oneself, during the daytime it is forbidden to have sexual intercourse (some informants denied this), or heave long fresh bamboos or canes into a house so as to leave a part protruding through the doorway into the light.

Taken with the animal prohibitions, this listing provides a fairly full account of what in the Perolak valley is formally regarded as *misik*. In other valleys, different species and acts are so regarded, as I discuss later in another context (see, for example, Benjamin 1966: 11). Despite these variations in content, the meaning of *misik* beliefs remains constant.

What, then, is this meaning? To attempt to divine a structural pattern behind the patently heterogeneous list of species and acts that constitute the content of *misik* behaviour would seem a thankless task, and one that I am not going to attempt. Indeed, apart from such obvious points as that most of the *misik* species (in the Perolak valley, but not necessarily elsewhere) correspond with what English-speakers loosely call 'insects' or 'bugs', and that daylight is a constant feature in the other behavioural prohibitions, there is little regularity to be discerned in the content at that level. The Temiars themselves do link together the various items that make up *misik* prohibitions, but not in terms of any internal structural features. For them the matter is simple. One may not draw attention to any *misik* animal because it belongs to Karey, and one must not perform any of the forbidden acts because they attract Karey's attention. I can say little on present evidence as to how the various species become so closely associated with Karey in Temiar thought. The distinct local variations strongly suggest that this is largely a matter of individual revelation that has been crystallised in myth, in much the same way as *sabat* stipulations vary from place to place. For the other behavioural prohibitions, the Temiars themselves provide us with a perfectly acceptable rationale: each of the restricted acts is more or less out-of-the-ordinary. The normal place for their performance would be within an inhabited house. In the open, the bright colours of dyed mats, the shininess of fresh bamboo, metal pots, fresh cane and mirrors, and the quick darting movements displayed in the various technical and sexual activities, all serve to attract the attention of Karey's ever-watchful malevolence. As an informant put it, 'he comes down to take a closer look'. The same applies to these activities newly carried out in a house that has not witnessed them for some time.

The common element in *misik* beliefs and observances is, then, Karey himself. But here there is a slight paradox: what is the point of instituting a whole series of avoidances having no intrinsic structural relationship to each other and serving only to lessen the danger of harmful supernatural intervention—an intervention called into question almost solely by those very avoidances? The answer must be that the institution of *misik* serves not so much to avoid Karey's intervention as to keep the thought of him alive in the mind of every Temiar. Karey exists *at all* precisely by virtue of the taboos instituted ostensibly to lessen the effects of his existence. Karey is a necessary concept that must be kept in the forefront of Temiar religious representations. For the Temiars, as we shall see, Karey is the highest embodiment of the concept of evil in their religious system. The function of *misik* taboos is to state clearly and repeatedly that evil is an ever-present component of the Temiar world—to serve, as I said earlier, as the everyday tropes of that concept.

Since the idea of evil represented by Karey is so basic in Temiar thought, it is hardly surprising to find that the concept of *misik* overflows its formal boundaries and is applied on the spur of the moment to acts that few Temiars would place in a formal paradigm of what is forbidden. Any act that is even slightly out-of-the ordinary may be greeted with cries of *ham-jɛʔ ʔa- ...*, *misik!*, 'stop ..., it's *misik!*' In other valleys, especially further south, the cry is *tɛrlaac* (Evans (1923: 206); Schebesta (1957: 95)). Playing games with domestic animals may go a little too far. To point out any slightly unusual natural phenomenon, such as a rainbow or a peculiarly shaped cloud, is considered foolhardy by many people. Even to laugh heartily, especially at another person, may be brought to an end for fear of stirring up Karey's curiosity. Indeed, it seems that any activity carried to excess, especially if it has an emotional content, may be terminated for fear that it might cause *misik*. At the other end of the scale, the greatest crime known to the Temiar, sibling incest,[25] even though it does not normally bear the label *misik*, invokes precisely the same sanctions as the lesser acts that are so labelled. Interestingly, parent–child incest does not invoke sanctions of this kind: see Benjamin (1967c: 16, 1968a: 127–128) regarding the relative conceptual importance of the filiative and consanguineal ties.

Joluŋ

Just as *gɛnhaaʔ* observances have their logical antithesis in the *joruuʔ* observances discussed above, so also do *misik* beliefs find their mirror image in a set of stipulations known as *joluŋ*. During a mediumistic séance and for a few days following it, the house is believed to be blessed by the continuing presence of the spirit-guides (*gunig*) called down by the mediums. Any act likely to scare them away (they are regarded as extraordinarily shy and elusive) is *joluŋ*, and puts the whole community in the unhappy position of losing their protective beneficence. Acts of *joluŋ* bear a remarkable relationship to some of the acts that are believed to lead to *misik*. For example, one should not heave a long freshly cut cane into the house, or leave a fresh bamboo pole protruding through the door, or bring freshly-plucked aromatic herbs into the house—herbs different, that is, from those used to attract the spirit-guides down in the first place.[26] It is clear, then, that acts which in one context (*misik*) serve to attract the unwanted attentions of Karey, serve in another context (*joluŋ*) to repel the desired attentions of the swarm of spirit-guides. The 'message' is that whatever Karey *is*, the spirit-guide is *not*. If Karey is the embodiment of evil then it follows that the spirit-guide is the embodiment of good. The function of the *misik/joluŋ* contrast is not to *define* these qualities, for

---

25. They claim that murder simply does not occur among them. [Added 2014] Historically, as we now know, this is not true.

26. [Added 2014] In 1968, I was told by respondents in two different villages that *joluŋ* also applies to the same acts carried out near fruit trees that contain tiger-spirits (*kɔnoruk*) and lianas in the vicinity of the village. The tree then calls on various *kɔnoruk* tigers to act. The small tigers emerge first, and then call on the progressively bigger ones to carry out a revenge (*doos*) attack on the persons who committed *joluŋ*, by pouncing on whoever is available. The tigers might also eat the prey caught in the villagers' traps or their chickens. A great medium would foresee this in a dream and perform a flower-spirit séance (*pɔɔh boot*) in darkened *kɔbut* style (see Chapters 7 and 10) at the request of his tiger spirit-guide. The latter would then take the flowers, preferably rare mountain ones, as appeasement to the *sarak*-tiger, thereby preventing the trouble. Etymologically, this set of ideas suggests a connection with the Javanese word *julung* used to label a child born in astrologically unlucky circumstances and therefore thought liable to become the prey of a tiger (Prawiroatmojo 1981: 194). This word is also occasionally employed in both Indonesian and Malay (Wilkinson 1932: 438), though not always with the tiger connection.

that is ensured by other components of the religious system, but to bring them into opposition through tying them in with contrasting elements of everyday behaviour. (We shall see shortly just how spirit-guide beliefs become a feature of everyday behaviour.)

One feature of the *misik* complex that has been commented on by several authors, such as Evans (1937: 'blood-sacrifice' in the index), Schebesta (1957: 88) and Needham (1964), is its close association with beliefs and observances related to blood. This is most explicit in the rite of the blood-offering to be discussed in the following chapter, but there are indications that the relationship between blood and thunder in Temiar thought is even closer. As was generally the case with ideas concerning blood, I failed to obtain a coherent account from my informants, but I was told that there is 'another type of *misik*' known as *misik lɔɔt*, 'blood *misik*'. This possibly refers to rules of right behaviour whenever human (?) blood is shed; certainly, it is a topic for further investigation.[27] More striking is the part played by the leech as a *misik* animal. Both Needham (1964: 141–142) and Freeman (1967) see much significance in this, but I shall not examine their arguments here. In any case, the ethnographic data available to these authors was incomplete; and, as we have seen, the leech is but one of many animals in the *misik* category.

However, both Needham and Freeman were right in assuming that the obvious association of the leech with human blood makes it something of a special case. This is borne out by several ethnographic references to a prohibition on burning the leech, from the Negritos to the west of the Temiars or the Semais to the south (Evans 1923: 199; Schebesta 1957: 99). As far as my information goes, this is the only animal for which burning is formally regarded as likely to cause *misik*, although to deliberately burn any other live animal would very likely be regarded as dangerous. Burning, as we have seen, is a crucial element in two other ritual complexes, *genhaaʔ* and *joruuʔ*. This immediately suggests a possible relationship between these concepts and leech-*misik* behaviour. Although it is normally forbidden to burn leeches, it seems never to have been reported in the literature that it is *obligatory* to burn them once they have been carried into a house on someone's body or clothing. To throw such leeches out into the open again is an act of *misik*. Therefore, the prohibition on burning the leech in the forest could be regarded as a sort of *joruuʔ* prohibition (more usually concerned with not burning seasonal fruits), whereas the requirement that it must be burnt once it is brought into the house may be seen as a form of *genhaaʔ* behaviour (more usually concerned with ensuring the complete consumption within the house of

---

27. [Added 2014] Some later information on the ritual handling of problems caused by out-of-place blood is presented in Chapter 12.

certain edible animals). The leech is thus ambivalent: the animal itself is clearly in nature, but the human blood inside it ensures that it is also part of culture, and must be treated as such. (As we shall see later, it is the *human* component that represents culture in this case, for blood alone as a symbol represents quite the opposite—nature.)

Summary

It has been no part of the present discussion to wonder why certain species and not others are drawn into the pervasive system of ritual categorisations. I have too little evidence on which to decide the matter. In any case, such a discussion would not necessarily add significantly to our knowledge of the primarily religious concerns that interest us here. The important thing is not the nature of the various species but the category-based calculus they serve to express. The calculus remains for the most part uninterpreted: interpretation is the function of such other components of the religious system as myth and mediumship. But before passing on to other topics, it will be as well to look again at the conceptual entities generated by the ritual categorisation of natural species described in this chapter.

We have seen that eating implies the setting-up of sharply distinguished conceptual categories. First, a tripartite division is set up between (1) species that eat humans, (2) species that humans eat, and (3) species that humans feed ('cause to eat', in Temiar). The first and third categories correspond to a set of conjoint oppositions:

Dangerous animals	:	Domestic animals
Village	:	Forest
Women-&-children	:	Adult men
Culture	:	Nature

On this basis, the edible species in Category 2 must effect a 'passage from nature to culture'; they are mediators between the two domains.[28] The mediation is ensured by a complex set of rituals—*pocuk*, *gɛnhaaʔ*, *joruuʔ*—that make play with elements recurring throughout Temiar religious behaviour. The essential opposition seems to be that between ground (*tɛʔ*) and off-the-ground (*baliik*). Associated with this are the oppositions between exposure and burial and those between various

---

28. There is a parallelism between these food categorisations and the informal categorisations of suitable sexual or marriage partners, just as Leach (1964: 42f) reported for the English and the Kachins. Category 1 corresponds to the women of other valleys, who are thought likely to entrap one with sorcery (Chapter 7, Benjamin 1966: 14). Category 3 corresponds to the women of one's own village, with whom sex relations would be incestuous, at least ideally (cf. Benjamin 1966: 17, 1967c: 5). And Category 2 corresponds to the eminently approachable women of other villages in one's own valley.

other elements discussed earlier. Important here is the implied opposition between head-soul and blood: the first is tied up with the ritual categories *sabat*, *gɛnhaa²* and *joruu²*, the second with *pocuk* and *misik*. (I enlarge on this in the next chapter.)

Second, we find a cross-cutting set of ritual practices concerned with the deity Karey. The opposition expressed in these *misik* practices is ultimately the basic opposition between good and evil. We shall see in the following three chapters, however, that these two systems of categorisation become one single system when approached from the wider viewpoint of Temiar culture as a whole.

| Chapter | *Temiar Religion (1967)—* |
| 6 | Souls |

This long chapter is in many respects the core of the present study. Here, I discuss the ways in which the wider categorisations of Temiar religious thought become internalised in humans as soul beliefs and then extended similarly to the rest of animate (and in some cases inanimate) nature. Much of the data derives from the dogma-like statements of Temiar informants when asked for a paradigmatic exposition of their beliefs. Although I use the 'dogma' to help order the argument, most of what follows is a description of the many ritual activities in which the soul beliefs become manifest. I shall accordingly discuss Temiar ideas about diseases, passage rites, mortuary practices and other related topics, such as the symbolism of blood and hair. At intervals, it will prove necessary to interpolate theoretical discussions to lay bare the underlying structure of these practices and prepare the way for a fuller discussion of Temiar theology in Chapter 8.

However, since the soul beliefs are themselves reflexes of the wider categorisations that pervade other fields of activity, I start by discussing certain 'totemic' diseases that directly reflect these categorisations.

'Totemic' diseases

In the last chapter, we learnt of the various misfortunes that are believed to afflict people as a result of certain voluntary actions. In this chapter, I examine diseases believed to result from acts that are mostly involuntary, in that the offenders usually do not realise that they have done wrong until they fall ill. Once the disease has been recognised, its cause may then be discovered and the harm undone through a variety of ritual acts performed by the patient or by a medium. Most diseases of this sort result from acts that threaten to override the hard-won category distinctions discussed earlier; but some of the disease beliefs serve to set up further category distinctions of a less universal kind.

The first group of diseases is concerned with the off-the-ground/ground (*baliik/tɛʔ*) distinction. These are frequently stated to be the causes of several minor bodily upsets.

Təracɔɔg

This is perhaps the most commonly cited group of diseases. The symptoms vary and are believed to depend on the nature of the offending act. In any case, the offending act is recognisable generally only after the event, when the disease symptoms appear. Nevertheless, there are certain precautions one should take for fear of coming into contact with any *təracɔɔg*-causing object or situation. The list of acts believed to cause *təracɔɔg*, and the respective forms taken by the affliction, are complicated. But as *təracɔɔg* is itself complex, we can best understand it by examining all of its manifestations.

One set of *təracɔɔg*-causing acts entails the penetration by the elements of the ground into the domain of off-the-ground. Here, soil is the operative factor. Violent headaches, followed by bodily shivering and ultimately death, are believed to result from bringing firewood or bamboo into the house with soil still trapped in the ends. Various types of ants build nests that project up from the ground. Sitting on or near the mound of the *takɔr* ant or the funnel of the *mɛrsəwar* ant may prove to have been the cause of an attack of boils over one's body. If this happens, the offending ants' nests should be searched out (they are usually hidden under a layer of leaves), then dug up and drenched in boiling water. At the same time, one should make oneself known to the ants: 'You, I've seen you and I know you're there. Don't *təracɔɔg* me. I'll pull you apart, I'll heat up some water, and I'll dig you up!'

Any hollow object that has been used as a container for food or water, especially the ubiquitous bamboo tube but also the increasingly common tin can (figure 6.1), should not be thrown into the river after use. If sand and gravel from the river bottom enter it, it is thought likely to lead to a form of *təracɔɔg*

Figure 6.1 Discarded cans at Jias (2010), deliberately punctured to prevent *təracɔɔg*
This community is now Christian, and the canned food was supplied by the missionaries who converted them. Nevertheless, there appears to be a continuing fear of the improper entrapment of on-the-ground items within off-the-ground items. (See also Jennings 1995: 65.)

in which the victim dies from respiratory failure (*səlood*, the word used also for 'to drown'). If a bamboo contains trapped water in its basal sections these should be carefully cut away before it is taken home for domestic use. Otherwise, maggots (which are normally ground-dwelling) might breed there and cause a form of *təracɔɔg* with deafness as its main symptom.

Second, there is a set of *təracɔɔg* afflictions that result from acts in which the ground (literally) is penetrated by elements belonging properly to the domain of off-the-ground. Temiar houses are built on wooden pillars, which necessarily penetrate several feet into the ground. To prevent a permanent state of *təracɔɔg* resulting from this, a rite is performed before the first insertion of each pillar. A pebble is placed at the bottom of the foundation hole and water is then poured onto it from a bamboo while the builder utters an imprecatory spell. The symbolism of this is obscure, but it is surely relevant that once the house is completed, pouring water away so that it flows down the pillar into the ground is then regarded as a possible cause of *təracɔɔg*. If, despite all precautions, the disease should occur (and it will be of the respiratory failure type), the offending pillar must be pulled up and replaced.

Care should be taken when eating in the open to avoid littering the ground with crumbs or remains of food. The danger is that ants of various species carry them below the ground, thereby possibly causing an attack of *təracɔɔg*. Similarly, many Temiars (this varies from valley to valley) believe that to bury a corpse along with belongings that have been used by someone else is likely to lead to *təracɔɔg*. For the same reason, many individual Temiars are afraid to bury their children's hair-clippings; instead, they keep them in a packet stowed on the wall of the house. They even fear to use water closets or earth latrines when these are available. If possible, one should defecate into running water so that fish may eat the stools before they become absorbed into the river bottom.

So far, the overall symbolism remains clear: any confusion of the primary categories of ground and off-the-ground is likely to be dangerous. *Təracɔɔg* beliefs serve, then, to maintain the distinctness of these categories. But for the Temiars, *təracɔɔg* refers primarily to a type of headache believed to result from actions or phenomena that are difficult to interpret in the foregoing manner. The head feels exceedingly heavy and as if tightly bound; the eyes are swollen and heavy, and the neck stiff. The 'type' case results from contact with a pair of trees whose trunks have become fused along part of their length. This fusion is known as *gerpid*, the name by which *təracɔɔg* in general is known in those valleys where its 'true' name is treated as ineffable. Similar beliefs are that *təracɔɔg* may result from contact with a tree intertwined with lianas, or from carrying home a bamboo the top of which was caught in the canopy-level foliage. Presumably, it is thought anomalous for a plant to be held off the ground by the associated forest growth on being felled, when it would normally fall to the ground. The form taken by the disease in these cases is that of severe continuing headache, which must be cured by the medium's felling and cleaving the offending fused growth. A dream leads him to the right place.

Tanig and *mamɛɛŋ*

Two other diseases are believed to result from actions that confuse the category distinction between ground and off-the-ground. *Tanig*, a gouty disease of the leg joints and feet is caused by the intervention of a demon of the same name who is black and hairy 'like a Tamil', and lives in the river rapids. It follows a first-time contact with the stones of an area of *teʔ sǝmɛryɛŋ* 'rocky outcrops', where the basal rocky element of the ground projects conspicuously into the off-the-ground space, thereby blurring the distinction between the categories.[1] The second disease, *mamɛɛŋ*, is a violent headache caused by the dripping of dew (*tɛŋmɛɛŋ*) onto one's head from the roof of a house or from a tree. (Both words are inflected forms of the same root **mɛɛŋ*, which I have not otherwise recorded.[2]) Clearly, the proper place for dew is on the ground; when transposed into an anomalous off-the-ground position, it becomes dangerous. This type of *mamɛɛŋ* is naturally contractible only in the early morning. From this point of view, it is concerned not only with delimiting ground from off-the-ground but also with a further category distinction between night and day, which is expressed in other disease beliefs too. The periods when the one is passing into the other are regarded as dangerous. At dawn and dusk, all sorts of malevolent influences are thought to be abroad. Indeed, *mamɛɛŋ* itself may also be brought on by shouting or talking too loudly in the morning just before dawn: an already unstable situation should not be made more so.

Mamǝʔ, paad and *bahyaaʔ*

Several other diseases serve as expressions of the dangers held to be inherent in dusk and dawn. *Mamǝʔ* is a severe itching of the legs that affects 'allergic' individuals only. It arises after one enters the water during the night, early morning or late evening, but not during the daytime. The cause is said to be the coldness of the water at that time, and the treatment is accordingly to give oneself a good warming at the fire. After a night spent catching frogs, for example, Temiars commonly stand right over the fire when they get home and

---

1. [Added 2014] Penghulu Dalam also described *tanig* to me in non-supernatural terms as a throbbing of the leg muscles making it difficult to walk, sometimes occurring after heavy exercise. Dr Malcolm Bolton identified one such case in Humid as gout. Phonologically, *tanig* looks as if it derives from Malay *tanding*; but the latter's usual meaning ('comparison') hardly seems to fit the Temiar usage. However, *tanding* can also mean 'a heap (of fruits or grains)'. This might just fit, in reference to the rough stones that Temiars associate with the disease *tanig*.

2. [Added 2014] I now suspect that the word *mamɛɛŋ* derives from the Malay *mambang*, the name of certain malevolent spirits thought to be associated with the glow of sunset (Skeat 1900: 428). The phonological shift would be perfectly regular, and the meaning would fit with the view that *mamɛɛŋ* is likely to strike at dusk or dawn. A less likely possibility is a derivation from the Malay *mamang*, which Wilkinson (1959) defines as 'a strong unnoticing stare; the eyes of a man fully awake'.

waft the smoke over their bodies and clothing for a few seconds. This, they hope, clears them of the possible ill effects of being in the wet late at night.

More serious are two types of water demons living in the sand of the river bed that send out creeping tentacles in early morning and late evening. These tentacles eventually come upon a human waist to attack, whereupon they liquefy and enter the upper body to eat away the blood of the person's *hup*, the seat of the emotions. The larger of these two demons is known as Bahyaaʔ, which in fact means 'crocodile'—an animal known to the Temiars by tradition only, as it does not occur within their territory. The smaller is known as Paad, a Temiar root meaning 'to suck dry', as when a person chews sugarcane or Karey, the thunder deity, sucks dry the flesh of people who misbehave. It occurs also in the curse *nam-pɛdpaad* 'may he suck (you) dry!' shouted at someone who passes wind inside the house. It is also believed that Paad afflicts the rump of a person who sleeps too close to his parents, and it thereby bears some relation to incest regulations.

There are yet other diseases considered to result from the dangers of dusk and dawn, but it will be best to discuss these after first examining the nature of Temiar soul beliefs.

Soul concepts

Needham (1964:148) has remarked that 'the opposition nature/culture is as aptly to be established within man as between him and the rest of creation'. This provides us with a clue to understanding Temiar ideas of the soul, for the oppositions between the various multiple souls that inhabit natural species and topographical features may be viewed, in part at least, as reflexes of the larger oppositions I have been examining.

Since the Temiars do not possess any single concept of 'the soul' in the abstract, the subject is difficult to discuss with them. The nearest I could get to asking for a complete inventory of the souls each human being is believed to possess was by employing periphrastic expressions containing the Malay word *semangat*, with the suggestion that for the Temiars there were perhaps several different types of *semangat* (not just one, as the Malays believe). The danger lies in the fact that the Malay concept of *semangat* corresponds rather well with one particular Temiar soul concept, that of the *rǝwaay* or head-soul. Nevertheless, continued probing did provide useful and detailed information on their soul beliefs.[3]

---

3. 'Soul' is used here in the non-committal sense of *Notes and Queries* (1960: 176): 'an immaterial aspect of human personality', with the proviso that it is extended also to the worlds of animate and inanimate nature. [Added 2014] As indicated in Chapters 2 and 12, I have since revised my ideas about 'soul', which I now see as referring to the animistic notion that entities contain communicable-with subjectivities (or 'minds'), usually thought of as lodged in particular parts of the body—and therefore less 'immaterial' than the *Notes and Queries* definition would suggest.

The human being possesses four identifiable souls: the head-soul, *rəwaay*; the heart-soul, *jərəək* (or *hup,* see below); the eye-soul, *kɛnlɔɔk*; and the shadow, *wɔɔg*. Of these the first two are by far the more important in Temiar affairs, although the latter, especially the shadow, do play some part. There is a certain amount of functional interplay between the various souls, but they seem on the whole to be independent of each other.[4] However, this does not accord entirely with the beliefs reported by Stewart (1947: 21–22), who describes four secondary souls under the sway of one primary heart-soul, the *sengik*. In the course of my fieldwork I did not come across any Temiar word that both corresponds with Stewart's spelling and fits into the context of this discussion.[5] Of Stewart's four secondary souls, only three correspond with the listing I obtained, but, as Stewart himself states, 'the degree to which the concepts were employed by individuals in different localities were [*sic*] extremely variable'. In defence of my own account, I can only say that my informants in very different areas gave explanations essentially similar to the one I give here.

The head-soul

The head-soul, *rəwaay*, dwells in the roots of the hair, which for the Temiars form a part of the brain.[6] Traditionally, the Temiars never completely shaved their hair for fear that the head-soul would find no resting place. This is still true of the children, who retain a small tuft of hair for the head-soul to reside in when they have their heads shaved, usually as a delousing measure. As already noted, this tuft (over the forehead for boys and at the crown of the head for girls) is known as the *wɔɔj,* the same word as is used for the roots of the hair (figures 2.2 and 6.2). This concern that the head-soul should be provided with at least a minimal resting place suggests that it is not fixed, but labile. Temiars do indeed believe that the head-soul may leave the body with ease. Dreaming is said to be one of its activities, as it leaves the body during sleep and travels far and wide to observe and perform a wide range of acts. Furthermore, one does not dream *directly* of someone in Temiar, but

---

4. [Added 2014] In my later studies of Temiar religion (printed here as Chapters 10–14) I have in practice reduced the soul-inventory to just two: the *rəwaay* 'head-soul' and the *hup* 'heart-soul'. While that approach differs to some extent from what is presented here, it corresponds better to the manner in which Temiars usually talk spontaneously about these matters. Roseman's and Jennings's accounts also mostly follow this procedure, with Roseman providing additional details about the other 'soul' concepts, the *wɔɔg* 'shadow' and *ŋɔɔy* 'odour'. However, I no longer consider these to be souls in the sense adopted in the rest of this volume, despite their undoubted relevance to Temiar daily practice. A further development is that I now regard what I described as a 'functional interplay' between the 'independent' *rəwaay* and *jərəək/hup* as constituting a single dialectical relation.

5. [Added 2014] On later visits, I did come across Stewart's *sengik* (as *sənjiiʔ*), but it seemed by then to have lost any of the importance he had ascribed to it. In any case, he mentions it on very few pages in the whole thesis. Moreover, some Temiars told me that *sənjiiʔ* was a Semai word, and that it was identical with the *hup*, 'that part of us which cares for the people we love and keeps them together'. I later confirmed this when speaking Temiar to collect a wordlist from a Semai-speaker, who gave *sənjiiʔ* as the Semai translation for *hup*.

6. [Added 2014] Significantly, Jennings (1995: 63) characterises the *rəwaay* as situated 'on' the body, in contrast to the *hup*'s position 'inside the body'.

Figure 6.2 Young girls with wɔɔj tufts at the back of their tonsures, Sengsaak (1964)
For a male example, with the tuft at the front of the tonsure, see the young boy in figure 2.2.

of that person's head-soul. Dream-encounters are therefore regarded as the encounters of disembodied head-souls.

Absence of the head-soul, however, puts one in danger. Only in sleep is one safe without it, and it is regarded as dangerous to wake sleepers from their slumbers. If it should prove necessary to do so, then it must be done as gradually as possible or the subjects may find themselves awake while their head-souls are too far away to return with ease. Prolonged absence of the head-soul while awake gives rise to the sickness known as rɛywaay ('to lose one's head-soul'), the imperfective verbal form of the word rəwaay. One description of this disease ran as follows. Three or four days without a head-soul leads to death, but before this happens or while undergoing a mediumistic cure, the sufferer is supposed to pass through quite recognisable stages, which tell us much about how the head-soul is believed to function. The patient begins to feel drowsy and loses any appetite for food, then sleeps fitfully for a day or two and becomes really ill, sometimes reaching a state of delirium and great weakness. The other villagers carry out mediumistic healing rituals, urging the patient to avoid falling asleep, and washing his or her body with cold water to prevent that from happening. If this meets with success then the patient recovers—the missing head-soul returns home—and, so my informants claim, is astonished to learn what happened, having been unconscious of his or her surroundings while in the *rɛywaay* state.[7]

Although the head-soul is regarded much as a free agent, its absences from the body are as likely to be caused by being enticed or snatched away under external influences as under its own volition. This usually occurs when someone has offended the *rəwaay* of a plant that is of some use to humans. (I shall discuss shortly just what it means for a plant to possess what in other creatures is regarded as the head-soul.) The offended plant's *rəwaay* takes away the offender's *rəwaay* and carries it off either to a swidden (in the case of cultivated plants) or to a stem or trunk. There, the two *rəwaay*s disport together until such a time as the human *rəwaay* is returned to its owner's body by the ministrations of a medium. The relationship between the two souls is conceptualised as that between elder and younger siblings, the plant *rəwaay* being the senior. In form, both sorts of *rəwaay* are thought to be like manikins, variously male or female according to species, but people can see them in this form only when they appear as *gunig* spirit-guides in dreams.[8]

The plants treated in this manner fall into three groups: *canaaʔ*, the staple food crops; *boot səlaay*, cultivated flowers; and *bərək*, seasonal fruits, whether wild or cultivated. The *canaaʔ ʔasal*, the 'food crops of the Creation' (sugarcane, banana, caladium, yam, millet and sweet potato), must not be allowed to float away downstream nor may they be sworn at—otherwise the plants' *rəwaay*s imagine that they are being abandoned from human care. The same applies at the beginning of their seasons to the non-'Creation' but economically more valuable crops, cassava and rice. Cultivated flowers, which the Temiars use as body decoration, must not be allowed either to float away downriver or be burnt on the fire. Depending on the species, they must either be eaten in a stew as a vegetable or be hung up in the house to die naturally. This applies even to the most recently introduced plants if they require tending as they grow. Seasonal fruit trees of any sort must not be burnt on the fire or sworn at, nor must their fruits be allowed to float away in the river. More casually, one should take care in all of one's dealings with cultivated plants to ensure that they receive the full benefit of people's care. Even if one drops a few crumbs of tobacco onto the floor by accident, one will be greeted by cries of *rəwaay hah!* '[watch out for] your head-soul!' Many people regard careless treatment even of manufactured confectionary in the same suspicious light. In

---

7. [Added 2014] Significantly, this is similar to the typical response of spirit-mediums when coming round from their trance state, as discussed further in Chapter 10. Appendix 1.2 presents a brief account by Noone (1937) of a séance at which the spirit-medium was described as bringing back a child's wandering *rəwaay* by sending his own *rəwaay* after it while in trance.

8. [Added 2014] Roseman (1991: 123–126) showed that the presumed sex of the *gunig* is significant, at least insofar as most mediums are male and at least two-thirds of spirit-guides are females, often thought of in erotic terms.

an alternative account of *rɛywaay*, the offended plant soul carries the human head-soul off to Tanig, the earth-demon. If this occurs, only the spirit-guides of powerful mediums are able to search out the lost souls and return them to the patient. In the Brok and Telom valleys, certain mediums are reported to make a speciality of dealing with Tanig in this way.[9]

The head-soul, then, is essential for the continuance of life. There exists a distinct term (*sakɔb*) for the purely physical body in the absence of the head-soul; this word is not the same as that used for 'corpse'. The general problem posed—when is a body not a body?—is mentioned by Firth (1955) in his paper 'The Fate of the Soul'. Death, finally, is the irreversible loss of the head-soul. Yet it should not be thought that the head-soul is treated with any great solemnity. Its characterisation as a manikin fits well with the easy-going attitude the Temiars seem to take in its regard. Jokes about it are not unknown: one man, for example, after giving his son's head rather too close a shave, remarked that his head-soul had probably gone down to his stomach, and this caused much amusement. It may be that its role in dreams is what allows the head-soul to be regarded in such a light-hearted manner— dreaming is so highly valued as a source of good. Also, spirit-guides are generally met with in the form of *rəwaay*, and this whole field of activity is for the Temiars a joyous one.

The heart-soul
Whereas the head-soul controls the emergence of the full vital functions, it is the heart-soul, *jarəək*, that is supposed to generate the initial thoughts, speech and motivations. As one informant put it, 'the heart-soul controls our thoughts while the head-soul enables their utterance'. I have referred to it as the 'heart'-soul, but it is not at all certain that the Temiars regard it as so tightly localised. Strictly speaking, the *jarəək* is the soul of the *hup* (the 'seat of the emotions', usually identified as the liver) and of the breath, *hənum*. Linguistically, *hənum* 'breath' is a derivative of *hup*; but the latter word is harder to characterise. Whatever its basic meaning, *hup* clearly has an anatomical reference. My informants used the word to identify both the heart and the liver. On the other hand, both the liver and the kidneys alike are known by another word (*ʔɛnrɔs*, *ʔɛnrʉs*). Stewart (1947: 21) regards the *jarəək* (which he spells *jereg*) as the *liver*-soul, but only one source (Adams 1922: 113) translates *hup* as 'liver'. At least

---

9. [Added 2014] In 1968, I was told that *rɛywaay* soul-loss is greatly feared during the flowering of seasonal fruit trees. The treatment is for the medium to obtain the offending flower and hang it up as a *tənamuuʔ* (ceremonial spirit-welcoming wreath). He then trances it and collects its *kahyɛk* (liquefied spirit-essence) in his outstretched hands and spreads it over the patient's head. The errant *rəwaay* then returns, the patient feels 'cool', and is immediately fed on waking up. A great medium can return a missing *rəwaay* in the daytime, but a small medium can only do so at night. I was told that in the old days the medium would collect the *kahyɛk* liquid in a china bowl and show it around. (Compare this with Noone's (1937) report in Appendix 1.2.)

three other published sources translate *hup* as 'heart' (Blagden 1906: 544, B380b; Schebesta 1931: 651; Carey 1961: 88),[10] and in view of the way in which the Temiars regard the *jərəək* it seems more meaningful to regard it as the heart-soul rather than the liver-soul. But the confusion remains, aggravated rather than simplified by the conscious equation of the Temiar *hup* with the Malay *hati*, which Wilkinson (1963: 92) glosses 'the heart and liver; the seat of the feelings'.[11]

However, precise anatomical location may be irrelevant to the present discussion. A possible solution was suggested by one Temiar, who claimed that the *jərəək* is nothing more than the *hup* that has left the body, either as mediumistic lycanthropy (when it takes the form of a were-tiger) or after a person's death, whether a medium or not. This view certainly fits well with much of what follows, but it did not seem to be shared (explicitly) by the majority of those I questioned. What is significant about the heart-soul is its association with the blood, and secondarily with the breath.[12] This will become clearer later. I have little information on the supposed form and function of the heart-soul in the living individual. Although Stewart's data (1947: 110–111, 1957: 22) differ on this point, my informants claimed that only the heart-soul of a medium has the power to leave the body.[13]

---

10. [Added 2014] To these should be added Means (1998: 53), who also (correctly) lists such meanings as 'mood, feeling, emotion'. But she seems unaware of the word's more specifically religious connections.

11. [Added 2014] Roseman (1991: 30–36) and Jennings (1995) provide further information on Temiar heart-soul ideas. Although I have translated *hup* as 'heart(-soul)', it also encapsulates 'liver'; but speakers do not usually bother to distinguish the two organs, except on the rare occasions when they are discussing them as meat, when *hup* means 'liver'. One respondent told me that the *jərəək* is in the blood as well as in the heart (*ʔɛnrŭs*) and the *hup*. This only increases the confusion, as *ʔɛnrŭs* in its narrowest anatomical sense means 'kidney'. The linguist Eric Oey (1990: 142–143) has added a comparative perspective to this semantic puzzle by pointing out that

> Malay and other Southeast Asian languages regularly employ expressions constructed primarily around the term for 'liver/heart,' but involving additionally the 'mind,' 'head,' 'blood,' 'mouth,' 'hands,' 'face,' or other body constituents. ... In Malay, much of what is regarded as conscious mental activity is thought to take place not in the brain, but in the heart or liver. The Malay word most commonly used to refer to such activity is *hati* literally meaning 'liver' ... but also frequently denoting 'heart'.... In older texts, *hati* also can refer to the liver, heart, gall-bladder, and 'viscera' collectively.

My own view is that what seems so confusing to observers operating in a non-dialectic framework (including Stewart 1947: 22) does not confuse those, like the Temiars, who subscribe to a dialectical mode of orientation, where an entity can indeed be thought of as simultaneously partaking of other entities.

12. [Added 2014] Later, in 1968, I was told that the seat of the *hup* is both the liver (*hup*) and the blood. The *hup*'s function is to tell us what activity we should do next. The same respondent said that the term *jərəək* was an older word for *hup*, with which it is identical. Another respondent said that the *jərəək* is the leaving-tiger aspect of the *hup* of old-time tiger-mediums. For further discussion of the complicated Mon-Khmer etymology of *hup*, which also links it with 'breath' and 'breathe' (both of which are *hemnum* in Temiar), see Benjamin (2012b: 211–212).

13. [Added 2014] In 1968, however, I was told that even a *halaaʔ* medium would die if his *hup* were to leave the body. This corresponds to Stewart's statement (1947: 110–111) that even a great medium's heart-soul (here, *sengik/səɲiiʔ*) must not leave his body. But this directly contradicts a statement by Noone (1937): 'the "heart-soul" may leave the body and journey fancifully in dreams, but when the "*ruwai*" or "head-soul" departs, it means death.' Given that I now see the head-soul and the heart-soul as partaking in each other dialectically, the apparent confusion is understandable. Indeed, I have heard Temiars themselves invert the terminology when speaking casually, which they would not normally do when speaking more carefully.

The heart-souls of ordinary people leave only at death. Like the head-soul, then, the heart-soul is necessary for the continuance of life.

The eye-soul

The eye-soul, *kɛnlɔɔk*, is rarely mentioned. It is the soul of sight and dwells in the eyeball. Its function is to enable people to use their bodies to the full and to guard over their various skills. Like the other souls, the eye-soul is believed to leave the body only at death and, while not exactly essential for the continuance of life as such, it is essential for the especially *human* way of life, involving as it does the use of special skills.[14]

The shadow

Although not situated within the body, the shadow, *wɔɔg*, is regarded as a permanent attribute of the human personality.[15] Little mention is made of the shadow (as a soul, that is) during a person's life, except in relation to illness. Sick people are often partitioned off by a curtain from all but their closest relatives (their parents or spouse) to prevent the shadows of any other people from falling upon them. This amounts to a taboo that puts the patient's life in danger if it is broken. However, no informant was able to explain the reason for this observance.

The souls after death

At death, all four souls are released from the body, whereupon they undergo various transformations. The head-soul, heart-soul and eye-soul proceed towards the sunset where they meet up with the deity known as Tohaat.[16] Like most Temiar Creator figures, Tohaat is conceived of as a sort of matriarch or *yaa?*, 'grandmother', and she is often known simply as *Yaa? Sɔy ʔis*, 'Granny Sunset'. Her name bears a double meaning. In the first place, Tohaat is transparently a Temiarised form of the (pre-Muslim) Malay deity Tuhan, best regarded simply as 'God'.[17] But it is also an hypostatisation of the term of address *tohaat*, 'healer', used towards a medium or midwife (or even a modern

---

14. [Added 2014] In 1968, I was told that *kɛnlɔɔk* was an old-fashioned term for the *hup*, and that the two are identical. The *kɛnlɔɔk* may be seen in the eyes, but it 'enters into our blood', and is what escapes when an animal's liver is butchered. Noone (1937) too explicitly refers to the *'kenlok'* as the 'heart-soul' (Appendix 1.2).
15. [Added 2014] In 1968, I was told that the *wɔɔg* is the same as the *sarɔɔʔ*, a word normally used for 'corpse'. Perhaps here it is just a way of referring to the physical source of the shadow. Unlike the *hup*, the *wɔɔg* does not tell us what to do. Roseman (1991: 40–45) provides significant new information on the *wɔɔg*. However, as already noted, I would not regard it as a 'soul' in the 'subjectivity-containing' sense adopted in this volume. In 2008, as if to confirm this suspicion, I heard a Temiar say *tɔʔ bar-wɔɔg* 'there's no *wɔɔg*' when his television set failed to show any image; they also use *wɔɔg* to refer to someone's image in a photograph.
16. [Added 2014] The common fate of these 'souls' suggests that all three are manifestations or aspects of the *rəwaay* 'head-soul'. However, in 1968, I was told that the *hup* proceeds to the tigers at the debouchment downstream (*mɛŋkah rɛh*), which I took to mean the east. The old people had said that the *hup* may return as a *kɛnlɔɔk*-tiger, but this was not what most people still believed.
17. [Added 2014] Here, I merely note without explanation the sex difference between the apparently female Tohaat and the clearly male Tohan.

doctor) who has previously taken responsibility for the subject's health. There seems to be no clear connection between beliefs about Tohaat and beliefs about the other Temiar deities. Several informants from different areas, after telling me of the more conventional deities, vouchsafed the information that, of course, if I really wanted to know who started it all in the first place, then surely it was Tohaat. Furthermore, they claimed, the Malays who once lived downstream held the same ideas. Tohaat's dwelling-place in the sunset is known as 'the Flower-Garden' (Kəbun Boot in Temiarised Malay), and this is the nearest that the Temiars get to any concept of a Land of the Dead.[18] With the exception of the shadow, all human souls proceed to the Flower Garden, but only the head-soul remains there with any degree of permanency.[19] The heart-soul of an ordinary person is ejected again by Tohaat and returns to the area where its owner was buried. There, it prowls about in the form of a small tiger (of which more will be said later). It may thereafter be met only by a 'great' medium, some of whom possess human heart-souls as spirit-guides, which are called up at a séance in the same way as any other spirit-guide of the tiger class.

The heart-soul of a 'great' medium, on the other hand, is ejected by Tohaat right to the sunrise at the opposite end of the cosmos. There it joins up with the heart-souls of earlier mediums, all gathered together as ground-dwelling tigers of the *sarak* type (to be discussed shortly) in a great rock bearing the ineffable name of Batuuʔ Baloʔ. Such a tiger prowls around the forest as a 'metamorphosed heart-soul tiger' (*mamuug lãᾱs jərəək*), which, since it may be met with in waking life by anyone, is greatly feared by the Temiars. One of the dangers of talking too openly about a deceased 'great' medium is the possibility that uttering his name will attract the evil attentions of his heart-soul's were-tiger.[20]

The eye-soul at death changes into a whitish stone (*batuuʔ tərolɛw*) that remains for part of the time in the Flower Garden and the rest of the time travels about in the world of humans. Great mediums occasionally dream of these eye-soul stones, but they do not seem ever to adopt them as spirit-guides.

The afterlife of the head-soul is more complicated. On entering the Flower Garden, it is reconstituted into a perfect manikin. It then undergoes a

---

18. [Added 2014] This account should not be taken as definitive; it is just one imaginative projection among many possible ones. Roseman (1991: 202), for example, later found that the idea of a Flower Garden afterworld was explicitly rejected by Temiars she spoke to in other valleys. She suggests several possible reasons for the discrepancy, relating to the segmentary, uncentralised, character of Temiar society. One further possibility, not mentioned by Roseman, is that the Flower Garden idea may already have been moribund when it was reported to me in 1965 (not only in the Perolak valley but also in the Brok and Plus valleys of Kelantan and Perak respectively), and was forgotten soon afterwards. However, the concept plays no significant part in Temiar religious practice as I have observed it. On the other hand, I have overheard statements at funerals that clearly implied an afterlife belief: *Sɛnʔɔɔy mɛj, ciib ma-sɔy mɛj* 'Good person, go to a good end [?=sunset]'; *Hãᾱʔ ma-tɛʔ səjuʔ, kanɛɛʔ bɛdbʉd; hãᾱʔ sənaŋ, kanɛɛʔ payah* 'You to a cool land, but we are hot; you are comfortable, we have it difficult.'
19. [Added 2014] In 1968, this was confirmed by a respondent who said that, unlike the *hup*, the *rəwaay* does not return to this world.
20. [Added 2014] See Chapter 10 for a later account of an event that was explained in this way.

protracted purification under the guidance of Tohaat. Some say that between the time it leaves the body and the time it enters the Flower Garden, the head-soul takes the form of a frog. This may well constitute a sort of theory of recapitulation, as there are myths that claim people were originally frogs. Interestingly, Schebesta (1957: 314) reports that there is a Jahai Negrito word *ćankay* (*ćankei*, *chankei*), meaning 'frog', which is so similar to the name of the Mountain-Creator Cɛŋkey (figure 4.2) as to suggest a tenuous connection between concepts of the soul and the larger questions of cosmology.[21]

Life in the Flower Garden is much the same as on earth except, some people claim, that the houses are of the forest shelter (*diŋ-rəb*) type, unlike the full-scale forest-clearing longhouses typical of the world of the living. Otherwise, the topography and natural phenomena are unchanged. One informant, however, suggested that the afterworld was inhabited by the head-souls of the Temiars only. In general, though, I believe that Temiars would claim that at least all the Senoi and Negrito groups of whom they have knowledge share with them the same afterworld. As far as I could gather, there is no restriction in the admission of head-souls to the Flower Garden. There was no talk of differential treatment for the souls of the wicked, such as Evans (1937: 256) and others have reported for some related Aboriginal groups. Paradise—for such is the Flower Garden—is open to all.

Perhaps the Flower Garden's most striking feature is that it is filled with seasonal trees, the importance of which in Temiar culture I have commented on several times. Chief among these trees is the perah (*Elateriospermum tapos*), which, as already noted, is the most visible sign of the year's passing. The annual cycle is believed to be under the control of the deity Yaaʔ Podɛɛw, an hypostatisation of the perah species. (I was told that *podɛw* is one of the names of the perah in the Jahai Negrito language.) Yaaʔ Podɛɛw also is said to live in the Flower Garden, but my Temiar informants claimed that it is the Negritos to the west, especially the Jahais, who really understand her true nature. Schebesta's account (1957: 321), on the other hand, claims that Yaaʔ Podɛɛw (his ya-Pudeu) is a typically Ple (i.e., Pəlɛh, the mixed Semang–Temiar population of north-west Perak) deity, regarded as the [female] ruler of the afterworld ('Herrscherin im Totenreich'). Although our two accounts differ in many details, there is some confusion here between Tohaat and Yaaʔ Podɛɛw, a confusion that extends to the different interpretations proffered by my informants.[22] It is generally agreed that the annual fruiting of the various species of seasonal trees is the direct result of some influence emanating from the Flower Garden in the west. In one version Yaaʔ Podɛɛw causes the perah trees to fruit, while another denizen of the afterworld, Ciɲcɛm (variously, the

---

21. [Added 2014] At Rening in Pahang in 1968, I was told that Cɛŋkey does indeed mean 'frog', and that its *pəterii* spirit takes the form of a frog.
22. [Added 2014] In 1968, for example, I was told that at death the *rəwaay* goes 'to our origin over there' at the sunset, and that this was known in Perak as Podɛɛw.

collectivity of ancestors (Stewart 1947: 224) or the hypostatisation of human corpses known otherwise by the ineffable name Sarɔɔʔ 'corpse') controls the fruiting of the other (and lesser) seasonal trees. Simultaneously, Tohaat sets free the deceased human head-souls that have been dwelling in the Flower Garden so that they may gather around the new fruits and disport themselves, as described earlier. It is believed by some that this leaves the Flower Garden empty for a while. If the year's new fruits are sweet, then they betoken the release of the head-souls of young men and women. If bitter, it is the turn of the head-souls of men and women who died later in life. A simpler version states that Tohaat sets free the head-souls under her care during the fruit season so that they may revisit the area where they were originally buried. There, they gorge themselves on the wild fruit trees and the nearby swidden crops. The head-souls return to the Flower Garden some time later in the season. There is some confusion between different informants as to whether the burgeoning fruits are themselves the returning head-souls or whether the two are simply associated together.[23]

Since the latter view came from individuals whose theological ruminations were usually profound, it seems likely that it is the more 'correct' version. Nevertheless, it is significant that the new season's fruits are sometimes known as the 'metamorphoses' (*sɛdnid*) or 'returning home' (*mɛʔnaaʔ*) of human head-souls. Certainly, the arrival of the new fruits creates great excitement among the Temiars, and they often camp out in the forest at this time to collect them more efficiently. Moreover, it is surely no coincidence that Temiar social structure depends so closely on the ownership of seasonal fruit trees (Benjamin 1966: 18).

The shadow-soul (*wɔɔg*), as already noted, does not pass over to the afterworld on the death of its owner. Instead, it remains in this world as the deceased's ghost, *lɔɔʔ*. In the west, the ghost is known as *yɔɔj*, which seems to be the same as the Lanoh word that Schebesta (1957: 175) spelled *yurl*. Among the Temiars of Pahang—where *lɔɔʔ* is also the normal word for pig!—the ghost is sometimes known as *kɛjmuuj*, obviously cognate with the Kensiw and Lanoh Negrito word *kemoid* or *kemoij*, 'Leiche [corpse], Totengespenst [ghost]' (Schebesta 1957: 318).[24] Whatever it is called, the ghost is thought to haunt the area around its old village, and may be met with suddenly by anyone at any time. If this should happen, the thing to do is to hide and try to beat it with a stick before it does any harm. Ghosts are intrinsically wicked, and even the ghost of one's own mother may attempt to kill the unwary interloper. Some people believe that human ghosts eventually change into the horned toad *sɛgnug kaŋkooŋ* (*Bufo melanostictus*). Even then it would remain

---

23. [Added 2014] On later occasions, the association between seasonal fruits and returning human head-souls was sometimes, but not always, reaffirmed in discussions with respondents.

24. [Added 2014] In 1968, I was told that *kɛjmuuj* is a Semai word, which would explain its use in Pahang.

dangerous, as this is one of the animals falling into both the *misik* (Karey-attracting) and *jɛrʔaar* (flood-causing) categories (table 4.1).

Non-human souls

It is not only humans that are animated by souls, for plants, animals and mountains possess them also. But humans are unique in possessing as many as four distinct souls; the other beings possess fewer, usually two only. We have here an important clue in our search for the overall meaning of Temiar religious categories: the expanded human soul concepts may be regarded as representing an 'elaborated code', in contrast to the 'restricted code' implied by the fewer soul types characteristic of non-human beings.[25]

Rɘwaay, kahyɛk and *pɘtɘriiʔ*

Temiars generally hold that whatever has life must possess a *rɘwaay*, which in humans takes the form of the head-soul, and that death follows on its absence for more than a short time. The form of the *rɘwaay* in non-human species seems to remain a mystery for the Temiars (but see below). Their argument is simple—life presupposes a *rɘwaay*. Their concepts begin to take firmer shape, however, when they think about the form assumed by the *rɘwaay* when apart from the body it normally animates. This is especially so in the context of mediumship. When a medium enters into a relationship with a natural species as his spirit-guide in dreams or in public séances, it is not the species as such that becomes the spirit-guide, but one of its separable soul-like principles. In most cases, the relevant principle corresponds to the *rɘwaay*, and a spirit-guide is often known as the '*rɘwaay* of such-and-such'. This is especially true of the titles of spirit-guide songs. In dreams, the *rɘwaay* of plants and mountains appear as young men or young women, according to the species or peak. I can discern no general rule, however, for this difference in sex-ascription.

Yet it is not in the form of a *rɘwaay* that a natural species makes its mediumistic appearance. Usually, the soul-principle involved is the *kahyɛk*, which more strictly is the name given to the watery form taken by most types of spirit-guide when they have been called up at a séance.[26] I deal with this point in more detail later, when discussing Temiar mediumship. All types of plants and animals generate *kahyɛk*. Many people assume that in plants the *kahyɛk* is none other than the sap.[27] In animals, it probably corresponds

---

25. [Added 2014] As noted earlier, as well as in Chapter 2, this is over-elaborate. In practice, all animate entities are thought of a containing just two 'souls', as shown in table 2.1.
26. [Added 2014] According to Gérard Diffloth (personal communication), the wider Mon-Khmer cognates of *kahyɛk* have such meanings as 'snot', 'earwax', 'froth on fermenting beer', with the underlying meaning perhaps of 'secretion'.
27. [Added 2014] In 1968, Wakil ʔabaaŋ was more specific. In dreams, the *kahyɛk* materialises as a young man or woman; in trance it is seen as a sap (*cɘboh kahyɛk*). Withered plants have lost their

entirely to the *rəwaay*, which, when the facts of anatomy allow, is homologous to the head-soul of human beings. Mountains too possess what the Temiars explicitly acknowledge to be a form of *kahyɛk*, except that it often bears the distinct name *pətərii²*, which I believe to be a Temiarised form of the Malay *menteri*:[28] they sometimes refer to the head-soul as *mɛntərii² kuy*, 'minister of the head'. The important point is that, whether it is called *rəwaay* or *kahyɛk*, the soul-principle under discussion is regarded as the head-soul of animals or the soul of the above-ground parts of plants and mountains. The parallels are in fact quite marked. The human *rəwaay* dwells just below the topmost surface of the body in roots of the hair; the plant *rəwaay* (*kahyɛk*) dwells in the sap primarily in the outermost foliage; and the mountain *pətərii²* resides in the layer immediately underlying the surface of the peak.

Kənoruk and *sarak*

The localisation of the *rəwaay* or *kahyɛk* in the upper parts of the species they inhabit suggests that there may be a conjoint but opposed principle residing in the lower parts. We have seen that this holds true for human souls, in the opposition between the upper head-soul and the lower heart or blood-soul. The Temiars acknowledge quite explicitly that many natural species and mountains also are infused with soul principles homologous with the latter. Again the terminology is confused: instead of calling the lower-body principles simply *jərəək* or *hup* on the human pattern, the Temiars refer to them instead by the terms used more strictly for their appearance in the context of mediumship (see table 2.1). These terms are of some interest, and they are both, I believe, borrowings from Malay. The lower-body principle of plants and animals is known as the *kənoruk*. (Not all species possess a *kənoruk*, though, as we shall see shortly.) I have no doubt that *kənoruk* is an infixal Temiarised form of the Malay *kurung* (the phonological changes are quite regular). If this is so, then *kənoruk* means 'an enclosure'. Similarly, the lower-body principles

---

kahyɛk. While it is still located within the plant, the *kahyɛk*—which is its *rəwaay*—has the form of a stone (*batuu² kahyɛk*). Some mediums, especially among the Jahais, can find these stones in the plant, and keep them as good-luck charms to ward off disease. This is probably related to the *batuu² tərolɛw* mentioned earlier and to the *talɛw* of the Jahai mediums mentioned later. Hitam Tamboh, also in 1968, told me that a *batuu² kahyɛk* found in the forest is known as a *təgas*, and this is ideally what should be held in a medium's palm when he carries out ritual blowing for healing purposes or for averting a thunderstorm, as described later. These ideas appear to be the Temiar version of the belief in bezoar or mustika stones supposedly used by shamans and mediums in other parts of Southeast Asia. A *təgas* is regarded as a kind of amulet (*taŋkal*), and the word is probably related to the Malay *tegas* 'firm, resolute, tough'. I was also told that mediums sometimes materialise their patient's illness in their hand in the form of a stone while carrying out a *tɛnhool* blowing (Chapter 7), but that this involves trickery if the medium is not a 'true' healer. (Cf. Freeman (1967) on a parallel example of shamanic 'trickery' among the Ibans of Sarawak.)

28. [Added 2014] The word *pətərii²* has an unusual phonology: its consonants follow Temiar patterns, but the irregular first schwa vowel marks it as a Malay word. This suggests that the Temiars who pronounced it this way had not decided whether the Malay source was *puteri* 'princess' or *mĕnteri* 'minister', consequently fusing the consonants of the former with the vowels of the latter. However, as already indicated in table 2.1, I now think that *pətərii²* (which Roseman, 1991: 192, writes as *potərii²*) could indeed have derived from the Malay *puteri* 'princess', often used in the sense of a fairy spirit. The most famous of these in Malay legend is Puteri Gunong Ledang, the Spirit of Mount Ledang.

of mountains are known as *sarak*, which Temiars acknowledge to be their borrowing of the Malay word *sarang*, '(animal's) hole, nest.' The similarity between the meanings of *kənoruk* and *sarak* is so striking that we are led to ask precisely what it is that they are believed to contain.[29] Our strongest clue is in the belief that the human heart-soul is capable of metamorphosis into a tiger. Indeed, it is *as* a tiger that the disembodied heart-soul is usually recognised. The same is true of the lower-body soul-principles of plants, animals and mountains: the Temiars could give me no information on their normal resting form, but as disembodied wandering souls they appear in the guise of various kinds of tiger.

There seems to be little regularity in the list of species believed to possess *kənoruk* souls. The details that I managed to obtain are displayed in table 6.1, but a few words of explanation are called for. Only a small number of non-seasonal tree species are believed to possess *kənoruk*, among them the

Table 6.1 *Kənoruk*-possessing species

Animals

ʔamboj	wild pig
jɛɛd	barking deer
pəgər	fireback pheasant
rosaaʔ	sambar deer

Certain birds play a role in myths in which they carry people off to their own domain. Most of these are believed to possess *kənoruk*. Examples are:

hohooy	an unidentified game bird
tərək	rhinoceros hornbill
taŋkəwɔɔj	bay owl

Certain fishes likewise occur in myths and are *kənoruk*-possessing. An example is:

lɛmyɔm	kelah (mahseer) (*Tor* sp.)

Plants

All the demoniac trees listed in table 4.2 are *kənoruk*-possessing. In addition, certain non-seasonal fruit trees fall into this category (e.g., *lɛʔ* 'oaks').

The following plants also fall into this category:

boot ɲiləəm	a cultivated decorative flower
boot cəriik	a wild flower used by a great medium in his hut
ʔajɛɛl	a rattan used in construction work
manar	a rattan used in construction work
pənoruuʔ	a rattan used in construction work

29. [Added 2014] In 1968, Wakil Ɂabaaɲ of Humid gave me a slightly different account of these terms. He said that the *sarak* is the lair and the *kənoruk* is the tiger itself. Nevertheless, *sarak* is used for rocks and mountains and *kənoruk* for trees. All mountains with *pətəriiʔ* also possess *sarak*, but only the highest mountains possess *pətəriiʔ*. The latter is usually regarded as a young woman or a young man, according to how it appears in one's dreams.

taxon *lɛʔ*, 'oaks'. My informants stated explicitly that the *kənoruk* is directly equivalent to the heart-soul of human beings. It is capable of leaving the roots of its tree in the form of a tiger (*mamuug*, the general undifferentiated term), but while still within the tree it has no physical counterpart.

Many seasonal fruit trees (table 4.3) possess *kənoruk*. In principle, it seems that these are the species about which there are traditional stories— stories that generally involve complex series of metamorphoses of fruits into humans, and vice versa. The *kənoruk*-tigers are feared. Just as the *rəwaay*s of cultivated plants and seasonal fruits may make off with the *rəwaay* of anyone who treats them carelessly, the *kənoruk*s of seasonal fruit trees are likely to devour anyone foolish enough to utter a curse at them, after tripping over their roots or falling from their branches, for example. Many *kənoruk*-possessing trees, both seasonal and non-seasonal, are believed to emit a dangerous giddifying emanation from their sap if cut carelessly. This giddiness (*wɛ̃ɛ̃d*) is said to have much the same symptoms as an attack of *pocuk* (Chapter 5). The implied connection between *kənoruk* and blood is an important point to which I return later.

As far as I could gather, the *kənoruk*s of trees, both seasonal and non-seasonal, are thought to emerge in the form of ordinary full-sized tigers, but the *kənoruk*-tigers of other natural species and mountains differ from normal tigers in various ways. Some flowering herbs possess small but otherwise normal *kənoruk*-tigers, among them a flower (*ɲiləəm*) planted by the Temiars in their swiddens and a wild flower (*cəriik*) used by 'great' mediums within their séance huts. Certain types of cane used in construction work possess *kənoruk*-tigers that emerge small in size—described variously as being the size of rabbits or cats—but enlarge gradually as they pursue their interlopers. The *ʔajɛɛl* cane was said to possess a *kənoruk* tiger that attains the size of a barking deer, with a whitish lint-like coat. The *kənoruk* tigers of the *manar* and *pənoruuʔ* canes are of the same size, but their coats are respectively striped and greyish.[30] These cane *kənoruk*-tigers are not in ordinary circumstances 'wanderers'. But if one should commit an act of *joluŋ* by drawing any of these canes conspicuously through the doorway of a house in daylight (Chapter 5), it is believed that the canes' *kənoruk*-tigers then become 'wanderers' and follow the offender about until they have exacted their penance. The same is believed to happen if one chops these canes indiscriminately or swears at them.

Among mammals, some of those that are liable to cause an attack of *pocuk* are also thought to possess *kənoruk*: the barking and sambar deers, the fireback pheasant, and the unidentified ground-dwelling bird *jərɛgpaag*.

---

30. [Added 2014] One respondent later said that domestic cats do not to have a *kənoruk*, but if they are treated badly their *rəwaay* after death may call on their 'grandfather', the tiger, to devour the tormentor. I suspect that this statement expressed a hitherto unformulated general concern about treating animals properly rather than a formulated 'belief' about cats in particular.

There is no complete correlation, however, as there are *pocuk*-causing species that do not possess *kənoruk*—the domestic fowl and the mousedeer, for example. Further, there are species, such as the pig, that do cause *pocuk* but possess no *kənoruk*.

Of birds and fishes, it is believed that those which appear in traditional stories possess *kənoruk*, at least potentially. The rhinoceros hornbill, bay owl and fish-owl all possess *kənoruk* and all appear in stories as birds that succeed in carrying people off to their domain. There are probably many more of this kind, but my data do not stretch so far. The red-fleshed kelah fish (mahseer, *Tor sp.*), about which there are stories, possesses a *kənoruk* that gives rise to a reddish tiger the size of a barking deer. It is only recently, though, that this became known, when a kelah fish at Kuala Ber in Kelantan was reportedly seen to leave the water, levitate, and change into a tiger. Previously the kelah had not been considered a *kənoruk*-possessing species. We can only guess at what really happened, of course, but this is probably an example of how so much of the detailed content of Temiar religious concepts comes into being: through the dreams of respected mediums being reported far and wide.[31]

The *sarak* tigers of mountains are the archetypal 'wandering' were-tigers. They are said to regularly emerge at night from their lairs in the basal parts of the slopes as large creatures of various colours—black, white, striped, etc. They travel over wide areas and are the prime reason why the Temiars prefer to stay indoors at night. Each mountain may possess several *sarak* tigers.

Non-human eye-souls

Before discussing further the ideas presented so far, it must be noted in passing that the eye-soul also has its counterparts in the animal world. Fish and larger mammals are believed to possess *kenlɔɔk* in much the same way as humans, and many Temiars believe that this is true also of those species of birds about which there are traditional stories. It may well be that this is simply a way of saying that these animals demonstrate motile skills of some complexity, for that is the function that the eye-soul is believed to control in humans.[32]

---

31. [Added 2014] In 1979, Penghulu Dalam told me about a more complicated case of tiger-transformation—from bees. We were talking near Lambok next to the massive limestone tor known as Batuuʔ Pɛnlaaw. Dalam's father and grandfather told him that in their time Menriqs used to live in the cave at the foot of this tor, from which they would regularly gather honey. Eventually, they gathered so much honey that the bees transformed into a tiger, and ate up all the people then occupying the cave—children, women, everyone except the shamans, who were able to escape by flying (*pəlaaw*) away. (Hence the current name of the outcrop, Pɛnlaaw 'flying'.) Dalam went on to say that the bees were not true bees, but the *kənoruk* of the cave itself, which had emerged as a tiger, annoyed that the Menriqs had been taking so much honey. The *kənoruk*-tiger then flew downstream into the area where the Menriqs now live.
32. [Added 2014] For further light on Temiar ideas about the self-mobility of animals, see my discussion (Benjamin 2011b: 23, 31–33) of the 'middle-voice' morphology embedded in the Temiar names for a large number of animals.

Non-human soul-diseases: *pacɔg*

We have seen how the equivalent of the head-soul in natural species is believed in certain circumstances to attack people and make them ill. This may take the form either of the abstraction (*rɛywaay*) of one's head-soul by the *rəwaay* of a cultivated plant or a more general bodily attack by the *rəwaay* of certain foodstuffs, especially certain meats (as with *gɛnhaaʔ*). In a similar manner, the serious disease *pacɔg* is caused by the attack of the *kənoruk*-souls of certain species at inauspicious times or under inauspicious circumstances. Strictly speaking, *pacɔg* are an aspect of the *kənoruk* of the rotted logs of those trees known collectively as the *jəhũʔ mɛrgəəh*, 'the demoniac trees'[33]—those listed in table 6.1 as *kənoruk*-possessing species. The attack involves the penetration of the victim's chest by needle-like emissions that 'eat away our flesh and suck our blood'. Schebesta (1957: 320) reports the equivalent Jahai word, *pacǫg* as meaning 'Brustschmerz, Rheuma' (chest pain, rheumatism). With a couple of exceptions, the inauspicious circumstances have little to do with deliberate human acts. The most dangerous times are at dawn and sunset (as already mentioned), when any sort of unusual occurrence is likely to attract *pacɔg*: shouting, red clouds (a generally feared state known as *ɲɛbɲaab*[34]), the strong aroma of such plants as the *ləbag* flower or freshly-cut bananas, or even unusually cold water. The so-called 'hot rain' (Malay *hujan panas*; Temiar *təəh bəralããj*) that falls while the sun is still shining is regarded as particularly likely to bring on an attack of *pacɔg*, and, just as when the sky is red, one should stay indoors until it is over.

Soul beliefs as nature/culture

This material is complex and not at all easy to understand, but beneath it lies a fairly simple calculus-like structure. If we look more analytically at this underlying structure, we should be better placed to understand what these beliefs represent.

The opposition between the diseases *rɛywaay* and *pacɔg* provides us with a model of the internalisation within humans of the overall nature/culture opposition mentioned earlier. In *rɛywaay*, humanoid plant upper-body souls (*rəwaay*) carry off the human head-soul manikin (*rəwaay*) to play together and gorge themselves in the swidden. In *pacɔg*, lower-body souls of plants enter the human lower body in the form of tigers and eat away the flesh and blood—the blood which is so closely associated with the heart-soul.

---

33. [Added 2014] The word *mɛrgəəh* is probably cognate with the Old Mon *mirguḥ* /*mərguh*/ 'stoutness, inflexibility' (Shorto 1971: 294), implying perhaps that the trees in question are resistant to rotting.
34. [Added 2014] According to Gérard Diffloth (personal communication), *ɲɛbɲaab* is cognate with Batek (Northern Aslian) *yãp* 'blood'. Dentan (2008: 72) shows that some Semais, employing the cognate term *ɲyaamp*, explicitly associate the red of certain sunsets with blood. Presumably, this is connected with the idea held in some Northern-Aslian speaking populations that Karey rubs the blood offered in the *somuk* ritual (see later) onto his chest.

The *rəwaay* souls are essentially playful and often the subject of jokes, whereas the lower-body souls, whether referred to as *jərəək*, *kənoruk* or *sarak*, metamorphose easily into greatly feared were-tigers. This last contrast is clearly the reflex of a nature/culture opposition. Upper-body souls make their appearance in the form of the most cultural of creatures, young men and women, while the various lower-body souls appear as the most natural of creatures, the tiger. And this ties in directly with the off-the-ground/ ground opposition that has appeared so frequently in the present study. For plant and mountain souls, the spatial arrangement is quite explicit: there is a soul (variously *rəwaay*, *kahyɛk*, *pətərii?*) for the above-ground parts and one or more distinct souls (variously *kənoruk*, *sarak*) for the below-ground parts. For animals and human beings, we have the evidence of the explicit association between their head- and heart-souls and the above- and below-ground souls of plants and mountains. What in the latter case is an opposition between above and below the ground becomes transformed in the animal and human cases into an opposition between hair and blood.

Soul beliefs and blood

The direct association between the head-soul and hair has already been commented on, but the relationship between the heart-soul (or its equivalents) and blood has yet to be made clear. Several examples have already been mentioned in passing: spilt human blood is believed to metamorphose into a headless were-tiger (*kəpej*); as the disease *pacɔg*, the *kənoruk* of rotted logs attack and suck dry the blood of human beings; and the personified afflictions known as Paad and Bahyaa? are believed to attack by eating the 'blood of our *hup*'—precisely the organ inhabited by the heart-soul. Two further examples concern the special case of menstrual blood. A menstruating woman, in addition to other restrictions, is forbidden to eat any of the foods that are believed to possess souls of the *kənoruk* type (see table 6.1). On the other hand, all men must avoid any contact with menstrual blood if they are not to contract the disease *təruu?* or *tɛnruu?*. A medium under such circumstances would further suffer the loss of his spirit-guides, and any menstrual blood that he touched is believed to enter his *hup* and change into a tiger—a straight case of lycanthropy. Earlier, I suggested that the heart-soul's most significant feature was its association with blood. Perhaps it would be more accurate simply to refer to it as the blood-soul. The otherwise unrelatable ethnographic data detailed above would certainly become more comprehensible if we took this step. We shall learn later of evidence that further confirms this association.

If we re-examine in this light some of the disease concepts discussed earlier, an interesting parallel suggests itself. The diseases *rɛywaay* and *pacɔg* are essentially attacks upon the head and heart-souls of humans by (respectively) the equivalent upper and lower-body souls of plants. In much the same way, the diseases *gɛnhaa?* and *pocuk* (Chapter 5) contrast in that they are caused by attacks by (respectively) the head-souls and blood-odour of animals—and, as we have just seen, blood is directly associated with the heart-soul.[35]

Souls: Summary

The foregoing may be summarised as a set of identities arranged in the form of a conceptual calculus. For reasons that will become apparent later, we may reduce the series of oppositions to a set of reflexes of the basic opposition off-the-ground/ground. (That this opposition may validly be considered the same as the opposition culture/nature is not of relevance at present.)

The soul types are interrelated in the following way:

Off-the-ground	:	Ground
Head-soul	:	Heart-soul
Upper-body soul	:	Lower-body soul
Kahyɛk	:	*Kənoruk*
Pətərii²	:	*Sarak*

The related diseases are interrelated in a similar fashion:

Gɛnhaa²	:	*Pocuk*
Rɛywaay	:	*Pacɔg*

We have seen also that these conceptual structures are filled out by a content that is itself in part structured on the same pattern:

Hair	:	Blood
Manikin	:	Tiger
Playful	:	Dangerous

Further regularities are discernible. It will be remembered that, for the Temiars, animals fall into three classes of edibility: species that eat humans, species that humans eat, and species that humans feed. We can now see that the domain of plants is categorised in a precisely parallel manner. Corresponding to the animals that eat humans are the trees whose *kənoruk* souls attack humans in the form of the disease *pacɔg*. The animals that humans customarily eat correspond as a class to the staple swidden crops (*canaa² səlaay*: cassava, rice and maize) and the various food plants collected in the forest (*canaa² ²en-bɛɛk*). The domesticated animals (the species that humans feed) correspond to the plant species that people must take care to tend properly—those plants (the 'crops of the creation', the cultivated flowers, and the seasonal fruit trees)

---

35. [Added 2014] Jennings (1995: 118–136) presents a more detailed account of Temiar concerns over blood.

that otherwise cause an attack of the disease *rɛywaay*. Here, I draw attention again to the parallelism between these sets of categories and those relating to preferred sexual relationships, commented on in Chapter 5. This series of parallels could be considered as an 'elaborated code' statement, by means of food categorisations, of a mediation between the two prime categories culture and nature. Equally, of course, they could be analysed as a statement of the *polarity* of culture and nature, categories that implicitly (and sometimes explicitly, as in Chapter 8) underlie the expression of Temiar theological understandings, discussed more fully later. There remain several other matters to discuss, however, before this contention becomes clear.

Occasional and ceremonial rituals

So far, I have discussed ritual acts that follow contingently on the events of everyday life: eating, excreting, disease, jungle-craft, and so on. But there are other important rituals that are performed in special circumstances, far less frequently, and in a more ceremony-like manner than these rather unelaborate ritual acts. The most highly developed rituals of this kind form an integral part of the mediumistic complex, discussed later. First, I discuss the passage rites that mark life-cycle changes and the special 'blood sacrifice' rites directed at Karey, the thunder deity.

On the whole, the Temiars treat life-cycle changes with little formality. As far as I could learn, only three particular stages are picked out as the occasion of special ritual activity, and even then they are sometimes performed in a diffuse manner. The stages in question are birth and the early weeks of life, first menstruation, and death and burial. Of these, I was able to collect first-hand data only for burial (but not the moment of death). Temiars find childbirth and menstruation highly embarrassing to discuss if men are present. The only times I noticed a blush suffusing the cinnamon-coloured faces of Temiar friends was when I turned the conversation in that direction. Otherwise, sexual matters are talked about freely in mixed company and in the presence of children.

Childbirth

My information on childbirth is sparse. A child was born only once during my stay in any Temiar village, and that occurred quite without warning. The villager who had cooked my midday meal returned to the almost empty longhouse only to run back a few minutes later to report that his wife had just given birth to a son, attended by the only other villager present, fortunately the midwife. I went to take a look and found the young mother sitting up, suckling the baby as if hardly a thing had happened.[36]

---

36. [Added 2014] For detailed ethnographic accounts of childbirth among the Temiars, see Jennings

Births are attended to by the village midwife, who holds her position not by hereditary succession but because she is 'brave' enough to undertake training in the job from an older woman.[37] No special restrictions affect the husband at this time, apart from the general dietary restrictions of parenthood, but he is expected to make himself helpful in tending to his wife's needs while she is confined to the house during labour and for a few days after the birth. This confinement clearly has ritual content when seen in the light of overall Temiar ritual categorisations. The mother and her young baby must not come into contact with the ground during the highly dangerous first few days: they must remain unambiguously in the domain of off-the-ground. It is the duty of the midwife at this time to wash the mother and child by pouring warmed water onto them from a bamboo container raised up in the air. I once chanced to see this happening: the midwife stood by the mother's outstretched legs and, raising the tube of warm water to about the height of her own head, she gently let it drip onto the mother's genital and perineal regions. Throughout this time the mother rests on the slanting piece of springy split bamboo that served in the first place to facilitate the birth.

This bathing continues regularly for two or three days until the mother may go out from the house for the first time, which I was told occurs only after the first flow of true milk. The act of pouring warmed water from a bamboo tube also forms a part of the ritual at first menstruation, as described below. Its meaning seems to be twofold. First, the water is warmed in a bamboo tube that has been carefully selected in accordance with the rules on avoiding *tɜracɔɔg*. This is an act of cooking, a making cultural, and it would be wrong to employ water in its unmodified natural state, cold and in an unprepared container. Second, the water is poured from a height, emphasising that it is coming from off-the-ground, so that it washes all the exuvia (which, on the analogy of menstrual blood, are presumably highly polluting) down through the slatted floor onto the ground below. The whole procedure is thus a bathing of the mother and child in the waters of culture so as to wash away all non-cultural polluting elements into the ground where they rightly belong, leaving the subjects more securely in the domain of culture.[38] Throughout this period, there is no strict prohibition on the approach of the husband (or any male) near the mother, but they should sleep apart until all is declared well and the mother has safely gone out of the house for the first time. In fact, the bamboo couch on which the confinement takes place is often right in the centre of the house, or at least next to the fire where everyone congregates.

(1995: 127–136, 149–151). Some related topics are also discussed in Chapter 12.
37. [Added 2014] Male 'midwives' are found in some Orang Asli communities, such as the Semelais (Gianno 2004), but I never heard of any among the Temiars.
38. [Added 2014] See Chapter 12 for a discussion of this practice from a rather different, more phenomenological, perspective.

Rituals of parenthood

Elsewhere (Benjamin 1967c: 14) I have commented how

> for the first year or so of his child's life the father is liable when the
> occasion arises to make placatory offerings to those spirits (actually plant
> souls) thought likely to run off with the child's rather labile head-soul
> (rəwaay). To a large extent parenthood is viewed as the protection of the
> baby's head-soul from its tendency to wander away (rɛywaay).

On reflection I am not sure that 'placatory offerings' properly describes
the barely noticeable ritual whereby the father (and perhaps the mother also)
of a very young child tears off a bunch of leaves and throws them on the
flowing water before he bathes or wades in the river. One man who dictated a
text to me on the subject after I observed him carrying out the ritual claimed
that he did it because he feared for the head-soul of his child. He was not
required to do it, though; he regarded himself simply as 'helping' his young
son. Furthermore, anyone else who wanted to 'help' in the same way was
welcome to do so, but no wrong was attached to any omission. No informant
was able to provide a rationale for this little ritual, and we are left only
to guess at one. Clearly, it has something in common with the belief that
allowing cultivated plants to float away downstream is thought likely to lead
to the abstraction of one's head-soul. Perhaps the logic in this case is that, by
throwing an uncultivated weed onto the stream and allowing the blame to fall
on anyone but the young child himself, any resulting harm would be mild and
not attack the delicate head-soul of the protected child. In short, the rite might
serve as a sort of spiritual counter-irritant.[39]

Menstruation

The only information I have on the rituals of first menstruation comes from
a male informant who was repeating what his grandmother had told him
when he was approaching puberty. (This seems to be the normal source of
information about female sexuality for a young Temiar boy.) At her first
menstruation, a girl is tabooed: she may not go down to the river, carry heavy
objects, nor cook for men throughout the period. She is taken into the forest
by her mother for a ritual bathing. The girl removes her old sarong and stands
naked under a tree of the type known as *sogiiʔ* (also: *tamud, yeeb* or *ləyɛs*), and
her mother heats up a large bamboo tube of water on a special fire. She then
hangs the full bamboo on a branch of the tree at head level, bends down the
surrounding branches and punctures the base of the bamboo so that the warm
water trickles slowly off the leaves onto the girl's head and over her body.

---

39. [Added 2014] In Chapter 12, I present an alternative explanation of this practice (yaŋyɔw), based
on later research.

When the water has emptied, the mother releases the leaves and places a new sarong on her daughter. They then return home, where the mother combs her daughter's hair and anoints it with oil.

The grammar of this ritual is obviously similar to that of the post-natal ablutions. The difference is that, because menstruation is shameful and generally polluting, its associated rituals are carried out in the forest and not in the house. Remembering that the leaves of a tree are where its *rəwaay* soul dwells, the significance of their use as a shower mechanism becomes clearer: it is a further example of a 'bathing in the waters of culture', for we have seen that both *rəwaay* and off-the-ground represent culture in the overall system of categorisations. The grooming of the girl's hair when she returns home seems to have much the same meaning, for that is precisely where her own *rəwaay*, or head-soul, resides.

The Temiars, at least the menfolk, regard menstruation as very polluting. They will not readily use the word (*ʔəd*) by which it is regularly known among the women, finding it more obscene than any other Temiar word they know. Instead, they refer to menstruation by a sort of avoidance term, *ʔɛsnʉs*, which is close to the word for 'badness, filth', *ʔɛsnəs*. A menstrual period may be known as *ʔis laʔəs* 'bad day' (the same root as in *ʔɛsnəs*) or *ʔariiʔ bɛʔbɔʔ* 'useless day'. Although a menstruating woman privately wears a piece of waste cloth, known variously as *ʔabat cənaweed* 'perineal cloth', *ʔabat pɛrcar* or *ʔabat gareed* (the latter is a tree that used to provide barkcloth), public statement of the fact is made by her avoidance of communal food. Instead, she eats food that contains no salt, no meat, or vegetables of the *kənoruk*-containing kind. Nor may she cook for any men. It is believed that if a menstruating woman should ignore these taboos the food will stick in her throat and cause violent coughing fits. After four or five days she again joins the rest of the household in eating the full range of normally salted food, and she is then regarded as 'well'. I was told that these taboos are observed at the expected time of the month whether or not menstruation has occurred by then; but, because the reckoning would soon get out of step, this claim must be doubted. Except for the avoidance of *kənoruk*-containing foods (which I have already commented upon), it is difficult to understand the symbolism, if any, that underlies these menstrual food taboos. Perhaps the explanation is no more complex than that salt and meat are optional components of normal Temiar meals.[40] Their avoidance simply expresses the abnormal social situation of a menstruating woman.

As to why menstruation should be regarded as dangerous, we can again only guess. It is doubtful whether sexuality plays any part in the avoidance, since normally there is no prohibition (outside the bounds of modesty) on

---

40. [Added 2014] See Chapter 12 for a later discussion of this issue, especially with regard to the place of salt in the diet.

seeing or touching the genital organs of the opposite sex. As suggested earlier, the significant feature seems to be the concern over blood as a potent ritual category. We have already seen how contact with menstrual blood is regarded as highly dangerous for men. The prohibition on the descent of a menstruating woman to the river in which everyone bathes should also be seen in this light, as should the requirement that she should bury her blood-soiled perineal cloth after use. This latter feature makes an explicit association between blood and the ground, an association that recurs elsewhere. This is made all the stronger by contrast to the general *təracɔɔg* prohibition against allowing bodily emissions or outgrowths to penetrate into the ground (although the watery emissions of urine, tears and saliva seem to be neutral in this respect).[41]

Death and burial

I have commented already on the logic of burial as opposed to exposure. Burial itself proceeds to the accompaniment of various rituals, many of which can be understood as expressions of the ideas I have been discussing. I attended two burials and collected data on a third, which had occurred a week or so before I arrived in the village where it took place.

Temiar burials vary in procedure from place to place and from occasion to occasion. Often, I found that the rituals followed were structurally the inverse of rituals found elsewhere. Since it might confuse the issue here to give over-detailed accounts of what actually occurred at the burials I attended, I shall concentrate on those ritual procedures that relate to the conceptual system I have been describing.[42] This is not to say that the rituals left undescribed are

Figures 6.3a and 6.3b A burial (from the documentary film *Timeless Temiar*, Malayan Film Unit, 1956)
First (figure 6.3a), the deceased's wrapped body is cut away from the pole from which it was suspended; the split-bamboo flooring is visible in the grave. Then (figure 6.3b), the prepared split-bamboo roofing is placed on the grave after the interment, before being covered with a mound of soil. (Digitisation by the Centre for Orang Asli Concerns.)

---

41. [Added 2014] See Jennings (1995: 119–127) for a fuller account of Temiar practices and ideas concerning menstruation, gathered from some of the same individuals who had found it difficult to talk to me about the topic.
42. [Added 2014] See Appendix 3 for further accounts of Temiar burials.

without significance—it is just that they refer more to the values of locality and community than to the more primarily theological questions that concern the present study.

The burial takes place as soon after the death and as early in the day as possible. Anyone who dies after mid-morning will normally be buried early the next day. But if the death occurs earlier, especially during the night, the burial will take place on the same day. From the moment of death (and even before, if the death is expected), the deceased's autonym (unique personal name) is strictly tabooed and replaced by 'the deceased' (*bɛɛs*), or 'the corpse' (*sarɔɔʔ*).[43] The body may then be washed in cold water (but not dried, it seems), and the eyes and mouth are closed. It is then well wrapped in the deceased's own used garments, and perhaps also in a sheet. The wrapped body is encased in a long piece of split-bamboo flooring sufficient to form a firm cylinder around it, and the whole is suspended from a pole (which may be a beam from the deceased's house) by string or cane (figure 6.3a). This provides an easy means of carrying the body to the burial site. A young child's body may be carried, wrapped, in the arms of a villager. The parts of the house that the deceased contacted while dying become a tabooed polluted area known as *sapɛʔ*. These will either be burnt along with the whole of the house (then known as *deek sənarɔj*), or partitioned off to be eventually dismantled and burnt separately.

Throughout this activity the close mourners (mainly those in the deceased's nuclear family, but occasionally others also) play little part in the proceedings: the job is taken out of their hands. The funeral procession leaves the village, with 'outsiders' (people from elsewhere or villagers not closely related to the deceased) carrying the body slung from its pole. Someone goes ahead to beat away the physical obstructions to the procession's passage. In one of the cases I witnessed, a bridge had been hastily built before the burial could take place. Sometimes, those in front carry burning bamboo torches, but whether this serves a ritual function in addition to providing the means of lighting the graveside fires I cannot tell. Following behind the corpse, a few people, usually women, carry the deceased's personal belongings bundled into back-baskets. The burial always takes place across a river from the village, even if the river is no more than a token stream a few feet wide. The site chosen is ideally in an old swidden once cultivated by the deceased. However, one of the burials I saw took place on the edge of a swidden bearing a new crop of cassava.

On reaching the chosen gravesite, the body is laid on the ground while people get on with their various tasks. The close mourners for the most part just sit silently, perhaps weeping; occasionally they may lend a hand with

---

43. [Added 2014] See Benjamin (1968a) for a detailed account of Temiar personal naming practices, including the changes that take place after someone dies. Cognates of *bɛɛs* in other Aslian languages mean 'ghost' or 'evil spirit' (cf. Benjamin 1968a: 116).

some lighter work. The main work is carried out by the 'outsiders'. First, the surrounding growth is cleared, starting from what is to be the head end (the west) of the grave: this is said to allow the head-soul greater freedom to travel away towards the sunset. The slashing is then continued all around the site, while others busy themselves with its excavation. In contrast to the restrained demeanour of the mourners proper, the gravediggers treat the whole occasion with some degree of levity. They talk about past burials and their difficulties, discuss the non-Aboriginal burials and cemeteries they have seen in the outside world, and even joke openly and laughingly when the opportunity presents itself. This seems to be in strict contrast to the way they behave before crossing the stream that divides the burial site from the village. Before setting out, behaviour is restrained and the village is silent except for the sobs of the mourners. A modern development, surely related, is that I was allowed to take photographs only after the cortège had crossed the stream. Unfortunately, my attempts at photography failed.[44]

The grave takes about two hours to dig to the required shape and dimensions, an oblong trench oriented along the sunrise–sunset axis and reaching a depth of about three-and-a-half feet. The details of its internal form differ, however, from place to place. The grave I saw in Cherber (Cɛrbɛr), a village in the Perolak valley of Kelantan, had an overall length of about nine feet and a breadth of about seven feet.[45] Its basic depth was about three-and-a-half feet, but in the middle of the floor there was a further box-like pit measuring about five-and-a-half feet long, two-and-a-half feet wide, and two feet deep. Finally, along the south side of the grave there was left a ledge measuring about one foot wide and one foot high; on the opposite side there was a slight overhang from the main floor of about nine inches. The grave I saw being excavated in the Pahang Temiar village of Rening had a simpler form. Its overall dimensions were much the same as those of the Cherber grave, but all around the bottom was a ledge about nine inches high surrounding a depression in the middle. The grave-diggers checked the measurements by gauging it against the body with a stick.

While the digging proceeds, others pile up the slashed undergrowth and use it to light fires around the grave. In both of the cases I witnessed, a fire was lit initially to the west (head) end of the grave. In Cherber, two more fires were lit at the other end to either side of the east–west axis, as if for the body's two feet. In Rening, on the other hand, a single fire was lit, at the foot end on the axis of the grave.

Before the body is let into the grave, flooring is placed along the bottom (figure 6.3a). This, with the split-bamboo covering placed over the body

---

44. [Added 2014] To make up for this deficit, I have inserted two stills (figure 6.3) from the colonial-period documentary film *Timeless Temiar*. The depicted funeral was clearly acted out for the film-makers' benefit, as the 'deceased' woman was alive and co-operating when the sequence started. But the details of the subsequent 'funeral' were otherwise wholly authentic.

45. [Added 2014] My detailed fieldnotes on this burial are presented in Appendix 3.3.

(figure 6.3b), ensures that it does not come into direct contact with the soil.[46] In the Cherber grave, the pit at the bottom was first laid with three transversely placed saplings. On this were laid two strips of split-bamboo flooring with the inner surface upwards, so that the bottom of the grave was completely covered. Finally, the deceased's plaited sleeping-mat was spread on top. In Rening, the grave was floored with a single layer of exactly-fitting split-bamboo sheet. In this case, however, the outer surface was left facing upwards, as in normal domestic flooring. In Cherber, the body was allowed to fall into the grave by cutting the restraining ropes from the carrying pole suspended over the grave mouth. It was left slightly uncovered as a result, but this did not seem to matter. Things were gentler at Rening, where the body was supported from beneath by two men while the ropes were cut. It was then slowly lowered into the grave and allowed to rest on the flooring.[47] The strings tied around the winding-cloth were cut away and the body was turned slightly onto its right side. In both cases, the bodies were buried fully extended with the arms at the sides and with the head at the westerly end.

Before the graves were closed, various grave offerings were distributed over the bodies. In Cherber, various pieces of new sarong cloth, freshly torn, were scattered over the body. The deceased's worn clothes, gold chain and some used steel axe heads were added. The village headman threw in about 30 Malayan dollars in banknotes.[48] In Rening, only the axe and bush-knives that had been used in the burial were placed alongside the body. Similar coverings were placed over the body, again to ensure that it rested freely in a space of its own and did not come into contact with the earth. In Cherber, about 15 saplings were placed across the grave from the ledge to the top of the overhang, forming a slanting palisade from one end to the other. This was covered with upturned split-bamboo sheeting (as in figure 6.3) held in place by a single stick, and over this were spread layers of banana leaves. The earth that had been heaped at the graveside was pushed rapidly but gently back into

---

46. [Added 2014] In 1968, Penghulu Dalam provided an historical rationale for some of these practices. He said that in the time of his father's father (which would place it in the nineteenth century), exposed tree 'burial' was the practice for all, not just *halaa'* mediums (other than stillborn babies, who were wrapped in a cloth and suspended from a tree with hands and feet bound). Exposure of this kind was known as *saŋkar* or *sənaŋkar*, from the Malay *sangkar* 'coop, cage'. Four suitable trunks were found in the jungle and a split-bamboo flooring built on their cut-off tops. The body was left there, with a roof made over the whole platform. The deceased's house was then burnt down and the whole village deserted while the people moved some distance away, 'as far as from Lambok to Kuala Betis' (about 30 minutes' walk). Dalam said that the present-day pattern of burial resulted from a command of the Malays, presumably the Mikong at Kuala Betis. The complicated pattern of split-bamboo flooring and roof within the grave—not in itself a Malay practice—was an attempt to please the Malays while still retaining a platform (*baley*) structure beneath the ground. Nowadays it is up to people themselves to say how they wish their bodies to be disposed. Some people fear burial (*kɛmnəm*) because they may in effect drown, and their *rəwaay* head-soul may have to fight its way out—if indeed it is not trapped.

47. [Added 2014] The space left around the body in these burial practices may explain the occasional cases of accidental live burial that were reported to me. One such incident involved a young girl whose poor speech in later life—which I witnessed—was explained as due to this experience, as was her preference for calling her husband 'father'.

48. [Added 2014] At the time, this would have been worth around 10 US dollars.

the grave until eventually a mound was formed, oval in shape and about two feet high in the middle. Stray plants were thrown aside and bits of root left in the earth were cut into pieces before the mound was stamped into a more firmly defined shape. In Rening, transverse bamboo slats were placed across the ledge over the body to provide a support for longitudinally placed split-bamboo flooring which completely covered the bottom of the grave. Both the slats and the flooring were placed with their green sides upwards. Piled-up earth was then placed carefully by handfuls onto the flooring so as to leave no gaps—one of the participants actually said quite clearly 'let you not see upwards!' Only then was the rest of the earth dropped into the grave; it was scraped fine, with the lumps crumbled out and pieces of root removed. The final layer, however, consisted of untreated earth, still lumpy and containing roots. This was not only taken from the excavated earth but was dug up, additionally, from the ground around the grave. (A suggested interpretation of these observances is proposed later.)

The last stage of the burial proper is the leaving of various funerary offerings on the grave, and in this regard there was some difference between the two villages. In Cherber, the deceased's personal belongings had already been buried with him and the offerings left consisted of food and refreshment for him in both real and representational form. Clods of clay were formed into grenade-like shapes and left at the head of the mound with the words 'here is food for you'. With it were placed a punctured tin cup, an upturned bowl, and a section of cut-open bamboo (the traditional Temiar eating vessel). A half coconut shell was placed at the foot end. Finally, at the head end were placed a few newly-rolled cigarettes, a complete betel masticatory apparatus, and a bamboo tube of water, which had to be specially punctured—as Evans so vividly states (1937: 268), on the principle of dead objects for dead people.[49] In Rening, on the other hand, the deceased's personal possessions had not already been placed in the grave. Her half-completed pandanus plaiting and her tin plates were placed on the grave, along with a bunch of bananas. Two large fires were prepared at the foot and head of the grave. On the former, they burnt a back-basket full of the deceased's personal sarongs, sheets and sleeping mats. On the latter, the deceased's father burnt off a large cast-net of his own. The fire at the head end was the first to be started.

In Cherber, the last act, overlapping with the offering of funerary goods, was the building of a palisade of crossed bamboo slats around the grave, completed by the planting of defoliated stems of cassava so that they would grow up around and into the palisade. In Rening, the final graveside acts were to complete felling the trees near the foot end of the grave and to strip the bark off the remaining stumps to leave them gleaming white. This was to allow

---

49. [Added 2014] It is more likely, *pace* Evans, that this puncturing was aimed at preventing *tɔracɔɔg*, as discussed earlier in this chapter.

the ground to dry out, and also to prevent the various evil spirits (primarily the trees listed in table 6.1 and the earth demons) from finding anywhere to settle. Instead, the spirits would be forced to dissipate their evil in the grave, rather than by following and pouncing on the living. The stripped stumps also served to frighten away the various malign influences emanating from the grave itself. This did not seem to be so explicit at the Cherber burial, but there, as the mourners left to return to the village, they plucked leaves from the pathside bushes and hit at the stumps with their bush-knives in a manner that suggested something of the ritual intent of the fuller practices followed at Rening. As the Cherber villagers left the burial site, they again addressed themselves to the deceased (or more strictly, perhaps, to the deceased's ghost). This they did in a manner reminiscent of the imprecatory statements uttered at Rening: 'you go to a cold land, we remain in a hot land'; 'you have it easy, we difficult—we gave enough sarongs'; and so on.

An interesting contrast appeared between the two villages with regard to the behaviour required of those returning home after a burial. In Cherber, all except the close mourners bathed in the river after leaving the burial site, giving their digging tools a good scrubbing also. The close mourners, however, did not bathe until they had re-entered the house. In Rening, the behaviour was the reverse. The close mourners there were required to bathe themselves before returning home (but they were not allowed to comb their hair on the day of the funeral). The non-mourners had to return unbathed, but before entering the house they had to dry off their sweat over a hastily made fire. This sweat, known as *semyaap ʔesʔəs*, 'polluting sweat' (both words are somewhat unusual and euphemistic), is believed to be closely associated with the evil propensities of the deceased's ghost,[50] and consequently to pose a special threat to the life of the children living in the deceased's house. If, on the other hand, they do bathe themselves before returning it is believed that the deceased, now referred to as *bɛɛs*—which means 'ghost' in other Aboriginal languages—somehow grabs hold of the offenders and bears them away.

The standard practice is for the whole village to join together in a feast immediately after the burial. If possible, the meat is supplied by killing the deceased's own chickens, and the rest of the food by gathering it from the swidden in which he or she was buried—which, ideally, was the deceased's in any case.[51] But often other people have to donate the food. Before beginning to eat, the headman utters a few words on the deceased's good qualities. The meal proceeds with few signs of mourning, except that the close mourners may weep quietly in a corner, occasionally giving out a less restrained wail.

---

50. In Pahang (and perhaps elsewhere), this is known as *kejmuuj*, a cognate of the various Negrito words for ghost, as discussed later. As already noted, the Pahang Temiars also use this word for 'ghost'.
51. [Added 2014] This led the women attending the funeral in Cherber to complain that the burial site had been badly chosen, because it was in plain view of the settlement 'like the graves in town'.

Interpretations of mortuary rituals

The days immediately following a burial are believed to place the village in a state of danger. This was especially apparent in Rening, which is situated in a valley where the mediums claim a special revelation of the nature of the death-causing agents. Their ideas, though not necessarily rejected in other valleys, are elsewhere accorded at most only partial recognition. But in the other valleys, people could offer little in the way of detailed explanation about the causes of death apart from a myth of its origin. This is apparently familiar to all Temiar groups, and was told to me often when the talk turned to mortuary behaviour.

It will be helpful to recount the myth here before discussing the more detailed beliefs current among the Temiars of Pahang, as it provides a rationale for some of the practices I have described. The chief character is ?aluj, Karey's younger brother and the First Man (and First Medium) of the Temiar creation stories (Chapter 4). We shall learn more of him in Chapters 7 and 8.

Now ?aluj was living on earth, and his people were very numerous. Karey looked from the heavens above and came down to ?aluj saying, 'Luj, how is it that your companions number so many and mine so few? What do you do about having them die?' ?aluj replied, 'I order them to carry the dead person slung from a pole.'

'How do they do that, Luj?'

'Oh, I order them to cut a pole off the *jarag* tree [an especially hard wood] and carry him on that.'

'How do your people make grave offerings, Luj?'

'No, my people do not make grave offerings. Instead, I order them to find a suitable frond on a *balaa?* palm and hang from it the deceased's nose-quill, beads, headdress, quiver, and blowpipe. Then they return home, where they sit and wait until the evening. Then the man who was dead returns from the earth below, carrying meat on his back and a blowpipe over his shoulder. He gives the meat to his wife for them to roast.'

Then ?aluj asked Karey, 'How, then, do you arrange people's deaths?'

'Oh, Luj, I order them to die completely and that they should be buried in the earth, and that grave offerings should be made of their loincloths, beads, knives, axes, blowpipes, quivers, spears. Their bodies should be wrapped in their own barkcloths, covered with their sleeping-mats, and with their pillow under their heads. Then we cut a pole and tie the dead man to it enclosed in split-bamboo, supporting him at the feet, the chest and the head. Then we carry him by the pole, one man at the feet and another at the head, and we set off.'

Then ?aluj asked Karey, 'How do you go?'

'Feet first, the head next. Then the people in the dead man's house burst out crying and uncontrolledly start pulling the house apart and embracing each other closely.'

'And what do you do with the dead man's house?'

'Oh, we burn it down.'

'And after it has burnt down?'

'Then we flee the place.'

'Flee? Why should you do that?'

'Because we fear the disease brought by the death-pollution [*sapɛʔ*] which tries to follow us everywhere. But we fell trees onto the path and the disease is frightened off—it flees back to its hole, the grave.'

'And what do you do about the grave?'

'Oh, we mash up wild ginger in water and sprinkle the fluid over it, and then we light fires at the head and foot. We take hold of the ginger-water in a bamboo tube and sprinkle it all over the place, saying, "Here, I sprinkle you, I sprinkle and cast you all off, you dead people. Go away elsewhere; go to the sunset: Don't keep us living people in mind, don't cause falling trees to crush us. Carry yourselves off, and don't bring death to us!"'

Then ?alʉj said, 'You feel no sympathy for people, whereas I do—it is up to you to order complete death.'

And Karey agreed, 'Yes, I want them to die, I want them to mourn, I want them to sorrow, and I want them to be love-lorn. I order that eventually they shall all die—men, women, junior aunts, senior aunts, grandmothers, grandfathers, senior uncles, junior uncles, fathers. I shall be the origin of death, and I shall order them to die in their ones, twos and threes. I shall order them to sing when the time comes to break the mourning taboo and make all well again—they shall trance, and then the women shall paint the men's faces with *kesumba* [*Bixa orellana*] dye and flirt with them. Then the men shall fall in love with the women and wish to take them as wives. Everyone will want an end to the death period so that they may get married.'

The initial message of this myth is that death exists not in the natural order of things, but because Karey made it so. Without Karey there would be no permanent death. Death, then, is just one of the necessary evils of this world—a point I follow up on later. The next part of the message is that, as long as death was not permanent, there was no need to make grave offerings; the various objects were just left for the deceased's use on returning to everyday life. Nowadays, the objects are buried with the deceased because death has become permanent. The obvious implication is that there is an afterlife in which the deceased will find the buried objects of some use—and we have seen that the Temiars do hold such a belief. But Temiar afterlife beliefs are more complex and variable than this simple view would suggest. Although the version of the myth just presented makes no mention of the point, only the head-soul seems to undertake the sort of afterlife in which the accoutrements of everyday life would prove useful. Yet, further on, mention is made of an imprecatory text in which the dead are urged not to bother themselves any longer with the living. As we shall see shortly, many Temiars believe that at the time of a death it is precisely the human head-souls that are likely to pose a danger to the living. The grave offerings may therefore be intended to provide the dangerous head-souls with sufficient material of interest within the grave, allowing them no reason to enter the houses of the living. However, this must remain conjecture: the Temiars gave as their reason for making grave offerings simply that they felt 'sorrow' for the dead and that they could best express this in funerary prestations.

A clear distinction should nevertheless be drawn between grave offerings of the deceased's own personal effects and those offerings that are funerary prestations made by other members of the community. Earlier, I noted how some Temiars fear to bury the used garments of people still alive, on pain of causing an attack of *tǝracɔɔg*. In Rening, it was noticeable that no personal belongings were buried in the grave, whether they belonged to the deceased or to those still living. Instead, they were burnt off on the ground above the grave. It is in this valley and its neighbour the Brok that the *tǝracɔɔg* complex becomes ritually elaborated so that the very name becomes ineffable, being replaced by such euphemisms as *gɛrpid*, 'fused tree growth'. Several of the mediums in those valleys even claim *tǝracɔɔg* itself as their spirit-guide. The Temiars of other valleys recognise this specialisation and, on occasion, they travel south to be treated by a practised *tǝracɔɔg* medium. It seems likely, then, that the fear of the Rening people about burying personal possessions— and they stated quite explicitly that that is how they feel—is a reflection of the greater concern in their area for the whole of the *tǝracɔɔg* ideology. Little more need to be said here about the efficacy of fire and burning as a means of keeping clear the ground/off-the-ground distinction, as I have discussed the point earlier.

In Rening, the grave offerings of goods belonging to persons other than the deceased were rather limited, amounting only to the father's cast-net burnt at the foot of the grave. In Cherber, on the other hand, many objects belonging to the villagers were placed right in the grave. Further down the same valley, in the village of Humid, I was given an account of the grave offerings made at the burial of a two-year old girl who had died of dysentery while I was away.[52] Twelve worn sarongs were given by many villagers, whose stated reason was that the dead child was some specified relative of theirs. The father and the headman each gave an old bush-knife 'because of the pity they felt'.

---

52. [Added 2014] A more detailed account of this funeral is presented in Appendix 3.1.

Many villagers gave money, amounting in all to about 40 Malayan dollars. But if the giving of grave offerings is any measure of sorrow, then the father must truly have been heart-broken. In all, he buried with his child a saucepan, a cauldron, an axe, a bar of soap, a sleeping-mat, a mosquito net, a tin of talc that his daughter used to play with, a tin of commercial dye, a cast-net chain, an electric torch, a domestic knife, and a wristwatch that had cost him 50 dollars. It is harder to interpret these personally felt grave-offerings as objects of use in the afterlife. Rather, they should be seen as expressions of the relationship held to obtain between the donor and the deceased. In life, the Temiars constantly express their relationships to each other through a flow of prestations. The moral obligations this entails seem to continue for a while when one of the partners dies. My informants in Humid expressed surprise on learning that Europeans do not make grave-offerings. They felt that since some form of mourning was to be expected on the death of a loved one, grave offerings were the obvious way of doing so. One might suspect, though, that in saying this they were in a less sophisticated frame of mind than usual, since they knew that there are other peoples in Malaya, let alone Europeans, who do not make grave-offerings.[53]

The next point in the myth relates to the orientational elements in the burial procedure. My version of the myth tells us only that the body is carried feet first, but Temiars regularly make the further stipulation that it should be buried with the head towards the sunset and the feet towards the sunrise. The symbolism of this prescription is clear: the afterworld to which the head-soul makes its way lies at the sunset. This concern for the correct orientation of the body is a further example of the establishment of the cosmic distinctions of nature and culture within the human being, and it follows logically from the soul beliefs. Granted that this is so, it is hardly surprising that there should also be a stipulation regarding the way in which the body is carried to the grave. Yet it is harder to see why the rule should be feet first, and not vice versa. In the absence of an explanation from the Temiars themselves, I suggest that since burial represents almost literally a passage from culture to nature, it makes sense that the head—the part of the body in which culture finds its corporeal embodiment—should be pointing towards the eminently cultural village when the body leaves it for good. And inversely, it makes sense that the lower part of the body, in which nature finds its reflex, should be the first to enter the natural domain of the burial ground.

After carrying the body out from the house, the myth tells us, the close mourners are left behind to weep and console each other. In other words, as we have seen, the task of burial is entrusted to the 'outsiders'. In life, as in the myth, no formal constraints are placed on the extent to which the mourners

---

53. [Added 2014] I now suspect that a further motivation for making grave-offerings is the feeling of guilt at not have suffered along with the deceased: if the deceased had lost life, then the survivors should lose something too.

express their sorrow—although in my experience they were usually quiet and turned in on themselves.

The burning of the deceased's house and subsequent fleeing of the village are classical pieces of Temiar custom that, as the myth says, have the overt function of avoiding the ghost-like polluting influence (*sapɛʔ*) that pervades all the materials with which the deceased customarily came into contact. In terms of its latent function, this custom has direct implications for the maintenance of the social structure, as I have discussed in more detail elsewhere (Benjamin 1966: 18). I pursue the point no further here. In fact, it is unusual nowadays for Temiars to entirely flee the site of a village after a death, or even to destroy the whole of the house in which it occurred. Usually it suffices to dismantle only the section in which the deceased lived, having first built a wall across the dividing line between it and the rest of the house. However, if they do decide to burn the house down, they plant tobacco and kitchen-garden herbs in the ashes, and move to a new site between 20 and a few hundred yards away.

The dangers accompanying a burial are believed to persist for several days. The ensuing ritual behaviour is partly aimed at obviating the effects of the deceased's ghost and the other malign influences abroad at the time. The myth mentions two ways in which people attempt to keep the dangers away: felling trees across the paths, and pouring ginger water on the grave. We have seen that burials are accompanied and followed by the felling, slashing or stripping of trees. Despite the claims of the myth, I have no report that ginger water is poured onto a newly made grave. Instead, the Temiars I questioned claimed to use the much more potent *rɔɔk*, the famous *ipoh* blowpipe poison of the Malayan Aborigines. This is burnt on the day after burial on and around the grave, when it is inspected for the first time. The Rening people believe that this prevents both the attacks of tigers and the undesired invasion of massed human head-souls. It is this last that calls for some explanation.

The ideology of death seems to be more highly developed in Rening than in the other valleys I studied. Death provides the occasion for the visit of Karey's death-dealing agent known as Wuuk, or euphemistically as Ɲam Baliik 'the Animal from Above'. Some claimed that Wuuk is the direct cause of death, others that he merely feeds on the flesh of the newly buried. Whatever the 'correct' version, one informant, a medium who had Wuuk as his spirit-guide, was able to give a graphic description of his appearance and behaviour. Wuuk has teeth the size of sugarcane internodes, arms that are grey below and ruddy above, and nails from which extend elephant-sized cords reaching to the tops of the mountains. He is the chief of all the aerial demons—principally the various dangerous trees listed in table 4.2—which are brought to action by his uprooting them with his cords. His travels are recorded by the falling of jungle trees—and indeed much of the Temiars' fear of falling trees is to be explained by this association. (Note how in the myth the dangerous grave emanations are urged, 'don't cause falling trees to crush us'.) Wuuk normally visits to feed on the flesh in a new grave, and much effort goes into the attempt to frighten him off. He is so evil that he poses an extreme threat to the living as well as to the dead.

My Rening informants claimed that associated with Wuuk are massed swarms of past human head-souls,[54] the direct agents of the decomposition of the deceased's body. The head-soul swarm arrives near the village in the late evenings throughout the six nights immediately following the burial, eating away at the deceased's flesh, thereby releasing the head-soul for its journey to the sunset. Large fires are lit at the village entrances to discourage their closer approach. At the same time, the medium goes around the village uttering spells while beating on the pillars of the houses with a rod. I was able to observe this in Rening. There, the medium, Paa[ʔ] Bali[ʔ], applied himself assiduously to the task and kept up the beating at all hours of day and night, suddenly jumping up and starting again after a respite of an hour or so. Only he could perform the task, as only powerful mediums specialised in the rituals of death can see ('meet') the ghosts and head-souls associated with a burial.

Two points arise out of this discussion of the beliefs about death current in Rening. First, they lend support to the widespread Temiar idea that ultimately Karey, the thunder god, is the cause of death. This is made clear in the myth I quoted, and I was told informally many times that this is so. In Rening, they say that Wuuk is under Karey's control, not ʔaluj's: it was at this point in the discussion that they produced the Origin of Death myth as evidence. But this can probably be taken further. The description of Wuuk given to me by a medium with revealed knowledge of him corresponds closely to some of the descriptions of Karey himself that have appeared in the literature on the Malayan Aborigines, although I myself failed to elicit such descriptions from the Temiars. Evans (1937: 144), for example, reports that the (Lanoh?) Negritos of Grik describe Karey as 'like a siamang monkey'. The siamang, with its two-coloured arms, is indeed the obvious model for the conception of Wuuk put forward by the medium in Rening.[55] In Humid, furthermore, I was told that the brachiating animals (Chapter 5), including the siamang, are regarded collectively as the bringers of death, known as Wuuk or Sɛlmɔɔl in Temiar. Although no Temiar made explicit any identification of Wuuk with Karey, the identity is present in an incipient form. Whether this represents a further refraction of one of Karey's characteristics into a distinct personality (as we

---

54. [Added 2014] This sounds very like the characterisation given elsewhere in this volume of the Cinʃcɛm cult first reported by Noone and Stewart.

55. [Added 2014] Dentan (2002: 208), who worked in the Telom valley shortly before I did, but among the Semais, has the following to say about the matter. (For Temiars, Nkuu' (ʔɛŋkuu[ʔ]) is the same as Karey; see also Baharon (1966).)

> As the storm rages, people shout incantations to it, to the Thunder God Nkuu' and his younger brother Pnooy, Wind. Semais visualise Nkuu' as a mammoth black animal, ghastly black, sometimes slashed with white or flame-red, a Malayan sun-bear, a giant pigtailed macaque, langur or siamang with a huge throat pouch that goes uuuUUUUUuuu or swells and releases quickly: BUU!

have already seen to occur) or a tendency for an otherwise very similar concept to fuse with that of Karey, it is impossible to say on the present evidence.

The second point that arises is the apparent confusion over beliefs about the fate and action of the head-soul. This is especially so when attempting to correlate the beliefs of the Rening people with those in Humid. Some Temiars, including those in Humid, believe that at death the head-soul leaves the body and proceeds to the Flower Garden situated at the sunset. But they fail to solve the inconsistency between the idea that death is permanent loss of the head-soul and the necessity to clear a path for the head-soul when it leaves the grave. Whether the body carries its head-soul with it to the grave, possibly in a loosely attached form, is not clear. I got the impression that the Temiars would like to have it both ways and forgo logical rigour. But it is the Rening beliefs that appear so surprising for, contrary to expectation, it seems that there the deceased's head-soul and the swarm of head-souls that it attracts are feared and treated as highly dangerous. Indeed, the Rening image of the head-soul after death corresponds rather well with what other Temiars describe for the 'ghost', the form taken after death by the shadow, wɔɔg. The Rening Temiars nevertheless do have a concept of the ghost, which they call kɛjmuuj. It may be that on occasion they employ the term rəwaay, which elsewhere normally means just head-soul, in a synecdochal manner to refer to 'soul' in general, without specifying any particular variety. The ghost could then justifiably be referred to under the rubric of rəwaay.[56] Yet, even so, the idea that the body of the deceased is eaten away by the mass action of returned human rəwaays does not fit at all with what we know of Temiar concepts of the ghost.

Even in regard to the rəwaay proper—the head-soul—the Rening people hold seemingly inconsistent beliefs. Although, like all Temiars, they believe that the head-soul leaves the body at death, in another context some of them claimed that part of the purpose of placing poison on the grave was to prevent the egress of the head-soul. Others claimed quite the opposite, namely that the head-soul after burial simply exists within the earth, with the possibility of changing into some unspecified disease. It is hard to choose between these various versions. One or more of the following reasons may account for the variation: my ethnography may be incomplete; the Temiars may themselves be muddled when it comes to theological problems; or the word rəwaay may have layers of meaning in Rening that it does not have elsewhere.

Mourning

Let us return now to the myth. Mourning and the eventual cessation of mourning are regarded as part of the proper order of things. It involves little alteration to the course of everyday life. As the myth suggests, the

---

56. [Added 2014] If valid, this would be an example of what I later came to regard as the 'dialectical' mode of orientation.

more occasional and ceremonial activities of singing and trancing are forbidden during the mourning period. This is a period of restraint on openly joyous activities, as implied by the myth's statement that courtship and lovemaking should recommence after the mourning is over. (There is, however, no ban on sexual activities as such during the mourning period.) The restrictions apply not only to the close mourners but also to all the inhabitants of the village in which they live. There seems to be no formally reckoned length of time attached to the mourning period. A few informants tried hopefully to make me believe that the correct period was six months for an adult's death and one-and-a-half months for a child, and that the village headman was responsible for the reckoning. But in reality, mourning periods vary considerably in duration, depending on the personal feelings of the closest mourner. The mourning period following the burial in Rening described above lasted just one month. In Humid, on the other hand, following the burial of a young child, the mourning period lasted for nearly three months. It is impossible to generalise from these figures. Just as there is no distinction between the amount of grave offerings required on the death of a baby or a headman, there is no regular variation in the length of the mourning period to accord with the formal status of the deceased. In the end, though, the decision to throw off formal mourning probably results from a balance between the mourners' desire to prolong their grief and the desire of the other villagers to recommence mediumistic and musical activities. Temiars feel that a village cannot go for long without calling down the spirit-guides: it begins to stagnate and become spiritually stale, and the people, as their dream songs so strikingly proclaim, become weary and listless.

The séance at which the mourning taboos are cast off makes these points clearly, and the ceremony is explicit in meaning. I leave until the next chapter a description of those parts that bear more on the subject of mediumship than on mourning. Here, I restrict myself to a brief account of the way in which the ceremony purges the village of the sorrows and restrictions of mourning. At the outset, it should be remarked that this ceremony (*tərɛnpʉk tɛnmɔɔh* 'the bursting of the mourning') cannot fail to strike the outside observer as very moving. It is certainly the most beautiful set piece in the whole round of Temiar religious activities. The following account is based on the ceremony held at Humid on 28 October 1964, bringing to an end the mourning for Malam's young daughter. Unlike other such ceremonies, this did not become an occasion for trance mediumship.

Preparations started early on the morning of the ceremony. The women were busy cooking special food—cakes of rice cooked in bamboo tubes, and a bread made of banana and grated cassava mashed together. The men meanwhile had gone hunting and fishing; some had even been out the previous night to catch frogs. One man was sent to the subsidiary

Sɛŋsaak village (figure 4.4) about three hours' walk upstream to fetch those who lived there, including the medium whom the headman regarded as especially skilled at performing the mourning-cessation ceremonies. Later in the day the more immediate cooking got under way, consisting of the meat and fish that had been caught, as well as some shop-bought foods such as sardines and noodles. Two of the women busied themselves with preparing the decorations and cosmetics. They plaited crowns and bandoliers of pandanus,[57] and set a large tray of herbs and flowers, such as citronella grass and hibiscus, on the mats they had spread in the centre of the dancing floor. Later they added freshly rolled native cigarettes, a bunch of red *kesumba* (annatto) fruits (*Bixa orellana*) for use as face-paint, and a bowl of sugarcane sections.

The food was then served in the late afternoon, and the 'mourning cessation feast' (*cɛʔnaaʔ lɛynəəy tɛnmɔɔh*) began. This was held in the 'old style', with the men eating communally in the middle and the women served separately in their own compartments around the periphery of the house. Those who ate were urged to close up the circle and leave no gaps. The close mourners, however, remained apart, some of them weeping, and ate only the remaining food after everyone else had finished. In contrast, the non-mourners seemed to be in forcedly high spirits. After the meal they turned on the radio for further amusement.

The ceremony proper started a couple of hours later, at dusk. The remains of the feast had been cleared away and the central area of the house had been rearranged. A line was stretched across the house at about head-level, and on it were hung six men's and seven women's sarongs that Malam had bought a few days before in the shops at Gua Musang, two days' march away. Two logs were set at right angles so that, together with the line, they formed an enclosure to the central space on three sides. Seven sets of bamboo beaters were placed at the ready. The women who formed the chorus seated themselves inside the logs, and the old man from upstream squatted in the middle. Many of the other men sat in a rough row under the line of sarongs. The mourners, though, remained out of things and sat in their own compartment, which looked directly onto the ceremonial area.

All the lights and fires were extinguished, and the wife of the master of ceremonies started beating out a steady duple rhythm with her bamboo stampers. The other women followed suit and the singing began, slowly and mysteriously. The song was a traditional one used throughout the Betis region as the means of ending a mourning taboo period. But since all Temiar song performances are extemporised it was only the tune and the recurrent verse that followed the standard pattern. The first lines ran:

---

57. [Added 2014] For an example, see figure 2.8.

Nam-bokaa? jərɛŋkaaŋ,	Let the dawn open up,
nam-yah baliik	let morning break in the sky
num-rɛh ma-doh.	from downstream [i.e., East] to here.

This beautiful lyric recurred as a refrain throughout the night's singing. This first song lasted about half-an-hour, while the dead girl's mother could be heard wailing in her room. The singers, however, were still treating the occasion lightly, interspersing the proceedings with laughter. As the song came to an end, the lights were slowly raised and they started to sing the second song. By now, the music had taken on the character of a normal evening's singing, such as the villagers of Humid often perform for sheer musical pleasure.

Without interrupting the proceedings, two of the men now began distributing the sarongs that had been hung above the singers. The first was tied around the head of the lead singer in the style of a simple Malay kerchief. The rest were then distributed to the other singers, by laying the cloths across their shoulders. At this point, the headman suggested to me that this was in part a return for the grave goods that several of them had earlier presented at the burial. Meanwhile, one of the women had brought in the tray of cosmetics, and the headman's sister proceeded to paint the faces of several of the men red. The main singer then placed some hibiscus blossoms in his own hair, stood up, and while still singing beckoned to everyone to gather round and squat close to him. Dancing around slowly, he waved his new sarong over their heads as if in blessing. Then, turning his attention to the mourners while still singing, he performed a ritual 'blowing' (*tɛnhool*; see the next chapter) on the heads and ears of the mother, father and mother's sister's husband of the dead girl. He then did the same for the headman's wife—the dead child's midwife—and the young girl that she was fostering. He was so buried in his task, uttering spells mostly beginning with 'do not ... ', that his wife, the leader of the women's chorus, complained they could not hear well enough for them to repeat what he was singing in the traditional canonic manner. After a short retirement in her room, the dead girl's mother moved over to one of the central fireplaces with her surviving daughter on her lap.

The assembled men meanwhile had begun anointing each other's hair with oil and folding ceremonial kerchiefs made out of the newly presented sarongs on their heads. These they decorated with herbs from the large tray. Also from the tray, they smoked the cigarettes that had been specially prepared. The singing was now taken over by another man, and this set the pattern for the rest of the night. He too began with the *Nam-bokaa? jərɛŋkaaŋ* refrain, but moved on to lighter songs, progressing steadily towards the style of a normal musical evening. Others took over in turn, and the singing went on until dawn, flagging occasionally. Some women danced half-heartedly, while some of the men performed ritual blowings because a few of the people were feeling unwell, and to rid the village of the last traces of mourning. People were alternately taking naps and singing. Others kept themselves awake by eating snacks. One man seemed to wander off into a spontaneous trance and jumped up, running off hooting into a corner, although this was not otherwise a séance.

And so the night proceeded: the music never completely stopped, and several of the men performed occasional ritual blowings on almost all the people in the house. At dawn the singing was again led by the man who had started the evening off, only he now rose to his full height to 'sing upwards' (*gabag baliik*). Still singing, he led the responding chorus of women down the steps, from the house to the central village space. The women continued to beat their bamboos on the ground as they moved along, crouching to do so. One of them had heated three bamboos of water in the house, and after the leading singer had finally sung *bokaaʔ jərɛŋkaaŋ, hɔj nam-yah, lah ʔɛ-mɛʔmaaʔ* 'let the dawn open, day is about to break, let us return home', they washed their faces in the water. Then, smashing both the beaters and the water bamboos and throwing them away with much mirth, they returned to the house. The mourning had formally ended.

Returning to the house at about 10:00 a.m. I found several people still sleeping, some back at work, and nearly all humming tunes as if in anticipation of the second song performance due for that evening. The headman's wife was returning with the dead girl's mother from collecting cassava. It was obvious that the load of sorrow, so evident the previous day, had lifted. The girl's mother had put on lipstick and was laughing uproariously. Most people were still in festive dress, and some were wearing bead bandoliers that they had put on since the previous night.

That evening, they sang again, this time without the formal layout and without feasting beforehand. Although the *Nam-bokaaʔ jərɛŋkaaŋ* was sung, the atmosphere was different. The singers were accompanied by women dancing and men playing musical instruments. At the same time, it was evident that all elements of mourning had not yet been expunged. The dead girl's mother could again be heard weeping and flailing about in her misery, and there was much ritual blowing performed throughout the house, especially by the dead girl's father. This time, the latter did much of the singing, in contrast to his seclusion the previous night. But there was a catch in his voice; and his wife, who was now one of the women's chorus, sobbed while he sang. As on the previous night, the performance was not halted until dawn. At one point, a woman prodded her brother-in-law into wakefulness so that he could take over when the last remaining woman singer had to go to the other end of the house to tend her crying child. He lay down to sleep again as soon as she returned.

The meaning of this ceremony as a passage rite needs little further explanation: the reincorporation of the initially separate group of mourners into the normal flow of everyday life is both acted out symbolically and made into a psychological reality. Certain of the ritual elements have appeared elsewhere in this study, and others will reappear later. The use of comb and hair oil recalls both the reintroduction to normal life of a newly menstruating girl and the prohibitions placed on mourners immediately after a burial. The same is true of the ritual bathing in warm water that brings the ceremony to its end. The contrast between darkness and illumination as well as the use of hair oil are features that recur as elements of the mediumistic complex.

Soul concepts in mortuary rituals

This discussion of Temiar reactions to death has shown how the associated rituals express important theological categorisations, in particular those most clearly expressed in the soul beliefs. Yet it would be forcing matters to claim that this provides a full understanding of Temiar mortuary behaviour. It is surely significant, for example, that the body must be buried in such a way as not to come into direct contact with the soil, while at the same time being completely surrounded by it. In acknowledging this to be so, my Temiar informants nevertheless failed to provide an explanation. It may be that the observance seeks to have it both ways, ambivalently treating the human corpse as a clearly cultural object that has been reduced to a state of nature. The grave effectively takes the form of an enclosed dwelling situated underground. Just as the houses of the living are isolated from the earth by their pillars, so is the grave-house isolated from the earth by its carefully made walling and roofing. Perhaps the similarly unexplained crumbling and cleaning of the first layer of soil should be understood in the same way. A layer of culturally processed soil in immediate contact with the roof of the burial chamber ensures that the latter does not contact the untreated (natural) vegetation-containing soil piled on top.

Yet, if these observances do not directly reflect the soul concepts, they nevertheless show a close dialectical relationship to them, insofar as both are transformable ultimately into the same calculus of culture and nature. I have already demonstrated in part how this is so, but we must wait until the final chapter (Chapter 8) before seeing how highly integrated is the total theological system built up from elements of this sort. Before closing the present chapter, however, there remains a final piece of occasional ritual for us to examine.

Thunder rituals

A so-called blood sacrifice among the Temiars and other Aboriginal groups has been widely reported in the literature.[58] I did not myself witness any

---

58. See especially Skeat & Blagden (1906 (II): 200), Schebesta (1927: 87–88, 1957: 78–104), Evans (1937: Chapter 17), Slimming (1958: 153–155), Freeman (1967) and Needham (1964).

Figure 6.4 Penghulu Dalam and his wife ʔahɔɔd with their foster-daughter ʔasɔɔd (1964)

ritual of this kind, but I was able to observe much of the informal reactions that the Temiars have towards close thunder, the context in which the 'blood sacrifice' is carried out. The Temiars greatly fear thunder, as shown by their actions when a storm comes near. A few anecdotes will illustrate the effect that thunder has on them. Once, while talking in my own house with an informant, a loud clap of thunder exploded overhead. Emitting a nervous giggle he shot up suddenly and rushed out of the house to join his people in the longhouse a few yards away. On other occasions, they would brandish their shotguns at the sky while shouting curses at Karey, the cause of it all. A more usual procedure takes on the appearance of a ritual act: the approach of louring thunderclouds serves as a signal for some people to blow forcibly at the sky through their clenched fists,[59] following through by throwing the hand upwards, open, in a gesture of defiance. This is repeated several times.

It was evident, though, that fear of thunder is something that Temiar parents find it necessary to teach their children. One 10-year-old boy reported to me, 'When Karey thunders Mother stops up my ears.' On another occasion, Penghulu Dalam's wife (figure 6.4) covered the ears of her very young foster-

---

59. [Added 2014] This kind of blowing is known as sɛnʔuh (verb: sɔʔuh). It can also be applied to various objects, turning them into curative amulets. Temiars usually distinguish sɛnʔuh from tɛnhool (verb: tɔhool), the kind of mediumistic blowing that is applied directly to a patient's body.

daughter as a clap of thunder sounded, but the girl treated the whole thing as a joke and laughed happily. At the same time, another young girl's father was busy shouting at Karey about his apparent attempts to kill us, but the girl blithely copied her father as if it was nothing but play.

I never witnessed the blood sacrifice, despite the fact that it was definitely known to my informants in Humid, who were able to give a brief description of the ceremony. Yet there is conclusive evidence that those same villagers have carried out the rite themselves. This occurs in Slimming's report (1958: 154–155) of the actions of Penghulu Dalam's wife during a heavy storm. When the thunder arrived immediately overhead, she

> bundled all her possessions in a piece of cloth and carried them to the doorway. She stood on the top step with several other women and they screamed and shouted at the storm, clenching their fists and shaking them at the sky. The men sat, silent, by the fire waiting for the storm to finish but the women defied it and cried out in anger and fear.
>
> 'Go away, storm: Go away: Either you go or we shall go:'
>
> 'Either you leave or we shall leave:'
>
> 'Go: Go:' And they clung on to their small bundles of possessions and shook them up at the sky. They had pulled out their hair combs and now their hair was hanging forward, plastered over their faces.
>
> The storm got worse and the people more frightened until finally Dalam's wife ran back into the room towards the fire .... and several of the other women followed her. She searched for a parang—pushing one of the men to one side as she reached for it—and cut her leg, lightly, below the knee. I suddenly realised that this was the blood sacrifice that I heard about and never seen. Blood from the wound trickled down her calf and she caught some of it in a bamboo cup—the other women were cutting themselves: one of them standing on the hot embers of the fire as she did so and not noticing it. Each carried a cup with blood in it and they slopped water in with the blood and ran out into the thundering darkness. The cleared space was lit up with flashes of blue-white light and the women ran about in the mud, scattering blood on the ground and calling out above the noise of the pounding rain.

Apart from telling us that they stayed outside until the storm began to move away, Slimming unfortunately gives us no more details. I can myself vouch for the initial behaviour he describes. In Rening, a violent storm accompanied by high winds once approached the village. Although it was night time, everyone suddenly left the house, carrying with them packs of personal possessions bundled in sarongs over their shoulders. Hastily lighting a fire right under the house and feeding it with splinters of dried bamboo, they threw onto it a tortoise carapace that had been stowed on the wall of the house for some months past, perhaps with just such an emergency in mind. The house above rapidly filled with dense foul-smelling smoke while people beneath stood and shouted threats at the sky. The aim was to make conditions unbearable for Karey, the cause of the storm. I witnessed this practice among no other Temiar group, and it may therefore have been a borrowed Semai custom. Evans (1923: 201), for example, was told that during very bad storms indeed 'the Behrang Senoi [i.e., Semais living in southern Perak] assemble under the house and burn *jadam* (extract of aloes (?)) and evil-smelling rubbish to scare away the storm'.

The blood-letting offering is called *somɔk* or *somuk* by the Temiars, an odd-appearing word that sounds as if it were borrowed from some other language. But the only possibly related form that I can find is the Malay (Indonesian) word *sumbang*, which apart from its more usual meaning of 'abomination' may also signify the act of 'contribution'.[60] And indeed, most of the published accounts—see especially Schebesta (1957: 88–89)—maintain that the blood is primarily an offering to the deity, in this case Karey. My informants confirmed that the blood is taken from the leg, mixed with water in a bamboo and thrown upwards then down on to the ground.[61] They added the further detail that it may also be mixed with charcoal from the fire. Unfortunately, they failed to tell me their views about the purpose of the rite, and made no mention of the range of underground deities that, according to Schebesta (1957: 89), part of the blood is supposed to go

---

60. [Added 2014] Schebesta (1957: 89) spells the word as *semug* and *somag*, the final *g* showing that these were in the Perak dialect of Temiar. However, judging by his variant and somewhat inaccurate glosses, Schebesta appears to have regarded them as two different words. At the *viva voce* examination of the thesis, Rodney Needham rejected the meaning 'contribute' for *sumbang* in favour of 'abomination'—a meaning that typically includes 'incest'. However, when once discussing incest (Temiar: gɛɛs) in Humid, the borrowed Malay word took the form *sumak*, in the phonologically expected pattern, rather than *somɔk*. In most Malay dictionaries, the 'contribute' meaning for *sumbang* is clearly marked as an Indonesian usage, even though it is now current in modern Malay. In support of this, I was later told by a Pahang Temiar who was also fluent in Semai that Temiar *somɔk* was equivalent to the Semai concept of *jamuu*². The latter is clearly a borrowing of the Malay word *jamu* meaning 'to entertain; to keep a familiar spirit' (Coope 1997: 137), but which can also be used, as *perjamu*, to mean 'offering to an evil spirit' (Wilkinson 1932: 443). I now think that *somɔk* is simply a Temiarised form of a Malay word meaning '(spirit)offering'. To confuse matters further, some Temiars use the apparently unaltered form *sumbaŋ* as the name of a variety of squash—a completely different meaning, not found in any Malay or Indonesian dictionary.

61. [Added 2014] In 1968, Saleh (pictured in figures 2.4 and 2.5) gave me some further details. Only the person who had done wrong performed the blood-offering, whether male or female, and whether the storm was near or far away. The blood is taken from either calf by tapping (not slicing) two or three times with a knife or bamboo sliver until the blood flows. A bamboo vessel containing a lot of water is then placed under the cut, and the blood is scraped off into the water and stirred. The mixture is then carried to the door of the house or to the ground below. The vessel is held horizontally while the following imprecation is pronounced: *Doh ²i-somuk ha-rii² hah, ham-dɛŋdək na², ham-jɛr²aar, ham-ba-hɔlɛjwij* 'Here, I *somuk* you—you who want to storm, cause floods, and send lightning right at us.' The liquid is then thrown strongly skywards. If the storm is especially violent and rain is falling, the blood-containing bamboo is forced into the ground so that the blood drips into the hole, while uttering *Ɲɔb Tanɔŋ, ɲɔb Cɛbrɛb, ɲɔb ²ɛɲ²ɔɔŋ, ɲɔm-tɛdteed na², ɲɔm-ba-hɔlɛjwij, ɲɔm-dɛŋdək, ɲɔm-²ɛr²oor, ɲɔm-ba-todoh na²* 'You Tanɔŋ, you Cɛbrɛb, you ²ɛɲ²ɔɔŋ, take it, you who are lightning right here, you order (him), you make it peaceful.' Those addressed include some of the underground deities mentioned by Schebesta; they also appear in some of the traditional stories about Karey, the thunder deity.

to. In other contexts, such as myth-telling, however, they displayed some slight knowledge of these deities. Faced with such a paucity of data (to be rectified by further fieldwork, it is hoped) I am forced instead to examine the external structural meaning of the blood-offering rite. Schebesta sees in it the core of Aboriginal religion, a sort of primordial sacrificial act. But, whatever the case, it is clear that there is a lack of repeated devotion to the act: Slimming's account makes clear that it is highly contingent. This should warn against building upon it any elaborate theories of the prevalence of sin ideologies among Malayan Aborigines. I would rather adhere to the view, at least until further evidence is forthcoming, that the blood-offering is a ritual means of relating everyday categorisations to the notion of evil when the latter is at its most manifest in the close approach of Karey during a violent thunderstorm.

As if to support this contention, I was told that Temiars do occasionally cut off a lock of hair during storms and burn it in the fire—just as do the Penans of Sarawak, according to Needham (1964: 143). This is done while saying *Doh ʾi-tɔɔd, ham-dɛŋdək* 'Here, I burn (it), you want to storm'; but this ritual is apparently not referred to as *somuk*. We have seen already how the opposition between hair and blood stands on the personal scale for the much larger opposition of culture and nature. Further, in terms of the logic of ritual acts, we have observed in many contexts an opposition between burning and dropping onto the ground— the first a retaining-in-culture, the second a returning-to-nature. This approach allows us also to pose an answer to Needham's significant question (1964: 148): 'and why, in any case, is the blood taken from the leg?' I have suggested that, on the terrestrial scale, the cosmic oppositions are reflected as oppositions between the upper and lower parts of those animate or inanimate entities in which they are thought to be established. It would follow that the ritual's blood—the reflex of the lower-body category—should be drawn from a point as far removed as is practical from the site of the hair which represents the other ritual pole. Most of the other points in Needham's listing (1964: 144) of characteristic features of this ritual complex can also be fitted into this scheme. That the blood is mixed with water is probably no more than a means of increasing its volume to allow of easy handling and throwing. The expiation of transgression is relevant insofar as Temiars assert that a whole range of tabooed acts (*misik*, Chapter 4) bring Karey's thunderings down to earth. These transgressions consist mainly of the mockery of animals that forms Needham's sixth listed characteristic. His eighth and ninth points deal with beliefs in the uprooting of trees and the prohibition on burning the leech, both of which I dealt with earlier. The only point I am not yet able to clarify is the reported belief that the thrown-up blood is applied to the deity's body (chest).

Conclusion

Readers who have followed the argument up to this point will see that there is indeed an ideological unity underlying all the various acts and beliefs discussed in this and the preceding chapter. The aim of Needham's study (1964) of older accounts of similar ethnographic data was to show that this unity probably holds, and that it reflects the sophisticated ordered set of categorisations upon which the Aborigines base their grasp of the world and its problems. Just *how* sophisticated is the theology that this entails, we shall learn in Chapters 7 and 8.

Chapter | *Temiar Religion (1967)—*
7 | Spirit-mediumship

Most of the activities discussed so far have little of the overtly 'religious' about them. Several months passed before I realised that the various dietary and other taboos related to concerns lying far beyond the mundane problems of subsistence. However, after I had eventually succeeded in mildly blackmailing[1] my informants into revealing the details of their mediumistic activities,[2] it became apparent that here was a whole field (at last) almost purely 'religious' in its scope and aims. Later, it became clear that mediumship is not only the prime religious activity of the Temiars but also that it serves as a focus in which all the different ritual strands are brought together in such a manner as to make obvious the connections between them.

'Blackmail' was necessary, not because mediumistic practices are in any way secret, but because my informants had yet to be convinced that I was a sufficiently serious investigator to warrant their taking pains to explain such a complex topic. I already knew from the literature that the Temiars had a highly developed trance behaviour. Furthermore, many of my friends in Malaya had witnessed their spectacular séances. Yet my informants in the village of Humid preferred to let me believe that, whatever was the case elsewhere, the inhabitants of the Perolak valley did not undertake mediumistic activity. But there were chinks in their armour. The children happily acted out for me the trance behaviour of their parents, telling me that trance séances had indeed been held during my absence. In any case, I did not remain in the one village. Travelling upstream along the full length of the valley, I met other Temiars who not only stated categorically that no community could survive long without mediumship, but also took the trouble to introduce me to its complexities. As Penghulu Hitam Tamboh (figure 7.1) put it, '*Tɔʔ ʔɛ-halaaʔ,*

---

1. By threatening to leave them, taking with me not only their ready source of tobacco, curry, cash, etc., but also threatening to destroy the trust between us, which as Temiars they greatly valued.
2. [Added 2014] The original version of the thesis talked mostly of 'shamanism' rather than 'spirit-mediumship'. According to Firth (1964: 247–248), the latter is 'normally a form of possession in which the person is conceived as serving as an intermediary between spirits and men'. The former is 'a master of spirits. Normally himself a spirit-medium, the shaman is thought to control spirits by ritual techniques, and in some societies, as in Kelantan (Malaya), he may not himself be in trance state when he does this, but be controlling the spirits in another medium'. Although there are occasional traces of shamanism in Temiar religious practice, I have now preferred to speak of 'mediumship', as that is the predominant component.

rɛʔ-lɔɔʔ ʔɛ-gɔɔsʔ. Macam ʔobad tɔʔ mɔʔ, tɔʔ ʔɛ-gɔɔs 'How could we live without mediumship? Just as if there were no medicine, we could not live.'

One thing became clear: that my friends in Humid were quite justified when they claimed later that mediumship is a topic not easily explained to the outsider. But, as with so many other topics, on realising that I was already partly initiated they readily undertook to instruct me as far as their own knowledge allowed, with apologies for having at first kept me in ignorance.

Full understanding of Temiar mediumship requires that it be examined from two different vantage points. Viewed from the inside, it resolves into the question of a person's relations with his or her spirit-guides and of the whole community's relations with the totality of its members' spirit-guides. From the outside, the features that differentiate between the various types of mediumship reintroduce us to the categorisations that enter ultimately into the overall theology of the Temiars. The study of the Temiars' relationship with their spirit-guides takes us into the realm of dream psychology, which (as if to compensate for my own lack of psychological training and sufficient relevant

Figure 7.1 Penghulu Hitam Tamboh (1964), next to his old-style house at Jak
Hitam Tamboh was the first Temiar to tell me any significant details about the workings of spirit-mediumship, a few months after my fieldwork began. Jak is now uninhabited, but in the 1960s it was a remote mountain-plateau settlement, notable for growing millet rather than rice as its staple crop.

field data) has already been the subject of intensive study by Kilton Stewart, in close association with H. D. Noone.[3]

Dreaming

My own experiences demonstrated that the Temiars place great value on dreams and dreaming. All dreams are charged with significance, which it is the duty of the dreamer and his fellows to try to decipher. One has only to say 'Last night I dreamt ...' and immediately the people sitting around enthusiastically urge the dreamer to tell all. Behind this enthusiasm lie two important ideas. First, it is always hoped that the dreams of one of the villagers may contain some revelation of importance to the community as a whole, ranging from a piece of technical advice to a new religious idea that may revitalise the spiritual life of whole valleys. Second, Kilton Stewart claimed that the process of maturation among the Temiars is closely bound up with the guidance given to the youngsters to direct their dreaming to the attainment of certain desired ends. The question of dream-given revelations is fundamental to an understanding of Temiar religion, and I shall discuss it shortly. First, I take a brief look at what Stewart had to say about Temiar dream education. Such data as I collected on the content of dreams are at least congruent with some of his ideas.[4]

Stewart on dream education

Initially, Temiar children's dreams are free-ranging, but often taking as their subjects the events of the preceding days. The dreamers may undergo frightening or pleasurable dream experiences, which they are encouraged to discuss with their parents and others—who make them feel that their dreaming is important. This is in marked contrast, says Stewart, to most other cultures, where dreaming is treated with much less concern, if at all. The things that terrorise the children in their dreams are overblown versions of everyday happenings: choking in the smoke of the fire, drowning in the river, falling from a tree, and so on. But on waking they are told by their elders that dream happenings are intrinsically good. It will be good for them in their later dreamings to move more deeply into the terror-ridden situation, even to die. In the end, they will find some sort of treasure, which they may bring back for all to share. They may even succeed in making a servant of whatever frightened them in their earlier dreams. If their dreams are pleasant, the same

---

3. Stewart (1947, 1951, 1953, 1954, 1962). A useful summary of Stewart's (Noone's?) views, written for the layman, will be found in Holman (1962: 91–102).
4. [Added 2014] I have left the succeeding remarks almost entirely unrevised even though, as already discussed in Chapter 2, I would today be much more critical of Stewart's later claims, especially those concerning dream *control*. In his thesis (1947: 112–117), Stewart is clearly referring to the *discussion* of the child's dreams with the father *after* the event, rather than to the dreams themselves *as dreamt*, even though he writes as if it is the latter that form his focus.

instruction is given them. If they find themselves soaring happily, they are told that in future dreams they must float to some definite place from where they will again bring back some treasure. Stewart claimed (1947: 155–7) that the dreams of Temiar children do in fact 'mature' along these lines as they grow older. The adolescents consistently dream to a definite end, destroying their enemies and bringing back treasures in the form of 'songs, designs, poems, stories, and mechanical inventions'.

The psychological consequences of this, Stewart later claimed (and psychology was his prime concern), are immense. Since all dream happenings are intrinsically good, the children may speak openly about matters that would otherwise have to remain hidden. If in their dreams they come into open conflict with, for example, their parents, and the next morning make this known to them directly (as they are encouraged to do), then the parents cannot fail to take note of what Stewart (1954: 399) calls this 'reaction against, or a protestation of, the very process of socialization'. Furthermore, since the dreams usually relate to some specific event of the previous day(s) the parents gain detailed warnings as to how they should react to their children's growing personal autonomy. In urging them to overcome their dream adversaries, even if these be the parents themselves, those who listen to their dreams ensure that ultimately the strains and conflicts that would normally arise in everyday waking life are removed to the realm of dream life, altered into a force for good, not evil. The almost total shunning of violence by the Temiars would, on Stewart's understanding, result from this process of dream education.

Stewart's own accounts (1947: 91–253) of the psychology of Temiar dreaming are detailed and subtle. I have done little more here than give a sketch of his work. My aim in introducing his material is simply to show that dreams and dreaming have for the Temiars a high value lying largely outside and independent of the domain of religion proper. It should not be thought, though, that the peaceability of the Temiar personality is to be explained only through the process of dream education. There are several other diffuse methods of social control, which Stewart seems to have been ignorant of. I discuss these in the next chapter. On the other hand, I can certainly adduce independent evidence of the importance of dreams in Temiar life. The children who clustered around me each morning as they played frequently offered, without prompting, to tell me their dreams of the previous night. In this way, I collected several children's dreams that correspond closely to the patterns described by Stewart in his dissertation (1947: 92–102, 452–457): full of deaths, drownings, tigers, poisonings, tortures, all retold openly and, apparently, happily.[5] It is true also that the Temiars discuss their dreams with each other, though to suggest that this attains the status of a formal breakfast-time council, as Stewart (1947: 103–118) did, is to make too much of the

---

5. [Added 2014] All 15 of the children's dreams I collected are presented in Appendix 4.

matter. Most Temiars believe implicitly in the validity of dream experiences. Occasionally, when something unusual occurred, such as my sudden arrival in a remote village, the inhabitants showed no surprise, for (they said) they had already dreamt what would occur. Moreover, the belief is maintained even against the evidence: one man spent the whole day worrying how it came about that the young men had returned from a hunting expedition laden with large fish and monkeys when he had dreamt that their bag would be two or more large deer. Another man felt certain that my Temiar cook, with whom I travelled, would one day become a great medium, as the cook's presence had caused him to dream that the village was surrounded with were-tigers. (I await the outcome of this prophecy with interest: there is reason to believe that it might come true.)

The spirit-guide relationship

The later stages of the dream maturation process described by Stewart (1947: 128–169) bring us back to the main topic. Some time after adolescence, many Temiar men (and sometimes women) begin to have a more positive involvement with their dream characters than hitherto, so that eventually some form of permanent personal relationship is set up between them. Such a dream character is known as a *gunig*, the 'spirit-guide' mentioned earlier. In Chapter 6, I showed that dream characters are usually constituted by the *rǝwaay* (head-soul or upper-body soul) of their originating selves. Less often, it is their *jǝrǝǝk* or *hup* (blood-soul, lower-body soul) that is involved. In the typical paradigm, the dream character appears as a young man or woman (some say a young child), yet somehow still identifiable as the representative of a definite species or other entity, natural or otherwise, in the real world. A special word, *cǝrɔɔʔ*, which seems not to occur in other contexts, is used for the 'arrival' of the *gunig* in a dream. In return for certain specified new observances as a token of the relationship, the spirit-guide offers to become the dreamer's child-cum-mentor. The new observances might include dietary restrictions or prohibitions, often aimed at the flesh of the spirit-guide's own species. Less often, the spirit-guide may institute linguistic taboos, such as forbidding the use of earlier names for certain animals or medicines. The relationship thereby established is explicitly mutual: the spirit-guide, while calling the dreamer *bǝǝh* 'father' and being regarded as *macam kǝwããs* 'like (my) child', is known also as the dreamer's *guruuʔ*, 'teacher'.[6] The spirit-guide's first teaching is usually a new song lyric for its 'father' to sing at the next communal singing session. But it could also be a new vocal or instrumental tune, a decorative blowpipe pattern, and so on.

---

6. [Added 2014] This characterisation of the spirit-guide as simultaneously 'child' and 'teacher' is a further expression of the dialectical mode of orientation discussed explicitly in later studies, including Chapter 12 in this volume.

The spirit-medium, *halaa²*

Many elaborations are built around this basic paradigm, but the majority of Temiars never get beyond the simple state of possessing just one spirit-guide who visits them occasionally in dreams. Most villages contain several such people, whom the casual informant would be unlikely to refer to as mediums proper, *halaa²*. Yet, in other contexts, anyone who has dreamt and continues to dream of a spirit-guide may be referred to as a *halaa²*. We therefore need to look more closely at this word before proceeding further. Linguistics gives little guidance, as *halaa²* is a mono-morphemic root occurring in no other context.[7] Cognate words are found in many Aboriginal languages, however, and these are usually glossed as 'medicine-man' or some close equivalent (Blagden 1906, II: 656). A more significant clue perhaps is that in the Telom dialect of Semai (a language contiguous with Temiar) *halaa²* is used for 'spirit-guide' as well as for 'medium'. Traces of such a usage occur in Temiar also: a man might say *halaa² yeh* non-committally to mean something like 'the state of my possession of a spirit-guide'. At the other extreme, questioners are likely to be told that 'there are no *halaa²* here', *halaa²* in this case referring to the most powerful of mediums, only one of whom is normally found in each major valley. The simplest way to resolve this terminological difficulty is to employ Dentan's suggestion (1964: 181) that 'all Senoi believe that people may be more or less "adept" (*halaaq*)', and to use *halaa²* in this sense. This has the advantage of fitting well with the Temiar way of looking at things: the casual dreamer and the great medium do indeed differ in their degrees of adeptness—their adeptness at turning to good use their essentially similar experience of possessing one or more spirit-guides. That the former meets his spirit-guide privately and informally and the latter publicly and formally should not disguise the essential similarity bound up in calling them both *sɛn²ɔɔy bə-halaa²*, 'people possessing adeptness'.

In a sense, there is a gradation between the two; but in the present study I am paying more attention to the public and formal aspects of the spirit-guide relationship than to its private and informal features.[8] Nevertheless, the congruence between public practice and private belief is an important

---

7. [Added 2014] This judgment was premature. It is now clear that *halaa²* and *bə-halaa²* are related to the Malay noun *berhala* 'idol, graven image, joss' (Wilkinson 1932: 127), though not necessarily by direct borrowing. The word derives ultimately from the Prakrit *bharāla* (Gonda 1952: 42), in which form it is found in the Old Malay Srivijayan inscriptions from Sumatra, and also on a fourteenth-century Buddhist statue from East Java (Reichle 2007: 89–90). Cuisinier (1936: 41, 44) reported that the Kelantan Malays also employed this word—pronouncing it [al:ɒ²], corresponding to the 'standard' Malay pronunciation [hala] or [halə])—to refer to the shaman's spirit-guide as well as to the were-tigers believed to dig up the corpse of a buried shaman. However, in an interesting etymological reversal, she claimed that the word had been borrowed from the 'Semang'—a Northern-Aslian-speaking Orang Asli population, whose version would have been *hala²*. Malays more usually, unlike the Orang Asli and the Kelantan Malays, do not treat the initial *ber-* of *berhala* as a detachable prefix, thereby holding true to its Indic original. Strangely, in an otherwise well documented article on the etymology of Malay *berhala*, Rivers (2010) makes no mention of these Aslian and Indic connections, treating it instead as a *ber-*prefixed form of *hala* 'direction'.

8. [Added 2014] I discuss the subjective aspects of mediumship in Chapter 10. Both Roseman (1991) and Jennings (1995) provide detailed material on the more private features of the spirit-guide relation.

feature, enabling the mediumistic cult to be fully integrated with the rest of Temiar life. Whereas mere dream meetings with one's spirit-guide rarely have relevance beyond the individual (or the individual's parents, if a child), mediumistic activities are aimed explicitly at making the good powers of the spirit-guides available to the whole community and beyond. This is the purpose of the communal musical séances for which the Temiars are famous throughout Malaya. As we shall see, séance procedures vary; but it will serve our purposes best to examine first the structure of an idealised ordinary séance, one at which no so-called 'great' medium officiates.

The séance

Much of what I described in the previous chapter for the ceremony ending the mourning period applies also to an ordinary séance. For example, the same eagerness is displayed by the women in preparing decorations, usually bandoliers (*tɛnwaag*) and headdresses (*tɛmpɔɔ²*) woven out of pandanus (figures 2.8, 10.3–10.5). More important are two special ritual objects that are also made by the women several hours before the séance. The first of these is the whisk, of which several may be made, that the medium uses initially to fan himself into a trance and then in his healing rituals (figure 7.2). This may consist of any convenient bunch of leaves, but it is usually made from unopened fronds of the *kɘwaar* palm cleverly cut so that the outer third of their length flares out into an attractive fan of zigzagging greenery. The whisk is commonly referred to simply as *kɘwaar*. A common alternative is a bunch containing leaves of the *calun* plant, presumably the same as the *daun chalong* (*Clausena excavata?*) that Cuisinier (1936: 58) reports to be used by Malay mediums. The second ritual object is a wreath, the *tɘnamuu²*, measuring about 20 inches across and consisting of a hoop or rectangle of cane with small bunches of flowers and sweet-smelling herbs hanging down at close intervals (figures 7.2, 10.3–10.7). The whole assemblage is then hung from a beam over the centre of the dancing floor. Like much else in the ritual field, the Temiars refer to this apparatus by a word that seems to be a borrowing from Malay altered by a Temiarising inflection. The source is probably the Malay *tamu*, suggesting the entertaining of a guest. If, then, *tɘnamuu²* means 'thing for the reception of a guest', it precisely describes the suspended wreath's function, for it serves as a sort of landing-ground for the spirit-guides called down in the later stages of the séance. (No Temiar informant directly suggested, however, that the word had this, or any other, meaning.) The various preparations are completed before night sets in and followed by the evening meal.

The séance starts casually with the dimming of the fires. A few women seat themselves with their bamboo stampers along a special log or a floor-level beam (figures 2.5 and 2.7) and begin beating out a steady, usually duple, rhythm. This, interspersed with a few words of encouragement, leads one of the men to squat in the middle, one ear resting on his hand. After a few grunted

Figure 7.2 *Kəwaar* whisk and floral *tənamuu^ʔ* at a mourning-
cessation ceremony, Lambok (1979)
See front cover for the colour version.

or sighed calls for inspiration—*ma-lɔɔ^ʔ, ma-lɔɔ^ʔ* 'where, where?'—he begins
his song. The women then follow him in canon (more or less 'close' according
to the valley), while still beating out their rhythm. The song is extemporised
but within limits, depending on how well known the melody is and the extent
to which the lyrics make use of standard poetic figures. (I have more to say
later about the ritual significance of musical styles and the meaning of the
sometimes highly obscure song lyrics.) One man may keep the singing all
to himself, or he may be replaced successively by as many others as wish to
sing. But once started, the music will continue with sporadic halts for hours,
often till dawn.

So far, little will have happened to distinguish the proceedings from an
ordinary musical evening when the villagers sing solely for pleasure. In my
main village of Humid, most of the song performances were of this type.[9] If the
evening is to proceed as a séance, however, the pace soon quickens and some
people may get up to dance. There is considerable local variation in styles of
dancing and in who dances—men, women, or both. Stewart (1947: 170–193),
presumably following Noone, claimed that the different dances had different

---

9. [Added 2014] I suspect that this apparent preponderance of entertainment performances in Humid
was because the villagers knew that I was interested in their music *as* music, and that I wished to record
it on tape. Also, for reasons explained in Chapter 9, they withheld their religious practices from me for
the first few months of my fieldwork.

ritual meanings. I summarise his views below. The sexual divisions seem to be patterned on a north–south axis. In the north, down to the latitude of the Perolak valley (I have no data for Perak), the distinction between women's and men's dancing is quite marked, whereas further south both sexes perform in the same manner. This is surely to be correlated with similar variations in sex-linked behaviour in other fields of activity; Temiars themselves make such a correlation. In the north, parent-in-law avoidance is much more stringent, and same-generation affinal sexual relations are much more free than in the south, where marriage takes on a greater degree of formality and stability. In the north, women never to my knowledge dance themselves into trance, whereas in the south such behaviour is quite institutionalised, even though it is rare for a woman to become a medium.[10]

In Humid, if the men dance they do so progressing anti-clockwise in a circle around the floor, with short double hops on alternate feet and much bending of the waist and flailing of the arms. As the atmosphere gets more excited, the dancers leap violently and the whole house shakes to their rhythm. Suddenly, one or more of them seem to lose control, staggering backwards but just failing to fall to the floor. They have reached a state of light trance, or as the Temiars say, they have *wəl hup* 'forgotten their feelings'.[11] Those more practised in attaining the trance state bother much less with violent dancing. Instead, they sway gently, fanning and slapping the air around their heads and shoulders, and sometimes inhaling forcibly through their clenched fists until a gentle undemonstrative trance comes over them. Temiars acknowledge that mediumship and the attainment of trance are not the same thing. Many people who have never succeeded in calling down a spirit-guide in full séance go into trance, and this often happens spontaneously (*na-kəjɨd*, the Temiars say: 'he is startled'). Others enter trance simply as a form of entertainment, although the eagerness with which women in the south insist on trancing suggests that there may be more involved than mere entertainment. A great deal of tension is released, and people are more relaxed during the succeeding few days.

If the séance is at all a serious one (and Temiars do distinguish between those that are just for play and those that have a more serious intent behind them, such as healing), the focus soon shifts to whoever is about to call down a spirit-guide. There is no incompatibility in the simultaneous presence of several spirit-guides; the more spirit-guides that can be made to swarm around the house, the healthier spiritually the village will be. 'Small', that is ordinary, mediums are able to call down only those spirit-guides that pertain to the off-the-ground (*baliik*). These make their appearance as the watery emanation aspect (*kahyɛk*) of the upper-body soul of their originating source, whether

---

10. There is some evidence that this patterning reflects the geographical position of the Temiars between the Negritos to the north and the Semais to the south. [Added 2014] For further information, gathered later, on areal differences in kinship organisation among the Orang Asli, see Benjamin (1985, 2011a).
11. [Added 2014] See Chapters 2 and 11, where the *hup* is analysed as the seat of one's will or agency.

human, animal, plant or mountain. The spirits need coaxing, however, and before entering the house they behave shyly, hovering over the nearby mountain peaks and jumping onto the flowers and fronds of the vegetation around the village. This is made explicit in the songs that welcome them. The lyrics, which are cast as the spirit-guides' own words, describe in detail how the approaching spirit-guide dallies on its chosen mountain tops, espying the village from afar and waiting until it notes that a real welcome awaits, as evidenced by the preparation of flowers and cosmetics earlier in the day.

In Temiar, the process of calling down a spirit-guide is known as *tərɛnhəwal* 'the act of causing to emerge', and this describes fairly what is involved. The spirit-guide, appearing to the medium as 'a rain-like object', is believed to station itself somewhere over the roof-beam of the house or on the *tənamuu²* wreath. From there it lets down (*pəjɛɛw*, the word that also describes a spider letting itself down on a thread) a bundle of cords or threads known as *pərɛɲjɛɛn*, a word that may just be related to *pəjɛɛw* but of which I have no separate record. These threads are caught sight of in trance only by the medium who called down the spirit-guide in the first place. He then holds out his hand to meet the freely hanging threads, which collapse into his palm, liquefying into the watery state of *kahyɛk*; the threads are not aimed by the spirit-guide. With this small pool of *kahyɛk* in his hand, the medium is now powerful to extend his spirit-guide's powers wherever he wishes, either in healing or in instilling someone else with the same spirit-guide. The spirit-guide may now in some way enter the medium's heart-soul, *jərəək* (or *hup*). This is the soul responsible for speech (Chapter 6), and it is usual for the medium to start speaking aloud as the vehicle of his spirit-guide. The fires may be raised once the spirit-guide has firmly arrived. The surest sign that the spirit-guide has taken over is when the medium addresses members of the audience by altered kinship terms. Since the spirit-guide is the medium's 'child', anyone the medium addresses is shifted up through one generation: 'elder brother' (*kəloo²*) becomes 'senior uncle' (*kooc*), 'wife' (*lɛh*) becomes 'mother' (*boo²*), 'grandchild' (*cacə²*) becomes 'child' (*kəwãã̃s*), and so on. As a result, the spirit-guide's relationships become entirely consanguineal: a possessed medium may happily speak directly even to his mother-in-law (*bələ²*), who thereby becomes 'grandmother' (*yaa²*), but whom he would normally entirely avoid (Benjamin 1967c: 10). This state of inspired non-responsibility provides an opportunity for the airing of a few home truths, and the occasion is rarely wasted.

An alternative method of calling down the spirit-guide is for the medium to collect its freely hanging *pərɛɲjɛɛn* threads on the ends of his leaf whisk. In this case, the *kahyɛk* fluid is said to 'enter' the leaves, from where it may then be sprayed over whoever wishes to be instilled with its influence. This method of passing on the *kahyɛk*, known as *cɛwnaaw* 'spraying', is used only on those

Figures 7.3a and 7.3b *Tɛnhool*, Lambok (1979)
First (figure 7.3a), the medium expresses kahyɛk *from his* hup *into his fist. Then (figure 7.3b), he blows it* (tɔhool) *into the* hup *of the patient through the latter's chest.*

who are already practised as mediums in their own right. In villages where almost everyone joins in the trancing, *cɛwnaaw* is employed by the leading medium as a means of extending it to those who have danced themselves into a highly suggestible state. The medium may even openly dip the whisk into a bowl of scented water to reinforce the suggestion.

Greater interest attaches, though, to the handing-on of the spirit-guide's essence when it has been collected as *kahyɛk* in the medium's open palm. This he does by ritually blowing through his fist, an act that takes different names in different contexts. The blowing pure and simple is known as *tɛnhool* (verb: *tɔhool*),[12] which can also be applied to the blowing aimed at warding off the approach of a violent thunderstorm, in an act otherwise known as *sɛnʔuh* (verb: *sɔʔuh*). The verb *tɔhool* is more usually applied, however, to the blowing done curatively when bringing a spirit-guide's influence to bear on a person receiving treatment (figure 7.3a and 7.3b). In parts of Perak, the verb *coos* is sometimes used for this. If the aim is actually to hand on the spirit-guide's essence and instil it *into* some other person, then the blowing is part of an act known as *pərɛnlʉb* (verb: *pɛrlʉb*), a word which I can analyse no further, beyond noting that it looks like the causative form of a root **pɔlʉb* or **lʉb*, which I have not recorded in any other context.

---

12. [Added 2014] Linguistically, *tɔhool* (verbal noun: *tɛnhool*) is possibly a doublet of *tɛrhɔwal* 'to cause to come out', the verb employed to refer to the calling down of the spirit-guide. *Tɛnhool*, however, is not necessarily connected with spirit-mediumship. The rationale for the practice was explained to me by Penghulu Dalam as being to heat the body of the patient by breathing (*hum, hɔnum*—words clearly related to *hup*) hot air directly onto the affected part, which is thought to be suffering from cold (*dɔkad*)—a diagnosis that seemed to include malaise, sadness and depression. He later elaborated that sicknesses, regarded as spirits and addressed as *hãã ʔ* 'you' when under such treatment, like to be cold and flee from heat. Any adult of either sex may perform *tɛnhool*, regardless of the patient's age, sex or age, and they do so because they want to 'help', not because the patient requests it.

The music continues throughout the healing rituals, led either by the healing medium (who leaves off singing for the few moments when actually performing a blowing) or by one of the other men, whether in trance or not. The dancing also continues during the healing rituals, but soon afterwards the pace lessens and the dancers' trances get shallower. To the outside observer, they might appear to be tipsy rather than dissociated. Their behaviour often causes amusement to those watching, even though the proceedings as a whole are regarded as serious. The whole cycle does not normally take long. If the intention is to trance, the first half-hour is taken up by the preliminary singing and dancing. Most men will have attained their deepest trance after about three-quarters of an hour. The deepest stage lasts about ten minutes, and the following half-hour may be spent in the healing procedures and in coming out of trance. From that point on, the evening is treated as an ordinary song performance, continuing just as long as at least two or three people have the will to sing. By this time, many will be fast asleep in their rooms around the central dancing floor.

Such is the course of a typical simple séance, but variations and extra procedures are often added to this basic pattern. The period of trancing may be prolonged as an end in its own right. This is often the case in communities lying in the south of the Temiar territory: in most of the séances I witnessed in the Brok and Telom valleys, the trancing was much deeper than it was further north. After about half an hour, one or two men would enter so deeply into trance while dancing that they would collapse onto the floor. Still prostrate, they would continue the dancing movements for a while before eventually appearing to pass out and lie motionless for about 15 minutes. At this stage, the dancing of the others usually became so violent that several non-dancers had to retain sufficient control of their faculties to prevent those in deep trance from doing serious damage to themselves or to others.

However, when the séance was led by a powerful medium, possessing many spirit-guides and well proven as a healer, he would typically remain in a more shallow trance. This was the case even when it was he who had instilled the spirit-guide essence that led the others to trance so violently. He would usually do this by direct *parɛnlʉb* rather than by *cɛwnaaw* sprinkling, approaching one of the dancers from behind and performing *tɛnhool* blowings on the latter's head. Still from behind, he would then put his arm around the dancer's body so that both swayed together to the rhythm of the music, with the medium's hand pressed tightly to his partner's chest. As soon as the latter felt that the spirit-guide had passed into his own heart-soul, he would usually enter into sudden trance, bouncing off on his own like an animated marionette—an action known as *kɛnrook* (verb: *kərook*), 'shuddering, losing bodily control'.

When this happens, especially in the southern valleys, it is not unusual to see as many as 20 people bouncing up and down as the excitement (*haab*) reaches a feverish pitch. Houses sometimes collapse under the strain. At this stage, all semblance of a formal séance is lost and little remains of the bamboo-beater orchestra. The women would have joined in the dancing, one of them singing out a scrap of traditional lyric, which is tossed to and fro until another woman sings out a different phrase. This may go on for up to an hour, with slight abatements followed by waves of excitement. It is this apparent fusion of all the participants into one singly reacting whole that provides the communion-like spiritual refreshment that Temiars seek, even yearn for, in their séances.

There is nothing forbidding or 'sacred' about these occasions. Indeed, some of the older men complained to me that the younger people too often treated séances as a form of entertainment or as an excuse for engaging in sexual flirtation. They condemned such elaborate practices as placing live coals in one's mouth as playing to the incredulity of impressionable young women. Flirting does indeed take place during these night-time sessions, with the women often taking the lead. Techniques include looking towards the man with eyes made conspicuous by reflecting the fire's flames, or falling into his lap while ostensibly in an uncontrolled trance. If the occasion is not primarily religious, the songs might carry witty and allusive sexual repartee, providing an institutionalised opportunity for courting. It is not easy, therefore, to decide whether it is enthusiasm for trancing or a desire to flirt that leads Temiars to spend so many of their evenings singing. This was well described in a text I recorded from Wakil Ɂabaaɲ (figure 4.1) early in my fieldwork (Benjamin 1967c: 2–3, modified slightly):

If we're singing at night and there's a woman there we desire, we look hard at her and then she comes and sits close. While the singing is going on she rolls a cigarette and gives it to us in the dark so that the others can't see us flirting. As we take the cigarette from her she grasps our hand, pinches it with her nails and strokes the palm. Then we think, 'This girl really wants me!' She moves to our side and sits close. We rub noses, we hug, and in the dark we kiss. If they should stir up the fire, she moves some distance away so that the others don't notice anything and fail to realise that we've been flirting. But of course we have been flirting, feeling her breasts in the dark. The singing goes on until daybreak. Then we leave the house, while the woman remains behind. We spend the day out and deck our waists with flowers, returning home in the afternoon. When she sees us she thinks, 'He looks good: I'd like to marry [or: "sleep with"?][13] him and have him as my husband.'

---

13. [Added 2014] 'Marry' and 'sleep (with)' are both expressed in Temiar by the verb *salɔg*, which also means 'lie down'; it can accordingly be used both transitively and intransitively.

Eventually, the singing comes to a stop, sometimes quite abruptly, and everyone goes to sleep. If anyone has succeeded in calling down one or more spirit-guides during the singing, then the spirits' influence remains and people must continue to behave accordingly. As long as they remain undisturbed, the spirit-guides do not return immediately to their distant starting points. They stay for about five days as an invisible swarm over the roof of the house, in the leaf whisks and in the *tənamuu²* wreath. However, as discussed under the rubric of *joluŋ* (Chapter 5), there is a range of acts thought likely to scare the spirit-guides away.[14] Since the spirits represent the element of good, the Temiars feel that harm may come to the village if this is allowed to happen. Séancing brings the whole village under the beneficent influence of the combined effect of its members' individual spiritual revelations. The effort expended in coaxing the spirit-guides to attend must therefore not be wasted through carelessly committing *joluŋ*: not only would the medium suffer, but so also would the whole community.

Healing outside of séance

If a new séance is not held within a few days, the spirit-guides may eventually leave the village; but this does not leave the mediums powerless to heal. Portions of their spirit-guide(s) are believed to remain in the heart-soul of every medium so that he carries his mediumistic powers with him, albeit in an attenuated form. While the public calling-down of the spirit-guides in a séance is believed to be the most efficacious way of turning them to good use, Temiars with even a slight degree of 'adeptness' feel obliged, if asked, to offer their services to anyone in his own village who was ill. (But, as noted below, they may not always be in a position to fulfil the obligation.)

The technique employed on such occasions is the same as already described: to bring the spirit-guide's power to bear by performing a *tɛnhool* blowing on the patient's skin. With intense concentration, the healer presses his fist tightly to his own chest and with slight milking movements makes as if to express the essence of his spirit-guide from his heart-soul into his hand. He then performs the blowing as usual, directing his efforts mainly to the patient's head and chest. This is repeated several times a day, quite informally and without diverting the attention of others in the house, even though it is usually accompanied by rapidly mumbled incantations known as *jampii²* (Malay, *jampi-jampi* 'spells'). The ritual may be performed at the request of the patient or because the would-be healer feels moved to 'help' his fellow in this way. But if the healer is a well-respected medium, a greater degree of formality emerges. Treatment is then less casual, and the medium may impose a taboo (*tɛnlaa²*) on the patient so that the latter remains indoors

---

14. [Added 2014] As noted in Chapter 5, some components of what is described here as *joluŋ* are also covered by the categories *joruu²* and *rəwaay bərək*.

for a specified number of days, usually behind a suspended blanket. In such a case, the medium will feel considerable responsibility towards his patient, and will stay nearby until he feels that he can influence the course of the sickness no further.[15] One of my travelling companions from Humid village was scandalised to be asked to undertake a healing ceremony for a young child in a strange village where we were spending the night. Although his reputation had gone before, he was not prepared to undertake the responsibility when everyone knew that he had to be on his way the next day. No amount of persuasion from the distraught mother could make him change his mind, and the child died in the morning of severe diarrhoea without the benefit of a final attempt to cure him.[16]

Becoming a medium

Although it is not possible to become a medium without personally experiencing dream revelations of a spirit-guide, two courses may be followed by the medium-to-be. He may rely entirely on his own dream revelations, becoming a medium after singing openly for the first time the new song lyric taught to him by his spirit-guide.[17] Such a medium is known as a *halaaʔ riiʔ* 'self-adept'. But since mediumistic adeptness carries with it much responsibility—such as avoiding the misleading 'deception' of false dream characters and ensuring the full compliance of patients involved in a mediumistic cure—many prefer to keep to themselves the fact that they have had spirit-guide dreams. Such persons are known as *halaaʔ kɛmloop* 'concealed adepts'. Other people may suspect what has happened, but they will not push him into revealing himself.

Temiars take the medium's calling seriously. It is certainly not restricted, as in many other cultures, to persons who are in some way socially inadequate. Part of the reluctance to reveal oneself is for fear that practising public mediumship might lead the initially spontaneous dreamings to become so frequent and rich that the medium is swamped by more spirit-guides than he can cope with. His dreamings may begin to populate the world around him with spirits of all kinds. As we shall see, this is the process by which a 'great' medium comes into being. The essential spontaneity of dreaming poses this

---

15. [Added 2014] In 1968, Hitam Tamboh provided some further information. If the medium is obliged to leave, he may perform a blowing directly onto the patient, squeezing the *kahyɛk* of his spirit-guide from his chest (as in figure 7.3), followed immediately by a similar blowing—now referred to as *səʔuh*, as with anti-thunder blowings—on some tobacco or turmeric. The patient keeps this as a *taŋkal* 'amulet' while the medium is away. If the illness has not abated after the medium returns, then he will *səʔuh* another such amulet, which the patient will keep in his tobacco pouch. A great medium will go further and perform a *sɛnʔuh* on a *batuuʔ mamuug* 'tiger stone' or *təgas*, a bezoar stone found in the *ʔajɛɛl* and *manaar* canes, and then give or sell it for use as an amulet against such dangers as storms, tree-falls or elephants.

16. [Added 2014] It is very unusual for a Temiar to refuse a direct request, as it is thought likely to cause harm to the person who was refused, as outlined later (Chapter 8). In this instance, the refusal must be seen as a measure of the even greater seriousness that the medium ascribed to the dangers of walking out on a patient once the healing rituals had been started.

17. [Added 2014] Female mediums also exist, but I did not have the occasion to observe any of them in action during my initial fieldwork. (See also Roseman 1991: 72.) To avoid complicating the writing, I have therefore continued to employ 'he' alone in this section.

ever-present threat, and most people prefer to behave very modestly in relation to their one or two spirit-guides rather than risk entering a situation that might overwhelm them. Some men, however, far from remaining apprehensive of the spontaneity with which dream characters enter their lives, take positive measures to bring new spirit-guides into their lives by seeking instruction from an established medium. The importance of this instruction lies not so much in the details of ritual behaviour as in the fact that the medium deliberately works to instil his spirit-guides into his pupil through the process of *pərɛnlub*. The established medium carries out ritual blowings on his pupil's head and chest over a period of time, usually while in trance at séances. The pupil learns the distinctive melodies and lyrics of his teacher's songs, and eventually carries on with the latter's methods after his death. Consequently, much Temiar music and ritual practice is recognised as having precisely defined sources. It is nevertheless essential for the pupil himself to have been visited in his dreams by the spirit-guide that his teacher is passing on to him.

Although Temiars usually give encouragement to the budding medium, his rise in public authority, which is of the 'charismatic' kind (Weber 1958c: 245), is marked by an increase in his ritual activities. Stewart (1947: 170–193) proposed that the different kinds of dances performed at séances are directly related to the degree of mediumistic maturity attained by the leader of the séance. I have no direct evidence that this is so, nor do I have information that would throw doubt on his interpretation. A brief summary of his views may nevertheless help to clarify my own account.

Stewart on dancing and the grades of mediumship

Stewart says that a young man who has just dreamt a spirit-guide for the first time is urged to lead the village in a dance of the *gɛnsaak* pattern during the coming night. The exact steps and flourishes will have been taught to him by the spirit-guide. What qualifies it as a *gɛnsaak* dance is not the steps involved but the fact that it is danced as a 'chain pattern' (Stewart 1947: 170), in which the budding medium leads with his newly learnt steps. The readiness with which others follow him is the measure of the authority he has gained through his dreaming, especially as they might have had to obey certain restrictions before the dance on the orders of the young man's spirit-guide. Once accepted, a new dance may have further elements added to it as a result of dream revelations, and this too is a measure of the new medium's gain in prestige.

The next grade is reached when the medium has been inspired to lead the dancers in the *jiɲjaŋ*, the round dance already described as typical of the normal Temiar séance.[18] Stewart (1947: 181) claims that they dance in a circle only when the séance is to proceed to healing ceremonies. It is only during

---

18. [Added 2014] In 1968, Penghulu Hitam Tamboh told me that Jiɲjaŋ was originally a distinct mediumistic cult of which only the round (*ciŋwɛl*) dance now remains. His account of its history is presented in Appendix 2.1.

Figure 7.4 Women dancing in *cacii²* style at Penghulu Cawan's house, Pulat, Kelantan (1970)
The similarity of these arm movements to those shown in the nearby prehistoric Gua Chawas cave drawings (figure 13.4) is remarkable.

the round dance that the various ordeals that some mediums like to undergo are carried out. In both *gɛnsaak* and *jiɲjaŋ* the basic steps are the double hops of the men (and sometimes the women) known as *sənisɛ²* (verb: *sisɛ²*), and these, repeated furiously, are what normally leads to the trance state. There are other less energetic but more expressive dances. If the emphasis is on the movements of the arms and upper body the dance is known as *cənacii²* (verb: *cacii²*). Often this is performed as a developed art form by the older women (figure 7.4), but it is sometimes also danced by mature mediums to add dignity to their performances.[19]

The highest grade of mediumship is notable for dispensing with dance as an element in its performance. We shall see shortly that this serves to emphasise the 'ecstatic' character of ordinary mediumship. The trance behaviour of the 'great' medium is markedly 'ascetic' in character.

Spirit-guide species

So far, I have discussed only the spirit-guide relationship and the ways in which it is brought to bear on public concerns, but I have said little about

---

19. [Added 2014] In 1968, I collected descriptions of some nine named dance types, including some of those also described by Stewart. See Appendix 2.1 for the details.

the spirit-guides themselves. In filling this gap, I move from mediumship viewed from the 'inside' to a consideration of its place in the overall theological system.

Ordinary Temiar mediumship is concerned with the possession of spirit-guides of the off-the-ground (*baliik*) type. This means not only that the spirit-guides are called down in séance from above, as the ritual and ideology make clear, but also that the actual species represented tend to fall into a related pattern. The typical spirit-guides among the Temiars are various flowers, but animals and mountains are frequently found too. In the village of Humid, for example, where several men were mediums (if only in a small way) the spirit-guides were as follows:

Dalam	*Boot Taŋjok* (*Hibiscus sp.*)
Pampɔɔh[20]	*Galɛɛŋ*, the mountain Gunong Ayam
Salɛh	*Padii²*, the rice plant
Siluŋ	*Nɔɔr*, coconut; *Boot Tampɔ²*, a wild flower
Malam	(a new *halaa²*, spirit-guide as yet undeclared)
Payaaw	*Kəbɔk*, otter
Kubuu²	*Boŋaa² Pəət*, a cultivated flower

The pattern discernible in this rather heterogeneous list is best defined negatively: it does not contain any species (apart perhaps for the otter) that can be regarded as being of the ground, *tɛ²*. The fact that the clearly off-the-ground seasonal fruit trees are also not represented is a point I return to shortly. The species actually represented are 'neutral' enough for dream revelation to place them without undue strain into the off-the-ground category.

A point of interest, which cannot be developed here for lack of data, is that the various spirit-guides appear in dreams as distinctively male or female. Hibiscus as a spirit-guide, for example, always appears as a young woman, and the mountain Gunong Ayam as a young man.[21] However, other flowers appear as males and other mountains as females. No rule is discernible. In any case, I have no evidence that further ritual or ideological play is made with these sexual distinctions.

'Great' mediumship

The further significance of the choice of spirit-guide species will become clearer only after I have discussed the highest grade of mediumship among the Temiars and the status of Temiar mediumship in relation to that of the

---

20. [Added 2014] For later information on Pampɔɔh (figure 10.8), who died in 1977, see Chapter 10.
21. [Added 2014] For a later study of Gunong Ayam (Galɛɛŋ) as a spirit-guide source, see Chapter 14 below and also Roseman (2007).

neighbouring Orang Asli populations. I have noted already that the activities of the 'great' medium (*halaa? mənuu?*) are marked by asceticism, but this is just one of several polar contrasts between ordinary 'small' mediumship (*halaa? ?amɛs*) and the highest grades. The essential difference is that whereas 'small' mediums deal only with spirit-guides that are the upper-body souls of various natural species, the 'great' mediums' spirit-guides represent the *lower*-body souls—variously the *jərəək*, *kənoruk* or *sarak*—of the chosen species. These make their appearances not as watery *kahyɛk* from above but in the form of tigers (*mamuug*, *?ataɲ*) from below, and the pattern of a tiger séance is set accordingly. Even other *jərəək*-possessing animals, such as the pig, emerge at such séances as tigers. Unfortunately, I witnessed only one such séance, and then without realising what was happening. The following account is therefore based on the paradigms of expected behaviour given to me by informants.

A tiger séance usually takes place preliminary to an ordinary séance later the same night, but special preparations are made. Instead of suspending a *tənamuu?* wreath of flowers from the roof, bunches of flowers are laid out on a mat spread on the central floor in front of the medium. Very often, a special hut will be built inside the house for the medium to sit in while calling up his tiger spirit-guide. This 'temple', as Stewart (1947: 192) picturesquely but misleadingly calls it, is constructed of long *bayas* palm (*Oncosperma horrida*) fronds with their bases stuck into the floor in a circle and overlapping at the top. The resulting conical structure is similar to the hastily constructed rain shelter or hide that the Temiars make while out hunting. When used in mediumistic ritual the hut goes under various names, none of which tells us very much about its origins or functions.

Commonly, the hut is called *paley*, the Temiar name of a palm from which it is often made. Even more casually it is referred to as *bumbun*, the Malay term for a hunter's hide. Of more interest are two terms which the Temiars share with many other Aboriginal groups, not all of whom are known to them traditionally. Along with the Negrito groups, some Temiars call the hut by a word variously transcribed in the literature as *panọ'*, *panọ*, *panọh* (Schebesta 1957: 320), *panoh* (Evans 1937: 191), and *pano* (Holman 1962: 101). But I only heard this word once from the Temiars themselves,[22] as the groups I lived with preferred to use the widespread term *kəbut*. According to Schebesta (1957: 317), *kəbut* is found as far south as among the 'Jakud'n-Krau'

---

22. [Added 2014] I later found out that this word does occur in Temiar, as *panɔɔh* (not *panɔh*). According to some Temiars this refers to the space in the centre of the house employed for trance-dancing, *pɔɔh*, but others do indeed use *panɔɔh* (or perhaps *panɔh*) to refer to the great medium's trancing hut. Linguistically, however, I suspect that there may be some confusion here. *Panɔh*, with a short vowel—the form I initially recorded—is probably a borrowing from Jahai (which has no vowel-length contrast). It would therefore refer to the trancing-hut, as indeed it does among the Temiars of Perak living closer to the Jahais and Lanohs. But *panɔɔh*, with a long vowel, could well be a wholly Temiar form, a 'middle-voice' nominalised derivative (Benjamin 2011b: 23–25) of the verb *pɔɔh* 'to trance', with the meaning 'trancing place'.

(Aboriginal Malays) of Johor, and my own data show it as current among the Semais. At first sight it looks as if this is a Temiarised version of the Malay word *kebun*. Unfortunately, the only such word in Malay means 'plantation, garden'. A likelier derivation is to be found in the list of very similar words under D22a in Blagden's massive Aboriginal vocabulary (1906: ii, 572): it would then mean 'shade, darkness'—precisely one of the functions that the hut is intended to serve.

As the session commences, the fires are entirely extinguished and the medium enters his hut through a small gap at the bottom.[23] The singing begins, with the medium leading in the distinctive 'tiger song' style—short, low, 'minor-key' phrases answered immediately by the chorus of bamboo-beating women. The lyrics, in which the possessing tiger-spirit describes its roaming through the rank vegetation, are interspersed with stylised growls (*ʔaaw yaaw*, etc.) that serve musically as a sort of ritornello. There is no dancing, nor even any movement, by the others in the house. They must sit quite still, and no one may leave or enter until the lights go up about half an hour later. The medium, squatting in his hut, works himself into a calm trance with none of the violent movements employed by lesser mediums. The spirit-guide tiger, attracted by the flowers laid out for it and by the singing, arrives at the edge of the village but stays on the other side of the river or half way up a nearby slope. It would be extremely dangerous if a spirit-tiger were to enter the house like the lesser spirit-guides called down from above. The Temiars do not doubt that it would then act like any other tiger, and devour the people within. Instead, the tiger sends out cords, essentially like those of other kinds of spirit-guides, that reach out under the house and up through the floor into the medium's hut. In some unspecified way, the cords now enter the medium's body so that he undergoes a partial metamorphosis into a tiger. The accepted sign that this has happened is that he starts scratching violently and his knuckles begin to sprout tiger's claws. Many Temiars swore to me that they had seen this happen—or rather, that they had seen the last vestiges of the disappearing claws when the lights went up. A slightly different version states that the medium's hand fills with a small pool of water containing the tiger's claws. In either case, he is now powerful to heal or to pass on the spirit-guide. This last is only carried out when instilling the tiger spirit-guide into the 'great' medium's likely successor.

Carrying out a ritual blowing or spraying on those—the majority—whose 'adeptness' is insufficiently mature would put their lives in grave danger. So potent is the tiger-possessed medium that it is too dangerous for him to have direct contact even with the patient whose illness was the reason for the

---

23. [Added 2014] Stewart (1947: 194–217) devotes a whole chapter of his thesis to the position and activities of the great medium, which he refers to as 'temple shaman', after the somewhat grandiose term he applies to the palm-frond hut. Stewart also emphasises the seriousness and sense of danger that attach to the great medium's activities.

séance in the first place. It is enough for the sick person to be brought into contact with the outer part of the medium's hut for the spirit-guide's curative powers to be made available to him. Assisting the medium in this task is his practised assistant, *sɔlantɛɛs* (Schebesta's *serlantes*, 1957: 321), who, without himself touching the medium or his hut, brings the patient into the correct position for healing.[24] As far as I could ascertain, tiger séances with a *kɔbut* hut are held only when healing is the aim of the evening's ceremony. I have no reliable data as to what, in detail, constitutes the act of healing, but it is clear that the Temiars regard the healing powers of a tiger spirit-guide as far greater than those of other spirit-guides. Doubtless, the atmosphere of imminent danger that surrounds the tiger séance reinforces the impression of the spirit-guide's great power.

Meanwhile, the singing goes on unabated in the typically 'tiger' style, led perhaps by some other man for part of the time. In a short while, usually less than half an hour, the medium begins to come out of his trance, although (apart from a cessation of his clawing activities) this will not be very obvious to the observer. The trance ceases as the tiger spirit-guide makes its departure. In contrast to the less powerful off-the-ground spirit-guides, tiger spirit-guides do not remain behind in the house; the slightest glow of fire is enough to keep them away. The only trace of their having been present is that the flowers and the mat on which they lie will have been consumed by the sucking of the tiger's cords. With the greatest mediums, all traces will have disappeared. This process, *jɔrɛnbɔɔt* (verb: *jɛrbɔɔt*), is frequently alluded to in the lyrics of tiger songs. The greater the consumption and the more shrivelled the remains (*jɔrasag*), the more successful the séance is reckoned to have been.[25] I have no idea as to how the trick is really carried out—if indeed it ever proves necessary for the physical facts to accord entirely with the beliefs. When it is clear that the medium's trance is over or at least that his tiger spirit-guide has left, the fires are raised and the singing moves on to the normal light-hearted songs that are sung at ordinary, spirit-guide-from-above séances. The dancing now starts, several men work themselves into a trance, and the move from the ascetic phase into the ecstatic is complete. The great medium leaves his hut and may now himself trance as any other medium, calling down his lesser spirit-guides from above.

Such is the paradigm of 'great' or 'tiger' mediumship, but since great mediums are few in number there is considerable variation from this norm. Most great mediums do without the *kɔbut* except for very special séances. Others prefer to build it on the ground outside the house, in Jahai Negrito fashion. The tiger mediums specialise in harnessing as spirit-guides the

---

24. [Added 2014] In 1968, I was told that *sɔlantɛɛs* is the name of a flower used by tiger-mediums, but that in song-lyrics (*hɔnelad*) it is used as a metaphor for the medium himself.
25. [Added 2014] In 1968, I was told that *jɔrasag* is the name employed in song-lyrics for the *kɔbut*-hut itself.

various diseases and demons associated with the ground. These too appear in trance as tigers, even though in dreams they appear in their normal guise—ogre, dragon, etc. We have already met examples of this, with mediums who specialise in the disease demon Tanig. There are very many demons, diseases and other troubles of this kind. Collectively, these are known as mɛrgɔɔh, which is used colloquially as if it meant 'extreme nuisance', but since most of them come into recognition through being dreamed by a great medium, the local variations are too complex to list here. Their names frequently crop up in conversation, only to fade into vagueness as soon as an attempt is made to define more clearly what sort of creatures are in question.[26]

Becoming a 'great' medium

A 'great' medium becomes great precisely because he has dreamt these many creatures into existence. For example, while I was living in the village of Fort Brooke (Bɔɔk Bəlatəp), a large rock lying in the nearby river, which had previously been regarded as perfectly innocuous, was dreamt by the valley's leading medium as animated by a sarak tiger. An immediate explanation was thereupon provided for recent raids by a tiger on the people's livestock. From then on, the rock was regarded as dangerous by all the Temiars who came to know about it.

The greatest mediums appear to be bombarded continually by the influence of previously unrecognised spirit-agencies in the world around them, until eventually they end up with 100 or more spirit-guides, as compared to the two or three of the ordinary little medium.[27] Yet there must be some control over this, for it seems that there is never more than one fully matured great medium in each major valley at any one time. At least, the Temiars believe that this should be so, and as far as my records show, they are correct in their belief. The pedigree of the great medium of each valley is usually known in detail, both there and elsewhere. Throughout most of Temiar country in Kelantan, the would-be great mediums are still increasing their powers after the deaths of the previous incumbents, whose positions they are openly taking over.

Although some of the earlier great mediums appear to have been 'self-adepts', their present-day successors were all instilled by them through the process of pərɛnlʉb blowings.[28] In my own 'home' valley, the Perolak, the

---

26. The same is true of other elements in Senoi and Semang religion, as can be discovered by looking at the complexity of Evans's (1937: 138f) and Schebesta's (1957: 10f) attempts to make order out of the many deities talked about by their informants.

27. [Added 2014] In 1968, Wakil ʔabaaɲ (not himself an active medium) told me that a 'beginner' tiger-medium finds that tigers begin to appear (carɛɛʔ, carɔɔʔ) to him in dreams. Initially, he dreams minor tree-kənoruk spirits; then the sarak-spirits of hills and ridges begin to appear; finally the powerful spirits of rocky mountains visit him. There is an obvious gradation of power here, suggesting that the dreamer needs to establish a sufficient degree of bravery before agreeing to emerge finally as a 'great' medium.

28. [Added 2014] The present tense in this section refers, of course, to the mid-1960s. The current republication dates from two or more generations later—twice the period of time that had elapsed between Stewart's and my own doctoral fieldwork!

great medium used to be Taaʔ ʔamaaw (a name that seems onomatopoeically to recall the tiger's growling), who was renowned throughout several neighbouring valleys. In addition to passing on his spirit-guides and knowledge to the present great medium of the Ber valley to the south, Busuuh ʔegiʔ who lives at Serau (Səraaw), Taaʔ ʔamaaw passed on the great mediumship of the Perolak valley to his own son Rɛmʔum, who now lives several miles below his father's old village. Rɛmʔum is still increasing his powers (he is a young man), but it is already being said that his successor will be another man who has recently been dreaming Taaʔ ʔamaaw's own special spirit-guide, Datoʔ Lɛŋriʔ, the vast tiger spirit guarding the debouchment of the Nenggiri river. This other man was my own cook, Malam, whom I mentioned earlier as likely to become a great medium in due course. Originally, Taaʔ ʔamaaw received his mediumship from the previous great medium of the Perolak valley, Taaʔ Jaan, who, although he lived and died in the uppermost village of the valley, was a Jahai Negrito born in the Gentes (Ɖɛntɛɛs), a tributary of the Piah river in Perak. He used to trance Jahai-fashion in a hut on the ground outside the house, but his then pupil Taaʔ ʔamaaw persuaded him to move indoors for fear that his own spirit-guide would eat him up. It is by such processes that the different Aboriginal culture strains diffuse from group to group, to be absorbed or altered, as the case may be. While he was at the height of his powers, Taaʔ ʔamaaw served as the leading medium for both the Ber and Betis valleys as well as his own. In time, however, the other valleys came to have their own great mediums. At present [1965], the only fully established great medium in the southern part of Kelantan—the only area I know in detail—is Taaʔ Pəlodɛɛw who lives at Təluur in the highlands of the Betis valley. He is a Jahai Negrito who married and settled into another tribe and state. If he is still alive when I return, I hope to get rich information from him about Temiar mediumship.[29]

Since a medium's 'greatness' depends initially on other people's allegiance to his revelation, it is not surprising that the great mediums' clientèles extend over a wide area. 'Clientèle' is the appropriate term: any stranger who wishes to have a special healing ritual performed expects to have to pay. I have more than once heard Temiars worrying about collecting enough cash to afford the best possible professional treatment for a sick relative.

'Great' and 'little' mediumship compared

'Great' and 'little' mediumship differ, then, in several contrasting features. The many little mediums call down their few spirit-guides from above, while the very few great mediums call up their many spirit-guides from below. (However, as we have seen, great mediums also practise as little mediums.) The different ritual procedures lead to a polarisation between little mediumship as an ecstatic

---

29. [Added 2014] Unfortunately, this never happened.

activity and great mediumship as an ascetic one. The presence or absence of illumination and dancing, and the contrasts in musical and trance styles sharply define this opposition.[30] Earlier, I noted that in death as well as life there is a marked contrast between great and little mediums. Little mediums are buried in the earth as normal human beings, but great mediums may choose to be exposed (*kɛrwaak*) in their deserted houses. Their afterlives differ also. The little medium's heart-soul changes eventually into a small prowling tiger of the *kɔnoruk* type, which only a great medium is able to meet. The great medium's heart-soul finds its way eventually to join all the other great mediums' heart-souls in a place, Batuuʔ Baloʔ (possibly the one in figure 7.5), from which it may emerge in a form visible and dangerous to *any*body, whether in trance or not.[31] Indeed this lycanthropic ability of the great medium, both during and after his life, is a feature made much of by many Temiars. Others are more sceptical. What holds constant is the belief that there *are* people, not necessarily Temiars, able to become tigers at will and sometimes spontaneously. I examine the importance of such beliefs in more detail below.

We may justifiably claim that the different types of mediumship serve as tropes of the larger category oppositions that I have discussed earlier: mediums are 'totems', whatever else they may also be. The opposition between the great and the little medium is equivalent to the opposition between the ground and off-the-ground in the first place, and consequently to that between evil and good—a matter I develop later. If we wished to take the analysis further we could say that the great medium—half man, half animal—represents the 'natural' pole of an overall nature/culture opposition. But that is a consideration not immediately relevant to the present argument.

Areal aspects of mediumship

The 'totemic' aspects of Temiar mediumship go deeper. As pointed out elsewhere (Benjamin 1966: 12), our understanding will be weakened by considering the Temiars in isolation from the neighbouring Orang Asli populations. It is now time to explain what I then left unclarified:

> the ritual activity of any one tribe attains its full meaning (for both participant and observer) only in relation to the rather different ritual

---

30. [Added 2014] In later research, Roseman (1984, 1991, 1995) has greatly expanded on the relation between musical genre and ritual style.

31. [Added 2014] On several later occasions I found that some Temiars, Menriqs and Bateks held that Batuuʔ Baloʔ is the limestone outcrop or tor known to Malays as Gua Janggut (figure 7.5), south of the present-day Menriq settlement at Kuala Lah (Bɔɔk Leew), commented on elsewhere in this volume as a ritually important locale. I visited it in 2008. This is not the same as the impressive Bukit Baloh outcrops nearby, on the south bank of the Nenggiri river, right next to the Temiar settlement of Pulat, where I visited Penghulu Cawan in 1970. Although Penghulu Cawan said that he sometimes held trance sessions in the caves of that Bukit Baloh, he also said that the 'real' Batuuʔ Baloʔ of Temiar mythology was situated in the Kemaman or Dungun districts of Terengganu, well outside Temiar territory.

Figure 7.5 Batu Janggut, Kelantan (2008)
This limestone tor, situated at the side of the road (D29) that now runs from Gua Musang to Dabong, is regarded by Menriqs and some Temiars as the Batuuʔ Baloʔ. Menriq mediums perform twice-yearly ceremonies inside a cave within this tor. (See the entry on Mojiiʔ in Appendix 2.2.)

activity of the other tribes. The structural interrelationships along an east–west axis (more strictly, the axis formed by the daily path of the sun) of the ritual categories implied by the ideal type of shamanism [mediumship] associated with each tribe constitute an expression in supra-tribal terms of those structural relationships conceptualised along a vertical (heaven-and-earth) axis that are implicit in the ritual activity within each tribe separately. In other words, for any one tribe the other tribes become in some contexts totemic categories (Lévi-Strauss 1963) expressing what in other contexts is expressed by the more conventional totemic species involved in the ritual activity of that tribe alone.

The polar opposites among the more conventional totemic species are, at the natural end, the tiger, and at the cultural end, the seasonal fruits. The latter are closely associated with the notion of off-the-ground and the former with the ground. If, as I have claimed, this vertical axis is rotated to the horizontal plane in the context of intertribal relations, we should expect the populations to the west to specialise in seasonal-fruit mediumship and those to the east in tiger mediumship—and indeed this is precisely what the Temiars claim to be the case. They take as their key types the Menriqs in the east and the Jahais and Lanohs to the west. These groups are conventionally classified as Negritos, but to the Temiars they are essentially 'hill people' (sɛnʔɔɔy sərɔk) like themselves who happen to speak different languages and observe slightly different customs. Where they abut on each other, as for example in the lower Nenggiri river of Kelantan or the upper Perak river of Perak, there is a considerable amount of symbiosis. Individuals are often unsure whether they 'belong' to one 'tribe' or the other. (For a similar case, see Benjamin (1966: 10) on Temiar–Semai relations.) Especially noticeable are the variations in mediumistic practices among the Temiars according to how close they live to the peripheral Negrito groups. These practices constitute the 'totemic' categories I am trying to isolate.

Some versions of the original creation myth tell of the Creator (Tohaat) ordering ʔaluj to teach each of the various human groups their respective type of mediumship. In the story, this comes between the allotting of each ethnic group to its rightful place on the ground and their subsequent instruction in the dietary observances. In Humid, the myth-tellers inserted into the story some extra material that was plainly not a crystallised text, but a piece of traditional knowledge served up as if it were time-honoured myth. This was obvious from the seminar-like circumstances in which the myth was recounted. Since traditional knowledge is more relevant to the present discussion than any formulaic text would be, the version I recorded is a useful guide to Temiar attitudes towards the mediumship of other Orang Asli populations.

The myth teaches that the various types of mediumship are distributed as in table 7.1. From this, several important interrelated points emerge. The populations fall into three groups, each with a distinct class of typical spirit-guides. The westerly Negritos (Group 1) are primarily concerned with the seasonal-fruit mediumship, and those to the east (Group 3) with tiger-mediumship. The Temiars express this more meaningfully by saying that mediums among the people living towards the sunset concern themselves with *baraŋ baliik*, 'off-the-ground things', and those living towards the sunrise with *baraŋ ʔɛn-tɛʔ*, 'things in the ground'. (I have several times remarked on the connection between seasonal fruits and off-the-ground, and between tigers and the ground.) In accord with this schema, the Temiars acknowledge themselves and the similarly placed Semais as possessing a

Table 7.1 Mediumship types

	Population	Medium's song genre	Typical spirit-guide
Group 1	Jahai	Bɛrwɛɛs (wild manggosteen?)	*Pənaaʔ* (annual fruit cycle)
	Lanoh	Pɛnhəəy (*perah* nut?)	*Podɛɛw* (*perah* nut)
Group 2	Temiar (Perak and Kelantan Rivers)	Kahyɛk (see Chapter 6)	*Boot* (flowers)
	Temiar (Kinta River)	Kahyɛk	*Jɛlmɔl* (mountains)
	Semai	Kədəŋ (?)	*Bədɔk* (a flower)
Group 3	Menriq, Batek	Mojiiʔ (?)	*Mamuug* (tiger)

mediumship concerned with *baraŋ ʔɛn-gagid*, 'intermediate things', typically the flowers and mountains that effect a sort of mediation between the ground and off-the-ground.

Fortunately, the question does not remain one of myth alone. I was told several times about the mediumistic practices undertaken among neighbouring groups. These were described in such a manner that it should prove possible to check objectively whether they really occur. Two particular claims are especially instructive. The Jahais and Lanohs in the west not only have seasonal fruit species as their typical spirit-guides but are also reputedly skilled in curing the sicknesses of such trees by mediumship. If a valuable tree (such as a durian or rambutan) fails to give fruit, one of their mediums may be called in to perform a ritual *tɛnhool* blowing upon it, often climbing up into the branches in the process. Through instilling the medium's own *pɔnaaʔ*-type (annual-cycle) spirit-guide into the tree it is hoped that its proper periodicity will be resumed. Apparently, the Jahai mediums are famed among the neighbouring country Malays as healers of ailing trees. At the other end of the scale, my informants claimed that the Menriqs (and the mixed Temiar–Menriqs) living to the east on the lower Nenggiri sometimes carry out mediumistic rituals actually under the ground, in the caves and potholes that are said to exist on the lower slopes of Gunong Berangkat. Taking bamboo torches with them, they then hold a tiger séance of great power.[32]

The scepticism of Penghulu Dalam, the headman of Humid village, provides a further interesting sidelight. For months, he had tried to persuade me that any claims that Temiar mediums could turn into tigers were quite unfounded, despite what was said by everyone else. But once, when discussing his visits to town, he described to my surprise how he had seen a Batek headman become tiger-like in his sleep, growling and clawing—*na-lãã̃s* 'he had metamorphosed'. This took place in the hotel room they were sharing in Kuala Kerai. When I challenged him about his earlier apparent disbelief in spiritual matters, which had expressed itself in other respects also, he replied that it was the Temiars he had doubts about. The people who lived *kɛɛd ʔis* 'at the base of the sun [i.e., the east]' most certainly could change into tigers, and frequently did. Furthermore, he was now afraid to have too much contact with the Menriqs and Bateks.

---

32. [Added 2014] I was later able to substantiate this information. In 1968, Wakil ʔabaaɲ gave me his Temiar view of this practice as followed by the Menriqs living to the east of the Temiars. The mediums enter the *gua* cave (figure 7.5), holding resin torches and singing songs in the Mojiiʔ genre (Appendix 2.2). The *gunig* spirit, said to be female, is *mamuug mɛŋkah* 'tiger of the debouchment downstream'. In 2008, I visited the mouth of the cave in question with Ading Kerah, discussing it immediately afterwards with the Menriqs living at Lah, their nearby resettlement village. They told me that their mediums enter the *gua* twice a year, climb up a series of named steps, and then descend on a rope into the cave, where they perform their all-night ceremony on its the sandy floor. (I was honoured with an invitation to attend one of these ceremonies, but the opportunity has yet to arise.) Ading insisted that this particular *gua* is the true *tiang dunia*, the 'earth column' that holds heaven and earth apart. He added that the other *gua*s in northern Malaysia that have also been declared to be the Batuuʔ Gɔrɛm world column are 'fake' (*gɛwgɔw*), including the impressive Gunung Reng at Batu Melintang in Jeli district near the Thai border that I had previously assumed was the prototype example—as also did Schebesta (1927: 163–164, and the plate opposite p. 137).

I have little information about the séance behaviour of non-Temiar Aboriginal groups, but some points of interest were told to me. The Temiars have both ecstatic and ascetic séances, depending on whether they are calling spirit-guides down from off-the-ground or up from the ground. In both cases, the performances are choral. This is in contrast to the séances of the easterly Negritos in which the leading medium sings alone, without even a beaten bamboo accompaniment.[33] From the Temiar point of view this is ascetic behaviour indeed, and among them this style of singing (*pɛŋjəwɔk*) is used only by the sad and lonely to console themselves or when singing in one's sleep the song just taught by one's spirit-guide. At the western end, among the Jahais of the upper reaches of the Perak river, the called-down spirit-guide is said to materialise in the medium's hand as a minute lump of cold resin (*talɛɛw*) which nevertheless makes his hand hot: this is supposed to be visible to anyone who cares to look. When the medium comes to perform a ritual blowing, the resin melts and changes into a fistful of hot water. The openness and the heat suggest that here we have séance behaviour more ecstatic than that of those Temiars (the majority) who do not follow Jahai practice.

This overall patterning, integrating the practices of people living up to 120 miles apart, should not surprise us. That the west is the domain of the seasonal fruits is clear to all Temiars. It is restated in many of their myths and forms an essential part of their afterlife beliefs. Furthermore, the west is the home of the creator forces. There live the deities Tohaat (God), Yaa' Cɛŋkey (Granny Chingkai, the mountain–Creator), ʔaluj (the first man and the teacher of culture), and Yaa' Podɛɛw (Granny Perah-fruit, the chief of the supernaturals in control of the annual cycle). In contrast to the positively life-producing character of the west, the east (sunrise) hides many of the most malign influences in the Temiar spirit world. Were-tigers of all sorts issue at night from there, among them the arch were-tiger Dato' Lɛŋriʔ.[34] The collectivity of deceased great mediums' heart-soul were-tigers live in the Batuu' Balo', which is to be found in the direction of the sunrise.[35]

'Malay-style' mediumship

The further east one travels, the more noticeable is the influence of Malay folk religion. Some Temiars on the main Nenggiri river live on sites once occupied by Malay peasants: it seems that the traditional chronological

---

33. [Added 2014] From later field trips among the Bateks and Menriqs, I discovered that this was not always so. They do frequently employ choral responses, but in a highly heterophonic and non-unified manner, contrasting sharply with the unison manner followed by the Temiars. For a brief discussion of the significance of this distinction, see Benjamin (2004).

34. Dato' Lɛŋriʔ may well be the heart-soul of the Mikong—the traditional Temiar–Malay go-between who held office at Kuala Betis, Kelantan. The last-but-one Mikong bore the title Dato' Lɛŋriʔ and lived probably around the year 1900. [Added 2014] See Noone (1936: 47–48) and Benjamin (1968b: 9–13, 1987: 142–143) for information on the Mikongs.

35. [Added 2014] It is unclear whether my informants regarded this Batuu' Balo' as purely mythological or as the one that I eventually visited, as Gua Janggut (figure 7.5), in 2008.

order of settlement in the lowland area (around Bertam) was first Negritos (Menriq), then upland Malays, and only finally Temiars.[36] In accordance with the Aboriginal stress on locality as the determinant of ritual forms, much of the content of Temiar mediumship on the lower river derives from the spirit-beliefs current among the Malays of that area. But those forms have been invested with a new meaning by assimilation to the traditional Temiar view of Negrito mediumship. The many demons in the Malay system are assimilated to the Temiar notions of ground-dwelling evil spirits, usually identified with the Daŋgaaʔ (the widespread *naga*, the dragon of Southeast Asia) and the Bahyaaʔ (or Boyaaʔ; the crocodile, *buaya* in Malay). I have little information, though, on the extent to which these beings enter into the Temiar mediumistic system as spirit-guides. More detailed studies in the lower Nenggiri may prove fruitful.

As far as I can trace, the chief earth demon, Səlumbaŋ,[37] of the eastern Temiars does not belong to any native Malay inventory of evil spirits. It is, rather, a sort of spirit of Malayness. The great flood of 1926 (Winstedt 1927: 306) led to many deaths in the lower reaches of the big rivers, and even for those Temiars who lived above the area of danger the flood is remembered with awe to this day. Soon after the flood, the mediumistic cult of Səlumbaŋ moved upstream from around Kuala Wias (Wiyas) (the present boundary between Temiars and Malays) and into the Yai (Yaay) valley. My informants, who sing Səlumbaŋ songs only at second-hand, described Səlumbaŋ variously as a huge snake-like dragon and as a dead Malay buried under water. This suggests that in their séances, Səlumbaŋ mediums (who still are active primarily on the main river and in the Yai valley) call up as their spirit-guides the collectivity of Malays who died in the 1926 flood. The Səlumbaŋ séance does not fit into the traditional categories of Temiar séances: it is a *pɛhnɔɔh gɔb*, 'Malay-style trancing', in which the ritual largely follows Malay models and the songs are in the Malay language.[38] Temiars elsewhere merely sing these now widely

---

36. [Added 2014] Since the 1980s, Malays have again moved into that area. Kuala Betis is now a substantial village on a paved road, with a complex of modern buildings housing the offices and staff housing of the JAKOA as well as a primary school attended mostly by Temiar children.

37. [Added 2014] The word *selumbang* is not found in modern Malay, but it is possibly related to *umbang* 'to voyage, float'; both *sə* and *l* are known formatives in Malay. An alternative or parallel etymology would relate it to the Hakka-Chinese phrase *ˌɛɛi ˍluŋ ˍvɔŋ* 'water dragon king' (Huang Phay Ching, personal communication), modified to sound appropriately Malay—a suggestion that was already reported in an alternative spelling by Roseman (1991: 103). This is not as far-fetched as it might seem: some Temiars formerly had close relations, including marriage, with the Hakka-speaking Chinese settlement of Pulai just outside the boundary of Temiar country (Middlebrook 1933; Carstens 1980), and I have known Temiars who could speak Hakka.

38. [Added 2014] In 1970, I was able to witness a distinctively Səlumbaŋ-style performance in the house of Penghulu Cawan at Pulat, far downstream on the main Nenggiri river. (The photograph of *cənaciiʔ* dancing in figure 7.4 was taken at this performance.) The session took place without a *tənamuuʔ* wreath; instead, the whole house was decked with flowers and leaves. The singing involved (as usual) a canonic women's chorus, here beating out a slightly unusual variant (known as *sənimbɔɔl*) of the 4/4 rhythm with their bamboo tubes, identical to the 'Rhythm II' notated by Roseman (1991: 102). They also used a *bəranɔʔ* drum of the type shown on Plate 10 of Roseman (1991). However, I was told that this was not the original form of Səlumbaŋ performance, which would have employed an open-weave medium's hut, known as a *cɛnlaay*, made of just four fronds of the *ləgook* palm. This was

known songs for pleasure. In other areas, such as at Lambok and Kuala Betis in Kelantan, the séances of some mediums follow the patterns taught to them by the Malay mediums who formerly lived there. Throughout the Betis and Perolak valleys, they still talk of the greatness of a Malay medium named Raning who lived at Kuala Betis until the Japanese war.[39]

Sorcery

Powerful mediums, in touch with the spirits of evil as well as of good, are ambivalent characters, sharing many of the features that in other societies would lead people to treat them as witches or sorcerers. But the Temiars seem to dissipate their social tensions by internalising them in dreams rather than by projecting them onto others in the classical witchcraft manner.[40] Nevertheless, they do hold a range of ideas as to how witches and sorcerers might set about their tasks, and they sometimes fear that certain mediums known to them but living elsewhere might try to do them harm. The belief that sorcery awaits those unwarily travelling through a strange area is often just an expression of the inter-valley suspicion that I have already commented upon (Benjamin 1966: 14), but it may sometimes be real enough to be focused on a particular medium. My travelling companions from Kelantan were certainly frightened on this account when we passed over the watershed into Perak, intending to pass down the Plus valley. They had heard that at one of the uppermost villages, Kuala Mu (Bɔɔk Muuk), there lived a woman medium by the name of ʔalɔb who, in addition to being a powerful *halaaʔ* of the Ciɲcɛm type (Chapter 6), was thought likely to bewitch fat children, handsome young men and other mediums. In her jealousy, she would rather have them die. Apparently, she harmed strangers only, and since my companions were unknown to her, they were especially afraid. Another informant who was brought up in ʔalɔb's valley maintained, on the contrary, that she was quite harmless, but this had not prevented Temiars in other valleys from fearing her. (I met her briefly myself: there seemed little about her to justify her sinister reputation.)

More detailed accusations are laid against the mediums of other Orang Asli populations, and sometimes against Malays. The supposed procedures are very similar to those reported from elsewhere, and this may explain why the

---

sometimes set up inside the house and sometimes on the ground. The Pulat Temiars were in contact with the nearby Menriq people, whose spirit-performances are regularly held on the ground, on a board of bark—a practice I witnessed among the Bateks on the Aring river in 1970. The lights were left on, so these were not *kɔbut* 'darkness' sessions. The chorus of women would sit in a circle around the *cɛnlaay* hut. The medium would then get up and dance the *siseʔ* within the circle, with the other men following him. Women would dance only if they felt particularly keen to do so.

39. [Added 2014] Roseman (1991: 99–104) later supplied further details on these Malay-style practices. For my own further information on the presumed sources of the Sɔlumbaŋ genre, see Appendix 2.2.

40. [Added 2014] Stewart (1947: 32) briefly mentions such a possibility, but does not provide any specific data. I would now say that if there is any truth in this claim—and I have no evidence that there is—it would result from *talking* about such dreams to fellow villagers rather than the dreaming itself.

Temiars place no great stress on malevolent mediumship: evil-doing is usually to be found 'elsewhere' or 'in earlier times'. The Semais and the Negritos are believed to specialise in three types of malevolent mediumship or sorcery: *pensuʔ*, *penlaaw* and *seŋnʉg*. *Pensuʔ* is the Malayan version of 'sending' (verb: *pəsuʔ*): the medium performs a ritual blowing on a sharp object (usually a sliver of bamboo), whereupon it turns to water, flies to the victim's throat and pierces his windpipe. This is carried out on receipt of a fee from a client who wishes to exact revenge for theft or adultery. *Penlaaw* is not, strictly speaking, sorcery; it is the ability to suddenly lose bodily form and fly away (*pəlaaw*) invisibly from whatever threatens. When combined with powers of sorcery, *penlaaw* is much feared. *Seŋnʉg* is the power of causing the victim's head-soul to leave (*səŋʉg*) his body so that the sorcerer–medium's spirit-guide (a flower) may squeeze it so hard that the victim dies. Some Semai mediums are said to carry out a form of sorcery known as *pacɔɔw* (possibly related to the Malay *pachau*, 'talisman to scare people away'). Pieces of the victim's left-over food or cigarette-ends are pounded with soil in the bottom of a bamboo and then stuffed with four sticks. The victims' *hup* (heart & liver, seat of the feelings) becomes like the wood, their bodies stiffen, and they die. The bamboo may then be lodged in the river as a talisman. *Pacɔɔw* is carried out for payment or for the medium's own fell purposes; there are two recognised grades of severity. Poisoning and blowpiping are said to be used by both mediums and ordinary members of other Orang Asli populations, but these are not regarded as specifically mediumistic activities, however wicked the medium.

Mediumship and culture change

I cannot leave this discussion of mediumship without noting that it serves as perhaps the greatest dynamic element in Temiar culture. Mediumship is the filter through which most new concepts enter the system, and in some cases it has led to considerable changes. It may yet happen that increased contact with the outside world will lead to an enhancing of the medium's role in digesting newer concepts so that Temiar culture may encompass them even more easily. Noone (1955: 4) suggested as much when he describes songs that 'tell the Temiar that the wind in the bamboos is the force that moves airplanes they see flying in the sky' or that the spirit of the Chinese *jelutung* tappers' outboard motor gives the medium a new dance and song.[41] Their acceptance of modern medicine has on the whole been complete, with the lead set by mediums who acknowledge its efficacy alongside their own methods. This has succeeded so well that the Aborigines Department hospital at Ulu Gombak near Kuala Lumpur has on its establishment Ngah Sidek (Ŋah Sideʔ), a well-known

41. Noone—assuming that the translations were by him—was actually wrong in stating in his acompanying notes that these were the meanings of the song-lyrics, but he clearly obtained views of this kind from the people he lived with and whose songs he helped record.

Temiar great medium from southern Perak, whose activities are found to be very reassuring to the patients under treatment in such strange surroundings. His photograph appears in Holman (1958: 46).

Mediums have authority: their position is based on public acceptance of the revelations they receive. Whatever a great medium claims to be the case is generally accepted as such. Knowledge of the spirits that inhabit the rocks, trees, animals and mountains in the environs is usually the direct result of the dreamings of a trusted medium. This obviously involves cultural change. Respected mediums introduce not only additional observances but also changes in traditional behaviour. For example, the names of the plants and animals important to the Temiars are very mixed, the confusion largely resulting from the localised changes in nomenclature following a mediumistic revelation. In the Brok valley, I once observed people carefully eating the flesh of a *genhaaʔ* animal that I could not identify. Because of the rule against uttering an animal's the name while eating its flesh, I was obliged to wait until the next day to ask them what it was. They told me that it was now known by the name *kɛɲwɛɲ*, after a respected medium had dreamt that its earlier name must be tabooed. Since the earlier name was the one I must have been using in the Perolak valley I still have no idea what species was intended by the name *kɛɲwɛɲ*. Within the Perolak valley, the names of blowpipe poisons show much variation. When I asked the headman of the valley's most upstream village for the name of his most frequently used poison, he replied that the now deceased great medium Taaʔ ʔamaaw had dreamt that its real name was not to be uttered, or tigers would devour the one who transgressed the rule. Instead, the poison was now known simply as *lɛɲriʔ* (Nenggiri), the name of the valley where it is found. Fortunately, he did manage to inform me of the name by which it was known in my own village further downstream. If animal and plant names can show such great local variation (see also Harrison et al. (1955) and Dentan (1967)) as a result of mediumistic revelations, then we may assume that the variation found in the larger features of Temiar culture—mythology, dietary observances, 'totemic' taboos, even sexual behaviour and kinship rules—also has a similar source.[42]

Occasionally, a religious movement will sweep over a large area as a result of one powerful medium's dreamings. The Səlumbaŋ cult discussed earlier is just such an example, but I was never near enough to its source to find out much in detail about its origins. More is known about the genesis of the Ciɲcɛm cult in Perak in the 1930s, as Noone and Stewart were on the scene at the time to observe it.[43] The details of Ciɲcɛm (which the authors spell Chinchem: Stewart 1947: 218f; Noone 1955: 4) do not concern us here. But we should

---

42. [Added 2014] Diffloth (1980) has pointed out that taboos of this kind are responsible both for the frequent polysemy of Aslian languages and for the subfamily's rather rapid rate of change.
43. [Added 2014] See Appendix 1.3 for a contemporary account of Noone's ideas, which I was not aware of when writing the thesis.

note that the cult, with its concern for the afterworld and its distinctive song and dance-forms, is still very much alive among the Temiars of the Korbu, Kinta, Plus, Ber and Brok valleys, and is occasionally performed elsewhere. Over 30 years, the dreaming of one man, Datok Bintang (Dato⁷ Bintaŋ), has thereby become an integral part of Temiar culture. To what extent religious movements of this kind will effect any deep change in the structure of Temiar society it is as yet hard to say. At both societal and cultural levels, the Temiar way of life is remarkably open-ended, and there seems to be little restriction in the sort of elements that Temiar mediumship can grasp hold of and make into integral components of the whole culture.[44] Mediumship itself seems likely to withstand greatly changed social circumstances simply because it is so deeply rooted in the intensely personal dream life of each individual Temiar.[45]

---

44. [Added 2014] Marina Roseman's continuing studies (1994, 2000, 2002, 2007, 2012a, 2012b) over the years have concentrated on this particular topic, and shown that mediumship is still a major means of managing cultural change among the Temiars.
45. [Added 2014] Chapter 14 tells the story of a much more recent endogenous cult, ?aluj Salamad, effectively a new religion still extant at the time of writing—although, strictly speaking, it employs only the *forms* of mediumship, not its content.

Temiar Religion (1967)— Theology

As demonstrated in the preceding chapters, the Temiars' ritual acts and attendant beliefs display a striking degree of integration. I now turn to the overall meaning of Temiar religion and the ways in which it relates to everyday life. A concern for overall meaning requires a shift from the minutiae of ethnography to what is more usually treated as theology. In this chapter I shall therefore attempt a statement of Temiar 'theology' and show how it generates a morality of direct relevance to the Temiars' everyday life, the organisation of which has been described elsewhere (Benjamin, 1966, 1967c, 1968a).

As it stands, we have just the bare bones of an ideational calculus: the calculus remains 'uninterpreted', making it necessary to search for those components of Temiar culture that inject values into the bare system to make it meaningful. First, however, we must look again at the information presented in the preceding chapters and extract the underlying calculus from it in such a way that its thorough-going consistency becomes clear.[1]

The three levels of ideology

In anthropological terms, most Temiar ritual activities display an implied basic opposition between nature and culture. To talk of nature and culture in this manner is, of course, to employ a sort of shorthand, referring to certain recent refinements of the Rousseau-an tradition.[2] The Temiars are more concrete: although their culture does indeed present them with conceptual tools for abstract thought, the major part of their categorisations are tied firmly into the activities of everyday life. Yet this is not a simple matter. The Temiar conceptual system holds together at three distinct levels, corresponding reasonably closely to the chapter divisions of the present study. First, I

---

1. [Added 2014] As indicated in Chapter 2, I no longer regard 'thorough-going consistency'—with its associated talk of 'calculus', and implication of 'system' and 'structure'—as the appropriate way of analysing this kind of material.
2. [Added 2014] The 'Rousseau-an' allusion was to the works of Claude Lévi-Strauss, which were just becoming known to British anthropologists as I was writing the thesis. I had gained an early introduction to his ideas by reading *Le Totémisme Aujourd'hui* (1962a) and *La Pensée Sauvage* (1962b) before they were translated into English, and before I went to Malaysia. Lévi-Strauss himself made an explicit linkage to Rousseau in the same year (1962c).

discussed the *cosmic* level of ideas, explicitly in Chapter 4 on cosmology and implicitly in Chapter 7 on mediumship. In dealing with species-directed behaviour (Chapter 5), the discussion related to the *mundane* level of ideas. Then, in Chapter 6, I showed how the complex of ideas and behaviours surrounding soul beliefs represents a reduction of the conceptual system to the *personal* level. Mediumship (Chapter 7) was given extended treatment primarily because it makes clear the underlying unity of the three levels of ideology. What starts as personal revelation is made public in communal séances, which in turn lead to an awareness of larger ideas extending far beyond the village order.

The cosmic level

The cosmic level of ideas is lent regularity by recognition of an underpinning celestial axis stretching from sunrise to sunset. The original spying-out of the land by the *beraay* bird, the magpie robin (Chapter 4), was first to the east then to the west. This pattern is repeated in other contexts. The Creator's home lies at the sunset, whither the head-souls of deceased humans repair to enjoy an untroubled existence. This is directly reflected in the care taken to orientate the body correctly at burial (Chapter 6). In contrast, the east is the source of many of the death-dealing agencies in the Temiar spirit-world (Chapter 7), including the malevolent influences that appear in tiger guise. The patterning of mediumship types in relation to locality also draws a clear distinction between east and west. An explicit association is set up between the west and seasonal fruit trees, and between the east and tigers. Since the same totemic identifications are also entrenched in the mythology, one of the prime elements in the calculus is the identity:

$$
\begin{array}{ccc}
\text{West} & : & \text{East} \\
\text{Seasonal fruits} & : & \text{Tigers}
\end{array}
$$

The mundane level

The opposition between seasonal fruits and tigers appears again at the mundane level of ideas, but less explicitly. They are polar opposites: the seasonal fruits are the archetypal example of natural species closely allied to human society, and tigers are those furthest removed from humankind. Seasonal fruits form an essential element in the maintenance of Temiar social organisation (Benjamin 1966: 18), and their ownability is exceptional among forest plants. The great care with which they must be treated shows that for the Temiars they have the character of plant 'pets'. Tigers, on the other hand, are greatly feared, in both their real and their symbolic forms. All the dangers of the forest are usually subsumed under the rubric of 'tiger'. As spirit-guides, the various malevolent powers make their appearances as tigers. The thought of eating or taming a tiger fills Temiars with revulsion.

More basic than the opposition between seasonal fruits and tigers is the opposition that underlies it on the mundane level of ideas, namely the opposition between the village and the forest. I discussed Temiar attitudes towards this distinction in some detail in Chapter 4, but a few points are worth recalling here. A key distinction is that the forest is overgrown with vegetation while the village is situated in a clearing. This suggests a further opposition, between the essential unownability of things in the forest against the ownability of things in the village. The clue is that, although seasonal fruit trees are potentially ownable, they become so in practice only after the jungle growth has been cleared from around them; they may not be claimed while the ground is overgrown. Ownability is also at issue in many of the complicated procedures involved in the correct treatment of meat. The *genhaaʔ* practices (Chapter 5) are concerned with the integrity of the village as a discrete category. The essential character of the typical *genhaaʔ* animal is that it is an unownable (untameable) part of nature when alive but an ownable part of culture when dead and properly brought into the domain of the village. As discussed in Chapter 5, other practices also mark a sharp ritual distinction between forest and village. The disease *pocuk* makes such an implication, as also does the opposition between the diseases *sabat* and *genhaaʔ*. We may now draw up a further identity as an element in the calculus:

> Seasonal fruits : Tigers
> Village : Forest
> Ownable : Unownable

However, these are subsidiary and rather abstract categories. In everyday life, the ritual practices operate in terms of a more important category opposition, and one that I have noted more frequently than any other in the present study: ground/off-the-ground. Let me first recall how deeply this distinction is embedded in the categories I have just been discussing. Seasonal fruits are ownable only for as long as they remain on the tree; anyone may pick them off the ground. The tiger is the ground-dwelling animal *par excellence* (although the Temiars are aware of its tree-climbing habits). The various kinds of were-tiger are believed to live below the ground. Huts built in the forest are normally on the ground, whereas permanent village houses are always raised off the ground on pillars. The complicated ritual requirements involved in eating *genhaaʔ* meat draw a distinction between the obligatory total consumption off-the-ground and the forbidden returning of any part of the meat to the ground.

Other observances are closely related to these. At least one seasonal fruit, the bramble *tɛgtag*, grows so close to the ground as to be considered unownable. The below-ground root crops are unownable and free for anyone to gather, while the above-ground crops are ownable and may be taken only with the owner's permission. *Genhaa²* observances find their logical inverse in the *joruu²* requirement (Chapter 5) that seasonal fruits must be thrown on the ground after eating and not burnt in the fire, off the ground. Both *genhaa²* and *joruu²* imply the distinction between exposure and burial that we find in the contrast between the proper ends accorded to great mediums and still-born babies and to normal people and domestic animals. (A more detailed summary of these practices has already been presented in Chapter 5.)

The importance of the ground/off-the-ground distinction is so great that much of Temiar ritual life seems as if it is concerned with little else than to maintain the two categories clear against confusion. Certain of the diseases discussed earlier (*təracɔɔg, tanig, mameeŋ*) are hardly to be understood on any other basis than that they are caused by acts that intermingle the two domains and destroy their discreteness. Mediumship, the most highly valued and purely religious of Temiar activities, is similarly the vehicle for a differentiation between ground and off-the-ground. Here, the Temiars are explicit in their ideas: 'little' mediumship involves *pɛhnɔɔh baliik* 'trancing of off-the-ground things', while the rarer and contrasted 'great' mediumship involves *pɛhnɔɔh num-tɛ²* 'trancing of things of the ground.' The characteristics of off-the-ground spirit-guides contrast point-by-point with those of spirit-guides of the ground.

However, ground and off-the-ground are not just neutral 'good-to-think' categories. It is clear that much of Temiar practice is aimed at obviating the influence of the former while maximising the influence of the latter. Here we have a valuable clue to the proper 'interpretation' of the conceptual calculus. We need only recall (Chapter 6) how the various disease-bearing spirits (*mamə², paad, bahyaa²*) that abound at twilight dwell in the ground, and how the ceremonies at childbirth and first menstruation make play with the act of washing pollution into the ground by pouring water from aloft. Above all is the requirement that settled villages should consist of *deek baliik* 'off-the-ground houses'. In short, in most contexts, off-the-ground is desirable and ground undesirable. That this leads directly to a theology of good and evil, I shall shortly demonstrate.

We may now add another element to the conceptual calculus:

Village	:	Forest
Off-the-ground	:	Ground
Desirable	:	Undesirable

The personal level

The same structuring can be discerned at the personal level of ideas. The human personality is regarded as partible, with the various parts carried by the multiple souls that animate the body. Although on some accounts human beings possess four distinct souls, only two of these have relevance to the present discussion—the head-soul (*rəwaay*) and the heart-soul (*hup*). Most of what the Temiars tell about their souls is dogma rather than an account of everyday behaviour. The dogma is anchored to lived experience primarily through mediumship and the various rituals connected with hair and blood. But these activities relate to the soul ideas as manipulable concepts rather than revealing much about their detailed content. The association of the head-soul with the hair and the heart-soul with the blood is explicit, but it is not so clear from the rituals alone that they form opposed categories. In only one ritual is the opposition made explicit: during a severe thunderstorm, blood is scattered on the ground and hair may be burnt in the fire. For the rest, we must turn for enlightenment to the ideology of mediumship.

The head- and heart-souls of humans are paralleled by the various upper and lower-body souls that animate non-human beings: the Temiars state explicitly that the two series of souls are homologous. Mediumistic ritual makes it clear that the upper- and lower-body souls are categorically opposed by associating them unequivocally with the notions of off-the-ground and ground. Upper-body souls become off-the-ground spirit-guides and lower-body souls emerge as spirit-guide tigers from the ground below. So important is mediumship that it would in itself be sufficient to maintain a constant awareness of the head-soul/heart-soul opposition, but people are also frequently reminded of their souls in everyday life. Hair—and hence the head-soul—is the object of special attention. It is frequently combed, oiled and decked with flowers by men and women alike—activities that are either enjoined or forbidden during first menstruation and mourning. During childhood, a ritual tuft (wɔɔj) of hair is left and the cuttings should not be buried.[3] Blood—and hence the heart-soul—is likewise the object of much attention, the details of which I discussed earlier.[4]

Any concern for the well-being of one's souls becomes, then, a reminder to people that they contain within themselves the very oppositions that pervade the rest of the Temiar world. The diseases rɛywaay and pacɔg result from attacks upon the head-soul and heart-soul respectively. Both are incurred by committing any of a range of seemingly trivial acts, all of which may be avoided by conscious effort. In this way, the purely epistemological aspects of soul beliefs come to have a moral cast through being made the object of individual free choice.

We may now add to the calculus a further element:

Off-the-ground	:	Ground
Upper-body soul	:	Lower-body soul
Hair	:	Blood

---

3. [Added 2014] I observed that some hair cuttings of pre-pubertal children were kept wrapped in paper and stuck in the wall-posts inside the house to prevent ants from carrying them underground and causing tɔracɔɔg (Chapter 6). Once the children reach puberty, their cut hair is not kept.
4. [Added 2014] See Chapter 12 for further information on Temiar concerns over blood.

A more detailed summary of these structures has already been presented in Chapter 6.

Nature and culture

The discussion so far has concentrated on the conceptual structures implied by the concrete activities of everyday life, but this does not mean that Temiars never get beyond a purely concrete level in their ideas. In certain contexts, they seem to talk directly about nature and culture in a manner not very different from that of some anthropologists. Much may be learnt about the Temiar concept of nature by studying how the frequently heard expression *hun-tɛ^ʔ* is used. Indeed, it would not be wrong to translate the phrase itself as 'natural', as long as the word is understood in the sense of 'pertaining to the category of nature, as opposed to culture'. Etymologically, the compound word *hun-tɛ^ʔ* is transparent. *Tɛ^ʔ* means 'earth, soil, country', and, most significantly, 'ground', as opposed to *baliik* 'off-the-ground'. *Hun-* is a proclitic form of the word *hup*, several of the meanings of which I have already discussed. In ordinary speech, *hup* refers to the autonomy of will: a person does one thing rather than another because it is 'their own *hup* to do so'; or a person's intentions will be referred to their 'good' or 'bad' *hup*, as the case may be. By extension, *hup* is used to mean 'in the manner of' some specific attribute of an animate or inanimate object; the composite expression *hun-tɛ^ʔ* thus means 'in the manner characteristic of ground'. Examining how *hun-tɛ^ʔ* is used in everyday speech should therefore help to reveal precisely which features qualify as 'characteristic of ground'.

Two key meanings seem to be involved. In the first place *hun-tɛ^ʔ* is used to describe a state of affairs in which things are quite literally dispersed over the surface of the ground. This refers most frequently to the various ways of life. The Temiars contrast their present-day life with that of their Negrito neighbours by claiming that they live in semi-permanent villages while the latter lead the *hun-tɛ^ʔ* life of nomadic gatherers, living in one place for no more than a few days at a time. Temiars use the same term for those of their own activities that require them to leave the village, and which could therefore be carried on in the absence of settled village life. In particular, hunting is often referred to as 'going *hun-tɛ^ʔ*'. They also refer to the way of life of their grandparents, who moved village more frequently than contemporary Temiars do, as 'living *hun-tɛ^ʔ*'.

Second, *hun-tɛ^ʔ* is used colloquially to mean 'disordered, untidy, lacking ensemble', in which sense it is one of the most frequently uttered words in the language. A man missing a target, women singing in an uncoordinated manner, someone who talks off subject, a baby who crawls all over the place—all are acting *hun-tɛ^ʔ*. Of particular interest is the idea that before ʔalʉj taught people the correct kinship appellations, they called each other and associated in a *hun-tɛ²* manner, without regard for proper social order. This allows the characterisation of ?alɨj as the bringer of order.

Such a widespread concept implies its own antithesis. In Temiar this is supplied by the phrase *hum-boo²*, which balances the concept of *hun-tɛ²* point-by-point in structure and usage. The first element *hum-* is again a clitic form of the word *hup* 'in the manner of'. *Boo²* is primarily the word for 'mother', but it has several other related meanings. In its inflected form, *baboo²* means 'female', but its most common other use as an unaltered form means 'stem, trunk (of a plant)'. The word *boo²* occurs both as a term of plant anatomy and as a numerical classifier in enumerating plants. In other words, *boo²* is the above-ground portion of the plant that gives rise, like a mother (*boo²*), to its offspring—the flowers and fruits.[5] Another use of *boo²* is in the expression *(deek) diŋ-boo²* 'communal longhouse'. The image here is of the central communal portion of the house somehow spawning the adventitious private rooms that crowd into its walls on all sides. In all these meanings, the keynote is normality and proper orderliness. Accordingly, I suggest that the basic meaning of *hum-boo²* is 'normal'. A usual way of doing something, an accustomed place, a correct form of speech, a valued tradition—all are *hum-boo²*.

The two concepts are opposed, then, in just the same way as order is opposed to disorder, village to forest, off-the-ground to ground, and, indeed, society to animality (if we take the evidence of the myth of the origin of kinship appellations). Yet the two single phrases deal adequately with a whole range of categories: just as an anthropologist might talk of culture and nature, the Temiars talk of *hum-boo²* and *hun-tɛ²*. Much is subsumed under both terms.

The conceptual calculus is now almost complete. The three levels of ideas—cosmic, mundane, personal—are associated with series of category oppositions the content of which is anchored to everyday life through a network of personal rituals. Each of these oppositions is the same as the opposition between nature/*hun-tɛ²* and culture/*hum-boo²*. But Temiar theology goes further: it is not enough just to point to the nature/culture opposition, or even to attach it to everyday affairs. Rather, one is to be *preferred* to the other. It is to this question of values that I now turn.

Good and evil

The foregoing discussion touches on points that necessarily involve human preferences. The opposition off-the-ground/ground, in particular, turns out to be equivalent to the opposition desirable/undesirable. Similarly, as evidenced by two further oppositions, Temiar behaviour displays a preference for the one element over the other: seasonal fruits are highly valued and readily

---

5. [Added 2014] For further discussion of the etymology and semantics of *boo²*, see the final section of Chapter 12.

sought after, while tigers are greatly avoided; and Temiars prefer the village to the forest, which they rarely enter without some specific purpose in mind.

However, the elements of these oppositions are neither desirable nor undesirable in themselves. Rather, the moral force that pervades the conceptual calculus derives from the fact that the calculus is itself composed of the moral categories of good and evil. The various oppositions examined earlier are all transformations of the basic opposition between good and evil. Indeed, the oppositions that underlie everyday practice are so closely interlinked— note especially the various paradigmatic presentations in the preceding chapters—that it would be sufficient for just one element of the calculus to be ascribed some moral value for the remainder similarly to take on moral values. The 'interpretation' of the calculus would then be a simple matter. But if only a single interpreting strand linked the empty categories to the moral ideology, it might fail to impress itself on most of the people it was aimed at. The difficulty is resolved through a repeated linking of the conceptual calculus with the moral ideology at different points and by a variety of means. Mythology, ritual and song lyrics all play a part in this 'interpretive' process, supplemented by various diffuse sanctions of social control.

Mythology

Temiar mythology is rich, seemingly inexhaustible, and variable from place to place. Many of the stories in this large corpus are entertaining fables in an Aesopian mould, and much of anthropological interest could be discovered by digging below their surface enchantment. Many of these are stories involving complicated serial metamorphoses between humans, animals and seasonal fruit trees. These carry a theological content, but are too complicated to discuss here. Instead, I shall discuss one of the many stories centring on the relation between Karey (the Thunder deity) and his younger brother ʔalɨj (the First Man).[6]

We met another of these stories, The Origin of Death, in Chapter 6. There, Karey's role as the source of death is made clear. In everyday life also, Temiars take pains to keep alive the notion of Karey as the ever-present source of evil: see especially the discussion of *misik* in Chapter 5. One of the significant features of the myth about death is the way in which, as protagonists, Karey and his brother ʔalɨj are set off as foils against each other. In that particular case the two brothers are structurally opposed, but the story nevertheless portrays them as cooperating in a joint task. Generally, however, in the Karey stories the two brothers are opposed in all respects, with ʔalɨj regularly acting towards Karey as any human being might—with trickery and deception. ʔalɨj is cast throughout as the apotheosis of humankind in general, and of spirit-mediums in particular.

---

6. [Added 2014] Further stories in this sequence are presented in Chapter 9, along with Edmund Leach's analyses of them.

In fact, Karey's activities in these stories often seem insufficient in themselves for him to be regarded as the embodiment of evil. Indeed, it is often the antics played upon Karey by ʔalᵿj that seem cruel. It is only through the repeated assertion that ʔalᵿj is the 'good' character that we see just how evil Karey must be! Often, as these stories were being dictated to me, the teller would insert explanatory phrases that would normally be omitted from the abbreviated versions recounted to audiences who already knew the tales by heart. These interpolations made the major points of the stories explicit, and are accordingly relevant to any discussion of the place of Karey in Temiar thought. Towards the end of one such story for example, after describing how Karey had interfered with ʔalᵿj and his companions, the teller added 'Karey is like that: an evil man, a fierce man.' It is significant that both 'evil' and 'fierce' were expressed here by the Malay loanwords *jahat* and *buas* respectively. In Temiar proper there does not seem to be any way of saying 'evil' except by using, for example, the heavily worked word for 'bad', *laʔəs*. The concept of evil is nevertheless implicit in almost all culturally patterned Temiar acts.

The Karey stories are organised as a succession of interludes in which Karey acts the rogue and ʔalᵿj gets his own back. Many of these interludes recur as motifs throughout the different stories. In the story presented in outline below, there are two of these motifs. First, women from ʔalᵿj's 'side' entice Karey into copulating with them, whereupon his penis swells unmanageably. ʔalᵿj, as a spirit-medium, is then called in to cure the affliction—only to use the opportunity to inflict further painful indignities upon his brother. Second, ʔalᵿj 'magics' things so that Karey gets stuck up a tree while hunting. Eventually, he has no choice but to throw himself off, whereupon he dies—temporarily, of course: the show must go on, and real death had not yet been invented! Both these motifs cause much amusement in the retelling whenever they occur. The first is the occasion for much bawdy elaboration of the text; the second puts Karey into a situation sometimes suffered by Temiars in real life. In the following text, the inserted parenthetical comments were added by the storytellers themselves in answer to my queries.

> Karey and ʔalᵿj were out constructing fish-weirs. Karey worked on the side of the river with a good flow of water, but ʔalᵿj had only a sand bank on his side to build on. When all was finished, Karey suddenly found the situation reversed—now it was ʔalᵿj who had the water while he was left without. So it was only ʔalᵿj who caught the desirable *kelah* fish.
>
> They then returned home and cooked some millet to make a feast of the fish. They spread out mats in the traditional manner, and Karey called out for his fine elbow-pattern-twilled tobacco pouch (a traditional design, now fast disappearing), telling them to give the ugly one to ʔalᵿj. They settled down to eat, but while eating Karey noticed that a trick had been played on him: he now had the ugly pouch and

ʔalɥj the fine one. He complained bitterly, but there was nothing he could do about it.

The next morning, the women (who were really the millet in a metamorphosed form) left the house and went out to work. Karey followed them and crept up silently, hoping 'to pounce, to grab, to copulate'. But as soon as he did so, he found that he had grabbed nothing but the buttress root of a tree. He puzzled how it was possible for a woman to change form so suddenly, but decided to give it another try. Again he pounced, and again. But each time, the woman became a tree. In the end, he gave up, literally hurt, and returned home. The women followed soon afterwards.

The next day, he had more success. He followed the ten women to where they were cutting bamboo, and pounced on each in turn, managing to copulate with all. Satisfied, he returned home, only to find that his penis had swollen 'as big as a column, as big as a tree'. He realised immediately that that is what comes of copulating with so many women. Finding no relief, he decided to send his son Cɛbrɛb (a dragonfly-like insect) to seek curative advice from ʔalɥj. Cɛbrɛb returned with ʔalɥj's advice that Karey should cure himself by beating his penis with a hammer. So Karey laid his swollen penis on the threshold of the house and beat it flat with a hammer. But, of course, ʔalɥj had deceived him, and Karey died on the spot.

They left him in the house on his sleeping platform for about ten days. Then Cɛbrɛb plucked the shoot of an *ʔapoos* plant [*Phaeomeria* sp.] and hurled it into the ear of his dead father. At this Karey suddenly revived, and got up saying 'Ah ah, I've been dreaming from source to estuary.' ('But he only pretended to have dreamt, for in reality he had been dead', the teller explained.)

Once again Karey and ʔalɥj set out together, this time to set snares. ʔalɥj concentrated on setting fall-traps at the base of the trees while Karey worked in the tree-tops. Then they went home for a night's sleep. But Karey got up and found that a pig was caught on the spears of ʔalɥj's trap. So he removed it and stuck it instead onto the spears of his own trap in the tree-top so that it would seem as if the pig was by right his own. Then he went home to sleep for the rest of the night. In the morning, he woke and told ʔalɥj he had dreamt that his own trap had caught a pig but that ʔalɥj's was empty. ('He was wicked and had played a trick with ʔalɥj's trap', the teller explained.) Karey then went off to collect his gains from the tree, but he found that it had now grown very much taller than before. He climbed up, released the pig from the trap and dropped it to the ground. But he could no longer climb down himself, so tall had the tree become: ʔalɥj had magicked it in return for his stealing the pig. Karey then tore off a shred of his loin-cloth, which called back to him that it still lived [*sic*] after the fall. Then he let drop one of his fleas, which likewise survived the fall. So he decided to jump himself, and of course, he died once more.

After ten days, his son Cɛbrɛb came along and revived him as before.
Karey woke saying, 'I dreamt of estuaries, I dreamt of sources.'
And there the story ends.

Nothing is resolved: the antagonism between Karey and ʔalɥj is to continue indefinitely. The interjections of the audience and storytellers when I heard these tales retold left me in no doubt that we were meant to be on ʔalɥj's side whatever happened. We humans were getting our own back on Karey for his malign attitude towards us.

Yet if we examine the mythology a bit more closely, it becomes clear that Karey is not always unambiguously polarised as the evil element of the opposition. Karey is merely one aspect of a composite deity. His better half is known as ʔɛŋkuuʔ (Chapter 4). In the Creation story, ʔɛŋkuuʔ is the last to come on the scene, long after ʔalɥj had been about his business. When finally he does come into being we are told nothing of his evil qualities, only that he was set in the sky to thunder. Furthermore, in some traditions ʔɛŋkuuʔ is said to be responsible for the fruiting of the seasonal trees.[7] In Temiar eyes, this must link him with the forces of good. The duality of ʔɛŋkuuʔ/Karey implies, then, that good and evil are not entirely distinct.[8] A detailed analysis of other myths (not about Karey) would show that the confusion between the two moral quantities poses a problem for the Temiars, though not necessarily an explicit one. Unfortunately, the analysis would be too protracted for discussion here.

Ritual

Karey as the embodiment of evil is, then, opposed to ʔalɥj as the apotheosis of humankind. But ʔalɥj is also the First Medium and it is therefore not surprising to discover that in certain contexts mediumship and Karey are opposed as good and evil. This is especially striking in two particular ritual contexts. Many of the *misik* acts that attract the unwanted attention of Karey are precisely the same as the *joluŋ* acts that scare away the protective swarm of spirit-guides after a séance. Karey and spirit-guides are ideally in complementary distribution: where evil is, good has no place. The ritual blowing (*tɛnhool*) employed by mediums against disease is used also as a means of warning Karey off during a thunderstorm. Here, a double identification of Karey with evil is made. First, Karey is directly associated with disease, which represents evil. Second, he is brought into obvious opposition to the spirit-guides, which, judging by their curative powers and the positive efforts expended by the Temiars in their direction, represent good. But the spirit-guides in question here are the typically off-the-ground

---

7. [Added 2014] There is an inedible bright-red liana fruit known as *kədɔɔr ʔɛŋkuuʔ* 'ʔɛŋkuuʔ's lady', presumably so called because its colour recalls the idea that sacrificed blood is transformed by the deity into fruit.

8. [Added 2014] Nowadays, I would characterise this as exemplifying the dialectical mode of orientation, discussed explicitly in Chapters 10–13.

sort, not the tiger-spirits that appear from below.[9] The latter do not remain behind as a swarm, and the corresponding ritual requirements therefore do not apply to them—just as a medium possessed by a tiger-spirit does not treat disease with ritual blowing. So it would be more accurate to say that certain rituals set up an opposition between Karey on the one hand and the conceptual category of off-the-ground on the other, making it clear that the latter category is to be interpreted as good.

The major part of Temiar ritual is concerned, however, with the setting-up of the conceptual calculus rather than with the interpretation of the values it represents. Once the category of off-the-ground has been so firmly attached to the notion of good, ritual practices then extend that evaluation into all areas of everyday life, as we have already seen in some detail.

Song lyrics

The complexity of Temiar song lyrics, in both language and meaning, would deserve extended treatment in itself. Temiar music, though attractive, is simple in structure and repetitive. As distinct elements, tunes and rhythms hold little interest for Temiars.[10] Their aesthetic judgments are aimed instead at the quality of the singing voice rather than the song's musical content. The reason is simple: singing is meant as the vehicle of the lyrics, which receive almost all the attention.[11]

At a serious séance, the words sung are either supposed to be the spirit-guide's own or to reflect directly the singers' feelings of spiritual lethargy at the spirit-guide's long absence. There is a certain amount of mutuality in this. The spirit-guide's own words often express querulous excitement about the preparations made for its arrival, while singer's words express longing for its coming. Two short samples, taken from my own tape-recordings in the village of Humid, will illustrate something of the character of these songs. The simple English versions of the lyrics give no indication of the poetry and

---

9. [Added 2014] In 1965, during my original fieldwork, two of my instructors—Jɔs, mentioned again in Chapter 10, and his friend ʔaman—agreed with my then emerging theory that everything is divisible into good and evil components on the *kahyɛk–kənoruk* pattern. They went on to say that all mediums have a portion of their *gunig*'s *kahyɛk* in their *hup* (*jərəək*), even when not trancing—hence the ability to 'blow' (*təhool*), carry out healing actions (*sooʔ*) and transfer (*pɛrlʉb*) spirit-guide power in the daytime without trancing. I take this to be confirmation of my claim that they viewed good and evil as constantly linked together in what I would now regard as a dialectical relation.

10. [Added 2014] In 1968, however, Penghulu Hitam Tamboh was able to give me names for three distinct rhythmic patterns beaten on bamboo tubes by the women at ritual song performances. The basic unelaborated duple rhythm was known as *cənantok*, derived from the default word *cantok* for 'to beat bamboo tubes'. More complicated duple and quadruple rhythms, in which each tube is sometimes beaten more than once in succession, are known as *sənimbɔɔl*; an example is notated musically by Roseman (1991: 102) in her description of the *Səlumbaŋ* genre. Hitam said that one variant of this was typical of old-time Semai practice. On one occasion, in Hitam's own house, I was amazed to hear the women's chorus beat out a septuple (7/4) rhythm. Hitam said that this was known as *pənɛmrum*, and that it was employed at the opening of a *Səlumbaŋ* trance session. Sadly, I have never again heard this performed.

11. [Added 2014] Later work, by Roseman (1984) especially, has shown that the musical *structures* of Temiar song-performances are nevertheless meaningful in their own right. (See also Benjamin 2004.)

allusive power of the original Temiar songs, the language of which is very different in register from that of everyday life.

The first example comes from the end of a song named after a hornbill spirit-guide. The earlier verses have described his swooping flight over the nearby mountains and villages, his alightings on the flowers in the village gardens and in the house, and his intention to come right in and land on the ritual wreath (*tənamuuʔ*) to hear the singing. He sings more specifically of the welcome that awaits him:

Samɔh dalam baley	Behold within the house
ʔim-ʔintey ca-yaar gənuruuʔ.	the medium and I will glance about.
Ma-lɔɔʔ tənamuuʔ ləbag?	Where is the wreath of *ləbag* flowers?
Gabag tɛrman	Sing in play!
Samɔh sənaŋ kəwaar	Behold the remains of (last time's) palm whisk
pɛnsaar molaŋ.	but hurry forward with the new barkcloth headdress.
Samɔh la-gɛlgəlɛɛl.	Behold the fine singing.
Na-muɲcoŋ ʔayaap.	Mount Ayam rises up.
Rɛʔ-doh yaar guruuʔ.	Like this are my medium and I.
Yəəh, ma-lɔɔʔ?	Oh where, where?

The spirit-guide sings of his pleasure in coming to the house and of the preparations that have been made (the wreath, the new headdresses, the fine singing). At one point, he complains about the villagers' negligence in leaving a worn-out palm whisk; but a new headdress immediately makes up for it. As if to emphasise his all-out intention to get to Humid village for the festivities, the spirit-guide sings of his flight along the full length of the mountain (Gunung Ayam, Galɛɛŋ; figure 8.1) at the foot of which the village lies. On arrival, he stresses his unity with his 'father', the medium. Then, at the end, the singer calls out seeking more inspiration (the songs are extemporised), but none comes and the song peters out.

Expressions of the singer's longing usually take the form of interpolated verses within a longer song. A typical verse is *ləteh lɛŋləmɔɔŋ dalam bodiiʔ*, 'Tired and weary in spirit'. (Most of these words are Temiarised Malay.) Or the singer may complain that without his spirit-guide's presence, he has nothing to say: *Doʔ doʔ ʔeeh, dɛmdəyam sayəəh*, '(nonsense syllables) I am left silent' (also in Temiarised Malay). Similarly, repeated exhortations that the women's chorus should sing more heartily also have the effect of suggesting that all is not well until the arrival of the spirit-guide:

ʔim-bokaaʔ təraŋ lantas,	I shall open up clearly forthwith,
lantas yɛdyɔɔd.	with much blasting forthwith.

Figure 8.1 Galɛɛŋ (Malay: Gunung Ayam) (2006)
Galɛɛŋ is highly valued in Temiar Religion as a spirit-mountain containing both pətərii? and sarak. Previously very hard to see and therefore rather mysterious, it has now become visible (here, from the south-west) following road-building and forest-felling, some of which can be seen in the foreground.

Ma-lɔɔ? səŋalaa? mɛn-waa??	Where are all the (spirit-guide's) aunts ?[12]
Səlaa? ?ɛm-mɛ?maa?.	Hurry, or we may as well go home.

The 'aunts' are of course the chorus of women essential to any song performance. They were singing well below standard at the point when I recorded them, and the lead singer acted out in his lyrics the expected reactions of any normal spirit-guide. The women must not give way to the lethargy that comes from the spirit-guide's absence or they will lose all hope of coaxing it down to stay with them.

The songs sung for off-the-ground spirit-guides thus express the mutual longing of villagers and spirit-guide for each other. Songs thereby become a rich way of stating that off-the-ground spirit-guides are to be interpreted as agents of good, serving as a reinforcement of one of the main functions of myth and ritual. But tiger spirit-guides associated with the ground also have their distinctive songs, which, though less frequently performed, attract more excited attention than the more usual off-the-ground songs. The tiger-

---

12. [Added 2014] I now believe that this was an homophonous pun: the word *mɛn-waa?* 'plural-aunts' could also have been transcribed as *mɛnwaa?* (without the hyphen), the Temiarised version of Malay *benua* 'country'.

medium sings of a restrained horror between his spirit-guide and the villagers. Interspersed with stylised growls, these songs frequently contain admonitory verses beseeching the tiger to remember its place and not go too far by eating up the people in the house. In a song of the tiger-spirit Dato⁷ Leŋri⁷ mentioned earlier, the following lines occurred:

ʔoy yəəh, ʔoy yəəh	(Growls)
Gunig tənataa⁷,	Spirit-guide of the old men,
ʔiŋad ha-lah ʔɛɛ⁷.	do remember us all.
Jagəəh, Dato⁷ Lɛŋri⁷.	Guard well, Dato⁷ Lɛŋri⁷.

My informants stated explicitly that this was aimed at reminding the tiger-spirit to remain safely in its proper abode. Other tiger songs commonly relate, in the spirit-guide's own words, how its prowlings take it through dank hollows filled with the rotting logs of the dangerous trees (those listed in table 4.2). The poetry of the lyrics then consists of rhythmic recitations of the names of those trees.

In both cases, the song lyrics help to set up an awareness of the core characters of the two types of spirit-guides—that off-the-ground spirit-guides are good, and ground spirit-guides evil. Temiars love singing, and they do so frequently: it provides them with a further means of determining how the conceptual calculus should be 'interpreted'.

Sanctions of social control

Temiar society is marked by informality at all levels. Nowhere is this more striking than in relation to the means of social control. The office of headman is not indigenous: the various 'penghulus', 'panglimas' and 'batins' are appointed by outside authorities, who were formerly the local Malay chief but nowadays the Department of Aboriginal Affairs. Although in some cases the office has become successionary, it has never derived its authority from *within* Temiar society, and headmen are merely officially recognised go-betweens carrying the outside authority's wishes to their fellows.[13]

Although there was no formal office of leadership in traditional times, there were nevertheless leaders of a charismatic kind. In addition to the religious authority acquired by a respected medium, there was usually an elder, known sometimes as the *tataa⁷ səlaay* 'swidden elder' or *tataa⁷ sɛrseer canaa⁷* 'food-distributing elder', whose lead was followed in matters of worldly wisdom. (The secular leader and the medium were sometimes the same person.) But even a leader respected by his own people had no means of implementing a decision if the people themselves disagreed with what had been decided.

---

13. [Added 2014] I later (Benjamin 1968b) examined Temiar political organisation, including headmanship, in detail. In the present century, Temiar headmen are increasingly reversing their orientation, by representing changing Temiar views of their situation *to* the authorities.

Neither formerly nor today has Temiar society had any organised sanctions in which the power of authority could be brought to bear on an individual. The autonomy of the individual's will is a cardinal principle of Temiar life. Even parents may reprimand their child only with the excuse of having lost their temper. If the child loses its temper, it is left to exhaust its tantrum while the adults look on impassively or with an air of helplessness. If I wished to photograph a child or if the flying doctor wished to carry out an examination, nothing could be done unless the child himself wished to comply. The parents certainly made no move to force the child to agree.

The same principle extends into adult life, but by that time the former child has ceased to have temper tantrums. Adult Temiars never so much as raise their voices to each other, though they do complain about other people's behaviour behind their backs. Points of disagreement are settled by dignified public discussion in which everyone is asked to air their point of view. It is here that the informal leader may make his influence felt—in bringing conflicting views into apposition and leading people to settle their own differences as they think best. It is true that many people talk as if there were a range of regulated fines to be paid to the headman by a miscreant, but although such a fine might be declared, it is never paid. Nor, I suspect, does anyone ever expect it to be paid. The conflicting parties usually solve the matter simply by moving to separate villages. Such trouble cases almost always arise out of marital problems.

It is clear that 'crimes' are not a regular element of Temiar life. Except for the occasional sexual intrigue, people simply do get on with each other peacefully. This is not due to the influence of modern values from outside the society, which in any case are much more likely to induce conflict than peacefulness.[14] An early (and charming) account of the Temiars (Brau de Saint-Pol Lias 1883: 281) shows that things have not changed in this respect during the course of almost a century:[15]

I continue my researches into the penal legislation of the Orang Sakai [Temiars]:
– And when a Sakai kills a man…
– *Tida!* (never!) Tolilò interrupted sharply.
– When he steals…
– *Tida!* he rejoined with the same energy.
– What! There are no thieves?
– *Tida!*
– When a man is hungry and has no *ubi* [cassava]…?

14. [Added 2014] On later visits, I have witnessed occasional verbal altercations with raised voices, and more noticeable unfavourable gossiping than previously. In the resettlement sites at least, I suspect that this is due largely to the mixing of people who came originally from different areas.
15. [Added 2014] This is my translation from the original French. At the time of this republication, 'almost a century' has become 'a century-and-a-half'.

- He asks for some or he buys some.
- If he has no money?
- That doesn't matter, someone gives him some. When someone from far away is in our country, he only has to ask and people give him food to eat. This is all said with the greatest simplicity and an air of sincerity that leaves no doubt.

My own experience bears out the truth of these remarks: murder and theft are almost unheard of among Temiars, and none of my informants was able to say what would be done to the delinquent in such circumstances.[16]

How, then is social order maintained in Temiar society? As a clue, we may take one of the remarks reported above: 'he only has to ask and people give him food to eat'. This is in fact one of the cardinal principles of Temiar society: if one is requested to give something to someone else, then one must give. However, this is more than just a moral precept. Failure to give when requested involves sanctions of a sort best described (*pace* Radcliffe-Brown, 1959: 206) as 'supernatural'. In this particular case, the sanction involved is that of *səlantab*. The person who asks but is refused is the one who suffers, being liable to attack by a whole panoply of misfortunes—the bites and stings of centipedes, scorpions or snakes, the cuts of sharp-edged plants, or the breaking of a limb through falling over stumps or the misdirected felling of a tree. Temiar informants identify *səlantab* with the Malay principle of *punan* (or *kempunan*), the dangerous state that arises through leaving one's desires unsatisfied. Evans (1923: 237–239) gives a useful account of such beliefs as he found them among various Senoi groups all over Malaya. He also suggests that the Temiar word *səlantab* may be a form of the 'royal' Malay word *santap* 'to eat'. This is indeed a likely derivation, and it would make sense both linguistically and semantically. While the stress among other Aboriginal groups is on the satisfaction of desires, among the Temiars it seems more important that one should share one's possessions. Evans himself (1923: 239) noted that the concept of 'shelantab' was in evidence among the 'Negrito–Sakai' of Ulu Temengor and the 'Sakai' of Ulu Kinta—both groups are Temiar—when food was brought out in the presence of other people. If one person had some, then

---

16. [Added 2014] Despite this remark, there are mentions in the earlier literature of occasional violence committed by Temiars, especially where different valley-populations or non-Temiars were involved. See Clifford (1897: 177–178; 1927 [1899]: 267), Noone (1936: 53, 55), Parsons (1941: 180) and Benjamin (1966: 8) for examples. Quadens (1990: 76–78), reviewing this and other evidence, claimed that the Temiars were neither more nor less given to violence than other populations in Asia; but she put most of it down to reactions against external interference. Tragically, as mentioned in Chapter 2, it is thought that Noone was himself blowpiped to death by a Temiar, or possibly two Temiars. According to Holman's third-person account (1958: 174–176, 237–238), as noted in Chapter 2, this would have occurred in 1943 near the Temiar settlement of Rening, Pahang, but by someone from Perak who had been travelling with Noone. In 1965, people in Rening who had known Noone asked me, in seeming innocence, where he was. If indeed Noone was murdered as described by Holman, then the Rening people must have known about it. However, Holman (1958: 238) says that after Noone's death the matter was placed under a taboo and was not to be talked about.

with murmurings of the word *shelantab*, he gave at least a token portion to everyone else. I can confirm from my own experience that this often happens.

Two features of *səlantab* ideas are crucial. In the first place, so far from being a means of assuaging desire, the rule is that one must accept what is offered whether or not one wants to. To avoid giving offence a token acceptance is required. Second, the sanctions that follow a breach of the proper behaviour fall not on the one who fails to give, but on the one who fails to receive. Together, these stipulations ensure a high degree of mutuality in social affairs, for they apply just as much to clothing and luxury goods as to food. The peculiar efficiency of a moral system in which harm rebounds onto the wronged rather than the wrongdoer has been commented on forcefully by Geddes. His account of the etymologically and functionally related Land Dayak principle of *panun* (1954: 54) makes it clear that such a system of sanctions so markedly other-directed can serve admirably as a means of infusing the whole community with a moral concern for one's fellows. We are told only of one such principle (*panun*) among the Land Dayaks, but among the Temiars there are several other sanctions of social control characterised by the same other-directed structure.

I have already discussed one of these sanctions more fully in Chapter 5, under the rubric of *gɛnhaaʔ*. As with *səlantab*, the danger of a *gɛnhaaʔ* death falls onto the person who is denied a share of the meat rather than the person who does the denying. In contrast, other sanctions of this sort are concerned with immaterial things. In one such sanction (the name of which I unfortunately failed to record), a child who has been wilfully hit by an adult is liable to meet with some bodily accident soon afterwards. Hence, Temiar parents refrain from hitting their children.[17]

An interesting case concerns the dangers of making promises too casually, as also reported by Evans (1923: 245). If one promises to join someone else at a specific time and place but then fails to arrive, the person to whom the vain promise was made is liable to meet with misfortune. Typically, it is believed that the offended party will be eaten by a tiger, which gives the institution its name, *sərɛnlɔɔk*. Evans, who recorded the word as 'sirlok', thought that it meant 'promise'. In fact, it refers to the way in which the tiger 'gets' the person who has been misled. The verbal form *sɛrlɔɔk* means 'to be successful in hunting'. In the myth that retells the origin of *sərɛnlɔɔk*, the tiger repeats a little refrain in which the word appears in a differently inflected form (*sɛnlɔɔk*) meaning 'successfully hunted': *Baglag rɛgjaag / ʔi-bəʔ kɛnrah / sɛnlɔɔk bubuuʔ* '[Nonsense syllables] / I carry the legs (of eaten people) / caught (as if) in a fish-trap'. Once, when passing through a strange

---

17. On the other hand, the reverse—committing an act of impoliteness by stepping over or snatching something from one's senior—is believed to cause a form of madness (*papɔɔʔ*) in the wrongdoer rather than in the wronged person.

village, I was about to say that I would return in two months' time, when the headman's wife cut me short with a briskly uttered '*sərenlɔɔk!*'. She thought it was unlikely that I would come that way again, and presumably did not wish to lay herself open to trouble from tigers.

One such sanction, *gɛɛs*, is thought to rebound upon both parties to the misdeed. *Gɛɛs*, though used normally as if it simply meant 'incest', is strictly speaking the name of the incapacitating swelling of the thighs and genitals of both partners to an incestuous act. The same sanction follows on the 'close approach' committed by young people past puberty who share a sleeping platform with their parent of opposite sex or the latter's 'siblings'. But so heinous is incest that it is believed to call down sanctions on the whole community as well, in the form of a violent thunderstorm. I myself witnessed such a thunderstorm, ascribed to the incestuous relation of two of the villagers in Humid (Benjamin 1967c: 10).

To return now to our original concern: how to derive further evidence for the proper moral 'interpretation' of the conceptual calculus from this discussion of the sanctions of social control? Although the discussion has had relevance to the overall thesis, and I shall refer to it again shortly, its connection with the information presented earlier in this section is not immediately obvious. The significant features of these sanctions, apart from their social structure, lie in the relation of the various resulting mishaps to what are elsewhere regarded as manifest expressions of evil. In two of the cases, the relation is obvious: with *sərenlɔɔk*, wrong behaviour brings a tiger into affairs; with *gɛɛs*, it is Karey himself who intervenes. These two social behaviours are thereby identified with two elements of the conceptual calculus that the Temiars clearly regard as evil. With *səlantab*, the sanctions (animal attacks, accidents) are those that Temiars in other contexts acknowledge to be sent by Karey in his role as the bringer of disease and death. *Gɛnhaaʔ*, as we saw in Chapter 5, is primarily concerned with the distinction between the village and the forest—the actual ritual observances taking the form of differentiating between the house and the ground below it. Social factors, such as the enforced sharing of the meat, seem to play a secondary part in this, but they do nevertheless play some part. Here too, social morality is directly tied to ritual observances.

A formulation of Temiar theology

We are now in a position to draw together the different threads of this extended discussion of Temiar religion. Taken singly, the various beliefs and practices would appear complex, to Temiars as well as to outside observers. Yet it is possible to discern beneath these details a considerable degree of regularity, as suggested in the structural analyses inserted at various points in the preceding chapters. But what does it add up to? We shall best find the answer by concentrating on two themes that have recurred throughout the analysis.

The major conclusion has been that behind the rich content of Temiar religion lies a constantly present organising principle—namely that, throughout, there is a basic conceptual opposition between two categories. From the conceptual viewpoint, these categories are culture and nature; from the moral viewpoint, good and evil. Here, it is the moral aspects of Temiar Religion that are in focus. In Chapter 3, I proposed that to a great extent conceptual concerns become moral concerns as soon as they enter a social context. For Temiars, the opposition between culture and nature is the same as the opposition between good and evil. The present study has shown how these oppositions confront them in most of their regular activities—hunting, cultivating, eating, travelling, giving birth, dying, explaining the world and, not least, ceremonial.

The second recurrent theme, the autonomy of the individual, has been paid less attention in the present study, but it has been mentioned several times; it has also been noted in my accounts of Temiar kinship and naming (Benjamin 1967c, 1968a).[18] To the outsider, the inability of the Temiars to enforce their wishes on others is perhaps their most striking characteristic, showing itself particularly in the way they bring up their children and in their lack of formal political organisation. In the religious sphere, autonomous individual inspiration plays a large part, including the high valuation placed on dreams. But the Temiars do not become wayward or anti-social as a result of this autonomy: it is by their own choice that they work well together in all contexts. The choice, however, is not primarily between either working with one's fellows or going one's own separate way. Their religious conceptions lead to a realisation that good and evil underpin all their activities, but they are also led to realise that good, specifically, is implicit in the various sanctions discussed earlier that regulate how they behave towards each other. In other words, each individual is faced with the choice between good and evil. If they choose good, their decision as to how to behave is aided by these few rather loose rules, which still allow a wide range of quite idiosyncratic behaviour.

The message of Temiar theology is, then: there is good and evil in all things, but individuals may by their own efforts increase the influence of the former while decreasing that of the latter. This follows directly from the coexistence within the one religious system of the two themes I have just discussed.

Religion and everyday life

What do the Temiars regard as the good life? We have seen that it largely consists of a proper give-and-take, a generalised reciprocity (Sahlins 1965: 147) of goods and services throughout the community. It consists too in a non-interference in the affairs of others. Dentan (1964: 180) makes the

---

18. [Added 2014] Further analysis of Temiar ideas about the autonomy of the individual can be found in Chapter 12.

point more strongly and talks about the 'strict taboo against violence' that characterises Senoi society. In discussing religion he reaffirms that, along with 'their belief in the autonomy of the individual', a basic factor is 'their fear of violence'. There is no need to labour the point further, but for more specific information on what the Temiars regard as good in everyday life, as opposed to purely ritual occasions, let us look at a text I collected. Temiars are fond of delivering exhortatory speeches when the occasion arises,[19] and they will expand at length on the qualities expected of the good person. An occasion that sometimes arises these days for them to make extended speeches is the presence of a tape-recorder, wielded by an ethnographer or by a reporter for the Temiar service of Radio Malaysia. I recorded the following text just four days after first entering Temiar country, when I requested a text for linguistic analysis. The speaker received no guidance whatsoever in his choice of topic.[20] As before, it is not possible to indicate anything of the speaker's marked declamatory style, with its repetitions and hesitations. What follows is merely the sense of his speech.

> Tomorrow we are going to fell a swidden. Let us not be lazy, for it is to be a single large one, on the Department's advice. All must pay attention and not be lazy or reluctant. We must agree to work a joint swidden, not several separate ones as we used to in the past. Now that we have joint villages and land that we work together, so must we be of one mind. To go separate ways is bad. In everything we do we should be of one mind, from hunting to cutting the grass for the Tuan, especially as they now call us *Asli* instead of *Darat* ['Inland Hill people'].[21] It's no good if one person is lazy, another is reluctant, one lacks diligence, or another says, 'I don't want unpaid work!'
>
> Women too, it's no good if they're out digging cassava and one of them says the other is stealing her tubers. They must dig jointly. And in the swidden, one must not keep others away. Such bad behaviour was all in the past. Nowadays we must do all our cropping together and for each other. Women, when they cook or go gathering banana shoots and sweet potatoes, must do it together. And the same holds for the men. If someone borrows a cast-net and tears it, then he must repair it before handing it

---

19. Cf. Dentan (1964: 180) on the Semais: 'Verbal facility, thought synonymous with intelligence, was ... the *sine qua non* of leadership.'

20. [Added 2014] Judging by his tone, it is possible that he thought I was employed by the Department of Aboriginal Affairs. Four days' residence in his village would not have been long enough for him to realise that I was not.

21. Recently [that is, the early 1960s], moves have been made by the Department of Aboriginal Affairs to bring about a change in the traditional lowly image of Malaya's Aborigines. One of the important changes has been in the general name by which they are known. Nowadays they are officially called Orang Asli which, though it means literally 'aborigines', has not the same undertones as that English word, especially in Malaysia. *Asli* in Malay carries the connotations not merely of 'indigenous' but also of 'well-born', 'pure', and 'classical'.

back. After hunting, whatever he gives his wife to cook she must share out to the others, even if it's only a rat. Women again, if they go to fetch water or chop bamboo, they must do it together without quarrelling, and behave like the people of a single village should.

There must be no playing around with married women. On the other hand, if a married woman decides to help a bachelor by cooking for him, then her husband must not make a fuss. She's doing what is right. In the past, we may have quarrelled, complained and gossiped about the sharing of food, but nowadays we must learn to share readily and without complaining.

If anyone receives some money, then let them remember the other kindly. If someone comes upon a pair of trousers, let him pass it on to some man—or if he should come by a blouse, then let him give it to some woman. We must no longer behave badly.

Be good to children. Number one is never to hit them. When they grow bigger then send them to school, while we remain at home to hunt and fish for them. But we must hold our land fast against the encroachments of outsiders. Otherwise, how would we manage to find food? Help them and trade with them by all means, for money, but do not give up our means of livelihood to them. But if one of *us* says 'My house is falling down, help me rebuild it', then do so without any thought of money or wages. We are not Malays that work for money. But of course, if the Tuans want to give us some work, it's only fair that they should give us some money too—we have always been people owning nothing. Things are developing, though, and outsiders are beginning to pay us for work.

If your friend empties your fish-trap, don't complain and ask for payment. If he takes it, just make yourself a new one. If he makes free with your bird-lime sticks, blowpipe or quiver, don't complain. After all, he might remember you kindly one day and bring you some meat or fetch your firewood for you. And whatever you might want, he will give, and his children too will help you. But if you borrow another man's blowpipe and quiver, then take care not to waste all his darts. Otherwise, he will rightly think that you have behaved improperly. Remember that. That's all.

Further comment would be redundant—except to remark that the ideas put forward in the speech are precisely those that the Temiars apply explicitly when discussing their problems. When, as sometimes happens, gossip goes on behind a defaulter's back, these are the very points that are called to issue.

In a society that places such a stress on the autonomy of the individual, it is hardly surprising that people should sometimes go their own way and do some of the things the speaker so deplored. He himself was accused of holding on to his money too firmly for one who was the community's only member with a regular, though small, monetary income as guardian of the first-aid hut. The point that stands out is that transgressions of the social norms are far more likely to cause unfavourable comment than transgressions of the purely religious rules. A mean person is readily identified as bad for the community. But someone who, for example, chooses to work on his crops during a lunar work-taboo period is regarded merely as foolhardy or brave, and not likely to harm anyone but himself. The individual variations in religious belief are striking. It does not seem to worry people that two or more openly expressed opinions on matters of 'dogma' may be entirely incompatible, or even diametrically opposed. Views that might be thought atheistic are not commented on with any disapproval. (The only avowedly atheistic Temiar that I met was a secondary schoolboy who was studying in a large town.) Indeed, their remarkable acceptance of the rather different practices of the other Orang Asli peoples as forming part of a single religious system along with their own suggests that the Temiars are not unduly concerned for the primacy of their religious representations. To them, it is more important to put the theological message into practice by living the good life than it is to worry too much about the way that message is expressed. If some of them are able to grasp hold of the idea of good and put it directly into practice without the bolstering help of Temiar religious representations, nobody thinks the less of them for it. Conversely, others find that it serves their purposes better to go along with the standard ritual practices, preferring to make full use of the conceptual tools offered to them by their religion. We should not forget that in all societies people differ markedly in their preferences for the religious way of life, as Radin (1953) and Bidney (1960) have both pointed out. That individuals differ in their use of Temiar religion provides us with a powerful clue to understanding the status that religion occupies in relation to Temiar society as a whole. It is to this problem, finally, that I now turn.

Religion and society

One of the points raised in the introductory Chapter 3 was the function of religion in making intellectually respectable the moral values that people live by. In the succeeding chapters I showed in detail just how an apparently disordered collection of ritual and dogmatic items—what an older generation of anthropologists might have called 'superstitions'—actually holds together as an ordered structure. The conceptual categories mutually imply each other in a manner far from haphazard. But we saw too that the conceptual system is more than a set of relationships between empty categories. Ultimately, its content is a moral one, involving both a calculus of good and evil and a direct link with sanctioned rules of good behaviour. A chain of implication and allusion therefore stretches between everyday interpersonal behaviour and the many ritual requirements that each individual meets up with in eating, travelling, working, and so on. The essential 'rightness' of the system, restated in different guises wherever they turn, can hardly fail to impress itself on individual Temiars. Their own behaviour both derives from and serves to generate the total system.

This is not to suggest that there is any determinate relationship between Temiar religion and Temiar society.[22] The religious system has such a degree of autonomy that it takes on a considerable objectivity for the Temiars themselves. We have seen how individuals do indeed make choices in regard to religious action, and though in sum their behaviour 'produces' both society and culture, the integrity of either is not necessarily threatened if any individuals choose to go their own way. Culture (and hence religion) and society are in any case in no more than a dialectical relationship to each other. The one is the result of recurrent human interaction and the other the tool that individuals make use of in order to act in a social manner. On this view, Temiar religion is a peculiarly well developed kind of tool that encodes societal information in a highly efficient manner. Nevertheless, it is a tool constantly open to re-examination and change—without however, for most people, destroying the 'aura of factuality' that Geertz regards as a key characteristic of any religion.

This study will have achieved its aim if, in addition to describing the religious system of an intrinsically fascinating people, it has taken away the mysticism that some anthropologists discern in attempts to treat conjointly both the relative autonomy of religion and its relationship to the society as a whole.

---

22. I use 'society' here to refer quite strictly to the system of social interaction between persons, following the useful distinction between culture and society that has been urged by Geertz (1957). See also my own remarks (Benjamin 1968a: 128–130). [Added 2014] While I would still reject the idea of a *determinate* relation between religion and social relations, I certainly now think that there is a close relation between them, as explored in much of the rest of this volume.

Chapter	Field-report Correspondence
9	with Edmund Leach

At this halfway point in the volume, I present some of the detailed correspondence that passed between Edmund Leach and myself while I was still in the field, between 1964 and 1965. As Leach remarked in May 1965, 'Just for the record please note that all your letters are being put together in a single file in my office in the Department.' I have that file with me as I write; it has proved to be an invaluable resource.

The correspondence was extensive. To conserve my supplies, the letters and field-reports were written tightly, with no margins, on very thin airmail paper. They were then usually picked up by Malcolm Bolton on his monthly flying doctor helicopter visits, and sent out by airmail from Kuala Lumpur. Leach received the letters between ten days and six weeks after I had written them, and usually replied immediately. As noted by Tambiah (2001: 66), to whom I provided copies of the letters, Leach's commentaries on the information I sent him 'convey some sense of the authentically pleased engagement with the research ... and his irresistible urge to order, analyze, and comment' on it.

This chapter provides a slightly different and more compact viewpoint on the account presented in Chapters 3–8, as well as some further ethnographic material that appears here for the first time. The necessity to keep within a word limit led me to exclude much of my data from the PhD thesis, including the texts of four longer myths, some of which were mentioned but not spelled out in the thesis. There is also additional information here on the circumstances of the research. This includes, of course, not only my own personal situation but also the broader intellectual and academic framework within which it was carried out. The mid-1960s were a crucial period in the development of social anthropology, in which Edmund Leach came to be regarded as the key figure. It is clear from Leach's letters that he was still mulling over many of the ideas for which he later became famous—or, as some might say, notorious. In particular, as noted below, he expressly acknowledged that my ethnographic findings were informing his response to the newer publications of Lévi-Strauss that were appearing while I was in the field, which he had not yet found entirely acceptable.

In other respects too, I was fortunate to have Edmund Leach as supervisor. Today, it is unthinkable for a PhD student in anthropology to be allowed to pursue such an unfocused 'general' ethnographic (and in my case, also linguistic) study. Bureaucratic accountability now requires the initial preparation of a detailed 'research proposal', accompanied not infrequently by a detailed outline of the proposed thesis—all before setting foot in the 'field'. The tightening-up that has taken place since—in which, as a university teacher myself, I have unavoidably been complicit—has undoubtedly produced some academic gains. But much has also been lost in the process, as indicated in the free-flowing yet closely attentive character of Edmund Leach's supervision of my research, at a point when we had not even discussed what the topic of my thesis should be. Indeed, the decision to focus on Temiar religion as the topic was not made until several months after I returned to Cambridge. I spent the preceding months instead on writing basic accounts of Temiar society,[1] as recommended by Leach in a letter dated 3 June 1965, before I had left the field:

> When you finally leave the field and draw breath, the first thing you should drive yourself to do, although it may seem extremely tedious at the time, is to write up an absolutely straightforward ethnographic account of the Temiar addressed to an imaginary audience who really know nothing about them at all. The point is that at that stage in your work, as perhaps never again, you will have an overall but very detailed feel for what Temiar culture 'really is'. Once you get buried into details of a PhD thesis the overall balance will get heavily distorted. At this stage you do not even need to bother about what the precise subject matter of your PhD thesis is going to be. You have enough stuff for about six different theses. But it is very important that the overall ethnographic framework is written up as soon as you leave the field so that you have something on which to base later decisions.

To integrate the correspondence more satisfactorily into the text, the different items are presented below without regard for chronological order. Apart from some corrective comments in the added footnotes, I proffer no further judgment on the appropriateness of Leach's analyses. I let these stand—along with reproductions of his sketched diagrams—as a witness to Leach's involvement as a supervisor experienced in Southeast Asian fieldwork and to his place in the intellectual framework of British anthropology at the time of my initial research.

I have divided the materials into four main sections, as indicated in the subheadings. These correspond to different issues I had raised or reported on, which Leach then responded to.

---

1. These papers were later published as Benjamin (1966, 1967c and 1968a). Before turning to the thesis itself, I also wrote a brief account of Temiar phonology and morphology. Several years later, this was expanded and published as Benjamin (1976).

On the apparent lack of Temiar religion in Humid

As mentioned in Chapter 3, my field reports from Humid village in 1964 were reporting that the people did not engage in overtly religious practices. Although I later discovered that this was not the case, the following extract from a letter I wrote to Leach on 15 September 1964 will give a clear impression of the situation at the time. Leach's reply to this a month later, printed here, occupied just one paragraph in a longer letter. But his recommendation turned out to be right on the mark. At the time, religion had not been specified as a key topic in my research plans, leave alone as a thesis topic, and I treated my seemingly negative findings as a matter of curiosity rather than as a threat to the completion of my research.

Kuala Humid, 15 September 1964

The Temiar of Humid turn out to be cynical atheists, much to my disappointment (although it raises further interesting problems). As the headman [Dalam] put it to me, 'I've never seen or heard Tohan, Karey, etc.—have you? No, they just don't exist; we don't believe in them. In my opinion when we die we just rot away, like trees.' Other men had previously given some very fragmentary after-life beliefs, but plainly without much faith in them. When I put this to the headman he explained that these beliefs reached Humid through their occurrence in the lyrics of songs of the next valley system to the north [presumably, the Perias and Yai valleys] (which I hope to visit in the next few days), ultimately stemming from the people of the valley in Perak that rises opposite to it. And I have every reason to accept this view.

All this ties in with what I now know to be the definite *absence* of any institutionalised spirit-medium cult in Humid (and probably in the whole valley). At first I thought they were keeping it secret from me, performing only when I was safely tucked up in bed. But 5½ months of careful clue-gathering has shown that there is no such cult here. Noone's statement— 'normally the Temiar will only sing and dance when they wish to summon their spirit guides to come down and possess them. In addition singing and dancing go together'[2]—is in neither particular borne out in Humid. Here they sing every two or three nights for pleasure only—no dissociation, no formality, and except in jest, no dancing; everyone sits or lies down. They have a well-developed aesthetic of music, and they put a high value on a good performance, being very critical of the performances by other villages that they hear on the Aborigine broadcasts. This last fact strongly suggests that other villages perform much less frequently. Indeed our 'top' singers frequently remark that their frequent performances are for *tareniŋ*

---

2. This quotation actually comes from Robertson's 'foreword' (1955: 1) to the printed version of a broadcast talk by Noone (Appendix 1.4).

(training) purposes—one of many English loan words, presumably from soldiers. They have actually been training me for a performance in some months' time!

Of course, singing has some ritual significance, e.g., the taboo on it during mourning, and the strongly normative moral ideology expressed in the lyrics (the mourning has prevented my properly analyzing these lyrics, but as soon as I can I shall get the recordings transcribed). Although most songs are extemporized, there seems to be a class of traditionally remembered lyrics which everyone knows. These may prove very interesting.

I'm not claiming that there is no ritual, or that they are not afraid of thunder (= Karey, etc., in some contexts) or of the various mishaps befalling taboo-transgressors in the jungle etc. What I do claim is that, far from being the typical 'animists' interpreting everything in terms of supernatural forces that Noone, Skeat and others state them to be, my Temiar view such ritual acts that they do perform as purely technical acts having no reference to supernatural beings/forces.

For example, their taboo on cutting pandanus until the padi has overgrown the felled logs for fear the latter will wither is to them simply one of the purely technical acts that the Malays taught them when introducing them to rice cultivation—it is an essential part of the Gestalt of rice cultivation, and no further explanation or rationalization is felt necessary. It may be a beautiful piece of Frazerian sympathetic magic (one in fact on which he comments—I've got the *Golden Bough* with me, and it's boring me to tears! I just feel it should be read while a 'captive audience'), but the Temiar do not see it that way. There are many taboos of this sort, the transgression of which incurs the automatic penalty of injury or sickness *without* the agency of anything supernatural outside the simple taboo—automatic sanction mechanism. The word for taboo is *tɛnlaaʔ*, the verbal noun of *tɔlaaʔ*, 'to impose a taboo', which takes a human subject and may be transitive; the headman uses it freely of his own actions.

It's interesting that two men who spoke to me in terms of supernatural beliefs were born in different valleys. One talked about disease as stemming from the actions of *ʔɛŋkuuʔ*, and the other clammed up completely when I caught him roasting a snake and asked him about it— one must not utter the snake's name and very few people can or will eat it. (He forbade me to, and a younger man smuggled me some later—it was delicious!) Snakes and tigers do seem to carry a highly-charged aura and their attitude is difficult to figure out—these two species in other Temiar groups are were-animals and spirit-guides, according to some reports. So perhaps there's a lead here. All the same there is a very real problem in explaining the absence of a spirit-medium cult here when all other accounts make it the central feature of Temiar life. A postscript: they tell me that in the days when Kuala Betis was a Malay village the Imam was the great bomoh whom they all went to consult when they felt the need (those that believed, that is!).

Leach's one-paragraph reply to this, dated 15 October 1964, reads as follows:

> It is certainly a pity that your particular Temiar do not seem to engage in Trance mediumship, but scientifically of course it is very interesting that you are able to report this negative fact. If you can later observe trance performances in another valley the comparison should be extremely interesting.

Leach on good and evil in Temiar theology

By 1965, all thought of the Temiars as a people without religion had dissipated. The following material, which presents the first account of the information that fills Chapters 5 and 6 of this volume, comes from a tightly packed and enthusiastic 20-page letter I wrote to Leach on 27 April 1965. This took five days to write, commencing at the JHEOA office at Bertam Baru and completing it, on the edge of the 'field', at the JHEOA-run school at Lambok, where my monthly airdrops were delivered. Leach's reply, which follows the extract from my own letter, was sent off two weeks later.

From my letter (27 April 1965)

In the last letter I mentioned a group of afflictions caused by contacts with certain types of vegetational abnormalities. There now prove to be many categories of these nature–person transgressions. Let me give a few examples, and we'll see if we both come to same conclusion about the underlying principle.

Tɘracɔɔg: caused by contact with or use of the following—ants that build clay houses sticking up from the soil; ants that bury the waste crumbs of our meals; burying a person in clothes belonging to and used by someone else; bamboos whose internodes are water-filled; bamboo or wood that has soil pressed into its ends; throwing any punctured container into the river to allow gravel to enter it; two or more trees or lianas tightly interwoven or fused—etc.

Mamɛɛŋ: severe headache caused by dew (*tɛŋmɛɛŋ*) falling onto one's head from the roof of a house or from a tree.

Tanig: gout-like disease from visiting sharply rising rocky outcrops for the first time.

Gɛnhaaʔ: very difficult to decipher, but I'll try: the removal from a house of objects that customarily belong to that house; carrying a mat from a house rolled over one's shoulder (resembling a wrapped-up corpse) instead of inside a back-basket; a whole group of animals (in which I can discern no zoological regularities) which when killed as meat must be brought into the first house that is passed, shared out to all those who are accustomed to eat it, must not be brought from the house once it has entered, and whose bones, serving bamboos etc. must be burnt up and not thrown below the house onto the ground; the requirement that any visitor be given some refreshment as soon as he enters the house, but not before.

Now in all these (and others) the operative Temiar word is *tɛʔ* 'land, soil, substratum, below, country'. The antithesis, reciprocal of *tɛʔ* is *baliik* 'upper regions, off the ground, sky'. *Tɛʔ* also includes, as normal elements, water, subterranean, aquatic and ground fauna, herbaceous non-woody plants; *baliik* includes trees, arboreal and aerial fauna, houses (always on piles). What these concepts seem to say is '*tɛʔ* is safe, *baliik* is safe, but any "mixing" of *tɛʔ* and *baliik* is dangerous.' Bearing in mind my earlier notes on *hun-tɛʔ* ('disorder, unorganized', which you yourself called 'Nature'), and that houses in villages are always on piles, i.e., are *baliik*, we may say

tɛʔ : *baliik* :: nature : culture

Note further that huts in the jungle are built directly on earth; going hunting during lunar taboos is 'going *hun-tɛʔ*', while the taboo expressly forbids work on housebuilding and swidden, i.e., culture. *Tɛʔ* is merely the unknowable substratum from which grow the ownable crops and on which stand all domestic possessions, all of which are *baliik*. This is only the beginning, I feel. Discussion with an English-speaking Temiar did seem to provoke some recognition in him.[3] But why should it be forbidden to throw seasonal jungle fruits on the fire? Their waste *must* be thrown on the ground—the exact antithesis of *gɛnhaaʔ* meat.

Many months ago you remarked that the Temiar were concerned in a very sophisticated way with the problem of evil. You were right.

Misik: the causing of thunderstorm (= Karey) by any one of a long series of transgressions: pointing at, laughing at or mocking a long list of insects (all of whom are regarded as Karey's *cɔɔʔ* 'familiars', and occur in myths—Talɔk is one of them),[4] many species of birds (many of whom

---

3. This English-speaking Temiar was ʔajɔm, and the conversation in question took place in Kuala Lumpur. Although ʔajɔm is now (2014) a senior citizen among the Temiars of Lambok, he was young at the time and not one of my fieldwork respondents. He had, however, worked as Gérard Diffloth's main linguistic 'informant' on Temiar, and was therefore not unused to answering researchers' questions.
4. By writing 'all of *whom*' (instead of 'all of which') I appear to fallen unwittingly into the animistic framework of the Temiars themselves. This, as noted at several places in this volume, attributes

occur in myth as the agents in the Creation); laying out dyed mats in the sun or in an unoccupied house; using a mirror outdoors or in an unoccupied house in daylight; washing an iron pot in the river; leaving fresh bamboo poles sticking out from the house; pulling a length of fresh rotan into the house; and many many others—any slightly unusual laughter or mockery is apt to be called *misik*, though not formally so.

Joluŋ: during, or for several days after, a séance to leave bamboo jutting from house, pull rotan into house, bring freshly plucked aromatic herbs to house, etc.

The explanations given are: *misik* is anything that attracts Karey's inquisitive attention and threatens to bring him down to earth to take a closer look (which he does by sending down cords~lightning; cf. Evans on shaman's cords) and put men in mortal danger. *Joluŋ* has the effect of frightening away the crowd of *gunig* that surround and protect the village during a séance and for about five days afterwards. Enough has been said earlier to show that Karey = evil (an equation explicitly stated by the Temiar). Now those acts that frighten away the *gunig*-swarm are precisely those that attract Karey; which is the same as saying

$$\text{Karey} : gunig \; :: \; \text{evil} : x, \text{ therefore } x = \text{good}$$

No Temiar has yet succeeded in explaining just how the healing power of the *gunig* works. The difficulty is obviously in finding a concrete Temiar expression for 'healing by the power of unalloyed good'! But their apparently superstitious behaviour shows just what they have in mind.

We can take this further. You will remember that you regarded the mythical ?aluj as being the 'good' antithesis to Karey. What you didn't know is that other myths state quite clearly that ?aluj was the first *halaa?*, that his various *gunig* created all the natural species and elements, and that he himself was the first man to order life according to the now-accepted rules (primarily kinship, which was ?aluj's teaching). Karey for his part was responsible for teaching ?aluj about death, i.e., the destroyer of culture. So our Temiar theology reads so far:

1) ?aluj : Karey   ::   culture : nature   ::   good : evil
2) culture : nature   ::   good : evil   ::   *baliik* : *tɛ?*

That Karey is nature was made more explicit to me when all the ineffables of the Temiar pantheon were whispered to me surreptitiously by one of my best informants. Karey (thunder) appears as the primus inter

---

personhood to natural species. Talɔk had already been discussed by Leach in his analysis of the *Story of Karey*, presented in the next section.

pares of the various apotheoses of Rain, Wind and Fire, all of whom have graded aspects of severity (including Karey, whom I should be calling ʔɛŋkuuʔ in this neutral context), and all of whom are closely interrelated by a 'chain of command' system.

BUT the expected 3) ʔaluj : Karey :: baliik : tɛʔ does not seem to hold. In fact the opposite is stated clearly in myth, and in popular belief—Karey is a non-human sky being; ʔaluj is a human earth-dwelling being. Any ideas?

The 'theologically' relevant point is that neither is believed autochthonous. Both were the creations of the original Creator, Yaaʔ Cɛŋkey 'Grandma Chingkai', which is a real mountain in Perak (Korbu valley), sometimes confused with the Malay 'Tuhan'; surely we can say that Mount Chingkai is both tɛʔ and baliik—hence the reconciliation of Good and Evil in a sophisticated theology. I wonder what abstract ideas would have been played around with in a literate Temiar culture in place of the concrete jungly symbols they are now forced to use. I spent this morning trying to demonstrate to three Temiar schoolboys (English-speaking; and removed from their cultural mainstream at around ten years of age) that all their fathers' superstitions were not as silly as they thought, but that they did after all add up to something quite impressive, both as a sophisticated way of thought and a personally satisfying way of life (for them, not me!).

Leach's reply (10 May 1965)

It is clear from Leach's reply to my 'Any ideas?' that he was actively mulling over—and perhaps still reading—Lévi-Strauss's recent publications, but had not yet made up his mind about them. It appears that it was my own field data, still fresh, that helped him accept Lévi-Strauss's ideas more readily than previously. A few years later, this acceptance (still not without reservation)[5] led to the publication of Leach's short book (1970) on Lévi-Strauss, aimed at the Anglophone world.

I can't sort out all your puzzles, but here are some suggestions. Lévi-Strauss in his recent monumental piece on South American myths called Le Cru et le Cuit (The Raw and the Cooked) claims that the transformation dichotomy raw/cooked is contrasted (in South American myth) with another transformation dichotomy, fresh/putrid. The first is a process under human control, i.e., a product of culture, while the second is process of Nature. The art

---

5. For example, in his interview with Adam Kuper (1986: 86), Leach still expressed misgivings: 'In the later volumes of [Lévi-Strauss's] Mythologiques the manner has become Frazerian. Any evidence will do; it can be drawn from any part of the map. The "structure" is imposed on the evidence; it does not emerge out of the evidence. But I remain fascinated by the great guru's ingenuity!'

of cooking must be elevated into a supreme symbol of the Culture–Nature distinction!

This struck me at the time as rather a fast one, but now you come up with this stuff about waste residue of fresh fruit being thrown on the ground and the wasted residue of meat being thrown on the fire and all these complicated distinctions about being in the house and outside the house—it all seems Lévi-Strauss down to the last word. But as you point out these nice antitheses ultimately run into a contradiction. Good versus evil should also stand for evil versus good. But this also is very Lévi-Straussian. In this new book of his the structure of myth is compared in a most involved way with the structure of music. You will appreciate this much better than I do, but I think I am right in saying that in any serious music the crux of the matter is the point at which the sensitive listener is led to a crisis, a kind of contradiction in which the next note is not what you expect but what you don't expect. This too is fundamental in myth.

One line of logic must lead to the hypothesis that the wild outside is the other world full of dangerous powers where are located the spirits of the dead. This wild outside is in this sense a source of evil. But from another point of view the tame inside is where the living human beings actually reside and suffer misfortune and the other world where things are perfect and which is a source of benefits must also therefore be located in the wild outside. So I did not find it at all surprising that it is in this area that you find the inconsistencies in Temiar myth and ritual. I find it especially interesting that it seems to be almost explicit that everything will be alright if you keep your categories distinct. On the other hand not only do illnesses result from confusing categories, but also the power of the *halaa’* seems to depend on his special abilities in bridging categories. The prototype deity who was the first *halaa’* is a human being who is also a non-human being, and he is an earth-bound creature who can visit the sky.

My reply (8 August 1965)

I replied to this two months later from Rening (Pahang), my final fieldwork site, after spending the previous weeks visiting other Temiar settlements, including some very remote ones, by accompanying Dr Bolton on his monthly helicopter visit.

Your notes about Lévi-Strauss's recent work helped me reduce a few more chunks of Temiar culture to order. The link you noticed, concerning the 'end' of foodstuffs, seems to me in Temiar culture to be strongly parallel to the distinction between burial and exposure as the 'end' of 'normal' and 'abnormal' human beings respectively. 'Abnormal' are great shamans (who have more than the normal complement of souls) *and* stillborn corpses (who have no souls). Thus, roughly speaking, seasonal fruits and cultivated plants, i.e., those that have manikin-like souls, must *not* be burnt but thrown to the ground—burial, *not* exposure. The *gɛnhaaʔ* animals have no humanoid souls, and are 'nature' par excellence—they *must* be burnt, not thrown on the ground = exposure:

$$\frac{\text{culture}}{\text{nature}} \cdot \frac{\text{normal human}}{\text{abnormal human}} \cdot \frac{\text{burial}}{\text{exposure}} \cdot \frac{\text{seasonal fruits,etc}}{\text{wild animals}} \cdot \frac{\textit{baliik}}{\textit{tɛʔ}} \cdot \frac{\text{ownable}}{\text{non-ownable}} \text{ etc.}$$

I've already pointed out how land tenure etc. fits in with this.

Leach on 'The Story of Karey'

To indicate yet further the extent of Leach's involvement with my field reports, I present in this and the next section two sets of myths that Leach commented on in letters to me. First, I present an important cosmogonic myth that I sent him in the early weeks of my fieldwork, which I had freshly translated from a tape recording, followed by his own detailed analysis of the text. In the next section, I then present three further myths that I sent to Leach a few months later, along with his commentary on them.

The mildly obscene trickster tale, 'The Story of Karey', was spoken into my tape recorder by ʔampɔɔh (figure 10.8) in April 1964. It relates to material on the thunder deity Karey presented in Chapters 4–6 and to the stories discussed in Chapter 8. The story figures both Karey and his trickster brother ʔalʉj. (This is the same ʔalʉj who was later to be re-invented as the central mono-god of the new ʔalʉj Sǝlamad religion outlined in Chapter 14.) At the time when I sent the text to Leach, he was studying Lévi-Strauss's newly published studies of South American mythologies: in his letter of 10 May 1965, he remarked enthusiastically, 'I must say that it really does look as if the Temiar could have been invented by Lévi-Strauss!'

Below, I present the English version of the story of Karey that I sent to Leach on 13 June 1964, followed by his response to it. My own (foot)notes and commentary on the story as sent to Leach are also presented. The main purpose is to illustrate Leach's enthusiasm for the materials I was sending him, but it also contributes some new material on Temiar culture. I have updated the orthography of Temiar words throughout, as I had not fully phonemicised the language at that stage. I was not yet a fully competent Temiar-speaker, and therefore relied to some extent on my respondents' translations into Malay of words that needed explaining. Nevertheless, despite what I now recognise as mistranslations (as indicated in the footnotes below), I have otherwise left my 2½-page English version exactly as I sent it to Leach. The explanatory sentences in parentheses were inserted by the interpreter when we went through the text. The footnotes added in this writing are indicated, as elsewhere in the volume, by inserting '[Added 2014]'. Some of these corrections would certainly have led to different responses by Leach, so he should not be blamed for some of the obscurity in his analysis.

The Story of Karey

Ɂalɥj is our ancestor and Karey is our *kɘloo*ʔ ['elder brother'].[6] Karey said to Ɂalɥj, 'Let us all make a house and live together in one village as a single community—we've been living apart.' So said Karey to Ɂalɥj, and Ɂalɥj obeyed him. (Ɂalɥj is our ancestor, but Karey is a wicked man and behaves badly towards us.)[7]

They built the house and when it was finished they moved in. When they finished moving he ordered them to live in separate households. Now they hadn't moved until the millet was cooked[8] and Ɂalɥj had given the word. After moving they ate the millet, and then left the house. At this, Karey took down his blowpipe and heated the inner tube to dry it out. Ɂalɥj's wife was present too, and when he had finished heating the blowpipe he aimed it at her. Whereupon, Karey's son said 'Wah, my father is heating and aiming the blowpipe at my *ʔawaa*ʔ ['parent's younger sister'].[9]

'You're mad', said Karey, 'I'm heating it to go out hunting; what you say is not true—it's bad to have anything to do with one's *mɛn-ʔun-waa*ʔ ['daughter-in-law']'.[10]

But Karey now feared Ɂalɥj, who returned and spoke to him. He moved house because Ɂalɥj told him to. We[11] now lived in separate houses, Ɂalɥj too, because Karey had behaved badly towards his wife. Karey now sat and waited, three, four, five days; and then Karey's wife paid him a visit. (Karey's own wife had grown old and unattractive, and she coughed—so he desired Ɂalɥj's wife.) Ɂalɥj had thought a while, and then ordered his wife, 'Go and ask him for a parang[12] [bush-knife], but deceive him by

---

6. *Kɘloo*ʔ—'classificatory elder sibling'.
7. The portions in parentheses refer to bits not in the original text, but supplied later. An example of the extreme ellipticism that demonstrates that everyone knows the story, and probably many others besides, although they hotly deny it.
8. [Added 2014] This should probably have been translated as 'ripened' rather than 'cooked'.
9. *ʔawaa*ʔ = 'parent's *mɘnɘɘy*'; *mɘnɘɘy* = 'sibling-in-law of opposite sex', a joking relationship with reciprocal terminology. [Added 2014] The basic meaning of *waa*ʔ is 'aunt younger than one's parent', regardless of relative sex (Benjamin 1999: 7).
10. *Mɛn-ʔun-waa*ʔ = 'child's spouse's younger sister', when a man is speaking to his *cacɔ*ʔ 'grandchild'. The relationship is one of avoidance. [Added 2014] Although the principles stated in this note were correct, the details were wrong. The relationship referred to is indeed one of tabooed avoidance, but *mɛn-ʔun-waa*ʔ ('collectivity of parent's younger sisters', a semantically 'plural' expression) is a standard way for a man to refer to his son's wife or her sisters, even in the singular, when speaking to other people (Benjamin 1999: 13). Moreover, as in this instance, *cacɔ*ʔ means 'younger sibling's child' as well as 'grandchild' (Benjamin 1999: 6).
11. 'We'—rather obscure, but possibly an identification of present-day Temiar with Ɂalɥj. [Added 2014] As made clear earlier in this volume, where Ɂalɥj is characterised as the first human, I would now accept this identification as obvious.
12. [Added 2014] I left the Malay word *parang* untranslated, assuming that Leach—who had done fieldwork in Sarawak—would know what it meant. But it means 'bushknife', rather than the 'sword' that he took it to mean in his comments.

pretending to chop up some bamboo. Deceive him.'

So away she went, a rice-bag on her back and leaf-decorations in her hair and ear-lobes. *'Tataaʔ, Tataaʔ*[13] ['old man', a polite term of address],' she cried, 'give me three parangs, give!'

'What are you going to do with them?'

'Oh, I'll coarse-grind them then hone them fine in case they're too blunt for chopping up bamboo.'

He gave her three parangs and down she went with her back-basket to fell some bamboo. And so she felled, *puŋpapuŋpuŋ*, down, down, down, *puŋpapuŋpapuŋ*'

'Ya', said Karey, 'I'm young yet; you women are making a great noise *"bərahəəy bərahag"*; I'll go and join them now.' And he went down and saw very many women. He grabbed and copulated *'hĭhahĭhahĭ'*. 'Ouch, they bite! he cried.

The women each cried out, 'Hey, I've got pubic hair, I've got pubic hair.' He grabbed each one in turn—each one who shouted out he grabbed. (But ants began) spilling out (of his foreskin[14]), and he returned home. Then he saw that his foreskin was gathering to a swelling. It was swelling to a large size, as big as this—as big as this, it swelled. When it had stopped swelling, he thought and said, 'Ya ya, go son,[15] go and tell Ɂalɨj to do something for my foreskin.'

His children[16] set off and came to Ɂalɨj, our ancestor—'What's wrong with father's foreskin? It's swollen and throbs with pain—father's near to death.'

'Spread out a mat near the door and tell your father to lie on it face upwards with his legs spread out; his chest like that.'

His father lay down, legs spread out, and said, 'What's he going to do to me, now that I've lain down?' But nevertheless, he took a mat and slept[17] on it near the door. Then down flew a bird, *titɨy!*,[18] The bird's name

---

13. *Tataaʔ*—literally 'old man', the equivalent of Malay '*tuan*', and the term by which they addressed me before extending kinship terms to me—I'm 'younger sibling' to the headman, and 'elder uncle' to most of the others.

14. The Malay equivalent they gave means 'foreskin', but I have observed the original Temiar word in everyday speech as if it meant 'penis' or 'genitals' rather than 'foreskin'.

15. The text used the word *lɛh* 'wife', but my informants all assured me that in this case it was short for the form *Ɂalɛh* 'son' in the addressive form. [Added 2014] If so, this would have been a case of teknonymy, in which the father or mother of a first-born daughter is addressed as *Balɛh* (Benjamin 1968a: 111). That would leave open here the choice between 'son' or 'daughter'. At this point in the research, I had been in the field for no more than ten weeks and was just beginning to drop Malay in favour of Temiar as the language of daily communication. Accordingly, there was still much room for confusion.

16. Inexplicable change to the plural.

17. [Added 2014] Or perhaps 'lay down'; the same word (*sələg*) does for both meanings.

18. *Titɨy*—an onomatopoeic expressive for flying things swooping down, including helicopters.

was Talək,[19] and he was Karey's *bisat* ['co-parent'].[20] He flew down and grasped the foreskin, which then began to bleed and spill out ants onto the ground. He was afflicted with ants nibbling away his foreskin.

'Oh,' he said, 'I think these ants are really women. Ha ha, that's it—I dreamt it.' (His mind[21]) had deceived him, pretending to dream. So Talək his *bisat* became his *tohaat*,[22] and Ɂɛŋkuu[23] recovered.

-x-x-x-

Note: The whole story was told in an extremely elliptical manner, and much had to be filled in by my translator [giving explanations in Temiar and Malay], although he still professes not to know any stories!

My interpretation as sent to Leach

This sad tale deals with the built-in contradiction of the Temiar *mənəəy* relationship (footnote 9):

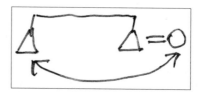

Figure 9.1 Diagram to explain the *mənəəy* relation

This is a joking relationship involving a reciprocal terminology and sexual rights; but it is in contradiction with the ideally good relations between siblings (asymmetrical terminology, *kəloo*[?] (footnote 6) ↔ *pə*[?]). In the story this is 'resolved' by a conceptual split of the *mənəəy* relationship through one generation so that it becomes the strong avoidance relationship of *mɛn-ʔun-waa*[?] (footnote 10), that is between a man and his son's *mənəəy*.[24]

19. *Talək* was described as having no meaning—'just a name'. [Added 2014] Actually, *talək* is the carpenter bee (*Xylocopa* sp.), a large black insect that typically lives in holes that it excavates in house-beams. The translation 'bird' is because the original word (*cɛp*) can be also be used generically for any winged animal, including flying insects.
20. *Bisat*—'child's spouse's parent', reciprocal, irrespective of sex; not classificatory, so far as I can see at present.
21. The word actually used, *hup*, like the Malay '*hati*', means heart or liver, both anatomically and in compound expressions as 'seat of the emotions'. It was supplied as a later explanation, not occurring in the text.
22. *Tohaat*—optional term of address towards a person who cured a disease, etc. My cook uses the term towards (a) his wife's midwife, (b) an old man who cured his wife of some old disease involving the cleaving of intertwined trees (which I'm now investigating), and (c) towards the flying doctor under whose aegis he attended an elementary medical course. Its use does not preclude the use of the regular kinship term also. [Added 2014] The disease referred to is *təracɔɔg*, discussed in Chapter 6. *Tohaat*, as a duplet of Tohan 'God' (and ultimately of Malay *tuan*) is mentioned in Chapters 5–7, 11 and 13.
23. Karey and Ɂɛŋkuu[?] seem to be two aspects of the same 'high god'; Karey is malevolent and associated with thunder; Ɂɛŋkuu[?] is benevolent. But I await further details—others have reported up to four aspects, all named. [Added 2014] See Chapters 4 and 8 for the information gathered later.
24. [Added 2014] As noted, this was overcomplicated: the relation referred to is primarily that between

Structurally, we have

(a) the sibling relationship between Karey and Ɂalʉj is set up through the association {'Temiar'+Ɂalʉj} having Karey as *kɘloo*[?] 'elder sibling'.

(b) Karey points a blowpipe at Ɂalʉj's wife, his *mɘnɘɘy*; this is very likely a Freudian way of saying that he was claiming his traditional sexual rights. But when his son points out the 'strain' that's likely to result,

(c) Karey immediately shifts the relationship with Ɂalʉj's wife by one generation—*ˀawaaˀ* (i.e., 'father's *mɘnɘɘy*') becomes *mɛn-ˀun-waaˀ* ('grandfather's son's *mɘnɘɘy*') (footnote 10). Thus, relative to Karey both his son and Ɂalʉj's wife are pushed down a generation.

(d) This is reinforced by Ɂalʉj's wife calling Karey *tataaˀ* 'one conceptually of an older generation'.

(e) Karey is forced to seek help from Ɂalʉj, thus demonstrating the 'strain' between them. It was Ɂalʉj in the first place who led Karey into trouble by engaging his wife to involve him in a disastrous sexual entanglement.

(f) The bird Talɘk is Karey's *bisat* (footnote 20), and thus becomes conceptually Ɂalʉj's wife's 'father'. Normally *bisat* is a reciprocal, easy-going relationship, but 'strain' has here entered into it. This strain is resolved by a further generational shift in which *bisat* becomes *tohaat* (footnote 22), and hence conceptually a *tataaˀ* (footnote 13) of the ascending generation.

(g) The final resolution is the dénouement that the malevolent Karey becomes healed ('resolved') into the no-longer angry, benevolent Ɂɛŋkuuˀ. All is well again with the moral pointed—'leave other men's wives alone!'

Anyway, that's how I see it! The Temiar say they don't understand the story, so I promised to explain it to them some day—at which they laughed, puzzled.

Leach's reply (undated, but probably late June 1964)

Clearly excited at receiving some completely fresh mythology to work on, Leach omitted most of the expected full stops in his typewritten response, and indulged in a completely irregular use of the space bar. I have therefore, with only partial success, put some order into the punctuation and layout. Leach's wording remains unaltered except for the corrections I have made to the Temiar words and the updated references to the footnotes originally appended to the text I sent Leach.

---

a man and his son's wife, but it would normally also be extended to relations with his son's *mɘnɘɘy* 'wife's sister' (Benjamin 1999: 18).

Comment by E. R. L on the 'Story of Karey' (version June 1964)

I think G. B. has seen a number of key points but there are others. Let us note certain structural features. The inversion of the 'normal' is more thorough than G. B. has recognised. Thus:

Page A. para 1: The two male siblings start living apart and, agree to join up. In normality they would start by living together and then separate. The initiative is taken by the elder brother; in normality?? the initiative would be taken by the younger brother.

Para 2: The cooking of the millet refers ?? to a rite preceding the occupation of a new house but in the myth they cook the millet and leave the house. In real use heat is applied to a blowpipe during manufacture; *not* I suspect as a preparation for use ??.[25] (The aiming of the heated blowpipe at the brother's wife clearly has a direct sexual significance.)

Para 4: Karey accepts orders from his younger brother (inversion of status).

Note effect of this first section is to start with a unitary group of siblings distinguished as 'we' and 'they' and to reaffirm the fact that 'we' and 'they' are related but somehow separate and opposite.

Bottom para: Text may be defective. If not, it is confusing. Whose wife visits Karey? Apparently, in last line anyway, it is the younger brother's wife visiting elder brother. She uses non kinship terms of address … thus implying the possibility of sex relations. But if she had used the kinship term this would also have implied sex relations (see your point (b)). The use of *tataa?* thus seems to emphasise the non-kinship. The groups represented by the sibling brothers are now fully separate.

Page B: Sharpening swords (parangs) is a male job ??? so is cutting down bamboo ???[26]

Footnote 14 says 'foreskin' = penis, presumably by same criteria 'pubic hair' = vagina.

The initial equation is ants = semen (which turns into women).

The younger brother Aluj appears in diviner role.[27]

The instruction is that elder brother Karey shall lie on his back … i.e., the woman's position in normal intercourse. This 'Karey as woman' is then 'raped' by the bird Talɔk who is spouse's parent to Karey.

The significance of this needs further investigation. On what ground is Talɔk rated *bisat* to Karey? As a result of this sexual attack, Karey bleeds at the genitals … another female attribute … and 'gives birth' to ants which are

---

25. [Added 2014] Here, Leach was mistaken. Heating—that is drying—a blowpipe before using it *is* normal practice.

26. [Added 2014] Here also, Leach's guess was incorrect. The sharpening of bushknives and the cutting of bamboo is done by women as well as men.

27. [Added 2014] Although I have written ?eŋkuu? and ?aluj in the transcription of my own materials, I have left Leach's versions, Engku and Aluj, unaltered.

"really women". (Is there a boy's initiation rite which entails mutilation of the penis?)

Note the gloss on *tohaat*, footnote 22. Note also that although Karey is credited with an 'old wife' she does not appear.[28] Karey in fact seems to give birth to women by a kind of schismogenesis and at that point is converted into a relatively benign figure Engku.

The structure seems to be a 'Garden of Eden story' in which the beginning is like this:

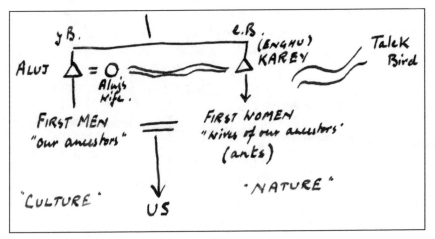

Figure 9.2 Leach's structural analysis of 'The Story of Karey', stage 1
This is Leach's original handwritten diagram.

The persistent inversion of normality might be significant in more than one way, e.g.,

This is a story about spiritual beings and spiritual beings belong to the 'other' world where everything goes backwards.

But the otherness seems to apply especially to Karey-Engku whom G. B. describes as a 'high god' (footnote 23) whereas Aluj is 'our ancestor' … more specifically 'human'.

This otherness of Karey merges him with 'nature' … he is a kind of totemic being in which man and nature are confused … his father-in-law/ sexual assailant is a bird, his daughters are ants. In contrast Aluj has an apparently human wife who only assumes male roles when in association with Karey … note also (footnote 15) where Karey's 'son' is muddled with Karey's 'wife'.[29]

The generation shift/joking relation—avoidance relation to which

---

28. [Added 2014] This mention of Karey's wife was not part of the story as told, but a gloss added later while I was being helped to translate it.
29. [Added 2014] As noted earlier, this was probably not so much a 'muddle' as an instance of regular teknonymy.

G. B. draws attention is certainly there but is complicated by the sexual inversions to which I have drawn attention in this note.

Indeed if we accept G. B.'s analysis we see that Karey really assumed three successive role-positions:

He is elder brother to Aluj and has an 'old wife'.

He is father to Aluj.

He changes sex and is raped by his 'father in law'. In this state he is presumably a generation senior to Aluj. In this capacity he produces women and presumably Aluj's wife is one of these women as indeed the myth itself implies. Page B middle.

Our diagram now assumes a new form:

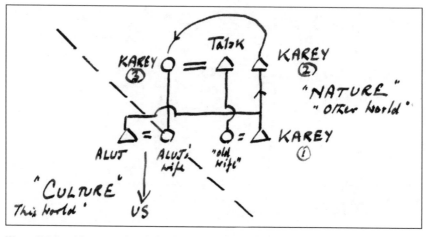

Figure 9.3 Leach's structural analysis of 'The Story of Karey', stage 2
This is Leach's original handwritten diagram.

For what it is worth it will be seen that Talək, in curing 'Karey 3' of his/her 'illness' is acting as a midwife (cf note 14) and perhaps the overall implication is that 'Karey 3' is 'wife' to 'Karey 2' so that 'Karey 3' is the equivalent of 'Karey 1''s old wife so in the words of the myth, last line: "Talək his *bisat* became his *tohaat*". This perhaps seems tortuously ingenious but does fit the record rather well!!!

NB: Birds + Ants are opposed to MEN. But also Birds are opposed to ants (Birds eat ants). Ditto, men have sex relations with women.

We could also turn the diagram round so that "Aluj is husband to the autogenerated daughter of Karey, elder brother of Aluj." This makes the myth a pure example of a Lévi-Straussian origin myth, for according to L. S. one of the 'contradictions' which origin myths are required to solve is the fact that our first parents must necessarily be both of one kind and of different kinds.

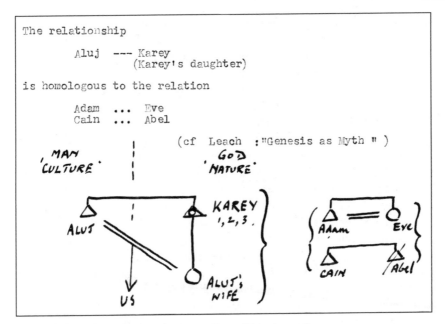

```
The relationship

        Aluj  --- Karey
                  (Karey's daughter)

is homologous to the relation

        Adam   ...   Eve
        Cain   ...   Abel
```

Figure 9.4 Leach's structural analysis of 'The Story of Karey', stage 3
This is Leach's original typed and handwritten diagram.

Leach on three more Temiar stories

I reproduce below the texts of some further stories as sent from the field to Leach on 6 October 1964. Parts of his response to these texts have already been published by Tambiah (2001: 80). Those portions are reproduced more fully here, below the complete texts of the three myths that Leach was commenting on.

I now see that there were some errors of translation in the texts I sent Leach, especially as regards kin-term usages. These caused some of the puzzlement he expressed in his notes, entitled 'Some Lévi-Straussian comments on your myth series'. Nevertheless, my corrections to the story-texts as presented here are limited to the newly added footnotes: the focus here is on Leach's analyses rather than the stories as such. The inserted section-numbers relate to Leach's diagrammatic analysis of the 'Rats' story presented at the end of this section.

The story of ʔɛŋkuuʔ

[1] Listen, I'm going to tell the story of ʔɛŋkuuʔ. Now, they (dual) were making a fish-weir. He [ʔɛŋkuuʔ] followed his *pəʔ* ['younger sibling'] ʔalɨj in making a fish-weir. When they (dual) had finished making it, they returned home—retuned home and slept, 'zzzz...', till morning. They woke early in the morning and went out trapping. They trapped and caught two bamboo-fulls of fish. They returned home and ate the fish after cooking it in bamboo. In this, ʔalɨj followed.

[2] 'Eh, let's fell our swidden!' So they went and felled the swidden, and then left it for ten or twenty days to dry out. Then they burnt it off and planted cassava, sugarcane, bananas, keladi, yams, and sweet-potatoes. When their crops had sprouted, ?aluj ordered, 'Eh, *tɔɔy* ['brother'], let's make a house for ourselves!' (Now ?ɛŋkuu? was the *kɔloo?* ['elder sibling'] and ?aluj the *pɔ?*. Things were well between them—they did not act wickedly towards each other.)

[3] When they had completed the housebuilding they moved into their new house. After they had moved in they had lived in the new house one or two months when some women turned up. There were two women— young women come to marry ?ɛŋkuu? and marry ?aluj. They had been married about two months when they conceived. Karey—eh! no, I mean ?ɛŋkuu?—became expectant [sic!] and so did ?aluj. Now they had many children, ?aluj and ?ɛŋkuu?.

[4] They (plural) had lived there for two years when they felled another swidden, and, as the people had become many, they (plural) built a bigger house, a longhouse. For the third and fourth years their crops sprouted—maize, sweet potato, cassava, bananas, sugarcane. When it was finished, they (plural) pondered. ?ɛŋkuu? thought, 'Eh, let us (dual) move to new land.' So they moved to new land, abandoning the old.

[5] But now Karey arrived on the scene—a wicked person, that. He arrived and sent the two of them, ?ɛŋkuu? and ?aluj, away. (?aluj and Karey are different; ?aluj and ?ɛŋkuu? are different—?aluj is distinct from those two.) He sent ?ɛŋkuu? away, and they (dual) fled, ?ɛŋkuu? [and ?aluj], elsewhere, to another river. And there they (dual) lived well. They (dual) hunted, blowpiped, limed birds, noosed rats, set tree-nooses, set ground nooses, and all was well with them. ?aluj trusted in ?ɛŋkuu?, a man of correct [behaviour]; ?ɛŋkuu? for his part trusted in ?aluj, a good man.

[6] And that's how things were—they lived, whittling blowpipe darts and bird slivers, and repairing their blowpipes. They were correct men. But Karey arrived and behaved wickedly towards them, culpably. He planned to blowpipe them, stab them, chop [their heads off]. Karey is, of course, a wicked person, a fierce person.

[7] Well, they (dual) fled, to another land. ?aluj then pondered to ?ɛŋkuu?, 'Oh, things are not correct with us (dual)—let's make things better and be correct persons. Karey imposes himself on us, chases us away, sends us away—he's not at all proper.' And so, at a time in the past, they fled. ?ɛŋkuu? fled to the sky above, and ?aluj fled to the earth below. That's it. I've told the story of ?ɛŋkuu?

The Origin of Rat(s)

[8] Listen, I'll tell the story of the origin of rats. The mother was a rat, the father a man—the man had slept with the rat, and the rat gave birth. Now,

they [the child-rats] went and stole cassava, the man's cassava. Every single day they would dig it up. The *tataaʔ* ['old man'] used to watch the cassava and say, 'Who's gathering this cassava?—Oh, those from the house across the river!' Well, he thought angrily, 'We [men] will meet and make a trap.' So they scraped lianas and made the trap. They caught twenty rats—a back-basket full. Then they returned home.

[9] The [rat-]mother died, but the father lived on. The father [went to another house, where they invited him —], 'Hey, *tataaʔ*, eat some of this rat-meat!' 'Oh no! I don't care to. Behold, those are my own children. I don't at all care to—they're my own children. And he looked [and thought,] 'Oh, they are my own children from before. And although it's true they stole my food, what can I, their father, do about it? For that is where their origin lies.'

[10] He didn't want anything to do with it, and returned home. He returned and slept till morning. 'I'll return to the house across the river!', he said. So he went and moved to the house of those many people. They married their *paʔ* ['younger sibling'] to him. He had slept with her for ten days to a month when she conceived. She gave birth to two, three, four, five children.

[11] Now that wife died, and they replaced her and married another woman to him. He slept with her and this time had three children. She too died and another woman took her place. The elder [of the house] thought, 'Something's not right about that man—all his wives just die. Things are not at all good with him around. That being so, what shall we do?—We'll kill him!'

[12] And so they killed him by beating him. They beat him until he died. When he had died they moved to another house. They moved and lived there for two, three months. But after three or four months he [the dead man] got up and awoke. He woke, and they saw him—'Eh, he's still alive! What shall we do?—We'll murder him again!' Then they fled to another house. They had lived there for two months when once again he got up and awoke.

[13] 'Eh, what's up? Before, he was dead; now he's awake. So let's blowpipe him ... I'll blowpipe him; yes I'll blowpipe him', [said his *kənuuɲ* 'wife's elder brother']. He died and they fled to another house. But five days later he got up and awoke. 'This isn't right. What shall we [dual, inclusive] do? Ten times he's woken up!' [said the elder]. 'Yaʔ, Ɂatɔw, I'll pay them back for murdering me!' [said the man]. So he went up into the house and hit them, and chopped them *cɛg cɛg*!, until the whole household was finished off. Then he went off in his real form [i.e., as a rat], and ran to join the rats, no longer a human being.

[14] They ate the cassava, and he dug up the sweet potatoes and yams. And so they lived on, until [men] from another house turned up. They

came and asked, 'Who has a fire going on the other side of the river?' 'Yah, it's my fire,' [answered the rat] 'come on over to my house!' They arrived [and asked], 'Where is your sleeping-platform?' 'No, I have no platform—I just live like that [i.e., on the ground].' He thinks 'It's likely that these men will be after killing me.' [And he ordered them,] 'Right, light a big fire, a fire to roast that cassava—light a big fire!'

[15] They were setting about lighting the fire when he grabbed them and cast them onto the fire to roast. They burnt up, and Taaʔ ['old man rat'] ate away until he had eaten them all up. Then their kɔlooʔ ['elder sibling'] started worrying, 'Where have they got to—it's three days since they set off to watch the smoke of that fire wafting upwards and ask "whose fire is that over there?"—Oh so that's where my younger siblings are—over the river! Come on, let's go!'

[16] [He goes and asks,] 'Whose fire is that?' 'Yah, it's my fire!' 'Where are your cacɔʔ ['grandchildren'; 'children of younger sibling']?' 'I don't know.—Eh, Tataaʔ, tell your wife to roast some cassava!' The woman made a fire and set about roasting the cassava. He [the rat] had planned to roast that wife, but her husband grabbed hold of him and beat him with a stick.

[17] 'Well, that's the end of you, you eater of my children!', and he beat him until he had killed him. Then he set light to him and cast him onto the fire, continually piling on firewood and leaves. The fire consumed away, peŋpɔlaŋ, jɛdjɛrlɔɔd,[30] away and upwards. And that was the end of him. Then they returned home. 'Oh, he has eaten my sons, quite without just cause has he eaten them. They were murdered, murdered, and they're dead, dead. But he [the rat] will feel [the consequences]!'

[18] Then they remained for ten days without their children returning, when suddenly in large numbers, they did return from the land downstream. They went out of the house [to meet them]. 'Oh, father, we're still alive!' 'But he ate you.' 'No, he didn't eat us. We were elsewhere.' So they returned home and chatted with their father.

[19] 'Right! Tomorrow, don't go about hun-tɛʔ [i.e., all over the place] as you used to do. Your mother and I worried and mourned for you. We cried for our children.' The old man then thought [and said,] 'That's it! We shall flee!' So they set out and fled to another house, a new house, a big house, a longhouse, a house with ten rooms. They arrived, and had stayed ten days, when their cassava ripened, and they ate it up. When they had eaten [he called out,] ʔalɛh ['(grand)daughter'], beat, beat, I'm going to sing! Beat out a rhythm! Beat, sing! Sing until dawn breaks in the sky!'

[20] They had lived in their large house for about two months when [the father ordered,], 'Sons! (i.e., grandsons!) build another house somewhere

---

30. Ideophones (expressives) for the noise and appearance, respectively, of a quick-burning fire.

else. Build it on a ridge!' They moved to the new house, felled a large swidden, planted cassava, sugarcane and bananas. Two swiddens they felled there at the end to which they had moved.[31] They lived there for two years and then [he again ordered,] 'Let's move again to a different land!'

[21] And so they moved again, to another river. They moved, and lived on that other river for two years. Then they went and moved to another river, where they lived for two years. [Then he said,] 'Let's return to our former house!'

[22] And so they returned to the old house [they had lived in] before. They returned and looked at the bananas and sugarcane. The bananas had ripened on the trees. The cassava would soon give tubers, and the bananas would ripen-in-storage. So they chopped them down and ate them up; dug up the cassava, roasted it, and ate it. They dug up the sugarcane, satisfying their bellies.

[23] They had lived there for two years when the rain started to rain, *cɛʔ cɛʔ cɛʔ*. It rained for two months, and *pəraʔaag*! it flooded them from upstream, it swelled over them and carried away their house. They died. The end.

The Origin of Fish

[24] Listen, I'm going to tell the story of the origin of fish. The old man ordered, *'Tɔw* ['grandson'],[32] cut down some rotan! I want to wicker a fish-basket trap.' The grandson went out to cut down the rotan, and brought it back. And then he [the grandfather] wickered, two traps he wickered. Five days later he ordered his grandson, 'Right! Cut down some rotan!' So he went and cut down some rotan, The grandfather then wickered three traps, and the grandson set them and caught some fish. He returned home and they ate it up.

[25] Then the grandfather wickered ten traps, and the two of them went off straight away to set them. They went far to set them, about two hours upstream. They slept till morning for two nights while trapping [i.e., in the jungle]. Then they returned home to eat the fish, [the grandfather] sharing it out to the grandson and *his* small child and wife, and to his *mensaaw* ['child's spouse'].[33]

[26] Then again they went trapping, the grandfather and grandson, staying for three nights. They caught two bamboos-full of fish, and returned home. 'Grandchild, cook them in bamboo!' So, taking bamboo, they cooked the fish. But when they poured them out they gave rise to

---

31. That is, to a new village-hereditary-area, or *sakaaʔ*, = Malay *pusaka* 'inheritance' etc.
32. [Added 2014] I now suspect that *cacɔʔ* 'grandson' here may be a mistranslation for 'nephew', i.e., younger sibling's son. Similarly, perhaps *mensaaw* (paragraph 28) should be '(male's) younger sister's husband'. These are possible alternative designations for the kin-terms in question, which might fit the story better.
33. Here, *mensaaw* refers to the elder brother of the grandson's wife.

women, young women at that! 'Eh, how can we possibly eat these human beings!'—they did not care to.

[27] But the women took them and settled down there, marrying the grandsons—to each grandson a woman. There were four of those women, and the male grandchildren were four also. And they slept together, *təhad tənaaʔ*.[34]

[28] And so they lived for two or three months. Then the women said, 'Come on! Let's move to father's place with his *mɛnsaaw* ['son-in-law'].' So they set off with their husbands to move house. But when they arrived [the husband exclaimed,] 'Yuh! How can we possibly live here. It's so cold!' So the women descended by themselves, and dived into the water. The men for their part turned back into the jungle, the jungle on the river-bank. For two days they sat there, and then the women appeared, saying, 'Follow us! We're returning to the place of our *mɛn-ɲanʉʔ* ['your parents'[35]]. They returned to the house.

[29] After they had stayed there for ten days they said, 'Come on, *mə-ʔum-beeʔ* ['father-in-law!'],[36] let's be moving house to our father's place—he asked us to last time.' And so they all set off and moved house, '*cɛŋgeew cɛŋgeew*'. When they arrived [the grandfather exclaimed] 'How, my children, can we live with *mɛn-ʔun-kəlamin?*[37] We would surely drown, cold, far down in the depths. Let's leave! Come on, let's go home!'

[30] So they set off and returned home for good. The fish, for their part, returned to the river. But a month later they rose up again and came back to the house. 'How is it that you preferred not to stay in our mother's house last month?' 'Oh, it was your *bələʔ* ['spouse's parent'] who didn't want to. You live in the water, and we're afraid we'd drown and die. We don't know how to live in water. Anyway, you've had your try at being married to us, and we would have been very happy for you to marry us if only you had been *real* human beings. But look, you are fish. It's not fish we want to marry, but women of our own kind. So, return to your own!'

---

34. This was explained as an ideophone (expressive) for 'a house full of couples indulging in intercourse, leaving none unpartnered'. [Added 2014] I now think that this was not an expressive, but an adjectival phrase meaning 'bodies tightly entwined' (*təhad* 'well-fitting'; *tənaaʔ* 'physical body').
35. [Added 2014] *Mɛn-ɲanʉʔ* (literally 'plurality of chiefs'), a woman's third-party reference term for 'husband's father', a tabooed avoidance relation. 'Your fathers' would therefore have been a better translation than 'your parents'.
36. [Added 2014] This is a rapid-speech contraction of *mɛn-ʔun-beeʔ*, which literally means 'plurality of parent's elder brothers'. Clearly, my translation as 'father-in-law' was either incorrect or I was wrong to treat it as a form of direct address. More likely, in this instance, it was an address to their husband's elder brother(s), which is not a tabooed relationship.
37. [Added 2014] In the version I sent Leach, I explained this expression as 'a household containing in-law relationships of more than one generation'. While this would fit the situation in the story, *mɛn-ʔun-kəlamin* 'plurality of they-couples' is more strictly a third-party expression referring to an avoided daughter-in-law.

[31] And they returned, changing into *təŋus*, *dawun* and *kəlah* fish [all edible species]. The real human beings, for their part, returned and settled down to fell swiddens, make ground- and tree-noose traps, make spring traps, set bird-limed fruits, and blowpipe squirrels. And that's the origin of fish. The end.

Leach's analysis

Leach's comments here refer to 'The Story of Karey' as well as the three stories just presented. The text is difficult to read, and completely illegible in places. My copy is a faded product of Leach's notoriously unreliable chemistry-based photocopy machine. As Tambiah (1998: 307) remarks, he 'took pride in displaying his practical skills, and his being a competent mechanic who was way ahead of other academics in using a personal photocopying machine (his students were eager recipients of the acid-smelling notes and queries he liberally distributed)'. I have rescued what I can from the faded parts of the document through digital photographic manipulation and by illuminating it obliquely with lights of various colours. Even so, a few words have resisted decipherment; these are indicated as [...illegible...].

Some Lévi-Straussian comments on your myth series

1. Running through the whole set is the theme that the 'first men' were male not female. This poses the question how do they reproduce without committing incest. The solutions offered are: first women are (a) ants (b) rats (c) fish (d) unspecified females. But in the case of (d) the puzzle is unresolved since it appears that these females are the 'same as' their male spouses ... Engku and Aluj *themselves* seem to become pregnant.

2. The identification of the first women as 'non-human' creatures of Nature seems to be linked with a very ambivalent attitude towards (a) women in general (b) affines. The 'rat' story especially seems to equate 'rats' with witchcraft of a destructive kind. If so there is a direct equivalence here with Kachin ideology where *yu* = affine (*mayu*) = rat = witchcraft. (The logic of this association is that rats work destructively in a mysterious way, destroying the food when it is safely in store or in the ground.)

3. Of these original non-human affines, the fish clearly fall into a normal 'edible' category. Do Temiar really eat either ants or rats?

4. A possible implication of your "Text I: Engku" where the original spouses are as in (d) above, is that the spouses in question are 'the same as' the fish which have been caught and eaten (ingested) in para. 1 of the story. This would make (d) a modified version of (c).

5. As you have observed yourself there is some odd kind of binary antithesis not only between Engku and Aluj as 'sky' and 'earth' but between these two brothers as 'good' and Karey as 'evil' but with a tendency on occasion to elide Engku and Aluj. (This seems to me very interesting, it suggests that the Temiar are concerned with the theological problem of the 'nature of evil' in a quite sophisticated way). On the other hand there is much more to Karey than just that.

Incidentally I see that Skeat and Blagden Vol. 2, p. 737, list both Karei and Engku under 'Thunder'. Vol 2 p. 177 they make Kari (Kare) 'the chief god'. He is the creator but not the creator of the earth and mankind who were separately created by Ple. At Vol.2 p.184 "we find the idea that man at first multiplied so fast as to make the earth too crowded. Kari the Thunder god slays them with his fiery breath and thus reduces the number of mouths to be fed ..." I.e., Karei is the 'origin of Death' rather than the 'origin of life' and this fits with your version.[38] The theological problem is an old one: How can both birth *and* death be 'god given'.

(As you probably know most of the Skeat and Blagden stuff about the myths and beliefs of the 'Semang' comes from writings in German by Hrolf Vaughan-Stevens. When the time comes it will probably be worth checking up on some of this stuff ... for bibliography see Skeat and Blagden Vol.1 pp. xxxviii/xxxix.)

6. At various places in Skeat and Blagden state/argue [?] in effect that 'souls' when dead take the form of birds Skeat and Blagden p.4f. Ditto p.761 gives the word *bisan* as meaning 'woman' or 'bird' [...illegible...] that the 'souls' of the dead especially of dead women become rats or fish or ants etc. Have you managed to unearth anything about an ideology of 'life after death'? A recurrent interchange between bird and human [... illegible...] an animal might make sense. But in that case [...illegible...] if at all aim at [...illegible...]. This might tie in with beliefs that there are specially endowed people of the 'shaman' category who can take the form of animals etc.

7. If you follow the sequence of events in the myth entitled the Origin of Rats distinguishing between those on this side of the river (true men) and those on the other side of the river (rat-men) there is an oscillation (see my diagram [figure 9.5] where the numbers in circles refer to the paragraph numbers of the text you sent me). But the man "A" who is a man at para 8 has by paras 10/11/12 become a *witch* and at para 13 a *rat* "whose home is on the other side." At para 14 he is a (rat)-man who is abnormal in that he sleeps on the ground. But although this rat-man-witch devours the human children at para 15 they return unscathed 'from downstream' at para 18.

Note that between para 10 and para 13 the man 'A' and his opponents change sides ... at para 10 A is a man and his affines

---

38. [Added 2014] Another version of this myth, gathered later than this correspondence with Leach, was presented in Chapter 6.

apparently are rats, but by para 13 the affines are men and A is a rat.

8. The last part of this story from para 19–23 seems to be a myth of origin of a system of shifting cultivation which justifies return to ancient house sites after an interval (because planted crops will be found growing there). It should logically be followed by a 'flood story' … Have you managed to record this?

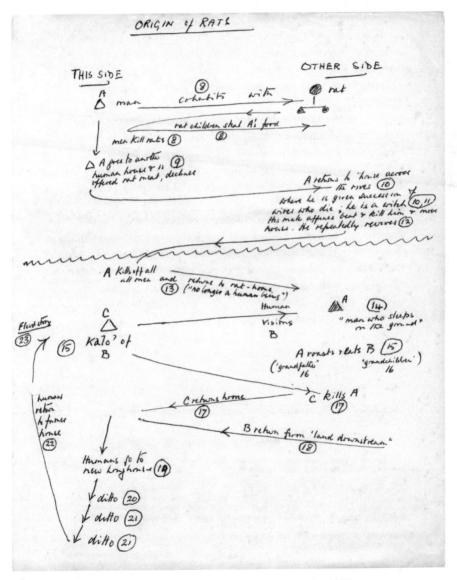

Figure 9.5 Leach's structural analysis of 'The Origin of Rats' (November 1964)
This is Leach's original handwritten diagram.

At this point, Leach added a few further thoughts and recommendations:

> May I repeat here a remark I made earlier: the worth-whileness of making detailed observations of how much children know about kinship etc. and also the value of recording the *mistakes* of children's speech which should be valuable to throwing emphasis upon what are the key distinctive features in the sound patterns.[39]
>
> Other points about the myths:
>
> Just what *is* the relation between Engku and Karey? I notice that even your informants seem to get muddled up and although they say "Aluj and Karey are different; Aluj and Engku are different;—Aluj is different from those two", no one actually says Engku and Karey are different ... Or do they?
>
> Fishing and hunting are represented as especially male occupations. Swidden cultivation is directly associated with living in houses and having wives and children.
>
> On hunting/fishing expeditions elder brother younger brother are shown as cooperative and also grandfather/grandchild but ? not parent child.
>
> Is there any verbal association between 'eating' and 'sexual intercourse'. In the myth, creatures which are eaten turn into women; if these women rate as 'my children' the man cannot eat them or sleep with them, but if they rate as unrelated human beings he cannot eat them but he can sleep with them.

---

39. [Added 2014] This unexpected piece of advice concerning linguistics was probably occasioned by Leach's interest in the work of Roman Jakobson, whose ideas (in simplified form) also influenced Lévi-Strauss in his use of binary opposition as a principle of structural analysis. Jakobson had given a well-attended lecture in Cambridge shortly before I went to Malaysia. Leach's own account of his connection with Jakobson reads as follows (Kuper 1986: 380):

> As is well known, Lévi-Strauss's structuralist thinking was greatly influenced by his contacts with Roman Jakobson in New York during the war. My own interest in linguistics also stemmed from Jakobson but much later. I spent a year at the Center for Advanced Study in the Behavioral Sciences at Palo Alto in 1960–61, when Jakobson and Halle were both there. Jakobson at that time was finishing off his work on distinctive feature theory in phonetics.

Chapter 10

Temiar Mediumship
in Context

In this chapter, I present some general comments on the phenomenology of spirit-mediumship, as well as further accounts and a discussion of Temiar mediumship in particular.

The phenomenology of mediumship

Spirit-mediumship is hard work, requiring time and effort, usually for little material reward. Mediums are therefore often reluctant to take the job on in the first place. Temiars, for example, as noted in Chapter 7, have a special term (*halaaʔ kɛmloop* 'concealed medium') for people who are potential mediums but do not want to be dragged into public mediumistic performance. In many religious traditions, the medium is not valued as such. Instead, it is the possessing spirit that is valued, and the medium is regarded as just an empty vessel. Thus, for mediums to continue their activities, they need to literally *feel* that what they are doing is authentic. This requires both external and internal validation—external validation to ensure that clients accept their mediums, and internal validation to enable the mediums themselves to authenticate their own experience.

External validation is normally achieved through the ritual transfer of spirit-power from an established medium *and* by being a medium's kin-descendent. Either of these factors alone is usually insufficient. In some mediumistic traditions, the initial intimations of authenticity depend on the public validation-through-discussion of the medium's lucid dreamings (dreams in which one supposedly knows one is dreaming), thereby 'proving' that one is both the producer and the experiencer of the dream. There is some slight evidence that lucid-dreaming ability—as opposed to the content of the dreams—might be 'trainable' through positive encouragement. Whether this corresponds to Stewart's later claims about dream 'control' among the Temiars has been examined by several authors, as already discussed in Chapter 2.[1]

---

1. I have had only two seemingly lucid dreams in my life, and they both occurred shortly after G. William Domhoff and I visited Stephen LaBerge's lucid-dreaming laboratory at Stanford University in 1985. I suspect that lucid dreaming is somehow related to the more common experience known in Malay as *tertindeh*: becoming conscious after sleep but not yet able to move one's limbs. This would

External authentication, of new mediums especially, often requires them to put on shows of transcendental power: piercings, playing with hot coal, acrobatics, grossly altered behaviour, and so on. Established mediums, who no longer need to prove themselves, require less of this and may consequently show no apparent sign of 'trance'-like behaviour.

Internal validation, although it has been less studied, is in some respects the more interesting side of the picture. Mediums could hardly continue practising unless they somehow managed to overcome their self-doubt. This they do by employing ritualised actions that engender within them the feeling of simultaneously *acting* (performing as a medium) and being *acted upon* (by a possessing spirit agency). Ritualisation—behavioural canalisation through repetitive stereotypy—is a feature of all religious activity, but it is especially important in mediumship. The automatising repetitiveness of the attendant ritual, whether external or internal, generates a sense that something additional to the performer's own conscious control is at work. A resultant degree of dissociative self-hypnosis usually accompanies such activities, adding to the effect, but it is not obligatory.

External stimuli might include percussion and other repetitive loud noises, such as the Temiars' stamping of bamboo tubes. (In modern circumstances, flashing 'disco' lights might serve the same purpose.) Internally generated stimuli involve a variety of bodily movements, such as juddering, sitting on swings, hyperventilation (through heavy breathing of leaf-switches or in mediumistic 'suckings'), dancing with repetitive movements, and reciting mantras, spells or other stereotyped texts. The latter are particularly effective when in a foreign or non-normal language, which can more easily trip automatically off the tongue. When joined together in a single context, such performances constitute what is usually labelled 'trance'.

Trance, then, is best regarded as a special kind of performance, often dissociative, incorporating the features just mentioned, and undertaken by mediums to convince themselves and others that an outside agency is acting on or through them. It constitutes a 'performance' insofar as the mediums must necessarily retain sufficient control over what they are doing if they are to act in the appropriate manner.[2] Consequently, *complete* dissociation, in which the medium totally loses awareness, is *not* trance; it is usually regarded as an unintended mishap, or even a religious emergency. 'Trance' therefore labels the various culturally established patterns that mediums must actively model their performances on. Consequently, to ask whether a medium is 'really' in trance or to assert that the actions might be 'fake', as observers frequently

---

further link so-called lucidity with the waking dreams in which Temiars can often be heard singing songs that they later ascribe to a spirit-guide. If so, as already suggested in Chapter 2, a distinction should be maintained between such lucid/waking 'dreams' and dreams as conventionally understood.
2. Opinions vary concerning the physiology of 'trance' and whether it constitutes a single identifiable state of consciousness. Whatever the case, it necessarily always involves an element of role-playing performance, which is the relevant issue here.

do, is to miss the point. In this respect, the English word 'trance' misleads. In other languages, including Temiar, mediumistic trance is typically described more directly as 'forgetting' (Temiar *wəl*, Malay *lupa*, Mandarin *wàng*) one's self (*hup, diri, jĭ*).[3] This widely encountered usage implies the entry of another subjectivity into the medium's body or immediate environment. To emphasise this view, mediums sometimes question observers after the event about what they did when they were in trance, indicating that they wish it to be thought that they had been unaware of what happened. It is reasonable to assume that this too is part of the performance.

An example from my own fieldwork illustrates the awareness of his circumstances that a medium retained while performing a trance procedure. In Chapter 7, I showed how the spirit-guide is regarded as the medium's child, and that the medium accordingly addresses people by raising their kinship-term through one generation: 'mother' becomes 'grandmother', 'brother-in-law' becomes 'uncle', and so on. In this way he indicates that it is the spirit-guide's words that people are hearing rather than his own. Normally, this proceeds without breakdown—proof enough that mediums are still consciously aware of their surroundings when in 'trance'. Sometimes, however, an even greater degree of awareness is exhibited, as illustrated in an occurrence I witnessed in 1979 during the séance shown in figures 2.8 and 7.3.

In Temiar, the kin-term *mɛnsaaw* has two different referents: (1) 'child's spouse' and (2) '(female's) younger brother's wife / (male's) younger sister's husband' (Benjamin 1999: 7). This means that *mɛnsaaw* also has two different sets of reciprocals: (1) *bəlɔʔ* 'spouse's parent' and (2) *kənuuɲ* 'wife's elder brother' / *mənɔɔʔ* 'husband's elder sister'. On the occasion in question, I noticed a medium addressing his own daughter's husband, his (type 1) *mɛnsaaw*. From the spirit-guide's standpoint, then, the latter should have been raised to some kind of '(male's) sister's husband'. The question was *which* kind of '(male's) sister's husband' to select, for in Temiar there are two different terms for this relationship: *mənaay* 'elder sister's husband' and *mɛnsaaw (2)* '(male's) younger sister's husband'. When addressed directly, these two kinds of brother-in-law differ in the required second-person pronoun: two men related reciprocally as *mənaay* address each other by the dual-number pronoun *kəʔan* 'you two', while a *mɛnsaaw (2)* and *kənuuɲ* address each other with the plural-number pronoun *ɲɔb* 'you all'.

---

3. The English word 'trance' derives from the Middle French *transir* 'to go beyond', in the sense of leaving normality behind. Several other activities, not usually considered to be trance mediumship, deserve mention here, as they too are aimed at generating through ritual the feeling that some spirit-agency is acting upon the performer. Christian 'speaking in tongues'—as the onomatopoeic term glosso*lalia* denotes—involves letting the tongue flap rhythmically, so that it modulates what is otherwise normal speech. Its practitioners, however, portray it as a special language spoken by the possessing Holy Spirit. The *dzikir* chanting of Sufi Muslims (in which they rock back and forth and make repetitive hand movements) and the whirling of Sufi dervishes are interpreted by the adherents as the immanent experience of an otherwise all-too transcendental God. The individual rocking back and forth in prayer by Orthodox Jews and Sufi Muslims serves a similar purpose, though they would not usually describe it in that way.

In the event, the medium addressed his actual son-in-law as *kə²an* 'you two', implying that his spirit-guide was now addressing him as 'elder sister's husband'. If, however, the medium had addressed him as 'younger sister's husband', the pronoun would have been *ɲɔb* 'you all'. But the pronoun would have remained *ɲɔb* even if the medium had *not* bothered to 'raise' the kin-term by a generation, for that is also the pronoun used between father-in-law and son-in-law. If the medium had employed *ɲɔb*, therefore, there would have been no apparent 'raising' of the kin-term, and hence no indication that it was the medium's spirit-guide rather than the medium himself who was purportedly speaking. By choosing the second-person-dual option, *kə²an*, the medium showed that although he was ostensibly in trance he still remained aware of his surroundings and how he should act.

Temiar mediumship as a theory of other minds[4]

So far, I have paid little attention to the wider context in which these activities take place. This too is a key element in generating the sense of authenticity essential for the continued practice of mediumship, but the details differ. Given the nature of the physical environment in which Temiar culture developed (figure 10.1), it is not surprising that plant and animal imagery plays an important part in their animistic worldview. Of particular salience, as noted in previous chapters, are the seasonal fruit-trees (such as rambutan and durian) scattered throughout the forest, and the tiger—the other animal besides human beings sitting atop the chain of predation. As illustrated in figures 2.2 and 10.2–10.5, Temiar material culture is, or was until recently, almost entirely plant-based. As is typical of many Southeast Asian cultural traditions (cf. Fox 1971), the Temiar way of talking about the world is accordingly mapped largely onto plant-based imagery.

Given the pervasive dialectic that underpins the Temiar worldview, plants and animals are thought to partake in this animistic interplay as fully as human beings do. Plants, animals and mountains, for example, are thought of as animated by the same kinds of subjectivity as human beings. As Roseman (1990: 231) puts it, 'all entities within the Temiar world are potentially *bə-sɛn²ɔɔy*, "having person", capable of becoming animated'. Several examples, including Galɛɛŋ mountain (figure 8.1), have been mentioned in earlier chapters. (For a fuller account of Galɛɛŋ as a Temiar spirit-mountain, see Roseman (2007).)

---

4. 'Theory of mind' is the established terminology. But, as the philosopher Daniel Dennett (2013) has pointed out, this is not strictly a *theory*—and, in any case, we do not need a theory in order to act. Dennett offers instead the phrase 'the intentional stance' to refer to the attributing of feelings, memories and beliefs to others as well as mindreading and predicting what someone will do next. It is in this sense that the attitude I am referring to here should be understood.

Figure 10.1 Aerial view along the Humid valley (1964), with the village near the river-mouth

The manner in which Temiars have responded to this imagery in their mediumship provides clues to their embedded theory of mind. As we have seen, they think of the intersubjective communication between themselves and their spirit-guides (*gunig*) as a mutually balanced two-way undertaking. As humans, they can communicate most successfully with something to which—for the moment of communication at least—they ascribe a human-like subjectivity. It is therefore appropriate that the Temiars should report that their (upper-body) spirit-guides take human form in dreams and trance performances, even though they are acknowledged at the same time to be plants, animals or mountains. In this respect, they are following the anthropomorphising pattern found in practical religion all over the world. What is unusual, however, is that the Temiars seem simultaneously to be taking the spirits' point of view. When trancing plant-spirits—their usual religious activity—they treat the

Figure 10.2 Detail of old-style Temiar house, Mengrod (Mɛnrɔɔd), Kelantan (2006)
The construction is entirely of plant-derived materials: wood, bamboo and cane.

Figure 10.3 Séance at Lambok (1979), showing the extensive use of plant materials, both as ceremonial garb and in the *tənamuuʔ* spirit-receiving wreath.

plants' subjectivities with as much consideration as they do their own, by decking themselves and their trancing spaces as virtual plants, in order to welcome their plant-derived spirit-guides into the house. And since the forest is also the environment of the animal- and mountain-spirits, dressing as plants should work just as well with them.

Figure 10.3, a photograph of a mediumistic performance, was taken at a séance at Lambok, Kelantan, in 1979, as was figure 2.8. What stands out is the way in which the Temiars dressed themselves and decorated the specially built house to welcome the spirit-guides. So much plant material was used that they had turned the house into a virtual forest and themselves into virtual trees. My fieldnotes on the occasion read as follows (with explanatory glosses inserted between brackets):

> **6 February 1979:** Last night there was a *pɛhnɔɔh* [trance session] at Tərolɔəh to celebrate the breaking of a taboo period after a child there had been cured of *rɛywaay*. The house was very traditionally decorated, with several rows of herbs hanging down, and a low-slung *tənamuu*ʔ [wreath to receive the spirit-guides]. The shaman was ʔaluŋ, Malam's *bəlɔ*ʔ [father-in-law] and it was a *kahyɛk* [watery spirit-from-above] performance. He frequently engaged his own *tɛmpɔɔ*ʔ [plaited crown] with the *tənamuu*ʔ, and also held onto it with his hands—an old general custom according to Dalam [the headman]; he was grasping the *pərɛɲjɛɛn* [the threads down which the spirit-guide arrives]. The *gunig* [spirit-guide] was *buŋaa*ʔ *tambus*, a flower planted in the village, and also *ɲɔɔr* [coconut] and *tərakɔ̃l* [monitor lizard]. The first two were *kahyɛk*, *num-baliik* [from above]. The *tərakɔ̃l* was in the form of a *talii*ʔ [cord] also from the *tənamuu*ʔ. It took the form of a *tərakɔ̃l* (not a tiger or human), and it was the *rəwaay* [head-soul] of the *tərakɔ̃l* that he *pɔɔh*'d [tranced].
>
> Later I saw him squeeze water from *boot carak* [*carak* flower] onto the child. ʔabur's mother said the water was ʔɔɔk *buŋaa*ʔ [flower water] from the *lisap* [monsoonal rain] that had been falling all day. Anyway, everything in the ceremony was symbolically clear for once: real water, real contact with the *tənamuu*ʔ.

Figures 10.4 and 10.5 show Abilem Lum performing in serious mode at the Cultural Centre of the University of Malaya in July 1995, as part of a series of educational sessions organised by Marina Roseman. (Abilem Lum, who has since died, was a significant source of information to both Jennings and Roseman.) These too illustrate that the vegetal basis of Temiar ritual performance must be maintained even when performing outside the forested area. Making further use of plant material, a special wreath or series of wreaths is suspended from the roof as the 'guest place' (*tənamuu*ʔ) for the spirits to land on. This can be made of shredded pandanus leaves (figures 10.4, 10.5), sweet-smelling herbs, or brightly coloured flowers (figure 10.6).

Nowadays, *tənamuu*ʔ-style decorations are also employed on non-religious occasions, as at the preparations for a wedding celebration shown in figure 10.7, at which the night-time music was to be supplied by a Temiar pop-group rather than a more traditional bamboo-stamping chorus. Much effort goes into

Figure 10.4 Abilem Lum and his fellow villagers at the University of Malaya (1995)

Figure 10.5 *Tənamuuʔ*, University of Malaya (1995)

Figure 10.6 Close-up view of *Tənamuuʔ*, Mengrood (Mɛnrɔɔd), Kelantan (2006)

Figure 10.7 *Tənamuuʔ*, Sɛŋsaaŋ, near Fort Brooke, Kelantan (2006)

the preparation of these plant-based decorations, and they are never disposed of until they have withered naturally many days later.

The healing benefit of *pɛhnɔɔh* séances

I have little to add to the detailed studies of the healing aspects of Temiar mediumship already published by Roseman and Jennings: their observations and explanations accord very closely with my own. Here, however, to exemplify the psychological relief generated by a successful *pɛhnɔɔh* séance, I present my fieldnotes on the first session of a two-night *tərɛnpuk tɛnmɔɔh* 'mourning cessation' ceremony held in Humid on 29 October 1964 and already outlined in Chapter 6. This marked the end of the mourning period for the baby whose death and burial is reported in Appendix 3.1. The key people in this account are: Malam and Pəleman, respectively the deceased baby's father and mother; Pəleman's sister Abong (ʔabɔŋ) and her husband Salleh; the main celebrant ʔajam;[5] and the headman, Dalam. The other people mentioned are less central to the account, but their names are given to indicate the intensely communal character of the situation.

After observing the many preparations for the night's performance, including the gathering and hunting of food and decorating of the longhouse, I wrote as follows:

> On returning at dusk I find everything cleared away and Salleh sweeping the floor. Dalam explains with a mixture of pride and cynicism that the singing will start in complete darkness—*ʔadad kanɛɛʔ* 'our custom'—and then the fires will be raised.
>
> A line had been stretched across the house and on it were hung six men's and seven women's sarongs, which Malam had bought in Gua Musang. Dalam explained that they were for the singers. The others would not receive any (although he suggested that some return may be made to those who gave grave goods).
>
> Salleh arranged two logs at right angles with seven bamboo beaters at the ready. The women were called to take their places: ʔajam's wife, Lɛmbeʔ, Jəmuuʔ's wife, ʔacɔb, ʔawããs. The men—ʔajam, Jəmuuʔ, ʔayaaw, ʔasuy, Səradiih, Rotiih—sat themselves inside the logs. Pəleman and ʔabɔŋ did not join the singing. Dalam remarked that the singing is by *sɛnʔɔɔy mɔy* ('other people') only [those not directly related to the deceased].
>
> The lights were all extinguished, and ʔajam's wife started beating and ʔajam singing. The song lasted about half an hour. Halfway through someone started blowing ritually, and with whooping ran off to ʔandɔʔ's

---

5. ʔajam is the man wearing a sarong in figure 2.2.

fireplace. It sounded like ?ayaaw—but he was in the centre when the lights went up. Pɔleman could be heard crying violently and beating the floor. The singers however found time to laugh. At the end of the first song the lights were slowly raised and the second song started.

Salleh then went round ceremonially distributing the sarongs, tying the first one, a flower-on-red, as a headpiece on ?ajam's head while he was singing. Then he and ?andɔ? distributed the others, laying them on the singers' shoulders. ?awããs had meanwhile brought in the cosmetic tray and Lɛmbe? painted the faces of ?ajam, Jɔmuu? and Rotiih with the dye. ?ajam then placed *taɲjok* flowers in his hair, stood up still singing, and beckoned everyone to gather round, including the mourners. He then danced around slowly waving his new sarong over the heads of all as if in blessing.

He then squats, and stands up again and, still singing, 'blows' onto the ear and head of Pɔleman, Malam, Salleh. Then after a pause, on the head of Dalam's wife ?ahɔɔd (Dalam remaining on his own threshold), running his hand over her chest and clucking his tongue. Then he did the same on baby ?asɔɔd lying in ?ahɔɔd's lap. The text seemed to be a set of imprecations beginning *jaɲan...* ('let not...'). ?ahɔɔd then returned to her compartment with ?asɔɔd. ?ajam's wife complained that she couldn't hear the text so as to follow his singing, when he was bent over Pɔleman.

Pɔleman, after a short retirement in her room, went with ?agɛŋ, her young daughter, to the upper fireplace. Some of the men began anointing each other with hair oil and placing ceremonially folded new sarongs decorated with herbs from the cosmetics tray on top. The men take tobacco from a big pile in the middle and smoke. Rotiih was combing his hair in the mirror he had just brought in. Then he rubbed oil into Jɔmuu?'s hair.

?aŋah and ?adɔn then arrived from the bottom edge of the house.

Dalam urges *ɲɔm-kɛrjɛɛr ?adeh; ɲɔm-cacii? bɛ?boo?, taa? nam-nɛɛh!* ('Dance the *kɛrjɛɛr*; you women, dance the *cacii?* for Taa? [me] to see!'). But there was no dancing.

Rotiih then sings, but this time amidst general mirth, beginning with the same lyric as ?ajam: *nam-bukaa? jɔrɛŋkaaŋ, nam-yah baliik, num-rɛh ma-doh* ('Let the dawn break, let morning appear in the sky, from downstream to here'). Dalam explains—'after this set formula the singer goes on *hun-tɛ?* (without order)'.

Jɔmuu? sang next, then ?ajam again. Salleh could be heard blowing strongly in his part of the house. Dalam said ?abur (Salleh's son) was a bit ill. Siluŋ eventually came in from the lower end of the house. Dalam refers to ?ajam's song as *sah kanɛɛ? ?anuh* ('authentically ours here')—a traditional Perolak song. The singing eventually loosened and became a normal *gɔnabag* song-session, with the normal motif [a triplet figure that I notated musically] playing a part.

The ceremony ended at daylight, around 6.30am with ʔajam standing up to *gabag baliik* ('sing upwards/to the sky'). Then he led the women out of the upper door, still beating (*təb*) their bamboos on the ground along the central village area to the jackfruit tree. ʔaboŋ meanwhile had heated three bamboos of water and brought them outside to the singers, who then bathed their faces with it. Then they all smashed the bamboos and threw them away—both the beaters and the warm-water containers, men and women—after ʔajam had sung for the last time *bukaaʔ jərɛŋkaaŋ, həj nam-yah, lah ʔɛ-mɛʔmaaʔ!* 'open the dawn, morning has broken, let's go home!' This took place in some mirth.

Returning to the house around 10.00am I found several people sleeping, some back at work, and nearly all humming tunes as if in anticipation of tonight's *gənabag*. ʔahəəd and Pəleman returned from foraging, the latter with lipstick, laughing uproariously—the load of sorrow seems to have lifted. Most were still in festive dress, and wearing bead-bandoliers which I didn't see last night.

Thus, the night's singing and trancing successfully lifted the mourners' depression, and enabled them to return, happier, to the normal round of daily life. Feasting and music are reliable means of healing sadness, but in this instance the intense involvement of the whole community in the process was, I suspect, even more important. Sessions of this sort do not necessarily require a crisis before they take place. As an example, I present below my account of a *pɛhnəəh* séance that took place in the same house in Humid a few weeks later, on 22 December 1964.

I suspect, but cannot be sure, that the real purpose of this session was to allow Penghulu Dalam to make amends for having previously told me that he didn't believe in spirits or the afterlife, and that no trancing ever took place in Humid. By then I had visited many more Temiar settlements, and in particular I had been put right about Temiar religious practices by Penghulu Hitam Tamboh in his highland village at the top end of the Perolak valley. A significant feature of the séance in question is that it illustrated three different degrees of mediumistic involvement. Dalam himself was serious, but not as practised as the others, and found it hard to draw his *gunig* into the proceedings. ʔampəəh was very practised, and had no difficulty. Ali (ʔaliih) was altogether less serious and less controlled. In this respect, he seems to have remained this way when Jennings (1995: 110) met up with him as a 'minor shaman' several years later.

My detailed notes on this singing (*gənabag*) and trancing (*pɛhnəəh*) session read as follows:

During the day there was talk of a séance during the evening. Ali went off early on Dalam's orders to fetch *boot* [flowers and decorative leaves].

ʔabɔŋ and Pəleman about 16.30pm, started preparing the leaves: first they were making zigzag cuts about one-third of the way down the leaves of unopened fronds of *kəwaar* to form a sort of fan. The cuts were made with a small sharp knife. Further slips were separated and woven into *tempɔɔʔ* crowns by *bɛnyɛr* ('interweaving') work, and the zigzags inserted to form the crown.

The performance began about 20.00pm with only a few lamps on. Ali and Salleh mainly led the singing. Activity was centred on the lower part of the house leaving the upper part empty. Dalam started singing, and eventually beat time with his *kəwaar* whisk; this changed into a haphazard fanning in front of his nose, with occasional flicks over his shoulder and back of the neck. It took him a good half-hour to get into a light trance—he seemed to be trying hard even to do that. It wasn't clear what *gunig* he had succeeded in calling up. He soon disappeared into ʔandaʔ's compartment and could be heard performing a *tɛnhool* blowing. He later explained she has *bɛdlɑɑd* ('needle-like pain in the chest caused by *pacɔg*') and *tɛnyɔr* ('headache').

While in trance he called me *ʔaɲuʔ* ('parent's younger brother'), and after asking me for a cigarette then threw it away as a *rokoʔ kədey* ('shop-bought cigarette'). Then he remarked *in Malay* that it was 'really very far away'—presumably referring to the *gunig* he had called up. There was a fair amount of shouted audience participation—exhortations to come back from 'afar' and call up nearby *gunig* only. Then Dalam was urged to *taaw* ('come down') or *maaʔ* ('come home')—return to normal. This he did quite soon, with sudden jumps and shudders. Throughout the performance he spoke in a higher voice than usual. Salleh had taken over the singing at the beginning of the trance. While in trance, Dalam asked me *ʔaɲuʔ, num-lɔɔʔ deek hah?* 'Uncle, where's your home?', to which the others replied *num-tuuy, num-ʔiŋlɛn* 'from far away, from England'.

Then Ali, who had been slowly working up into a trance by violent dancing, seemed to call up several relatives—*yaaʔ, yaak* ('grandfather, grandmother'), and towards the end he shouted several times *Səlamad ʔakooc!* ('Greetings, Father's elder brother'). While in trance, he performed a *tɛnhool* blowing on ʔandaʔ, ʔabɔŋ and Pəleman—the two latter were singing right through the procedure. Ali called me *yaak* ('Grandfather') several times while in trance. Both he and Dalam seemed merely tipsy—and several people remarked '*jɛhwah* (playing around, joking)'.

ʔampɔɔh came to the centre and started singing after Ali was in trance and just before Dalam came out. He went into trance sooner than the others, but with much less waving of his *kəwaar* whisk. He seemed to breathe deeply with the *kəwaar* right on his nose; then he would slowly brush it all over his head. He gave the most violent starts of all, and seemed to alternate stillness with strong dancing. He too performed a *tɛnhool* blowing on ʔanda^ʔ and also on his wife ʔajɛɛh, who Dalam explained had a cold. Then he returned, and standing over Pəleman very concentratedly squeezed his *kəwaar* towards the tip, as if expressing a liquid onto Pəleman's head; then he *təhool*'d her. He repeated the performance for ʔabɔŋ. When I asked, Dalam explained that they weren't ill—ʔampɔɔh was doing it as a sort of payment for their having made the *tɛmpɔɔ^ʔ* crowns, ornamental flowers for the waist, and *kəwaar* whisks.

ʔampɔɔh continued in trance for some time. During his trance he asked several times who the stranger—myself—was. ʔandɔ^ʔ and Dalam explained loudly as if to a child that I was *təwan ^ʔɛɛ^ʔ; nam-nɛhnɛɛh pɛhnɔɔh ^ʔɛh* 'our tuan; he wants to watch our trancing'.

The whole performance, from Dalam's first trance to Ali's sudden waking and throwing away of the *kəwaar*, took about one-and-a-half hours. At the end, Dalam proclaimed that this has been a 'small séance' and that tomorrow *^ʔɛm-pɔɔh rayaa^ʔ* 'we'll trance big'. [This form of 'we' included me.] Singing went on normally for a couple of hours afterwards. Other points that I noticed:

- The singing was not allowed to flag but was handed on, mainly between Salleh, Dərin, Ali and Dalam.
- While in trance all three seemed to insist on smoking.
- There was much joking by the audience at the antics of the trancers— rather as people encourage tipsy friends at a party.
- Dissociation seemed very slight—except perhaps with ʔampɔɔh. They all avoided obstacles, although they made stumbling movements.
- It seemed essential to them to move aimlessly about, especially backwards.
- Salleh started waving his *kəwaar* whisk as if to trance, but did not proceed with it.
- Most people came up especially to watch, except Malam and ʔabur, who went to sleep after an initial look, to his father Salleh's surprise.
- Dərin brought a large lump of glowing wood from the fire right up to ʔampɔɔh's chest while in a trance, as if to tempt him to touch it. I couldn't see if he did so.

Several points emerge from this description. First, in the terms outlined earlier, the occasion was clearly a *performance*: the trancers knew what they were doing, and remained aware of their circumstances throughout. Second, Dalam's addressing me in Malay while in trance—he normally spoke to me in Temiar—implies that his possessing *gunig* at that moment was a purportedly Malay spirit. Given Dalam's historical connections with the Kuala Betis area, that would not be surprising. Third, the occasion involved healing, *gunig-*

relations and entertainment—all treated as completely compatible with each other. Presumably, any one of these purposes alone would be a sufficient reason for holding a *gənabag* song-session, which accordingly may or may not actually involve spirit-guides.

Tiger-mediumship

In the preceding paragraphs I have discussed the occasions on which mediumistic séances are directed towards upper-body spirit-guides of the *kahyɛk* type. As we have seen, these are mostly plant-derived. But the same concern for intersubjectivity also marks the far less frequent occasions when a lower-body spirit is welcomed in tiger form, as described in Chapter 7. These performances (usually known as *pɛhnɔɔh kəbut* 'séancing in the dark') take place with fires dimmed, with the medium sitting inside a specially constructed palm-leaf hut set up inside the house, singing melodies in a distinctly 'minor' musical mode and low tessitura. Prototypically, such a spirit-medium is regarded as a *halaaʔ rayaaʔ* or 'great medium', but I have heard reports of lesser mediums also performing in this manner. (Unfortunately, I have no photographs illustrating this, nor have any been published elsewhere to my knowledge.) The arrival of the tiger-spirit is indicated by the medium's scratchings and growlings, which is sometimes described as his transforming (*lãã̃s*) into a tiger. This suggests that the actions also serve to encourage the tiger-spirit's attention, by behaving in the way that a tiger might be expected to respond to peaceably.

I obtained accounts from different valleys of what supposedly was happening during a tiger-mediumship séance. These vary in a few details but agree in their main features. In June 1965, while making my second visit to the Brok valley upstream and downstream from Fort Brooke, I held detailed discussions on Temiar religious life with Josh (Jɔs), an unusually well-travelled Temiar. He was originally from the Plus valley in Perak, but was now mostly settled in Kelantan. (Decades later, in 2006, I met him again briefly at the historic Temiar settlement of Jalong in the Korbu valley, Perak.) Josh's account overlaps to some extent with what has already been presented in earlier chapters, while offering many details that I have not yet covered. By mid-1965 I had finally gained some familiarity with Temiar religious life and was therefore able to interview him in a focused manner.

Josh told me that *all* spirit-guides that emerge from below (*gunig num-tɛʔ* 'gunigs from-ground') did so in the form of a tiger; even a pig-spirit would appear as a tiger. The only exception to this was with spirits that originated from Malay territory or whose ritual treatment followed a Malay pattern, as with the Səlumbaŋ cult. Tiger spirits do not emerge wholly, but by extending their cords (*taliiʔ*) to the medium from across the river or from a hillside. (If such a tiger arrived in complete form, it would devour the inhabitants just like any other tiger.) The tiger's cords cause the medium to *lããs* 'transform', which I understood in this context to mean that he took on the tiger's behaviour rather than its bodily shape. Tiger séances must take place in the dark, hence the use of the *kəbut* hut to decrease the chance of dangerous light causing a transformed medium to startle (*kəjɨd*) and die. However, Josh stated that employing a hut was optional; it was the darkness that was obligatory. The whole session takes place without dancing and with the people seated quietly. Flowers (*boot*) are laid out on mats and, before departing at the end of the séance, a great medium's tiger will consume these by a process of *jərɛnbɔɔt*— direct absorption through its extended cords. In the case of a great medium (such as Taaʔ ʔamaaw, discussed in Chapter 7), these flowers and even the mat will be seen to have disappeared when the lights go up.

In contrast to the frequent use of direct *pərɛnlɨb* blowing to transmit a *kahyɛk* spirit-from-above from one person to another, this process is employed with a tiger-spirit *only* when handing it on to a designated great-medium successor. The process is then thought of as being effected by the tiger-claws that supposedly emerge within a pool of liquid in the medium's hand. If the recipient should consequently display actively dissociated behaviour (*kərook*), this is regarded as dangerous. Similarly, it is strictly forbidden for the medium to spray (*caaw*) the water over the participants, as is commonly done in a *kahyɛk* session. During a *pɛhnɔɔh* session, the tiger part of the proceedings must be carried out first. The *kahyɛk* part can commence only after the tiger has returned to its forest abode or to its *kənoruk* and *sarak* lairs (Chapters 2, 6 and 7). If the lights are raised during such a séance, it causes *joluŋ*, allowing the tiger to observe the various bright objects in the house, and so depart. In any case, unlike *kahyɛk* spirits, tiger spirits are thought not to hang around the house for several days afterwards.

A later account (March 1968), gathered in another valley (the Betis– Perolak system) from Wakil ʔabaaɲ, amplified some of these details. He said that tiger-based trancing in the dark is carried out not for curing, but because the spirit-tigers themselves ask their 'father'-medium to allow them to visit him, so that they may enjoy the special treats—flowers and special saps to drink—prepared by the villagers. The tiger-spirits inform the medium of their wishes in a dream, which leads him to hold a *kəbut*–type séance about once a month. To do so more frequently than this, however, is dangerous, as it is thought likely to attract 'other' tigers to the house. (The arrival of such unwanted tigers can also be precipitated by instances of 'blood *misik*', such as cutting one's finger while eating, or squashing lice or leeches in the house.) When this happens the medium's spirit-tigers are thought to act collectively in guarding the village against the approach of 'other' tigers, from whom the spirit-tigers keep secret their special relationship to the world of humans. Through the medium's dreams, the spirit-tigers warn the villagers of trouble in the broader tiger world, allowing the medium to tell the people to stay at home and keep away from danger. If, however, insufficient attention is paid to the spirit-tigers' desires by not welcoming them to séances often enough, this protective quality will be lost. Should that happen, they will flee elsewhere and become a danger to people in other villages.

Wakil said that the power of a great medium stretches only over two or three villages, even though in principle there is supposed to be only one great medium per river. Indeed, in 1965, Josh had given me a list of the sole great mediums who were operating in each of several named valleys. Each of these *halaaʔ rayaaʔ* was regarded as the successor to the earlier one, from whom he had received 'a portion of his tiger-spirit' (*ʔɛn-suk gunig ʔəh*) by *pərɛnlub* blowings, as described above. I present Josh's list here (table 10.1) for both its ethnographic and historical value. Note that knowledge of these great mediums had spread beyond their own valleys, and sometimes even beyond the boundaries of Temiar country.

Wakil gave me a description of how the special darkened tiger-séances are (or perhaps *should* be) performed. As noted below, his account differs in

Table 10.1 The great mediums (*halaaʔ rayaaʔ*) of the southern Temiar valleys, according to Josh (at Jɛgjɔg, Brok valley, Kelantan, June 1965)

River valley(s)	Name, Village	Remarks
Brok (between Belatop and Mering)	Taaʔ ʔabaaɲ, Jɛlgəək	Still increasing his *gunig*s after *pərɛnlub* by Taaʔ Paŋgan of ʔɛmpeed, who was a 'self'-*halaaʔ*.
Ber	Busuuh ʔegiʔ, Səraaw	A mature great *halaaʔ*. He was *perlub*'d by Taaʔ ʔamaaw (below), before which the Ber people trusted in the Perolak valley for access to a great medium.
Perolak	Rɛmʔum	Still increasing his *halaaʔ* powers, received from his own father, Taaʔ ʔamaaw.[1] ʔamaaw in turn received his from Taaʔ Jan, a Jahai from Dɛntɛɛs who lived and died at Jak. Jan *pɔɔh*'d in Jahai fashion in a ground *kəbut*, but ʔamaaw asked him to change this and *pɔɔh* inside the house for fear he would be eaten by *gunig*.
Betis	Taaʔ Pəlodɛɛw, Təluur	A Jahai from Boboŋ, married into the Betis valley. He *pɔɔh*'s Jahai fashion on the ground. Before that, the Betis people went to ʔamaaw (above).
Perias, Yai, Panes	—	Each of these valleys has one great medium (unnamed).
Plus	Taaʔ Bɔŋ	Their former great medium.

1. Josh said that he had dreamt during my previous visit to the Brok valley that Malam, with whom I was travelling from Humid, was to become a *halaaʔ rayaaʔ*, taking over ʔamaaw's Datoʔ Lɛŋriʔ spirit-guide.

certain particulars from Josh's. This is hardly surprising: with a procedure so relatively rarely performed, and with only one *halaa⁷ rayaa⁷* per valley, such differences are to be expected. According to Wakil, the medium's *bumbun* hut inside the house is prepared by spreading flowers on its floor and hanging some of the same flowers as a *tənamuu⁷* wreath into it from the roof of the house. (Josh, on the other hand, had said that no *tənamuu⁷* was employed at such séances.) While the medium sleeps and dreams in preparation, the other villagers collect the sap of the *ceŋcɔɔk* liana (which is thought to possess a *kənoruk*-tiger) in about ten small bamboo containers as drink for the tiger. They also weave *tempɔɔ⁷* crowns out of flowers. The medium, not yet in trance (*tii⁷ mad mʉn ⁷əh* 'still with his true face'), sings one or two *kahyɛk* songs outside the *bumbun* hut, with the lights not yet extinguished. (This too differs from Josh's insistence that a tiger-séance must come first in the proceedings.) The medium then enters the *bumbun* hut, the fires are dimmed, and he trances his plant-derived spirit-guides as *kahyɛk* onto the *tənamuu⁷*. He continues singing *kahyɛk* songs, three or more times, depending on how far away he judges the spirit-tiger to be.

Suddenly, the medium scratches the hut in a tiger-like fashion. This is the sign that the first tiger-spirit has emerged. The medium stops singing, and someone carefully pushes the previously prepared *ceŋcɔɔk* liana sap through the hole in the hut, without actually touching the hut. If the hut *were* touched, the medium would be startled (*kəjʉd*) and supposedly transform (*lããs*) into a ('real'?) tiger. This was explained as resulting from the spirit-tiger pulling the medium out to the forest by his cords, first in human form, then gradually with tail, claws, etc. This startled response in a possessed tiger-medium can also be caused by fighting dogs or by someone opening a light. If the sap is successfully pushed into the hut, it is then drunk by the medium—or rather, the tiger-spirit drinks the sap through the medium (its father) by means of its cords. These enter from below, in front, then into the medium's head and *hup*: the tiger song (*nɔŋ mamuug*) is realised through that channel. At the same time, the *pərɛŋjɛɛn* cords of the *kahyɛk* spirit are connected through the *tənamuu⁷* wreath to the medium's *tempɔɔ⁷* crown, from where they soak his head with the *kahyɛk* liquid. On asking whether there might be a conflict between the *kahyɛk* and the tiger, I was told that this would not occur 'as they both consider the medium to be their father'. If the session proceeds well and free of disturbance, the medium can call up as many as five spirit-tigers.

The above accounts were told to me as third-party descriptions. But in 1979 I obtained some first-hand and more subjective information about events relating to tiger-mediumship that had occurred since my first period of research 15 years earlier. Penghulu Dalam told me that he too could now hold a darkened séance, but that others in the community (Lambok) where he was now living did not know how to do so. After some further enquiry he admitted that he was now trancing not only upper-body *kahyɛk* in his *bumbun*

Figure 10.8 ʔalus (ʔampɔɔh) retrieving a fish-trap from the Perolak river, Humid (1964)
Having died in 1977, he is now referred to as Taaʔ Pəralaaw, after the site where his body was ritually exposed.

hut, but a tiger-spirit as well. The latter was the underground (*sarak*) spirit of Mount Galɛɛŋ (figure 8.1), that had 'returned home' to Dalam after its previous 'father'-medium ʔalus (figure 10.8), whom I had known as ʔampɔɔh (and listed as such in Chapter 7 and earlier in the present chapter), died two years previously. As Dalam expressed it, *ʔun-cɛn ma-sɛnʔɔɔy, ma-bəəh ʔun* 'they [the spirit-tigers] love humans, their fathers'.

Apparently, ʔalus used to carry out darkened séances in Humid during my first period of research, but he never did so in my presence. Dalam said that ʔalus had no specific intention of hiding his tiger shamanism from me; he just happened not to want to perform at the time I happened to be in the village. From earlier experience with him, however, I suspect that ʔalus was afraid that I might use certain words wrongly and cause some undefined mystical trouble. I now think it significant that I was told during my first few days of fieldwork in 1964 that he was afraid of tigers. When I interviewed him in 1964 after seeing him perform at a trance session the previous night, he said that his *only* spirit-guide was Galɛɛŋ. At the time I assumed that this meant solely the mountain's upper *kahyɛk*-manifestation, as he had said that his leaf-whisk had been connected to the peak by cords that the mountain itself has sent down to him. I now think he was also referring to Galɛɛŋ's underground tiger-manifestation, but was reluctant to reveal any further details to me. On the other hand, he also invited me to put questions to him—that is to his spirit-guide—the next time I witnessed him perform at a séance.

Dalam said that when ʔalus died, he was not buried in a grave, but laid on the ground with a split-bamboo flooring beneath, a fence around, and a thatch above, in the process known as *kərɛnwaak* 'exposure'. (This appears to be a causative derivation from the borrowed Malay word *kuak* 'to force an opening'.) This took place in the small Pəralaaw tributary of the Humid river, the regular burial site for Humid people, where ʔalus used to spend days alone enjoying the isolation. After leaving his body there, the villagers fled, both upstream and downstream. Later, two of them went back to Humid to spend a few days in the old houses, but ʔalus's spirit-tiger came wading downstream, growling (*paʔuum*), and teasing (*pɛgyoog*) them. According to Dalam, this was ʔalus's *jərəək-gunig*-tiger that had come to complain that the people had run away straight after the funeral instead of staying to guard his home. (At his death, a tiger-medium's heart-soul, his *jərəək*, is said to emerge as a tiger.) The encounter scared the visitors, and everyone had stayed away from Humid since.[6]

Closing comments

The Temiars' mediumistic practices thus display their knack for peering sympathetically into the 'minds' of quite different species, and acting towards them appropriately. This presents us with valuable insights into their implicit

Figure 10.9 Singapore's Deputy Prime Minister, Tharman Shanmugaratnam, together with Malaysia's Finance Minister II, Dato' Seri Ahmad Husni Mohamad Hanadzlah, and their wives, wearing *tempɔɔ́* crowns at a Temiar village in Perak. *(Photo courtesy of Muhammad Faizal Othman)*

---

6. The site of Humid has indeed remained uninhabited by Temiars ever since, although it is occasionally revisited for sentimental reasons; I did so myself in 2010. The site had been converted by outsiders to a commercial oil-palm estate some years previously (figure 14.2), without the villagers' permission and without granting them any significant compensation or employment opportunities. It is therefore no longer habitable by Temiars.

theory of mind—including their theory of *other* species' minds. Organised animism, by its very nature, requires that its practitioners have *in mind*, if not in their talk, a theory of mind. Other species too are thought of as *halaa²* mediums in their own right, and explicitly so in some of the traditional stories (Chapter 9). And, I suspect, at mediumistic séances the other attending species (albeit in spirit form) are themselves also thought to be trancing the humans' souls into *their* world.

As an afterword, I should note that the woven *tɛmpɔɔ²* crowns that transform night-time séance-attendees into virtual trees have taken on a new and additional function in Orang Asli culture. In modern nation-state contexts, these crowns are now also worn freely in the daytime when the people wish to display their distinctive ethnicity *as* Orang Asli,[7] especially in the overtly 'modern' contexts that now arise more frequently. When negotiating over their land rights, for example, they regularly wear *tɛmpɔɔ²* crowns. The crowns are also sometimes worn by non-Orang Asli (as in figure 10.9) as a matter of politeness and solidarity, but presumably unaware of their original significance as a device for connecting with the spirit-guides' let-down threads (*pərɛɲjɛɛn*).

---

7. An early example of this practice occurs in the colonial-period documentary film *Five Faces of Malaya*, shot in 1937, in which the Temiars (probably at Jalong, Perak, with Noone's help) are seen wearing abbreviated *tɛmpɔɔ²* while going about their daytime subsistence activities. The film can be viewed at http://www.colonialfilm.org.uk/node/1840. For another early example of wearing *tɛmpɔɔ²* in daylight, see figure A1 in Appendix 1.4.

Indigenous Religious Systems of the Malay Peninsula

' Indigenous' here refers to those cultural traditions that have evolved within the Malay Peninsula, namely those of all the Orang Asli (Aboriginal) groups except the originally in-migrated Orang Kuala and Orang Kanaq of Johor, and of all the Malays except such immigrant groups as the Minangkabau and the unassimilated Javanese, etc.

This chapter is concerned with a problem in ethnology. Malayan Aboriginal religion and Malay 'folk'-religion, sometimes referred to as 'Malay magic' following Skeat (1900), are ethnologically cognate in the sense that they derive in large part from a common cultural matrix, but they differ in the organisation and uses made of their otherwise very similar animistic ideas. In the following pages, I attempt to explain these differences in terms of social and historical factors that have somehow acted to transform the underlying animistic framework into the different patterns of animistic belief and practice that exist in Peninsular Malaysia today.

Animism

Evans-Pritchard's discussion of the term 'animism' (1965: 24–6) is enlightening. He points out that it has been employed ambiguously in anthropological writings, sometimes to refer to the belief in a pervasive life-force or personality that attaches to creatures and inanimate objects (i.e., belief in ghosts and spirits); and sometimes, more simply, to refer to the belief that creatures and inanimate objects have souls. As Evans-Pritchard reminds us, many writers have put forward the theory that belief in spirit somehow derived from belief in soul, and that ultimately spirit-belief evolved into the belief in 'supernatural beings' that Tylor (1871) took to be criterial of religion proper. Now it is easy to agree with Evans-Pritchard when he dismisses these evolutionary guesses as 'just-so stories', totally without support. What is not so easy to agree with is his contention that these theories must be false because 'the two conceptions, spirit and soul, are not only different but opposed, spirit being regarded as incorporeal, extraneous to man' (1965: 26).

The mention of corporeality brings to mind Mary Douglas's work (1966) on the sources of ritual power, based on her insights into the importance of categorial boundaries and their transgression. More to the point, Douglas's ideas have been applied to the Malay animistic system by Endicott (1970) in a study that makes it clear, for Malay beliefs at least, that souls are indeed manifestations of the same thing as spirits and ghosts. In Endicott's analysis, 'essence' may be either incorporeal, in which case it manifests itself as spirit, or corporeal, in which case it forms the 'soul' of the body that houses it. Analysis of my own data on Temiar religion (Chapters 3–8) and careful examination of the rather sparse literature on the other Orang Asli groups suggest that the same holds true for all the indigenous religious systems of the Malay Peninsula, for which we may set up the following identities as of general applicability:[1]

$$\text{spirit} = \text{free soul}$$
$$\text{soul} = \text{bounded spirit}$$

But what is the nature of the 'essence' of which both soul and spirit are manifestations? The animistic worldview posits the division of the cosmos into two dialectically conjoined planes of existence: the plane of things, matter, categories; and the plane of essence, spirit, soul. Entities on the two planes are readily conceivable as independent autonomous manifestations. But the normal 'resting' state of the cosmos is one in which for each entity on the plane of matter there is an equivalent entity on the plane of essence, and vice versa, in a one-to-one relationship. Any disturbance of this relationship, whereby essence escapes the bounds of matter, will introduce a dynamic imbalance into the system which may come to be regarded as the source of such things as power, danger, pollution, *mana*, and so on.

This fundamentally dynamic view of the cosmos would accord well with a more general dialectical theory. It is fitting, therefore, that such a skilled dialectician as Georg Simmel—here as summarised by Weingartner (1962: 83)—should best express this kind of relationship:

> Life is more-life—it is a process which pushes on, seeking to follow its own development laws. But life is also more-than-life; it is formative and produces objects that are independent of it. For life as a process to continue, it requires the aid of form, which in its stability is the antithesis of process. Hence, life as process stands the risk of being shattered on the surface of the very object it has produced.

---

1. [Added 2014] Since the original publication of this chapter in 1979, the literature on Orang Asli cultures has become considerably less sparse, especially in relation to their religions. In particular, the discussion of Semang religion in the original version contained some inaccuracies and was in any case out of date. I have therefore modified it where necessary, to take account of Endicott's monograph (1979). The discussion of Temiar and Malay animism remains mostly unchanged, in keeping with the 'historical reprint' character of this book, leaving later developments for Chapters 12 and 13.

If for Simmel's 'process' we read 'essence' and for his 'form' we read 'matter', we have here in a nutshell the fundamental premises of Malayan animism. (This analysis may well apply also to the animistic systems of the other parts of Southeast Asia; but this chapter is confined to a discussion of the Malay Peninsula.)

In Malayan animism this dialectic works itself out in the following manner: matter (or better: 'categories') tends to anchor essence progressively such that each category has its corresponding 'soul'. On the other hand, essence tends to break through the categorial boundaries to coalesce and form free spirit (or 'Soul'). Tightly bound soul implies health, neutrality, safety, profaneness; free spirit implies un-health, activity, danger, sacredness.[2] The major dimension of difference between the various forms of animism in Malaya lies in the different categorial systems that partition spirit into souls. For the purposes of exposition I will outline below only those systems that have yet been subjected to detailed study—Malay, Temiar and Semang—and hang the rest of the argument upon the contrasts that appear between them.

Malay animism

In the Malay system almost every recognised thing in the environment has the power to concentrate essence in itself, and hence to come to possess a soul. In older Malay usage, both 'essence' and 'spirit' in the general sense and 'soul' in the specific sense were referred to as *semangat*. In modern Malay, *semangat* usually refers only to the 'spirit' of the nation and to the 'soul' of a young baby, but its specifically animistic meanings are well reported in the older literature. Wilkinson's encyclopaedic dictionary entry on the word (1932: 1053) is an excellent guide to these various usages (here, abridged):

> *Sĕmangat*. Spirit of life; vitality; 'soul' (in the old Indonesian sense). The Indonesian 'soul' is a bird of life, timorous and easily scared; its flight is synonymous with weak vitality. It leaves the body in sleep, and when absent from the body may be seduced or captured by other persons; magic is used sometimes to attract and so win a girl's *sĕmangat* or to 'attach' it to oneself.
>
> Malays believe that this spirit of life is found in all nature, even in things that we consider inanimate. Thus the 'soul of iron' is responsible for the special merits of iron; and due homage has to be paid to it if a kris is to retain its virtue. This animistic belief underlies the special reverence paid to certain weapons and comes out clearly in the harvest rites associated

---

2. [Added 2014] As already noted in Chapters 1 and 2, I now regard 'soul' as a label for the communicable-with subjectivity associated with the various entities that are the object of animistic religious practice. This suggests a more restricted use of the word 'soul' than sometimes occurs in the literature, where a variety of other components of the human personality (such as the shadow or light of the eye) are also frequently referred to as 'souls', even though they do not serve as objects of religious activity.

with the 'rice-soul'. If the seed-rice is to give a good crop the following year it must retain its spirit of life; and every care is taken to honour it and to see that reaping is done so as not to lessen its vitality.

The bird-like character of the *sĕmangat* leads to its being addressed as a bird (*kur sĕmangat*); and this form of address has become a term of endearment. In Malay as in English the word for 'soul' has many tender associations. It is supposed to reside in the stomach and to enter the body by the mouth. But the beliefs of the aborigines—even of the Proto-Malayan aborigines—may mean a man-like soul; the offerings left on graves suggest a human existence; the 'soul-ladders' on a Jakun grave are alien to the 'bird' idea and other ideas must be linked to the belief that the soul of a wizard becomes a were-tiger and that a wizard's head is projected in sleep in the form of a *pĕnanggalan*.

The degree of differentiation and fixity of the soul depends upon the degree of specificity with which the category that houses it is known. Hence, a continuum exists from the bare differentiation of the vital principle (*semangat*) by attachment to nothing more concrete than the experiences that frighten the Malays, to its almost complete differentiation by incorporation within an identifiable human frame. The less differentiated forms of spirit fall

Table 11.1 The Malay animistic framework, after Endicott (1970) and McHugh (1955)

	Defining category	Manifestation		
Individuals	Humans: (i) individuality	(i) *semangat*	Souls	**Bounded,**
	(ii) life/death	(ii) *nyawa*	(*semangat*)	**safe**
	(iii) humanity/ animality	(iii) *roh*		
	Negritos: (i) individuality	(i) *semangat*		
	(ii) life/death	(ii) *nyawa*		
	Were-tigers	*belian*		
	Familiar spirits	*pelesit, polong*, etc.		
	Outstanding members of class	*keramat, daulat*, etc.		
Classes	Childbirth dangers	*pontianak, langsuir, penanggalan, bajang*	Birth demons	
	Species: trees, animals, etc.	*hantu tinggi, hantu berok*, etc.		
	Roughly bounded realms: mines, fishing grounds, etc.	*hantu pemburu, hantu rimba*, etc.	Free spirits, ghosts	
	Major realms: earth, water, etc.	*jembalang, jin tanah, hantu raya*, etc.		
Unbounded entities	God	Tuhan, 'Allah	Deities	**Unbounded, dangerous**

into the category labelled *hantu* ('ghost') in Malay, while the more highly differentiated forms are treated as the 'souls' (*roh, semangat, penenggalan,* etc.) of the various entities containing them. Note that in this system, mediums' spirit-guide familiars occupy an intermediate position between souls and ghosts.

The full Malay schema of spirit-differentiation is illustrated in table 11.1. The details will primarily be of interest to specialists in Malay studies, but the general pattern is significant for my present argument. As one moves out from the human end of the continuum (that is, down the table), there is a progressive change in the character of spirit-manifestations from bounded to unbounded, from safe to unsafe, from 'soul' to 'ghost', and from well-defined to vague. In the Malay system, then, the degree of differentiation varies with the distance from humans of the defining categories. This implies a degree of differentiation in the Malay-animist conception of humankind's place in the cosmos: humans can look on the rest of the cosmos as distinct from themselves. In other words, the Malay cosmos is not a projection of ego-centred conceptions. Rather, it has a quality of givenness, which for reasons that will become clear later, I shall refer to as 'sociocentric'.

Temiar animism

In principle, every 'thing' that the Temiars recognise in the world may become imbued with soul. In the case of plants, animals (including humans) and mountains, this is accepted as being so without further question. But in the case of other things, such as large boulders, natural phenomena, or less material entities such as diseases, dragons, or even modes of cooking,

Table 11.2 The Temiar animistic framework (Corrected from Benjamin 1979: 13)

	Upper-body soul	Lower-body soul
Humans, animals	*rəwaay* Mon-Khmer: 'soul', 'sing', 'tiger'	*hup* Temiar: 'heart', 'liver' (Mon-Khmer: 'breath')
Plants	*kahyɛk* Temiar: 'mystical watery substance'	*kənoruk* Malay: *kurung* 'enclosed space'
Mountains	*pətərii?* Malay: *puteri* 'princess'	*sarak* Malay: *sarang* 'nest', 'lair'
Spirit-guides	*cənɔɔy* (Semang), or *gunig*	*gunig* Malay: *gundik* 'concubine', 'spirit-guide'
Appears as	Young man, young woman	Tiger (or occasionally as *daŋgaa?* 'dragon')

the presence of a soul has first to be revealed to a spirit-medium or proven dreamer before other people become aware of the fact.

According to Temiar ideas (Chapters 2 and 6), souls are not simple unitary entities. Through the operation of a cosmically based oppositional principle, all soul manifestations are split into two dialectically opposed parts. Depending on the context, this opposition appears morally as good/ evil, cosmologically as culture/nature, and locationally as above/below. To take the latter first, the differentiation of soul is normally expressed as a distinction between the upper- and lower-body souls of the object so animated—respectively, the leaf- and root-souls in plants, the head and heart-souls in man and animals, and the summit and underground-souls of mountains. Though the various souls of each of these classes of objects are called by distinct names (see table 11.2, a repetition for convenience of table 2.1), their underlying homology is demonstrated by the fact that they are normally reported to appear in the same guise to dreamers and mediums, regardless of their derivation. Upper-body souls almost always manifest themselves as humanoid manikins, and lower-body souls as tigers. It is these dream- and trance-based soul manifestations that constitute the spirit-guides among the Temiars. In this respect, Temiar animistic beliefs are different from those of the Malays, in that the various 'things' recognised by the Temiars do not differ in the degree to which they can fix and differentiate soul. Humans' souls are neither more nor less labile, nor better known than, for example, the souls of mountains. In other words, in contrast to the Malay system, Temiar cosmic distinctions are established within humans in the same way and to the same extent as in anything else.

In Chapter 8, I argued (1) that this apparently neutral oppositional principle becomes imbued with moral and cosmological content, and (2) that it is not a merely dichotomous binary oppositional principle, but a dialectical one. To paraphrase Murphy (1972: 175), the opposed entities generate each other, cut against each other, clash, and pass into each other in the process of being transformed into something else. For example, Temiar respondents state quite explicitly that, although their head-souls and heart-souls are regarded as different at one level of discourse, they become identical at another level and labelled just 'soul'. In such contexts, they use the words for 'heart-soul' (*hup*) and 'head-soul' (*rəwaay*) indiscriminately to stand for either. The theological message carried by this dialectic is: good and evil are immanent in everything; good implies evil, evil implies good.

Semang animism

The following comments are based mainly on the large body of descriptive material by Evans (1936) and Schebesta (1957). I have also utilised information from Endicott's study (1979) of the Bateks (who had been the least-studied Semang population) as well as from some of my own more superficial field investigations of Semang topics. My conclusions nevertheless remain tentative.[3]

Just as in Malay and Temiar animism, almost everything that the Semang recognise in their environment may come to anchor spirit and possess a 'soul'. Unlike the Temiar case, however, souls in Semang ideology are not usually regarded as partible. They exist in one main form, which in humans and animals is associated with the liver and heart (also *kəlaŋes*), and in stemmed plants with the pith. Endicott (1979: 89) clarifies this as follows: 'Lessons given to me by the Batek in the internal anatomy of monkeys have shown that *kelangès* means the heart alone (Malay *jantung*) in mammals. But the term *kelangès* is also used to translate Malay expressions in which states of emotion are indicated by reference to the *hati*, which means heart and liver together.' These comments apply equally to the various meanings surrounding the Temiar *hup*, which (as in the rest of this volume) I have usually labelled 'heart-soul'.[4] Unlike the Malay case, on the other hand, Semang soul-conceptions do not imply any differences between the soul-embodying properties of humans as opposed to those of plants or animals. In this respect, Semang conceptions run parallel to those of the Temiars.

When present, the Semang conception of the spirit-guide appears to differ from that of both the Malays and the Temiars. The Semang cosmos is ordered into a three-level hierarchy: the mundane level of the soul-possessing entities (humans, animals, plants, etc.), the celestial level of the many nature-gods and godlings that fill the Semang pantheon, and the intermediate level of the *cənɔy*.[5] These *cənɔy* are functionally equivalent to the spirit-guides of Malay and Temiar

---

3. [Added 2014] When this chapter was first drafted in the early 1970s, Semang religion had been little investigated in terms of modern anthropological approaches. In particular, Endicott's account of Batek religion (1979) had not yet been published. Moreover, in the intervening years I have been employing the label 'Semang' in a more restricted sense, to refer to a particular pattern of social organisation—one that the Bateks happen not to exhibit (Benjamin 2011a: 176–180; 2013: 455). On the other hand, the label 'Negrito', which has in the past been treated by anthropologists as synonymous with 'Semang' in the previous sense, is nowadays employed primarily in reference to a particular somatic phenotype, i.e. as an ostensibly biological term. The biology of the 'Negrito' phenotype, however, has recently been shown to be less distinctive than the former typological approach suggested. (This is discussed in Benjamin 2013, as well as in several papers by other authors that appear in the same issue of *Human Biology*.) To confuse matters further, Malaysian governmental agencies employ the label 'Negrito' in their official communications to label one of the three major divisions that they classify the Orang Asli into. There is no *single* solution to this terminological indeterminacy, but since this chapter does not depend on such a solution, I have left the label 'Semang' unaltered. And because it is an analytical category rather than an ethnonym, I have avoided supplying it with a pluralising *s*.
4. [Added 2014] Endicott also mentions some Batek ideas about accessory souls, just as the Temiars (Chapter 6) sometimes also talk of an 'eye soul' (*kenlɔɔk*) or a 'shadow soul' (*wɔɔg*). In my view, as already remarked, such accessory 'souls' are something other than souls as understood in this volume, in that they are not treated as seats of communicable-with subjectivity. However, in his report on the soul ideas of the Menriqs, a Semang population (in my societal-tradition sense of 'Semang') who live next to the Bateks, Endicott (1979: 96) shows that they do indeed have a unitary concept of soul, which they call by the Malay term *semangat* or by the widespread Mon-Khmer (in this case, possibly Temiar-derived) term *rəway*.
5. [Added 2014] The Bateks (Endicott 1979: 124–128) refer to these as *hala' 'asal* 'original superhuman beings' to distinguish them from the ordinary mediums and shamans, who are referred to as *hala' te'* 'earth *hala''*.

mediumship in those Semang populations where spirit-mediumship occurs.[6] They are elf-like creatures associated with various natural (especially plant) species, but conceived of as having an objective existence in their own right. They do not seem to be regarded as the manifestations of spirit set free from natural or imagined objects, as among the Malays and Temiar. Exactly what the relationship is between essence and category in the case of these *cənɔy* creatures is not yet clear, as there appears to be significant variation among the different Semang populations. One possibility is that they represent a distinct class of beings, possessing both body and soul on the 'mundane' pattern, that can be cajoled by humans into releasing their souls in the form of powerful free spirit, which can then be used in a mediumistic manner, where that practice is present.

We see then that Malay, Temiar and (to a sometimes lesser extent) Semang animism fit into the general model of animism presented earlier in this chapter, but that there are significant differences in the ways in which they structure the cosmos and the spirit domain:

> **The Malay cosmos** is structured upon an in/out (or human/world) axis, differentiation along which is continuous.
>
> **The Semang cosmic** axis is up/down (or deity/human), differentiation of which is into three discrete levels.
>
> **The Temiar cosmos** is structured upon a complex in/out :: up/down matrix (as Temiar ritual makes clear), which is established within humans to the same degree as it is in the rest of nature. Humans, accordingly, are not completely differentiated from the rest of the cosmos.

The spirit-guide in these three animistic systems also exhibits significant differences:

> **Malay spirit-guides** (for which there is a variety of names) are drawn from the released souls of entities intermediate between humans and ghosts on the in/out axis of differentiation. The spirit-guides are thus formed of the souls of species remote enough from humans to be set free as spirit relatively easily, but not so remote as to be dangerously uncontrollable.

---

6. [Added 2014] Endicott (1979: 161–215) presents a comprehensive survey of the supernaturals, both spirits and deities, of all the Semang populations. The spirit-guide idea appears not to be universally present among them, and in those places where it is found there is evidence that it has been borrowed from the Temiars (Endicott 1979: 214). Some of the Batek ritual activities should more properly be regarded as shamanism, in that the performer is regarded as setting his own soul to travel to the domain of the spirits, rather than himself serving as a conduit for the spirits. This is true also of practices among the Orang Asli in the south of the Peninsula and the Malays, who follow what I have elsewhere (Benjamin 2011a) characterised as the 'Malayic' societal tradition. (See, for example, Laird (1979) on the Temoqs.) However—except for certain comments on the Bateks—it will not significantly affect the argument presented here if shamanism is subsumed under mediumship.

Semang spirit-guides, where the idea is present, are derived from the souls of beings intermediate between humans and the various deities on the up/down cosmic axis.

Temiar spirit-guides may derive from the souls of any category whatsoever, material or immaterial, animate or inanimate, human or non-human. Furthermore, mediumistic powers are ascribed not only to humans but also to any entity believed to possess the power of setting the soul free from other entities and manipulating the resulting spirit for a specified end.

The practice of animism in Malaya

Whatever the structural position of the source of spiritual power within these Malayan animistic systems, use of the spirits involves the freeing of 'soul' (bounded essence) from the restraints of material or categorial boundaries. As long as the quiescent, one-to-one relation between soul and 'things' remains undisturbed, no religious action is possible. For that to happen, it is necessary first for some imbalance to have occurred in the system, spontaneously or by deliberate human intervention. Only then is the quiescent soul set free as potent spirit, becoming available for use in achieving various desired ends. The deliberate use of free spirit in this way forms the basis of mediumship, which shares broadly similar features across the three traditions discussed here.

However, these ideas have a darker side: if, with skill, people can control the spirits and make them into allies, with carelessness they may well find themselves controlled instead *by* the spirits. There are two ways in which this control may be exerted: just as soul may be lost, spirit may invade. Therefore, any entity in the environment that has lost soul may become powerful, through the valency of its own soul deficiency, to abstract soul from humans (or, in the Temiar case, from other species as well) in an attempt to regain equilibrium. Conversely, soul that has been set free as invasive spirit may attack humans (or other species) and cause serious disturbance of their individual body-soul balance.

In humans, soul-loss and spirit-attack are both regarded as resulting in sickness. The appropriate therapeutic actions take the form of soul-recall and spirit-abstraction rituals, respectively. In Malayan animistic practice, then, there are two crosscutting dimensions, giving rise to four different frameworks of explanation and action:

- Soul-*loss* and spirit-*invasion* as the reputed causes of sickness
- Soul-*fixing* and spirit-*manipulation* as the bases of ritual action

Soul-loss is an important cause of illness in all three systems, and the ordinary healer (Malay: *bomoh*, Temiar and Semang: *hala(a)*?, which also refers to mediums) spends much time in finding and returning souls. If they do this by means of power gained from some aiding spirit, they are employing mediumistic methods; but the methods employed are frequently non-mediumistic, involving magical procedures only. (The Temiars also have to watch that their actions do not cause non-humans, such as fruit-trees, to lose soul.)

Spirit-invasion, in all three traditions, is regarded as a more serious cause of disease, requiring the healer to identify and 'fix' the invading spirit. In the Temiar case, however, the aetiology of such diseases is immensely complex, as the number of possible combinations of invading spirits and attacked souls is very high. An invading spirit may derive from disembodied upper-body souls, lower-body souls, or plain undifferentiated soul, acting variously upon a human's head-soul, heart-soul, or undifferentiated 'soul'. The same applies, but in reverse, to cases of soul-loss or -abstraction. To complicate matters further, simultaneous spirit-invasion and soul-abstraction may occur, to generate monstrous composite soul-manifestations the material embodiments of which are regarded by the Temiars as particularly dangerous. An example is the headless tiger (kəpej) mentioned in Chapter 5. The majority of the recognised soul-hazards and transactions involve humans, as one might expect, but there are a considerable number that involve non-humans only. As far as I know, Malay and Semang animism is spared this florescence of spirit-based conceptions, probably for two reasons: they do not regard the soul as partible; and they focus all their attention on humans alone as the object of spiritual attack.

Soul-fixing is the major element in Malay magical practices, and involves the use of spells and magical substances. Spells characterise, make 'known', and hence place conceptual bounds around, the disturbing spirit. Magical substances are used to harden boundaries to prevent soul-escape, or to soften any boundaries across which a spirit straddles ambiguously, and hence dangerously. These practices, however, play little part in Temiar and Semang religion, except where the mediums are adopting Malay techniques. It is interesting to note, though, that members of all three traditions sometimes hold the mediums of the other two in high regard when they find it necessary to undertake soul-fixing magic.

Soul-manipulation is the basis of mediumship in all three traditions. (Some of the Semang practices probably deserve to be called 'shamanism', but I shall stick with 'mediumship' to avoid complicating the writing.) Despite some superficial similarities in how they are practised, the details diverge considerably. This is even truer of the *aims* of these practices in the three traditions. Malay mediumship is rarely employed for any other function than to relieve individual suffering, usually sickness. Malay mediums are professionals whose identity is public knowledge, and whose patients come to them as clients. Only rarely (as in the village-wide *bela kampung* ceremony) do they undertake ritual action to ensure the well-being of the whole community. There is evidence that they have sometimes also been employed as sorcerers, to put their powers to nefarious use (Gimlette 1929).

Although Semang mediums sometimes act as healers of individual sickness, their main function seems to be to use their power over the *cɛnɔy* spirits so that the latter will intercede with the deity in ensuring continuity of the seasonal cycle of thunder, flood and (plant) fertility. The Semang deity is closely associated with thunder. It is thought that if people's actions annoy him, they can be expiated by an offering of human blood, which the deity stores up and transforms in due course into the blossoms of the seasonal fruit trees (cf. Endicott 1979: 158–160). In Senoi and Semang symbolism blood stands for 'soul'. Semang religion seems therefore to be concerned largely with maintaining a proper circulation of the vital essence between the celestial and mundane levels of the cosmos, through the joint mediation of the *cɛnɔy* and their earthly representative, the medium. Failure to carry out these observations would lead, the Semang fear, to a failure of the natural seasonal cycle upon which their life so closely depends. For this reason, Schebesta (1957: 134) makes a case for the interpretation of Semang mediumistic ceremonies as a form of prayer.[7]

Temiar mediumship (Chapters 7 and 10) is neither primarily concerned with therapeutic action nor at all with any deity. Rather, the Temiars cultivate the spirit-guide relationship as a self-sufficient religious activity in which they enter into highly personal mystical relationships with the disembodied souls of various natural species and of other entities. These relationships range in degree from mere acceptance of the advances made by spirits in dreams to full-scale intense public mediumship. There is, then, a gradation from the private and slight degree of 'adeptness' (*halaaʔ*) that all Temiars are believed to be capable of, to the public declaration by an acknowledged full medium that he is prepared to make the power-for-good of his many spirit-guides available to the whole community. The Temiar medium's duty is neither towards a clientèle nor towards a deity, but to his own personally revealed spirit-guide (*gunig, cɛnɔɔy*). What this intense cultivation of the spirit-guide achieves, in the Temiar view, is the maximisation of the influence of good over that of evil within a cosmos in which, as we have seen (Chapter 8), the one is part of the other. It is striking that among the Temiars, but not among the Semang and Malays, mediumistic séances are held when circumstances are healthy and untroubled as well as when there is disease or misfortune.

Even though Temiar religion appears superficially to have less in common with Malay spirit-religion than with Semang religion, I believe the two spirit-

---

7. [Added 2014] At this point in the original (1979) text, I presented a view of Semang religion that can no longer be sustained. This included a degree of acceptance of Wilhelm Schmidt's view (1912) that the Semang (and what he called the 'Pygmy' peoples, more generally) exhibited monotheistic tendencies—a view that Schebesta (1957: 308–311), his pupil, later failed to support.

religions are nevertheless 'transforms' of the same basic animistic framework, and that they represent two poles of the same continuum. To demonstrate this, let us now turn attention to the socio-political context of these cultures, to see how far it has affected their religious patterns.

The societal dimension

The most obvious contrast between the Malay and Temiar patterns of animism lies in the differing characters of their religious representations: Malay animism is 'sociocentric' in structure while Temiar animism is 'egocentric'. This contrast may be tabulated as follows:

> **Malay animism** is based on a fixed number of nationally known spirits (McHugh 1955); Temiar animism is based on a potential infinitude of personally revealed spirits.
> **Malay cosmology** sets humankind apart from the rest of the cosmos; Temiar cosmology establishes the same distinctions within humans as in the rest of the cosmos.
> **The Malay spirit-medium** manipulates 'society'-given spirits for the benefit of a private client; the Temiar spirit-medium uses his own personally revealed spirits for the benefit of the community.
> **In Malay cosmology**, the major axis of spirit differentiation is divided into discrete categorial units; in Temiar cosmology, the major spirit-differentiating oppositions are dialectically part of each other.

These contrasting features imply a difference in the pattern of *differentiation* acknowledged by the two cosmologies. Malay cosmology views the individual as differentiated from, and acted upon by, the rest of society, and it views humankind as sharply differentiated from the rest of creation. Temiar cosmology, while acknowledging that the individual has a degree of personal autonomy from society, and humans from the rest of creation, represents that autonomy as no more than a muddled, dialectical pattern of differentiation between the major elements of the cosmos. Various theories of religious evolution, such as Bellah (1964), make much of this notion of differentiation, a point I discuss further in Chapter 14.

Translated to a political mode of expression, these differences imply that, whereas Malay cosmology sees humans as acted upon by society and nature, Temiar cosmology sees humans as freely participating in society and nature. This contrast provides a clue to the transforming variable responsible for the difference. The most obvious contrast between Temiar and Malay socio-political organisation is that the former is segmentary and egalitarian in structure, while the latter is centralised and hierarchical.[8] Now, from the point of view of the local (village) community, centralisation implies that power will be perceived as exogenous, deriving from a locus outside of the villagers' control. Segmentary organisation, on the other hand, implies that power will be perceived as endogenous, being in the hands of the villagers themselves. This is paralleled in the two cultural traditions, as we have seen, by their differing perceptions of the nature and source of spiritual power. In Temiar animism, spiritual power is endogenous, deriving from personal revelation and being used at the individual's own discretion. In Malay animism, on the other hand, spiritual power is exogenous, deriving from socially maintained spirit knowledge and being used at the behest of others.

What, then, of my claim that Temiar and Malay animism form the two poles of a chain of cultural transformations? To support this argument, it will be necessary to show that as the degree of centralisation and hierarchy increases in the socio-political domain, so also does the degree of 'sociocentricity' in the religious domain. Full documentation of this possibility must await the results of ethnographic research now being undertaken by several workers among a variety of Malayan Aboriginal populations.[9] Nevertheless, I believe that it is possible to provide some evidence for this argument from the data so far available from some of the more southerly Aboriginal groups.

Figures 11.1a and 11.1b Orang Asli woodcarvings, early 1960s
Figure 11a: Jah Hut carving of a Bes Tua *(Old Demon) by Kok. Figure 11b: Mah Meri carving of* Moyang Hombot *(Whirlpool Spirit) by Mi bin Awas.*

---

8. [Added 2014] For a detailed analysis of the background to this egalitarian/hierarchical contrast, see Benjamin (2011a).
9. [Added 2014] This sentence was originally written in 1973. Since then, several important studies of Orang Asli religion have been published, but there is no room to introduce their findings into the present discussion.

Two Aboriginal groups, the Mah Meri and the Jah Hut, have become famous in recent years for the high quality of their woodcarvings (figures 11.1a and 11.1b). Although the techniques of Mah Meri and Jah Hut woodcarving result from the deliberate introduction of foreign art styles in the late 1950s, the subjects of the carvings derive from wholly indigenous symbolism and ritual practice. The carvings mostly represent spirits of disease or misfortune, and they are characterised by visual attributes that immediately identify the spirit for anyone versed in the relevant culture. This holds true regardless of which individual artist produced the carving. In other words, the Mah Meri and the Jah Hut possess a developed, 'sociocentric' iconography (see Werner 1973, 1974).[10] In this respect, they contrast strongly with the Temiars, for whom spirits are a matter of great mystery, but align themselves with the Malays (and Semang, for that matter), for whom spirits' attributes are a matter of public knowledge (McHugh 1955). In socio-political organisation the Mah Meri and Jah Hut, along with most other central and southerly Aboriginal groups, possess an institutionalised system of political ranking that seems to be more genuinely indigenous in character than the 'headmanship' structures of the Temiars and their neighbours. It is a matter of simple observation that their economies are much more closely tied in to the outside world than that of the Temiars. They are not Muslims, however, and they bear a much less central relationship to the traditional state than the Malays. They appear therefore to occupy an intermediate position on both the religious and socio-political continua between the Malay and Temiar poles.

We have yet to fit the Semang into this picture. In fact, as I suggested earlier, the Semang do not really fit onto the Temiar-Malay continuum just discussed, but sit disjunctly apart from it. However, a few relevant points can be made. Semang deities and cənɔy-spirits have a considerable degree of objectivity about them, as Evans's, Schebesta's and Endicott's accounts make clear: their identities and attributes are well formulated (though very complex), and are known to all. In that sense, Semang religion qualifies as 'sociocentric' in structure. In terms of their experience of power, however, the Semang diverge significantly from both the Temiars and the Malays, in that their conditions of life lead them to perceive power as not deriving from any human agency at all, whether within or outside the community. Since their relationship to the human societies around them is opportunistic (Benjamin 1973: viii), they have not felt constrained by human agencies— at least, not until the military influences that commenced in the 1940s. Rather, the Semang have usually seen the constraints on their behaviour as deriving from the forces of nature, especially as manifested in the various deities. Hence, it is possible to maintain that the Semang too illustrate

---

10. [Added 2014] Couillard's account (1980) of Jah Hut carving contains fewer pictures than Werner's account, but it presents much more information on the cultural, social and economic background to the enterprise.

the correlation between sociocentric religious representations and the experience of power as extrinsic; the difference here is that it is the deities they fear, not humans.

Malayan animism and world religions

Several universalising or world religions have been present historically in the Malay Peninsula. In chronological order, Brahminism, Mahayana Buddhism, Islam, Christianity and recently Baha'i have all had varying degrees of influence on one or other of the indigenous populations. Of these, Islam requires more detailed discussion, as it is the only one to have maintained a close syncretism with animistic religion in Malaya for any length of time, though not among the Orang Asli. Some brief discussion of Brahminism will also be useful at this point.[11]

Brahminism (along with Mahayana and Tantric Buddhism) was associated with the Peninsula's increasing contacts with Indian religion and patterns of political organisation from the early centuries of the first millennium CE. The extent to which these influences spread among the indigenous populations is still a matter for debate. It seems probable, however, that Brahminism as a functioning religious system did not spread far beyond the boundaries of Indianised settlements or beyond the courts of the simple states that later developed in the region (Stargardt 1973). This is not to say that component elements derived from the Brahminic complex did not diffuse out and form part of the practices of non-metropolitan populations. There is evidence to suggest that this happened to early Malay culture, and surprisingly (according to Schebesta, 1957: 116–119) to Semang culture also. But neither the Malays nor the Semang could be said to have been Brahminists in any overall sense. If it is true that Brahminism in the Malay Peninsula was closely associated with the development of the state, then it would hardly be surprising that it remained closely associated only with the political centre. Heine-Geldern, in a seminal paper (1956), pointed out that Brahminic religion implies that the here-and-now is a microcosm of the cosmos, as evidenced in the cosmological underpinnings of such architectural complexes as Angkor Wat. In terms of Heine-Geldern's argument, the Brahminic worldview would therefore imply a geographically 'endogenous' model of the source of power, which would be unlikely to have been taken up by people dwelling beyond the pale of the court and its immediate environs. Their experience of power would have been 'exogenous' in character.[12]

---

11. [Added 2014] The final two chapters of the present volume provide detailed information on the more intense interaction that the Temiars have had with Islam, Baha'i and Christianity since the original version of this chapter was written.

12. [Added 2014] For a revised version of the argument presented in this section, incorporating more recent findings on early Southeast Asian society, and treating Mahayana Buddhism too, see Benjamin (forthcoming (a), Chapter 2).

It is this last point that provides the major clue as to why Islam was so much more widely adopted than Brahminism and Mahayana Buddhism had been. Like Christianity (which in the Southeast Asian context is relevant to a discussion of the Philippine situation), Islam is centred away from the local scene (in Mecca and other places in West Asia) and thereby, in terms of the present argument, it may serve as a further analogue of the 'exogenous' model of power already embedded in Malay culture. However, matters are not so straightforward. The ancient spirit-religion provided a perfectly good analogue of 'exogenously' experienced power at the level of the local village community—as, for many people, it continues to provide. But the fact that Islam was adopted by both the rulers and the ruled, replacing the Brahminism and Mahayana of the former while syncretising with the animism of the latter, suggests that a further level of analysis must be pursued if we are to understand why the Malays adopted Islam, and why most other indigenous Malayan groups rejected it. Obviously, there is more to this question than the mere presence or absence of the centralised state.

Viewed historically, the most significant change that Malay society underwent parallel to its adoption of Islam was its progressive peasantisation. By this I refer to the emerging socio-economic situation through which ordinary Malays came to feel themselves not only under the political sway of the rulers of their own state, but also under the sway of indirect and only vaguely understood economic forces emanating from the world at large. If we accept the standard version of Malayan history, this would have started with the establishment of Melaka as an international trading post.[13] I am suggesting, therefore, that Islam, through historical accident, was the first religion to arrive on the Malayan scene that could provide an adequate cosmological analogue of the socio-economic circumstances that were developing at the 'real world' level. Closely similar arguments have also been put forward by Geertz (1956: 90–91) and Wheatley (1964: 185). Catholic Christianity, centred as it is in Rome, could equally well have served the same purpose, as indicated by the similar historical and ethnological situation of the Philippines. There, Islam and Christianity now each survive in those areas where they were the first such religion to arrive on the scene—discounting the large band of territory (including even Manila) where Christianity replaced the previously established Islam.

To support this argument we must (1) demonstrate that the spread of Islam went hand-in-hand with the spread of the economic system that defines the 'peasant' social type, and (2) explain why many Malayan societies have never accepted Islam. The first of these is a problem for the historians. The second problem forms the subject matter of the next section. I shall deal only briefly

---

13. [Added 2014] The standard histories as told in Malaysia usually neglect the significance of the wider Malay World, which also includes parts of Sumatra and Borneo. Andaya (2008) reunites these places as part of the same story while also finding a key place for the Orang Asli in that story.

with the reasons why the Temiars and Semang have rejected Islam, despite many continuing attempts to convert them to that religion.[14]

First, the socio-economic situation of the Temiars and the Semang does not bring them so fully into the wider world system that they would be predisposed to seek a world religion. They remain even now substantially in control of their own day-to-day economic undertakings, through the ease with which they can fall back on traditional, non-cash, 'subsistence' methods of livelihood. In other words, they do not feel more swayed by exogenous forces than by endogenous forces.

Second, those Orang Asli who have become peasants do indeed show a tendency to seek membership in a world religion, which is precisely what the above argument would lead us to expect. However, exactly *which* world religion they choose is the result of a variety of factors, some historical and some structural. In the north, where there is a long history of animosity between Orang Asli and Malays (resulting mainly from the slave raiding which went on until well into the 1930s in some areas), such peasantised Orang Asli as the lowland Semais have almost completely rejected Islam. This is despite the fact that, in almost every other respect, they are now barely distinguishable in lifestyle from their Malay neighbours. Instead, they have taken readily to the Baha'i religion and to various forms of Christianity: there is some evidence to suggest that, in addition to the reasons expounded above, they have done this as a deliberate attempt to protect themselves against pressures to convert them to Islam. Furthermore, they are strongly resistant to circumcision and to the giving up of pork, a major item in their diet.

Third, the Semang still have an essentially unitary worldview despite their ancient and continuing relations with the outside world, and despite the fact that these relations have deeply influenced the details of their social organisation. Contrary to the problem that peasants have of finding a balance between the pulls of the Great and the Little traditions (see below), the Semang maintain an essentially opportunistic 'foraging' approach to all their contexts of activity. On settling down, then, they are unlikely to take up a world religion freely. Those Semang who have nevertheless adopted a world religion have become Muslims, which suggests (correctly, I believe, for most cases I have examined) that they have done so as a result of forced enculturation rather than through the choice implicit in the Christianity and Baha'i of the lowland Semais.

---

14. [Added 2014] This is no longer the case. The following paragraphs therefore represent the situation as it was in the early 1970s, when the original version of this chapter was written. Since then, all the Orang Asli, including the Temiars, have experienced much social and economic change, accompanied by the conversion of many to Islam. However, as explained later (Chapters 13 and 14), the conversion has so far been nominal, involving hardly any Islamic religious *practice*. It has been pursued primarily as a means of ethnic engineering.

Malay religious syncretism

One problem remains. As in the rest of Southeast Asia, almost all the communities that claim allegiance to Islam, Christianity or Buddhism also have recourse to animistic beliefs and practices. Why is it, in Malaya, that Islam did not oust the spirit-cults?

Here we may follow a clue provided by studies in Burma and Thailand by looking for internal contradictions of the theodicy kind in the world religion. Buddhism, of course, has its own peculiar theological contradictions (see especially Obeyesekere 1968), and the specific details of the arguments that have been developed to explain syncretism further north in Southeast Asia will not help us directly in looking at the Malay case. Nevertheless, I believe that Islam contains at least three internal contradictions of the theodicy kind that might have relevance to the retention of animistic religion among the Malays:

> How are the declared omnipotence, omniscience and all-benevolence of Allah to be maintained in the face of the ordinary person's experience of daily suffering?

> How is the conflict to be resolved between the doctrine that every Muslim has direct, unmediated access to Allah (there is no priesthood), and the doctrine that it is the duty of the State to organise the Islamic church? (Cf. Gellner 1969.)

> Islam imposes organisational responsibilities (such as the 40 adult men needed for the Friday mosque service and the obedience to rational bureaucratically maintained laws) that are only fully to be satisfied in an urban sophisticated milieu (cf. Hassan 1972). Malay culture is still rural in its orientation, and the maintenance of Islamic practice among them is therefore likely to be strained.[15]

In a manner parallel to what has been observed in the Buddhist countries of Southeast Asia, these theodicies can be resolved, or at least made less apparent, by recourse to the animistic system. For example, a Malay has only to declare that suffering derives from the action of the spirits for the all-benevolence of Allah to remain unchallenged. If any qualms remain about having thereby challenged the omnipotence of Allah, the situation can be eased somewhat by declaring (as Malays nowadays frequently do) that spirit beliefs have nothing whatever to do with 'religion' (*agama*), but are simply 'beliefs' (*kepercayaan*) deriving from the domain of 'Malay culture' (*adat, budaya*).

---

15. [Added 2014] The rural orientation of Malay society was still dominant in the 1970s, but massive urbanisation since then has had consequences for Malaysian Islam that could not have been foreseen earlier. In particular, Islam has become an explicitly managed issue in the country's political and cultural life, as discussed in Chapter 14.

The way in which the second of the two theodicies is resolved by appeal to the spirit-cults requires a far closer examination of the sociology of Malay life than it is possible to undertake here. The close relationship between Islam and Malay ethnic identity in modern Malaysia would play a large part in such an explanation. In any case, the too open declaration of the doctrine of unmediated access to Allah could come to be regarded as potentially subversive from a political point of view in contemporary Malaysia. Hence, this element of Islamic theology is unlikely to be of much concern to the average Malay peasant.

As to the mechanism of syncretism between Islam and animism, two points are of relevance. First, the power of the Word in Islam is much the same as the power of the word in *semangat*-based spells, which would allow of easier syncretism between the two in practice. Second, the use of the Arabic language in spells and in talking about religion prevents the explicit use of the *semangat* soul-concept. But this does not mean that rituals, especially those surrounding life-cycle transitions and crises, are not structured 'as if' the *semangat* beliefs held true. Third, as James Peacock has hinted (1986: 345), some Muslims may focus on the monotheistic aspects of their religion as a means of neutralising the power of the various spirits that they still suspect might exist.

Last, a parenthetical point. A further reason why the Temiars and the hill Semais resist Islam, even when they are drawn into the world cash economy, may well be that their religion obviates the need for theodicy-resolution because it makes the *dialectical* confrontation of good and evil the very centrepiece of the theology.

Chapter	Danger and Dialectic
12	in Temiar Childhood

Temiar childhood and socialisation differ significantly from many of the patterns followed elsewhere. On the Temiar view, parents and children are neither fully autonomous persons, as Westerners or Malays might think, nor are they component parts of a single compound person, as Chinese tradition often seems to insist.[1] Instead, the Temiars regard parent and child as tied together *dialectically*—as being simultaneously of the same and of different personal substance. In this chapter,[2] I discuss how, given the animistic framework of Temiar thought, this dialectic has led them to regard childhood—early childhood, in particular—as peculiarly dangerous for both parents and child.[3]

My hypothesis is that, since Temiars think of a child's personhood as being formed by a process of differentiation out of its parents' soul-substance, the same soul-stuff must be shared between two, three or more bodies at various stages between conception and maturation. (See figure 12.1 for a diagrammatic representation of this idea.) For this to be possible, those bodies must either have sufficiently permeable boundaries to allow such soul sharing or they must each make do with a reduced amount of soul-stuff.[4] Moreover, the growth and source of the child's souls are problematic. In the womb and during infancy, these souls are thought of as dependently shared with those of the parents. Once safely out of infancy, however, the child ends up with stably bounded souls of its own. There must be a point in the process, therefore, when the parents could come to be thought of as dependently sharing in their child's souls, rather than the other way round.

---

1. There is no space here to elaborate on these cross-cultural assertions, which are made simply to emphasise the specifically dialectical character of the Temiar cultural regime. The comparative theory of the different modes of cultural coherence—the immanent, the transcendental, the Zen and the dialectical—to which these comments refer is discussed more sociologically and in greater detail elsewhere: see Benjamin (1985, 1993a).
2. Passages taken from my PhD thesis (Chapters 3–8 in this volume) or which are used again in Chapters 12 and 13 appear here in précis form, so as to leave the continuity of those chapters intact.
3. These dangers were not simply the result of 'cultural' imagination. Some years after the research reported on here, death from childbirth was by far the greatest threat faced by a woman of child-bearing years among the neighbouring Semais (Fix 1971: 72). It must be assumed that the same was true for Temiar women too. The possibility that this was due largely to the anaemia resulting from parasitic infestation is raised by Dentan (1978: 111–112). See also footnote 27 in this chapter.
4. Is this why multiple births are regarded uneasily in so many human communities? For a Southeast Asian example of the animistic complications caused by twinning, see Kawai (1991).

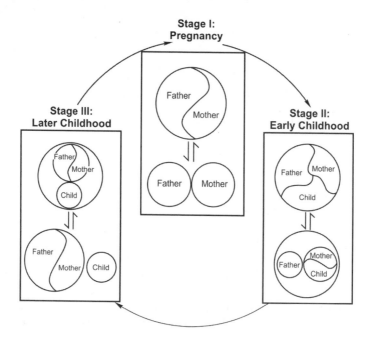

Figure 12.1 The dialectical soul-economy of Temiar parenthood. Drawn by Lee Li Kheng.

Viewed in this way, pregnancy and early parenthood are mystically problematic. To think of a person's souls as merging with those of others is to imply the possibility of soul-loss or its reciprocal, soul-sharing. Soul sharing, in turn, can readily be regarded as a form of soul-invasion.[5] Thus, although pregnancy, childbirth, infancy and parenthood are regular and desired features of Temiar life, they also have much in common with the many syndromes of abnormal soul-loss and spirit-invasion that Temiars recognise. It is hardly surprising, therefore, that soul-abstraction and spirit-invasion should provide much of the idiom that Temiars employ when talking of the special troubles thought likely to beset young children and their parents. Until the child has begun to crawl, parents and child alike are attended by a battery of closely connected dietary taboos aimed at preventing such troubles. These taboos and certain other special ritualised actions form the main focus of this chapter. I shall attempt to explain them in terms of the peculiar economy of soul-relations that holds at this period of the developmental cycle.

---

5. As noted in the preceding chapter, the approach to animism taken here was first developed by Kirk Endicott (1970). In particular, the theoretical insight that SPIRIT = UNBOUNDED SOUL and SOUL = BOUNDED SPIRIT, which is fundamental to my argument, derives from Endicott's work. I discuss the content of Temiar animism in more detail below. For an analysis of differences between the various Malayan patterns of animism, see the preceding chapter.

Temiar child-rearing

The interplay of communality and individual autonomy so characteristic of Temiar society is especially apparent in their child-rearing. The job is shared evenly between the two parents and with other kin, which often gives the impression that all the villagers are jointly responsible for the care of all the children. Fathers undertake the same care-giving activities as mothers, with the obvious exception of suckling—and even then, they frequently hold children to their chests in a manner that, from a distance, could be mistaken for suckling.

Children are allowed a great deal of freedom. Disciplining is limited to verbal advice or warnings of possible intervention by the thunder deity, Karey. Physical punishment or constraint is expressly avoided, even when the child throws a tantrum: it is regarded as leaving the child open to illness. This non-violent approach is absorbed into the child's emerging personality. Children may threaten each other in play, but their blows freeze in mid-air. They play soccer or other ball games, but no teams are formed: instead, they jointly cooperate in helping one of the players land a goal.

There is little educational or initiatory formality.[6] The rituals at childbirth and first menstruation (Chapter 6) are private, and weaning is so gradual that even six-year-olds might be given the breast if they ask. There are no rites of adulthood (apart from first menstruation). Children are allowed to learn by experimentation, whether it involves using knives, building rafts, having sex or smoking.[7] Other matters are explained, as the need arises, by citing the appropriate portion of Temiar mythology.

By the time they become adults, Temiars have learnt to feel anxious that their actions might cause someone else to suffer unsatisfied desires, for this is thought to leave that person open to accident, disease or misfortune. This conception is backed by a set of named, but diffuse, sanctions to ensure that people should always share food, accede to requests for a service or object, and avoid setting up a definite future meeting for fear that the arrangement cannot be kept to. (See Chapter 8 and Roseman (1991: 47–51).)[8]

---

6. Nowadays, most Temiar children attend government-run primary schools set up within their own territory. These have achieved basic National-language (i.e., Malay) literacy, with an increasing number now proceeding to secondary and tertiary education. This process was just beginning during the period of my initial field research, 1964–65. For a more extended account of Temiar child-raising at that time, see Benjamin (1967c: 13–18). For a study of socialisation done among the same people a few years later, see Jennings (1985, 1995). For accounts of child-rearing in a neighbouring and similar cultural framework, see Dentan (1978: 94–143; 1979).

7. I once heard a man who had just seen a group of children openly play-acting at sexual intercourse tell them off by saying 'you'll be smoking next!' For a photograph of Temiar children smoking, see Jennings (1995: 63).

8. An accessible account of the very similar set of sanctions as they operate among the Temiars' neighbours may be found (under the heading *punan*) in Dentan (1979). Dentan (in Dentan & Nicholls 2011) has since revised his ideas about the mechanism of these sanctions, favouring a psychological rather than supernaturalist explanation.

Naming

The different stages in the emergent parent-child relation are marked by changes to the personal names of the persons involved. The naming system thus comes to serve as a cultural paradigm—an indigenous normative sociology—of the maturational process. Infants are usually called by a unique 'true' personal name (*kənʉʉh mʉn*) or *autonym*.[9] These names are derived from the several thousand unused but phonologically possible syllables available in the Temiar language; they thus constitute, in effect, an open class.[10] When children later progress from baby to toddler and youngster, they gradually drop their autonyms in favour of names taken from a closed class of birth-order names. These *fratronyms* are really titles, positioning the bearer socially with reference to his or her sibling-set. Typically, the parents will now take over the child's autonym as their joint *teknonym*, though they may continue to be called by a variety of other kinds of name too—but never by their own childhood autonyms, of which they claim to be 'shy'.[11] For a period then, mother, father and child will all bear the same personal name, in an elegant native modelling of the dialectical merging of the three persons in one. In addition, parents are normally addressed by special parental titles as soon as their latest child is born: *Balɛh* 'Parent of a daughter' or *Litɔw* 'Parent of a son'. These titles too are often shared by both parents, again transforming them effectively into a single merged social person.

In my earlier study of Temiar names, I argued that these (and other changes not discussed here) serve to image the child's maturation as a progressive 'key-of-life' merging into his or her sibling-set, while the progenerative affinal and filiative links are simultaneously declared to be in the key of death. This image—the forging of active siblingship out of the simultaneous dissolution of filiative and affinal links—is a fitting representation of the developmental cycle that underlies Temiar domestic groups, and it also underlies the structure of Temiar kinship terminology (Benjamin 1999: 15). I shall return to this idea later, in discussing the 'tree' imagery that seems to underlie Temiar ideas about parenthood.

Before pursuing the discussion further, though, we must first take a closer look at Temiar ideas and practices concerning souls and spirits.

---

9. For an extended discussion, see Benjamin (1968a). The term *autonym* is taken from Lévi-Strauss (1961).

10. Because I had not at that stage recognised nasal vowels as phonemically distinctive in Temiar, the calculation of 'phonological space' given in footnote 6 of Benjamin (1968a) was an underestimate. The correct figure should be 10,350, which is close to the total size of the Temiar population at the time of my original fieldwork.

11. This 'shyness' is related to the fear of causing a startle response, resulting from head-soul loss (*rɛywaay*) in persons (and other entities) addressed by their true name. See also Roseman (1991: 27–29).

Temiar animism

A brief restatement of the underlying features of Temiar animism will be useful at this point. Temiars picture the cosmos, and the religious and social relations that occur within it, psychocentrically—that is, in terms of their direct experience of their own subjectivity. This derives its plausibility from individual Temiars' experience of their own subjectivity as simultaneously a controlling actor and an undergoing patient. These dialectically linked roles are talked of as being situated corporeally in the *hup* heart(-soul) and *rǝwaay* head-soul, respectively. Similar properties are ascribed to the rest of creation: any salient entity—a person, animal, plant, mountain, etc.—that appears capable of attracting to itself the attention of a human being is regarded as being able to do so by virtue of the simultaneously *hup*- and *rǝwaay*-like subjectivities situated within it as its 'souls'. Non-human entities can thus become aware of, or act upon, the subjectivity of individual human beings, and vice versa.[12]

This dialectical mutuality of agent and patient, subject and object, serves as the tacit, pre-reflective notion out of which coherence is constructed: the Temiar Self can be focused on and talked about, not as an autonomous entity, but only in ways that also implicate Other (and vice versa). As remarked earlier, ordinary social relations exhibit a complicated balance between communalism and individual autonomy, which would be difficult to maintain under any non-dialectical mode of orientation.

Temporarily disembodied upper and lower-body souls of mountains, animals and plants become powerful invasive spirits. Reciprocally, entities left depleted of soul thereby gain powerful valency to abstract soul from other entities. Soul-loss and spirit-invasion, separately or combined, are the mechanisms underlying a large number of the disease-like misfortunes discussed in this chapter.

The body

Temiars thus appear to feel that their body boundaries are so highly permeable to the passage of soul and spirit that, on occasion, body and person may cease to coincide. The reason for this, I believe, is that Temiars are much more concerned with body-insides (*rǝwaay* and *hup*) and with the space around the body, than with body surfaces. Concern for this space around the body is articulated in a complex set of ideas and practices relating person to odour (*ŋɔɔy*) and shadow (*wɔɔg*). Although they bathe frequently, and although they decorate themselves with face painting, earlobe ornaments and belt-bouquets, Temiars do not otherwise show much interest in the body surface as such. The Temiar ceremonial dress of plaited

---

12. Rich accounts of the animistic permeability of Temiar personhood are presented by Roseman (1990; 1991: 24–51).

head-crowns and bandoliers crossed over the chest (figures 2.8, 10.3, 10.4) is less a form of decoration than an externalisation of what lies within. This costume, which I earlier interpreted as a virtual tree-disguise, also serves as an intersubjective device to make human habitations more inviting for the spirit-guides.[13] The head crowns are extensions of the *rəwaay*, the seat of undergone experience, lodged in the imperceptibly growing hair roots under the scalp. The bandoliers refer to the *hup*, the perceptibly active heart and blood, the seat of will, agency and memory.[14]

On the other hand, Temiar spatial and directional symbolism generally attaches to external, environmental features—houses, fields, trees—and to the various environmental entanglements people get into, such as the affliction known as *təracɔɔg* (Chapter 6). Temiar speech is peppered with deictic particles that relate the various participants to the terrain or to temporality: 'the upstream man' (*sɛn²ɔɔy teh*), 'across-the-river Singapore' (*Suŋay Purəəh tuuy*), 'the just-now goat' (*kambik ²atɛɛ²*), 'you-in-a-moment' (*hãã² ²akaal*), and so on. Longer periods of time are recounted in terms of the people's

Figure 12.2 Temiar allo-decoration (early 1960s?)
(Wavell, Butt & Epton 1966: Plate 3)

---

13. For other photographs of Temiar ceremonial dress, see Wavell et al. (1966), Roseman (1991: Plates 6 and 10–13), Jennings (1995: Plates 14 and 20). The 'camouflaging' role of ceremonial dress is discussed by Roseman (1991: 82).
14. This implies that, for Temiars, remembering is something they *do* rather than simply undergo. See also Roseman's discussion (1991: 30–36).

territorial history: not '1968', but 'the year of the swidden at X'. Most important, the attachment of Temiar groups to land was mediated traditionally through their corporate ownership of physical entities standing off the ground, pre-eminently houses and trees (Benjamin 1966: 18–20; 2002a: 127–128).

These features presumably relate to the fact that the Temiar view of the cosmos is not materialistic, but spiritual or psychocentric, being calqued on their own internal experience of their own self-consciousness. In this respect, they seem to contrast with the much more body-surface and pollution-conscious cultures that fill many ethnographic reports. Why should this be? I suggest that it is because, in Temiar culture, the empirical self must be expressed by projection onto Self and Other in a *simultaneous* dialectic, leaving the 'empirical' body-surface relatively unremarked and unritualised. Indeed, Temiar body-decoration may well be a means of encouraging transition across the body boundary, since it is always carried out in a mutual and interactive manner, thereby downplaying the boundary as such in favour of a more highly marked self–other transaction (as in figure 12.2).

Childhood and parenthood

Conception and pregnancy

Despite my attempts to draw Temiars into discussion of the mechanism of conception, I obtained just three explicit statements on the topic. First, a man should refrain from having sexual intercourse with a girl whose breasts have not yet developed, to avoid making her bear a child she cannot suckle. Second, some Temiars claimed that if a woman has had intercourse with more than one man, then her child would resemble all of the men (as well as the woman herself). Third, one man said that girls resemble their mothers in appearance, but that boys resemble their fathers. These remarks are sufficient to confirm that Temiars understand the connection between sexual intercourse and pregnancy, and that the father has a role in conception.

Once a woman becomes pregnant, she and her husband should begin to follow many of the sexual and dietary restrictions that will continue until their child leaves infancy. For example, there is a general rule that a man should refrain from sexual relations with his wife for two months prior to the delivery until the child begins to crawl, at the age of six or seven months.[15] 'We search elsewhere' (*ki-kɛɛ² ma-mɔy*), as one man put it, referring to the widespread Temiar institution of permitting sexual relations between opposite-sex siblings-in-law, whether married or single, classificatory or 'true' (Benjamin

---

15. As far as I could tell, Temiars distinguish terminologically between the earlier and later stages of pregnancy. The first signs are known as *maŋkɔɔ²*, *²aŋkɔɔ²*, or *²akɔɔ²* and the later stages as *kayood*. I suspect that *kayood* is a polite doublet of *(bar-)kəd*, the more usual overall term for 'pregnant'. As a noun, *kəd* was said to refer to both the foetus and the mother.

1967c: 12). If the man has sex with a woman outside this category, however, he is expected to keep the affair secret from his wife. Husband and wife may resume sharing the same bed two months after the delivery, but they must not yet have sexual intercourse. Some claimed that if the rule about intercourse during the last two months of pregnancy were broken, the woman's abdomen would swell with blood. Most of the dietary taboos that will later affect the parents—mothers especially—also apply during pregnancy, as well as to menstruating women.

Childbirth and confinement

As already remarked, Temiars generally treat life-cycle changes with little formality. As far as I could learn, only three stages—birth and the early weeks of life, first menstruation, and death and burial—are picked out for special ritual attention, and even then in a rather diffuse form. My direct observation of childbirth and its sequels is rather limited, for only one birth took place during my time in any Temiar village (see Chapter 6). Most of my information on childbirth comes from a text dictated by the husband of the midwife who attended that birth, as well as from many casual statements thrown out by Temiars in different villages when I questioned them on ritual matters.

The mother and her young baby should remain in the house, off the ground, during the first few days after the birth. This accords with the general patterning of Temiar ritual categorisations around an opposition between off-the-ground and on-the-ground. The various confinement practices must therefore be regarded as having ritual content. The afterbirth is helped out by the midwife's firm massaging. Later, it is wrapped in a cloth and hung from a branch outside the village. The tree must first be examined carefully for any fused branches or trunks, as this would cause the mystical affliction known as *tɛracɔɔg*, in which the miscreant might suffer various illnesses or accidents. For the first few days after the birth, the midwife regularly bathes the mother and child by pouring warmed water onto them from a bamboo container, an act that I analysed in Chapter 6 as a passage-rite of enculturation. Although this takes place near the hearth, it does not have the institutionalised character of the widespread Southeast Asian custom of 'roasting' the newly delivered mother. The Temiars know the latter to be a Malay practice, but they do not follow it—even if its 'enculturating' rationale is similar to that of their own practice.

After the first such washing of the mother and child just after the delivery, the midwife puts the child to the mother's breast so that it will 'know' the nipple and learn to feed. After suckling is established, the midwife heats some special leaves in water, places them still hot onto the mother's belly and, with her foot, massages the mother through the leaves.[16] Then she binds the damp leaves firmly in place with a piece of cloth, to reduce the pain. The mother can now leave the house if necessary, but the baby remains inside (and thus off the ground), where it is frequently bathed and put to the breast. The hot-leaf massage and binding continue for five days, after which the mother is considered to be physically nearly recovered.[17]

For the first eight days after the delivery, the mother and the midwife must both refrain from eating meat, nor may they bathe in the river. If they break either rule they are thought likely to suffer *sabat* (Chapter 5, and further discussion below), with consequent difficulty in breathing. Other villagers catch fish for them to eat instead.

When the baby's umbilicus drops off after about seven days, the mother keeps it in a small plaited pouch. Later she burns the pouch and its contents on the ground and plants a few maize seeds in the ashes. When the maize ripens months later, she takes the cobs home, roasts them on the fire, and gives them to her child to eat 'because its own umbilicus-ash is in it'. This ritual sequence echoes the Temiar custom (now little practised) of burning down the house of a deceased adult and planting a crop (usually tobacco) in the ashes. It also brings to mind the Malay custom of burying the afterbirth—regarded as the new-born's 'elder sibling'—at the base of a tree near the house.

Throughout the confinement, there is no strict prohibition on the approach of the father or other males near the mother. The sloping bamboo couch on which the confinement takes place is often placed in the centre of the house, or at least near the hearth where everyone congregates. The father and mother should nevertheless sleep apart until all is declared well and the mother has gone out of the house for the first time. No other special restrictions affect the father at this time, apart from the general dietary restrictions of parenthood discussed below.[18] But he is expected to make himself helpful in tending to his wife's needs while she is confined to the house.

At the end of the confinement, the mother asks her husband to present the midwife with ten pieces of sarong cloth in payment for her services. The midwife then hands two of these to the mother 'because of the child's *rəwaay*'. This is a recognised way of showing that she is bound to the mother

---

16. A photograph of such a massage—without leaves, in this instance—appears in Roseman (1991: 107).

17. The various numbers of days given here should not be thought of as rules; they are simply what I was told in the accounts I collected. In practice, Temiars would be unlikely to count the number of days between events so officiously, or to observe rigorously any 'rules' that might seem to be based on such counting.

18. According to Marina Roseman (personal communication), a man should not do any fishing with a cast-net while his wife is pregnant, for fear that it might cause the foetus to become 'tangled'. A variant of this is reported by Sharifah, Nilan & Germov (2012: 245–248), who state however that only fish caught by someone *other* than the women's husband is forbidden to her, including also fish caught by line or by *bubu* fish-trap. She is allowed to eat such fish if caught by her husband. As noted several times in this volume, such differences of opinion are not unusual, given the changes that take place over time, and the different ideas that attach to different localities. In my own fieldwork I never came across these ideas, despite the fairly rich information I gathered on food prohibitions.

by a feeling of care, and not just as the provider of a service. For the rest of their lives, the mother calls the midwife by the pseudo-kinship term *tohaat* 'healer'; the child too may later come to call the midwife by the same term. The reciprocal term is *cɔɔʔ* 'pet; former patient'.

Yaŋyɔw

In Chapter 6, I described how the fathers of young children regularly make inconspicuous placatory offerings by throwing leaves into a flowing river before bathing or wading in it. The explanation originally given to me was that the offering was made for fear that the child's labile *rɘwaay* soul might be taken away by some plant-spirits.[19] This suggested that Temiars view parenthood as largely concerned with protecting the baby's head-soul from its tendency to 'wander away' (*rɛywaay*).

Some years later, however, I was given a rather different account. The leaf-throwing ritual was now portrayed as an offering to a river spirit known as Yaŋyɔw who, despite being regarded as a Malay, looks like a water-skater insect. The act is accompanied by a spell in Temiarised Malay, aimed at preventing Yaŋyɔw from stealing away the child's head-soul to play in the whirlpools. The key phrase in the spell is *sɘmaŋad budaʔ jaŋan lariiʔ, tɘdoh sɘkaliiʔ* 'don't run away with the child's *semangat*, remain calm'. The Malay word *semangat* 'vital force; soul' is often used by Temiars to translate their word *rɘwaay*, and Malays too hold very similar beliefs about the dangers of *semangat*-loss in young babies.

Whatever the explanation, this ritual underpins a notion that I examine in more detail below: the extreme lability of the infant's soul. In one sense, this expresses the quite rational fear that the baby may not survive, for the infant mortality rate was quite high at the time these data were gathered. But the ritual also expresses specifically animistic ideas, concerned with Temiar notions of the economy of souls.

Infancy and childhood

As already noted, Temiars generally feel that they have no right to command the behaviour of others, even their own children.[20] Presumably, this is because one's will is thought to be situated in one's *hup*. To exercise control over someone else could therefore be seen as a form of *hup*-invasion and/or *rɘwaay*-suppression. Although no Temiar offered me such an explanation for not controlling other individuals, I was expressly told that this is indeed what happens in spirit-mediumship (which is desired) or in spontaneous trance (which is undesired). The same explanation was

---

19. This presumably belongs with a wider set of Temiar ideas about the harm that can result from letting certain cultural objects, menstrual blood or the blood of certain game animals flow downriver.
20. The episode reported in Chapter 6 in which a child was explicitly taught to fear thunder serves as an example of what might happen when a parent does try to control a child's actions.

also given for most of the soul-abstraction and spirit-invasion misfortunes that, they claimed, threaten them.

In early childhood, however, the child's parents may legitimately tell it what to do, but only with regard to food taboos. This exception can be explained through an examination of the way in which the child's increasing maturation is given animistic expression. As we have seen, the dangers thought to attend infancy are most commonly expressed in the fear that the baby may lose its *rǝwaay* head-soul, especially through the inadvertent actions of its mother. This fear may be expressed in other ways too: parents often refuse, for example, to let their young child be photographed, in case the camera steals its *rǝwaay*. Consequently, the baby is sustained by a set of practices aimed at preventing *rǝwaay*-loss and any resultant *hup*-invasion; the *Yaɲyɔw* ritual is one of these. The dangers to the mother and child are frequently referred to collectively as *lagɛ⁷*, literally 'caul', the term used to refer to a new-born baby. This term is often applied as well to the restrictions followed by the father and midwife, further muddying the dialectical relation of personhood that holds between the people most closely involved in the baby's earliest months.[21]

A young baby's relation to its mother is so unitary that it is not even severed by the baby's death. If this should happen, the mother must bathe the baby's corpse with hot water dripped from a bamboo and then wipe it dry, so as to prevent herself from falling ill too. The rationale for this procedure seems to be that, since mother and baby share the same soul-substance, the baby's death will put the mother in great danger of soul-loss and spirit-invasion.

It is while the child is still a new-born that the mother and child come most firmly under the various dietary restrictions discussed in the next section. As the child grows older, however, the restrictions are gradually lifted, in step with the parents' fading ability to exert control. In other words, the erstwhile personal unity of mother and child (and/or father, and/or midwife) moves towards a more differentiated set of relations, as if between autonomous persons. The transition is never straightforward, though, for neither the initial unity nor the final autonomy are absolute. It is as if the parents—separately or jointly—and their child constituted a single physiological and psychological entity, at least until the child becomes mature enough to walk around by itself. The process constitutes a persistent dialectic, in which the players never separate wholly into self-sufficient 'individuals'.

Successive stages in this dialectic are marked by the establishing of new behaviours. The new-born and its parents follow the full range of dietary restrictions. As the child first begins to crawl around the house, and again

---

21. The slightly adversative connotation of *lagɛ⁷*—the word is only employed when the child is being thought of as vulnerable or as needing protection—may link it with the similarly adversative meaning of a cognate form in the closely related Semai language: *bǝlagɛ⁷* 'dirty' (Gérard Diffloth, personal communication).

when it begins to walk on the ground, the restrictions are progressively lifted. By then, a degree of autonomy has been established, and it is now more difficult for the parents to tell the child what to do. They still try to hold the child to some dietary restrictions, however, as the dangers are not yet over. For example, the child's head can now safely be shaved, which is done for cosmetic or health reasons. But the continuing lability of the *rəwaay* requires that a special tuft of hair (the *wɔɔj*) must be left on the child's scalp—over the forehead in boys (figure 2.2) and at the crown of the head in girls (figure 6.2)—to prevent soul-loss. This can be the source of some amusement: in 1964, a small boy whose head had been shaved the day before told me that his *rəwaay* had gone off into the forest, but that it would return later that day. (His father had told him that his *rəwaay* had gone to his belly.) By this time, children spend much of the day out of their parents' sight, playing with other village children. Their increasing ability to talk now enables them to discuss their own response to dietary restrictions—an important step in reassuring the parents that the child has become more responsible. The last stage in the progression is usually marked by changes in the personal names of both child and parents, as noted earlier.

Even after the child has grown out of immediate danger, the mother may choose to keep her own diet restricted, especially if she is still of child-bearing age. Her husband and child, on the other hand, are free to experiment with the hitherto forbidden foods. The child should first be judged sufficiently 'brave' (*galag*) to try the new food, preferably following an appropriate dream. (A more comprehensive account of these issues, as well as of those in the next section, was presented in Chapters 5 and 6.)

The dietary restrictions

Temiars hold that a large number of misfortunes are related to their behaviour towards various natural species. Of these, the afflictions known as *sabat*, *pocuk* and *tɛnruuʔ* are of special importance, for they separate out young children and their parents as a distinct social category, more restricted in what they may eat than any other members of the community.[22] The exact referents of these words are not always easy to specify, for they are often used interchangeably. As one Temiar put it when I asked him the difference between *sabat* and *tɛnruuʔ*, 'one disease, many sounds [i.e., names]'. Such an apparent—though not real—confusion results from the highly dialectical framework of soul-ideas on which these ideas lean. It is nevertheless possible to discern some focal meanings for each of the terms.

Sabat is the most widely used of the three terms (see also Chapter 5). It refers primarily to sickness in children, women of child-bearing age and the

---

22. The words *sabat*, *pocuk* and *tɛnruuʔ* are also used on other occasions, with reference to other social categories or individuals. Here we are concerned only with the 'unmarked' varieties, which relate primarily to parenthood and childhood.

fathers of young children, caused by eating foods forbidden to them; it also applies to both spouses during the wife's pregnancy. The same food taboos usually apply also to women while they are menstruating, whether or not they have young children. (For a chart of the social distribution of these dietary restrictions, see Roseman (1991: 139).) In the prototypical case, a young child suffers an attack of *sabat* if his mother eats pig flesh, although the term is normally used more broadly to include salt and chicken as well. In practice, though, the definition of a food as *sabat*-causing depends on the person, not the source it derives from. Any one kind of food may be *sabat* for one individual, but not for the next. Moreover, the list of foods regarded as *sabat*-causing is open-ended, showing considerable variation in time and space.

Temiars generally claim that *sabat* is their version of the Malay word *sawan* 'convulsions'.[23] Although this folk-etymology may be correct in a more general sense, *sabat* does not derive directly from the modern form of the Malay word. Phonologically, Temiar *sabat* should derive from an earlier **saban* (Gérard Diffloth, personal communication). If the word is indeed related to Malay *sawan*, it must therefore have come from a much earlier stage of the language, before **aba* changed to the current *awa* (Alexander Adelaar, personal communication). Another possible etymological linkage of Temiar *sabat*, however, is with the (Perak?) Malay *seban* (perhaps with an added 'undergoer, middle-voice' *-a-*) 'protracted (of labour in childbirth)'—a meaning that might fit better with that of *sabat* than does 'convulsions'.

Sabat is regarded as an 'illness' (*jani²*), the main symptoms of which were variously identified as vomiting, giddiness, shortness of breath, cold, shivering or headache—but not convulsions. The cause was described to me in several different ways. One man said that the *sabat* of game animals appears to spirit-mediums in trance as a baby version of the animal in question. This is the animal's *rəwaay*, and it attacks the victim's *hup*. Another said that *sabat* is the animal's *kɛnlɔɔk*—i.e., its *rəwaay* as seen in the eye's twinkle—and that it attacks human beings through the head; from there it consumes the rest of the body. It is also widely held that some plants, mainly certain tree-borne fruits, can cause *sabat*. These species possess *kənoruk* (root-souls that manifest themselves as tigers), which are the plant equivalents of *hup*. One man said that in this case, the *sabat* disease is caused by the *kənoruk*-tiger sucking blood from the victim's chest through its magical cords, then removing the *hup* and pulling the *rəwaay* out after it. A milder version had it that if a child were to eat *sabat* fruits, it would simply 'fail to grow fat'—a quite appropriate way of characterising the result of soul-abstraction, at least in the short run.

---

23. In their otherwise informative study, Sharifah, Nilan & Germov (2012), presumably working in Malay rather than Temiar, report only the word *sawan*. They make no mention of *sabat*, thereby treating 'convulsions' as merely one of the results of what I have reported as the much larger class of prohibitions that Temiars refer to as *sabat*. Sharifah et al. give details of several of these other prohibitions, including some newly developed ones, but without giving labels.

As already outlined in Chapter 5, *pocuk* and *tɛnruuʔ* are regarded as more acute forms of *sabat*. These afflictions are quite commonly mentioned in casual conversation, but from the varied descriptions I obtained it is difficult to define them clearly. Instead, let me provide a sampling of the opinions I gathered and then try to draw out the common themes they express. *Pocuk*, like *sabat*, is the name of a bodily affliction believed to attack those who fail to observe certain rules of behaviour. The list of causative animals always includes the sambur and rusa deers and the mousedeers. Some Temiars said that these were the only *pocuk* animals, while others provided much longer lists that included many ground-living game-birds, along with such exotic (even to Temiars) animals as tapir, rhinoceros and elephant. Some thought that certain plants too, especially certain seasonal fruits, might cause *pocuk*. In the latter case the affliction may also be referred to as *wɛdwẽẽd* 'giddiness'.

Women and children are the main targets of *pocuk*. I was told that if the father of a young child were to eat *pocuk*-causing food, it is the child who would die. The source of danger was thought by some to be the animal's *jərəək*, a term often applied to the reportedly tiger-like shape taken by animals' lower-body souls when envisioned in trance or dreams. The cause of *pocuk* in children, however, was more commonly ascribed to *cəʔaay* (sometimes called *ŋɔɔy lɔɔt* 'blood stink'), an emanation or vapour that originates from the blood of larger animals while they are being butchered. Young children must be kept away from this—which is why the initial butchering of hunted animals is usually done outside the village, and why meat is usually washed in the river before being distributed for cooking.

The mildest account of *pocuk* that I obtained described it as starting like an ordinary *sabat* attack and then progressing to giddiness, unstable vision and staggering fits. More severe accounts had the victim falling into a paralytic state in which his or her limbs get fixed in a posture characteristic of the causative animal. Victims may even begin to move about the house for an hour or so, making sounds like the animal; they are then said to have 'metamorphosed' (*lããs*) into the animal. If not treated, and especially in the case of a child, the victim dies. The preferred treatment is for a spirit-medium to remove the offending agent ritually in the form of a *batuuʔ kahyɛk*, supposedly a stony or crystalline—and therefore neutralised—form of the spirit-agency, which is normally thought of as a mystical liquid (*kahyɛk*) when still active. This accords with the claim that *pocuk* is caused by an emanation from the blood or the unbounded lower-body soul of the offending species. In other words, *pocuk*—like *sabat*—results from invasion by a stray spirit (that is, unbounded soul) attracted by the valency of the soul-deficit generated by the dialectically overlapping personhood of early childhood. *Pocuk* is thus the lower-body-soul (*hup* or *kənoruk*) counterpart of *sabat*, for the latter has its source in unbounded upper-body soul (*rəwaay*).

Tɛnruuʔ, the third of these afflictions, seems to be even more severe in its effects.[24] Grammatically, the word is a verbal noun, describing a state rather than a causative agent; the verbal forms *tɔruuʔ* and *teʔruuʔ* 'to undergo *tɛnruuʔ*' are also used. Pigs were mentioned as causative agents in all the accounts I obtained, but some people said that other animals, including certain red-fleshed fish, might be involved as well. The symptoms were variously described as 'vomiting, shivering, loss of appetite', 'blood in the urine' or 'the body becomes like rubber, and one cannot sleep'. However, the most dramatic description, obtained from several different sources, characterised *tɛnruuʔ* as a kind of transmogrification in which the patient both transforms into the animal concerned and flees the house to join the wild herds. For example, if pigs (and perhaps other herd animals) are sighted in the evening brazenly digging up swidden crops near human habitations, they are thought by some to be *tɔruuʔ*-ed humans in animal shape. Such pigs are regarded as very dangerous.

In cases of this sort, the cause is assumed to be the feeding of *sabat* meat to the parent of a *lageʔ* infant or to a menstruating woman. In some accounts, a newly delivered mother will *tɔruuʔ* not only if she eats pork, but also if she eats any meat, fish, salt or seasonal fruit—and so will her husband if he eats with her for the first week after the delivery. I was told that one way of curing this type of *tɛnruuʔ* is to perform the special blood-offering known as *sɔmɔk* (Chapter 6). This rare ritual more typically takes place in response to violent storms occurring right overhead, when it is performed by those who feel that their actions caused the storm in the first place. The aim is to appease the thunder deity Karey. They collect some of their own blood by cutting their shin (or calf, in some accounts) with a bamboo sliver, mix it with water, and throw it into the air and onto the ground, uttering appropriate imprecations.[25] If the ritual is done in response to a case of *tɛnruuʔ*, it should be carried out by the person who fed the wrong food to the patient. The blood-and-water mixture is collected early in the morning and flicked from the end of a leaf-whisk two or three times onto the patient's throat. Other treatments, especially when the victim is a child, include special 'blowings' (*tɛnhool*) by a spirit-medium. Since the source of power in the medium's breath is usually explained as deriving from his *hup* (which Temiars regard as the organ of breath), and since *hup* and blood stand for each other in Temiar symbolism, it is clear that these two 'cures' are very similar in their cultural logic.

The connection of *tɛnruuʔ* with blood is apparent also from its association with menstruation, as mentioned above. But menstrual danger

---

24. For another account of *tɛnruuʔ*, see Roseman (1991: 137–142).
25. For Slimming's graphic published account (1958: 154–155) of this ritual, performed by the midwife mentioned earlier in this chapter, see Chapter 6. Several scholars have debated the significance of the Orang Asli blood sacrifice since my thesis was written: see Freeman (1968: 353–359), Endicott (1979: 155–160), Robarchek (1987: 273–300), Dentan (2002), and (more obliquely) Nagata (2010).

is contagious. If a woman starts to menstruate while eating meat and then gives it up because of the taboo, anyone who unknowingly eats the left-over meat is thought likely to suffer *tɛnruuʔ* and transmogrify into the animal that caused the trouble. The cure for this, I was told, is for the menstruating woman to cut her leg and *sɔmɔk* her own blood onto the chest of the sick person. These seem to be rather archaic beliefs, for some Temiars did not know them at all, while others said that such things used to happen generations ago but do so no longer.

It is clear, then, that *tɛnruuʔ* (like *sabat* and *pocuk*) is thought of as involving soul-invasion. Its special feature seems to be that—in severe cases at least—it is the victim who becomes invasive, by fleeing into the animal realm. The precipitating states (childbirth and menstruation) both involve loss of blood, and the cures involve replacement of that lost blood in material or symbolic form. In soul-economy terms, this means that the affected person becomes temporarily *hup*-deficient, a state that generates a powerfully soul-attracting valency. Soul-invasion is the almost inevitable accompaniment to such an image, whether the victim is the one who is invaded or who (reciprocally) does the invading. Moreover, given the mutual dialectical involvement of mother, father and young child, it is hardly surprising that the dangers should be thought likely to befall them all.

A somewhat related case occurred in 2010, at the resettlement village of Təroləəh (Lambok, Kelantan). Although the community was now living in permanent houses supplied with electricity and clean running water, a concern over out-of-place blood was still present, even if handled in a new way. I was told that a woman had recently given birth with the shedding of much blood, which one of the *halaaʔ* mediums had somehow 'seen' transforming into human shape. He had since forbidden this humanoid spirit to enter the village, and had made it flee into the forest. He had reacted similarly when someone slaughtered a chicken in the village space. He then asked that in future women should give birth in hospital, and that chickens should either be bought already slaughtered or be slaughtered well away from the village.

I attended the special ritual feast held to repair the harm supposedly caused by the spirit and to ensure that it stayed in the forest. This was performed at midday in Malay style, with mentions of the well-known Malay spirits *Hantu Raya* and *Iblis* accompanied by instructions on how to rid the community of them. The mumbled spells were mostly in Malay. When discussing the events with me, people referred to the spirit itself not by any specific Temiar terms but by Malay avoidance words meaning 'thing': *benda* (Temiarised as *mɛndəəh*) and *barang*. It seemed to me that in this episode the people had fused their traditional concerns over the dangers of spilt blood with newer concerns over their increasing involvement with

Malays. They sensed that their troubles were Malay-originated and that they had to be dealt with in an appropriately Malay manner.[26]

Phenomenology, physiology, imagery

The discussion so far may have given the impression that I am concerned, in a cognitivist or structuralist manner, with the 'meanings' of the various practices that attach to Temiar childhood and parenthood. Where ritual is concerned, however, the Temiars seem not to share a body of explicit meanings, nor do they always agree about the referential content of the more mystical words in their lexicon. I suggest therefore that the analysis should not proceed solely on the level of articulated meanings, but should deal also with the more embedded level of unspoken *feelings*. We need to ask not only what these rituals and restrictions 'say' to the people who perform them, but also what they *do*. In this section I show how notions as basic as the dialectic of autonomy and communalism, or the dangers that attend early parenthood, come to be *felt* rather than just cognised. These notions are not so much 'expressed' or 'articulated', as *condensed* at one and the same time onto (1) directly felt bodily processes, (2) a view of kinship in which sibling ties are generated out of the simultaneous degeneration of affinal and filiative ties, and (3) the cosmogonic imagery that sustains it all. The discussion must therefore bring together psychological, cultural and linguistic data, within a generally phenomenological framework of interpretation.

Blood and thematicisation

Earlier, I argued that Temiars show more concern for body-insides than for the body's surface. I now examine this proposition more closely, with special reference to a topic that has underlain much of the preceding discussion—the phenomenology of blood. That will lead in turn to a consideration of the possibility that physiological issues might underpin the material presented earlier.[27]

As we have seen, the Temiars use blood ritually or refer to it symbolically in a range of different contexts. Examples include the offering of one's own blood in a *somɔk* ritual, or the symbolic hint of blood that lies behind the spirit-medium's *hup*-derived 'blowings'. In other contexts, however, blood is

---

26. The religious interaction between Temiars and Malays is dealt with in more detail in Chapters 13 and 14. It is possible that in future only the Orang Asli will keep Malay-derived animistic practices alive, as the Malays themselves increasingly drop them under the pressure of reformist Islam. If that comes to pass, it would certainly constitute an historical paradox.

27. It is probable that other physiological processes are involved besides those discussed here. Dentan (1978: 122–123), for example, suggests that the anaemia resulting from the typically heavy helminthic infestation in Semai communities plays a major role in generating the kind of 'startle' responses that the Semais talk of as soul-loss. Following Dunn (1972), there is reason to suspect that the same was true of Temiar communities during the period reported on here. If so, blood is the key to much of what I discuss here, not only conceptually but also materially. See Lim et al. (2009) for a later report indicating that such infections still affect Orang Asli communities.

avoided, as with the dangerous *cɔʔaay* blood-vapour of certain animals, or in menstruation.[28] In Temiar imagery, blood is the concentrate or trope of agency and will. It is therefore thought of as possessing inherent power to bring about new states-of-affairs. The importance accorded to blood as a trope of agency is especially apparent in the embarrassment that attaches to menstrual blood in Temiar culture. Why should this be?

As a trope of free *hup*, blood is in effect a form of spirit. Free (i.e., bleeding) blood is acceptable when used deliberately to achieve some balance in the world, as in the blood-offering rituals. But since free blood is normally uninvolved in any such complementarity, it is not usually acceptable. Menstrual blood is the most troublesome form that free blood can take, being inherently without counterbalance. First, although menstrual blood is in effect a form of spirit, it is nevertheless shed regularly in normal contexts of life. Second, unlike *hup* under normal circumstances, menstrual blood is not counterbalanced by any *rɔwaay*-token, since hair (the trope of *rɔwaay*) is not shed regularly from the body. Third, menstrual blood is not balanced by any male equivalent: this does not sit well with the usual Temiar concern for complementarity between males and females. Fourth, as free *hup*, menstrual blood has power but no apparent ritual use: it is therefore a danger that must be contained. So, not only is menstrual blood polluting and treated as 'dirt' (*ʔɛsnʉs*, *ʔɛdnid*), it is also profoundly *embarrassing*, as evidenced by the blushing and verbal evasion generated by my attempts to discuss it. It simply cannot be either explained or 'understood' by the means through which the Temiars normally approach their world.

This brief discussion raises the possibility that the dietary taboos discussed earlier might be concerned with the psychological thematicisation of physiological processes. Could it be that meats, salt and 'commercial' foods are forbidden by the rules of *sabat* because they increase the heart-beat and raise the blood-pressure? That would have the effect of making the mother's own *hup* and blood a thematic object of her attention at precisely the times when she has the most reason to be worried about the 'economy' of her soul-stuff. These same foods are also the ones that children should avoid until they have become 'brave' enough (through dreams?) to eat them.

To make something thematic is to make it the object of attention, thereby shifting it from the plane of the taken-for-granted to that of articulated and worrying concerns. Thematicisation in this sense is a common feature of Temiar culture, and it sits right at the core of the psychocentric mode

---

28. There are several other domains of Temiar life where the management of out-of-place blood proves troublesome. I found that the following events are all associated with complicated rules of behaviour: the removal of blood-engorged leeches from one's body; the treatment of bleeding that occurs while one is eating; the escape of blood from monkey meat while it is being butchered on the shore of a river. Jennings (1995: 119–136) devotes a whole chapter to Temiar concerns over blood and women. See also Dentan's account (1978: 110) of the careful precautions taken in some Semai communities against letting the afterbirth and other effluvia fall to the ground.

of surrogation mentioned earlier. Temiar ideas imply that the cosmos too maintains its own existence in this way, by subjectively holding itself within its own span of attention. (See Chapter 4 for the mythological data on which this claim is based.) It is hardly surprising therefore that the same concern reappears in regard to soul-based maturational processes.

As already noted, Temiar parents get away with telling their children what to do only during the children's early years and only with regard to the food-avoidances that mark the children's maturation. When the children grow a little older, the parents avoid interfering with their actions. This suggests that for the first few years of life the child is felt to be a part of the parents' Self, rather than an Other. But the dialectical character of Temiar thought implies that Selves are also Others, and vice versa. Having a child, becoming a parent, is a process that starts with the generation of a dialectical other out of one's own Self, but ends as the dialectical regeneration of one's Self out of the Other it originally produced. Phenomenally, the child's maturation—the transformational differentiation of the child as 'Other' out of the parents' Self—therefore amounts to a process of *changing emphasis*.

This makes sense if we assume that during the earliest stages of childhood the mother and child constitute the *hup-* and *rəwaay*-vessels, respectively, of the dialectical 'whole' that they jointly form (see figure 12.1). Later, by the time they become autonomous individuals, the mother must somehow have obtained her own *rəwaay*, and the child its own *hup*. I suggest that this can be achieved only through the appropriate focusing of the mother's attention. She must be made as aware as possible of *rəwaay* in her imagination, just as she must not imagine *hup* if she is to redress the balance between them. This, I suggest, is what underlies the rituals and dietary restrictions discussed earlier. By avoiding foods that might act physiologically to bring her *hup* (her heart and blood) into thematicised attention, she will be better prepared to bring *rəwaay* into her awareness. The ritual washing at first menstruation commences this process early, by prefiguring the *rəwaay*-enhancing properties of the same ritual as performed after childbirth. The child's situation, as might be expected, is directly linked to this. While the mother is protected against focusing her attention on *hup*, the child's well-being is protected by a battery of ritual restrictions aimed at preventing *rəwaay*-loss.

The mother as tree

In Southeast Asia, vegetal imagery is widely employed in talking about consanguineal relations; for example, the child is often seen as a kind of plant (Fox 1971). The Temiar material seems to share this characteristic, but it implies the view that mother and child together form a *tree*.

As noted in Chapters 2 and 6, the pouring of water forms part of the rituals at first menstruation, childbirth, and the setting of new house-posts. These acts are very similar to the ordinary watering that Temiars carry out when caring for a newly planted fruit tree. Temiars explicitly say that a tree's *kənoruk* (its *hup*-equivalent) is situated in its roots and that its *rəwaay* is found at the growing points of the leaves, where the petioles join the blades. Thus, if a 'tree' image were applied to human reproduction, the mother would be the roots (the *hup*-container) and the child the leaves (the progressively emerging *rəwaay*-container). For this image to work, however, it would be necessary for the trunk eventually to die off, so that the two parts—mother and child—that were initially joined together may achieve their proper autonomy. At first glance, this interpretation must seem over-imaginative, but it is supported by some remarkable features of the Temiar lexicon.

The most obvious of these is the fact that the ordinary word for 'mother', *boo²*, also means 'tree-trunk, stem'. But there is additional evidence, of a more opaque historical-linguistic kind, in support of this mother-as-tree view. Comparative studies in the Austroasiatic and Austronesian language-families show that the Temiar words *boo²* 'mother; trunk', *təp* 'formerly' and (just possibly) *suul* 'navel' have undergone a linked set of lexical transformations. The proposed linkage is based on the following findings. In *boo²*, the meaning 'trunk, tree' is a secondary elaboration from the 'mother' meaning (Shorto 2006: 96). In *təp*, the meaning 'former' derives from Proto-Mon-Khmer *təm ~ *təəm (Shorto 2006: 368), with such meanings as 'plant', 'tree', 'base', 'foot', 'beginning', 'trunk', still found in Monic (Diffloth 1984: 84), but which subsequently dropped out of use in Temiar.

The meanings 'trunk' and 'formerly' *can* be connected if we link them to the World-Tree image of cosmogenesis that is widely distributed in Southeast Asia, including aboriginal Malaya. The trunk of the World Tree, in holding heaven and earth conditionally apart, is maintaining the 'now' of the human world-space against the threat that it might dissolve back into the former primal state of undifferentiated mud. This parallels on the macrocosmic level the microcosmic image linking the 'mother' and 'trunk' meanings of *boo²* in Temiar. As remarked earlier, the mother–child filiative tie is what holds the key-of-life tie of siblingship apart from the key-of-death tie of affinity (namely, the child's father and mother viewed as husband and wife) that generates it. (For more on this image, see Benjamin (1968a: 126–128).

Thus, in Temiar motherhood, when the 'trunk ~ mother' (*boo²*) filiative tie enters the key of death, it becomes *təp* ('former ~ trunk'). Only when that stage is reached can mother and child become relatively autonomous individuals and cease to imply danger for each other. In so doing, they are re-enacting the primal separation that the cosmos maintains in providing human beings with a here-and-now life-space.

What then of the Temiar word *suul* 'navel'? This word possibly derives from a Proto-Mon-Khmer word meaning 'body hair' that Shorto (2006: 466) tentatively reconstructs as *ksuul* and which seems to have replaced some earlier Aslian word for 'navel'.[29] An alternative Temiar word for 'navel' is *panik*, which is probably a loan from a pre-modern form of the Malay word *pending* 'ornament worn in front of body; belt clasp'. (The phonological changes involved are all quite regular.) But the original Mon-Khmer word for 'navel, placenta' was probably **suǝk* (Shorto 2006: 170), now represented in Temiar by the word *sǝwag* 'afterbirth'. These shifts imply that 'navel' words in Temiar have been subject to linguistic avoidance, for reasons that might be linked in some still obscure way with the semantic shifts outlined in the previous paragraphs.

What of father?

In the last few sections, I have concentrated on the relation between mother and child. Earlier, I presented evidence to suggest that the father is entangled in the mystical dangers of parenthood almost as much as the mother is. At first sight, this almost equal, non-differentiated contribution of the mother and father is puzzling: it runs counter to the fact that motherhood is physiologically a much more involving situation than fatherhood. But, as we have seen, Temiar 'equality' or 'identity' is always fundamentally composed of a self–other dialectic. Temiars can thus easily claim that two things are the same while also being aware of the dialectical complementarity between them— especially when the two 'things' are both the dialectical transforms of the 'same' precursor. This is the case when (as Temiar idiom has it) mother and father are seen as the 'backwards' transforms (*sid*) of their child. To express the idea 'she looks like her mother', Temiars say *na-sid ma-boo? ?ǝh* 'she is transforming into her mother'.

Thus, if the mother is *hup* (heart-soul) to the child's *rǝwaay* (head-soul), as Temiar imagery would have it, then the father should indeed be *rǝwaay* to the mother's *hup*. But he could also be seen as *hup* to the child's *rǝwaay*— as is suggested by the way he shares in his wife's *hup*-related taboos (figure 12.1). These views are not formed 'structures', dogmas or explicit statements. Rather, they are my formulations of an attempt to represent the range of meanings that individual Temiars can, if they so choose, construct for themselves. They are projective formulations precisely because this particular domain is unformulated and thus open to the play of imagination. Just as with the component parts of the cosmos, the different elements here can be seen variously and in different combinations as sometimes the same and sometimes as different.

---

29. I originally presented this suggestion on the basis of the final syllable of reconstructed Proto-Austro-Tai **[(m)po]sol* 'basis, trunk (of tree, body), origin' as proposed by Benedict (1975: 226). This would have clinched my 'tree'-linked argument, but few, if any, linguists would be prepared to accept Benedict's identification. Blust & Trussel (2010), for example, reconstruct the etymon that Benedict had in mind as Proto-Malayo-Polynesian **puqun* 'base of a tree; cause; source, origin; beginning, first wife' etc. This is clearly not relatable to Temiar *suul*.

The father, however, would seem to be slightly more peripheral than mother or child. In phenomenal terms, of course, his peripherality is understandable: it is the mother, not the father, who physically produces and suckles the child (despite male attempts to 'suckle'). It is the mother, who through menstruating, bears the obvious relation to *hup*—the 'best' male equivalent to which is semen, which might just be seen by some individuals, therefore, as a trope for *rǝwaay*. The only evidence I have for such a view is that Temiars regard semen, despite its congealing properties, as a liquid, referring to it either as *ʔɔɔk* 'water' or *nɔɔm* 'urine': *rǝwaay*-derived spirit-guides are also thought to materialise in the spirit-medium's hand as a watery liquid (*kahyɛk*).

Remaining questions

The above discussion raises as many questions as it answers. There remains, for example, the problem of where the child's-cum-parents' soul-stuff is thought to come from. If it is formed by differentiation-plus-merger of the parents' soul, then the 'dangers' are understandable. But we still need to ask how the soul-stuff is thought to grow—what feeds it, and what is the substance in which it is transmitted to the child?

Also, it should be noted that blood has the property of clotting, which makes it suitable as a trope of 'unrestrained solid/constrained liquid', like the primordial mud (Limbaŋ) out of which, in Temiar myth (Chapter 4), the cosmos differentiated itself into being. This suggests a further cosmic connection: perhaps babies are imaged as being formed, like the world itself, out of the clotting of blood (~mud). A closer examination than I have been able to provide here of Temiar notions of cosmogony, the 'fate of the soul', dreaming, physiology and reproduction might provide some answers to these questions.[30]

---

30. For a richer account of Temiar concerns with blood, especially menstrual blood, see Jennings (1995: 123–136), which incorporates her responses to the original versions of the present chapter and Chapter 6, thereby complementing them. After discussing relevant data and ideas concerning women and blood from a range of different cultural and theoretical traditions, Jennings organises her own account around the assertion (with which I agree) that 'for the Temiars, *all spilt blood* is dangerous'.

Rationalisation and Re-enchantment: Temiar Religion, 1964–94

Introduction

In this and the following chapter the emphasis shifts from the culturally embedded ethnography of Chapters 3–12 to a more sociologically orientated approach, occasioned by the changes in Temiar religious life that occurred in the decades following my earlier fieldwork.

A recurrent theme in the sociology of religion, deriving from the work of Max Weber, has been the question of rationalisation. It may seem strange to associate religion—supposedly the most non-rational of all activities—with rationality. The connection can be explained by noting the following four key features. First, religious rationality is associated with the repackaging of religion so that it becomes *teachable*. Second, this is linked in turn with a high regard for *written* sources as the guarantors of religious truth. Third, the adoption of a formally rational approach to religion involves intellectualisation and what Weber's translators called 'disenchantment'. Recent religious sociology has paid much attention to this process, largely under the rubric of 'fundamentalism'. Fourth, through a dynamic 'pendulum-swing' inherent in formalised religion, disenchantment regularly generates a reactive 're-enchantment', in which people seek to re-establish a more emotionally satisfying set of practices.

Sociological studies of religious disenchantment and re-enchantment have typically been carried out in urban situations. Indeed, it has often been suggested that urbanism itself is the main factor precipitating these developments. In this chapter, however, I am concerned not only with a very rural situation, but with events situated on the tribal–peasant (or tribal–proletarian) transition. Approaches deriving from Weber's sociology of religion have rarely been applied to this domain, even though Weber's own account (1958a [1922–23]) covers a wide range of situations, from tribal ('savage') through peasant to urban ('civil'), both ancient and modern.

Implicitly or explicitly, writers dealing with such a wide range of circumstances have tended to take an evolutionary approach to their materials. Weber, on the other hand, is careful to note that changes of the type to be discussed here do not necessarily form stages in an evolutionary sequence:

> The increasing intellectualisation and rationalisation [as compared to the forms of practical knowledge found in simpler societies] do *not* ... indicate an increased and general knowledge of the conditions under which one lives. It means something else, namely, the knowledge or belief that if one but wished one *could* learn it at any time. Hence, it means that principally there are no mysterious incalculable forces that come into play, but rather that one can, in principle, master all things by calculation. This means that the world is disenchanted.[1] One need no longer have recourse to magical means in order to master or implore the spirits, as did the savage, for whom such mysterious powers existed. Technical means and calculations perform the service. This above all is what intellectualisation means. (Weber 1958b [1918]: 139.)

Weber also pays great attention to the social position of the individuals who instigate religious change. He argues (1958a [1922–23]: 268–269) that an economic or religious ethic is initially usually propagated and borne by a particular socially decisive stratum, even though its effects may be more widespread. He also strongly implies that the stratum in question will be literate, and may not always approve of the life-conduct and status of those in other strata. Whatever the initial character of the ethic in question, however, it tends to be adjusted to the religious needs of the succeeding generations (p. 270).

Weber (p. 284) goes on to claim in effect that urban ('civil') life is a major force for the generation and maintenance of the more disenchanted views of the world, since it is there that the 'practical rationalism in conduct' is at its most developed, in the lives of artisans, traders, cottage-industrialists, and others. This results largely from city-dwellers' detachment from economic bonds to nature. Instead, they rely on technological or economic calculations and on the mastery of nature and people. This predisposes them to an ethical and rational regulation of life, as preached variously by 'exemplary' or 'emissary' prophets (Weber 1958a [1922–23]: 285–286; 1978: 447–448).

The exemplary prophet is associated with a view of deity as supreme but static, in relation to whom one tries to achieve a personally satisfying

---

1. Weber's word for 'disenchanted' is *entzaubert*: literally, 'un-magicked'. In this extract, the distinction between practical and intellectualised knowledge corresponds to what Weber discusses elsewhere under the labels 'substantive' and 'formal' rationality. It is often overlooked that when Weber uses the term 'rationality' without further qualification, he is referring solely to *'formal* rationality' as opposed to all the other kinds, which he places under the general label of 'substantive rationality'. This point is important, for the distinction between 'substantive' and 'formal' rationality relates to a wider range of issues (including power relations) than is hinted at here. I return to this theme in the final part of the chapter.

psychological state. The emissary (or 'ethical') prophet, on the other hand, is associated with a view of deity as creatively active in the world, and of people as his active, rational vessels. Emissary prophecy is thus linked with the notion of God as transcendental, personal and ethical, as in the monotheistic religions of West Asian origin. Clearly, the emissary or ethical approach fits better with the views propounded by the powers-that-be in most modern states in their concern for economic development and the shaping of participatory citizenship. It certainly accords well with the religious style currently encouraged by the federal government of Malaysia—the country in which the events recounted here took place.

Baha'i and rationalisation among the Temiars

In the late 1970s, many of the Temiars became followers of a highly rationalised version of the Baha'i (strictly, Bahá'í) religion. The religion was taught to them by young Temiars whose actions were rather like those of Weber's emissary prophet. As described in the preceding chapters, I had studied the Temiars' indigenous animistic religion in detail some 15 years earlier, and their decision to embrace Baha'i surprised me when I first encountered it. On later visits, from the 1980s onwards, I discovered that their involvement with Baha'i had waned.[2] Instead, some of them were continuing to practise their earlier religion in much the same way as before, while others—acting more like exemplary prophets—had begun to follow innovative cults that synthesised the old religion with a variety of other sources. (One such innovative cult, ʔalʉj Salamad, is examined in detail in the next chapter.) For reasons that will become apparent later, I shall refer to these three phases as 'enchantment', 'disenchantment' (or 'rationalisation'), and 're-enchantment'.

Baha'i receives no mention in the published studies of Temiar religious life by Marina Roseman (1991) and Sue Jennings (1995), even though they worked in the same part of Kelantan as I did. Jennings's fieldwork in the early 1970s was carried out before Baha'i entered the scene, and Roseman's started in the early 1980s, after Baha'i had begun to weaken. If I had not chanced to visit the Temiars myself in 1979, at the height of the Baha'i period, the religion might have gone completely unnoticed. Consequently, the present chapter is the only published account of Baha'i among the Temiars. It is therefore worth asking: would it have mattered if Temiar Baha'i had gone unnoticed? Indeed, should any importance be ascribed to an episode so brief that it could have gone unnoticed? The answer, I believe, is that despite its apparently fleeting nature, Baha'i among the Temiars was indeed significant—and that it is the

---

2. When talking to Temiars from Kelantan, I have heard little mention of Baha'i since the mid-1980s, but there have been occasional references to its continued practice in a few places. In 2002, Colin Nicholas informed me that some Temiars of the Piah and Plus valleys in Perak were still active followers of Baha'i. In 2010, I was told of a few people in remoter parts of Kelantan who were reportedly still following the religion.

sociology of Max Weber, rather than conventional ethnological analysis, that best helps to delineate that significance.

Since the Baha'i religion has rarely been the object of ethnographic or sociological study,[3] I shall take this opportunity to give a fairly complete account of my field materials. My main concern, however, is not with Baha'i as such, but with the general sociology of Temiar religious life over the 30 years that led up to its adoption. I must confess at the outset that, because I did very little fieldwork in Temiar country between 1979 and 2006, my data get thinner as they get more recent. My materials on the 'rationalisation' and 're-enchantment' parts of the story are therefore spotty: in particular, I have no quantitative data on the number of people who converted to Baha'i. Nevertheless, I was able to observe Baha'i practice directly among the Temiars in 1979, and to talk to several of the primary actors (as well as dissenters), during the early stages of the 'rationalisation' phase. Thus, while it may lack sociological rigour, the following account should nevertheless contribute to the study of Temiar (and broader Malaysian) social history, and help to relate events in one small part of the world to processes that were occurring elsewhere.[4]

Analysis: Temiar animism as many-stranded

As portrayed in the previous chapters, the indigenous religion of the Temiars exhibits a unitary, monophysite—but dialectical—view of the person and the cosmos: what goes for people goes for everything else in nature too (cf. Needham 1964: 148). Elsewhere, I have discussed why the Temiars should have opted for such a highly dialectical approach to life (see especially Benjamin 1985, 2002a, 2011a). There is no room to re-state the arguments here, except to note that the reasons relate to the Temiars' long-term relations with other Peninsular populations, considered in archaeological, linguistic, ecological, social-organisational and political terms. It should be noted, though, that the general shape of Temiar ideas is typical of traditions that have not been reorganised to fit the dualistic, salvationist approaches propagated by most of the historical world religions. Moreover, it is even less congruent with the 'rational', intellectualised religious styles favoured by governments

---

3. An excellent brief account of Baha'i, incorporating much sociological discussion, is provided by MacEoin (1985), whose study I refer to later. He has also written in detail on the sources of Baha'i ritual (MacEoin 1994). The most accessible monograph on the history of the religion is by Smith (1987), a sociologist of religion who is himself a Baha'i. The well-known sociologist Peter Berger wrote his PhD thesis (1954) on Baha'i origins; regrettably, this is unpublished (but see Smith 1978).

4. It is precisely because of the dearth of historical writing on the Orang Asli that I have presented so many footnotes referring to publications and documents not readily available to most readers. The same applies to those footnotes where I have tried to relate my empirical materials to a range of theoretical issues discussed in the broader sociological literature. Weber's work looms large here, not simply for its intrinsic merits but because this chapter was originally prepared for a conference whose terms of reference derived directly from Weber's work. (If, like one of Lat's Malaysian cartoon characters at a hawker's stall, I am guilty of having *semua taruh* 'piled a bit of everything on my plate', so be it.)

concerned with economic 'development' and 'nation-building'. In this respect, Temiar religion is an archetypal example of the kind of activity identified by Ernest Gellner (1988: 43–49) as 'many-stranded'.

For Gellner, the classical sociological distinction between *many-stranded* and *single-stranded* activities provides the key to explaining the 'primitive'/'modern' distinction.[5] Moderns wrongly assume that 'primitive' many-stranded activities are single-stranded. Thus, Gellner says, the Nuers' ritual identification of cucumbers with sacrificial animals as reported by Evans-Pritchard (1956: 141–142, 203–204), has been interpreted single-strandedly by modern-minded scholars *either* as making statements about empirical reality *or* as recording the Nuers' loyalty to a given social order. But the many-stranded Nuers themselves had no need for such distinctions; indeed, they probably *depended* on the absence of such distinctions. For moderns, on the other hand, the division of labour, the separation of functions, is 'inscribed into the very constitution of nature and thought'.

This leads Gellner to re-define Weber's ideas about rationality. Where Weber talked of (formal) rationality as the belief that one can in principle master all things by calculation, Gellner re-states it as 'the single-minded pursuit of a single aim (say maximum economic gain)'. This, of course, is precisely what is precluded in many-stranded situations. Thus, a direct connection can be drawn between division of labour, population size and rationality. The fewer the people, the *more* conflated things get, whereas 'large societies can afford the luxury of neatly separated activities'.[6]

Whenever Temiar life gets increasingly single-stranded—as it did for many of them in the 1970s, and has continued to do so since—the indigenous religious framework comes to be seen as too complex to be put into words and talked about explicitly. From a modernist point of view, indigenous Temiar religion measures up poorly against the more easily expressible ideas of the various monotheistic religions, with their written sources and ready catechisms. Temiars who have taken up more modern ways of life therefore find it harder to talk about the older religion, and far from easy to maintain its details in their own minds. Temiar religion does not even

---

5. In this, Gellner is explicitly following a well-established, yet far from exhausted, sociological tradition. Although he does not say so, he is also in part re-working issues that were touched on rather differently by Marx (1986 [1844]: 35–47, 'species-being' and 'alienation'), Maine (1907: 172–174, 'status' and 'contract'), Durkheim (1902: Chapters 2 and 3, 'mechanical' and 'organic' solidarity), Tönnies (1955 [1887], *Gemeinschaft* 'community' and *Gesellschaft* 'society'), the later Lévy-Bruhl (as implied in 1975 [1938], 'participatory' and 'discursive' mentalities), Mauss (1938, the evolution of the various notions of the Self and the person), Fortes (1962, 'multiplex' and 'simplex' social relations), and several others, including Bellah (1964, 'compact' and 'differentiated'). However, Gellner adduces more features of social and cultural organisation than those authors do, and in a manner that allows direct connections to be made with more conventional sociological and demographic issues. In sum, his approach enables us to bridge the gap between cultural anthropology and hardcore sociology, and between interpretive and more positivist approaches.
6. A similar approach is taken by Bellah (1964), in distinguishing between (on the one hand) the undifferentiated 'compact' character of Aboriginal Australian and Dinka religions and (on the other) the 'differentiated' transcendental character of the religions found in more complex societies.

possess a name, let alone a formulated doctrine. At best, its followers would be thought of as possessing 'superstitions' or 'beliefs', but not a rationally ordered book-based 'religion'.

As Gellner (1988: 43–49) points out, the ease with which things can be talked about relates directly to the shift from many-stranded to single-stranded activities. In many-stranded situations, language-use conflates several different purposes and meanings, without privileging any one of them.[7] But the single-stranded situations typical of modern life privilege the *referential* use of language; all other modes of language-use are demoted to secondary status or treated as 'metaphor'. Such referential language-use may lack excitement—'without absurdity, no logical fireworks' (Gellner 1988: 49)—but it is an eminently more amenable form of discourse for those who wish to lead rationalised 'modern' lives, and it is accordingly favoured by the proponents of the more intellectualised varieties of religion.

This does not mean that individual Temiars were never capable of standing apart from their religious institutions to pass critical or even dissenting comments on them (cf. Bellah 1964: 364–365). In 1965, for example, Penghulu Dalam, the headman of my home village of Humid, expressed scepticism about spiritual matters.[8] He asserted, for example, that he did not believe in an afterlife, and that when we die we just rot like logs. The conversation was couched in terms that would have been thought atheistic—or at least single-strandedly rational—in other contexts. Yet even in those days, Dalam would sometimes perform his own spirit-guide's songs; and later, in the 1970s, he began practising as a 'big' tiger-spirit medium. (He figures as a medium in both Roseman's and Jennings's accounts.) To my mind, this shows that, even if Dalam may not in *all* senses have 'believed' what he was saying, it was at least possible for him (and hence others) to mount a rhetoric of standing apart from Temiar culture in a manner usually thought more typical of disenchanted situations.

But the situation was even more complicated than this. In Chapter 7, I reported a further conversation with Dalam on a similar theme. This conversation was indeed full of 'logical fireworks'. For months, he had been telling me that it was untrue that Temiar mediums could turn into tigers, even though this was widely believed to be so. However, he went on to say that once, when sharing a hotel room in town with a Batek headman, he saw him metamorphose (*na-lãã̃s*) into tiger-like behaviour in his sleep. When I asked how this squared with his previously expressed disbelief in spiritual matters, he said that those comments had referred only to the Temiars; the people

---

7. For an analysis of the effects of many-strandedness on the grammatical and lexical organisation of the Temiar language, see Benjamin (2014).
8. Penghulu (or 'Panglima') Dalam son of Bejau was the senior government-recognised headman of the area, and one of my own chief mentors in Temiar matters since 1964. He was born around 1910 and died in 1985. Some details of his background and reminiscences appear in Benjamin (1966: 19; 1968b: 9–10; 1987a: 142–145), and (in some detail) in Benjamin (2001).

living further east certainly *could* change into tigers, and frequently did. This was why he was somewhat afraid of the Menriqs and Bateks.

What are we to make of this apparently vacillating way of talking? Gellner (1988: 52) notes that, although traditional society has many domains of discourse that are impermeable to empirical evidence, it also has a few areas that *are* so permeable. So, while the bulk of traditional language use may indeed be ritualistic—what Malinowski called 'phatic communion'— there is still the possibility of a more referential usage. 'A nature independent of society cannot be avoided; but there is no need normally to systematise it into a single socially independent, unified system.' However, encounters with reality under such circumstances are themselves many-stranded and the pure 'empirical' content can therefore easily be over-ridden by the other, more 'ritualist' dimensions.

Gellner's argument about language use relates directly to proposals I have made myself (Benjamin 1988: 27–29) with regard to the emergence of the modern state. Gemeinschaft (local community) and Gesellschaft (wider society) were *both* present in pre-modern societies; but, through the deliberate *suppression* of Gemeinschaft, only Gesellschaft has been allowed to persist. Thus, we may assume that rationality or disenchantment in Weber's sense is not simply the outcome of certain circumstances of life, but that it needs also to be constantly engineered by those who have an interest in its maintenance. *Keeping* people disenchanted and formally rational requires the expenditure of political energy—a point I return to at the end of this chapter. But there was no such pressure on Dalam when he made the comments reported above. He could pass in and out of disenchantment with such ease precisely because his broader situation remained many-stranded. Feelings of 'bad faith' at talking like this (cf. Berger 1966: 164–171) were unlikely to trouble him, as they probably would if he had been living in a single-stranded situation—like the modern intellectuals for whom this chapter is written or like some of the younger Temiars I am about to discuss.

As already noted, a degree of single-strandedness did eventually emerge in Temiar country. Many Temiars—though not Dalam himself—responded to this new circumstance by embracing apparently 'rational' religions that were easier to put into words. Some became Muslims, especially in Perak, where the state government had been organising conversion activities among the Orang Asli for many years. Here, however, I am concerned with those Temiars, especially in Kelantan, who turned to the highly monotheistic Baha'i faith during the 1970s. As far as I could tell from my discussions with them (see below), they were looking for an organised religion comparable to those that the Malaysian authorities had been urging all citizens to follow. Baha'i, as I shall show in the next section, satisfied these mostly younger Temiars' desire for an easily explained religion, as well as for one that suited their emerging sense of individualistic modernity.

Disenchantment

The original push for the Temiars to embrace a named religion came from regular exhortations on the government-run radio stations that every citizen should have an *agama* (or *ugama*), a religion-of-the-book. In Malaysia (as in Indonesia), a citizen with no officially accepted religion—no *agama*—is liable to be considered an atheist, and hence a Communist. In practice, *agama* is defined as a named religion, with a founding prophet, a sacred book, a clergy, and formal places of worship. It is little wonder that the Malaysian authorities have regarded the Orang Asli as having no religion—at least, not until they become Muslims (the preferred choice) or Christians. At best, they have been spoken of as having 'beliefs' (*kepercayaan*). The requirement for belief in God (*Tuhan*, a non-denominational usage) is inscribed as the first clause in Malaysia's official national ideology, the *Rukun Negara*. Despite this, the situation of Baha'i in the authorities' eyes is more complicated, as I shall show in the next section.

Since the 1970s, articles in the JHEOA's in-house magazine, *Nong Pai* (Temiar, *nɔŋ paay* 'new way'), had made it clear that the Orang Asli should preferably choose Islam. At that time, almost every issue contained a section on Islam entitled *Sudut Ugama* 'religion corner'. Among the relevant news reports it contained were the following:

> *Unit Pembangunan Rohaniah mula menjalankan kegiatannya* ['The Spiritual Development Unit gets under way'], August–December 1979: 23–24. This gives details of Islamic training programmes organised for Orang Asli in several states.

> *Perasmian surau Orang Asli Sungai Badok* ['Official opening of the Orang Asli prayer-house at Sungai Badok'], January–February 1984: 1. This front-page article gives an account and colour photograph of events at a small Temiar village near Ulu Chemor, Perak, at which the Director-General of the JHEOA officiated.

In most of the Peninsular states, both the JHEOA and the state Muslim missionary authorities were mounting conversion campaigns in the more accessible Orang Asli communities. Details of the federal strategy behind this plan were laid out in a 31-page internal JHEOA document (1983), which stated that it would cost more than RM14.2 million to implement.[9] Table 13.1 shows the increasing percentage of the Orang Asli (not just Temiars) converting (or converted) to Islam and Christianity over the decades.[10]

---

9. I do not know whether this particular scheme is still in operation or whether it was carried out exactly as stated in the document. Gordon Means (1985–86) presents an account of the earlier phases of Islamisation among the Orang Asli. He also summarises the story of Christian missionary work among the 'Sengoi' (that is, Semais), based on his parents' account, Means & Means (1981).

10. Nah's figures are derived from Carey (1976) and Department of Statistics (1997). The sharp swings in the percentages for 'tribal/folk religion', 'no religion' and 'others' over the years are probably due

Table 13.1 Distribution of the Orang Asli population by Religion, per cent (Nah 2004: 106; Norfariza 2008: 31)

Religion	1968	1980	1991	2000
Tribal/folk religion	95.0	66.0	45.7	53.8
Islam	3.0	5.3	11.2	16.8
Christianity	1.3	4.3	5.1	7.4
Others	0.7	3.9	12.4	4.5
No religion	–	20.4	25.6	17.6
Total	100.0	100.0	100.0	100.0

The conversion led to the building of *surau* prayer-houses in the villages (see Chapter 14), and in many cases, the giving of preferential welfare to those individuals who had become Muslims. This is probably in line with the official treatment of the Orang Asli as potential or incomplete Malays, for they have usually been included within the 'Malay' figures in the published versions of the national censuses. Governmental policy towards the Orang Asli has long proposed that their integration into the broader Malaysian community should be brought about by assimilating them into the Malay community, which by local custom and national law is Sunni Muslim by religion. JHEOA officers have been heard to comment that the Orang Asli 'problem'—usually defined as that of poverty—would disappear if they became Muslims, and hence Malays. In September 1996, for example, the Secretary-General of the Ministry of Land and Cooperative Development (Datuk Nik Mohamed Zain bin Nik Yusof), gave the following justification for the federal government's newly announced review of legislation relating to Orang Asli land rights (*Straits Times* [Singapore], 3 September 1996: 16): 'If these amendments are made, Orang Asli can be more easily integrated into Malay society. It will help them to embrace Islam and follow Malay customs too.' This statement was made at what was described as 'the first national conference of aborigines from Peninsular Malaysia, Sarawak and Sabah', representing '95 tribal groups with a combined population of over two million people in Malaysia'.[11]

---

to differences in the definitions of these terms. According to Carey (1976: 324–325), of a total Orang Asli population of 53,000 in January 1968, the JHEOA reported that 1,600 had adopted Islam, 700 Christianity, and 350 Baha'i. Of the Christians, there were about 50 Catholics, 230 Methodists, 360 Lutherans and 20 'Church of the Gospel'. Presumably, 'Others' in table 13.1 includes Baha'i, as that would account for all of the 0.7% figure in the '1968' column. Hasan (1994) presents an historical account of Christian missionising among the Semais, based partly on Means & Means (1981), along with his own analysis of the reasons for the Perak Semais' relatively welcoming attitude to conversion.
11. The figure of two million cited here for the 'tribal' population of Malaysia included only a small number who would normally be considered tribal in terms of their current socio-political organisation. The surprisingly high figure also includes the 'native' peoples of Sabah and Sarawak, whose often large populations constitute the majorities in those states. Their circumstances are in almost all respects different from those of the approximately 190,000 Orang Asli of Peninsular Malaysia (estimated 2014 figure), for they possess legislation that (in principle, at least) guarantees them land rights, and they are not currently under official pressure to become Muslims.

It must be assumed, then, that religious assimilation of the Orang Asli to Islam remains a goal of federal policy.

This preference for talking about religion and economics as if they were a single issue probably derives from the evolutionary view of culture that still informs much of Malay social thought. As McKinley (1979) and Wee (1987) have shown, in Malay imagery, progress is monitored by regularly glancing back at what has been left behind. There is no shame in having ancestors who were pagans, 'Hindu-Buddhists' or tribal indigenes (*asli*) in a former era (*zaman*), so long as one consciously moves forward into the era of proper religion (*agama*), purified (*murni*) culture and 'modern' citizenship. For those who hold this view it is a foregone conclusion that economic improvement will follow religious improvement. There would therefore be no point in considering other possible outcomes.

It is clear then, that the Malaysian government's pro-religion stance is driven not simply by piety or cultural ideology, but also by a quite instrumental concern with administration, social control, ethnicity and modernisation. For example, campaigns on Malaysian television used to urge that it is one's *religious* duty to keep clean or to arrive at work on time. On the other hand, over-enthusiastic displays of Islamic piety that go beyond the bounds of the regularly required practices have either been contained or co-opted by the authorities. The officially supported forms of Islam correspond to the rational, urban type, and not to the mystical, charismatic types, which have a history of being suppressed in Malaysia as *ajaran sesat*, deviant teachings.[12] On the other hand, the federal government also avoids the more legalistic approaches: they have consistently opposed the application of Shari'a law to anything other than marriage, divorce, inheritance or—optionally—Islamic banking practices. They have also opposed the imposition of social constraints on women of the sort that typify some other Muslim countries. Indeed, the government has portrayed itself as a positive example of a society that can be both Muslim and gender-blind. Yet, at the same time, official Malaysian Islam has also tended to support a hierarchical, state-connected orientation, rather than the activist egalitarianism more typical of urban Islam further west.[13]

---

12. Public discussion in Malaysia has suggested that the government's attempts to prevent Malays from adopting Shi'ite Islam are based on the fear that they might be attracted to the revolutionary theocratic model followed by Iran. It is more likely, though, that the underlying reason relates to the Sunni tradition's preference for 'rational' bureaucratic organisation, which is much more congruent with 'modernity' than the charismatic structure of authority followed in Shi'a, and especially in Iran. To employ Gellner's terms (1969), the Malaysian government has elected to go with 'P-type', not 'C-type', Islam. (Though he does not explicitly say so, Gellner's imagery here clearly relates to the parallel, though anachronistic, Protestant/Catholic divide.)

13. Gellner (1992: 6–22) provides an excellent outline of the Islamic sources for such diverging views, though his primary focus is on the West Asian and North African countries. For a subtle account of the historical connection between Islam and Malay kingship, see Milner (1981). Lyon (1979) and Nash (1991) discuss the situation of reformist Islam as an element in Malaysian national politics a few decades ago.

There is a further complication: Malaysia is a federation of partly autonomous states, mostly sultanates, each with its own local government in control of land policy and Islamic institutions. The JHEOA too operates at the state as well as federal level. The situation of the Orang Asli with respect to Islam therefore varies from state to state. The Temiars (discounting the very few who live in Pahang) are roughly divided into those who live in Perak (66 per cent) and those who live in Kelantan (34 per cent). Many Perak Temiars have converted to Islam, at least nominally, but until recently the number in Kelantan was significantly lower.[14] On the other hand, it seems that the majority of the Baha'i conversions took place in Kelantan. Given that Islam has played a bigger political role in Kelantan than elsewhere in the country— it has been ruled for two periods by an overtly Islamist party, the PAS—why should this be?[15]

As of August 1996, Kelantan state politics was in turmoil. The 'Partai Melayu Semangat 46' (PMS46) partner had recently decided to withdraw its support for the dominant Islamist party (PAS) in the ruling coalition, in favour of rejoining the main nation-wide Malay party, UMNO, from which it had split several years previously. Semangat 46 then decided to dissolve itself nationally, and encourage its members to join UMNO. Temiars form an active and significant portion, around 11 per cent, of the electorate in the Gua Musang constituency of Tengku Razaleigh, the national leader of Semangat 46 and uncle of the wife of the Sultan of Kelantan. In the 2010 elections, the Kelantan Temiars were politically divided between those (the relatively well-off) who supported the Islamist PAS party that continues to rule Kelantan and those (the less well-off and the employees of the JHEOA) who supported UMNO. I suspect that the UMNO-supporters outnumbered the PAS supporters, and that they are partly responsible for the Gua Musang federal and Galas state constituencies remaining continuously in UMNO hands—a rarity in Kelantan. In the general election of 2013, Tengku Razaleigh again held the federal seat with a substantial majority. The Galas and Nenggiri state seats, situated within the Gua Musang parliamentary constituency, were also won by the UMNO candidates.

One reason for the difference between Kelantan and Perak is that in the latter state many more Temiars have lived near road-heads than in Kelantan, where the bulk of Temiar villages have lain beyond the access of land

---

14. Until the year 2000, after which the number of conversions greatly increased, I had known of only two instances among the Kelantan Temiars. One was a former field officer of the JHEOA who in the 1970s claimed to be a Muslim; but he continued to live in the community as an ordinary Temiar, following no Islamic observances that anyone was aware of. The other case concerned a married couple I met by chance in Kuala Lumpur in 1965, who had not only converted to Islam, but had fully entered the Malay community. The husband, in particular, was embarrassed that I had discovered his Temiar background and that I knew many of his unconverted, still-Temiar kinsfolk quite well. His wife, on the other hand, was quite pleased to learn of my connections with her Temiar relatives.
15. See Kessler (1978) for a detailed account of Islamist politics at the grass-roots level in Kelantan during the first of these periods. For further information on the Temiars of Kelantan in relation to national politics, see Noraini (1992).

transport until recently.[16] But this is not the only reason. It seems that it was perhaps the very strictness of organised Islam in Kelantan that allowed the Temiars there a higher degree of religious choice in the 1970s than had been available in practice to their cousins in Perak. The relatively greater piety of the Islamist politicians in Kelantan made them more aware of the formal Islamic doctrine that conversion is acceptable only if the converts understand what they are doing and are acting of their own free will. Conversions brought about for other reasons would presumably have been less acceptable to the Islamic clergy in Kelantan. These very opinions were expressed by Temiars at Lambok when I visited them briefly in April 1994—which shows that they had some understanding of the broader situation. Two days later I paid a brief visit by road to a Temiar village in Perak, where the population (and to some extent the housing) was clearly divided into those who had become Muslims and those who had not. Despite this, the prayer-house (*surau*) was unused. The contrast with Kelantan was striking.

I do not mean to imply, however, that the Temiars at Lambok had necessarily gained a *true* assessment of their situation. In the 1970s and the immediately following decades, the Temiars were neither concerned nor familiar with what was going on in the urban parts of Kelantan, where the state government had imposed restrictions against, for example, physical contact (whether deliberate or accidental) between unrelated men and women. One state ordinance requires men and women to join separate queues at supermarket checkouts; another rule has banned 'unisex' hairdressing salons. On several occasions, the same government has declared that 'good-looking' women and those who wear 'excessive' lipstick would find it harder to get jobs in the public service than plainer-looking ones, so that the male officers could concentrate better on their work. And in any case, they claimed, lipstick was banned in the *Qur'an* (*Straits Times* [Singapore] 2 September 1996: 28). Against such a background, therefore, the position of the Temiars in Kelantan with regard to Islam cannot be stated with any certainty. It may simply be their non-urban situation, rather than any specific policy of the state government, that left them in the 1990s relatively untroubled at their situation in this respect. Indeed, as detailed in the final chapter, the Kelantan state religious authorities are no longer content to leave the Temiars undisturbed to follow their own choices. The differences in this regard between Perak and Kelantan have now all but disappeared.

Even for those Orang Asli who *were* interested in adopting a formal religion, political push-factors and linguistic pull-factors made the choice between Baha'i and Islam less than neutral. First, the push-factors. Some of

---

16. The new highway (routes A181–C185) running from just south of Ipoh in Perak to Gua Musang in Kelantan passes almost entirely through Temiar country, bringing many more of them into contact with modern transportation. See Appendix 1.3 for an account of religious change among the Temiars at a road-head community in Perak 80 years ago.

the authorities in Malaysia continue to regard Baha'i as an Islamic heresy, although it has been officially recognised as a religion. And, as already noted, Baha'i is sometimes seen as inappropriate for adoption by the Orang Asli—a population usually viewed by government officers as Malay-like, and hence as potentially Muslim. As I shall show later, these factors did indeed cause problems for some of the Temiars who adopted the Baha'i faith.

The main pull-factor concerned language. In addition to English, Baha'i employs Malay (the national language) and various Aslian languages in its liturgy and catechismal literature, which can therefore be more easily understood by the Orang Asli. Islam, on the other hand, employs Arabic, a language that is understood by none of the Orang Asli nor by most of those Muslims who seek to convert them to Islam. While the use of an opaque language usually does not matter to those born into a religion—especially Islam, with its great emphasis on the *sound* of its liturgy—it is likely to weigh heavily on anyone wishing to convert to a new religion.

While Temiar conversion to Islam is mostly a recent phenomenon, this is not the first example of religious communication between Temiars and Malays. Many of the Malays currently living in the Kuala Betis area are the descendants of those who, two or three generations ago, regularly engaged in joint animistic practices with the Temiars living there.[17] On the Temiar side, this led to the development of a ritual genre known as *pɛhnɔɔh gɔb* 'Malay-style mediumship' (Chapter 7). As Roseman has pointed out, this genre, at least as practised around Kuala Betis, involves solo singing accompanied only by a drum and bamboo stampers—but no female chorus. Given the importance that Temiars normally ascribe to the females' 'following' (*wad*) in canon along the *nɔŋ* 'melody' (literally, 'path') of the medium, this probably marked a significant break in their view of things. In Roseman's words (1984: 427):

> The suppression of the chorus in the 'Malay-style ceremonies' heralds the emergence of the audience in Temiar musical events. It presents a marked contrast with the choral response of Temiar-type ceremonies, which actively integrate the *halaa?* and the community. The emergent audience of Malay-type ceremonies polarizes the participant and the nonparticipant. This process finds its parallel in the formalization of leadership into ranked headmanship with the concomitant increase in the distance between the leaders and the led. Both trends arise through historical interactions with hierarchical Malay society.

---

17. In 1979, Penghulu Dalam told me that he had recently fallen ill during the fruit season. For ten days he could eat only fruit, not ordinary food. Eventually a Malay traditional healer (*bomoh*) named Da'eng came from Kuala Betis and treated him with spells, saying that the *jin tanah* 'land demons' had given him *penyakit buhmin* 'earth disease', which can be caught at any time by walking along the ground. (Perhaps, in Temiar terms, this is another example of the equating of on-the-ground with evil.)

Thus, the Kuala Betis Temiars had already received intimations of single-strandedness before the Second World War. It is therefore not surprising that this area has since witnessed a greater intensity of spontaneous religious developments, towards both rationalisation and re-enchantment, than most other parts of Temiar country.

The rest of this section concentrates not on Islam but on the Baha'i religion, with special attention to the ethnography of its brief implantation among the Kelantan Temiars in the 1970s. This is followed by a discussion of the significance of the episode from the sociological point of view. (I return to the question of Islam among the Temiars in Chapter 14.)

Baha'i: an outline

There is space here only for a summary account of the history, doctrine and general sociology of Baha'i. The 'new' religion of Baha'i arose as an offshoot of a Shi'a sect (the Babis) in Persia during the 1860s. By a series of transformations it has now become a highly rationalised monotheistic religion, considered to have been founded by the prophet Baha'a'llah (or Baha'u'llah). Baha'i is attractive mainly to members of the urban middle-classes in various parts of the world, although rural communities also exist. MacEoin's account (1985) notes that there are underlying social strains in Baha'i, between egalitarianism and authoritarianism, and between theology and ritual practice. It is not clear to what extent that insight is yet relevant to the situation in Malaysia, however.

According to MacEoin, the Baha'i view of history is very linear, and it deals in long time-spans (500,000 years). It regards itself as the current, but not the final, manifestation in a long series of monotheistic revelations. For Baha'is these include Buddhist, Hindu and Confucian sources alongside the more conventionally monotheistic traditions, from which it clearly in fact derives. (Together, these constitute the 'Nineteen Religions' mentioned in Baha'i texts.) Baha'i nevertheless claims explicitly to be a new religion, not a sect of Islam. Baha'i teachers preach obedience to the state, but they also proclaim the oneness of humankind. As a corollary, Baha'i ideology insists on education and equal rights, especially of women and men. It rejects priesthood. It approves of science, preaches monogamy, treats public service as a form of worship, enjoins hard work, and supports the search for an institutional basis for world peace. Accordingly, it claims that its universality makes it *the* world religion of the future.

Baha'i makes much use of local languages in its printed materials. In practice, its major texts consist of English translations, rather than the original Arabic and Farsi. The texts are thus relatively accessible and not too mysterious, even if the English is often portentous and 'biblical' in style. The religion has been the most successfully missionised of the new religions in Africa, India and East Asia, although in the latter region it has recently received competition from other even newer religions. The first Westerners to convert to Baha'i did so as long ago as 1894.

The religion's earlier more charismatic mode of organisation lapsed with the death in 1957 of Shoghi Effendi, the last hereditary Guardian. Since then it has established a formally routinised structure of authority and local organisation. The National Assemblies are regulated by the Baha'i World Centre. Tight control is maintained over Baha'i publications. Since 1918, Baha'i has emphasised social and moral issues, rather than esoteric ones.

Baha'i in Malaysia

Baha'i is recognised by the Malaysian authorities as an autonomous and permitted religion. For example, since 1974, Baha'i adherents in government service have been allowed to take leave on up to five of their nine annual religious holidays (*Malaysian Baha'i News*, vol. 9 (4): 38). Membership of the religion, however, is permitted only to the non-Malay sectors of the population.

The Baha'i headquarters in Kuala Lumpur, which I visited in 1979 just after encountering the religion among the Temiars, was situated quite openly on a busy urban street. The men and women in charge of the centre were mostly Malaysian Chinese and Indians, and I got the impression that there was a significant proportion of school-teachers among them. The considerable amount of literature available there was mainly in English, but there was also some in Malay (as the national language) and in several Sarawak languages. Baha'i also has followings among other Malaysian communities, in particular Indian estate workers, the Ibans of Sarawak and the Semais of Perak. A Semai man, Bah Deraoh, served as a Malaysian representative at the international Baha'i Congress in London as early as 1963 (*Malaysian Baha'i News* 6 (2), 1970: 5).[18]

The only source available to me in reconstructing the history of Baha'i among the Orang Asli is the aforementioned *Malaysian Baha'i News*, a restricted-circulation publication that appeared between 1961 and 1974. The details that follow come from its pages.[19] Baha'i began its spread in Malaya around 1950;

---

18. Writing around 1963, Dentan (1964: 181) stated 'Baha'i missionary activities among the Semai are just beginning.' Other Perak Semais have been Lutheran Christians since the 1930s (Means & Means 1981; Means 2011), although they still form a small minority within the total Semai population, which mainly adheres to indigenous religious practices.

19. An especially useful account is the anonymous article on pp. 49–51 of vol. 9 (4), July 1974, entitled 'Milestones in W. Malaysian Baha'i history.' Other articles (mostly anonymous) in the *Malaysian Baha'i News* relating to the Orang Asli are:

   1970: 'Asli teaching course', vol. 6 (1): 4
   1970: '[An] Asli marriage', vol. 6 (2): 5
   1970: 'A greenhorn crosses the Main Range' by A. Machambo, vol. 6 (3): 33–34
   1971: 'Aboriginal participation [at the 8th National Convention, Kuala Lumpur]', vol. 7 (1): 19
   1973: 'A tenderfoot's experience' by G. A. Naidu, vol. 9 (2 and 3): 16–17
   1974: 'When the Aslis came to [National] Convention' by Shantha Sundram, vol. 9 (4): 17–18

the first Malayan to convert, Mr Yang Kee Leong, did so in Seremban in 1953. In 1959, a few Orang Asli in the Semai village of Chang, Perak, converted to Baha'i under Mr Yang's guidance. In 1964, the first 'Aborigine Teaching Committee' was formed, and the 'first translation of Baha'i into Asli dialect' (Semai) was done, by K. Krishnan. In the same year, there was an attempt to ban the religion in Malaysia, but this was 'averted through legal action'. The 'first course for teachers to teach in Asli areas' was held at 'Teaching Institute Malacca' in 1969. In 1971, the Local Spiritual Assembly in Seremban became the headquarters of the 'Asli Committee', and 'Asli training courses' began. Translation of literature into five 'Asli dialects' was completed in 1971 by Lim Kok Hoon, as part of the worldwide Nine Year Plan. The same Lim Kok Hoon was reported in the December 1968 issue, p. 15, as having translated the talk of a visiting Baha'i leader into the 'local dialect', presumably Semai, at Kampong Chang. Most significantly, the first two 'Asli' Local Spiritual Assemblies were registered in 1973, at Kampung Sungai Jentong and Kampung Menderang, Perak—both, presumably, Semai settlements.

Baha'i among the Temiars

First reports

Although I had previously heard rumours of large-scale conversions of Temiars to Baha'i, the first sure information I received was at the end of January 1979, while carrying out exploratory fieldwork among the Lanohs and Temiars living at the large relocation settlement at Kuala Dala (Dɛnlaaʔ), Perak. There, I was told by a Special Branch officer that the Kelantan Temiars had converted to Baha'i, especially in the Yai, Perias and Lambok areas—the latter being situated in the downstream portion of the area in which Carey, Jennings and I had done most of our Temiar research. A Semai man from the Baha'i 'headquarters' in Kampar, Perak, had been telling the Temiars that Baha'i was the 'Asal' ('original', but also 'Aboriginal') religion. The converts were giving frequent cash donations to the Baha'i headquarters; they practised a fasting period (*puasa*); they ate vegetarian food on Fridays; and they had been told that the original Baha'i people may be seen in Lasah (a village in Perak, on the borderland between Temiar and Malay country); their bodies were bear-like above, but human below. The Officer had sent a report about this to the Police in Ipoh, who in turn had sent a summary of it to the JHEOA.

Having previously encountered Baha'i as an urban religion in other parts of the world, and knowing that there were indeed some Semais who had become

---

1974: 'Asli [Local Spiritual] Assemblies officially registered' and 'First Penghulu's Conference', vol. 9 (4): 38
These articles are almost entirely about Perak Semais; they contain no mention of Temiars.

Baha'is (Chapter 11), I was able to recognise this account as a mixture of truths, half-truths, and downright fantasy. But I was unable to investigate the claims further until, a week later, I moved to the aforementioned Lambok, to re-visit the Temiars I had been working with since 1964.

The testimony of a non-Baha'i

At Lambok, Penghulu Dalam (who had moved there from Humid some years earlier) told me all he knew about Baha'i, even though he had not converted to the religion himself. He said that the first Temiar to bring the Baha'i religion into the area was Cik Gu Kermal (Kɛrmal, official name Kamaruddin), from the village of Cherber, a day's walk upstream. Kermal had that very day arrived at the settlement across the river from Lambok. The Baha'i leaders were all called 'Cik Gu'—the normal Malay title for a teacher—and there were many of them.

Kermal had first heard about Baha'i in Cherber. The news had reached there about three years previously (i.e., around 1976) from Temiars in Ulu Brok (the headwaters of the Kelantan/Nenggiri river), two valleys away to the south. They had brought the religion from Brok through the intervening Ber valley, to villages upstream from Cherber. The Ulu Brok people had studied Baha'i, at a place I was not able to identify, after some Semais from Bidor (Perak) had taught them that Agama Baha'i was 'their own' religion. The religion came from their own original god, Tohan (who was 'not the same as Allah').[20] They should now pray to Tohan by saying: *Alɔɔh bəhaaˀ, bəhay ˀalah*—presumably a Temiarised version of the Baha'i phrase *Allaahu abhaa* 'God is Most Glorious' (MacEoin 1994: 43) and of Baha'u'llah, the name of the founder of Baha'i.

Kermal had gone to Tapah town in Perak to work with the Baha'i centre ('HQ') there some two or three years earlier. When he first arrived in the Lambok area after his period in Tapah, he said he would collect 50 cents from each person. People willingly contributed, especially in the villages of Belawan (Bəlawan), Bawik (Bawiˀ), Jias, Chengkelik (Cɛŋkəliˀ) and Lambok. The Kuala Betis people refused, however, as they feared the reactions of the Malays living nearby, who were the descendants of the Malays who had

20. The assertion that Tohan is not the same as Allah contravenes formal Baha'i teaching—just as the frequent public assertion (even on television) by some Malaysian Muslim preachers that Allah is not the same as the Christian God contravenes formal Muslim teaching. That assertion was nevertheless given the force of law by a Malaysian court of appeal in October 2013, when it prohibited Peninsular Catholics from using the word Allah in their Malay-language publications. Such statements are not simply matters of ignorance; they directly reflect the complicated partial fusion of religion with ethnicity in Malaysia. In Temiar, the Austronesian term *Tohan* or *Tuhan* 'God < Lord' is usually assimilated to *Tohaat*, which also means 'healer'. In these Temiars' unselfconscious but explicit identification of the Baha'i Tohan with Tohaat/ˀaluj, we assert that an 'otiose god', such as Tohan (Tohaat) used to be, may cease to be otiose in a situation of religious change. There are probably many other features of Temiar religion ripe for reworking under new circumstances. As we shall see in Chapter 14, this is precisely what happened later with the emergence of the new ˀaluj Səlamad religion, in which ˀaluj *has* indeed come to be worshipped as God or Tohan.

lived there before the Second World War. Kermal had said he would take the money to Bidor or Tapah to contribute to a fund, from which each man would get a return of RM500 for each RM10, if he needed the money, as a kind of bank loan. (Penghulu Dalam said he had heard that the Temiars in Telur (Təluur) village, Ulu Betis, had bought a battery-powered TV set from their contributions.) Kermal had also travelled north to the Yai valley, but Dalam did not know how much money was collected there. Kermal then went to the town of Cameron Highlands, later returning with calligraphically inscribed plaques (*pɔlɛk*: see figure 13.1) for the donors to wear around their necks as an overt sign that they had become Baha'i adherents.[21]

They were then taught to eat a communal feast once a week; but there were no food taboos. Before eating they were to pray by putting their hands together and raising them to their foreheads while chanting *ʔalɔɔʔ bəhay*, and so on. Dalam had seen this once for himself, in the village across the river from his own, where the main group of Baha'i followers in that part of Temiar country lived. Further upstream at Cherber, Dalam said, everyone had converted, including one of my main helpers during my initial fieldwork in 1964 and an old man whom I had known well years before. At Hau (Haw), yet further upstream, the converts included Penghulu Hitam Tamboh (figure 7.1)—whom I had also known very well in the 1960s, and who figures as a singing medium in the published field recordings of Temiar music made by Marina Roseman (1995: Band 17). (It was Hitam Tamboh who took the photograph printed in Chapter 4 as figure 4.5.) According to Dalam there was no Baha'i prohibition on trancing, and many of the converts were still keen *halaaʔ* mediums, as I was able to confirm for myself a few days later. Apparently the Baha'i leaders had warned people not to throw their plaques into the fire or there would be a flood; if they laughed at the pictures of the prophet Abdul Baha there would be a serious thunderstorm. (These views obviously derive from the indigenous religious framework, especially the concerns over *misik* and *joruuʔ* discussed in Chapter 5.)

Figure 13.1 Calligraphic design on the *pɔlɛk*

---

21. Talismans are still very important in Baha'i practice, despite the ostensibly 'rationalised' character of the religion (MacEoin 1994: 48–51).

Dalam said that Kermal had claimed that the three most senior officers of the JHEOA—all of them Muslims whom he listed by name—had ordered the Orang Asli to become Baha'is. It had also been put around by some of the Baha'i followers in Hau that two of those officers and myself had actually become Baha'is. (Later, I found out from Kermal himself that people had mistakenly confused our knowing *about* Baha'i as constituting actual membership of the religion.)

As the appointed chief of the area, Dalam had been visited the previous year by the authorities from Gua Musang, the nearest town and administrative centre. The Imam (mosque leader) and Kadi (Muslim judge), as well as the District Officer and the Malay headman asked whether it was true that Temiars had 'entered' the Baha'i religion. Dalam replied that he had heard about it but had hardly yet seen it for himself. He added that 'it was the Aboriginal (*Sərɔk*) custom to "follow" anything that came from outside'. The visitors then declared that Baha'i was 'deceiving', and came from outside the country. Islam was the proper religion of this area and, what's more, it did not collect any money from people. (They apparently made no mention of the Arab sources of Islam or of the collection of *fitrah* and *zakat* religious tithes. Nor did they acknowledge that Malaysians—though not Malays—are legally free to practise the Baha'i religion.)

The Baha'is at Lambok present themselves
The next day, a young man called Jamel (Jamɛl), whom I had known since he was a child, brought me all the Baha'i literature that was in the hands of the local leader, Cik Gu Damak.[22] There were eight items in all, published by the Majlis Rohani Kaum Baha'i Malaysia [The Baha'i Spiritual Assembly of Malaysia], 32 Jalan Angsana, Setapak, Kuala Lumpur:

Majlis Rohani Tempatan ['Local Spiritual Assemblies'], 1977, 12pp., proper printing. Instructions on forming local Baha'i groups, with rules of proper behaviour.

Bɛs [badge] or *pəlɛk* [plaque] with writing in Arabic script. (See figure 13.1.)[23]

Ajaran-ajaran Baha'u'llah ['The Teachings of Baha'u'llah'], 16pp. A catechism, with hymns at the end.

Marob Kalimat-kalimat Tjab-tjab Baha'i Lenglek: bahasa

---

22. Many years later, Jamel told me that he had stopped practising Baha'i (probably before 2000), and had indeed ceased to practise *any* religion.
23. This was the same as the calligraphic device illustrated by MacEoin (1985: 491), composed of the Arabic words *Ya baha' al-abha* 'O splendour of the most splendid'. Other sources refer to this as *The Greatest Name*, and transcribe it slightly differently as *Yá Bahá'ul 'Abhá* ('O Glory of the Most Glorious!'). However, few if any Temiars seemed to know the literal significance of what was written on their plaques.

Malaysia (Malay), Loghat Temiar (a Malayan aboriginal dialect)
[Subtitled 'Some facts every Baha'i knows', in Temiar and Malay],
26pp. A few prayers, followed by a catechism. (See figure 13.2.)[24]

Kalender Baha'i ['Baha'i Calendar']. Shows that there should be
a feast-day (Khenduri) every 19 days; and it lists the 'Hari besar
Baha'i', the Baha'i religious festivals.

Surat Khenduri Hari 19 ['Letter for the 19th-Day Feast'] 3pp.
Cyclostyled, 24 June 1978. A newsletter, including news of a
Kuching Chinese who had been expelled for contravening the
Baha'i marriage laws [which are strictly monogamous].

Photographs of 'Abdu'l-Bahá.

A discussion with Dalam and the mostly young Baha'i adherents then
produced the following points. First, the proselytising of Baha'i among the
Kelantan Temiars was done by Temiars only. Literate Temiars were keener
than the non-literate ones in performing their prayers and other duties.
Second, there was a general fear that the JHEOA would cause trouble if the

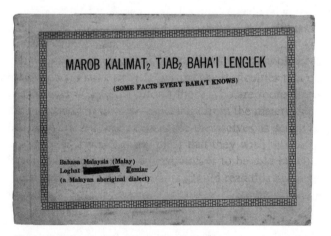

Figure 13.2 Front cover of a Baha'i book in Temiar

---

24. This rough and ready piece of book production was printed at The Ganesh Printing Works Penang,
and 'approved for publication by the National Spiritual Assembly of the Baha'is of Malaysia'. Its 26
pages contain a catechism and some quotations from Baha'u'llah, with the Malay text on the left and
a Temiar translation on the facing page. To my knowledge, this is the only printed book in Temiar. The
bracketed subtitle was printed from a rubber stamp, as is the word 'Temiar'. The latter replaces the
crossed-out 'Jahai', the name of a language spoken by about one thousand Orang Asli in the far north
of Peninsular Malaysia: this suggests that some Jahais too may have converted to Baha'i, but I have
no other relevant information. (Note also that whereas Malay is referred to as a 'language' (*bahasa*),
Temiar is labelled a mere 'dialect' (*loghat*)!) In my field notes I wrote 'the Temiar is pretty bad, both in
its transcription and choice of words; it is probably a Semai's attempt to write Perak Temiar'. (Certain
tell-tale grammatical features identified it as Perak, not Kelantan, Temiar.) However, I now think it
likely that the translation was done by Lim Kok Hoon, mentioned in the *Malaysian Baha'i News* as a
translator of Baha'i materials into five Aslian languages.

Baha'i icons were displayed openly, as the JHEOA officers downstream had already declared the religion to be *haram* 'religiously forbidden'. They had been hit especially hard at the collecting of money. Third, Jamel himself preferred Baha'i to Islam for two reasons: it did not involve any food taboos (he simply ignored the Baha'i prohibition on tobacco), and the prayers could conveniently be said in Malay. (Though literate, he couldn't read the so-called Temiar versions.) Fourth, no one recognised any conflict with older Temiar practices. Baha'i seemed to syncretise easily. Fifth, Jamel, at least, knew that the claim that Baha'i was the *asal* ('original') religion was meant to be a universal one, and not just for the Orang Asli. (But the possibility of deliberately confusing *Asli* 'Aboriginal' and *Asal* 'original' must have seemed too attractive to ignore.) Sixth, the claims that flood and thunderstorms would result from wrong treatment of the icons were, he said, merely supposition on the part of the ignorant. It was not part of Baha'i as taught here.

Kermal, the subject of Dalam's account the previous day, then turned up at the house with a host of his people. I immediately took the opportunity to talk directly with him, the first local Temiar to become a Baha'i. Kermal had left school in 1965, 14 years earlier. He heard of a new religion among the Semais of Sinderut, in Pahang, so he went there to learn about it. At Fort Brooke, in Ulu Brok, there were both Semais and Temiars who had been on the Baha'i course at Tapah, and in 1975 he went there himself at their direction. He took a three-day course, under a Chinese named Leong Choo,[25] and then returned to Cherber, his wife's village. There he taught people to 'pray' (for which he used the Malay word *sembahyang*), to follow the laws of the Malaysian government, and to follow the laws of Tohan, who was the creator of all—and who was the same as ?aluj ('Last-born': the mythic hero who created Temiar culture) and Allah.

They prayed in Temiar, 'like when we perform healing rituals (*soo?*) and utter spells (*jampii?*)', three times a day. Kermal himself taught them the words. He also taught the religion in Hau and the rest of the Perolak valley. After about a year, he came downstream to Lambok, and taught the religion there. Jamel and Kermal's younger brother, Angah (?aɲah), then also went on courses. Later, Ulu Betis was proselytised, but from Perak, over the watershed; from there, Baha'i spread across to the Perias and Yai valleys in Kelantan. Kermal had since been on courses in Berinchang (near Cameron Highlands), Kuala Lumpur, Port Dickson and Seremban. There he told the various Baha'i assemblies about the threats issued by the JHEOA officials that Baha'i was not only 'religiously proscribed' (*haram*) but also 'Communist', and that they might be arrested by the Police or the Special Branch. Consequently, they had concealed all the signs of their religion. Kermal said that although there were

---

25. This Leong Choo ('Master Leong' in Chinese) was probably the 'Mr Yang Kee Leong' mentioned earlier as the first Malayan to convert to Baha'i.

some Chinese Baha'i followers in Kelantan at Kuala Kerai and Gua Musang, he had met them only when attending courses in the towns on the western side of the Peninsula.

I asked about the co-existence of Baha'i with indigenous Temiar religion. He explained this as being the gift of Tohan, for it is Tohan who gives (spirit-) dreaming (*pɛʔnɔʔ*) to the *halaaʔ* mediums. I then asked about Karey, the Temiar thunder-deity: if Tohan is the same as ʔalɯj (Karey's younger brother), and if there can only be one god, then what about ʔalɯj's elder brother? To this, he replied that we must drop belief in Karey, because Karey only gives death, whereas ʔalɯj/Tohan gives life.[26]

They then turned to me for advice. In face of pressure from the Kelantan JHEOA, should they secretly hold on to their books and pictures or should they simply give up the Baha'i religion? I replied that what really mattered was their own commitment, how *they* felt about it. Then Kermal's father said that they did want to keep their religion, but were afraid. Also, as Orang Asli, they were in the habit of merely following whatever outsiders offered them. But in the case of Islam, no one had ever properly *explained* the religion to them, nor were they in any position to give up the hunting and eating of game animals forbidden to Muslims. The Baha'i religion, on the other hand, was presented to them in plain Malay; it fitted well with their beliefs; and it involved no change of ethnicity from Temiar to Malay.

My general impression was that they had no real interest in the content of the Baha'i religion, but that they dearly wanted to have an '*agama*'. They certainly were cavalier about some of the rules (such as no smoking), and their prayers, I suspected, were probably perfunctory. (Later, I found that this was not necessarily so.) They were not able to tell me *why* they wanted a religion, however—despite my attempts to demonstrate that they already had a religion, namely the one I had described in my PhD thesis.

A Baha'i prayer session and discussion

The following day (9 February 1979) I went with Dalam to a Baha'i prayer session across the river; Dalam too was curious. Strangely, although I had been in Lambok many times in the previous 15 years, I had only once before crossed to the village on the other side, the inhabitants of which were literally within hailing distance of Lambok but belonged to a rather different kin network.

It took some time for people to turn up, and the women were away harvesting rice. Eventually, with about ten men sitting around the edge of the floor and with Kermal sitting on a mat at the centre, he read out the first

---

26. This view does indeed accord well with the roles of these personages in Temiar mythology (Chapters 8 and 9). Moreover, coupled with Kermal's identifying of ʔalɯj with Allah and Tohan, this prefigures the monotheistic teachings that were to be propagated 30 years later by the founders of the endogenous ʔalɯj Sɔlamad religion (Chapter 14).

few prayers in the little *Doa Baha'i* prayer book. Although he had excused himself for using Malay, he did in fact read the Temiar version (perhaps for my benefit, or to impress me). The others, however, merely listened in silent respect, but with no signs of assent or of joining in. Kermal read in a quiet but clear voice. Afterwards there was a long, somewhat embarrassed silence, as they seemed not to know of any formal closing ritual. Eventually they started chatting and smoking furiously (Kermal included).

A discussion began on the possibility that the government might suppress Baha'i among the Temiars. It transpired that nothing had been heard from the JHEOA for over a year, so I suggested that the authorities must have accepted the *fait accompli*. At this, they mentioned that even the Special Branch officer (a Malay) at Kuala Betis, just downstream from Lambok, had been along and examined their books and icons, and done nothing. The discussion also showed to what extent these Temiars were in fear of the outside world. There was much talk of 'head-chopping' (*pɛŋpɔk kuy*, a reference perhaps to the notorious *kapak kecik*, 'little axes', of Kelantan), and some said that JHEOA officers had deliberately tried to put fear into them by referring to the towns as gangster-ridden. Their self-ascribed ignorance came through when they acknowledged that, although Baha'i was openly—and hence quite legally— practised in Malaysian towns, they would readily believe the claims of the Kelantan JHEOA officers that it was nevertheless *haram* ('proscribed').

Kermal then declared that, of the 'nineteen *agama*s' in the world, this was the one that he had fallen for, just like he might fall for a woman even if she was old and covered with skin disease! In other words, he could not explain why he chose Baha'i, and it may well have its faults as a religion. Islam simply had never been made attractive enough by its proponents. Some of the other men commented that, although the government had frequently dropped hints that they should adopt an '*agama*', no one had ever bothered to explain Islam properly. They talked as if they were regretful at a missed opportunity.

Analysis: disenchantment

I spent the next few days upstream at the village of Pedpod (Pɛdpɔɔd), where I recorded a Baha'i hymn-singing session. Not only was the singing performed in a diatonic 'hymn-tune' style quite different from the scale-structure of the Temiars' own music, but it was strictly homophonic, not canonic. Sociologically, this implied a concern for uniformity, overriding all social distinctions, and it thereby contrasted with the dialectical overlapping between the men's and women's voices, and between the *halaaʔ*'s and the non-*halaaʔ*s' voices, that is normally so highly valued in Temiar music.[27] However, the session took place directly beneath the ritual

---

27. For an extended discussion of the social organisation of Temiar musical performance, see Roseman (1984).

paraphernalia left hanging from the previous night's mediumistic séance (like those illustrated in figures 10.3–10.7). After returning to Lambok, I replayed the recording to Dalam and Jamel, which led to a brief discussion between them. Dalam, who had never been tempted to become a Baha'i, claimed there was nothing new about Tohan. Tohan was the source of the *halaa?*'s powers, so what was so special about Baha'i? Jamel replied that now *everyone* could understand clearly what it was all about, while 'you bomohs' (*ɲɔb buhmɔɔ?*) had a specialised knowledge that was not open to everyone. (*Bomoh* is the usual Malay word for 'traditional healer', including those who act as spirit-mediums.)

Here, in a nutshell, was the essence of rationality and disenchantment: a clearly stated, preferably written-down, framework of ideas that could be understood by anyone without reference to their social background. As Weber put it (1958b [1918]: 139), rationality is the knowledge or belief that if one but wished, one *could* learn anything at any time. In Gellner's terms, this is a single-stranded ideal. But Dalam, himself a practising spirit-medium, was quite happy to remain entangled in a many-stranded framework of ideas that required not explanation and propagation, but simple *doing*. How then are we to explain these intimations of rationality and disenchantment in Malaysia's social and geographical hinterland?

This was not the first appearance of a world religion among the Orang Asli. As already mentioned, some Semais had been Lutherans for decades as a result of missionary activity in the 1930s. Further south, there have been a few Catholic communities among the Temuans (a Malay-speaking group) for over a century (Borie 1886: 137–151). The so-called Portuguese of Melaka are probably descended from former Besisis and/or Malays who converted to Christianity in the sixteenth century, when religion and ethnicity were less tightly connected than they are now. Other Orang Asli groups, such as the Mah Meri (i.e., the Besisis) and the Jah Hut (see Chapter 11), re-formed their indigenous religions to accord better with the sociocentric pattern appropriate to those whose lives had fallen more completely under the sway of external political and economic forces. Thus, in turning to Baha'i, the Temiars too seemed finally to be taking the same route. Several factors were involved, some of which made the situation increasingly many-stranded, while others resulted from the Temiars' closer connection with broader Malaysian society. There were also factors that derived from events peculiar to the particular corner of Kelantan state inhabited by the Temiars.

Why did the Temiars not turn instead to Christianity or Islam?[28] Unlike the situation in Sabah and Sarawak, and despite the few cases just mentioned,

---

28. In the succeeding years, however, a significant number of Kelantan Temiars have become Muslims, while a smaller number have become Christians. See Chapter 14 for information on these later developments.

Christianity has not been a significant option among most of the indigenous populations of Peninsular Malaysia, where the Malay (and hence Muslim) presence is much stronger. As part of its agreements with the Malay sultans, British colonial practice in the nineteenth century avoided interfering with Malay religion, and protected the Malays from missionary activity by other religions (Yegar 1979). This pattern persists today in Peninsular Malaysia. In any case, the Temiars have been almost completely insulated by geography from Christian influence. As for Islam, the Temiars have probably avoided this in the past because conversion would almost certainly have made them not just Muslims, but Malays. In the Malay world, 'entering Islam' (*masuk Islam*) is usually synonymous with 'entering Malaydom' (*masuk Melayu*), and the Temiars were far too secure in their own very different cultural and linguistic framework to entertain such a radical change. It would have meant giving up their tribal autonomy for peasant dependency, thereby losing the economic advantages they derived from the complementarity between themselves and the Malays. Moreover, it would have meant joining the people who had often raided them for slaves, as shown by Clifford (1927 [1899]) and Endicott (1983). The much later conversions to Baha'i discussed in this chapter took place under very changed circumstances, after the Temiars' physical isolation had been reduced somewhat. Baha'i spread among them, not from external missionary activity, but from the autonomous initiatives of some younger Temiars.

The timing of the advent of Baha'i is significant. As best I can reconstruct, the religion arrived in Temiar country in 1976, just as the area was being opened up by the construction of wide tracks to allow the extraction of timber by private companies. Several things resulted from this: many Temiars gained an extra source of cash income as labourers in the (mainly ethnic-Chinese) logging camps, and they also learnt a few new technical skills. (However, they did not receive any royalties for the timber extracted from their land, which was regarded as the state's to dispose of, and they received only one-third of the amount that the Chinese workers were paid.) At the same time, large-scale 'relocation programmes' (*rancangan penempatan semula*) had most of the Temiar population of the Perolak and Betis valleys resettled in just two custom-built villages, with zinc-roofed, plank-walled houses arranged in streets, at a fairly high population density. These were built by the JHEOA as a compromise, aimed at preventing the Orang Asli from being removed wholesale from the forested areas by the military authorities. The latter wished to have unimpeded access to allow easier combating of the Communist insurgents who were still operating in the area. (The insurgency was declared to have ended in that area only in 1989.)

The relocation settlements greatly restricted the amount of land available for farming, so the Temiars living there became reliant on handouts and shop-purchases for their daily needs. Moreover, commercial logging activities muddied the rivers so badly that fishing ceased to be viable. Consequently, the new settlements became relatively dense concentrations of people who could no longer produce their own food. From a Temiar point of view, these new circumstances represented the closest approach to civic urban life, short of migrating to a city. This 'civic' development was reinforced by the younger people's literacy (in Malay) and their increased worldly sophistication, for most of them had by then received some elementary schooling. As noted earlier, Weber (1958a [1922–23]: 284) regarded rationalisation as being most characteristic of civic strata precisely *because* of their removal from direct contact with nature—that is, removal from food production.

Linked with these changes was the growing importance of the cash nexus. Previously it was just possible for Temiars to live entirely without cash if they worked hard at subsistence activities, but now it was no longer possible. Cash is the single most salient factor in the generation of single-stranded society, for it allows social relations to become anonymous, context-free and, above all, purely instrumental. The scene was thus set for experimentation with a religion that promised modernity, rationality, universality, and a learnable theology. The literacy of the younger Temiars was obviously a factor here. Baha'i reversed the usual order of authority in the community: the young people were now in charge, and making use of the one thing that most of their elders did not possess—literacy and the experience of book-learning. This explains their preference for Malay as the new liturgical language over Arabic or Temiar. The national language was transparent, whereas Arabic was opaque and Temiar ritual language was too allusively condensed. They had finally done what the government had been urging them to do—they had got themselves a religion-of-the-book, an *agama*.

Unfortunately, the Temiar Baha'is met with uncomprehending resistance from most of the governmental agencies who had dealings with them. They could not have known that the peculiar historical ancestry of Baha'i would lead many better-educated Muslims to see it as a heresy that must be stamped out. But there was a further complication, which had nothing to do with Islam as such. The Baha'i teachers' enthusiastic claims that this was the eventual universal religion of humankind got transformed into the idea that it was the *asal* 'original' religion—a view shared by some Muslims about their own religion.[29] Unfortunately, to the Malaysian authorities, the word *asal* in this context called to mind the 'Asal cells' that the Communist insurgents had

---

29. The assertion that Islam is the 'original' (*asal*) religion is based on the claim that God predates all other religious institutions. This view runs parallel to Wilhelm Schmidt's idea of *Urmonotheismus*, mentioned in Chapter 11, that Schebesta set out to explore but failed to find among some of the Temiars' Orang Asli neighbours in the 1920s. Currently, *Orang Asal* (as opposed to *Orang Asli*) has been a favoured term to refer to the tribal and recently-tribal populations of Peninsular Malaysia along with those of Sabah and Sarawak, presumably because it obviates the problems that arise from using the label *Bumiputera* 'indigenous' which, for a variety of peculiarly Malaysian reasons, sits uncomfortably with tribality—and which has recently (2012) been officially declared by some government officers to exclude the Orang Asli.

formed among the Orang Asli during the Emergency, to which a very high proportion of the people had belonged (Leary 1995: 101–108). The Special Branch officers still operating in Temiar country in the 1970s can therefore be excused for initially thinking that this '*asal*' religion was the creation of a Communist front organisation. It seems that it took about two years before the matter was cleared up, but by that time the damage had been done, and the Temiar followers of Baha'i had learnt that it was not advisable for them to be too open about their new-found allegiance.

Further opposition came from the local rural Malays, relatively unknowledgeable in Islamic history, doctrine and language, despite their devotion to the religion. For them, the problem of the Temiars' adoption of Baha'i was rather different. They had hoped, of course, that the Temiars would eventually become Muslims, and they had sometimes urged this directly. But, as Malays, they had themselves all been *born* into Islam, and had never experienced it as a matter of choice, rational or otherwise. Consequently, they had had no experience of *explaining* their religion to non-believers—which is exactly what some of the Temiars were hoping they would do.[30] Moreover, if sociability and *communal* religion were what counted for the Malays, then it follows that to be surrounded by non-Muslims might have made them doubt their own allegiance to Islam—a religion that relatively few of them understood intellectually, anyway. This would have enhanced their eager wish to make the Orang Asli into Muslims as well. Ethnicity was not the main issue here; rather, the Malays seem to have regarded it as a genuine puzzle and cognitive threat that the Orang Asli could not see the point of Islam.[31]

---

30. This contrast between the socially peripheral but religiously adventurous Temiar Baha'is and the socially more central but religiously conservative Malay Muslims recalls one of Weber's key passages (1952 [1917–19]: 206):

> Rarely have entirely new religious conceptions originated in the respective centers of rational cultures. Rational prophetic or reformist innovations were first conceived, not in Babylon, Athens, Alexandria, Rome, Paris, London, Cologne, Hamburg, Vienna, but in Jerusalem of pre-Exilic [times], in Galilaea of late Jewish times, in the Roman province of Africa, in Assisi, in Wittenberg, Zurich, Geneva and in the marginal regions of the Dutch, Lower-German and English cultural areas, like Frisia and New England. To be sure this never occurred without the influence and impact of a neighbouring rational civilization. The reason for this is always the same: prerequisite to new religious conceptions is that man must not yet have unlearned how to face the course of the world with questions of his own. Precisely the man distant from the great culture centers has cause to do so when their influence begins to affect or threaten his central interests. Man living in the midst of the culturally satiated areas and enmeshed in their technique addresses such questions just as little to the environment as, for instance, the child used to daily tramway rides would chance to question how the tramway actually manages to start moving.

The scale of Weber's references is much greater than the issues under discussion in this chapter, but the principle is the same—and it would surely apply to differences in religious orientation within the culturally assimilatory Malay community as well. (It is unfortunate that the published English translation reads so clumsily.)

31. I am grateful to Vivienne Wee for most of the ideas just presented. Years ago, when I gave a talk on Orang Asli at Universiti Sains Malaysia (Penang), a Malay student questioner raised this very question: Why couldn't the Orang Asli see how beautiful and desirable it was for them to become Muslims? I replied that they already had religions that they thought beautiful and desirable. But, because of the mismatch between the English word 'religion' (i.e., *any* religious activity) and the Malay word *agama* (an institutionalised, named religion-of-the-book, with a historical founder), my point was lost.

The rejection of the Temiars' involvement with Baha'i by governmental agencies and the nearby Malays thus placed them under a great deal of strain, as reported earlier. At other times and places, people in such a position might have responded with defiance or renewed religious involvement, but this seems not to have happened here. Instead, the Baha'i following among the Temiars began to wither, perhaps because there were yet other, more home-grown, reasons why they could not sustain their devotion. For one thing, they remained peripheral to any sophisticated contact with Baha'i teaching. The Baha'i religion is primarily urban in its situation, and few Temiars had any direct contact with the Spiritual Assemblies in the towns.[32] The life-blood of the religion seems to have dried up, for, like any monotheistic religion, it needs constant re-affirmation if its credibility is to be maintained. Such 'urbanisation' as the Temiars did experience began to fall away as the pressure to house them in relocation settlements lapsed for a few years after the remaining Communist insurgents capitulated in 1989. The Kelantan Temiars therefore remained rural, and many returned to live in their old village sites, newly rebuilt in forest clearings upstream. (This process has since reversed again, with consequent further changes in their religious alignments, as outlined in Chapter 14.)

Their position in the cash economy was also tenuous. Some individuals, especially those living downstream near the main Nenggiri river, did quite well economically and became entrepreneurs in a variety of activities, such as rattan trading and eco-tourism. Those who remained upstream were sometimes able to revert to a forest-based subsistence, by growing and finding their own food. Thus most of the conditions that had seemed ripe a few years earlier for the propagation of a rationalised form of religion had now fallen away, and the religion itself went into abeyance, perhaps permanently, perhaps temporarily.

Economic hardship, including considerable hunger at times, seems to have hit mostly the people living in the middle stretches between the highlands and the lowlands, because they had access to neither set of opportunities. Lambok and the nearby villages fall right in this zone, and it is precisely there that the next, 're-enchantment', part of my account took place.

---

32. Also relevant is the commonly expressed belief that, under Malaysian law, new religions may be proselytised among the Orang Asli only by other Orang Asli. In fact, no such law is stated in any of the relevant legislation—the *Aboriginal Tribes Enactment, Perak, 1939*, the federal *Aboriginal Peoples Ordinance, 1954* that replaced it, or the revised (and still current) *Aboriginal Peoples Act, 1974*. But the belief that there is such a law seems to have prevented any access by urban Baha'i catechists into Temiar communities, as the following item from a 1974 issue of the *Malaysian Baha'i News* (vol. 9 (4): 38) suggests:

> The first Asli Penghulu's Conference was held in July at Trolak, Perak, where about thirty penghulus (headmen) met with members of the National Assembly and the Auxiliary Board. The meeting was of great importance *as Asli teaching work is carried on entirely by the Aslis themselves*. [Emphasis added.]

However, no such belief has prevented outsiders from attempting to propagate Islam or Christianity among the Orang Asli.

Figure 13.3 Ancient Buddhist votive tablets found in Temiar country (1992)
Jacq-Hergoualc'h (2002: 332) states that the unexplained blue pigmentation is peculiar to tablets from Gua Berhala cave.

Re-enchantment

In 1992, terracotta Mahayanist votive tablets began to be found in large numbers in cave sites a few kilometres from Lambok. Additionally, some of the caves contained charcoal drawings, which Adi Haji Taha (2007: 232–241), the archaeologist in charge of the excavations, judged to be prehistoric but not yet dateable. This was a completely new development, as the sites in question had only just been made accessible along tracks constructed by the logging companies. (The sole advantage of deforestation in Kelantan is that archaeology will be easier there in future.) The tablets (figure 13.3) are similar to those previously found in Kedah, Perlis and Isthmian Thailand, as described by Lamb (1961: 76–78; 1964), but Adi (2007: 207–223) showed that this was the first time they had been found so far inland. The tablets are of red clay, and some have an inset blue coloration on the face. They may not be strictly terra*cotta*, in that they were probably just dried, not baked. Most are broken, but the iconographic details are reasonably clear. They appear to be authentically ancient, however, dating from so-called 'Srivijayan' times. The sites were probably used by Buddhist monks for meditation; they presumably came to know of the area because gold was being obtained from the nearby rivers. The Indic elements in the Temiar religious vocabulary, mentioned in Chapters 4 and 7, may well derive from associated sources.

After examining some half-dozen photographs I showed him, Professor Stanley O'Connor of Cornell University suggested, in a letter to me dated 26 April 1993, that the tablets are in an iconography, style, and type that comes into the Peninsula sometime in the late eighth or ninth centuries. Previously in the Peninsula, votive tablets were rectangular in form, Theravada in religious intention, and were carefully stamped and baked. [These tablets] reflect a later tradition in which the tablets are round or pear-shaped, unbaked, and Mahayana in content. These later tablets seem to have been formed rapidly and repetitively, as if they were the plastic equivalent of reciting a mantra or other efficacious formula.

These later tablets are usually associated with 'Srivijayan' influence, thus intruding a political entity into what is really a change in style, type, and religious content. I am not persuaded that this is, in fact, the case. Certainly the style is to be associated with that of Pala India and that is an international idiom. Similarly, the tantric-tinged Buddhism of India spread widely throughout the Buddhist world leaving its impression as far as Japan. In a cultural cross-roads like the isthmian tract of the Peninsula, a flux of ideas may be present without being imposed by military or political domination.

Presumably some of the rectangular and arched tablets found in the Peninsula are matched by tablets found in Dvaravati sites in Central Thailand. Either they are part of a broadly shared Mon visual culture or both areas drew their style and iconography from a common Indian source.

It is clear, then, that Temiar country was open to wide-ranging contacts at least a millennium ago, the specific details of which were later investigated by Adi Haji Taha. His conclusion was that the tablets are associated in a general way with the extensive goldfields of the area, which had been mined for centuries. More specifically he suggested that a Mahayana Buddhist polity may have been situated in the interior of Kelantan 'until quite late, say the thirteenth to fourteenth century', and that this might relate to the persistent Malay legend of Puteri Sa'dong, which local folklore associates with the slopes of Gunung Ayam (Galɛɛŋ in Temiar: figure 8.1). That an ancient kingdom could have been situated 200 kilometres upstream from the coast may seem improbable, but the collocation of gold with a highly navigable river (the Nenggiri) makes it just possible.[33] The other archaeological feature of note is

---

33. Regardless of this slight possibility, Adi (2007: 244) was mistaken in linking it with the 'Red Earth Land' kingdom of Chitu (Ch'i-T'u, 赤土国). According to Wheatley (1961: 36, 105), description of this short-lived Buddhist/Hindu kingdom appeared in the *Annals of the Sui Dynasty*, 636 CE, based on the account of two Chinese envoys who had visited it 30 years earlier. It used to be thought that the *Annals* placed Chitu 'more than one month' upstream from the coast (the reading accepted by Adi), but Wheatley later suggested (1983: 252) that the phrase in question should be 'amended' [*sic*] to read 'more than one day'. This would place Chitu far downstream in Kelantan's lowlands (where no relatable archaeological remains have yet been found). Nevertheless, the votive tablets from Temiar country may indeed be connected with some such polity, for the Chinese envoys' visit occurred just two centuries prior to the dates that have been ascribed to the tablets. For a recent discussion of the evidence for Chitu, see Jacq-Hergoualc'h (2007: 229–231). However, contrary to Jacq-Hergoualc'h's assumptions, any such polity is more likely to have been Mon-speaking than Malay-speaking at that

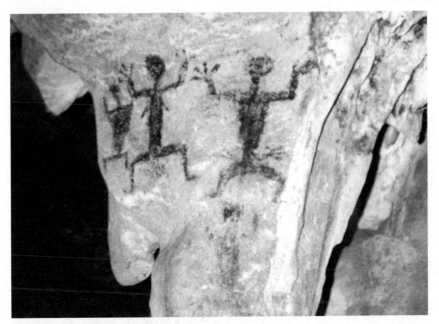

Figure 13.4 Prehistoric cave drawings, Gua Chawas, Kelantan (1994)
The drawings depict a child, a woman and a man, with a feinter figure below, presumably all dancing.

that the charcoal drawings on the walls of the caves depict ceremonies very similar to those currently performed by the Temiars who live in the area. Adi (2007: 236) reproduces drawings that appear to show people dancing next to a *tənamuuʔ*, and other drawings (2007: 241) of people wearing *tempɔɔʔ* crowns on their heads. To these, let me add my own photograph (figure 13.4) of cave-drawings from Gua Chawas (Cawã̃ãs) that depict dance poses identical to those shown in figure 7.4.

Marina Roseman, who was in the Lambok area in 1992 soon after the discovery of the tablets, told me that some of the Temiars had been placing them in shrines, and that they had become objects of religious veneration. Through the kindness of Adi Haji Taha, I visited the sites myself in April 1994.[34] On my way back to town I visited the Temiar settlement at Lambok, and noted a red-painted, fenced-off wooden shrine built on a polished cement platform on the ground near the house of Ading Kerah (ʔadiŋ Kərah), Dalam's successor as senior chief. Ading told me that he had built the shrine himself. Inside he had placed a variety of objects: not just Buddhist votive tablets, but also Hindu objects that he had been given in the town of Kuala Kerai. He said

period; see Benjamin (1987: 122–126) and Bauer (1992).
34. Regrettably, Adi died in 2012. He had been Director of the National Museum in Kuala Lumpur for many years. In his undergraduate days he had carried out ethnographic fieldwork among the Orang Asli, and retained an awareness throughout his later research of the important place of the Orang Asli in Malaysian studies; see, for example, Adi (1989). His very detailed PhD thesis (2000) on Ulu Kelantan was published as Adi (2007).

that this was his own place of worship, and then showed me how he did it: wearing a Temiar-style woven crown on his head, he sat on the ground as a Temiar spirit-medium might, but waved a bundle of joss sticks, Chinese style (figure 13.5).[35] He uttered a few words, and left some offerings of fruit and oil in the shrine. The shrine was Chinese in general appearance, although there were no Chinese images inside. It immediately brought to mind the much less elaborate, but genuinely Chinese shrines that I had seen 15 years earlier at Lambok, placed there by Chinese loggers to placate the local earth spirits. Those earlier shrines, though very rudimentary, were probably the prototypes for the one that Ading had built. The unboundedly syncretic character of Ading's shrine was evident: wearing a Temiar medium's crown while waving Chinese joss sticks and placing them in a Chinese urn. The objects of ritual attention (not all visible in the photograph) also included ancient Buddhist votive tablets, Hindu ritual objects obtained from town, and a swordfish's 'sword'. There were no Chinese-derived objects of worship, but the offerings of fruits and oil were typical of Chinese practice.[36]

Figure 13.5 Ading Kerah at his shrine, Lambok (1994)

---

35. In 2007, Jamel told me that in the 1960s, Temiars and Chinese used to hold joint mediumistic séances in the famous (and at the time isolated) Chinese temple in the old Hakka settlement of Pulai, south of Gua Musang. Abilem Lum also reported these sessions to Roseman (1991: 201), while placing them at a time before the Second World War.

36. For an account of what makes a shrine 'Chinese' see Wee (1977: 80–82). For a later and more elaborate Chinese shrine built in Temiar country, see figure 14.5.

Ading is not an ordinary Temiar. In the 1960s, he single-handedly ran the then twice-weekly Temiar-language broadcasts from Radio Malaysia's studios in Kuala Lumpur. He translated the world news bulletins into Temiar, played his own field recordings of Temiar music, and conducted interviews (including two with me, in Temiar, that were broadcast in 1965). In the 1970s, however, tired of life in Kuala Lumpur, he moved back to Kelantan to conduct business and live again in his home area. After the death of Penghulu Dalam in 1985, Ading was appointed by the JHEOA to succeed him as senior chief of the area. Despite his literacy and familiarity with urban life, Ading had continued to be a Temiar-style spirit-medium, singing his own spirit songs (some of which relate to his part-Menriq ancestry): he performs on Marina Roseman's published recording (1995) of Temiar music (Band 18). Regrettably, my 1994 visit to Lambok was too short to allow any proper investigation of what the innovative shrine meant. It is reasonable, however, to see it as representative of a re-enchantment motive on Ading's part.[37]

One other Temiar responsible for religious innovation was the well-known spirit-medium Abilem Lum (ʔabiləm Lum), who lived on the main Nenggiri river at the village of Bawik, right on the eastern edge of Temiar country, and therefore close to some recently re-established Malay settlements. Abilem figured as a major source in the monographs of both Roseman and Jennings, and his voice can be heard on Roseman's CD recording (1995: bands 3, 15). I met Abilem only once (although we already knew of each other), and that was at the special occasion in July 1995 when Marina Roseman organised a three-day Workshop on Temiar Dance and Music at the Cultural Centre, University of Malaya. The star of this Workshop was Abilem, with his troupe of accompanying singers and dancers (see figures 10.4, 10.5 and 13.6), all from Bawik, and all of them new to performing under the theatre-like circumstances in Kuala Lumpur.[38] I heard that he too had a shrine in his village, similar to Ading's. The importance of Abilem is that in recent years he had received a dream revelation, Temiar style, of a new and much less localised spirit that he identified as *Seri Kelantan* 'the Glory of Kelantan'. The new spirit was none other than the State of Kelantan itself. Old-style Temiar spirits are usually animal or plant species, or are associated with specific places. Although the dance and song genres associated with this new cult fell recognisably within Temiar tradition, Seri Kelantan related to a territory, not a place, thereby marking a considerable shift of reference from the here-and-now to the there-

---

37. Ading, who still (2014) lives in the Lambok area, has since ceased to follow these practices. The shrine had disappeared by the time of my succeeding visit in 2006, when he told me that he had placed the various ritual objects in an isolated and barely accessible place.

38. This event was made possible by the enthusiasm of Professor Mohd Anis Md Nor, Director of the Centre. Accounts by Alina Ranee (1995a, 1995b) of the workshop and the attendant performances and panel discussion were published in the *New Straits Times*. An account by Joseph Edwin (1995) of his experiences while visiting Ading Kerah and Abilem Lum at their homes in Kelantan also appeared in *New Straits Times*. These excellent pieces of journalism included interviews with both Ading and Abilem.

Figure 13.6 Abilem Lum (dancing, right) performs at the Cultural Centre, University of Malaya (1995)

and-then. Abilem, like Ading, was also not an ordinary Temiar. He worked for many years as a field assistant in the JHEOA, and was therefore used to receiving a regular wage. He too had now retired, and his Seri Kelantan cult should therefore also be considered as a form of re-enchantment.

Figure 13.6 shows Abilem with his relatives and friends dancing and trancing while singing in Temiar style. He had earlier allowed members of the audience to join in, but after a few minutes he asked them to return to their seats as he felt that they were not sufficiently attuned to the seriousness of the occasion. Although the session was 'staged' to a small degree—the troupe bowed to the audience at the beginning and end of the proceedings—it was for the Temiar participants an authentically spiritual occasion. Over the previous few days, Abilem and the others, under the cultural mediation of Marina Roseman, had been training some postgraduate students of ethnomusicology and Asian dance in all aspects of the performance: preparing the ceremonial clothing and decorations, making the bamboo stampers, and getting the subjective feel of the dance steps. The workshop was important because this was the first time that any Orang Asli performance art had been presented seriously and in depth to a broader Malaysian audience.

Analysis: re-enchantment

Why should there have been any re-enchantment in Temiar religious life? It is dangerous for me to draw conclusions on the basis of such thin data, but let me try. As already discussed, the young Temiars who acted as emissary prophets of Baha'i could not sustain their position on their own: the lack of close contact with more formal Baha'i sources and the general egalitarianism of Temiar society made that difficult. The Sri Kelantan cult and the cultic shrines were thus, in part, a return to what Weber (1964 [1920]: 20–31) would have called 'magic'—but one led by individuals (Ading and Abilem) who were in a better position to serve as (exemplary) prophets, since they were older men who had worked successfully in broader Malaysian society.

But that was not the only reason. 'Development' had failed to alleviate the economic and social position of most of the Temiars. With few exceptions, they were—and remain—at the bottom of the heap. But now, the relative prosperity and security of non-Temiars had become more clearly visible to them. Malays had moved back into the Kuala Betis area, and a plantation economy had emerged in parts of Temiar country—obliterating in the process any trace of my original 'home' village at Humid (figure 14.2). For sophisticated older Temiars like Ading and Abilem, the relative disparities must have seemed even greater than for those who had not 'progressed' so far in the past.[39]

The reappearance of Malays in the Kuala Betis area may well have stimulated the Temiars to develop their own nativistic response—but one which (with its obvious iconography and institutionalised 'places of worship' represented by the shrines) would be more congruent with what outsiders might expect of a 'religion'.

Related to this was Ading's use of *objects* (figures 13.5 and 13.7),[40] which contrasted sharply with the absence of objects from both traditional Temiar mediumistic practice (other than perishable plant materials) and from Baha'i practice (except for the plaque amulets). As I argued in Chapter 11, there is in the Peninsula an association between peasantisation and the use of an overt 'sociocentric' iconography. On the other hand, the discovery of Buddhist votive tablets in Temiar country in the 1990s may have played a special part too, for Temiars have always treated culture as pertaining primarily to *place* rather than people. The tablets, coming right out of the floor of caves, would for that very reason have been accorded a heightened transcendentalising power by any Temiar seeking a new religious orientation.

39. See Zawawi (1996: 89–94) for the directly-reported views of four young Temiars from Kelantan on the current socio-economic situation there. Zawawi (1995) has also written more broadly on the current situation of 'tribal' populations in Peninsular Malaysia. His general finding is that the Orang Asli do want 'development'—on their own terms—but that, for reasons beyond their control, they have mostly found themselves misunderstood and frustrated in that respect. Much the same was reported nearly 20 years earlier by Endicott (1979c). Zawawi also presents a valuable analysis of how the meanings of 'tribal' and 'peasant' should be rethought under contemporary circumstances. See also Benjamin (2002b) on this issue.

40. Of the brass object in figure 13.7, Ading said only that it had been given to him in Kuala Kerai, and that it had come out of the ground. My colleague, the late Ananda Rajah, identified it as a *vel* (Tamil: 'spear'), normally used as a tongue or cheek-skewer in the more ecstatic versions of popular Hinduism, such as during the Thaipusam festival. Thus, the object was not unconnected with medium-like practices, and may well have been given to Ading by someone who knew of his reputation as a spirit-medium. Kuala Kerai, known to the Kelantan Temiars as Bɔɔk Kərɛɛl, but situated many miles away from Temiar country, was formerly the only real town that they had dealings with. It marked the furthest point to which they would raft downstream to sell forest products—a major journey taking several days.

Figure 13.7 Ading Kerah holds up a ritual object presented to him by a Hindu in Kuala Kerai (1994)

Most importantly, the newer Temiar cults are more congruent with the continued practising of traditional Temiar religion than Baha'i ever was. Neither Islam nor Baha'i could answer the deeper-felt *religious* needs of people living in the manner still followed by most of the Temiars.[41] Any universalising features that were present in Baha'i must have come to seem illusory, as its Temiar followers realised that they were still being treated primarily and paternalistically as Orang Asli, and hardly at all as individually responsible and religion-bearing Malaysian citizens. They appear to have felt that they might as well live with this by 'going under' religiously, through developing their *own* cults of re-enchantment—in a process that brings to mind Weber's

---

41. As Weber (1958a: 270) put it: '[religious] reinterpretations adjust the revelations to the needs of the religious community. If this occurs, then it is at least usual that religious doctrines are adjusted to *religious needs*.' As already discussed in Chapter 1, I agree with van Baal (1971: 214–241), Polanyi (1975: 149–160) and other such writers that being *human*—and not simply social—does indeed generate specific communicative needs in individuals that can validly be thought of as religious. Just how these needs are met—through conventional 'religions' or through other means—is a different question.

version (1958a [1922–23]: 270) of Nietzsche's theory of 'resentment':

> As is known, this theory regards the moral glorification of mercy and brotherliness as a 'slave revolt in morals' among those who are disadvantaged, either in natural endowments or in their opportunities as determined by life-fate. The ethic of 'duty' is thus considered a product of 'repressed' sentiments for vengeance on the part of banausic men who 'displace' their sentiments because they are powerless, and condemned to work and to moneymaking. They resent the way of life of the lordly stratum who live free of duties.

The Temiars, of course, have lived under very different conditions from those of the urban proletariat that Weber was writing about, and their religious style has been different. But with due regard for the special circumstances, these remarks appear to apply just as well to the Temiar case.

Closely related to this is an important set of contrasts that lie implicit in most of Weber's writings. For Weber, the choice between formal and substantive rationality was not a neutral matter. He asserted, other things being equal, that formal rationality favours those who already hold power or might wish to gain power. Substantive rationality, on the other hand, favours those on the losing end of power relations. In Weber's words (1978: 979–980), talking here of law and administration,

> 'Equality before the law' and the demand for legal guarantees against arbitrariness demand a formal and rational 'objectivity' of administration .... . If, however, an 'ethos'... takes hold of the masses on some individual question, its postulates of *substantive* justice, oriented toward some concrete instance and person, will unavoidably collide with the formalism ... of bureaucratic administration. [....] .
>
> The propertyless masses specially are not served by the 'formal equality before the law' and the 'calculable' adjudication and administration demanded by bourgeois interests. Naturally, in their eyes justice and administration should serve to equalize their economic and social life-opportunities in the face of the propertied classes. Justice and administration can fulfil this function only if they assume a character that is informal because 'ethical' with respect to substantive content (*Kadi*-justice).

Formal rationality is typically associated with intellectualised discourse of the sort made possible not only by single-strandedness, but by literacy. In the religious sphere, this is most obviously manifested in the book-based *theology* favoured, among others, by emissary prophets. This approach leads rapidly to the characterising of certain religious practices as *correct* and others as *incorrect*—a distinction fundamental to the schoolmasterly authority that underpins the position of the clergy in many religious traditions, and especially in the more bibliolatrous ones. Thus, we might expect that, under conditions of religious change, actors would choose one or other of the following chains of elective affinity:

Formal rationality	Substantive rationality
Domination	Autonomy
Emissary prophecy	Exemplary prophecy
Disenchantment	(Re-)enchantment

The emissary implantation of Baha'i among the Temiars was therefore unlikely to succeed: it would have required a far greater display of interpersonal power than Temiars can normally stomach. On the other hand, the 'autonomy' later espoused by the exemplary prophets of re-enchantment was far more congruent with the general tenor of social life as led in most Temiar villages. Ading's shrine was 'his': he had no obvious will to organise other people around it, and his cultic activity remained as esoteric as that of the indigenous mediumship that he and others continued to practise. But Kermal's preaching of Baha'i *was* intended to organise people, in relation to an exoteric teaching available to all. It could not have worked unless a sufficient number of individuals agreed to do what he and the other teachers told them to do—and it seems that most Temiars, despite their increasing exposure to education and the cash nexus, were still not sufficiently ready to follow the path of rationalisation and disenchantment for long.

Temiar Religions, 1994–2012: Islam, Christianity, Paluj Səlamad

Introduction

At the time of my initial fieldwork in Kelantan in 1964, Temiars were regularly performing the ethnographically observable religious practices described in the preceding chapters, but without claiming any overt religious *identity*. Today many—perhaps most—Temiars claim one or other overt religious identity, while displaying little in the way of religious *practice* to substantiate those identities. Meanwhile, the pre-existing Temiar Religion has continued to be practised, without attracting to itself any named religious identity, or even the label 'religion' (Malay, *agama*).[1]

In the previous chapter, I presented a detailed account of the initial stages in these religious changes, when a substantial number of Temiars in Perak and Kelantan took up the highly rationalised Baha'i religion in the late 1970s. This was succeeded in turn by a degree of religious 're-enchantment' in the form of small-scale revivalist and syncretic cults, partly in abreaction to the 'disenchantment' of Baha'i rationality, and which I was able to witness during a brief visit in 1994. Baha'i has since almost disappeared from Temiar life, but the extraordinary enthusiasm that it aroused in many Temiars at the time set me thinking hard, and in an explicitly Weberian manner, about the broader social and political context in which they were living.

This final chapter carries the story forward from there, based on visits to Temiar country in 1994, 2006, 2007, 2008 (twice) and 2010. Because these visits have been relatively short and mostly to Kelantan rather than Perak, my newer information is uneven. As detailed in the earlier chapters, I have extensive first-hand information on indigenous Temiar Religion as it was in the 1960s and 1970s. My information on Baha'i in the 1970s and on the Paluj Səlamad cult (see below) in 2008 is also largely first-hand, but much less extensive. My information on Temiar Islam, while moderately extensive—considering, as we shall see, that there are no *practices* to observe—is based

---

1. Although the title of this book refers to Temiar 'Religion' in the singular, this chapter bears the title 'Temiar religions' in the plural, in accordance with the current situation.

mostly on second-hand information. My information on Temiar Christianity is unfortunately even thinner, being based on a brief encounter with Christian Temiars in 2010, along with some later information supplied by Eduardo Hazera, hearsay, and a few published sources.

In writing this chapter, I have met with a problem that hardly concerned me in my earlier research. In the past, I have regularly stated my respondents' real names when writing about the Temiars to ensure that my reports retained their value as history. This has become increasingly difficult. Because of their accelerating absorption into broader Malaysian society, both state-generated and otherwise, the Temiars are now differentiated among themselves, economically, religiously, and politically (figure 14.1). Newer tensions have emerged that are more difficult to report on as openly as I did formerly. In 2008, however, some Temiars explicitly gave me permission to identify them by name in future publications, which I have done. But in some cases I have used their Temiar names written phonemically rather than by the 'official' names inscribed on their Malaysian identity cards. In this way, readers on close terms with the individuals mentioned here will know who is being referred to, while outsiders with less access to the culture and language will find it much harder to identify them. Nevertheless, this chapter still contains

Figure 14.1 The house of a Temiar supporter of Partai Islam, Kuala Betis, Kelantan, during the General Election campaign (2008)
The banner reads 'Vote for PAS. Develop with Islam. Balance change with blessing.' PAS won almost all the seats in Kelantan, but this constituency (Gua Musang) fell to UMNO, which was widely supported by other Temiars.

a few statements made by respondents or about individuals who remain unidentified, for a variety of reasons.

Temiar society, 1994–2010

Until the 1970s, most Temiars were tribal (segmentary and autonomous) in social organisation, subsisting by swidden farming, hunting, fishing and the trading of forest products in some of the most isolated parts of the Peninsula.[2] Very few Temiars had received a secondary education or gained employment in the modern sector. Since then, however, most of them have experienced considerable change in their economic and social circumstances. Some individuals continue to live as tribespeople, subsisting off rice and cassava

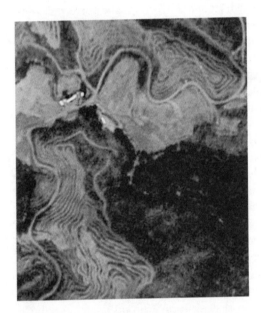

Figure 14.2 Vertical aerial view of the former Humid village, looking south-west (2010)
Photograph from Google Earth. Compare this with the view shown in figure 3.2 of the same location as it was in 1964. This recent view is relevant to the social changes discussed in this and the previous chapter. The terraced areas are clearings for the commercial planting of oil palms. The plantation is operated by a company located in Muar, Johor. The conspicuous tracks are unsurfaced roads, providing access to heavy lorries. The zinc-roofed buildings house estate workers, who include migrants from Lombok, Indonesia. No permission to utilise their land was sought from the Temiars who lived there, and no significant compensation has been paid to them.

from their own swiddens, but the majority have had to face the encroachment of broader Malaysian society. This has led to an imposed permanency of settlement and widespread access to primary and secondary education. On the other hand, their land and forests have been progressively alienated for logging and the monocrop planting of the non-foods rubber, oil palm and *Jatropha* (figure 14.2). Increasingly, they have been exposed to modern patterns of political activism. Since the 1970s, therefore, the Temiars have had much less access than formerly to the forested land they needed to sustain themselves, and their rivers have become so polluted with chemical run-off

---

2. For a discussion of 'tribal' as it applies to the Temiars and other such populations in Southeast Asia, see Benjamin (2002b: 12–17). My ethnographic accounts of the Temiars as they were in the 1960s (Benjamin 1966, 1967b, 1968a, 1968b) will be incorporated into a forthcoming book, *Temiar Society* (NUS Press, Singapore), along with newer material. For a later general account of Temiar society, see Benjamin (1993b).

and mud that their supply of fish has greatly decreased. Despite the existence of state and federal programmes aimed at alleviating their hardships, these changing circumstances have led the Temiars to become increasingly dependent on cash, even to obtain food.[3]

Consequently, many Temiars (possibly the majority) can no longer be regarded as tribespeople. The increasing differentiation exhibited by Temiar society means that most of them are now better thought of as peasants, rural proletarians, or petty commodity producers. Others are small provision-shop keepers or salaried employees, while a few are entrepreneurial business people, commercially recording pop-music performers, or salaried professionals. The latter include Nisra Nisran Asra Ramlan @ Angit, a Temiar from Kelantan and a trained accountant, who is the current Deputy Director-General (Development) of the federal Department of Orang Asli Development (Jabatan Kemajuan Orang Asli, JAKOA).[4] Nevertheless, most Temiars currently live in difficult economic circumstances, with much less access than they once had to autonomous subsistence sources of food or house-building materials. Along with most other Orang Asli, they fall within the poorest sector of the Malaysian population, and they now experience a much increased dependence on those kinsfolk and friends who have access to cash.

The physical circumstances of Temiar life have changed too. The government, through the Jabatan Kemajuan Orang Asli (still colloquially known as 'the JOA'), has built much permanent housing, broadly similar in pattern to that provided in development schemes for rural Malays, although often of poorer quality. These have met with variable success: the earlier pattern of purpose-built houses, constructed on raised pillars with plank walls and floors (figure 14.6), accorded better with Temiar preferences than the more recent cement versions, built right on the ground. A major consequence has been the emergence of permanent settlements, sometimes quite large, arranged in a linear pattern and possessing formal postal addresses (figure 14.3). This enforced entry into modernity will pressure the Temiars into a more formally rational mode of confronting the world. For example, many now have to pay regularly for mobile phone usage along with monthly bills for their domestic electricity supply and television service (see below). This increasing rationalisation of daily life has begun to colour their religious style.

The provision of modern housing has not prevented many Temiars from continuing to build houses in the traditional style (pillared, thatched, with

---

3. Official information on these programmes is available on the website of the Department of Orang Asli Development, JAKOA (http://www.jakoa.gov.my). For informed and up-to-date non-governmental reviews of these programmes, consult the website of the Centre for Orang Asli Concerns (www.coac. org.my). For critical assessments of the earlier stages of these changes see Mohamed Tap (1990) and Dentan, Endicott, Gomes & Hooker (1996).

4. See http://www.nst.com.my/Current_News/NST/Sunday/Focus/2354040/Article (*New Straits Times Online*, 20 September 2008).

Figure 14.3 A street of modern Temiar houses, Pos Blau, Kelantan (2006)
This settlement contains a well-equipped and permanently staffed school complex (including computer facilities), but also several traditional houses (not shown) erected by those who prefer not to live directly on the ground. The houses shown here tend to have persistently damp floors.

woven-bamboo walls), sometimes interspersed among the more modern houses. These are more comfortable but less permanent, and therefore not amenable to the supply of modern facilities (figure 14.4). Building houses off the ground in this way is an essential element of the indigenous Temiar Religion, as noted earlier. The modern houses are increasingly being supplied with electricity through the national grid or solar panels, which allows for refrigerators, better illumination at night, and electric fans during the day. It also enables the people to run radios (so they can listen to the dedicated Orang Asli channel of Radio Malaysia), video players and television sets—the latter fed by satellite dishes. It also allows them to recharge their mobile phones; many Temiar settlements are now within range of newly built communications towers. The sending of SMS text messages in Temiar has become common. Previously, the Temiar language was not written down by the people themselves, so this may turn out to be one of the most significant, though unintended, consequences of the basic literacy (in Malay) that primary education has brought to most young Temiars. Motorcycles are widely owned, and are used on the unsurfaced tracks in the village areas, as well as on the surfaced public roads (including a major highway, as shown in figure 14.4) that now run into Temiar country. This has made it much easier for younger Temiars to commute to cash-based jobs while continuing to live in their own settlements. Some Temiars own cars, though these are often in too poor a state of repair to be allowed on the public roads.

Figure 14.4 Traditional Temiar houses (2006) near Pos Blau, Kelantan, next to interstate route C185
Note the motorcycles owned by the people living there.

The increased ease and density of communication beyond the village have greatly altered the relationship between the Temiars and wider Malaysian society. Temiars are now much more a part *of* that society, where previously they lived mostly apart *from* it. Unfortunately, these modernising developments have not been accompanied by any parallel improvement in the land-rights situation, which remains in a confused legal and economic limbo, and which (like the religious situation) varies from state to state.[5] Nevertheless, the social differentiation that characterises Malaysian society in general has worked its way into the Temiar sector too. It is not surprising, therefore, that the character and context of Temiar religious life have changed considerably since I wrote my first account in 1967 (reprinted here as Chapters 3–8). As retold in Chapter 13, the first major sign of modernising religious change became apparent during a field visit I made in 1979, when I discovered that a significant proportion of the Temiar population had espoused a version of the Baha'i religion—which the majority of adherents have since dropped.

The near-failure of Baha'i to make a permanent impression did not, however, put a stop to further religious change and experimentation among the Temiars. The religious landscape, once relatively homogeneous, has become variegated. In addition to a remnant Baha'i following, there are now Muslim and Protestant Temiars. There have also been revivalist 're-enchantment' cults. Initially, these were small-scale and private (as with Ading Kerah's shrine described in the previous chapter), but they now also

---

5. On the distinctive legal situation of the Orang Asli, see Rusaslina (2010, 2011) and Subramaniam (2012).

include the new and endogenous monotheistic religion known as ʔaluj Səlamad, discussed below, which was still spreading widely throughout the Temiar population as of 2010.[6] At the same time, the older Temiar Religion continues to be practised, both by those who reject the new developments and by most of those who have accepted them. In this chapter I examine the social and cultural trajectories that characterise these religious developments, in relation to the broader changes that have taken place in Temiar and Malaysian society.

One consequence of these changes has been that Temiar religious alignments are now largely an individual matter, not a group matter. As we shall see, variations exist not only within settlements, but within households and families. Moreover, the different religions that Temiars have taken up in recent years vary in the extent to which they are self-motivated or introduced by others, and whether they are actually practised or just a matter of nominal identity.

Temiar religions and the state

In Malaysia, and especially with regard to the Orang Asli, the state is not a single agent. Temiars experience the state's authority and power through a variety of different agencies, which do not necessarily act in concert. These include

The central federal government, which has strong ideological control over issues that affect the Orang Asli.

The various federal agencies that interact directly with the Orang Asli. Foremost among these is the JAKOA, currently a division of the Ministry of Rural Development. (Its ministerial placing has changed several times in the past.) Additionally, the Ministry of Education, the Ministry of Health, the Forestry Department, and other such federal agencies, all have inputs into the circumstances of Orang Asli life.

The security agencies, especially the Field Force of the Special Branch, which used to have officers stationed at the various isolated 'posts' (*pos*) situated in Temiar country. In the past this agency had a considerable control over ingress into, and movement around, Temiar country, which remained 'black' with regard to Communist

---

6. In 1979, at the mixed Lanoh-Temiar settlement at Dala (Dɛnlaaʔ) on the Perak river, I listened to a home-made cassette recording of ritual singing in what was described as belonging to a new 'Maɲjar' cult, based on the name of a *siseʔ*-style dance, that had been started two years earlier at Fort Kemar by a medium named ʔitam. I have no further information, and cannot even be sure that 'cult' is the appropriate description. In 1968, I was given the names of at least 16 such named Temiar 'cults', with detailed descriptions of their specific performance characteristics, as well as of at least nine distinct types of ceremonial dance pattern; these are listed in Appendix 3. As we shall see, however, the ʔaluj Səlamad cult is more truly a new religion in its organisation and pattern of spread.

insurgency for many years after the Emergency was declared over in the rest of Malaysia.

The separate state JAKOA departments. These act with some degree of autonomy from the federal headquarters.

Various other (non-federal) state agencies that under the Malaysian Constitution are responsible for land and religion (Islam) issues. The Temiars, depending on where they live, are variously affected in this regard by the state governments of Perak, Kelantan and Pahang.

Apart from these state agencies, non-governmental agents are involved as well. These include individual Temiar entrepreneurs, cooperatives run by Orang Asli, external missionary organisations (both Protestant and Muslim), and some 'internal' conversion activities (Baha'i, ʔalʉj Səlamad) carried out by Temiars themselves. I suspect also that the Chinese Religionist shrines (figure 14.5) built in Temiar country by timber workers had an influence on the re-enchantment practices that some Temiars turned to in the early 1990s.

The officially maintained Malaysian view, applied to all citizens (including Orang Asli), is that they should belong to one of the recognised 'authentic' (*sah*) religions. The holders' religion is stated on the national identity cards, including the newer 'high-tech' Mykad version introduced in 2001. Islam is clearly the preferred religion; according to the Constitution it is Malaysia's sole official religion. Section 11 of that same Constitution,

Figure 14.5 Chinese shrine (*tokong*), since enlarged and beautified, built by loggers at the former site of Humid village, Kelantan (2006)

however, guarantees citizens freedom of religion, and (except for those born as Muslims or converted to that religion) Malaysians will not normally meet with problems if their identity cards label them as 'Christian', 'Hindu', 'Buddhist', etc. As long as the religion in question possesses the criterial properties of a proper 'religion' (*agama, ugama*), it will qualify as 'authentic'. In practice, this means that it should possess a name, a founding 'prophet' (which is a problem for Hinduism), holy scriptures, formal places of worship, and a body of clergy. These, of course, are the characteristic features of Islam, which thereby provides the ideal-type example of 'religion' that the others should replicate. Malaysian Islam, especially that of the Malays (who are obligatorily Shafi'i Sunnis), is closely policed for signs of deviation.[7] But the other religions are allowed a considerable range of manifestation, and run their own affairs with little governmental interference. Christianity among the ethnic Chinese and Indians, for example, is notably more variable in Malaysia than it is in Singapore, where it has been subject to some degree of constraint. In recent years, in an apparent shift of official practice, it has also become possible to have the labels *tiada beragama* ('no religion') or *agama animisme* ('animist') inscribed on one's identity card, at least for Orang Asli.

As we shall see, however, the situation of the Temiars and other Orang Asli in these regards is not so straightforward. Baha'i and (Protestant) Christianity among the Temiars have met with varying degrees of official blockage, while state agencies have strongly supported pressures for them to convert to Islam. I say more about these issues later. First, let me make some general points relating to the recent spread of new religious allegiances and identities among the Temiars.

A recurrent theme in official circles is the indecision as to whether state policy should aim at the 'integration' or assimilation of the Orang Asli. The declared official policy is for integration (*integrasi*), but—due perhaps to an intolerance of sociocultural *difference* in some Malay/Muslim circles— governmental discourse has consistently found it hard to separate integration from assimilation. This fusion seems to be motivated by the long-established preference of institutionalised Islam—as with the other monotheisms, Judaism and Christianity—for bounded-off social *sameness* (homogeneity) as the default way of life. As noted in the previous chapter, the cognitive dissonance of confronting a *Bumiputera* ('sons of the soil') population, such as the Orang Asli, who can achieve modernity without becoming Muslim, is psychologically hard to take for many Malay Muslims.[8] 'Assimilation'

---

7. At the conference at which the first version of this chapter was presented, Andrew Willford pointed out that this kind of *objectification* of religion leads inexorably to religious *identity*, and hence (adapting Weber) to an 'iron cage of religion'. A similar argument has been proposed for Singapore by Vineeta Sinha (1999).

8. This may partly explain the occasional but still occurring assertions in Malaysian public life that the Orang Asli are not 'indigenous' (*orang asal*, and presumably therefore not *Bumiputera*), on the peculiar grounds that they were not the bringers of 'civilisation' (the state?). This was stated several times by two former Prime Ministers, Tunku Abdul Rahman (*The Star* newspaper, Malaysia, 6 November

here refers to the idea that the Orang Asli should simply *become* Malays, primarily through conversion to Islam. The 'problem' posed by the existence of a still-Aboriginal element within the wider Bumiputera population, speaking different languages and following different religions from the Malay mainstream, would supposedly then disappear. After all, Malay culture itself has a long history of accretion by the assimilation of individuals and populations who were not originally Malay (*Melayu*) by culture or language (Benjamin 2002b: 37–54).

As already mentioned, the government's preference for resettling the Temiars into larger, permanent villages, along with the growth of transport and telecommunications, has greatly magnified the density of communication. This has facilitated the spread of new ideas. New religions, beginning with Baha'i in the late 1970s, did not gain any foothold among the Temiars until after the JHEOA's permanent resettlement programme (*rancangan penempatan semula*) had started. Before that, and in the 1960s especially, weeks could pass in a typical Temiar village before anyone from elsewhere made an appearance. The people went for long periods without news: there were no roads, no telephones, and no letter-writing—just several hours of jungle-bashing walk between villages.[9] The contrast is illustrated in the differences between figure 3.1 and figure 14.6. Figure 3.1, which I took by courtesy of a visiting helicopter pilot, indicates the isolation of one such village at that time—Kuala Humid, the 'home' site of my doctoral fieldwork. Figure 14.6 shows the village that has since replaced it, slightly upstream, near the conspicuous triangular swidden shown in the earlier photograph. The inhabitants of Humid in 1964 followed no other religion than their own Temiar Religion; their local descendants had all converted to Islam before 2006.

Individual Temiars, of course, have their own separate views of these changes and of the choices they face. As an example, consider the situation of a somewhat agnostic Temiar man whom I have known since he was a

---

1986) and Mahathir Mohamed (1970: 126–127); see also Teoh (2011). More strikingly, it was repeated by Nisra Nisran, the (Temiar) Deputy Director of the JAKOA, while this volume was in preparation (COAC 2012).

9. This isolation is the probable rationale for the older Temiar custom that one should remain silent for a while (say, 20 minutes) before entering into conversation when newly arrived in a village. The newly arrived people could not know what had happened (a death, for example) since the last meeting, and might end up speaking inappropriately. Noone (1937) also observed the same behaviour, and gave a similar explanation for it:

> Hardly have we returned to the house when three men come in. They were strangers from another group of Temiar on the Blatop river, but no greeting passed between my hosts and them. Without a word they sit down quietly near the doorway. The people of the house seem unconcerned and for a while the newcomers are ignored. Then Along, our leader, silently holds out sundried tobacco and the strangers rise and squat down near his fire-place. As they roll their cigarettes, Along asks casually if the rains of a few days before had made their path slippery. That is Temiar etiquette at a meeting. No brusque, hearty greeting, no handshakes: even the bringer of news, good or bad, must not offend with startling information. It is not only a matter of politeness, it is also because anyone strange to the surroundings may re-act as a dangerous influence on the group unless delicately handled.

child and who has spent most of his working life employed at the Orang Asli hospital just outside Kuala Lumpur. His wife and one married son are Christians; his recently married daughter is Muslim; he himself and his other married son remain Temiar Religionists. He said, 'Islam restricts food, but allows *sɛʔsooʔ* [mediumistic healing]. Christianity allows us to eat anything we like, but forbids *sɛʔsooʔ*. *Pa-mɔy pa-mɔy* [each is different].'

Baha'i

In the previous chapter, I explored the emergence of Baha'i among the Temiars as a disenchantment movement, suiting the desire of the younger, primary-schooled Temiars for an easily explained religion that better suited their emerging sense of individualistic modernity. Here, I outline the declining fortunes of the Baha'i religion among the Temiars since its heyday in the late 1970s.

Recalling the events of the 1970s to me in 2006 and 2008, several Kelantan Temiars told me that the religion had first been taken up in 1975, but that there were already fewer Baha'is by 1979 (when I had nevertheless been able to witness and record some Temiar Baha'i prayer sessions). The religion had finished its run in the downstream Temiar settlements by 1983 (or 1989, according to other respondents), having been forbidden by officials of the state Islamic Department and the JHEOA on the grounds that Baha'i was not a

Figure 14.6 Modern housing at Galaaŋ, just upstream from the former site of Humid village (2006) *Note the solar panels and satellite dishes, as well as the earlier pattern of modern housing on the left, plank-built on concrete pillars. The headman in the middle of the photograph, the son of Penghulu Hitam Tamboh, appeared earlier as the young boy in figure 4.5.*

recognised 'authentic' (*sah*) religion. (This is an example of the way in which Orang Asli are treated differently from other Malaysian citizens, as Baha'i is still openly and legally practised elsewhere in (mostly urban) Peninsular Malaysia, and also fairly widely in Sarawak.)

Reportedly, there were still a few Temiar Baha'is in 2010, mostly upstream and relatively out of contact, practising it as an *?agamaa? kərɛndɨ?* 'an undeclared religion'. There were also said to be some Baha'is among the Semais of Sinderut in Pahang (reachable only by 4-wheel-drive) and the Temiars of Cadak in Perak. Downstream, around Kuala Betis and Lambok, I was told that there were no Baha'is left because many of their leaders had died. I was also told that some of the Baha'i leaders had collected tithes in cash, which led to bad feeling. In 1979, a Field Force officer had told me that this was a further reason why the authorities wanted to stop the religion's spread.[10]

Jamel, who had been one of the most active propagators of Baha'i among the Temiars of the Betis and Perolak valleys in the 1970s, told me that he was now, 30 years later, 'without religion'. Many of the other former Baha'is have since converted to Islam or to the new ?alɨj Səlamad religion. The lack of Baha'i teachers was also mentioned in the villages around Jalong and Lasah in Perak as the cause of the religion's demise there. But they also told me that, in the face of Malay-led conversion campaigns (*kɛmpen*), the former Baha'is are now entirely Muslims because they feared they would otherwise not have received such modern facilities as housing and electricity.[11]

The rapid rise and fall of Baha'i among the Temiars raises interesting questions. First, is Baha'i the kind of religion that (like Christianity and Islam) can continue to function only if it receives continued support of its formal institutions? In the current Temiar case, such support necessarily has to come from external sources. As we shall see, Temiar Christianity receives such support for the moment, but Islam is less intensively supported even though it is more widespread.

Second, could the brief Baha'i period have been a precursor of the monotheism that characterises the new ?alɨj Səlamad religion, discussed below? In the preceding chapter, first drafted before ?alɨj Səlamad had emerged, there was already clear evidence that this is probably the case:

> [Kɛrmal] taught people to 'pray' (for which he used the Malay word *sembahyang*), to follow the laws of the Malaysian government, and to

---

10. No modern religion can subsist without cash. Muslim and Christian bodies also regularly collect tithes, in Malaysia as elsewhere. Whether this is regarded as legitimate or exploitative depends on whether one views the religion in question as 'authentic' in the first place. Conversely, declaring a religion to be inauthentic automatically redefines its tithe-collecting as exploitation, or even corruption.
11. A difference in the quality of housing between Muslim and non-Muslim Temiars was already visible when I visited a resettlement village in Perak in 1994. At the time, this may have been a distinctively Perak feature: I am not sure this difference exists in the Kelantan settlements, or whether it still applies in Perak. I have no information on the current situation of the Temiars in Pahang.

follow the laws of Tohan, who was the creator of all—and who was the same as ʔalɥj (ʔalɥj 'last born': the mythic hero who created Temiar culture) and Allah.

Islam

My first field encounter with Islam in a Temiar context was in January 1979, when I made the following entry in my notebook.

> The man who walked me back to Grik said that he considered the nearby kampung Malays to be *susah* 'difficult'. Around 1963, they had threatened to chop off the heads of the Orang Asli if they didn't *mɔɔj ʔaslam* 'enter Islam'. (This must have been when Kampung Ulu Grik was first opened.) He said the *kadhi* of Grik had also, recently, three times come to Kampung Ulu Grik to persuade them to convert, on the grounds that since they now were living near town in proper houses and had money, it was only proper that they should become Muslims. Each time, Penghulu ʔadiʔ had refused, on the grounds that they couldn't give up eating jungle game. The whole discussion arose spontaneously—I hadn't mentioned anything about Islam.

Since then, there has been a considerable increase in the number of Temiars who have converted (usually nominally) to Islam. I have no updated figures for the number of Temiar Muslims in Perak or Pahang, and the published figures for Kelantan in 2006 are confused:

> The latest figures show that in the past five years, 2,904 of some 3,000 orang asli who reside in Gua Musang and Jeli districts, embraced Islam on their own free will. (*New Straits Times*, 27 June 2006.)

> Hassan [Chairman of the State Religious Affairs Committee] said that 2,094 of the State's 12,000-strong Orang Asli community converted to Islam last year. (*The Star/Nation*, 27 June 2006.)

Clearly, the numerals '2,904' and '2,094' in these reports are jumbled (leading to a 28 per cent difference), as is the time-span ('last year' *versus* 'the past five years') over which the conversions are said to have taken place. The geographical spread of the conversions is also indeterminate: the '3,000' Orang Asli in Gua Musang and Jeli Districts would also include some non-Temiars, even though the Temiars are by far the majority Orang Asli population in Kelantan. The second report says that the figures relate to all of the '12,000' Orang Asli said to be living in all of the state's districts. Given this confusion, I prefer to stick with the rounded figures I was given by a (non-Muslim) Temiar employee of the JHEOA in December 2006, who said that there were then 8,000 Temiars in Kelantan, of whom some 2,000 were Muslims.

My own initial impressions of Islam among the Temiars were summarised in the fieldnotes I recorded after visiting some Perak Temiars in December 2006:

> **Temiar Islam:** In general, everywhere I go, the Islam is described as *kənʉʉh he²* 'in name only'. Reasons given for conversion are: (1) monetary payments, (2) better facilities, (3) weariness at resisting Malay pressures. Not once did I hear of anyone who had converted out of conviction. On the contrary, I heard assertions from non-converted Temiars that those Malays who insisted on the conversions were acting inappropriately, when they must know that *agama* (religion) is the last thing on Temiars' minds. Certainly, the picture is very different from the motivations I recorded in my Baha'i study, and from what I am told of the Christian Temiars' religiosity (which involves some 'healing', not just empty prayers).

By their own accounts, then, Temiars have been converting to Islam over the last decade or more because they have got weary of resisting Malay-Muslim missionising, and because they believe that conversion brings financial benefits. Nevertheless, I was told that there are indeed some praying Muslims, in Lambok, Kuala Betis and Hendrop (Hɛnrʉp), among other places. Some Temiars have reportedly even gone on the minor *Umrah* pilgrimage to Mecca, their fares paid by the Kelantan government's Department of Islam (Jabatan Agama Islam). At least one Kelantan Temiar is said to be an *ustad* (religious teacher) who has studied Arabic, and there are also said to be Temiar *ustad*s in Perak. (I was told that the latter defer to Malay *ustad*s when more difficult questions arise.) However, I myself saw no direct evidence that any Muslim Temiars actively perform their prayers. I was also told that, apart from some avoidance of pig-flesh, they do not follow Islam's *halal* dietary rules. I did see a few Temiar women wearing Muslim-style head-caps, but I was told that not all of these were Muslims, and that they were doing so simply out of stylish affectation. (The Islamist state government of Kelantan has made it compulsory for Muslim women to cover their hair. This is actively policed in the densely populated lowland areas; but in the less densely populated upland areas, even Malay women can sometimes be observed in public with their heads uncovered.) A further sign of the lack of Islamic practice among the converted Temiars is the parlous condition of the *surau* prayer halls that have been constructed by the state government in most of the permanent Temiar settlements. These suraus are by far the best built and most solid structures in the villages, being individually designed, with tiled walls and roofs, running water, and sanitary facilities (figure 14.7). Yet they are unused and often falling into disrepair.

The Temiars I talked to in Perak and Kelantan were correct, therefore, in asserting that Temiar Islam was more a matter of formal identity than of religious observance or belief. Malays, on the other hand, are not allowed to get away with such religious laxness, especially in strongly Islamist Kelantan. Why then is the non-observant behaviour of the Temiar Muslims in Kelantan (and presumably also in Perak) not similarly policed? The JAKOA, under the state and federal religious development plans, is supposed to have placed special Islamic workers known as *pembantu masyarakat* ('social helpers') in every Orang Asli village. These *pembantu* are not always as plentiful on the ground as the authorities might wish, but they are certainly in a position to observe what is going on. (One *pembantu*, a Malay woman, was described to me as being able to speak Temiar, but as doing little otherwise than just passing pleasantries.)

Given the presence of these field officers, as well as the increasing ease of communication already commented on, it cannot be that the authorities do not know what is going on—or rather, what is *not* going on. After I discussed this puzzle with other researchers, including educated Orang Asli, several possible explanations came to mind. There is agreement that the reasons for converting the Orang Asli to Islam are not in the first place religious at all, but

Figure 14.7 Surau at Mengrod, Kelantan, mostly in good repair, but unused (2006)

political. Conversion appears to be aimed at future generations, as a means of eventually assimilating the Orang Asli into the Malay sector of the population. The latter will then be able to counter the charge raised by the Malaysian Chinese Association (MCA) that the Malays too are migrants (*pendatang*)— as some Malay politicians regularly assert the Chinese to be. Since no one could seriously claim that the Orang Asli are migrants, assimilating them into the Malay fold would reinforce the latter's claim that they too are indigenous, not migrants.[12]

As already mentioned, Article 11 of the Malaysian Constitution (*Perlembagaan Negara*) states that religion is a private matter, so these conversions could be regarded as illegal, unless they are freely entered into (which is very hard to monitor). The conversions are organised jointly by the federal and state religious departments, with the open help of the JAKOA. The very active federal department is known as JAKIM (Jabatan Kemajuan Islam Malaysia, the Malaysian Department of Islamic Development). According to one Orang Asli observer (not a Temiar), the initial push was through the 'front door', by attempting to convert the educated Orang Asli. This mostly failed, so conversion now takes place through the 'back door' of the ordinary villagers.

The following two reports published in Malaysian newspapers provide further information on the state-organised Islamic conversion activities that were formally instituted in 2006 and aimed at the Orang Asli of Kelantan. These echo the age-old Southeast Asian practice by which a dominant population employs marriage as a means of assimilating a hitherto autonomous population.

Kelantan State Assembly: Cash and car among incentives for missionaries

Sheridan Mahavera, *New Straits Times*, 27 June 2006

As part of its efforts to convert more Orang Asli to Islam, the Kelantan Government is offering RM10,000 to its missionaries who marry Orang Asli women. They were also expected to settle down in Orang Asli communities in Jeli and Gua Musang [districts] to spread Islamic teachings and act as spiritual figures, the State Assembly was told yesterday.

Other incentives offered include free housing, a monthly allowance of RM1,000 and a four-wheel-drive vehicle. State Islamic Development and Dakwah [missionary] committee chairman Hassan Mohamood said

---

12. This would clash with the declaration by the (Temiar) Deputy Director of JAKOA in March 2012 that the Orang Asli—even if they are not migrants—are not 'indigenous', in the special sense of the word employed in some sections of Malaysian officialdom (COAC 2012). He said that 'indigenous' applies only to Malays. In an extraordinary reversal of the intended meaning of the word in the *United Nations Declaration on the Rights of Indigenous Peoples*, which clearly refers to dominated *tribal* populations and which Malaysia has signed, this was given as the official reason for Malaysia's exclusion of the Orang Asli from coverage by that *Declaration*.

the incentives were offered to the six missionaries registered with the State Government's Orang Asli Dakwah Unit. 'We are offering this as part of our efforts to increase the number of Orang Asli converts,' Hassan said in reply to a question from Abdul Halim Abdul Rahman (PAS–Chetok).

To a supplementary question from Mohd Adhan Kechik (BN–Bukit Bunga), Hassan said these incentives were introduced after the establishment of the Orang Asli Dakwah Unit last month. 'Our campaign to convert Orang Asli has never slowed down. In the past, it was performed on an ad-hoc basis by the State Islamic Affairs Department, State Religious Council and the Malaysian Islamic Dakwah Foundation (YADIM). 'But we only recently established a separate unit with dedicated personnel to focus specifically on converting Orang Asli.'

Outside the State Assembly later, Hassan said the incentives were provided to ensure missionaries stayed permanently in Orang Asli communities as imams, hold Quran and Fardhu 'Ain [Islam for Beginners] classes and conduct funeral rites.

Hassan said that 2,094 of the State's 12,000-strong Orang Asli community converted to Islam last year.

Incentives for marrying and converting Orang Asli
The Star, 27 June 2006

Kelantan will offer RM10,000 to each Muslim preacher who marries an orang asli woman and naturally [*sic*] converts her as part of renewed efforts to propagate Islam among the 3,000-odd community in the state. State Religious Affairs committee chairman Hassan Mahamood (PAS–Tawang) said the same incentive was applicable if the preacher was a Muslim woman who took an orang asli husband. Asked if the preacher may court the orang asli as a second or third wife, Hassan said it depended on the individual.

The latest figures show that in the past five years, 2,904 of some 3,000 orang asli who reside in Gua Musang and Jeli districts, embraced Islam on their own free will. Hassan said the state government was unhappy with the conversion rate of the orang asli, who traditionally did not subscribe to any main religion.

Besides the monetary incentive, the preachers would also receive free accommodation, a four-wheel-drive vehicle and a fixed monthly allowance of RM1,000.

On criminal activities and social ills among youths, Hassan said these were due to the influence of the western media. 'The Federal Government allowed sex-oriented movies, music and magazines to be accessible to the masses.' 'Crime can only be controlled through the Syariah Criminal Procedure Code,' he said.

Since the focus of these conversions is on the future rather than the present, and since Temiar Islam is more a matter of identity than religious practice, how exactly is that identity engineered? My enquiries suggest that the key mechanisms come into operation at three main junctures: when registering births, issuing identity cards, and burying the dead.

In Kelantan, Temiar births are registered at the government registry office (Jabatan Pendaftaran Negara) in Gua Musang and other towns. Many births now take place in hospital. Children are given their national identity cards at 12 years; these are changed again at 21. Birth certificates state the holder's specific Orang Asli ethnicity ('Temiar', 'Semai', etc), but the identity card only states that the holder is a *Warga Negara Malaysia*, a Malaysian citizen. The identity card also has an *agama* 'religion' slot, but this can be filled with 'no religion' (*tiada beragama*) or 'animist' (*agama animisme*).[13] Proper practice in Malaysia is to insert the phrase *anak lelaki* (*A/L*, 'male child of') or *anak perempuan* (*A/P* 'female child of') into the names of non-Muslim citizens if these contain a patronym. However, officers frequently insert the Muslim usage *bin* or *binti*—'son of' or 'daughter of'—into the child's name instead, without first checking whether it proper to do so. This 'lazy' practice (as it was described to me) later leads to the holders' identity cards labelling them as Muslims, whether or not that is the case. This can have serious consequences, since a 'Muslim' identity in Malaysia carries with it specific legal and customary restrictions that are not borne by non-Muslims. This gratuitous religious assignment *can* be changed by any Orang Asli who will make the effort, although the ease with which it may be done depends on where they live. The JAKOA is not necessarily involved directly in such a 'removal' of Islam, but it has occasionally lent its services.

Muslim Temiars must now be buried according to Muslim rites in an authorised Muslim burial ground, presumably alongside the Malay graves. The graves will therefore be permanent rather than left to be overgrown by resurgent forest, as was the historical Temiar practice. Non-Muslim Temiars in the more permanent settlements have recently, of their own accord, begun to bury their deceased relatives in permanent graves covered by cement. But the new requirement for a formal Muslim burial will presumably mean that future generations of Temiars will be urged to see their buried ancestors as Muslims—and probably also as Malays.

The following fieldnote extracts present the mixed views of several villagers concerning Temiar Islam as told to me in Kelantan and Perak. I have altered the language in places to retain the anonymity of most of the respondents.

---

13. This last option implies an interesting shift in the accepted meaning of *agama*, which normally refers only to named religions-of-the-book. Previously, animism would have been regarded as indicating the absence of *agama*.

Mengrod (Mɛnrɔɔd), Kelantan, December 2006: The surau [figure 14.7] seems unused. The Headman says that about ten couples are Muslims. Two women at the mediumistic séance last night wore Muslim head-caps. One respondent asserts that Islam is an 'Arab' religion, which Malays just 'copy', since they don't know Arabic.

Galaaŋ, above Humid, Kelantan, December 2006: There's a forlorn surau on the hill, even though all the villagers became Muslims in 2001. The late Hitam Tamboh converted first (leaving his Baha'i faith), followed by his family and the other villagers.[14] There was a 'campaign' led by JAKIM. Their officers return sometimes to run courses, and to give cash aid (*duit bantuan*) of RM400 every four months, for the people to eat together and for them to hold a Muslim meeting. There's also *bantuan Hari Raya*, cash to help celebrate the end of Ramadan. The JAKIM officers use the surau for courses, but those villagers who pray do so at home. One of the headman's daughters is said to pray regularly and has attended a course run by ABIM, the prominent Malaysian Islamic youth movement. Her Islamic certificates are proudly displayed on the wall (figure 14.8). The villagers avoid pig meat, but do eat other hunted animals that Malays would avoid. The headman says he *pǝgak naar budayaaʔ*, holds to two cultural traditions—the *ʔadad manah* 'the old way' [i.e., Temiar Religion] and Islam. He trusts them precisely *because* they are both old. He rejects the ʔaluj Sǝlamad religion because it is *new*.

Landap, Jalong, Perak, December 2006: There were Baha'is here before, but now there is no *guru*. In the face of Malay 'campaigns' they are now entirely Muslims. They became so because they otherwise would not have received facilities. The same is true of nearby Kampung Kenang (Kǝnaŋ). They converted in 1990. They get RM60 per family from the Perak State Religious Council to celebrate Hari Raya. They got RM100 for each parent on conversion, which was a mass event. 'Religion in name only, but not followed', a respondent said in Malay (*nama ada ugama, taʔikut*). They still eat wild meat. The surau remains unused. They still hold mediumistic dance performances and follow all other Temiar religious practices. But burials must now be arranged by the Muslim authorities. The *ustad* might cause trouble if they attempt their own kind of burial. Although there are Temiar *ustad*s, these defer to Malay *ustad*s on such matters.

Bendang Kering, Kg Bukit Chermin (Lowland Perak), December 2006:[15] Everyone here is a Muslim, because when the Malays asked

---

14. As noted several times in earlier chapters, Hitam (figure 7.1) was a headman whom I had known very well in the 1960s and who taught me much about the traditional Temiar Religion. With this new information, I have therefore followed him through Temiar Religion, then Baha'i, and finally Islam. (I tape-recorded a Baha'i service at his house in 1979.)

15. Before visiting Bendang Kering, a settlement distant from most other Temiar villages, I had assumed

Figure 14.8 Certificates of attendance at Islamic training courses displayed in a Muslim Temiar family's house, Galaaŋ, Kelantan (2006)

them to convert, it was too troublesome (*susah*) to refuse. They became Muslims in 1979. Attempts to get Muslim Temiars and Malays to celebrate (*raya*) together have failed. They still hold *sewang* singsongs, performing in Ciɲcɛm style (Chapters 6, 7, 13).

Tərolǝǝh, Lambok, February 2008: A young woman says most of the Temiars (in Lambok?) are Muslims, but not 'real' ones. They do it for the money. JAKIM pays RM400 to each family that converts to Islam. There are no further payments, except to widows and widowers, to whom JAKIM pays RM100 every month. The disabled receive this too. Her father calls this payment *hɔj bǝ-daʔwah* 'been *dakwah*'d' (undergone missionising). He himself did not convert, but his six children did. The young woman herself converted before her breasts had grown. Nobody prays here, she said. The surau is unused and falling into disrepair. After attending an Islamic *kursus* they get a certificate; hers is displayed in a frame on the porch wall.

As a closing comment on this drive for Islamisation, consider this warning by Colin Nicholas (2008) of the Centre for Orang Asli Concerns:

---

it was the 'lowland Temiar' village that in the 1970s I had been told was a Christian community, but there was no evidence of Christianity when I finally got there.

[T]he current active Islamic missionary activity among the Orang Asli is, in large part, a reaction to the equally active (and somewhat successful) efforts of the Christian missionaries. All missionaries, however, treat the Orang Asli as 'lost, unsaved souls' and do not recognize their indigenous religions as being on par with theirs.

It is to Christianity among the Temiars that I now turn.

Protestant Christianity

Until 2010, I had very little first-hand information on Temiar Christianity or Christians. I had met a few Christians at Lambok, but did not discuss their religion with them. They seemed to live slightly apart—at least insofar as the other Temiars living there did not know much about them. I was told that some of them were Temiars from Perak who had married Semais and subsequently moved across to Kelantan. This is significant, because there have been Lutheran Christians among the Perak Semais since the 1930s (Noone 1936: 57–58; Means & Means 1981; Means 2011), and their churches have survived since then, reinforced by input from so-called 'Sengoi' (Semai) missions based in Singapore and elsewhere. The Christians at Lambok appeared to be wealthier than their non-Christian neighbours, since their houses were better maintained and better furnished. I was told that they were regularly transported to places of worship elsewhere in vans run by outside missionary organisations.

While there were relatively few Christians in the parts of Kelantan that I had previously concentrated my researches on, there were said to be more Christian Temiars further down the Nenggiri (as the Kelantan River is known in Temiar country). In 2010, I eventually briefly visited two of these settlements, as reported below. First, I present what was known about Temiar Christianity before that visit.

In 2008, a Christian missionary website dealing with 'unreached peoples' gave the number of Temiar 'church members' (whom they strangely referred to by the century-old label 'Northern Sakai') as 1,010, which they stated amounted to '5%' of the population.[16] They also provided the following unsourced figures on the Temiars:

- Mission agencies working among this people: 1
- Persons who have heard the Gospel: 5,100 (31%)
- Those evangelized by local Christians: 2,200 (13%)
- Those evangelized from the outside: 2,900 (18%)
- Persons who have never heard the Gospel: 11,500 (69%)

---

16. *Bethany World Prayer Center*, http://kcm.co.kr/bethany_eng/p_code3/1528.html (retrieved 10 December 2008). This website also gave the largest Temiar religion as 'Islam (Sunni)', at 33.5% of the population; but no source was provided.

One such group, who converted as recently as February 2007, became embroiled in national news reports when their church at Jias was torn down by Kelantan state government agencies a few months later.[17] The basic facts of the case are as outlined in the following Internet posting.[18]

Another Orang Asli church demolished by authorities

Centre for Orang Asli Concerns (COAC), 6 June 2007

On Monday, 4 June 2007, a building erected by the Orang Asli of Kampung Jias in Kelantan to serve as a place of worship was demolished by the Gua Musang District Land Office. The Temiar community recently embraced Christianity and in February this year, their Penghulu (headman), Pedik bin Busu, made a written request for help to erect a church building in their village.

In March, the Village Development and Security Committee (JKKK) and the Department of Orang Asli Affairs (JHEOA), agreed to build a hall with concrete floors and wooden walls. Work on the site began on early March to clear the site and by 19 March, steel and concrete work was started on the ground beams and footings. On the same day, a person claiming to be an officer of the JHEOA arrived and demanded that work be stopped as permission was not granted to build a church building. Since conflicting signals were being given by the JHEOA, the community decided to build a brick and concrete building instead, as a structure like this was deemed to be more difficult to pull down.

On 11 April, three officers from the Gua Musang District Land Office served a stop-work order demanding that work be halted and the structure demolished. The order also accused the Penghulu of erecting a building on state land without permission under Section 425 (1)(a) of the National Land Code 1965. A penalty of one year's imprisonment or a fine of RM10,000 would be incurred if the Penghulu were to be found guilty. The National Evangelical Christian Fellowship (NECF) responded the following day with a letter disputing the legality of the stop-work order arguing that the property was native customary land by virtue of Section 2 (7)(1) and (8)(1) of the Aboriginal Peoples Act 1954. With this in mind, the community proceeded to continue their work on the building.

---

17. http://www.nst.com.my/Current_news/NST/National/2132585/Article/index_html, 'Orang Asli file suit over church demolition', *New Straits Times* (retrieved 12 February 2008). As of December 2008, this webpage was no longer available, perhaps because the case was by then *sub judice*. (Older news stories about the Orang Asli are still retrievable from the *New Straits Times Online* website.) This particular news item was also reported internationally, as for example in *USA Today*: http://www.usatoday.com/news/religion/2008-01-15-malaysia-tribe_N.htm (retrieved 10 December 2008). There is also a privately circulated video DVD on this affair.
18. http://www.coac.org.my/codenavia/portals/coacv2/code/main/main_art.php?parent ID=11374493258660&artID=11814707293830. (As of June 2013, this webpage was no longer retrievable.)

On 19 April, four officers from the Gua Musang District Council served another stop-work order, this time under Section 72 of the Street, Drainage and Building Act 1974, demanding that work be halted and threatening a fine of RM250 per day for non-compliance. On 24 May, notice was served by the Gua Musang District Council informing the Penghulu that the building be demolished within seven days. NECF immediately followed up with a letter disputing the legality of the notice and this was again followed up by a letter of demand by the legal counsel of the Penghulu to the District Council asking for a withdrawal of the said notice, failing which an injunction will be applied against the Council.

Unfortunately, despite various efforts to halt the demolishment, the church building was demolished on 4 June. This turn of events made it necessary for the Penghulu to make a police report asking for an investigation on the incident.

A brief news report on 13 June 2007, headed 'Kelantan government to rebuild church', stated that the state government was going to 'replace' the building.[19] It turned out that the eventual replacement was not a church, but a 'multipurpose hall', which is not what the villagers wanted. A suit against the authorities was then filed in the Kelantan High Court on 1 July 2007 with the help of lawyers acting *pro bono publico*. The case was eventually heard in chambers on 14 January 2008, but with no decisive result:

Submissions ordered in church demolition suit

Fauwaz Abdul Aziz, *Malaysiakini.com*, 15 January, 2008, 3:10pm

Parties to a dispute over the demolition of a church in Gua Musang [district], Kelantan, have been given a month each to provide written submissions to the Kota Baru High Court. Temiar Orang Asli villagers are suing the Gua Musang District Council head, the Gua Musang Assistant Land and District Officer and the PAS-led state government over the demolition of their church on June 4 last year. According to Lum Chee Seng, a lawyer for the villagers, Justice Mohd Azman Husin issued the order this morning after deliberations in chambers. Lum and N Subramaniyan—who are representing Kampung Jias village head Pedik Busu and three other plaintiffs—will have to deliver their submission next month, followed a month later by lawyers for the respondents. The court has fixed May 26 for the hearing.

The villagers—who were baptised around February last year—contend that the land on which the church had stood had been in Pedik's family for generations. Their legal action follows the failure of the authorities to keep a pledge to rebuild the structure. In their suit, they

---

19. http://www.malaysiakini.com/news/68585 (retrieved 10 Dec. 2008).

have applied for declarations that they have a right over the land as well as the constitutional right to practise their religion, which includes the right to set up a church on the land. They are also seeking a declaration that the issuance of notices against Pedik and the other villagers by the Gua Musang District Council head and Assistant Land and District Officer was unlawful. The plaintiffs further want a declaration that the demolition was unlawful and that it was an act of trespass on Pedik's property, an 'abuse of power' and amounting to intervening in the religious rights of the Orang Asli. They also filed for damages and other costs.

In their defence, the Gua Musang authorities cited the application of Section 425 of the National Land Code and Section 72 of the Street, Drainage and Building Act 1974, both of which pertain to structures built without the permission of the authorities.

The affected Temiars also sought a declaration under Article 11 of the Constitution of Malaysia that they had the right to practise the religion of their choice and to build their own prayer house. In response, the authorities claimed that the demolition had no relation to religion: the building had been put up without formal planning permission, and had contravened the land-use regulations as stated in two different acts of Parliament. According to news reports, the Kelantan High Court ruled in favour of the Temiars in October 2009, stating that they had the right to use the land to hold church services. However, the Kelantan state government then appealed that decision, and the case remained unresolved as of 2012 (Colin Nicholas, personal communication).

Temiar Christians are clearly under pressure, at least in Kelantan. In any case, given the religion's institutionalised character, it requires continuous outside support—from Semais, Chinese, Temuans and the odd European, as I found out later—in order to survive. The published reports mention that the Christians at Jias were represented by Pastor Moses Soo, an ethnic Chinese from outside the Orang Asli community. According to the several Christian websites dealing with Orang Asli, the external missionaries' motivations are tied up with the idea of 'unreached peoples'. This tells us little, however, about the motivations of the Temiar converts themselves. In a few cases, individual Temiars appear to be drawn by the close attention that some established Christians pay to the emotional needs of the converts. I know of one Temiar woman, for example, whose chronic depression appears to have been eased by attending church services in the Kuala Lumpur area. I have not witnessed any such services myself, but it is said that they involve 'healing' (sɛʔsooʔ), which implies that at least some of them are Charismatic in orientation. If that is indeed the case, then it would be relatively easy for Temiars to accept, as it would be similar to the mediumistic ceremonies that form the core of indigenous Temiar religious practice. But this is only a suggestion, and I have no solid data to support it.

With these and other questions in mind, I paid a brief visit in January 2010 to two of the Christian Temiar settlements whose situation had been publicised in news reports and brought before the law courts. My intention was to get behind what had been reported and talk to the people in their own language about the religious changes they had caught themselves up in.

First, I went to see the church at the tiny settlement of Kampung Pariʔ (also known as Sᴐtawar). I was told that there were eight Christian couples there, and that their visiting Pastor was Lisun, a Temiar-speaking Semai from Gopeng in Perak. As their own church was still being built (figure 14.9), they currently went to Jias (the next village I visited) to pray, on Wednesdays. But when their own church was completed, they planned to pray there, on Sundays. They had some books in Malay or Indonesian on display, but I could not tell whether these were bibles or prayer books. The villagers had been Christians for about two years, having been converted by the Chinese pastor who had also been serving at Jias, presumably the aforementioned Moses Soo. The man I talked to (ʔasim) said that he had decided to be a Christian because he loved to eat pork. (Presumably, he saw his choice as being between Christianity and Islam—the latter would have forbidden pork—as he made no mention of the possibility of *not* undergoing

Figure 14.9 The uncompleted new church at Pariʔ (2010)

any form of conversion.) One of the women had been a Muslim previously, but she too converted to Christianity.

The local religious council, the Majlis Agama in Gua Musang, objected to these developments and wanted to destroy the half-built church, which was being sponsored by an ethnic-Chinese businessman. The officials turned up with some policemen to 'report' on the situation, but apparently they decided that since the church was on Orang Asli land there was nothing they could do, and that the people's religion was their own concern, and the building was left standing.[20] The pastor had gone to Gua Musang to request to have their identity cards changed to read 'Christian', but without success. I looked at my respondent's identity card: it stated neither 'Christian' nor 'Islam'.

I then moved on to Jias, a larger and older settlement that I had visited occasionally during my initial research in the 1960s, and which had become the focal point of the legal proceedings just reported. Most of what Penghulu Pedik (Pədiʔ) told me accorded with the details revealed in those reports, but I was able to supplement these with information on the villagers' own views of the matter. Regardless of what happened after the police and the religious authorities had ordered the destruction of the first concrete-floored church he had built in 2007, he was now building a new wooden church without waiting for permission. He regarded the land as his, and in any case was not aware of any final legal decision. He showed me that the site of the destroyed church now had an all-purpose building (*balai serbaguna*) on it, as stated in the press reports.

Pedik became a Christian because he wanted his own religion (*ʔagamaaʔ haʔ riiʔ* 'religion in my own right'). He first heard about it from Pastor Moses, who said it came from Korea.[21] He has also been visited by a young unmarried English pastor, who stayed here and who speaks some Temiar and Semai.[22] He eats Temiar game food, and rejects his own food. Pedik said that a Semai pastor, Razali (Rəsaliih), from Pahang leads the services at several different Temiar settlements: at Enching (ʔɛɲciik) on Friday, Balar (Balaar) on Saturday, Jader (Jadɛɛr) and Bihai (Bihaay) on Monday, Tapey, Barooŋ and Jias on Wednesday. Other places he serves at are Post Simpor (now

---

20. This unexpectedly mild response must have followed the success of the Jias case in the Kelantan High Court the previous year. It is nevertheless surprising that the village should have been declared 'Orang Asli land' by people acting in an official capacity. As far as I know, no such standing yet exists under the law. Land rights are currently the major source of conflict in the area, as in most other places where Orang Asli live. Nearly 80 years ago, however, Noone (1936: 68–69) made it clear that the Temiars in this general area outnumbered the population of the few Malay and Chinese settlements by more than four to one, and that an Aboriginal reserve should be established there.
21. I am not sure how to interpret this statement. Was Moses Soo himself proselytised or trained in Korea? Or has someone been referring to Korea as a way of asserting Christianity's 'Asian' credentials?
22. Apparently, this 'Pastor David' had not heard of me. This suggests that he had not done his homework, so to speak, by studying the published research literature on the Temiars before working among them. (But then, who among missionaries, Muslim or Christian, has ever read the literature on the Orang Asli? The only exceptions known to me are those who are also engaged in linguistic research.)

half Christian, half Muslim), Pasiig (now Christian). Razali was said to live outside Gua Musang. He prays (preaches?) in Semai, Temiar and Malay, and spends one week each month in Pahang, at Cheroh and Raub, teaching bible. He has run a three-week course at Jias, at which literate students above the age of 18 wrote notes as he taught. Non-literate villagers have also attended these classes, just to listen.

They pray in Malay, led by their peripatetic pastors, who read from a thumb-indexed Indonesian-language bible published in Jakarta. These activities have introduced a new word into the Temiar language: *rejɔɔj* ~ *rejɔɔy* ~ *rejɔy*, meaning 'to pray collectively', derived from the English 'rejoice'. (The word has also entered the lexicon of non-Christian Temiars, as the equivalent of the Malay word *hibur* 'to entertain, amuse'.) Apparently, the preachers make the bible stories relevant to *səjarah kanɛɛʔ sərɔk* 'the history of us Aborigines', but I could not discover how they do this. Every Wednesday, Pastor Moses supplies them with rice, sugar, milk, oil, onion, salt and salt fish, so they can have a good feed. No money is taken by the pastors, 'because we are poor'.

Previously, the Jias people all followed *halaaʔ riiʔ* 'our own mediumship'; none of them were Muslims, ʔaluj-followers or Baha'is. When most of the villagers converted to Christianity, there were two Muslim couples who refused to do so. They had previously become Muslim 'because they did not have enough food to eat'; they then 'fled' (*dadoʔ*) the village. The Christians no longer hold traditional-style song-sessions (*gənabag*). (In this respect, they differ from almost all the Muslim-converts.) About half of the former *halaaʔ* mediums converted to Christianity, having 'set free' (*tɛrsɛʔ*) their *gunig* spirit-guides. On questioning this, I was assured that they do not fear that their former *gunig*s will exact revenge on them. The other *halaaʔ* mediums have kept to the old religion, but it was not clear whether they had to move elsewhere, for I was also told that the tendency is for whole villages to become Christian.

Marriages between Christians are solemnised by a prayer (*do'a*, the Malay-Muslim word) from the pastor. (I do not know whether this is also recognised as a formal marriage registration, or whether the authorities continue in practice to recognise Temiar customary marriage as valid.) A Christian burial ground is being readied in Kampung Garɔʔ, which I was told is an 'historic' village site. The only other Christians whom they know personally are ethnic-Chinese, who come here sometimes from Pahang and Kuala Lumpur. Penghulu Pedik once attended prayers at a large church in Kuala Lumpur, but the prayers were in English and he went just to observe. Some Malays from nearby Kuala Betis have come to Jias a few times to try and convert them to Islam, but the villagers refused. Their understanding is that Muslims cannot interfere with another *agama*. (This suggests another reason for their becoming Christian—to prevent further Muslim missionary activity.)

Pedik said that there were 2,000 Christian Temiars in Kelantan, by their own counting, and that the ʔalʉj-followers (see the next section) in Bihai, Tapey, Balar and Enching villages had now all rejected that religion in favour of Christianity. On the other hand, he said that ʔawis, the main propagator of ʔalʉj Səlamad, and himself a former Christian pastor, had stuck with the ʔalʉj religion.

Following my brief visit to Jias, I talked about it to the young Temiar man who accompanied me there, and who was well-informed about religious developments in both Kelantan and Perak, despite his own uninterest in taking up any of the offered religious affiliations. He said that only one-half of the ʔalʉj-followers in the previously named villages had left the religion. Of those who had done so, some had become Christians or Muslims, but others had returned to *halaaʔ riiʔ manah* 'their own old-time mediumship'. He also said that the Christian and Muslim converts do not understand their new religions. The Muslims converted for the sake of the RM400 that they supposedly receive, but he made no suggestion as to why others had chosen Christianity—as his own mother had done.

Since I wrote the above account, Eduardo Hazera has provided me with further information about Temiar Christianity in Kelantan. He confirmed that there are now several churches, built in Temiar style, at various downstream and upstream sites, and that these are indeed serviced by Moses Soo. Pastor Soo preaches in Malay, with an immediate translation into Temiar by a man named ʔaluŋ, supposedly for the benefit of the older women. Following the earlier practice (see Chapter 6), God is sometimes referred to as Tohaat. However, in their sermons (recordings of which I have listened to) the preachers refer to God as Tuhan—a form acceptable also to Muslims. But it is Jesus (pronounced Yesus) rather than God who is more frequently mentioned.

The sermons make much reference to the salvationist claim that eternal life (*hidup kekal* in Malay) will be granted to those who 'believe'. However, this is accompanied by darker, presumably sectarian, concerns with 'false prophets (*nabi palsu*)', 'the Anti-Christ', the 'hatred' that Christians supposedly experience, and even the future of contemporary Jerusalem. It is hard to know what, if anything, Temiar congregants make of these references. According to Eduardo Hazera (personal communciation) there is no evidence that they converted out of salvationist concerns. Rather, they see Christianity as providing them with God's protection against their worldly, rather than spiritual, troubles; and they welcome the pastors' provisioning of material benefits.

The preachers forbid their followers to continue practising séances (*pɛhnɔɔh*) and the wearing of *tɛmpɔɔʔ* crowns. However, there are reports that Christian Temiars still wear the latter, removing them only when the pastors are thought to be around. Significantly, this implies that they are wearing the crowns *in the daytime*—a non-traditional practice characteristic primarily of the new ʔalʉj Səlamad religion, as described in the next section (figure

14.16). This is hard to interpret: are they former ʔalɥj followers who have chosen to syncretise the two religions, or do they see the daytime wearing of *tɛmpɔɔʔ* as a marker of modern 'Asli' identity (cf. figure 10.9)? Similarly, at least one church (figure 14.10) is decorated with *tǝnamuuʔ*-like hangings. Along with the evidence of continuing fears of *tǝracɔɔg* (figure 6.1), this indicates that the adoption of Christianity has certainly not done away with traces of the older religion—which the Temiars, at least, probably see as custom rather than 'religion'.

Unlike the Muslim missionaries, the Christians have attempted to develop Temiar-language materials in propagating the religion. An example is the Lord's Prayer, posted in both Temiar and Malay versions on the wall of a church at a village in the upper Betis valley (figure 14.11). As with all attempts by non-linguists to reduce Temiar to writing, this shows some awkward features, although it is more accurate in some respects than most other such attempts. My own phonemic transcription and word-for-word glossing (above) indicates the extent to which this succeeded.[23] (Temiars are not regularly literate in their own language, except for the ad hoc sending of SMS messages; I suspect that they would find the Malay version easier to read.)

Figure 14.10 Temiar church near Bihaay, 2012 (Photograph by Eduardo Hazera)
Note the electric guitar and the tǝnamuuʔ-like hangings made of woven plastic obscuring the cross hanging on the end wall.

23. I am unable to identify or properly transcribe the word written as *behej*, presumably intended to mean 'Heaven'. The text contains several other unusual linguistic features, including the use of *riiʔ* 'self' as a relative pronoun. These probably result from the need to recast a very foreign subordinating sentence structure into Temiar, with its normally paratactically organised sentences. I shall not comment further on the language here, beyond noting the unusual word *tǝmelʔɔɔy*, which I had previously met with only in the special vocabulary of the ʔalɥj Sǝlamad religion. See footnote 24 in this chapter for further discussion. It would be interesting to determine in which direction the borrowing, if any, took place between the two religions.

Figure 14.11 The Lord's Prayer in Temiar (black) and Malay (red) at Təluur [?] village, Betis, Kelantan, 2012 (Photograph by Eduardo Hazera)

Two further points about Temiar Christianity deserve attention. First, as far back as the 1930s, Noone (1936: 58) predicted precisely the sort of difficulty that has now arisen. He wrote that if Christian missionaries were to have their way among the Temiars, it would lead to their estrangement, both from other Temiars and from broader (Malay) society. Second, as the news reports presented earlier show, the connection with Christian missionaries has become a major channel through which ideas about land rights are spread. Loggers, plantation managers and others are becoming aware that Temiars are beginning to know the relevant laws and wish to see them changed. Further problems may yet result from both Christianisation and Islamisation, if the example of the formerly nomadic Orang Suku Laut of the Riau archipelago in Indonesia can be taken as a parallel. Chou (2010: 101–117) reports that Indonesian state agencies hold that the Orang Suku Laut will not adapt to modern ways unless they are so *directed* from outside. The chosen modality of that 'directing' is religion—specifically the monotheism (belief in *Ketuhanan Yang Maha Esa* 'the godhead who is the great oneness') enjoined in the *Pancasila*, Indonesia's official state ideology. This has reached the Orang Laut in both its Muslim and Christian forms, the former with government support, the latter more privately supported and in several different versions. In both cases, however, the effect (intended or otherwise) has been a reduction in the self-sufficiency of the Orang Laut, formerly derived from fishing. This has been coupled with a marked fall in

The Lord's Prayer in Temiar (transcribed from figure 14.11)

ORIGINAL: Abe kandeek rik n' behej / termej la kene Heak.
PHONEMIC: ʔabəəh kandeeʔ riiʔ ʔɛn-[behej] / tɛrmɛj la-kənɨɨh Hãã̃ʔ.
GLOSSING: Father our who in-[heaven] / make.good EMPH-name Your.
ENGLISH: 'Our Father, which art in heaven, hallowed be thy Name.'

Laj la kerajaan Heak / perhej la nenchen Heak / n'tek gerek n'behej.
Laj la-kərajaʔan Hãã̃ʔ / pɛrhej la-nɛncɛn Hãã̃ʔ / ʔɛn-tɛʔ gərɛʔ ʔɛn-[behej].
Arrive.suddenly EMPH-kingdom Your / bring.about EMPH-wanting Your / on-earth like
   in-[heaven].
'Thy kingdom come, Thy will be done in earth, as it is in heaven.'

Og la kandeek ma is doh / nekcak kandeek rik secukub eh.
ʔog la-kandeeʔ ma-ʔis doh / nɛʔcaaʔ kandeeʔ riiʔ səcukub ʔəh.
Give EMPH-us for-day this / eating our which sufficient it.
'Give us this day our daily bread.'

Bok ampun elah ma teren seek kandeek / gerek kandeek hejek ki ampuni / Senoi rik
   eng terek seek ma kandeek.
Bɔʔ ʔampun ʔə-lah ma-tərɛnsɛɛʔ kandeeʔ / gərɛʔ kandeeʔ hijɛʔ ki-ʔampuni / sɛnʔɔɔy riiʔ
   ʔun-tərɛʔsɛɛʔ ma-kandeeʔ.
And forgive EMPH to-causing.stray.NMLZ our / like we also we-forgive / people who
   they-cause.stray to-us.
'And forgive us our trespasses, as we forgive them that trespass against us.'

Bok agok lah hain kandeek makeluj tenarek / tetapi tersek lah kandeek nom rik
   jedhad.
Bɔʔ ʔagoʔ lah ha-ʔɛn kandeeʔ ma-kəlɔɔj tənareʔ / tətapiiʔ tɛrsɛʔ lah kandeeʔ num-riiʔ
   jedhad.
And don't EMPH you-bring us to-within pulling / but set.free EMPH us from-which
   wicked.
'And lead us not into temptation, but deliver us from evil.'

Kerana heak lah rik berpunya kerajaan / bok kuasak bok temeloi loi ma bel-bel eh.
Kəranaaʔ hãã̃ʔ lah riiʔ bər-puɲaaʔ kərajaʔan / bɔʔ kəwasaaʔ bɔʔ təmɛlʔɔɔy lɔy ma-beel
   beel ʔəh.
Because you EMPH who possessing kingdom / and power and goodness reach to-
   when when it.
'For thine is the kingdom, the power, and the glory, forever and ever.'

(kemen, Amin)
(kəmɨn, ʔamin)
(true, Amen)

the status of the women, which was previously based on their equal role in fishing. The new religious allegiances have also introduced tensions between different local groups of Orang Laut, where none existed before. There are hints that the same problems have also arisen among the Temiars, and for similar reasons.

A new religion: ʔaluj Səlamad

ʔaluj Səlamad is a new endogenous, monotheistic and named religion that first emerged, as far as I can reconstruct, around 1998 or 1999 in certain Temiar communities. Exactly *which* communities it emerged in and in which state, Perak or Kelantan, is now a matter of disagreement among the Temiars themselves. The religion's name is not easy to translate into a single English phrase. In the Temiar myths I collected in the 1960s, ʔaluj (which means 'last born') is the younger sibling of the Thunder deity, Karey, on whom he is always playing tricks (Chapters 8 and 9). As noted earlier, Karey is a trope for the cosmos itself; but his brother ʔaluj was regularly spoken of as the first human being, and as the inventor of such cultural institutions as the Temiar kinship terminology. Səlamad is the Temiar pronunciation of the Arabo-Malay *selamat* 'security, peace, safety', but it also has the force of a greeting, as in *selamat jalan* 'goodbye' (literally 'journey safely'). Thus, the phrase ʔaluj Səlamad could mean variously 'ʔaluj is safe', or 'There is safety in ʔaluj', or perhaps 'Greetings, ʔaluj'. As Gellner (1988: 43–49) pointed out, the ascription of a *single* referential meaning to an utterance is not a desideratum in relatively less differentiated ('many-stranded') societies. Therefore, to impose a single unambiguous translation on this religion's name would be to distort the meaning that it must have for its own practitioners, as well as for other Temiars. More significant is the fact the religion actually *has* a name, and that its followers explicitly regard it as a 'religion' (*agama*). Neither of these features characterised the older indigenous body of practices that I—but not they—have been referring to as 'Temiar Religion'. (The upper-case R is intentional here.)

I first heard mention of ʔaluj Səlamad several years before making any first-hand acquaintance with it, through gathering a few shreds of third-party information. In December 2006, I began to collect information from Temiars who were not followers of the religion but who had witnessed some of its ceremonies in Perak and Kelantan. In December 2007, I managed to make field recordings of songs that were said to be in the ʔaluj Səlamad genre. But it was not until February 2008, at Lambok, that I finally managed to talk in some depth to any of its followers and to witness its practices. My main source of information was a Temiar man named Jidaʔ, whom I had known well 44 years earlier, when he was a small boy living

Figure 14.12 Jidaʔ and his father ʔayaaw, Humid, Kelantan (1964)

in Humid village (figure 14.12), a day's march upstream from Lambok. His late father, ʔayaaw (a widower), was then a 'big' *halaaʔ*, with a tiger spirit-guide whose songs he sang darkly, in a rich quavering bass voice. Jidaʔ, who went to primary school at Lambok in the late 1960s, became a Baha'i in the 1970s.

Opinions on the new ʔalɥj Sɘlamad religion vary greatly. The following account is therefore unavoidably preliminary. I shall commence with the 'insider' view presented by some of its practitioners, mainly Jidaʔ, and then proceed to some of the 'outsider' views I gathered from Temiars and others who were not followers of the religion, and use these as a basis for analysis. I also present some raw field data from several different places, to indicate the flux that has characterised the ʔalɥj Sɘlamad religion.

ʔalɥj Sɘlamad: Insiders' views

I talked to Jidaʔ in some depth at his house on 24 February 2008, with several other followers of the religion sitting in on the conversation. Two other Temiars who knew them well, but who were not themselves followers of the religion, were present too. The following night, Jidaʔ held an ʔalɥj Sɘlamad ceremony for me to witness directly for the first time.

Jida² said that the origin of the '?aluj' in ?aluj Səlamad is '?aluj Gɛrlɔɔk', in the old Temiar myths. In former times, he said, the people did not pronounce the true name of ?aluj, which is 'Gɛrlɔɔk'. (In 1965, I had recorded Gɛrlɔɔk as the name of a mountain on the Cəlapag river in the Ber valley, but Jida² did not mention this.) He then gave the following account of the ideas and practices underlying the ?aluj Səlamad religion—or as he put it, the reasons for singing to ?aluj Gɛrlɔɔk. The account, which I wrote down in the original Temiar, contains a fair sprinkling of words that are peculiar to ?aluj Səlamad usage, and which therefore had to be explained, both to me and my non-?aluj Temiar companions. Throughout his explanation, Jida² placed a lot of emphasis on people's feelings. (My translation attempts to retain Jida²'s sermon-like tone.)

Us humans in general, regardless of ethnicity (*baŋsaa²*)—he cares for us and looks after us. ?aluj looks after all Malaysians, and the whole world. ?aluj made us, he gave us knowledge (*²ɛlmuu²*), good fortune, food, cars, and so on. That is the purpose of singing to ?aluj Gɛrlɔɔk. We go together to the Dewan Sənindul prayer house. He doesn't mind who comes along: everyone is included under ?aluj Gɛrlɔɔk's rule (*hukum*).

At the proper times we come together at the Dewan. According to the rules of goodness (*hukum təmɛl²ɔɔy*), we mustn't behave badly (*jahad*). The fifteenth, twentieth, thirtieth and thirty-first days of the month are *təmɛrlɔɔy* (= *mɛjmɛj* 'very good') days.[24] We mustn't go anywhere, but stay at home working together, cooking bamboo-tube rice, grated-cassava bread, fish and frog over the fire, and then we eat it all from split-bamboo containers.

We, all of us, put our life-soul (*səmaŋad*) to rights, as commanded by ?aluj. Never mind those who died in the past or those who died recently—our *səmaŋad* is still alive. We are together under ?aluj's rule—?aluj whose origins are in Bɔɔk Bər [the confluence of the Ber and Brok rivers, in the next valley to the south, near Gɛrlɔɔk mountain].

?aluj followers still believe in dreams as a sign of our means of livelihood (*rezeki*). You will get what you dream. If we reject it, we don't get it. Even non-?aluj-followers will receive ?aluj.

?aluj followers mustn't say *boot* [the normal Temiar word for 'flower']; they must say *mɛɛ²* instead. The ?aluj greeting is *Səlamad ²ooy ²amɛɛ²!* or *Səlamad ²ooy ɲu²!*,[25] which functions like the Muslim

---

24. I am not sure whether *təmɛl²ɔɔy* and *təmɛrlɔɔy* are two different words, or the same word wrongly transcribed. Whatever the case, they bear an obvious phonic-iconic similarity. Etymologically, they seem to have some relation with the causative verb *terlɔɔy* 'to make something cross over (a river)', except that the *m* infix is not a regular part of Temiar morphology in this position. Note that *təmɛl²ɔɔy* also occurs in the Temiar version of the Lord's Prayer presented earlier, where it translates 'the glory'.
25. Literally, this would mean 'Greetings, Oh aunts! / Greetings, Oh uncles!' But, for ?aluj followers, *mɛɛ²* also refers to 'flowers', presumably those that the women's chorus wear during the song ceremonies. And I was told that *ɲu²* (literally, 'parent's younger brother') here also refers to ?aluj himself.

'*salaam aleikum!* and *wa-aleikum salaam!*'. ʔalɥj followers don't say that someone has *kəbɥs* ['died'] or *hɔj hɔy* ['has become no more']. Instead, they say *pəlɔɔw*.[26]

The following night's *Pɛhnɔɔh ʔalɥj* ceremony took place in the special Dewan Sənindul building, not used for anything but ceremonies (figures 14.13–14.15).[27] Except for its partly zinc roofing, this was an entirely Temiar-type construction. There were two doors on either side, one for women, one for men, each leading to a raised platform along the insides of the building. In the middle was a broad space. The floor and platforms were of springy split-bamboo. There was a *tənamuuʔ* wreath high up (cf. figures 10.5, 10.6), barely visible through the dense tracery of *calun* leaves at face height. Jidaʔ said this was done on purpose, so that the celebrants' heads would be in the leaves (figure 14.14).

Jidaʔ began with a spoken imploration to ʔalɥj.[28] Then the oil lamps were extinguished, and Jidaʔ began singing in Temiar style, with a chorus of six

Figure 14.13 The Dewan Səndindul at Lambok, with Jidaʔ looking on (2008)
By 2010, this was no longer in place.

26. Later, I was told by a non-*ʔalɥj*-follower that the verb *pəlɔɔw* is normally used for an insect's rotting away to its exoskeleton after it dies.
27. *Sənindul* looks like a borrowing from a Malay word of form *sindul, senendol* etc., but no such word appears in the dictionaries. I could no longer see the building when I revisited Lambok in 2010, and I suspect that it might have been replaced by a newly constructed traditional-style building high on the slopes of a nearby hill that was being lived in by a group of *ʔalɥj*-followers, despite the inconvenience of being so far from a source of water.
28. I recorded this and the rest of the ceremony, but I have yet to study the spoken words or song-lyrics.

Figure 14.14 Preparing the *calun*-leaf hanging at head-level inside the Dewan, just before the *Pɛhnɔɔh ʔalɨj* ceremony (2008)

Figure 14.15 The ʔalɨj celebrants, wearing distinctive crowns and holding ritual posies, before extinguishing the lamps to perform their songs in the dark (2008)

women. He stood up throughout. Three other men, standing and doing a minimal left-right *sisɛʔ*-dance shuffle, then sang in turn, passing the same song between themselves. There was no break in the singing, which lasted just one hour, and which I recorded in a single take. It ended when Jidaʔ bounced loudly in place a few times, rather like some Chinese mediums at the end of their trancing. But there had been no trancing, and afterwards Jidaʔ confirmed that they do not trance (*wəl hup* 'forget their *hup*'). They nevertheless referred to the ceremony as a *pɛhnɔɔh*, which normally refers to trancing. Perhaps the ʔalɥj followers now regard the word as referring to *any* ritual that involves singing and dancing.

The lamps were then re-lit, and I started questioning Jidaʔ about *whose* words the song lyric (*hənelad*) consisted of. I suspected that this was a prayer *to* ʔalɥj, rather than mediumship *of* ʔalɥj regarded as a spirit-guide. Regardless how carefully I phrased myself, Jidaʔ insisted that the words were not his own but ʔalɥj's, since ʔalɥj had created everything. Even when a non-ʔalɥj companion who understood the point of my question tried to help out, the answer was the same. Later, however, my friend confirmed that I was right, and the song-lyrics were indeed addressed *by* Jidaʔ *to* ʔalɥj. This was therefore a case in which Temiar mediumistic *forms* as traditionally practised were now reshaped so that the content served innovatively transcendental ends. Regular Temiar *pɛhnɔɔh* performances are thought of as the spirit-guide singing *through* the singer, who is therefore a *halaaʔ* medium.[29] In this performance, however, the singers were performing their own songs of praise to their new deity, ʔalɥj, but doing so in manner that to the uninformed observer would appear no different from a normal Temiar Religion ceremony, except for its brevity.

ʔalɥj Sɔlamad: Outsiders' views

The following day, I discussed the ceremony with the non-ʔalɥj-followers who had been present with me. These were a JHEOA employee who belonged to no named religion and his son, who had recently become a Christian. They were critical of what they had witnessed, not because they were opposed to the ʔalɥj Sɔlamad religion, but because they thought that things had not been done 'properly'—that is, according to what they had seen in Perak. There should have been a second pair of doors at the other end of the house (they said) for the men and women to exit by. The local ʔalɥj-followers had followed others' teachings (they said), getting some of it wrong, and not relying on any personal revelation. My friend's father had earlier worried that my friend might himself join ʔalɥj Sɔlamad precisely *because* it did not depend on the genuine revelation of one's own *gunig* spirit-guide. Temiars

---

29. See my discussion (Benjamin 2011b: 19–20) of the semantic underpinnings of the deponently 'middle-voice' shape of *gabag*, the word used for ritual singing, implying that it means 'to sing and be sung through'.

can sing other people's *gunig* for fun, but it is their own *gunig* that makes the *hənelad* song-lyric authentic and powerful to heal (*sɛʔsooʔ*). The ʔalɨj followers were inauthentic, precisely because they had trusted to someone else's teaching without truly experiencing it.[30] Similarly, they further objected to the way in which the ʔalɨj followers regularly perform their ceremonies by passing the same song between themselves. Presumably, this feels wrong to the traditionally minded because the song is then transcendentally 'out there' rather than 'in us'. They also disagreed with what I had been told about where the ʔalɨj Səlamad religion first developed, saying that the real founders lived in the headwaters of the Betis valley, to the north-west, and not in the Ber valley to the south-west. (I say more about the question of origins and leaders below.)

On this and previous visits, and before I finally managed to witness the ʔalɨj Səlamad ceremony, I had gathered as much information as I could about the religion from Temiars who were mostly not followers but who claimed to know something about it. Their views are interesting, in that they point to the ways in which ʔalɨj Səlamad deviates explicitly from the practices of Temiar Religion. I suggest that these differences were deliberately instituted to mark ʔalɨj Səlamad off as a formally bounded religion. The following ethnographic notes indicate something of the social situation of ʔalɨj Səlamad at the time of my earlier visits. The statements may well be out of date by now, but they are nevertheless of some historical significance, and relate to a new religion that has otherwise never been researched.

Galaaŋ, Kelantan, December 2006: The headman informs me that at Balar there are followers of a new religion, ʔagamaaʔ ʔalɨj, started by ʔawin Pədiʔ, a former Radio Malaysian broadcaster and former Christian *padri*. He orders that the ʔalɨj ceremony should run from 8.00 to 9.30 every night, exactly! (As a former professional broadcaster, ʔawin would indeed have learnt the necessity of following the clock.) There are lots of followers in Bihai, Lambok (one couple), and Taŋkɔɔl Gɛrtas, just below Lambok. The *pembawa* ('bringer') there is Jidaʔ son of ʔayaaw. This new religion overtly rejects the old taboo practices and beliefs. They even forbid mourning and crying: they perform the mourning songs straight after the death, with a seclusion period. (Normal Temiar practice is to forbid song ceremonies for the several weeks of the mourning period.)

Landap, Perak, December 2006: The new ʔalɨj religion has not reached here, but it has reached Lasah. In Sungai Pelantuk, near Chemor, there

---

30. My critical Temiar companions were in effect pointing to the distinction between 'magistral' and 'pupillary' understandings of allusive metaphor drawn by C. S. Lewis (1939), mentioned in Chapter 1. They were also, in their own way, indicating the transcendental character of relying on *others'* opinions instead of one's own. This approach is of course a fundamental feature of all monotheistic religions. ('Modern'-minded people who claim to reject this approach to God prefer to call themselves 'spiritual' rather than 'religious'.)

are 500–600 Temiars, many of whom are followers of the ʔalʉj religion, in addition to eight households at Kampung Pisang, near Landap. They celebrate *Hari Jadi ʔalʉj* ('ʔalʉj's birthday') on the 20th and 21st of each month. This follows from a story about *ʔasal ʔugamaaʔ* 'the origin of religion', which (like everything else) was given by ʔalʉj.

Sungai Pelantuk, Perak, December 2006: Half of the people follow ʔalʉj Səlamad, and half Islam. There are no Christians. ʔalʉj Səlamad arrived there in 1999, and ʔawin visited in 2003. Their practice involves normal Temiar-style performance with bamboo-tube accompaniment, but employing a different song-genre than Ciɲcɛm.

Sɛŋsaaŋ, Kelantan, December 2007: Christians, Muslims and ʔalʉj-followers still all carry on the *pɛhpɔɔh* ceremonies in the old style. ʔalʉj Səlamad has provided new melodies and lyrics too.

Lambok, Kelantan, December 2007: *Pɛhnɔɔh ʔalʉj* is done in the dark, after which they wash their heads in the 'water' squeezed out of the *maŋsiiʔ* shrub. The women's percussive accompaniment must be performed using bamboo tubes of the *sogiiʔ* variety. The *pɛhnɔɔh* lasts from 8.00 p.m. to 11.00 p.m. ʔalʉj followers wear old-style crowns (*tɛmpɔɔʔ*) wherever they go, even in town. [I later found this to be true: see figure 14.16.] They also decorate their vehicles with flowers. ʔalʉj-followers have lots of rules. Examples are: (1) the fixed times of ending the *pɛhnɔɔh*, and (2) that at feasts, they eat only 'original'

Figure 14.16 A Temiar follower of ʔalʉj Səlamad from the Jenera (Jɛnrɔɔl) valley, wearing a distinctive crown (*tɛmpɔɔʔ*) in Gua Musang town, Kelantan (2008)

(*ʔasal*) foods, including just the leaves of the cassava plant, but not the tubers. The fixed times vary from village to village. One of the local headmen has forbidden his followers from joining ʔaluj Salamad because he fears it will lead to a loss of original Temiar culture.

Lambok, February 2008, information from an ʔaluj-follower: An ʔaluj-follower named Yaah arrives. (He turns out to be the son of the woman seated on the right of the cover photograph of Benjamin & Chou (2002), which I took in Humid in 1964.) There are ʔaluj followers in several villages: Paralɔɔk, Kampung Tɛrrej, and Kampung Haag (but I did not know where these are, and had never heard of them before). The authorities have not tried to stop ʔaluj Salamad (unlike with Baha'i previously), even though they know about it. The ʔaluj Salamad people hold rituals only for ʔaluj, who is indeed the younger brother of Karey in the old myths. The new ruling (*hukum*) is that they have stopped holding ceremonies for other spirit-guides (*gunig*). (I took this as confirmation that ʔaluj Salamad is indeed monotheistic.) When someone joins ʔaluj Salamad, they then fuse (*tɛrmɔɔj*, 'cause to enter') the other *gunig*s to ʔaluj; they don't throw away (*bəs*) their previous *gunig*s. (Contrast this with what I was told had been done by the Christians at Jias, who reportedly just set their *gunig*s free.)

Lambok, February 2008: A well-travelled Temiar says that some Temiars are afraid of other Temiars for following ʔaluj, and they then drop the religion. In Banun, Perak, where there are Christians and Muslims, there has been some tension. The women there will not marry ʔaluj-followers. One of ʔawin's relatives, a follower, died in a road accident. People said that if ʔaluj Salamad was true, the victim would have survived.

ʔaluj Salamad as monotheism

At first glance, ʔaluj Salamad appears to be a wholly endogenous development, despite its monotheism. But is this the whole truth of the matter? While its god, ʔaluj, is indeed derived from indigenous Temiar sources, its monotheism shares features with the other better known monotheisms: Christianity, Islam and Baha'i, all of which have had a presence in the Temiar world. Those monotheisms, however, differed from each other in their manner of arrival on the scene. Temiars who deliberately *chose* monotheism did so through their own religious search—through Baha'i and ʔaluj Salamad. Conversely, those Temiars who have taken up Christianity or Islam did so for reasons having little to do with monotheism as such. As we have seen, Temiars experience Islam as a politically imposed change of identity. Christianity, on the other hand, attracts because of its 'healing' activities, for not imposing food taboos and for supplying material goods, rather than for any theological message it has to offer. In neither case is monotheism *as such* a salient issue.[31]

Some of the similarity between ʔalɨj Sǝlamad and the other monotheisms results from structural causes. To assert belief in just one god is to declare that the god is singular, and therefore unique and wholly *other*. The god is therefore in principle unlike anything else in our experience, making belief in him difficult to hold.[32] A greater than usual 'leap of faith' is therefore required to maintain monotheistic belief. This is eased by ensuring that the followers are surrounded by like-minded people all re-asserting the same belief. In turn, this leads to a social-psychological necessity for group-maintenance and boundary-formation, to ensure that the believers hold together. Rules must be imposed, to ensure that the followers *do* act similarly to each other, as far as possible. A parallel requirement is *separation* from those who do things differently. This frequently leads in turn to the generating of fault-lines between and within the different monotheistic religions—especially when they see the other versions as presenting threats to their own particular 'truth'.

These tendencies are clearly apparent in Islam and Christianity (Protestantism especially, and increasingly in Sunni Islam). Similar features have been put in place (but by whom?) in ʔalɨj Sǝlamad. These include the running of ceremonies according to clock time, the deliberate flouting of normal Temiar custom, the special forms of greeting and lexical usage, the regular wearing of distinctive headgear, the construction of a special non-domestic building only for ʔalɨj Sǝlamad ceremonies (a 'church' so to speak), and so on. Above all, ʔalɨj Sǝlamad constitutes a named social *identity*, a kind of ethnicity—just like the other monotheisms. Needless to say, the very uniqueness of a creator god also implies his universality. The claim of universality and the desire to eliminate difference are major drives for engaging in missionary work, a practice deeply embedded in both Christianity and Islam. As we shall see shortly, missionising has formed part of ʔalɨj Sǝlamad too. In all these respects, ʔalɨj Sǝlamad has clearly borrowed much of its organisational pattern from Baha'i, Christianity and Islam. It is no accident, then, that many of its followers were indeed formerly Baha'is or Christians, or both. Islam, of course, is a constant presence in Malaysia anyway.

---

31. My view of Temiar Christianity is based on limited evidence, and is therefore incomplete. It is also necessary to investigate exactly *what* messages, if any, the bringers of Christianity and Islam employ when they seek Temiar converts, events that I have not witnessed directly.

32. It seems that the singular gods of the monotheistic religions are always male. This is not a matter of patriarchy, as many writers still assert: societies with female deities are just as patriarchal as those with male deities. Mono-gods lie unaltered and outside their creation, just as fathers play an 'external' role in the procreation and rearing of their children, and remain physically unchanged by it. For the same reason, Earth deities are usually female: the earth is undeniably changed by the activities of human beings—the agents of 'God the father', under his command to enjoy the fruits of the earth—just as mothers are undeniably changed by bearing and rearing children.

Alongside these structural features, ʔalɥj Səlamad also has a distinctive *content*. We should therefore consider the possibility of some specific input from the other monotheistic religions. After all, no religion is ever freely invented out of nothing: all are formed either by transformation or by abreaction from already existing religions. (Christianity and Islam, for example, are both derived from earlier Hebrew religion, as their own better-informed authorities openly recognise.) In the case of ʔalɥj Səlamad, specifically Christian parallels are so striking that the connection cannot be wholly accidental. In particular, the Deity/Man parallelism between Karey/ʔalɥj and God/Jesus is patently obvious. It turns out that ʔawin (also known as ʔawis), one of the major propagators of ʔalɥj Səlamad, is a former Christian. He is reported to have once given a talk at the Orang Asli hospital at Gombak, just outside Kuala Lumpur, in which he taught that ʔalɥj had died and come back to life at Easter time. One of my Temiar friends, not himself a 'member' of any religion, also noticed the Christian-ʔalɥj similarities when he attended a service at his wife's church. What is significant is that he knew about ʔalɥj Səlamad first, and only then noticed the Christian parallels; he had no prior knowledge of Christianity. Another possible Christian element is the forbidding of older practices: this is reminiscent of Saint Paul's assertion that from now on believers live by faith, not law.

These suppositions also throw new light on the original Karey/ʔalɥj mythology that I collected in the 1960s. It is Karey ('Thunder', the elder brother of ʔalɥj) who reversibly 'creates' the cosmos, through the bootstraps of his own consciousness. But, as the old-timers explicitly told me, it is ʔalɥj who creates human culture and institutions. By dropping Karey from the picture, the reversible dialectic that previously held between world, animals, plants and people has thereby been replaced by a unidimensional and transcendental concern solely for *people*, through worshipping the mythic First Man, ʔalɥj, as god.

ʔalɥj Səlamad: Origins, history and sociology

It is futile to search for a *single* truth about the origins of ʔalɥj Səlamad. Although the religion is a very recent development, the Temiars I talked to all had different versions of its history and background. It seems that a mythology of sorts is rapidly developing, remarkably like the variant origin stories that occur in the New Testament gospels or surround the earliest manifestations of Mormonism, Baha'i or Melanesian cargo cults. But with regard to ʔalɥj Səlamad, those on the 'outside', Temiar and non-Temiar alike, seem to present a more uniform picture—one that implies a certain degree of possible exploitation by the founders and/or some of those who succeeded them. One non-Temiar observer suggested to me that the original founders had been supporters of the now defunct Semangat 46 political party mentioned in Chapter 13, which began as a break-away movement from the nationally dominant UMNO party. This party was led by Tengku Razaleigh, the Kelantan royal who is still the MP for Gua Musang (2014), the constituency in which most of the Kelantan Temiars live. He was popular because he was thought not to be opposed to traditional Orang Asli culture, and had supposedly promised that if Semangat 46 won the election the Orang Asli would be given their own seat in the state assembly. The Islamist PAS party had also made promises to the Orang Asli, but these were not kept after they won the election. As suggested in Chapter 13, I gained the impression that there was a degree of party-political alignment associated with these religious changes. Those who actively opposed the ʔalɥj Səlamad religion were supporters of PAS and had converted to Islam, at least nominally. Some of those who had led the ʔalɥj Səlamad religion had formerly supported the Semangat 46 party. Those who were neither Muslims nor ʔalɥj-followers voted variously for PAS or UMNO on an individual basis.

The general view among those Temiars and non-Temiars who know about ʔalɥj Səlamad is that the current leading personality in the religion is the aforementioned Kelantan Temiar known as ʔawis or ʔawin. ʔawis is his 'true' name; ʔawin is the name he used when working as a broadcaster in the Orang Asli service of Malaysian radio. ʔawin, who speaks English, appears in the Halonen & Wellman (1998) documentary video as the main interpreter of Temiar Religion. At the time of the filming, he was managing the Orang Asli Cooperative (Koperasi Kijang Mas) in Gua Musang, which deals mainly with handicrafts and forest products. In the video, he makes several pleas for the preservation of Temiar religious culture, and is shown as being equally at ease in the modern and village sectors. I was told that he once used to argue forcibly for spiritual rights to be considered along with land rights. More recently, he has been the headman (*penghulu*) of Bihai village—the same settlement from which the present Deputy Director-General of the JAKOA comes. This is said to be still an old-style village, because the people are reluctant to move to the larger resettlement villages. (As noted earlier, the people of Bihai are reported to have since become largely Christian.)

As I have not succeeded in talking directly with ʔawin, I have had to rely on information provided by others. This has not been entirely consistent and may be unreliable, but a general pattern has emerged. At the time of the filming of the Halonen & Wellman video in 1997, the ʔalɥj Səlamad religion had not yet emerged. By 1999, however, the religion had already made its appearance in Sungai Pelantuk, Perak, a large Temiar resettlement village that I visited in 2006, half of whose inhabitants were by then already ʔalɥj followers. (The other half were Muslims; there were no Christians.)

Many of the people I talked to in 2006 claimed that it is ʔawin himself who started the ʔalɥj Səlamad religion. Others claimed that it was one of

ʔawin's cousins who started it, and that ʔawin himself had initially tried to stop its spread. (This sounds very like the Saul/Paul account in Christianity!) They also claimed that when he was working at the radio studio and later at the Cooperative in Gua Musang, he was a Christian. (He began managing the Cooperative after the Halonen & Wellman video was filmed.) His wife at the time was a Christian Semai from Geruntom, a community that had been missionised in the 1930s by Paul and Nathalie Means. As a Christian preacher (*padri*), ʔawin had tried to convert the Gua Musang Temiars, but failed, because the people were unwilling to give up their song-based séance sessions (*pɛhnɔɔh*). He then gave up Christianity and started to *pɛhpɔɔh* himself, with ʔaluj as the focus, thereby in effect inventing a new religion. Despite the Christian elements, he apparently hoped it could be accepted by the government as a recognised 'authentic' (*sah*) religion.

Other stories are told. A follower of the religion gave me a completely different account, namely that the origin (*ʔasal*) of the religion was at Halak (Halɔʔ) village in the Yai valley, more than ten years previously.[33] The founder, now dead, was replaced by his son Salɛ̃w, who had also died. The current leader was Salɛ̃w's younger brother, by the name of ʔasal ('Origin'!). ʔasal was said to be still living in Halak. *His* younger brother, Kəjɔʔ, was also an ʔaluj leader. They all went to primary school in an Orang Asli settlement, but not to secondary school. (Some Singaporean friends of mine had visited this area frequently, and confirmed that there were many ʔaluj followers there. I have not been to that valley myself since the 1960s.)

Let me try to put these pieces together. If ʔaluj Salamad was already present in 1999 in Sungai Pelantuk, Perak, that was within two years of ʔawin appearing in the Halonen & Wellman video. In the video, he certainly spoke in favour of Temiar religious revelations, but with no hint either of ʔaluj Salamad or of his own earlier Christianity. This supports the view that someone other than ʔawin invented the religion, as some of my respondents claimed. (But where, then, would the obvious Christian elements have come from?) If so, it may be that ʔawin has since taken it over, at least in the areas he regularly visits, and adapted it to his own aims, religious or otherwise. This would, of course, explain why there is no single account of its origins, even though it began just ten years before I studied it at first hand.

I must emphasise that the above account of the religion's origins is based on hearsay. It almost certainly needs correction in many of its details. Nevertheless, a few general issues arise from these accounts and from what I observed. Given that the *forms* of ʔaluj Salamad are very close to traditional Temiar Religion even though the content differs, it will be interesting to see whether in the long run it (1) retains its distinctiveness,

---

33. As on the Frontispiece map, I have here and elsewhere followed the Temiar river-naming practice, which reverses the names Perias (Pɛryas) and Yai (Yaay). This difference between local-Malay and Temiar practice was also noted by Noone (1936: 18).

or (2) disappears (like Baha'i?), or (3) merges with Temiar Religion to become just another song-genre (like Ciɲcɛm). Like Baha'i, ʔalɥj Səlamad is patterned on the model of Islam and Christianity. Under pressure from the authorities, most of the Baha'i followers eventually went over to Islam. Christians, at least in Kelantan, are now clearly under pressure too, but the outside support they are receiving—which was not the case with Baha'i—may well decrease the likelihood that they will shift to Islam.

Afterword

I hope that the slight lack of tidiness in this collection of studies has been compensated for by its unusually extended first-hand reportage and analysis. Few single-author studies have followed the religious trajectory of the same tribal and then post-tribal society for a half-century, as I have attempted to do in this volume. There are still gaps in the story, but I have been privileged to chance upon the scene at various times when the Temiars were undergoing profound re-orientations in their social and religious lives. From a scholarly point of view, the findings feed into several of the theoretical approaches that fill the social-science literature, both old and new, as I have pointed out at several places in the text.

Equally important is the hope that this volume might contribute constructively to the history and appreciation of a population who, with rare exceptions, have been written out of Malaysian and Southeast Asian studies (while being written gratuitously *into* the founding mythology of Western 'Senoi' Dreamwork). I have tried to portray the difficulties that confront the Temiars in a manner that might inform those who are more directly able to alleviate their situation. It is clear, especially from the materials presented in the final two chapters, that the Temiars see themselves as active members of Malaysian society. But it is equally clear that they wish this to be on equal terms, and not as dependents who need always to be told by others what is good for them. If in future some Temiars should read this account and make use of it, I shall be especially happy.

Four accounts of H. D. Noone's work on Temiar religion

1.1 An article in *Nature* (1937)

The following account of Noone's work appeared in the journal *Nature* (139: 241) on 6 February 1937. It accords with the few other sources on Noone's researches into Temiar mediumship and ritual healing practices. The article appeared just after Noone's primary publication (1936) on the Temiars, which contained very little information on religious matters. Apart from the outdated physical anthropology and cultural hierarchisation, this account seems close to the reality. However, the distinction drawn between 'Temiar' and 'Sakai' is puzzling, as the professional literature of the time regularly considered the Temiars to be the 'Northern Sakai'. The writer may have been identifying 'Sakai' with the Semais, as the latter would fit the text slightly better.

Aboriginal Tribes of the Malay Peninsula

WHILE of the aboriginal tribes of the Malay Peninsula the Sakai, the Semang and the Jakun, though by no means well known, have been the subject of careful investigation by a number of observers, the Temiar, a hill people of Perak, are virtually untouched in an anthropological sense. Yet they number nearly one half of the aboriginal population of 25,000. They have, however, been made the subject of a considerable study by Mr. H. D. Noone of the Perak State Museum, who has given some years to the investigation of their culture, their ethnic affinities, and their language, which is said to belong to the Austro-Asiatic group, and to show Indo-Chinese affinities. A preliminary outline of Mr. Noone's results in *The Observer* of January 24 is cabled from Singapore, where a number of the tribe are staying at present for the purpose of a record of their speech. It is there stated that Mr. Noone finds that the Temiar show traces of negritic influence and also an Australoid type, akin to the Vedda, but that, essentially a hill tribe, they link up with the hill Stocks of Sumatra and other parts of south-east Asia. They are lighter skinned than the Sakai and belong to a higher order of intelligence and culture. They build communal long-houses instead of the rude shelters of the Sakai, use the bow, and hunt with the blow-pipe. Their religion is animistic. For driving out the spirits of disease, they make use of the religious dance, in which the medicine man is an important figure. These dances are performed in the event of an epidemic, the dancers becoming 'possessed' by a tiger spirit. Eventually they fall into a state of trance, which sometimes ends in complete rigidity.

1.2 Noone's Singapore radio lecture on the Temiars (1937)

As mentioned in the *Nature* article (above), Noone brought a group of Temiars to Singapore in January 1937. Among their activities was a radio lecture, broadcast on 15 January by the newly instituted ZHL station and accompanied by live music performed in the studio by three Temiar men. The full text of Noone's lecture, amounting to around 3,500 words, was printed in *The Straits Times* the following day; it can be read on the National Library's website (http://newspapers.nl.sg/Digitised/Article/straits times19370116-1.2.85.aspx).

The lecture was mostly taken up by an account of the daily round of subsistence activities. However, it also contained a few observations on Temiar religion—making up for Noone's relative silence on the topic in his few other writings. I present the relevant paragraphs here, which refer to observations made in the then remote Ber valley of Kelantan. It is clear that practices and ideas were much the same in the 1930s as I later found them to be in the 1960s, but a few explanatory comments may be useful. (I have left Noone's wayward punctuation unaltered.)

Noone refers to 'gunigs or tiger familiars'. The term 'gunig' is, or was formerly, restricted to tiger-spirits only in certain areas. As discussed in this book, *gunig* more generally refers to *any* kind of spirit-guide. Furthermore, Noone's report that tiger-spirits played a part in normal 'garlanded' dance-based seances differs not only from the ascetic hut-based tiger-spirit trancing reported in this book, but also from Stewart's account of 'temple' shamanism in his PhD thesis. Noone's talk of the 'kenlok' (*kɛnlɔɔk*) as the heart-soul (*hup*) should be compared with my comments in Chapter 6 on the currently somewhat rarer use of the word. His mention of the 'ruwai' head-soul is, of course, the entity referred to in my text as *rəwaay*. However, I am unfamiliar with the phrase 'Os Nieng': the first word is probably *ʔoos* 'fire', but I am unsure how to phonemicise 'Nieng' or discern its meaning.

Noone employs the unusual English word 'fey' when describing the medium's trance performance. I suspect that he had the word's former meaning in mind—'fated to die, doomed, dying'—as a metaphor for 'leaving the normal world and entering trance'. His mention of 'foam' appearing in the medium's healing hand corresponds to what Jennings, Roseman and I refer to as *kahyɛk*; but it would be interesting to know what, if anything, Noone actually *saw*.

Medicine Man Dreams. Then the rhythm of group discussion changes: an old man who is known as a "hala" [*halaaʔ*] or medicine man is recounting in slow, level tones a dream which he has had: he is telling the adventures of his heart soul, the "kenlok," who has brought back to him from the high summits of the hills, the notes and words of a new song. All inspiration, invention and novelty in Temiar life is the result of dreaming.

[…]

As darkness draws near, the last meal of maize potage, fish and brinjals is eaten, and soon the rhythm of the bamboo stampers beaten by the women is heard from the hearths, and then taken up by the Chief on a Brunei gong, which has been handed down from father to son for centuries, whilst the men beat against the rhythm on their monkey-skin drums.

[…]

Garlanded Men. The garlanded men move round in the dance and soon pass out of the work-a-day world of reality into that half light of the world of the spirit. They sway and stumble and stiffen as one by one they become possessed by their "gunigs" or "tiger familiars". Now they are "fey" they are "possessed" and powerful to heal sickness, and to foretell and renew the "luck" of the group.

A sick child is brought forward and laid on a mat in the middle of the springy bamboo floor. A "hala" or medicine man kneels over the child and chants his spells with the laying on of hands. Then he joins in the dance again and with the palm of his right hand up-turned he kneels again over the prostrate child.

The "ruwai" or head-soul, the "hala" proclaims had left the body and was on its way to "Os Nieng," the abode of the spirits of dead people. But the "hala" had sent his familiar spirit to bring it back before it had gone too far, and now it appears on the palm of his hand like foam from the bottom of a waterfall.

He presses it into the child's forehead, and so gives it back the life it so nearly lost. The "heart-soul" may leave the body and journey fancifully in dreams, but when the "ruwai" or "head-soul" departs, it means death.

Now the measure has changed to the "gersek" [cf. *gɛrsaak*?] in which men sing whilst they dance, and the women rise and with breasts uncovered, sway gracefully in the "chanachit [*cənaciiʔ*]", only one hand moving at a time.

1.3 Noone's lecture on *Chinchem* (1939)

The following summary of a lecture given by Noone appears among the reports of the Proceedings of the Royal Anthropological Institute (*Man*, April 1939: 57). I reproduce it here for several reasons. First, it is almost unknown to writers on Orang Asli religion; I was unaware of it myself when writing my PhD thesis and some of my later papers. Second, it appears to report an earlier instance of 'prophet'-led re-enchantment among the Temiars, consequent on cultural transition. Third, although the text was written by an anonymous rapporteur, it is probably as close as we will ever get to an account of Temiar religion by Noone himself, along with the account in Appendix 1.4. Fourth, the Chinchem (Cincɛm) complex still survives, although it has now become routinised as just one of the many Temiar song- and dance-genres, rather than as a distinct cult in either the anthropological or sociological sense. (For more details, see Chapter 7, Stewart (1947: 218f), Noone (1955: 4), Roseman (1995: band 3 and pp. 10–11 in the accompanying notes), and Appendix 2.2 below.)

Finally, Noone's account provides valuable material for discussion of Temiar religious change in terms of broader 'secularisation' theory. Do the last 75 years of Temiar religious history exhibit a long-term (secular?) tendency to rationalisation and disenchantment (cf. Wallis & Bruce 1995)? Or do the pendulum-swing approach of Gellner (1969) and/or the 'religious economy' approach of Stark & Bainbridge (1985) better apply?

Chinchem: a Study of the Role of Dream-Experience in Culture-Contact amongst the Temiar Senoi of Malaya. Summary of a communication by H. D. Noone, M.A., Field Ethnographer, F.M.S. Government, 7 March 1939.

Mediums amongst the Temiar Senoi find their spirit-guides through dreams of association, in which they are endowed with powers, usually for healing sickness. A leading Shaman in a border group has introduced a ceremonial dance-and-song complex called *Chinchem* [Cincɛm], obtained from a dream revelation on the tribal pattern. This has mobilized the morale of his group towards more effective adjustment in the contact situation. There are certain similarities with the Ghost Dance Revivals of North America.

Analysis of the behaviour of symbols in ordinary Temiar dreams showed when a chief symbol could become a potential spirit-guide; this could be expressed in terms of the degree of its identification with the dreamer, and other symbols in the dream. Some dreams of aspiring Shamans give additional evidence of this process. The power of spirit-guides depends upon what kinds of diseases they promise to aid in healing, whether caused by intrusion (treated during Round-dance) or soul-loss (treated through Medicine-hut). In very few dreams, a spirit guide also identifies himself with the welfare of society as a whole, or even with a veritable Cosmogony; the Shaman being chosen as interceder. *Chinchem* has developed from such a dream of intercession.

The originator of *Chinchem* was a Shaman and leader of a community

[Jalong, Perak] settled in the foothills close to Malay, Chinese, Hindu, and even European contacts. From the point of view of their economy, the group had survived the transition stage; herding tame elephants and buffaloes, and 'panning' for alluvial tin, whilst still maintaining their plantations and trade in jungle produce. Signs of social disintegration and spiritual conflict, however, appeared:—frequent divorces; quarrels for leadership; increasing death-rate, especially among younger children.

In this situation, *Chinchem* became established. Both individual and cultural antecedents to the central dream experience of Datok Bintang are assessed; in particular, the impact of Moslem ideas of conduct. The spirit of his dead wife becomes his spirit-guide, giving him new ethical values and therapeutic powers, which are now focused in the *Chinchem* dance and its cycle of songs. Although based on Temiar tradition showing Malay influences, *Chinchem* exhibits vital features new to both cultures. It is an instance of a force towards a new social integration, in which the stress of culture-contact, which has arisen through the medium of dream-experience.

1.4 Noone's *Commentary on Temiar Dream Music* (1941)

This is Noone's typewritten radio script, prepared to introduce a broadcast of Temiar songs from the Singapore station of the Malayan Broadcasting Corporation. No recording of the broadcast has yet been traced. The producer, E. D. Robertson (later to become Deputy Managing Editor of the BBC's General Overseas Service), reported that the disc on which Noone recorded his comments was later lost. The songs themselves, however, were later transferred from their original 78 rpm discs to long-playing 33 rpm discs by Folkways Records (record no. P150), now available again on an audio CD from the Smithsonian Museum (http://www.folkways.si.edu/temiar-dream-songs-from-malaya/islamica-psychology-health-world/album/smithsonian). Noone's notes were republished in the sleeve insert to that recording.

In 1965, at Rening (Pahang), I met some of the men who had sung on these recordings, and re-recorded some of the same songs with the same singers. Noone's commentary on the songs reads as follows.

A casual traveller among the Temiar tribes who inhabit the jungle-covered mountains of the Malayan main range will readily observe the material side of their way of life. He would see that they planted dry padi and root crops in their clearings, and also that most of their material needs could be satisfied by collecting the natural produce of the jungle, or by hunting with the blowpipe, fishing and setting traps. It would not be so easy to find out how their interest in life is organised, or how the motives which maintain their cooperative enterprise are reinforced. In short, how there can be food for the spirit as well as for the flesh, in such a way of living. Indeed, the routine of their workaday world is transfigured and inspired by the way they interpret the heart of reality.

Behind the material form and function of their jungle surroundings, the Temiar, like most primitive peoples, believe that a spiritual world also exists. The bare formula that the Temiar religion consists of a belief in spiritual beings, that is animism, would, however, be inadequate. Temiar religion, if it must have a label, is best described as 'shamanism', a system which may be found among primitive peoples and peasants from South East Asia northwards across Siberia, and throughout North America and parts of South America. For, to the Temiar, the world of spirits is not the exclusive domain of demons, ghosts and bogey-men. There are also spirits friendly to man, willing to be guides and guardians. The Temiar shaman, or 'hala' is the medium between the tribe and the spirit world. The 'hala' secures his sanction during dreams. In a 'hala' dream, a special relationship is set up between the 'hala' and a particular spirit who promises to become his guide. These guides may be spirits from trees, crops, stones, mountains, wild animals or even ancestors. A spirit gives a revelation, according to a traditional tribal pattern, to the dreaming 'hala'. A typical revelation includes a verse of poetry, music for song and dances, and an offering in the form of leaf and flower decorations to be worn by the performers. The 'hala' can summon any of his spirit guides to come down and possess him by performing according to the special instructions, and during the performance he can pass on the spirit in possession to his fellow dancers.

Some spirit guides may only give advice on the hunt, others, new art patterns for wood carvings or the plaiting of mats, or new songs and dances which are particularly recreational; others again may convey special powers by transfiguring the bodies of the dancers, so that they can withstand injuries and pain and perform extraordinary feats. A few may endow the 'hala' with the power of healing sickness; again, a very few spirit guides may identify this with a messianic message affecting the welfare of the group or a tribe, or even mankind as a whole. Some of these master spirits can claim cosmic or universal significance. These spirit guide inspirations are open to most Temiar men in the tribe. There are many small 'halas' who can claim a few spirit guides, and a very few big 'halas' who can claim who can summon ten or a score. To communion with these master spirits many strive but few attain.

Religious ritual among the Temiar is singing and dancing for grace or for power to heal, help or guide their neighbours. It is worth noting that among a people so cooperative in their way of living the only original and traditional idea of rank is the title of 'Tohat', an address of respect accorded by a man, who has been sick in body or soul, to the 'hala' who has restored his health and peace of mind. A successful song, or dance or poem was spread from valley to valley through the Temiar mountains, and each performance was given the name of the 'hala' who dreamed it, suffixed by the name of the particular spirit guide.

This evening you will hear some of this music sung by a people among whom inspiration is still very much a living thing. It is night in a Temiar longhouse. The house is like a whole village under a single roof; in the centre is the dancing floor of split bamboo, framed along four sides by twenty separate family compartments, each screened off and opening on to a fire hearth of beaten earth. The rhythm from the bamboos beaten by the women is taken up by the deeper notes of the drum and the gong. The dancers take the floor and the bamboos vibrate to the measured tread of their feet. The flare from a score of fires lights up the gloom and plays on the moving frieze of the dancers, whisks of fragrant lemon grass in their hands, plaited strands of gold green grass on their heads and round their shoulders, their waists and their ankles; the leading 'hala' quickens the rhythm, and then he is stark in the middle of the magic circle. The spirit is in him, he stretches and bends with the power of it, like Laocoon in the coils of the serpent. He is in a state of grace and powerful to heal.

The circumstances of the field recordings, which were made with Noone's help on 3 and 4 December 1941, are described in a letter by Peggie Broadhead (who later became better known as Peggy Robertson) to a friend in Australia. The letter was dated 7 December, just one day before the Japanese invasion force landed in Kelantan to begin Malaya's entry into the Second World War: the recording personnel were ordered to return immediately to Singapore. (In the following extract from Broadhead's letter, I have corrected a few obvious typing errors.)

We have just come from Grik near the Siamese frontier where we have been making records of tribal music of the original people who first came to Malaya thousands of years ago. These people are not Malays who are fairly civilised and live in the cities nowadays and work in white men's jobs. But they are the jungle people who only wear bark loincloths, and who have blow pipes and who live in longhouses and whose religion is to perform dances to their spirits. They believe that these spirits come from the trees from motor boats from aeroplanes, etc. In the tribes there are special men who are called halas. They get messages from the spirits and they interpret them in songs and dances. These dances are some of the most beautiful I have seen.

Figure A.1   The 'great white recording van' of the Malaya Broadcasting Corporation at Grik, 8 December 1941
The Temiar singers stand in front of the specially constructed 'longhouse' where their performances were recorded. Photograph probably by Peggie Broadhead (http://www.dspace.cam.ac.uk/handle/1810/230153)

They are so rhythmical that they beat the Russian ballet easily. They dress up in gold and green palm leaves and while the women beat hollow skin drums (tell Ken with a really swing rhythm) and the old men beat gongs and hollow bamboo sticks, the male dancers sing and dance on the bamboo matting floor of their longhouse. I stayed up all night listening and watching the Temiar dance. In the corner of the longhouse was a fire and during the dance the dancers took live hot pieces of coal and danced with them in their mouths. There were rush light torches stuck in the wall, and the whole effect was most eerie. I think I am the first white woman that these people had ever seen. They were most friendly, and one mother gave me her baby to hold. The smell lasted in my hair for days, but it was only a jungle smell, and not really unpleasant—just different from the smells we generally like around. There was a small boy of about seven—stark naked, who danced with the grown ups. He was the liveliest thing I have seen for a long time, and did all the steps just as well as the others. Some of the women when they dance, get themselves into a hysterical state, and rush round laughing and crying. But you don't wonder much when you get to know them. They are just like very small children who smile at you in a simple and very lovely way. Some of the smiles of the men

when they were told that the job they had done was good, would have
made Hollywood very envious. The Malays and Chinese gape at our
recording van, but the Temiar, when they listened to their songs being
played back, just began to dance. Pat Noone, the protector of Tribes
in North Malaya, and who lives with them in the jungle, said that very
probably a hala would be visited by a spirit who would tell him a
dream dance about the great white recording van that came north, and
of the spirit that came inside it, and probably the Temiars would make
up a new dance all about us.

Appendix 2 | Dance types and spirit-guide song genres

Stewart, Jennings and Roseman all discuss Temiar dance patterns and song genres in some detail. I have said relatively little about these topics in this volume, but I did nevertheless gather relevant material at various times during my fieldwork. The following brief descriptions present the various diagnostic features of each dance or song type as told to me. Much of the information came from Wakil ʔabaaɲ (figure 4.1), whom I interviewed at Humid village in March 1968. Others who answered my queries, in April 1970, were Penghulu Hitam Tamboh (figure 7.1) at Humid, Penghulu Cawan at Pulat near Bertam, and three Menriq men (including Penghulu Buloh) whom I interviewed at Bertam in the same month. I also obtained some information from a man called ʔawaay Tənabaag, who said he was from the Kelian (Kɛlyɛt) valley in northern Perak; but he may have meant the Kelaik valley, between the Perolak and Brok valleys in Kelantan, which is also Kɛlyɛt in Temiar. The various listed characteristics of each genre are what they chose to tell me. I cannot be sure therefore that the details, especially those concerning the supposed places of origin, are historically correct in all respects. For that reason I have provided references also to Roseman's later accounts of some the song genres, which she obtained mostly from Ading Kerah.

An especially interesting aspect of these descriptions is that they point to features that appear to have disappeared as the various genres became assimilated to the more regular pattern described by all ethnographers of Temiar ritual life, from Stewart and Noone onwards. It is also significant that several of the dance types and song genres are said to have originated among the Semais of Pahang, as well as from former Semai communities in parts of Kelantan, such as the Ulu Galas, where they had not lived for many decades.

2.1 Dance types

Gɛrsaak

A fast round-dance (*ciŋwɛl*), the men proceeding first and the women following, with arms swinging slowly back and forth. It is found in all Semai settlements; the Temiars just 'borrowed' it. It is not danced while in trance, but may be danced preparatory to trance, led by the medium. Healing may then follow. (This is probably the same as Noone's 'gersek', mentioned in Appendix 1.2.)

Kinɔd

This comes from the Korbu valley, Perak. It involves flexing at the knees, done slowly or fast, in a circle.

Kɛrjɛɛr

This originated in the Temengor valley, Perak. (Since I gathered this information, the Temengor settlements have been permanently drowned under the man-made Temengor Lake.) The *kɛrjɛɛr* dance is done for fun by both men and women, with everyone joining in. It does not depend on the presence of a spirit-guide. The feet make the basic *kinɔd* shuffle slowly, while the main action is in the hands weaving back and forth. The dancers do not form a circle, and the men and women are not separated. (*Kɛrjɛɛr* is also employed as a general term for 'dance'.)

Sisɛ², sənisɛ²

Said to have originated among the Semais and Temiars of the Telom and Sua (Səwaar) valleys of northern Pahang, this is the standard shuffle-and-skip dance, with body bent forwards, but no special arm movements. It is danced, usually slowly, by men, women and children, but not in a circle. It is not necessarily associated with trance. (I have also seen people break into this dance movement out of doors for a few seconds when in a celebratory mood.)

Cacii²

This 'classical', rather Southeast-Asian-looking dance, supposedly originated in the Piah valley, Perak. It involves the hands, arms and torso only, with the feet kept in place on the floor (figure 7.4). A variant is to keep one hand on the hip and put all the movement into the waist and other arm, very slow and Balinese- or Thai-like. In principle, both men and women can *cacii²*, but I only ever saw older women do so, as an especially artistic performance. It is regarded as an 'old time' dance, now dying out. It usually precedes trancing, but the dancers do sometimes sing.

Susut

This originated from the Semais of the Serau valley, Pahang. It is a slow circle dance, with a wand of *susun calun* in the dancers' hands. Apart from this, it is like the *sisɛ²*. A variant known as *pənosiŋ* ('spinning') is danced while twirling a *kəwaar* helicopter-style over one's head.

Sila*ʔ*

This originated with village Malays, and is the style of *sisɛʔ* danced, fast and in a circle, as part of the Səlumbaŋ cult.

Gayoŋ

This is danced in a circle, slowly, while waving one's hands straight back and forth. Widely found; even Malays danced it.

Picəəʔ

This originated in Perak, from where it spread to the Perolak, Betis and Yai valleys of Kelantan. It is not so much a dance step as an occasion: the people stand at the edge of the dance floor and order '*cəəʔ, cəəʔ, cəəʔ!*' to those dancing, in *caciiʔ* style. It is regarded as an old-time style.

A song-and-dance genre: Jiɲjaŋ

Jiɲjaŋ

In April 1968, Penghulu Hitam Tamboh gave me an account of the Jiɲjaŋ dance genre and its associated ritual practices. As mentioned in Chapter 7, Stewart (1947: 181) had portrayed this round-dance as a significant component of Temiar ritual performance, preparatory to mediumistic healing ceremonies. Hitam said that the Jiɲjaŋ was the usual genre of mediumistic performance in his home area at the headwaters of the Perolak river, near the Perak border. However, it originated with the Malays of Kuala Betis, far downstream. At the time of his account, he said it was still the form of Malay-style trancing (*pɛhnɔɔh Gɔb*) on the north bank of the river at Lambok—that is, among the people who later converted to Baha'i and whose prayer session I reported on in Chapter 13.

Wilkinson (1959 (I): 473) confirms that Jiɲjaŋ is indeed known to the Malays. Two of his four definitions of *jinjang* include the following:

> I. Attachment. Esp. (Mal.) of the attachment of a familiar spirit to a wizard; *jinjangan raja* (prince's medicine-man); cf.: *hantu ta' bĕrjinjang* (masterless familiar).
> II. *Main jinjang*: a form of dancing.

The Jiɲjaŋ cult, Hitam said, was started by a Malay known as Janggi, from the same community at Kuala Betis as Raning, the famous medium mentioned in Chapter 7. Janggi's grandson Kasing was still living at Gua Musang, Hitam said. Janggi instilled (*pɛrlub*) it into a Temiar named Lanaak, who was living on the Pəralaaw river, near Humid. Lanaak then took it southwards into the Ber valley, from where it spread to the upper reaches of the Brok, and over the watershed to Perak.

The *gunig*-spirit seems to have been the *ləbay*, the ineffable name of the *bɛrbɔw* tree (Malay: *merbau*). This tree must not be chopped with a knife, or a Malay would emerge from within it and stab people to death. (This is somewhat similar to the ideas about *genhaaʔ* held by the people of the Telom valley, Pahang, mentioned in Chapter 5.) The original form of séance involved solo singing by the drummer (*gədiŋ*), without a chorus of women. (Hitam said that if there *is* a chorus then the session is sure to be a normal *kahyɛk* séance, not a Jiŋjaŋ one.)

Nowadays, however, Hitam said that Jiŋjaŋ had been absorbed into the normal *kahyɛk–tənamuuʔ* method of séance, and that only a medium named ʔanəəh on the north bank of Lambok, still tranced in the Malay fashion. The present-day *gunig*s of Jiŋjaŋ are various flowers (*boot*). All that remains of the original Jiŋjaŋ is the round dance in an anti-clockwise (*pusing kiri*) direction. Thus, Hitam's version of the history of Jiŋjaŋ tells of a distinctive cult becoming routinised, as also happened to the Ciŋcɛm cult mentioned at several places earlier in this volume. Stewart recognised the Ciŋcɛm cult as having very recently emerged, since he met Datok Bintang, its founder. But, assuming that Hitam's account is reliable, Stewart seems not to have recognised either that Jiŋjaŋ was a cult, and not just a dance-pattern, or that it too was of recent origin. Indeed, I calculate that it must have just reached the Perak Temiars at around the time when Noone began his researches in the early 1930s.

2.2 Spirit-guide song genres

Wakil said that the major source of the various genre-names was Ading Kerah and his colleague Ali, who were in charge of Radio Malaysia's Temiar broadcasts throughout the 1960s and later. Roseman (1995: 88) agrees with this assessment of Ading's importance. Ading regularly took recording equipment into Temiar and other Orang Asli villages to collect the musical performances that formed the most popular part of his broadcasts. (Unfortunately, the studio authorities have not properly archived these irreplaceable tapes.) Roseman's accounts (1995: 87–105) form the only detailed published information on some of the Temiar song genres, including some of those described below.

Taŋgəəy

This is the (possibly Jahai) name given by the Perak Temiars to the typical song genre of the Temiars of the Təmuur valley in Perak and the Perolak, Ulu Betis and Ber valleys of southern Kelantan. The spirit-guides are typically flowers, but not seasonal fruits. They refer to the medium's hut as *paley*. However, a Temiar from the Kelian valley of northern Perak told me that Taŋgəəy was the *sɔc* 'perah' nut.

There is some possible confusion in Roseman's account (1991: 92–96). She distinguishes between Taŋgɔɔy and Taŋgəəy as two different genres. But her Taŋgɔɔy should probably have been written Taŋgooy, which I was told *is* a different genre, presumably the one that Roseman reports as having been started by Abilem Lum, which would make it a rambutan- rather than perah-directed genre. Wakil could provide little further information about this, but in 2006 other respondents told me that Taŋgɔɔy (pronounced as such, and not as Taŋgooy) and Taŋgəəy are the same.

Pɛnhəəy

Roseman (1995: 87–90; 2000: 39–47) presents extended accounts of this genre, based largely on information from Ading Kerah. Her investigation locates its origins in the Grik area of Perak, around 1941. The following, more abbreviated, information predates her account and contains some interesting differences of detail, while conforming in general terms to Ading's account.

This genre, Wakil said, originated in the Belum valley in the north of Perak, inhabited mostly by Jahais. It is also followed in the Temengor, Lanweng (Lɛŋwɛɛk), Ringat (Rəŋaaj), and Piah valleys of Perak, and in the Puian (Poyan), Ulu Jenera (Jɛnrɔɔl), Yai and Panes valleys in Kelantan. The spirit-guides are the rambutan (*ləgɔs*), the perah nut (*pərah*) and planted flowers (*boot səlaay*). The practitioners refer to the *tɛmpɔɔʔ* crown as *jəralɔd* and to the *kəbut* hut as *jərasɛm*. A Temiar from Perak told me that Pɛnhəəy means 'rambutan', presumably in that genre's special ritual language, but Roseman's respondents identified it with the perah nut.

Slightly different versions are also found. In 1970, Penghulu Cawan said that Pɛnhəəy began around 1955, when Iskandar Carey became the Protector of Aborigines for Kelantan at Kuala Kerai. In 1979, at the mixed Temiar–Lanoh settlement site of Kuala Dala (Dɛnlaaʔ) in Perak, I was told that Pɛnhəəy, the local genre, originated in Kemar, also in Perak. There, the spirit-guide terminology differed slightly from that in use elsewhere, especially Kelantan: *gunig* referred specifically to tiger spirits emerging from below, whereas spirits 'from above' are known as *cənɔɔy* (or *cənɔy* in the northwest dialect). Clearly, this is the same word as the *ćenoi* or *chinoi* referred to by both Schebesta and Evans in their 'Negrito' studies.

Talɛŋ

Roseman (1995: 90–91) presents Ading Kerah's detailed account of the history of this genre, which he regarded as an offshoot of Pɛnhəəy, starting in the 1950s near Gerik in Perak, and as having some relation to the Cənolɛɛs mountain near there. (See the following entry.)

Wakil said that Talɛŋ was practised in the Yai valley, upstream from Chabai. In 1978, Hitam Tamboh added Temengor (Tumŋɔɔʔ) and Piah, both in Perak, to the list. Talɛŋ is the name of the spirit-guide, which is the totality of seasonal fruits (bərək), including the durian, considered as dead souls. (This makes it somewhat similar to the Cincɛm cult, below.) The word talɛɲ means 'deceased's ghost' (yəəj). The performances are held in the dark, with the kəbut hut sometimes set up by sticking the leaves straight into the ground. It is described as pɛhnɔɔh hɔl, yəəj kɛsbʉs 'trancing the ghosts of the dead in a hole'. (It was unclear whether the hut on the ground had a hollow underneath it.) They referred to the hole as tabɔh.

Cənolɛɛs

Wakil knew little more of this genre than its name. He thought that the gunig-spirits might be the seasonal fruit trees that 'guard' the tops of certain mountains. Of these he mentioned Batuuʔ Cənolɛɛs (a limestone tor?), Merooy, Rəlaay, and the Hɛnwid mountains in Perak (which I am unable to identify). They also engage in tiger-mediumship.

ʔawaay was more specific: he said that Cənolɛɛs was a Lanoh genre, but that the original medium had died. Cənolɛɛs was their word for sɔc 'perah', presumably the source of the spirit-guide.

Səlumbaŋ

Wakil's account differs slightly from those given in Chapter 7. While he agreed that Səlumbaŋ was associated with the great flood of 1926 and that it was a landslide-wreaking dragon, he thought that the cult began in the Temengor valley of northern Perak, possibly among the Jahais. It then passed via the Keniar (Kɛnyɛr) and Sara (Sarah) valleys across the watershed to the Perias and Pergau (Pɛrgɔw) valleys in Kelantan. From there it was passed on by pərɛnlʉb to both Temiars and Malays living along the main Nenggiri river. The sole spirit-guide is Səlumbaŋ itself, which Wakil described as a Gɔb Laleeʔ, a Malay with a Temiar mother and a Malay father, looking like a Temiar but speaking Malay. (Note that he said Gɔb Laleeʔ, 'a mixed Malay', not Sərɔk Laleeʔ, 'a mixed Temiar'.) The song lyrics are accordingly in kuy laleeʔ 'mixed language', mostly Malay. There is no kəbut-trancing in the dark.

ʔawaay, on the other hand, said that the Perak Temiars regard Səlumbaŋ as a specifically Kelantan genre. The medium starts by dancing in caciiʔ style, before passing the spirit on to the others by pərɛnlʉb, whereupon they dance in Jiŋjaŋ style. In possible confirmation, Hitam Tamboh, after hearing it on one of Ading Kerah's radio broadcasts in 1964, told me that the Səlumbaŋ genre began at Kuala Yai. (On published maps, this is marked as Kuala Perias.)

A more detailed account was given to me in 1970 by the senior chief Penghulu Cawan, when I stayed briefly in his house at the far-downstream settlement of Pulat on the main Nenggiri river. Cawan was himself a practitioner of the Səlumbaŋ cult, which he said had begun on the Embeu (ʔɛmbeew) river, a tributary of the Səpɛɛg, itself a tributary of the Yai, during the heavy rains of 1926. (I cannot trace any river named Səpɛɛg, and the

Embeu actually flows directly into the Yai.) This caused severe floods and landslides that destroyed houses and left the people cut off in the Səpɛɛg valley while the rain continued unabated. Jam, the elder brother of Busuuh Sədin, had a dream in which he asked 'Are we here going to live or die?' The spirit then sang to him in the dream, saying 'When you wake, light some benzoin incense next to the collapsed houses and down on the river where it is blocked. Then go home and sing the song I just taught you. Tell them to fetch flowers, and then you hold a trance session and sing my song. Then it will stop raining. That's all.' They then sang the song all night long, and people continue to sing it today.

Cawan went on to say that Səlumbaŋ originated as a *daŋgaa*ʔ (*naga-dragon*). Its body, according to the few people who had seen it, was like a snake's. Originally, it lived in a pool on the Səpɛɛg river, but this was swept away in later floods in accordance with its promise that if its 'father'-medium should die it would flee downstream to the sea, from where it had originally emerged during the 1926 flood. The dragon had promised not to kill the medium as long he continued to sing the Səlumbaŋ spirit's song. This is why Səlumbaŋ is a Malay-speaking spirit. As a result of the travels of Sədin, the younger brother of the founder, who was still alive, the Səlumbaŋ genre had by now (1970) spread to the Perias, Yai and Puian valleys, and on the main Nenggiri river all the way up to Kuala Betis and Lambok.

Roseman (1991: 104–105) later obtained a closely similar account of the origins of the Səlumbaŋ genre from Ading Kerah. Ading admitted that he was less than directly involved, and was therefore unsure about some of the details. Nevertheless, he too ascribed its origins to the elder brother of Sədin (who by that time had recently died), except that Ading referred to him as Səliloh, not Jam. But Temiar names are notoriously unfixed. Roseman presents further ethnographic details of the Səlumbaŋ genre as an example of 'Malay-style séancing' (*pɛhnɔɔh gɔb*).

Ciɲcɛm

Wakil's account corresponds closely to what was presented in Chapter 6 and Appendix 1.3 as the cult of the same name that Stewart and Noone witnessed in the 1930s. It is followed mainly in the Plus and Korbu valleys of Perak. The spirit-guide Ciɲcɛm is *sarɔɔ*ʔ, the souls of dead people considered as a collectivity. No tiger-mediumship is involved. But Wakil went on to say that Ciɲcɛm was a *new* cult. Does this mean that it took 35 years to reach Kelantan? Or perhaps it was restricted to Perak until Ading spread knowledge of it through his broadcasts in the 1960s. Noone's unpublished notes (1940) to a Ciɲcɛm recording describe it as 'a ritual dance ..., which is on the highest level of Temiar dream inspiration. The song and dances were given to a chief on the Korbu River in Perak, by an ancestor's spirit. It is now the symbol of a new order of life growing out of the traditional tribal pattern.'

Kədəŋ

Wakil said that this is a Semai genre, which they took over from the Jahais. This sounds improbable, as Semais and Jahais are not known ever to have been contiguous populations. However, if by 'Jahai' Wakil was referring to Menriqs or Bateks, such contacts could have occurred two or three generations previously. The spirit-guide *gunig* is the *bədɔk* flower. The celebrants tie a cord around the house, from which they hang flowers and shredded *kəwaar* leaves; they also hang a *tənamuuʔ* in the middle. (This is presumably the source of the decorations I saw in Mengrod and upstream from there in 2006, as illustrated in figure 10.7.) This genre does not involve *kəbut*-trancing in the dark.

Mojiiʔ, Bəlajur

Wakil gave me a Temiar view of the genre, which actually belongs to the Menriqs of the Lebir (Ləbir), Pergau and Lah (Leew) valleys in Kelantan, to the north-east of the Temiars. Mojiiʔ proper does not involve *kahyɛk* trancing. Bəlajur, which also means 'sing' in that tradition, is the *kahyɛk*-trancing version. The *gunig* spirit is *mamuug mɛŋkah* 'tiger of the debouchment downstream'. The celebrants enter the rocky *gua* outcrop while singing (*bəlajur*), then go into the cave, holding candles made of resin. Only the *halaaʔ* mediums go in, singing in unaccompanied (*pɛŋjəwɔk*) style, with no bamboo-tube percussion and no women. (See figure 7.5 for a recent photograph of Gua Janggut, also known as Batuuʔ Baloʔ, within which the cave in question is situated.)

In 1970, the Bateks of the Aring valley (later studied by Kirk and Karen Endicott) told me that the Menriqs had the same *gunig* as themselves, but that they (also?) held secret trance sessions inside the cave of Gua Janggut, to celebrate an earth spirit (*hantu buhmin*) called Mojiiʔ. They also said that the Temiar Penghulu Cawan (then still alive) was a Mojiiʔ medium and held trance sessions in the caves also—as indeed Cawan had told me himself. The Bateks said that Bəlajur meant *ilmu* 'mystical knowledge' and was a variant of the Malay word *belajar* 'to learn'. After ceremony has finished they *kuɲciʔ* 'lock' the cave with a stone.

Kuɲciiʔ

This is presumably related in some way to the *kuɲciʔ* just mentioned. (Northern Aslian languages such as Batek lack the phonemic contrast between long and short vowels.) But Wakil's account of Kuɲciiʔ as a genre presents a very different story. He said it originated a long time ago in the Tiang (Təyaŋ) valley in Ulu Galas, from among the mixed Temiars and Semais who used to live there. Their *gunig* spirit is the *bədɔk* flower, tranced as *kahyɛk* from above; no seasonal fruits or tigers were involved. Their typical lyric runs: '*Kuɲciiʔ kuɲcab / ʔalɔɔh Kəlantan*', which I cannot fully translate. The Temiars of Blau still 'borrow' this genre in their trancing sessions.

Bɛrwɛɛs (ʔLɛrwɛɛs)

Wakil knew little more about this genre than its name. It has seasonal fruits (bərək) as its spirit-guides, and originated in the Belum valley of Perak (among the Kensiws he guessed—obviously wrongly). ʔawaay was more specific: he said that bɛrwɛɛs was the word used for kahyɛk by the Semnams, a Lanoh subgroup.

Gamɔʔ (Pəgamɔʔ)

This is a new genre, originating with the Semais of the Təkal valley, Pahang. Wakil said that the founding medium, Bah Səwin, had 'recently' (that is, during the 1960s) been killed by sorcery of the pɛnsuʔ ('sending') type. The spirit-guide is the rɔɔk flower, but he also mentioned some connection with dɔɔg, the *Antiaris* blowpipe poison.

At Lambok in 2006 I made an audio recording of a song that was described as 'Gamɔʔ, not Pɛnhəəy'. It was identified as the style typical of Rening in Pahang and Mengrod in Kelantan. The performance mode was described (in Malay) as *terlewat* 'later, behind (in time)', that is with the women singing their response after the medium had finished his verse. This was acknowledged as being more common among the Semais, who *mesti tunggu* 'must wait', and also as a feature of so-called Malay-style trancing when performed by the Temiars. This was contrasted with the overlapping-canon more usually employed by Temiars, which was described (also in Malay) as *sambung-sambung* 'all joined up'. The canonic mode was identified as the norm from the Ber valley northwards, where the Pɛnhəəy genre is more usual, even if less known at Lambok.

Riɲjoŋ, Poŋey

This originated in the Temiar and Semai settlements of the Kinta valley, Perak. The *gunig*-spirit is Poŋey, also known as Riɲjoŋ, which is a sɛnʔɔɔy ʔen-tɛʔ 'earth person'. They perform their trances with a tənamuuʔ and a *calun* whisk, but the spirit emerges from the ground, not as kahyɛk, but as a human rather than a tiger. They commence their ceremonies in the dark, but then light the fires once the spirit emerges. Roseman (1994) provides further information, including a musically notated example (pp. 132–133) from a Poŋey song that she recorded in the field.

Rɔŋgɛŋ

This genre was started by a Semai named Bah Jərakaag in Ulu Serau, Pahang, from where it spread to the Semais in Ulu Galas, Kelantan, when they were living there. These people used to visit the Temiars around the Jeram Gajah area on the upper Nenggiri (Brok) river. The *gunig*-spirit is Rɔŋgɛŋ, a water-spirit that appears in human shape. This is tranced 'from above', with a suspended frame known as a *maloŋ* from which three tənamuuʔ hang like a propeller. Their performances involve neither seasonal-fruit- nor tiger-spirits, but they do involve the *gunig*-spirits of what were described as *jɛlmɔl rɛʔyaaʔ* 'big mountains', which in this context I took to mean limestone tors.

Pawun (?=Tawun)

This possibly corresponds to the genre that Roseman (1991: 91–99) reports on extensively under the name Noŋ Tahun 'the Way of the Annual Fruits', but there are differences between that and the genre described to me, as follows, by Wakil and ʔawaay.

Pawun is a Temiar genre, presumably originating in Perak. The *gunig*-spirits are *mənɛhlɛh tɛhtəəh* 'young women of the rain', that is the rain itself making its appearance as young women. Pawun ('*phone* wires'?) was said to be name of *pərɛɲjɛɛn* cords by which the *gunig*s let themselves down in the trance sessions. They practise some tiger-trancing, but no seasonal fruit spirits are involved. ʔawaay said that the word *pawun* referred to *wɔɔg sɛnʔɔɔy kɛsbʉs* 'the shadows of dead people', more usually called *yəəl* 'ghosts'. The genre began in the Jemheng (Jumhɛɛŋ) valley, from where it passed to the Temengor and Yum (Yuup) valleys. Their ceremonies are similar to those of the Səlumbaŋ genre, with no *kahyɛk* or tiger trancing.

Səribuuʔ

This is a Temiar and Lanoh genre, originating in the Piah valley of Perak. The *gunig*-spirit is ʔɛŋkuuʔ, the Thunder deity himself. In the Piah valley, it is forbidden to utter the name ʔɛŋkuuʔ; Səribuuʔ (Malay: 'one thousand') is substituted. The medium employs a *kəbut*-hut, but the spirit emerges from above, not below. A *tənamuuʔ* is also used. There is no seasonal-fruit or tiger trancing. Their typical song lyric is '*Səribuuʔ ʔim-ʔacuuʔ bɛybəweey cəboh bəweey* (= *cah*)*, cəboh bəlanteey* (= *taliiʔ ʔɛŋkuuʔ*). (Or is it *bəwɛɛy*? My handwriting is unclear.) I find this almost impossible to translate. An attempt is: 'Səribuuʔ, I'll threaten *bɛybəweey* the sap of the *cah* tree, the sap of the *bəlanteey* (= ʔɛŋkuuʔ's cords).'

ʔawaay was a little more specific. He said the genre began among the Lanoh Jɛŋjɛŋ people of Dala on the Perak river, from where it moved to the Piah valley. (He also said that the Lanoh Jɛŋjɛŋ were the people who spoke a dialect of Temiar that I have elsewhere referred to as Northwest Temiar: they say *deeŋ* instead of *deek* for 'house', for example.) He agreed that Səribuuʔ was an avoidance name for ʔɛŋkuuʔ and also for Karey, both of which may not be uttered at Dala. (Hitam Tamboh said that they also employed Kerəəy as an avoidance form for Karey.) A trancing hut was used, but the spirit-guide appeared in human, not tiger, form, while extending its cords into the *panɔh* hut. (He also said that only tiger-mediums employ a *panɔh* hut, so it must be assumed that a Səribuuʔ medium also served as a tiger-medium on other occasions.) The genre has since died out as a distinctive practice, having assimilated to the more usual performance, dancing in the *kerjɛɛr* manner while wielding a *kəwaar* whisk.

Kəladiih

This is an old-time Semai genre from the Telom valley, Pahang. The *gunig*-spirit is ʔawɛn 'bamboo'. The medium had a trick of causing bamboos to burst. The genre has almost died out. They tranced neither seasonal fruits nor tigers, but they did dance. Their typical lyric ran *ʔim-tuntaŋ buloh kəladiih* 'I shall sing the *kəladiih* bamboo', with *tuntaŋ* (cf. Malay *dondang*) replacing the more usual word for 'sing', *gabag*.

Pərɛŋgan

This is a Temiar genre, originating from the Korbu valley, Perak. The *gunig* is an earth spirit, emerging in human form. They employ flowers and a *tənamuuʔ* in their ceremonies, which are held with the fires lit and with *kerjɛɛr*-style dancing. They do not use *kəbut*-huts, nor do they trance seasonal-fruit or tiger spirits.

Further accounts
of burial practices

As mentioned in Chapter 6, I witnessed two human burials directly. I also gathered detailed third-party information on burial practices, and witnessed a group of children burying their pet cat. Information of this kind is relevant to the fuller understanding of Temiar religion, but is hard to come by, especially concerning children's burials (cf. Halcrow et al. 2008: 394). I therefore present some of it here. (A Lanoh funeral is described in detail by Williams-Hunt (1954–55), along with some comparative notes on the funerals of other Orang Asli. Schebesta (1957: 157–174) also provides some information on the graves of northern Orang Asli.)

3.1 A baby's funeral

While I was away from Humid village in August 1964, the death of a baby girl occurred. On returning a few days later, I gathered as much information as I could from those who had witnessed the baby's burial and the preceding attempts at healing her. My edited field notes are presented below. The account is especially interesting for the information it provides on the practice of grave offerings, *pɛnsoor* (from the verb *pɔsoor* 'to make a grave offering'), already described in Chapter 6. These do not seem to have been merely ceremonial. The parents' offerings were overtly explained as indicating their wish to memorialise the baby's fondly recalled behaviour. The *pɛnsoor* offerings given by the villagers were too disparate yet too valuable to be explained as mere ritual formalities. Although I was given no overt reason, it seems safe to assume that part of the motivation for the offerings was a wish to share in the suffering caused by the death. The account also presents a few brief mentions of ideas about an afterlife.

> I asked one of the villagers about the baby's death. She had been ill for five days, vomiting blood and suffering diarrhoea. They gave her a medicine consisting of *cɛdrɔd* leaf pounded in a bamboo tube and then anointed over her whole body; but the illness remained. On the third day the baby's father took her to Penghulu Dalam's house for further treatment. Dalam then uttered healing (*sɛʔnooʔ*) incantations while waving a *kɔwaar* leaf-

whisk. Several other people were present, including the man who was reporting these happenings, but he doesn't (or won't) remember the words of the incantations. The healing *sɛˀnooˀ* had been held three times on the third day of the illness, first around 3–5 a.m., then about 2 p.m., and then about 5 p.m.

The baby died on the fifth day about 5 p.m. and this was announced by Penghulu Dalam, who then ordered everyone in the village to prepare items for the burial. The items were:

- Twelve worn sarongs, presented by eleven different relatives.
- Two parang knives, presented by Penghulu Dalam ('because the baby was his *cɔɔˀ*', as his wife had supervised the birth) and by the child's father ('out of sorrow').
- Money, in the following amounts: Malam (the father) RM10, Dalam RM4, Wakil (the deputy headman) RM4 and his wife RM3. Ten others gave amounts varying between 50 cents and RM3. The total left on the grave was RM38.50. [At the time, this would have been a considerable sum for any Temiar community to amass.]
- The baby's father, Malam, gave: a cooking vessel, a drinking cup, a bar of scented soap, an axe head, a decorated mat, a pack of face powder previously given to the baby as a toy, the chain from a cast-net, a large electric torch, a paring knife. He wrapped all of these in the sarong cloth in which she had died, and placed them into a back-basket.

The two parents then washed the body in cold water, leaving it undried. They closed the mouth and eyes. No medicaments were applied. They then wrapped the body in one of the father's own sarongs, leaving no part visible. One of the men (not an immediate relative) carried the body cradled in his arms, walking in the middle of the procession formed by many of the villagers, including children. They walked up the Humid valley to the edge of the former swidden site at Pəralaaw, the primary burial site for the Humid community. On arrival, the body was placed on the ground, while the man who had carried it then dug a thigh-deep hole, aided by the sister's husband of the baby's mother. Three other men chopped bamboo to make a criss-cross fencing around the grave, while others cleared the surrounding ground. The baby's mother sat weeping nearby. Malam, the father, placed his prepared basketful of goods onto the floor of the grave, which was then covered by a split-bamboo flooring. The two men who had dug the grave then stood at the edge and lowered the body onto the platform by the cloth in which it was wrapped. They then covered it with leaves ('no particular species'), and filled the grave with soil, using a mattock. Finally, they burnt some old bamboo at the site.

Two days after recording this account, I visited the gravesite with the man who had given me the above details. (His name was ʔaliih; his photograph appears as Plate 12, 'Ali Songkok', in Jennings (1995).) A space measuring approximately 50 feet by 50 feet had been cleared around the fenced-off grave. The grave itself was about 5 feet in diameter, with a mound of soil about one foot high in the middle. On the mound were two kettles, a cauldron and an axe-head ('because the baby had seen and played with them'). The father had broken the vessels and removed the axe-head from its haft 'because the baby had earlier damaged these objects in play'. Also placed on the grave were some skeins of screwpine plaiting material ('because the baby liked to play with it'), and some *cog bambeeŋ* fruits ('because they are shaped like a mother's breast'). A small bamboo water-vessel was placed at the side, 'so that the baby could drink in the other world'.

A ring of plants had been inserted around the grave, about two feet away from it; these included pineapples and various flowers. My companion made me plant a flower, while he burnt three piles of dead wood as a customary procedure. The burial was orientated with the head to the west and the feet to the east. (I was told that the body had been laid on its back with arms at the sides.) One pile of dead wood was burnt at the head end, about 12 feet away from the grave. The other two piles were burnt on each side of the feet, also about 12 feet away. I was told that the burning must *not* be done at the feet, but no reason was given.

3.2 Children's burial of a pet cat

The children involved in this episode figure again as adults in the later chapters of this book—Jidaʔ as a leader of the ʔalɨj Səlamad religion, and ʔabur as my most recent helper in organising the logistics of Temiar research. Although the burial was abbreviated, and no grave offerings were made, the general pattern of the procedure was the same as that for a human being. After the burial I discovered that the village's cats were all given names, mostly of the unique autonym type, and that their genealogies could be recited when asked for. My account, only slightly edited, reads as follows:

1 October 1964
The cat ʔampul died at around 13.00, Dalam's cat. Around 14.00 Pəleman [the mother of the deceased child in the above account] and her sister ʔaboŋ [the mother of ʔabur] arrived and told the children to see to it. ʔabur was afraid. Jidaʔ then brought some *ləbət* cane and bound the corpse's hind legs and neck by nooses at either end.

They then carried it across the Humid river, ʔakɔw first with a parang, then Jidaʔ with the cat. Jidaʔ exhorted me not to laugh—it would cause a storm. At the top of the old path ʔakɔw dug a hole about two feet deep and stuffed the corpse in with his feet, shovelling back the earth with his hands. Then he cut some branches and banana leaves and made a roofing over the grave on a frame of two sticks. Then we returned down the hill and the children bathed *pasal ʔɛ-babəʔ ʔolah səʔɛɛk* 'because we carried a stinking/rotting body'.

Tomorrow, ʔabur and Jidaʔ plan to burn off the surrounding land.

All the time, the women and Wakil were shouting instructions from the other side.

The overall principle seemed to be that having fed the cat during life, they should treat it properly at death (*hɔj ki-bɛrcaaʔ, kalɔɔn lah* 'we fed it, feel pity').

3.3 A full account of the funeral at Cherber

In Chapter 6, I presented a brief outline of the funeral I witnessed at Cherber village on 23 November 1964. Published accounts of Orang Asli funerals are very rare, which justifies presenting my fieldnotes of the occasion here, verbatim and *in extenso*, slightly edited for clarity. (There is still some unavoidable overlap with the account in Chapter 6.)

I chanced upon this funeral when travelling upstream from Humid with several people, including Malam (my main helper at the time), his wife Pəleman and ʔandɔʔ, who all had close kin in Cherber village. The headman of Cherber was Busuuh, a man who had visited Humid often during my residence there. Apart from the deceased's wife, his closest surviving relative was a man named Bardʉs ('Bulldozer'), also a frequent visitor to Humid.

The notes read as follows:

22 November 1964
We arrived at Cherber around 13.00 to find that a man [whose name I failed to record, perhaps because it had been immediately tabooed] had died earlier in the day. The burial would be tomorrow, and Busu [one of the men travelling with me from Humid] said that undoubtedly we would wait, since the deceased was Malam's *yaak* 'grandfather'. (Actually, *kooc* 'parent's elder brother', said ʔandɔʔ.)

23 November 1964
The funeral: Malam tells me I can take photographs only after crossing the river. [In the event, for unknown reasons, my photographs of the funeral all failed.]

They started around 09.00 by selecting a beam from the deceased's house. I couldn't see what was going on in the deceased's house, but ʔandɔʔ says he had a wife, and presumably it was her I heard wailing out loud.

The body was wrapped in a *gərɛmpɛh* sheet of split bamboo and suspended from the beam in a cradle with cane strips. It was borne by Malam, the deceased's elder brother ʔaluŋ, and a man visiting from the Bər valley. The deceased's daughter brought a bundle of stuff from the next house, and several women brought packed plaited bags.

Two lighted bamboos were carried across the river, along a freshly erected bridge. We had to take our shoes off first, and some people plucked leaves as we entered the swidden. We crossed into a new cassava swidden (made in primary forest, no rice planted), where there were some remarks from one of the women about not planting the body in the cassava.

A fire of cleared bamboo was lit towards the landward side of the grave site. The main work of digging was done by Malam, with the man from Bər, Busuuh and ʔandɔʔ. The body was rested near the fire on the downstream side. I could now see the details of the wrapping. Innermost was a sheet, then a plaited mat, then some bundled sarongs, and then the split-bamboo sheeting, all tied in four places to two stout staves.

The women meantime sat smoking or chewing, even laughing. The only man not taking part was Bardus [a close relative of the deceased], weepily sitting to one side. Another fire had been lit by ʔaluŋ at 90° to riverwards of the first, and then a third a was lit opposite to it by Bardus's friend. Two women then go off and fetch a bunch of (betel-chew?) leaves.

They then set about seeing to the stuff brought in a bag. They were dismayed to see that the deceased's betel-chew lime had almost run out. Sticking out from the bag I could see a pouch for betel-chew lime, some ordinary tobacco pouches, a bowl, some brass betel-chew apparatus.

The women started complaining about the bad site chosen for the burial—in the cassava and where it can be seen just as in the *kədey* ('town', literally 'shops'). All this time the digging had been going on. ʔandɔʔ was felling some distance from the head end of the trench. He brought back stout saplings. The short-haired women and Bardus's friend each fetched a bamboo of water. ʔaluŋ makes jokes about other, harder, funeral digs he's had to do. Malam remarks on the amazingly large graves he saw in Kuala Lumpur. ʔandɔʔ then mentions a Chinese towkay's burial in Gua Musang.

They measure the length of the largening hole with a pole.

Busuuh loads his rifle.

Everyone except Bardus joins in the conversation.

Bardus's wife restarts a fire that had gone out. His friend makes split-bamboo sheeting.

Malam defoliates the surrounding cassava plants.

ʔandɔʔ relights the head fire.

The grave itself seems to have a wide mouth, about seven by nine feet, with a box-like pit at the bottom with vertical sides, about 5½ feet by 2½ feet by 2 feet. The overall depth is between 3 and 3½ feet. Earth is heaped up all around.

It starts to rain as the work nears the end. The sun comes out at the same time. [Such 'hot rain', *tɔəh bəralããj*, is regarded as unlucky.]

Malam asks where is *sɔy ʔis* (the west)—*ʔandɔʔ* then tells him where to place the body's head.

But the final form of the grave is different. To the riverwards side there is a ledge left, about 1 foot by 1 foot, occupying the length of the grave. On the other side a slight overhang of about 9 inches is excavated.

ʔaluŋ places three transverse saplings on the bottom and two upturned strips of flooring on top, the full length of the grave. Then he unrolls a woven mat onto it. The body was then suspended over the top and the string cut, allowing the body (not completely covered) to fall into the grave. Then standing on the ledge, ʔaluŋ distributed the grave goods over the body, covering it in freshly-torn cloth, mostly new. Others then put in the deceased's worn clothes, some axe-heads, a gold chain. Busuuh put in about RM30.

The deceased's wife then started weeping. Malam stood in the ledge and uttered a few imprecations—*sɛnʔɔɔy mɛjmɛj, ciib ma-sɔy mɛj* ('good person, go to a good end'), etc. But he laughed soon after. It was all informal.

About 15 saplings were then placed transversely from the ledge over the body to the top of the overhang. This was covered with upturned split-bamboo sheeting (Malam: 'its front to the top!'), held down by a single stick. This was done by ʔaluŋ. He and Bardʉs's friend then covered this over with banana leaves brought by the visitor from Bər. Then speedily the earth was filled in by Malam, Bardʉs's friend, ʔaluŋ and the man from Bər. When it was fairly covered the deceased's wife and Bardʉs's wife shovelled the earth on with their hands from the edge. Gradually a mound was formed, oval and about 2 feet high in the middle. This was then pressed hard by the same men with their feet. Plants were thrown aside and the earth was searched for stray roots, which were cut. Then with a shovel the shape of the mound was improved by flattening around the edges, and making the mound more sharply defined.

ʔaluŋ forms clods of clay into grenades in his hands, placing them over the head—*doh canaaʔ hãã*! ('here is your food!'). ʔandɔʔ and the man from Bər start making the palisade at the head end on the outer edge of the flattened earth—about 2 feet from the mound. ʔaluŋ then placed a tin cup (after puncturing it), a whole bowl upturned on the head of the mound, and a half coconut-shell at the tail end. A section of bamboo cut open was placed next to the clay-food (as a dish?).

The fencing meanwhile went on, meeting from both flanks at the foot of the grave. Malam stuck a skewer of six new-rolled cigarettes (given to him by the short-haired woman) near the 'food' on the flat earth. ʔandɔʔ poured water from a bamboo into the 'dish', but they shouted to him to split the bamboo—which he did, and then placed it next to the 'dish'. ʔaluŋ placed a leaf of betel-chew, *doh kapur hãã̃ʔ, doh bəyaʔ hãã̃ʔ* ('here's your lime, here's your chew') so that it formed a group—food, water, tobacco, betel, at the head. Long stems of surrounding cassava were then partially defoliated, and some planted on the landward side. Busuuh said that people would return to 'guard' today and tomorrow, especially Bardɨs.

They leave the site saying variously *haã̃ʔ ma-tɛʔ səjuʔ, kanɛɛʔ tɛʔ bɛdbɨd* ('you to a cool land, we to a hot land'), *cah nɔŋ rayaaʔ* ('cut a broad path'), *hãã̃ʔ sənaŋ, kanɛɛʔ payah—ki-ʔog ʔabat cukub* ('you have it easy, we have it hard—we gave you enough sarongs'). As we leave the area they pluck leaves from the trackside plants, and take swipes with their parangs. A woman takes a bag of cassava back from the site.

On reaching the other side the men strip and bathe, at the same time scrubbing the shovels and mattocks that had been used in the burial— all except Bardɨs and Busuuh. The latter bathed on reaching the house. Bardɨs waited for everyone and came last in the line of men. I found that the deceased's house had been partially dismantled when we arrived back. Malam said later that it would be burnt.

The cassava brought from the burial was being prepared for a funeral meal, and Malam killed two large cockerels ('old style'—with bare hands) belonging to the deceased. Pəleman and Bardɨs's wife were doing most of the preparation of the cassava.

Meanwhile the walls had been stripped off the deceased's house and two small fires lit beneath. Bardɨs was hanging around the adjoining house. An old man who did not attend the burial seemed to be seeing to the fires.

ʔandɔʔ, Malam and ʔadɔn (ʔandɔʔ's young son) take the chicken's feet to be roasted in another house, wrapped in leaves. Malam says it's because there is not enough room in Busuuh's house—it has no ritual significance. When all had been seated Busuuh said in a matter-of-fact voice *ʔis doh ha-wɛʔ; ʔiŋad lah ma-kanɛɛʔ, cacɔʔ cənɔɔʔ hah* ('today you departed; remember us, your grandchildren and great-grandchildren'). Busuuh then urged Bardɨs who was sitting aside to join the circle and eat, which he did.

After the meal Busuuh distributed sarongs, sheets and money to the gravediggers. These belonged to the deceased's son, and some were handed over to Busuuh for distribution:

- ʔandɔʔ received two sheets, one sarong, three finger-rings
- Malam received two sheets, one sarong, one parang blade

- The man from Bər (Taaʔ Hitam) received two pieces of unsown batik cloth, one sarong, RM10 in cash, five finger-rings
- Ɂaluŋ refused to receive anything, because the deceased was his own *kooc* ('uncle')
- Ɂaɲjaŋ, Bardus's younger brother, received two finger-rings.

The idea seems to be that all physical reminders of the deceased must be removed from the cognizance of near kin.

3.4 Hitam Tamboh on old-time funeral practices

On 1 December 1964, after I proceeded further upstream from Cherber, Penghulu Hitam Tamboh filled in some gaps in my information about death customs. His account confirms some of the assumptions made earlier, especially about the nature of grave-offering behaviour—as for example his assertion that a dead child receives no less than a dead headman, thereby emphasising that it has to do with the pity that the survivors feel. Here are my notes of his account:

> In the old days burials were carried out far from the houses, not near them. This was especially so in the case of sudden death. The custom was to bury a person in one of his own previous swidden sections, so that he truly returned 'to his land'. Children and wives were buried in the swidden sections of their respective households.
>
> *All* the houses in the village were burnt down and everyone moved with their possessions on the morrow, early in the day. But the acquisition of a *kampung*, namely fruit trees and coconuts which are essentially permanent, changed this to the contemporary truncation of these practices.
>
> A funeral feast (*ʔewɔh*) is customary—the deceased's chickens are eaten if available; if not, then someone else's; or just vegetables are consumed.
>
> He explained that the custom of making grave offerings (*pensoor*) is because of the feeling of pity (*kalɔɔn*) for the deceased. He was surprised to learn that the British do not do this. The custom is only for house-heads, the men of property, to make such offerings. In a longhouse, it is the elders (*teʔtaaʔ*) who do so. In Hitam's own house, for example, only he would make offerings, not his various sons-in-law; in the other houses, only two other men (whom he named) would do so. Each gives according to his means, and no one thinks badly of a poor man giving little or a rich man much. A dead child receives the same amount of grave offerings as a penghulu.
>
> Also buried with the body are possessions of the deceased—*baraŋ hɔj na-tənaaʔ* ('things he had recognised'). These were all the less durable

goods which he either used or possessed without using—betel apparatus, tobacco pouches, mats, cloths, knives ('they rust away'), etc. However, fine or old examples of durable objects become hereditary possessions and are not buried. In this class are blowpipes, quivers, metal spears, krises, crockery (not tin?), and especially gongs. (Poorer blowpipes or quivers might sometimes be buried.) Such hereditary objects (*baraŋ sakaaʔ*) *must* be retained by the recipient, to be passed on as *sakaaʔ* at *his* death. Hitam seemed to think that the obligatory handing-on of inherited articles, that I had been told about in Humid, was a lowland (*baroh*) custom, but he was sure that highland (*jɛlmɔl*) custom was as he had stated.

Children's accounts
of their dreams

The topic of dreams has emerged at various places in this book. As discussed in Chapter 2, the view latterly attributed to Kilton Stewart that Temiars can *control* their dreams has been shown to be unfounded. It nevertheless remains true that Temiars place great store by their dreams—or at least by the *idea* that dreams are important. They listen to each other when recounting what they dreamt; they explicitly regard dreams as the primary vehicle through which they come to know their personal *gunig* spirit-guides; and they regard their dreams as having predictive qualities. Examples of these practices occur throughout this book.

However, an aspect of Temiar dreams that Stewart discussed in detail but which I have merely touched on is their *content*. As the following accounts show, the dreams of Temiar children, at least, were as full of fallings, deaths and other violent happenings in 1964 as they appear to have been when recorded in the 1930s by Stewart. Other dreams—at least as remembered the following day—were free of such features, and stolidly prosaic. As against the 312 dreams of adults and children that Stewart précised in his PhD thesis, I gathered a mere 15 dream accounts, solely and directly from two young children. These are presented below. Since I am still in touch with the dreamers five decades later, I shall not embarrass them by giving their names. Instead I shall refer to them simply as A (a young boy about seven years old) and B (his cousin, a young girl about four). The dreams were told to me spontaneously in mid-October 1964. The style was very abbreviated and made more difficult to follow because, as children, they sometimes used word-forms not always occurring in adult speech. My notes read as follows, except that the original Temiar has been freshly translated into English. I have added reference numbers in brackets to identify the different dreams.

> It was obvious that they remembered the dreams very sharply—they
> came out in a torrent of words. Also, they obviously discuss them among
> themselves, if not with their parents, and told me each other's dreams.
> Their mothers turned up to listen, and no one seemed embarrassed
> (except me).

A tells me that last night he dreamt, [1] 'I was carrying a big rock.' Then he dreamt, [2] 'I was climbing a fruit tree. I kept lopping off some branches. They fell onto a woman and she died. We grabbed her, we went up, up, then buried [her] up there.'

A says that yesterday he dreamt, [3] 'I was playing around on a fish-weir.' Then he dreamt, [4] 'I climbed a bamboo, I chopped it down, it fell, I lopped it.'

B had just told A of her dream: [5] 'I chewed some chilli pepper, it made my breast [or milk?] smart, she [or 'he'?] suckled, suckled, suckled, she rejected, she cried.' She also dreamt, [6] 'she rolled a rock onto my (A's) foot.'

Yesterday, B had told A that she dreamt she was carrying four cans: [7] 'I went, went, I submerged myself [in the river], I bombed fish, it died. I roasted the fish, the fire burnt my hand, I wept at the fire, I died, I buried myself.' Later, A gave me a more elaborate version: [7a] 'I carried cans, two bottles I carried. I bombed fish, they died. I brought them, roasted them, ate them. I gave one to A. The fish burnt me in revenge, I hit it and it died. I wept, I died, I buried myself. I opened up [the grave], entered, suffocated and closed it up. I opened it to the daylight.' A added, 'She opened it up, she had suffocated.' The end was lost here, but she seems to have awoken and returned to life and the village.

After that B dreamt, [8] 'She was plucking leaves, she was carrying a bag, a back-basket, a tiny bag, woven of cane. She threw it on the swidden. She built a raft, she felled a paddle, she travelled downstream, to below the rapids, alone she travelled, to Lambok. In Lambok, they grabbed people [Temiars] to go back up to Tuan Biles's place.[1]

A asked me what I dreamt. Yesterday, he said, [9] 'I dreamt of a chicken, I cut it sharply, I cut its throat. It died, I buried it.' [10] 'I dreamt I stole a chicken, I cut its throat with a small knife. I threw it away, it wriggled in the water. It flowed down into the rapids.'

A says that yesterday [11] 'I dreamt of a big bamboo. I dreamt of a big tree. I felled it. I went at ease.' [12] 'I dreamt of a big glass. I was drinking. I finished it.'

The following day, A reports that last night he dreamt, [13] 'My father cut some vegetables, and put them in a back-basket.' [14] 'I dreamt I was planting cassava.'

A reports that B had dreamt, [15] 'She fell on top of me. Her father bought some *sawit* [unclear: probably 'leafy vegetable' (Malay: *sawi*), but possibly 'bangles' or 'oil-palm']. He gave me a lot, to little B a small amount, to A a lot. She wept, "he gave a lot to him".'

---

1. At the time, Howard Biles was the head of the JHEOA in Kelantan state. He had occasionally visited me at Humid, where I was living in a rest-house (*sətawus* in Temiar) originally built for him and where these dream-retellings took place.

One thing missing from this small sample is any mention of entering into a personal relationship with a new dream character. In other words, it would be hard to tell from these accounts that there was any presaging of the idea that dreams were the medium through which one gained *gunig* spirit-guides. For example, I once overheard Penghulu Dalam remark *gunig ʔi-pɔʔ paay doh* ('I recently dreamt a *gunig*') while chatting to a group of men. This could be seen as supporting Stewart's view that Temiars exhibit dream-maturation as they grow older; but it would be wrong, I think, to see this as a purely psychological progression occurring outside of any institutional framework. As this book has documented, that institutional framework is immensely rich in content and supported by an unusually close communal input. In such a context, meeting a *gunig* in a dream is effectively something *expected* of an adult Temiar.

Bibliography

Adams, T. S. 1922. 'A vocabulary of Pangan.' *Journal of the Straits Branch, Royal Asiatic Society* 85: 97–123. [This wordlist is not Northern Aslian, as the title suggests, but Temiar.]

Adi Haji Taha. 1989. 'Arkeologi Orang Asli.' *Akademika, Journal of Southeast Asian Social Sciences and Humanities* 35: 113–124.

———. 2004. 'Ulu Kelantan: archaeological evidence of ancient outside contact.' *Heritage Asia* (June–August): 34–37.

———. 2007. *Archaeology of Ulu Kelantan.* Kuala Lumpur: Ministry of Culture, Arts and Heritage Malaysia, Department of Museums Malaysia.

Ahmad Ezanee bin Mansor. 1972. 'Kampong Lubok Legong: a Negrito resettlement community in Kedah.' Unpublished honours thesis. Penang: Universiti Sains Malaysia, School of Comparative Social Sciences.

Amran Kasimin. 1991. *Religion and Social Change Among the Indigenous People of the Malay Peninsula.* Kuala Lumpur: Dewan Bahasa dan Pustaka.

Andaya, Leonard Y. 2008. *Leaves of the Same Tree: Trade and Ethnicity in the Straits of Melaka.* Honolulu: University of Hawai'i Press / Singapore: NUS Press.

Baer, Adela. 2012. 'Contacts and contrasts: the British vs. the Orang Asli in Colonial Malaya.' 24pp. Typescript, Oregon State University. http://hdl.handle.net/1957/29700.

Baharon Azhar bin Raffie'i. 1966. '"Engku"—spirit of thunder.' *Federation Museums Journal* 11: 34–36.

Baker, A. C. 1933. 'An account of a journey from the Cameron Highlands to the East Coast Railway and of a visit to the Temiar settlements in the valleys of the Sungai Blatop and S. Ber.' *Journal of the Malayan Branch of the Royal Asiatic Society* 11: 288–295.

Bauer, Christian. 1992. 'Mon–Aslian contacts.' *Bulletin of the School of Oriental and African Studies* 55: 532–537.

Becker, A. L. & I Gusti Ngurah Oka. 1974. 'Person in Kawi: exploration of an elementary semantic dimension.' *Oceanic Linguistics* 13: 229–255.

Bellah, Robert N. 1964. 'Religious evolution.' *American Sociological Review* 29: 358–374.

Bellwood, Peter. 1993. 'Cultural and biological differentiation in Peninsular Malaysia: the last 10,000 years.' *Asian Perspectives* 32: 37–60.

————. 2004. 'Aslian, Austronesian, Malayic: suggestions from the archaeological record.' In *Southeast Asian Archaeology: Wilhelm G. Solheim II Festschrift*, ed. Victor Paz. Quezon City: University of the Philippines Press, pp. 347–365.

Benedict, Paul K. 1975. *Austro-Thai: Language and Culture*. New Haven: HRAF Press.

Benjamin, Geoffrey. 1966. 'Temiar social groupings.' *Federation Museums Journal* 11: 1–25.

————. 1967a. 'Temiar Religion.' Unpublished PhD thesis, University of Cambridge. [Reprinted, slightly revised, as Chapters 3–8 in this volume.]

————. 1967b. 'Lévi-Strauss and anthropology.' *Cambridge Review* 89A: 122–123, 149–151.

————. 1967c. 'Temiar kinship.' *Federation Museums Journal* 12: 1–25.

————. 1968a. 'Temiar personal names.' *Bijdragen tot de Taal-, Land- en Volkenkunde* 124: 99–134.

————. 1968b. 'Headmanship and leadership in Temiar society.' *Federation Museums Journal* 13: 1–43.

————. 1973. Introduction to *Among the Forest Dwarfs of Malaya*, by Paul Schebesta. Second impression. Kuala Lumpur: Oxford University Press, pp. v–xii.

————. 1976. 'An outline of Temiar grammar.' In *Austroasiatic Studies, Part I*, ed. Philip N. Jenner, Laurence C. Thompson & Stanley Starosta. Honolulu: University Press of Hawaii, pp. 129–187.

————. 1979. 'Indigenous religious systems of the Malay Peninsula.' In *The Imagination of Reality: Essays in Southeast Asian Coherence Systems*, ed. Aram Yengoyan & Alton L. Becker. Norwood NJ: Ablex, pp. 9–27. [Reprinted, revised, as Chapter 11 in this volume.]

————. 1985. 'In the long term: three themes in Malayan cultural ecology.' In *Cultural Values and Human Ecology in Southeast Asia*, ed. Karl. L. Hutterer, A. Terry Rambo & George Lovelace. Ann Arbor MI: Center for South and Southeast Asian Studies, University of Michigan, pp. 219–278.

————. 1987a. 'Ethnohistorical perspectives on Kelantan's prehistory.' In *Kelantan Zaman Awal: Kajian Arkeologi dan Sejarah di Malaysia*, ed. Nik Hassan Shuhaimi bin Nik Abdul Rahman. Kota Bharu: Perbadanan Muzium Negeri Kelantan, pp. 108–153.

————. 1987b. 'Notes on the deep sociology of religion.' National University of Singapore, *Department of Sociology Working Papers* no. 85.

————. 1988. 'The unseen presence: a theory of the nation-state and its mystifications.' National University of Singapore, *Department of Sociology Working Papers* no. 91.

————. 1993a. 'Grammar and polity: the cultural and political background to standard Malay.' In *The Role of Theory in Language Description*, ed. W. A. Foley. Berlin: Mouton De Gruyter, pp. 349–392.

————. 1993b. 'Temiar.' In *Encyclopedia of World Cultures, Volume V: East and Southeast Asia*, ed. Paul Hockings. Boston: G. K. Hall, pp. 265–273. http://www.everyculture.com/East-Southeast-Asia/Temiar.html.

————. 1994. 'Danger and dialectic in Temiar childhood.' In *Enfants et Sociétés d'Asie du Sud-Est*, ed. Jeannine Koubi & Josiane Massard-Vincent. Paris: L'Harmattan, pp. 37–62. [Reprinted, revised, as Chapter 12 in this volume.]

————. 1996. 'Rationalisation and re-enchantment in Malaysia: Temiar religion, 1964–1995.' National University of Singapore, *Department of Sociology Working Papers* no. 130. [Reprinted, revised, as Chapter 13 in this volume.]

————. 1997. 'Issues in the ethnohistory of Pahang.' In *Pembangunan Arkeologi Pelancongan Negeri Pahang*, ed. Nik Hassan Shuhaimi bin Nik Abdul Rahman et al. Pekan: Muzium Pahang, pp. 82–121.

————. 1999. 'Temiar kinship terminology: a linguistic and formal analysis.' Penang: Academy of Social Sciences, *Occasional Papers* no. 1.

————. 2001. 'A Temiar chief remembers: the early 20th century as recalled in tribal areas of Kelantan and Perak.' Paper presented at the Fifth ASEAN Inter-University Seminar on Social Development, Singapore, 23–25 May 2001.

————. 2002a. 'Process and structure in Temiar social organisation.' In *Minority Cultures of Peninsular Malaysia: Survivals of Indigenous Heritage,* ed. Razha Rashid & Wazir Jahan Karim. Penang: Malaysian Academy of Social Sciences (AKASS), pp. 121–144.

————. 2002b. 'On being tribal in the Malay World.' In *Tribal Communities in the Malay World: Historical, Cultural and Social Perspectives*, ed. Geoffrey Benjamin & Cynthia Chou. Leiden: International Institute for Asian Studies (IIAS) / Singapore: Institute of Southeast Asian Studies (ISEAS), pp. 7–76.

————. 2004. 'Music and the cline of Malayness.' Paper presented at the *International Symposium on Thinking Malayness*, Research Institute for Languages and Cultures of Asia and Africa, Tokyo University of International Studies, Tokyo, 19–21 June 2004.

————. 2005. 'Consciousness and polity in Southeast Asia: the long view.' In *Local and Global: Social Transformation in Southeast Asia. Essays in Honour of Professor Syed Hussein Alatas*, ed. Riaz Hassan. Leiden and Boston: Brill / Kuala Lumpur: Dewan Bahasa dan Pustaka, pp. 261–289.

————. 2011a. 'Egalitarianism and ranking in the Malay World.' In *Anarchic Solidarity: Autonomy, Equality and Fellowship in Southeast Asia*, ed. Kenneth Sillander & Thomas Gibson. New Haven: Yale University Southeast Asia Studies, pp. 170–201.

————. 2011b. 'Deponent verbs and middle-voice nouns in Temiar.' In *Austroasiatic Studies: Papers from ICAAL4 (Mon-Khmer Studies,*

Special Issue no. 2), ed. Sophana Srichampa & Paul Sidwell. Dallas: SIL International / Salaya: Mahidol University / Canberra: Pacific Linguistics E-8, pp. 11–37.

———. 2012a. 'The peculiar history of the ethnonym "Temiar".' *SOJOURN: Journal of Social Issues in Southeast Asia* 27: 205–233.

———. 2012b. 'The Aslian languages of Malaysia and Thailand: an assessment.' In *Language Documentation and Description, Volume 11*, ed. Peter K. Austin & Stuart McGill. London: Endangered Languages Project, School of Oriental and African Studies, pp. 136–230.

———. 2013. 'Why have the Peninsular "Negritos" remained distinct?' *Human Biology* 85: 445–484.

———. 2014. 'Aesthetic elements in Temiar grammar.' In *The Aesthetics of Grammar: Sound and Meaning in the Languages of Mainland Southeast Asia*, ed. Jeffrey Williams. Cambridge: Cambridge University Press, pp. 36–60.

———. Forthcoming (a). *Between Isthmus and Islands: Studies in Malay-World Ethnohistory*. Singapore: Institute of Southeast Asian Studies. [This incorporates revised versions of Benjamin (1985, 1987a, 1997, 2005, 2012a).]

———. Forthcoming (b). *Temiar Society*. Singapore: NUS Press.

Benjamin, Geoffrey & Cynthia Chou, ed. 2002. *Tribal Communities in the Malay World: Historical, Social and Cultural Perspectives*. Leiden: International Institute for Asian Studies (IIAS) / Singapore: Institute of Southeast Asian Studies (ISEAS).

Berger, Peter. 1954. 'From Sect to Church: A Sociological Interpretation of the Baha'i Movement.' Unpublished PhD thesis. New York: New School for Social Research.

———. 1966. *Invitation to Sociology: A Humanistic Perspective*. Harmondsworth: Penguin.

Bidney, David. 1960. 'Paul Radin and the problem of primitive monotheism.' In *Culture in History*, ed. Sol Diamond. New York: Columbia University Press, pp. 360–379.

Blagden, C. O. 1906. 'Language.' In *Pagan Races of the Malay Peninsula*, Volume 2, ed. W. W. Skeat & C. O. Blagden. London: Macmillan, pp. 379–775.

Blust, Robert A. 2013. 'Terror from the sky: unconventional linguistic clues to the Negrito past.' *Human Biology* 85: 401–416.

Blust, Robert A. & Stephen Trussel. 2010. *Austronesian Comparative Dictionary*, Web Edition (Revision 19 May 2012), www.trussel2.com/ACD 2010.

Bolton, Malcolm. 1972. 'Food taboos among the Orang Asli in West Malaysia: a potential nutritional hazard.' *The American Journal of Clinical Nutrition* 25: 789–799.

Borie, P. H. D. 1886. *La Presqu'île de Malacca, les Malais et les Sauvages*. Tulle: Imprimerie J. Mazeyrie.

Brau de Saint-Pol Lias, Xavier. 1883. *Pérak et les Orangs-Sakèy: Voyage dans l'Intérieur de la Presqu'île Malaise*. Paris: Plon.

Bräunlein, Peter. 2000. 'Auf der Suche nach den "träumenden Senoi": Ein Beitrag zur Faszinationsgeschichte des Traumes.' *Träume/n. Kea: Zeitschrift für Kulturwissenschaften* 13: 45–90.

Broadhead, Peggie. 1941. Unpublished letter to 'Brenda' from Perak, 7 December 1941. In *Aileen Margaret Robertson: Senoi Collection*, World Oral Literature Project, http://www.oralliterature.org/collections/probertson001.html.

Bulbeck, David. 2004. 'Indigenous traditions and exogenous influences in the early history of Peninsular Malaysia.' In *Southeast Asia: From Prehistory to History*, ed. Ian Glover & Peter Bellwood. London: RoutledgeCurzon, pp. 314–336.

———. 2011. 'Biological and cultural evolution in the population and culture history of *Homo sapiens* in Malaya.' In *Dynamics of Human Diversity: The Case of Mainland Southeast Asia*, ed. N. J. Enfield. Canberra: Pacific Linguistics, pp. 207–255.

Burenhult, Niclas. 2008. 'Streams of words: hydrological lexicon in Jahai.' *Language Sciences* 30: 182–199.

Burenhult, Niclas, Nicole Kruspe & Michael Dunn. 2011. 'Language history and culture groups among Austroasiatic-speaking foragers of the Malay Peninsula.' In *Dynamics of Human Diversity: The Case of Mainland Southeast Asia*, ed. N. J. Enfield. Canberra: Pacific Linguistics, pp. 257–275.

Burridge, Kenelm. 1967. 'Lévi-Strauss and myth.' In *The Structural Study of Myth and Totemism*, ed. E. R. Leach. London: Tavistock, pp. 91–115.

Carey, Iskandar. 1961. *Tengleq Kui Serok: A Study of the Temiar Language, With an Ethnographic Summary*. Kuala Lumpur: Dewan Bahasa dan Pustaka.

———. 1976. *Orang Asli: The Aboriginal Tribes of Peninsular Malaysia*. Kuala Lumpur: Oxford University Press.

Carstens, Sharon. 1980. 'Pulai: memories of a gold mining settlement in Ulu Kelantan.' *Journal of the Malaysian Branch of the Royal Asiatic Society* 53: 50–67.

Chou, Cynthia. 2010. *The Orang Suku Laut of Riau, Indonesia*. London: Routledge.

Clifford, Hugh. 1897. 'In a camp of the Sĕmangs.' In *In Court & Kampong*. London: Grant Richards, pp.171–181.

———. 1927 [1899]. 'The flight of the jungle folk.' In *The Further Side of Silence*. Garden City NY: Doubleday, Page & Co., pp. 244–271.

COAC [Centre for Orang Asli Concerns]. 2012. '"Orang Asli *bukan* orang asal".' http://www.facebook.com/note.php?note_id=361422953901637.

Cole, R. 1959. 'Temiar Senoi agriculture: a note on aboriginal shifting cultivation in Ulu Kelantan, Malaya.' *Malayan Forester* 22: 191–207, 260–271.

Coope, A. E. 1997. *A Malay–English English–Malay Dictionary*. Revised edition. London: Macmillan.

Corner, E. J. H. 1940. *Wayside Trees of Malaya*. Singapore: Government Press.

Couillard, Marie-Andrée. 1980. *Tradition in Tension: Carving in a Jah Hut Community*. Penang: Penerbit Universiti Sains Malaysia.

Coxhead, David & Susan Hiller. 1976. *Dreams: Visions of the Night*. New York: Crossroad / London: Thames and Hudson.

Cranbrook, Gathorne. 2006. [Obituary:] 'Dr J. Malcolm Bolton: Flying doctor in Malaysia who later, with the WHO, assisted in the final eradication of smallpox.' *The Independent*, 26 October 2006.

Cuisinier, Jeanne. 1936. *Danses Magiques de Kelantan*. Paris: Institut d'Ethnologie.

Dawkins, Richard. 2006. *The God Delusion*. London: Bantam.

De Josselin de Jong, P. E. 1981. Review of *The Imagination of Reality: Essays in Southeast Asian Coherence Systems,* ed. A. L. Becker & A. Yengoyan. *Bijdragen tot de Taal-, Land- en Volkenkunde* 137: 486–491.

Dennett, Daniel. 2013. 'Daniel Dennett: "I don't like theory of mind"— interview.' http://www.guardian.co.uk/science/blog/2013/mar/22/daniel-dennett-theory-of-mind-interview.

Dentan, Robert Knox. 1964. 'Senoi-Semang.' In *Ethnic Groups of Mainland Southeast Asia*, ed. Frank M. Lebar et al. New Haven: Human Relations Area Files Press, pp. 176–186.

———. 1965. 'Some Semai Senoi dietary restrictions: a study of food behaviour in a Malayan hill tribe.' PhD thesis, Yale University. Ann Arbor: University Microfilms.

———. 1967. 'The mammalian taxonomy of the Senoi Semai.' *Malayan Nature Journal* 20: 100–106.

———. 1968a. *The Semai: A Nonviolent People of Malaya*. New York: Holt, Rinehart & Winston. [Expanded *Fieldwork Edition*, 1979.]

———. 1968b. 'Semai response to mental aberration.' *Bijdragen tot de Taal-, Land- en Volkenkunde* 124: 135–158.

———. 1978. 'Notes on childhood in a non-violent context: the Semai case (Malaysia).' In *Learning Non-aggression: The Experience of Non-literate Societies*, ed. Ashley Montagu. New York: Oxford University Press, pp. 94–143.

———. 1983. 'A dream of Senoi.' State University of New York at Buffalo, Council on International Studies, *Special Studies Series* no. 150.

———. 2000. 'Ceremonies of innocence and the lineaments of ungratified desire: an analysis of a syncretic Southeast Asian taboo complex.' *Bijdragen tot de Taal-, Land- en Volkenkunde* 156: 193–232.

————. 2002a. 'Against the kingdom of the beast: Semai theology, pre-Aryan religion, and the dynamics of abjection.' In *Tribal Communities in the Malay World: Historical, Cultural and Social Perspectives*, ed. Geoffrey Benjamin & Cynthia Chou. Leiden: International Institute for Asian Studies (IIAS) / Singapore: Institute of Southeast Asian Studies, pp. 206–236.

————. 2002b. '"Disreputable magicians," the Dark Destroyer, and the Trickster Lord: reflections on Semai religion and a possible common religious base in South and Southeast Asia.' *Asian Anthropology* 1: 153–194.

————. 2008. *Overwhelming Terror: Love, Fear, Peace, and Violence among Semai of Malaysia*. Lanham MD: Rowman & Littlefield.

Dentan, Robert Knox, Kirk Endicott, Alberto G. Gomes & M. B. Hooker. 1996. *Malaysia and the 'Original People': A Case Study of the Impact of Development on Indigenous Peoples*. Boston: Allyn & Bacon.

Dentan, Robert Knox & David Nicholls. 2011. 'Stress, equality and peaceability among east Semai: a preliminary account.' Paper presented at the Annual Meeting of the American Anthropological Association, Montreal, November 2011.

Department of Statistics (Malaysia). 1997. *Profile of the Orang Asli in Peninsular Malaysia*. Population Census Monograph Series No. 3. Kuala Lumpur: Department of Statistics.

Diffloth, Gérard. 1980. 'To taboo everything at all times.' *Proceedings of the Sixth Annual Meeting of the Berkeley Linguistics Society*: 157–165.

————. 1984. *The Dvaravati Old Mon Language and Nyah Kur*. Bangkok: Chulalongkorn University Printing House.

Domhoff, G. William. 1985. *The Mystique of Dreams: A Search for Utopia Through Senoi Dream Theory*. Berkeley: California University Press.

————. 2003. *Senoi Dream Theory: Myth, Scientific Method, and the Dreamwork Movement*. http://dreamresearch.net/Library/senoi.html. [Updated version of Domhoff (1985).]

————. 2005–06. 'Dream research in the mass media: Where journalists go wrong on dreams.' *The Scientific Review of Mental Health Practice* 4: 74–78.

Douglas, Mary. 1966. *Purity and Danger*. London: Routledge & Kegan Paul.

Dunn, F. L. 1972. 'Intestinal parasitism in Malayan aborigines (Orang Asli).' *Bulletin of the World Health Organization* 46: 99–113.

Dunn, Michael, Nicole Kruspe & Niclas Burenhult. 2013. 'Time and place in the prehistory of the Aslian language family.' *Human Biology* 85: 383–400.

Durkheim, Émile. 1902. *De la Division du Travail Social*. Second edition. Paris: Félix Alcan.

————. 1912. *Les Formes Élémentaires de la Vie Religieuse*. Paris: Félix Alcan. (Translated as *The Elementary Forms of the Religious Life*. London: George Allen & Unwin. Many editions since 1915.)

————. 1953 [1898]. *Sociology and Philosophy*. Translated by David Pocock. London: Cohen and West.

Eccles, John C. 1977. 'Evolution of the brain in relation to the development of the self-conscious mind.' *Annals of the New York Academy of Sciences* 299: 161–179.

Edwin, Joseph. 1995. 'Dying art of the Temiar in treating their sick.' *New Sunday Times*, 11 June 1995, p. 10.

Endicott, Kirk M. 1970. *An Analysis of Malay Magic*. Oxford: Clarendon Press.

————. 1979a. *Batek Negrito Religion: The World-view and Rituals of a Hunting and Gathering People of Peninsular Malaysia*. Oxford: Clarendon.

————. 1979b. 'The Batek Negrito thunder god: the personification of a natural force.' In *The Imagination of Reality: Essays in Southeast Asian Coherence Systems*, ed. A. L. Becker & A. Yengoyan. Norwood NJ: Ablex, pp. 29–42.

————. 1979c. 'The impact of economic modernization on the Orang Asli (Aborigines) of northern Peninsular Malaysia.' In *Issues in Malaysian Development*, ed. J. C. Jackson & Martin Rudner. Singapore: Heinemann, pp. 167–204.

————. 1983. 'The effects of slave raiding on the Aborigines of the Malay Peninsula.' In *Slavery, Bondage and Dependency in Southeast Asia*, ed. Anthony Reid. St Lucia: University of Queensland Press, pp. 216–245.

Endicott, Kirk M. & Karen Endicott. 2008. *The Headman Was a Woman: The Gender Egalitarian Batek of Malaysia*. Long Grove IL: Waveland. [Reprinted, 2012, Subang Jaya: Centre for Orang Asli Concerns.]

Evans, I. H. N. 1923. *Religion, Folk-lore and Custom in British North Borneo and the Malay Peninsula*. Cambridge: Cambridge University Press.

————. 1937. *The Negritos of Malaya*. Cambridge: Cambridge University Press.

Evans-Pritchard, E. E. 1956. *Nuer Religion*. Oxford: Clarendon.

————. 1965. *Theories of Primitive Religion*. Oxford: Clarendon.

Faraday, Ann & John Wren-Lewis. 1984. 'The selling of the Senoi.' *Lucidity Letter* 3: 79–81. http://www.sawka.com/spiritwatch/selling.html.

Firth, Raymond. 1955. *The Fate of the Soul: An Interpretation of Some Primitive Concepts*. Cambridge: Cambridge University Press.

————. 1964. *Essays on Social Organization and Values*. London: Athlone Press.

Fix, Alan. 1971. 'Semai Senoi Population Structure and Genetic Microdifferentiation.' PhD thesis, University of Michigan, Ann Arbor: University Microfilms.

————. 1995. 'Malayan paleosociology: implications for patterns of genetic variation among the Orang Asli.' *American Anthropologist* 97: 313–323.

————. 2011. 'Origin of genetic diversity among Malaysian Orang Asli: an alternative to the demic diffusion model.' In *Dynamics of Human Diversity: The Case of Mainland Southeast Asia*, ed. N. J. Enfield. Canberra: Pacific Linguistics, pp. 277–291.

Fortes, Meyer. 1962. 'Ritual and office in tribal society.' In *Essays on the Ritual of Social Relations*, ed. Max Gluckman. Manchester: Manchester University Press, pp. 53–88.

————. 1966. 'Totem and taboo.' *Proceedings of the Royal Anthropological Institute for 1966*: 5–22.

Fox, James J. 1971. 'Sister's child as plant: metaphors in an idiom of consanguinity.' In *Rethinking Kinship and Marriage*, ed. Rodney Needham. London: Tavistock, pp. 219–252.

Freeman, Derek. 1955. *Iban Agriculture*. London: HMSO.

————. 1967. 'Shaman and incubus.' *Psychoanalytical Study of Society* 4: 315–343.

————. 1968. 'Thunder, blood, and the nicknaming of God's creatures.' *The Psychoanalytic Quarterly* 37: 353–359.

Galin, David. 1977. 'Lateral specialization and psychiatric issues: speculations on development and the evolution of consciousness.' *Annals of the New York Academy of Sciences* 299: 397–411.

Garfield, Patricia. 1995 [1974]. *Creative Dreaming: Plan and Control Your Dreams to Develop Creativity, Overcome Fears, Solve Problems, and Create a Better Self*. Second edition. New York: Simon and Schuster.

Geddes, William R. 1954. *The Land Dayaks of Sarawak*. London: HMSO.

Geertz, Clifford. 1956. *The Development of the Javanese Economy*. Cambridge MA: Harvard University Press.

————. 1957. 'Ritual and social change: a Javanese example.' *American Anthropologist* 59: 32–54.

————. 1966. 'Religion as a cultural system.' In *Anthropological Approaches to the Study of Religion*, ed. Michael Banton. London: Tavistock, pp. 1–46.

Geertz, Clifford & Hildred Geertz. 1964. 'Teknonymy in Bali: parenthood, age-grading and genealogical amnesia.' *Journal of the Royal Anthropological Institute* 94: 94–108.

Gellner, Ernest. 1969. 'A pendulum swing theory of Islam.' In *Sociology of Religion: Selected Readings*, ed. Roland Robertson. Harmondsworth: Penguin, pp. 127–138.

————. 1988. *Plough, Sword and Book: The Structure of Human History*. Chicago: University of Chicago Press.

————. 1992. *Postmodernism, Reason and Religion*. London: Routledge.

Gianno, Rosemary. 2004. 'Women are not brave enough: Semelai male midwives in the context of Southeast Asian cultures.' *Bijdragen tot de Taal-, Land- en Volkenkunde* 160: 31–71.

Gimlette, J. P. 1929. *Malay Poisons and Charm Cures*. London: J. & A. Churchill. [Reprinted 1971, Kuala Lumpur: Oxford University Press.]

Glenister, A. G. 1959. *The Birds of the Malay Peninsula, Singapore and Penang*. London: Oxford University Press.

Gonda, J. 1952. *Sanskrit in Indonesia*. New Delhi: International Academy of Indian Culture.

Goody, J. R. 1961. 'Religion and ritual: the definitional problem.' *British Journal of Sociology* 12: 142–164.

Halcrow, Siân E., Nancy Tayles & Vicki Livingstone. 2008. 'Infant death in late prehistoric Southeast Asia.' *Asian Perspectives* 47: 371–404.

Haldane, J. B. S. 2001 [1927]. *Possible Worlds and Other Papers*. New Brunswick NJ: Transaction Publishers.

Hallowell, A. I. 1960. 'Self and society in phylogenetic perspective.' In *Evolution After Darwin, Volume 2: The Evolution of Man*, ed. Sol Tax. Chicago: Chicago University Press, pp. 309–372.

Halonen, Arto & Jan Wellman. 1998. *A Dreamer and the Dreamtribe*. Videotape, 53 mins. Helsinki: Jan Wellmann/Mandrake Productions and Art Films Production. [For information: http://www.artfilmsproduction.com/Unelmoija-engl.html.]

Harris, Roy. 1980. *The Language-makers*. Ithaca: Cornell University Press.

Harrison, J. L. et al. 1955. 'Aboriginal names of animals.' *Malayan History Journal* 2: 53–58.

Hasan Mat Nor. 1994. 'Christianity and the peripheral community: a Malaysian case.' *The Journal of Sophia Asian Studies* 12: 143–58. http://repository.cc.sophia.ac.jp/dspace/handle/123456789/5125.

Hassan, Riaz. 1972. 'Islam and urbanization in the Medieval Middle East.' *Eastern Anthropologist* 25: 107–122.

Heine-Geldern, Robert. 1956. 'Conceptions of state and kingship in Southeast Asia.' Revised version. Cornell University, Department of Far Eastern Studies, *Southeast Asia Program, Data Paper* no. 18.

Hickson, Andy & Sue Jennings. Forthcoming. 'Order and challenge in education and therapy: the influence of Temiar beliefs and practices.' In *Malaysia's 'Original People': Past, Present and Future of the Orang Asli*, ed. Kirk Endicott. Singapore: NUS Press.

Hitchens, Christopher. 2007. *God is Not Great: The Case Against Religion*. London: Atlantic Books.

Holman, Dennis. 1958. *Noone of the Ulu*. London: Heinemann.

———. 1962. *The Green Torture: The Ordeal of Robert Chrystal*. London: Robert Hale.

Hood Salleh. 1978. 'Semelai Rituals of Curing.' Unpublished PhD thesis, University of Oxford.

Horton, Robin. 1960. 'A definition of religion and its uses.' *Journal of the Royal Anthropological Institute* 90: 201–226.

Howell, Signe. 1984. *Society and Cosmos: Chewong of Peninsular Malaysia.* Singapore: Oxford University Press.

Jacq-Hergoualc'h, Michel. 2002. *The Malay Peninsula: Crossroads of the Maritime Silk Road (100 BC–1300 AD).* Leiden: Brill.

Jennings, Sue. 1985. 'Temiar dance and the maintenance of order.' In *Society and the Dance,* ed. Paul Spencer. Cambridge: Cambridge University Press, pp. 47–63.

———. 1995. *Theatre, Ritual and Transformation: The Senoi Temiars.* London: Routledge.

JHEOA. 1983. 'Strategi Perkembangan Ugama Islam di Kalangan Masyarakat Orang Asli.' 41 pages, duplicated. Kuala Lumpur: Jabatan Hal Ehwal Orang Asli.

Karim, Wazir-Jahan. 1981. *Ma' Betisék Concepts of Living Things.* London: Athlone.

Kawai, Toshimitsu. 1991. 'The navel of the cosmos: a study of folk psychology of childbirth and child development among the Bukidnon.' In *Kinship, Gender and the Cosmic World: Ethnographies of Birth Customs in Taiwan, the Philippines and Indonesia,* Second edition, ed. Yamaji Katsuhiko. Taipei: SMC Publishing, pp. 105–129.

Kessler, Clive. 1978. *Islam and Politics in a Malay State: Kelantan 1838–1969.* Ithaca NY: Cornell University Press.

Kroes, Gerco. 2002. *Same Hair, Different Hearts: Semai Identity in a Malay Context—An Analysis of Ideas and Practices Concerning Health and Illness.* Leiden University: Research School of Asian, African, and Amerindian Studies.

Kuper, Adam. 1986. 'An interview with Edmund Leach.' *Current Anthropology* 27: 375–382.

LaBerge, Stephen. 1985. *Lucid Dreaming: The Power of Being Awake and Aware in Your Dreams.* Los Angeles: Tarcher.

Laird, Peter. 1979. 'Ritual, territory and region: the Temoq of Pahang, West Malaysia.' *Social Analysis* 1: 54–80.

Lamb, A. H. 1961. 'Kedah and Takuapa: some tentative historical conclusions.' *Federation Museums Journal* 6: 69–88.

———. 1964. 'Mahayanist Buddhist votive tablets in Perlis.' *Journal of the Malaysian Branch of the Royal Asiatic Society* 38: 47–59.

Leach, Edmund R. 1954. *Political Systems of Highland Burma.* London: Bell.

———. 1964. 'Anthropological aspects of language: animal categories and verbal abuse.' In *New Directions in the Study of Language,* ed. E. H. Lenneberg. Cambridge MA: MIT Press, pp. 23–63.

———. 1967. Introduction to *The Structural Study of Myth and Totemism,* ed. E. R. Leach. London: Tavistock, pp. vii–xix.

———. 1970. *Claude Lévi-Strauss.* New York: Viking.

———. 1983. Unpublished letter to G. William Domhoff, 23 June 1983.

Leary, John D. 1995. *Violence and the Dream People: The Orang Asli in the Malayan Emergency, 1948–1960*. Athens OH: Ohio University Center for International Studies.

Lee, Dorothy. 1963. 'Freedom and social constraint.' In *The Concept of Freedom in Anthropology*, ed. David Bidney. The Hague: Mouton, pp. 61–73.

Lévi-Strauss, Claude. 1958. *Anthropologie Structurale*. Paris: Plon.

———. 1962a. *Le Totémisme Aujourd'hui*. Paris: PUF.

———. 1962b. *La Pensée Sauvage*. Paris: Plon.

———. 1962c. 'Rousseau, the father of anthropology.' *The Unesco Courier*, March 1962: 10–15.

———. 1963. *Totemism*. Translated by Rodney Needham. London: Merlin.

———. 1964. *Le Cru et le Cuit*. Paris: Plon.

Lévy-Bruhl, Lucien. 1975 [1938]. *The Notebooks on Primitive Mentality*. Translated by Peter Rivière. New York: Harper and Row.

Lewis, C. S. 1962 [1939]. 'Bluspels and flalanspheres: a semantic nightmare.' In *The Importance of Language*, ed. Max Black. Ithaca NY: Cornell University Press, pp. 36–50.

Lim Y. A. L., N. Romano, C. Nicholas, S. C. Chow & H. V. Smith. 2009. 'Intestinal parasitic infections amongst Orang Asli (indigenous) in Malaysia: Has socioeconomic development alleviated the problem?' *Tropical Biomedicine* 26: 110–122.

Lindskoog, Kathryn. 1981. 'A dream come untrue: the amazing story of Kilton Stewart's amazing story.' *Journal of the American Scientific Affiliation* 33: 180–182.

———. 1993. *Fakes, Frauds and Other Malarkey: 301 Amazing Stories and How Not to be Fooled*. Grand Rapids MI: Zondervan.

Linton, Ralph. 1936. *The Study of Man: An Introduction*. New York: Appleton-Century.

Lye Tuck-Po. 1994. 'Batek Hep: Culture, Nature, and the Folklore of a Malaysian Forest People.' Unpublished MA thesis, Honolulu: University of Hawai'i.

———. 2001. *Orang Asli of Peninsular Malaysia: A Comprehensive and Annotated Bibliography*. Kyoto: Center for Southeast Asian Studies, Kyoto University.

Lyon, M. L. 1979. 'The Dakwa movement in Malaysia.' *Review of Indonesian and Malayan Affairs* 13: 34–45.

MacEoin, Denis. 1985. 'Baha'ism.' In *A Handbook of Living Religions*, ed. John R. Hinnells. Harmondsworth: Penguin, pp. 475–498.

———. 1994. *Rituals in Babism and Baha'ism*. Pembroke Persian Papers, volume 2. London: British Academic Press.

Mahathir Mohamed. 1970. *The Malay Dilemma*. Singapore: Asia Pacific Press.

Maine, Henry. 1907. *Ancient Law*. New impression. London: John Murray.

Malaysian Baha'i News. Quarterly magazine ('for internal circulation only'). Kuala Lumpur: National Baha'i Spiritual Assembly.

Manickam, Sandra Khor. 2010. 'Taming Race: The Construction of Aborigines in Colonial Malaya, 1783–1937.' Unpublished PhD thesis, Canberra: Australian National University.

Marx, Karl. 1986 [1844]. 'Estranged labour.' From *The Economic and Philosophical Manuscripts of 1844*. In *Karl Marx: A Reader*, ed. Jon Elster. Cambridge: Cambridge University Press, pp. 35–47.

Massard, Josiane. 1983. *'Nous' Gens de Ganchong: Environnement et Échanges dans un Village Malais*. Paris: CNRS.

Massard, Josiane & Jeannine Koubi, ed. 1994. *Enfants et Sociétés d'Asie du Sud-est*. Paris: L'Harmattan.

Mauss, Marcel. 1938. 'Une catégorie de l'esprit humain: la notion de personne, celle de "moi".' *Journal of the Royal Anthropological Institute* 68: 263–281.

McHugh, J. N. 1955. *Hantu Hantu: An Account of Ghost Belief in Modern Malaya*. Singapore: Donald Moore.

McLuhan, Marshall. 1964. *Understanding Media*. London: Routledge & Kegan Paul.

McKinley, Robert. 1979. 'Zaman dan masa, eras and periods: religious evolution and the permanence of epistemological ages in Malay culture.' In *The Imagination of Reality: Essays in Southeast Asian Coherence Systems*, ed. Aram Yengoyan & Alton L. Becker. Norwood NJ: Ablex, pp. 303–324.

Means, Gordon P. 1985–86. 'The Orang Asli: Aboriginal policies in Malaysia.' *Pacific Affairs* 58: 637–652.

Means, Nathalie. 1998. *Temiar–English English–Temiar Dictionary*, ed. Gordon P. Means. St Paul: Hamline University Press.

Means, Paul. 2011. *The Story of the Sengoi Mission*, ed. Gordon P. Means. Singapore: Genesis Books.

Means, Paul & Nathalie Means. 1981. *And the Seed Grew*. Toronto: University of Toronto Press.

Middlebrook, S. M. 1933. 'Pulai: an early Chinese settlement in Kelantan.' *Journal of the Malayan Branch of the Royal Asiatic Society* 11: 151–156.

Milner, A. C. 1981. 'Islam and Malay kingship.' *Journal of the Royal Asiatic Society*: 46–70.

Mimica, Jadran F. 1981. 'Omalyce: An Ethnography of the Ikwaye View of the Cosmos.' Unpublished PhD thesis, Australian National University.

Mohamed Tap Bin Salleh. 1990. 'An Examination of Development Planning Among the Rural Orang Asli of West Malaysia.' Unpublished PhD dissertation, University of Bath.

Murphy, Robert. 1972. *The Dialectics of Social Life*. London: Allen and Unwin.

Nagata, Shuichi. 2010. 'Cəmam or sexual prohibition among the Kensiw of Kedah, Malaysia.' *Moussons: Recherche en Sciences Humaines sur l'Asie du Sud-Est* 16: 133–155.

Nah, Alice. 2004. 'Negotiating Orang Asli Identity in Postcolonial Malaysia.' Unpublished MSocSc thesis, Department of Sociology, National University of Singapore.

Nash, Manning. 1991. 'Islamic resurgence in Malaysia and Indonesia.' In *Fundamentalisms Observed*, ed. Martin E. Marty & R. Scott Appleby. Chicago: Chicago University Press, pp. 691–739.

Needham, Rodney. 1964. 'Blood, thunder, and mockery of animals.' *Sociologus (New Series)* 14: 136–149.

———. 1966. 'Age, category and descent.' *Bijdragen tot de Taal-, Land- en Volkenkunde* 122: 1–35.

New Straits Times. Daily newspaper, Kuala Lumpur.

Nicholas, Colin. 2008. 'The Orang Asli of Peninsular Malaysia: a brief introduction.' http://www.coac.org.my/codenavia/portals/coacv2/code/main/main_art.php?parentID=11497609537883&artID=11509699100857. Retrieved on 10 December 2008.

Nobuta, Toshihiro. 2006. *Living on the Periphery: Development and Islamization Among the Orang Asli in Malaysia*. Subang Jaya: Center for Orang Asli Concerns.

Nong Pai. Bimonthly magazine and newsletter, published by the Department of Aboriginal Affairs, Kuala Lumpur.

Noone, H. D. 1936. 'Report on the settlements and welfare of the Ple-Temiar Senoi of the Perak-Kelantan watershed.' *Journal of the Federated Malay States Museums* 19: 1–85.

———. 1937. 'Sakai drum heard on radio. Tribal life described in Singapore broadcast. Mr. H. D. Noone tells of Temiar customs.' [Text of a broadcast lecture.] *The Straits Times*, 16 January 1937, p. 13. Retrieved from: http://newspapers.nl.sg/Digitised/Article/straitstimes19370116-1.2.85.aspx.

———. 1941. 'Commentary on Temiar dream music.' Unpublished typescript for a radio broadcast, Malayan Broadcasting Corporation. In: the Robertson Senoi Collection, Museum of Archaeology and Anthropology, Cambridge University, http://www.dspace.cam.ac.uk/handle/1810/226416. [These notes were later incorporated into the booklet accompanying the following recording.]

———. 1955 [1941]. 'Introduction and notes' accompanying *Temiar Dream Songs from Malaya*. 12-inch 33 rpm gramophone record. New York: Ethnic Folkways Library album no. P. 140. Reissued on compact disc by the Smithsonian Museum, http://www.folkways.si.edu/temiar-dream-songs-from-malaya/islamica-psychology-health-world/album/smithsonian. [Reprinted as Appendix 1.2 in this volume.]

[Noone, H. D.] 1939. 'Chinchem: a study of the rôle of dream-experience in culture-contact amongst the Temiar Senoi of Malaya. Summary of a communication by H. D. Noone, M.A., Field Ethnographer, F.M.S. Government, 7 March 1939.' *Man* (April 1939): 57. [Reprinted as Appendix 1.4 in this volume.]

Noraini Awang Mat. 1992. 'Penglibatan dan Kesedaran Orang Asli Dalam Politik: Fokus Pilihanraya 1990 Kawasan Gua Musang, Kelantan.' Unpublished academic exercise, Department of Sociology and Anthropology, Universiti Malaya, Kuala Lumpur.

Norfariza Hanim Kassim. 2008. *Population and Housing Census of Malaysia 2000: Orang Asli in Peninsular Malaysia*. Monograph Series No. 3. Kuala Lumpur: Department of Statistics, Malaysia.

Notes and Queries. 1960. *Notes and Queries on Anthropology*, 6th edition. Prepared by a Committee of the Royal Anthropological Institute. London: Routledge & Kegan Paul.

O'Connor, Stanley. 1993. Letter to the author, 6 April 1993.

Obeyesekere, Gananath. 1968. 'Theodicy, sin and salvation in a sociology of Buddhism.' In *Dialectic in Practical Religion*, ed. E. R. Leach. Cambridge: Cambridge University Press, pp. 7–40.

Oey, Eric M. 1990. '"Psycho-collocations" in Malay: a Southeast Asian areal feature.' *Linguistics of the Tibeto-Burman Area* 13: 141–158.

Onfray, Michel. 2007. *In Defence of Atheism: The Case Against Christianity, Judaism and Islam*. Translated by Jeremy Leggatt. London: Serpent's Tail.

Parsons, Claudia. 1941. *Vagabondage*. London: Chatto & Windus.

Peacock, James L. 1986. 'The creativity of tradition in Indonesian religion.' *History of Religions* 25: 341–351.

Polanyi, Michael. 1959. *The Study of Man*. Chicago: University of Chicago Press.

———. 1964. *Personal Knowledge*. Revised edition. New York: Harper Torchbooks.

Polanyi, Michael & Harry Prosch. 1975. *Meaning*. Chicago: University of Chicago Press.

Prawiroatmojo, S. 1981. *Bausastera Jawa–Indonesia*. Second edition. Volume 1. Jakarta: Gunung Agung.

Quadens, Olga. 1990. *L'Architecture du Rêve: Du Cerveau à la Culture*. Louvain: Éditions Peeters.

Radcliffe-Brown, A. R. 1929. 'The sociological theory of totemism.' *Proceedings of the Fourth Pacific Science Congress, Java*, Volume II: 295–309. [Reprinted in Radcliffe-Brown 1959, pp. 117–132.]

———. 1945. 'Religion and society.' *Journal of the Royal Anthropological Institute* 75: 33–44. [Reprinted in Radcliffe-Brown 1959, pp. 153–177.]

———. 1951. 'The comparative method in social anthropology.' *Journal of the Royal Anthropological Institute* 81: 15–22.

————. 1959. *Structure and Function in Primitive Society*. London: Cohen and West.

Radin, Paul. 1953. *The World of Primitive Man*. New York: Schuman.

Randall, Alex. 2010. 'Comment from Alex Randall—1996.' *Sweet Dreams from Dr-Dream*. http://www.dr-dream.com/Senoi.html.

Ranee, Alina. 1995a. 'Integrating Orang Asli arts, culture.' *New Sunday Times*, 6 August 1995, p. 15.

————. 1995b. 'Tuning in to Temiar culture.' *New Straits Times*, 7 August 1995, 'Heritage', p. 8.

Reichle, Natasha. 2007. *Violence and Serenity: Late Buddhist Sculpture from Indonesia*. Honolulu: University of Hawai'i Press.

Rivers, P. J. 2010. 'Whither berhala?: The search for an idol.' *Journal of the Malaysian Branch of the Royal Asiatic Society* 84: 47–101.

Robarchek, Clayton A. 1987. 'Blood, thunder, and the mockery of anthropology: D. Freeman and the Semang thunder-god.' *Journal of Anthropological Research* 4: 273–300.

Robertson, E. D. 1955. 'Foreword.' In the enclosed notes to *Temiar Dream Songs from Malaya*, 12-inch 33 rpm gramophone record, New York: Ethnic Folkways Library album no. P. 460, pp. 1–2.

Roseman, Marina. 1984. 'The social structuring of sound: the Temiar of Peninsular Malaysia.' *Ethnomusicology* 27: 411–445.

————. 1990. 'Head, heart, odor, and shadow: the structure of the Self, the emotional world, and ritual performance among Senoi Temiar.' *Ethos* 18: 227–250.

————. 1991. *Healing Sounds from the Malaysian Rainforest: Temiar Music and Medicine*. Berkeley: University of California Press.

————. 1994. 'Les chants de rêve: des frontières mouvantes dans le monde temiar.' *Anthropologie et Sociétés* 18: 121–144.

————. 1995. *Dream Songs and Healing Sounds: In the Rainforests of Malaysia*. Compact disc recording with accompanying notes. Washington DC: Smithsonian / Folkways Recordings, no. SF CD 40417.

————. 2000. 'Shifting landscapes: musical mediations of modernity in the Malaysian rainforest.' *Yearbook for Traditional Music* 32: 31–65.

————. 2002. 'Engaging the spirits of modernity: the Temiars.' In *Tribal Communities in the Malay World: Historical, Cultural and Social Perspectives*, ed. Geoffrey Benjamin & Cynthia Chou. Leiden: International Institute for Asian Studies (IIAS) / Singapore: Institute of Southeast Asian Studies (ISEAS), pp. 185–205.

————. 2007. '"Blowing 'cross the crest of Mount Galeng": winds of the voice, winds of the spirits.' *Journal of the Royal Anthropological Institute (N.S.)*, S55–S69.

————. 2012a. 'Temiar cosmopolitan: indigenous knowledge in a globalising world.' In *Social Science and Knowledge in a Globalising World*, ed.

Zawawi Ibrahim. Petaling Jaya: Malaysian Association of Social Sciences (PSSN) *and* Strategic Information and Research Development Center (SIRD), pp. 389–407.

———. 2012b. 'Have the movements changed? Hybridity in the forests of Malaysia.' In *Dancing Mosaic: Issues on Dance Hybridity*, ed. Mohd Anis Md Nor. Kuala Lumpur: Cultural Centre University of Malaya *and* National Department for Culture and Arts (JKKN), Ministry of Information, Communication and Culture, pp. 286–298.

Rusaslina Idrus. 2010. 'From wards to citizens: Indigenous rights and citizenship in Malaysia.' *Political and Legal Anthropology Review* 33: 89–108.

———. 2011. 'The discourse of protection and the Orang Asli in Malaysia.' *Kajian Malaysia* 29 (Supp. 1): 53–74.

Sahlins, M. D. 1965. 'On the sociology of primitive exchange.' In *The Relevance of Models for Social Anthropology*, ed. Michael Banton. London: Tavistock, pp. 139–236.

Schebesta, Paul. 1926. 'The Jungle Tribes of the Malay Peninsula.' Translated by C. O. Blagden. *Bulletin of the School of Oriental Studies, University of London* 4: 269–278.

———. 1927. *Among the Forest Dwarfs of Malaya*. Translated by A. Chambers. London: Hutchinson and Co. (Second impression, 1973, with an 'Introduction' by Geoffrey Benjamin, pp. v–xii. Singapore: Oxford University Press.)

———. 1928. *Orang-Utan: Bei den Urwaldmenschen Malayas und Sumatras*. Leipzig: Brockhaus.

———. 1931. 'Grammatical sketch of the Ple-Temer language.' Translated by C. O. Blagden. *Journal of the Royal Asiatic Society 1931*: 641–652.

———. 1954. *Die Negrito Asiens, II (1): Wirtschaft und Soziologie*. Wien–Mödling: St Gabriel Verlag.

———. 1957. *Die Negrito Asiens, II (2): Religion und Mythologie*. Wien–Mödling: St Gabriel Verlag.

Schmidt, Wilhelm. 1912–55. *Der Ursprung der Gottesidee. Eine Historisch-kritische und Positive Studie*. 12 volumes. Münster: Aschendorff.

Scott, James C. 2009. *The Art of Not Being Governed: An Anarchist History of Upland Southeast Asia*. New Haven: Yale University Press.

Sharifah Zahhura S. A., P. Nilan & J. Germov. 2012. 'Food restrictions during pregnancy among indigenous Temiar women in Peninsular Malaysia.' *Malaysian Journal of Nutrition* 18: 243–253.

Shorto, H. L. 1971. *A Dictionary of the Mon Inscriptions from the Sixth to the Sixteenth Centuries*. London: Oxford University Press.

———. 2006. *A Mon-Khmer Comparative Dictionary*, ed. Paul Sidwell, Doug Cooper & Christian Bauer. Canberra: Pacific Linguistics.

Sinha, Vineeta. 1999. 'Constituting and re-constituting the religious domain in the modern nation state of Singapore.' In *Our Place in Time: Exploring*

Heritage and Memory in Singapore, ed. Kwok Kian-Woon, Kwa Chong Guan, Lily Kong & Brenda Yeoh. Singapore: The Singapore Heritage Society, pp. 76–95.

Skeat, W. W. 1900. *Malay Magic.* London: Macmillan. [Reprinted 1966, London: Frank Cass.]

Skeat, W. W. & C. O. Blagden. 1906. *Pagan Races of the Malay Peninsula.* Two volumes. London: Macmillan. [Reprinted 1966, London: Frank Cass.]

Slimming, John. 1958. *Temiar Jungle: A Malayan Journey.* London: John Murray.

Smith, Peter. 1978. 'Motif research: Peter Berger and the Baha'i faith.' *Religion* 8: 210–234.

———. 1987. *The Babi and Baha'i Religions: From Messianic Shi'ism to a World Religion.* Cambridge: Cambridge University Press.

Sorokin, P. 1957. *Social and Cultural Dynamics.* Boston: Porter Sargent.

Sperber, Dan. 1975. *Rethinking Symbolism.* Cambridge: Cambridge University Press.

Spiro, Melford. 1966. 'Religion: problems of definition and explanation.' In *Anthropological Approaches to the Study of Religion,* ed. Michael Banton. London: Tavistock, pp. 85–126.

Stacey, Tom. 1953. *The Hostile Sun: A Malayan Journey.* London: Duckworth.

Stargardt, Janice. 1973. 'The extent and limitations of Indian influences on the protohistoric civilizations of the Malay Peninsula.' In *South Asian Archaeology,* ed. Norman Hammond. London: Duckworth, pp. 278–303.

Stark, Rodney & W. S. Bainbridge. 1985. *The Future of Religion: Secularization, Revival, and Cult Formation.* Berkeley: University of California Press.

Stevens, Hrolf Vaughan. 1892. *Materialien zur Kenntniss der Wilden Stämme auf der Halbinsel Malâka.* Berlin: Veröffentlichungen aus dem Königlichen Museum für Völkerkunde. Berlin: W. Spemann / Georg Reimer.

———. 1894. *Materialien zur Kenntniss der Wilden Stämme auf der Halbinsel Malâka. II Theil,* ed. A. Grünwedel. Berlin: Veröffentlichungen aus dem Königlichen Museum für Völkerkunde. Berlin: W. Spemann / Georg Reimer.

———. 1902. 'Namengebung und Heirat bei den Ôrang Tĕmîa auf der Halbinsel Malaka.' *Globus: Illustrierte Zeitschrift for Länder- und Völkerkunde* 82 (16): 253–257.

Stewart, Kilton. Ms (ca. 1936). 'Journey of a psychologist.' Unpublished draft (by Nancy Grasby?) of an autobiography. [Chapter 7, 'Malaya', pp. 467–559, recounts his time among the Temiars with Noone during their first trip together.]

———. 1947. 'Magico-religious Beliefs and Practices in Primitive Society:

A Sociological Interpretation of their Therapeutic Aspects.' PhD thesis. London School of Economics. http://ethos.bl.uk/DownloadOrder. do?orderNumber=THESIS00529310.

———. 1951. 'Dream theory in Malaya.' *Complex* 6: 23–41 (Reprinted 1972 in *Psychological Perspectives: A Quarterly Journal of Jungian Thought* 3: 112–121.)

———. 1953. 'Culture and personality in two primitive groups.' *Complex* (Winter), 22 pages, unpaginated.

———. 1954. 'Mental hygiene and world peace.' *Mental Hygiene* 38: 387–403.

———. 1962. 'The dream comes of age.' *Mental Hygiene* 46: 230–237.

———. ca 1962. [Reprints of the above and other papers, along with some further discussion.] New York: The Stewart Foundation for Creative Psychology.

Strunz, Franz. 1985. 'Die Legende vom Wundervolk des Traums und die Wirklichkeit einer neuen Therapie.' *Gestalt Theory* 7: 182–200.

Subramanian, Yogeswaran. 2012. 'Orang Asli Land Rights by UNDRIP Standards in Peninsular Malaysia: An Evaluation and Possible Reform.' PhD thesis, University of New South Wales.

Svalastog, Anna-Lydia & Stefan Eriksson. 2010. 'You can use my name; you don't have to steal my story—a critique of anonymity in indigenous studies.' *Developing World Bioethics* 10: 104–110.

Tambiah, Stanley J. 1998. 'Edmund Ronald Leach, 1910–1989.' *Proceedings of the British Academy* 97: 293–346.

———. 2001. *Edmund Leach: An Anthropological Life*. Cambridge CA: Cambridge University Press.

Teoh, Shannon. 2011. 'Dr M: Malay claim to country stronger than Orang Asli's.' www.themalaysianinsider.com/malaysia/article/dr-m-malay -claim-to-country-stronger-than-orang-aslis. (Retrieved 1 March 2012.)

The Straits Times. Daily newspaper, Singapore.

Tönnies, F. 1955 [1887]. *Community and Association*. London: Routledge & Kegan Paul.

Twain, Mark. 1898. *Following the Equator*. Hartford: The American Publishing Company.

Tweedie, Michael W. F. & John L. Harrison. 1954. *Malayan Animal Life*. London: Longmans, Green.

Tylor, E. B. 1871. *Primitive Culture*. London: John Murray.

Van Baal, Jan. 1971. *Symbols for Communication: An Introduction to the Anthropological Study of Religion*. Assen: van Gorcum.

Wallis, Roy & Steve Bruce. 1995. 'Secularization: the orthodox model.' In *The Sociology of Religion, Volume I*, ed. Steve Bruce. Aldershot: Elgar, pp. 8–30.

Wavell, Stuart, Audrey Butt & Nina Epton. 1966. *Trances*. London: Allen and Unwin.

Weber, Max. 1952 [1917–19]. *Ancient Judaism*. Translated and edited by Hans H. Gerth & Don Martindale. New York: Free Press.

———. 1958a [1922–23]. 'The social psychology of the world religions.' In *From Max Weber: Essays in Sociology*, ed. H. H. Gerth & C. Wright Mills. New York: Oxford University Press, pp. 267–301.

———. 1958b [1918]. 'Science as a vocation.' In *From Max Weber: Essays in Sociology*, ed. H. H. Gerth & C. Wright Mills. New York: Oxford University Press, pp. 129–156.

———. 1958c. *From Max Weber: Essays in Sociology*. Translated by H. H. Gerth and C. Wright Mills. New York: Oxford University Press.

———. 1964 [1920]. *The Sociology of Religion*. Translated by Ephraim Fischoff. Boston: Beacon Press. [Revised translation in Weber 1978: 399–634.]

———. 1978. *Economy and Society: An Outline of Interpretive Sociology*, ed. Guenther Roth & Claus Wittich. Two volumes. Berkeley: University of California Press.

Wee, Vivienne. 1977. 'Religion and Ritual Among the Chinese of Singapore: an Ethnographic Study.' MSocSc thesis, University of Singapore.

———. 1987. 'Material dependence and symbolic independence: constructions of Melayu ethnicity in island Riau, Indonesia.' In *Ethnic Diversity and the Control of Natural Resources in Southeast Asia*, ed. A. Terry Rambo, Kathleen Gillogly & Karl L. Hutterer. University of Michigan Center for South and Southeast Asian Studies, pp. 197–226.

Weingartner, Rudolph. 1962. *Experience and Culture*. Middletown: Wesleyan University Press.

Werner, Roland. 1973. *Jah-Hut Art and Culture*. Kuala Lumpur: University of Malaya Press.

———. 1974. *Mah Meri of Malaysia: Art and Culture*. Kuala Lumpur: University of Malaya Press.

Wheatley, Paul. 1964. *Impressions of the Malay Peninsula in Ancient Times*. Singapore: Donald Moore.

———. 1983. *Nāgara and Commandery: Origins of the Southeast Asian Urban Tradition*. University of Chicago, Department of Geography, Research Papers no. 207–208.

Wilkinson, R. J. 1959 [1932]. *A Malay–English Dictionary*. Two volumes. London: Macmillan.

Williams-Hunt, P. R. 1952. *An Introduction to the Malayan Aborigines*. Kuala Lumpur: FMS Government.

———. 1954–55. 'A Lanoh Negrito funeral.' *Federation Museums Journal* 1&2: 64–74.

Winstedt, Richard O. 1927. 'The great flood, 1926.' *Journal of the Malayan Branch of the Royal Asiatic Society* 5: 295–309.

Worsley, Peter M. 1956. 'Émile Durkheim's theory of knowledge.' *Sociological Review (New Series)* 4: 47–62.

———. 1967. 'Groote Eylandt totemism and "Le Totémisme Aujourd'hui".' In *The Structural Study of Myth and Totemism*, ed. E. R. Leach. London: Tavistock, pp. 141–160.

Yegar, Moshe. 1979. *Islam and Islamic Institutions in British Malaya: Policies and Implementation*. Jerusalem: Magnes Press.

Zawawi Ibrahim. 1995. 'Regional development in rural Malaysia and the "tribal question".' University of Hull, Centre for South-East Asian Studies, *Occasional Paper* no. 28.

———. ed. 1996. *Kami Bukan Anti-pembangunan! Bicara Orang Asli Menuju Wawasan 2020*. Kuala Lumpur: Persatuan Sains Sosial Malaysia.

Index

Temiar words are alphabetised in the following order: ʔ (ʔ), a, aa, b, c, d, e, ee, ə, əə, ɛ, ɛɛ, g, h, i, ii, j, k, l, m, n, ŋ, ɲ, o, oo, ɔ, ɔɔ, p, r, s, t, u, uu, ʉ, ʉʉ, w, y

ʔalʉj (deity), 64, 138–139, 143, 180, 182, 193–198, 221–223, 225–226, 229–230, 317, 321–322, 351, 365–367, 370, 372–373, 375–378, 380–382
ʔalʉj Səlamad (new religion), 13, 32, 40, 82, 187, 221, 339, 345–346, 350, 357, 366–367, 370–383, 407
ʔeŋkuuʔ (deity), 60–61, 90, 143, 198, 215, 224–226, 229–230, 403
see also Karey

Abilem Lum, xvi, 245–246, 332–334, 398
ABIM (Malaysian Islamic youth movement), 357
Aboriginal Malay (ethnic group), 44, 174, 298
Aboriginal Peoples Act, 24, 328, 360
Aboriginal Peoples Ordinance, 328
Aboriginal Tribes Enactment, 328
Aborigines, Malayan, 44, 78, 142–143, 153, 263, 272
see also Orang Asli
Adi Haji Taha, 20, 329–331
Ading Kerah, 181, 331–332, 336, 344, 394, 397–400

afterlife, 95, 117–119, 139–141, 144, 182, 187, 250, 306, 405
animals in Temiar religion, 76–105
animism, 6, 7, 10–11, 14, 16, 34, 215, 259–262, 264–272, 274–278, 283–285, 289, 304–307, 347, 356, 390
Malay animism, 262–264, 269, 271–272, 274–278

Baha'a'llah (founder of Baha'i), 314, 317–318
Baha'i (religion), 8, 11–13, 40, 274, 276, 303–304, 308–309, 311–328, 334–336, 338–339, 344, 347–351, 357, 365, 371, 378–380, 383
outline of Baha'i, 314–315
Baharon Azhar bin Raffie'i, xiv, 60, 143
Batek (ethnic group), 9, 57, 60, 125, 178, 180–182, 184, 265–267, 306–307, 401
Batuuʔ Baloʔ (reputed world column), 117, 178–179, 182, 401
Batuuʔ Gərɛm (reputed world column), 55–56, 58, 181
Becker, Alton, 10
Bellah, Robert, 7, 10

Ber valley, 124, 177, 187, 255, 317, 372, 376, 386, 396, 397, 402

Berger, Peter, 18, 304, 307

Bɛrwɛɛs (song genre), 180, 402

Biles, Howard, xiv, 415

Blagden, C. O., 15, 115, 160, 174
  see also Skeat, W. W.

blood, x, 77, 80, 85–86, 98, 105, 106, 110, 115–116, 121, 123, 126–128, 192, 198, 254, 270, 284, 286, 288, 291–297
  blood-offering, 103–104, 125, 128, 149–153, 293–295, 296
  menstrual, 126, 129, 132, 288, 296, 300

blowing (as a ritual), 121, 147–148, 150, 165–166, 168–170, 174, 176, 181, 182, 185, 198–199, 248–249, 251–252, 254, 255, 293, 295
  see also ritual

blowpipe poisons, 142, 144, 186, 402

Bolton, Malcolm, xiv, 2, 81, 109, 212, 220

bomoh (Malay traditional healer), 216, 268, 313, 324

Brahminism, 274–275

Brok valley, 41, 61, 114, 117, 140, 166, 186–187, 213, 255, 394

Buddhism, 20, 274–275, 277, 329–330, 347
  votive tablets, 329–331, 335

Bumiputera, 326, 347–348

burial, *see* death, burial

cacii² (dance type), 171, 183, 249, 387, 395, 396, 399

Carey, Iskandar, xiv, 32–33, 60, 115, 308–309, 316, 398

cash, 23, 155, 177, 276, 278, 316, 325, 326, 328, 338, 342–343, 350, 354, 357, 412

cassava, 22, 63, 67, 75, 87, 113, 127, 133, 136, 145, 148, 203, 208, 230–233, 341, 372, 378, 409, 411, 415

Cawan, Penghulu, 55, 171, 178, 183, 394, 398–401

Centre for Orang Asli Concerns (COAC), 132, 342, 348, 354, 358, 360
  see also Nicholas, Colin

cə²aay (harmful emanation from a slaughtered animal), 86, 292, 296

cənacii², *see cacii²*

Cənolɛɛs (song genre), 399

cənɔy (spirit-guide, Jahai), 266–267, 270, 273, 398
  see also spirit-guide

cənɔɔy (spirit-guide, Temiar), 35, 264, 270, 398
  see also gunig, spirit-guide

Cɛŋkey (spirit-mountain), 63–65, 93, 118, 182, 219

childbirth, 11, 128, 263, 280, 291, 294, 297
  confinement 286–288
  death from, 279, 288
  post-natal ablutions, 129, 131
  rituals, 128–129, 281

childhood and parenthood, 285–295

child-rearing, 281–282, 379

Chinchem (song genre), *see* Ciŋcɛm

Chinese (ethnic group), 183, 185, 279, 315, 321–322, 325, 330, 332, 346, 347, 354, 362–365, 364, 393, 409

Chitu (ancient kingdom), 330

Chou, Cynthia, 368

Christianity, 11, 13, 40, 274–277, 308–309, 324, 340, 347, 350, 358–370, 378–380, 383

Chrystal, Robert, 26

Ciŋcɛm (song genre), 118, 143, 184,

186, 358, 377, 383, 387–389, 397, 399–400
Clifford, Hugh, 24, 204, 325
Communists, 1, 21, 26, 308, 321, 325–329, 345
conception and pregnancy, 81, 279–280, 285–287, 291
Constitution of Malaysia, *see* Malaysian Constitution
conversion, 13, 107, 276, 304, 307–321, 324–325, 346–352, 355, 360–366, 379, 381–382, 396
Corner, E. J. H., 43
cosmology, x, 55–75, 118, 189, 271
creation myths, 62–65, 73, 74, 88, 89, 90, 92, 93, 95, 99, 113, 127, 138, 180, 198, 218–219, 379
crime, 102, 203–204
culture and nature, xi, 3, 53, 68, 71–73, 79, 84, 92, 96–97, 104, 110, 125–128, 141, 149, 153, 178, 188, 190, 193–194, 207, 216–218, 221, 227, 265

Dalam, Penghulu, 94, 109, 124, 135, 150–151, 165, 181, 214, 245, 248–252, 256–258, 306–307, 313, 317–322, 324, 331, 333, 405–407, 416
dance types, 394–396
Dato' Leŋri' (Kelantan state *as* a spirit-guide), 177, 182, 202, 255
Datok Bintang (well-known 1930s spirit-medium), 187, 389, 397
death and burial, 96, 106, 132–144, 149, 405–413
    exposed burial, 96–97, 104, 132, 135, 191, 220–221, 257–258
demoniac trees (*mergəəh*), 71, 95, 122, 125, 176
demons, 57, 109, 110, 114, 137, 142, 176, 183, 263, 313, 390

Dentan, Robert, 5, 31–33, 44, 60, 125, 143, 160, 186, 207–208, 279, 281, 293, 295–296, 395, 342
Department of Aboriginal Affairs, *see* JHEOA
Department of Orang Asli Affairs, *see* JHEOA
dialecticism, 7–9, 14–15, 19, 23, 34, 37, 40, 70, 111, 115, 144, 159, 198, 199, 242, 261–262, 265, 278, 279–280, 282–283, 285, 289–290, 292, 295, 297, 299, 304, 323, 380
dietary rules, 65, 76–80, 82–84, 129, 155, 159, 180, 186, 280, 285–297, 352
    see also food taboos
Diffloth, Gérard, xvi, 11–12, 34, 87, 99, 120, 125, 186, 217, 289, 291, 298
diseases, totemic, 106–110
disenchantment, 12, 301–303, 306–314, 334–338, 339, 349, 388
    see also rationality, re-enchantment
domestic animals, xi, 65, 77–80, 96, 101, 104, 123, 124, 127, 191
Domhoff, G. William, xvi, 25–27, 29–32, 239
Douglas, Mary, 6, 53, 260–261
dreams and dreaming, 11, 14, 53, 63, 82, 84–85, 102, 109, 111–114, 115, 117, 120, 122, 124, 145, 156–159, 184, 186–187, 197–198, 224, 239–240, 243, 254–256, 265, 270, 290, 292, 296, 322, 333, 372, 387–393, 400, 414–416
    'dream control', 26–27, 29–32, 157, 239
    dreams, and *gunig* spirit-guides, 159–161, 169–170, 172, 176–177

Senoi Dreamwork, 26–40, 82, 384

Durkheim, Émile, 5, 31, 48, 51–52, 305

Endicott, Kirk, 6, 10–11, 16, 60, 68, 261, 263, 265–267, 270, 273, 280, 293, 325, 335, 342, 401

Evans, I. H. N., 31, 43–44, 52, 56, 59, 101, 103, 118, 136, 143, 149, 152, 173, 176, 204–205, 218, 260, 265, 273, 305, 398

eye-soul, 111, 116–117, 124, 266
  see also kɛnlɔɔk

Fire, as deity, 62, 219

fire, 37, 61, 62, 64, 72, 88–89, 92, 94–95, 100, 109, 113, 129, 130, 137, 146, 151, 153, 157, 161, 164, 167, 174, 175, 191, 192, 217, 220, 232, 248, 252, 253, 256, 318, 386, 391, 392, 402, 404
  graveside fires, 133–136, 139, 140, 143, 409, 411

Firth, Raymond, 28, 114, 155

food crops, 23, 47, 63, 65, 73, 75, 77, 87, 113, 119, 127, 156, 190, 210, 217, 230, 237, 389–390

food taboos, 65, 81, 82, 84–85, 88–89, 131, 155, 186, 280, 286, 289, 291, 294, 296, 318, 321, 378
  see also dietary rules

Fort Brooke, xv, 42, 176, 247, 253, 321

Fortes, Meyer, xiv, 41, 53, 54, 305

forest, attitudes towards, 66–72, 77, 83, 86, 94, 96–97, 100, 103–104, 118, 119, 127, 131, 189–191, 195, 244–245, 294, 356

fruit trees, seasonal, see seasonal fruit trees

Galɛɛŋ (spirit-mountain), 58, 172, 200–201, 242, 257, 330
  see also Gunung Ayam

Gamɔʔ (song genre), 402

gayoŋ (dance type), 395

Geertz, Clifford, 6, 47–48, 50–52, 76, 211, 275

Gellner, Ernest, 6, 12, 60, 277, 305–307, 310, 324, 370, 388

gender relations, 23, 37, 68, 73, 81, 83–84, 86, 104, 116, 131, 146, 161–163, 165, 208–209, 287, 292, 310, 312, 314, 352, 370
  see also sexual relations

gɛnhaaʔ (disease), 11, 72, 80, 84, 86–98, 102–105, 125–127, 186, 190–191, 205–206, 217, 221, 397

gɛrsaak (dance type), 387, 394–395

good and evil, xi–xii, 53, 60, 77, 101–102, 105, 143, 153, 158, 178, 184, 191, 194–199, 202, 206–207, 210, 265, 270, 278, 313
  Leach on, 216–220, 235–236

Great Flood of 1926, 99, 183, 399–400

ground/off-the-ground distinction, x, 23, 71–72, 75, 80, 87–89, 92–98, 104, 106–109, 121, 126–127, 129, 131–133, 140, 163, 172, 175–176, 178–182, 190–194, 198–199, 201–202, 217, 220–221, 285–287, 313, 343

gunig (spirit-guide), 35, 40, 84, 102, 113, 159, 181, 199, 202, 218, 243, 245, 250–253, 255, 258, 264, 270, 365, 375–376, 378, 386–387, 397–399, 401–404, 414, 416
  see also spirit-guide

Gunung Ayam (mountain), 200–201, 330
  see also Galɛɛŋ

hair, x, 106, 108, 111, 121, 126–127,
131, 137, 147, 149, 151, 153,
192, 223, 226, 249, 284, 290,
296, 352
halaa² (spirit-medium), 35–37, 40,
115, 135, 155, 160, 169, 172–
173, 184, 218, 220, 239, 253,
255–256, 259, 270, 294, 313,
318, 322–324, 365–366, 371,
375, 387, 401
see also mediumship, shamanism
Hantu Raya (Malay forest ghost),
263, 294
Hazera, Eduardo, xvi, 13, 340,
366–368
head-soul, *see rɔwaay*
heart-soul, *see hup* and *jɔrɔɔk*
heaven and earth, constitution of,
55–62
Hinduism, 20, 335, 347
Hitam Tamboh, Penghulu, 38, 72,
94–95, 121, 155–156, 169–170,
199, 250, 318, 349, 357, 394,
396–399, 403, 412–413
hum-boo² (normality/culture), 64,
194
Humid (village, river), xv, 1, 2, 22,
36, 41, 42, 46, 55, 62, 67, 69,
73, 81, 85, 88, 99, 122, 140–
145, 147, 151, 152, 155–156,
162–163, 169, 172, 180, 181,
199, 200, 206, 214–216, 243,
248–253, 257–258, 306, 335,
341, 346, 348–349, 371, 394,
396, 405–408
hun-tɛ² (disorder/nature), 68, 193–
194, 217, 232, 249
hup (heart-soul), 11, 34–37, 40,
75, 110–111, 114–117, 121,
126, 159, 163–165, 185, 191,
193–194, 199, 224, 241, 256,

264–266, 283–284, 288–289,
291–300, 375, 386
see also *jɔrɔɔk*

identity card, 340, 346, 347, 356,
364
incest, 6, 63, 102, 104, 110, 152,
206, 235
infancy and childhood, 11, 84, 192,
279–300
Islam, 11, 13, 20, 40, 45, 274–278,
295, 308–314, 323–324, 326,
336, 339, 347–348, 350–359,
363–364, 378–380, 383

Jahai (ethnic group), 9, 44, 55,
57–58, 60, 64, 66, 118, 121, 125,
173, 175, 177, 179, 180–182,
255, 320, 397–399, 401
Jah Hut (ethnic group), 1, 10, 272–
273, 324
JAKIM (Jabatan Kemajuan Islam
Malaysia), 354, 357–358
Jakun (ethnic group), 44, 173, 263,
385
Jalong (village), 27–30, 63, 253,
259, 350, 357, 388
Japanese occupation, 26, 184, 391
JAKOA, *see* JHEOA
Jennings, Sue, 4–5, 29, 31–34, 37,
40, 79, 95, 107, 111, 115, 127,
132, 160, 245, 248, 250, 281,
284, 296, 300, 303, 306, 316,
333, 386, 394, 407
jɔrɔɔk (heart- or blood-soul), 111,
114–115, 117, 121, 126, 159,
164, 173, 199, 258, 292
see also *hup*
JHEOA (Department of Orang Asli
Affairs), 2, 25, 32, 183, 216,
308–309, 311, 316, 319–323,

325, 333–334, 342, 345–346,
348–349, 352–354, 356, 360,
375, 381, 415
Jidaʔ, 82, 370–376, 407–408
Jiɲjaŋ (song genre, dance type),
170–171, 396–397, 399
joluŋ (disease), 38, 80, 87, 102, 123,
168, 198, 218, 254
joruuʔ (acts that scare spirit-guides
away), 80, 95, 97, 102–105, 168,
191, 318

kahyɛk (watery spirit-guide
manifestation at séances), 35,
40, 114, 120–121, 126–127,
163–165, 169, 173, 180, 199,
245, 253–254, 256–257, 264,
292, 300, 386, 397, 401–403
Karey (thunder deity), 34–35, 58,
60–61, 65, 71, 98–99, 101–102,
105, 110, 120, 125, 128, 138–
139, 142–144, 150–153, 195–
199, 206, 214–215, 217–219,
230, 235–236, 238, 281, 293,
322, 370, 378, 380, 403
story of, 221–229
see also ʔɛŋkuuʔ
Kensiw (ethnic group), 9, 57, 64,
119, 402
Kermal, Cik Gu, 317–319, 321–323,
338
kəbut (séance in the dark; tiger-
medium's hut), 102, 173, 175,
184, 253–255, 398–399, 401,
403–404
Kədəŋ (song genre), 401
Kəladiih (song genre), 404
kənoruk (lower soul of trees and
animals), 35, 102, 121–127, 131,
173, 176, 178, 199, 254, 256,
264, 291–292, 298

kɛnlɔɔk (eye-soul), 111, 116, 124,
266, 291, 386
see also eye-soul
kɛrjɛɛr (dance type), 395
kinɔd (dance type), 395
kinship, 21, 23, 41, 45, 47, 54, 79,
89, 163–164, 186, 193–194, 207,
218, 223–224, 226, 238, 241,
282, 288, 295, 370
Kintaq (ethnic group), 9, 59
Kuala Betis (village), 135, 182–184,
216, 252, 313–314, 317, 323,
335, 340, 350, 352, 365, 396,
398, 400
Kuɲciiʔ (song genre), 401

Lambok (village), 39, 40, 58,
124, 162, 165, 184, 216, 217,
244, 245, 256, 294, 312, 316,
317, 319, 321–324, 328, 329,
331–333, 350, 352, 358, 359,
370–371, 373, 376, 377–378,
396–397, 400, 402, 415
Land rights, contemporary, 24, 97,
259, 309, 341, 344, 364, 368,
381
land rights, traditional, 73, 75,
96–97, 119, 190–191, 285
Lanoh (ethnic group), 9, 44, 58,
60, 62, 64, 95, 119, 143, 173,
179–181, 316, 345, 398–399,
402–403, 405
Leach, Edmund, x, xiv, 2–5, 8–9,
17, 25–26, 28, 30–32, 41, 53, 57,
104, 195, 212–238
Lee, Dorothy, 48–50
Lévi-Strauss, Claude, 5–6, 8, 53–54,
179, 188, 212, 219–221, 228–
229, 235, 238, 282
Lewis, C. S., 18, 376
Limbaŋ (primordial flood), 63, 99,
300

Lim Kok Hoon, 316, 320
linguistic etymologies, 11, 34, 35,
    64, 79, 81, 85, 87, 98, 102,
    114–115, 160, 165, 173, 183,
    193, 194, 204, 291, 298–299,
    367, 372
literacy, 281, 326, 333, 337, 343
Lord's Prayer in Temiar, 367–369

Mah Meri (ethnic group), 1, 10,
    272–273, 324
Malay (ethnic group and cultural
    tradition), 2, 6, 9–11, 20–23, 27–
    28, 32, 34–35, 44, 56–58, 60, 67,
    71, 73, 74, 77–78, 81, 85–88, 90,
    94, 96, 98, 102, 109–110, 115–
    117, 121–122, 125, 135, 147,
    152, 160–161, 168, 173–174,
    178, 181–185, 196, 200–202,
    204, 208–209, 215–216, 219,
    221–224, 233, 239, 241, 251–
    253, 258, 260–264, 266–279,
    281, 286–288, 291, 294–295,
    299, 309–311, 313, 315–317,
    319–328, 330, 333, 335, 339,
    342–343, 347–348, 350–354,
    356–358, 363–368, 370, 373,
    382, 388–389, 391–392, 396–
    397, 399–404, 415
    Malay animism, 15, 161, 184,
        260, 267, 269–271, 277–278
Malay (national language), 23, 281,
    313, 315, 326
Malayan Emergency, 1, 21, 327, 346
Malaysian Baha'i News, 315, 320,
    328
Malaysian Constitution, 346, 354,
    362
Malaysian Department of Islamic
    Development, *see* JAKIM
Malaysian Islamic Dakwah
    Foundation (YADIM), 355
Malaysian Islamic youth movement
    (ABIM), 357
*mamə*ʔ (disease), 109, 191
mamɛɛŋ (disease), 109, 191, 216
many-stranded and single-stranded
    relations, 60, 314, 324, 326, 337,
    370
    Temiar religion as many-
        stranded, 60, 304–307, 370
McKinley, Robert, xvi, 7, 310
Means, Gordon, 308, 315, 359
Means, Nathalie, 61, 115, 308, 309,
    315, 359, 382
mediumship, xii, 3, 9, 14, 18, 30,
    32, 33, 35–40, 53, 57–58, 61,
    63, 64, 79, 102, 104, 106, 109,
    112–115, 120, 121, 124, 126,
    138, 140, 143, 145–146, 155–
    187, 191–192, 195–196, 199,
    200–202, 214–216, 239–259,
    266–271, 288, 292, 293, 294,
    318, 322, 324, 332, 333–334,
    335, 357, 362, 365–366, 375,
    385–386, 388–390, 395, 396–
    397, 399–404
    areal aspects of mediumship,
        178–182, 189
    great (tiger-)mediumship, 37,
        77, 96, 115, 117, 123, 173–
        176, 179–181, 191, 199,
        201–202, 253–258, 306,
        399–400, 403
    'Malay-style' mediumship,
        182–184, 313, 396, 400, 402
    phenomenology of mediumship,
        239–248
    *see also halaa*ʔ
Menriq (ethnic group), 9, 44, 55, 57,
    64, 124, 178–184, 266, 307, 333,
    394, 401
menstruation, ritual bathing and,
    130–132, 297
mental illness, 33

mɛrgəəh, *see* demoniac trees
millet, 22, 63, 74, 87, 113, 156, 196–197, 222, 226
misik (thunder-attracting acts), 35, 38, 69, 80, 95, 98–103, 105, 120, 153, 195, 198, 217–218, 254, 318
missionaries, 325, 346
    Baha'i, 315, 325
    Christian, 61, 107, 324, 359, 362, 364, 367–368, 379
    Muslim, 308, 354–355, 358–359, 364, 365, 367, 379
Mojiiⁱ (song genre), 401
monotheism, 13, 16, 40, 270, 278, 303, 305, 307, 314, 322, 326, 328, 345, 347, 350, 368, 370, 376, 378–390
moon, 57–60
    lunar-cycle work taboos, 59–60, 68, 210, 217
mourning, 39–40, 139, 141, 144–149, 161, 192, 215, 248–253, 376
mythology, Temiar, 43, 55, 59–65, 81, 84, 88–93, 95–96, 118, 122, 138–144, 178, 180–182, 189, 194–198, 205, 217–238, 281, 321–322, 370, 372, 378, 380

naming system, 47, 79, 133, 207, 282
nature and culture, *see* culture and nature
Needham, Rodney, 54, 67, 84, 103, 110, 149, 152–154, 304
Negritos, 3, 44–45, 57–58, 103, 118, 173, 177, 179–180, 182–184, 193, 204, 266, 398
Nenggiri river, 64, 177, 178, 180, 181, 182–183, 186, 311, 317,

328, 330, 333, 359, 399–400, 402
Ngah Sidek (well-known 1960s medium), 185
Nicholas, Colin, xvii, 303, 358, 362
    see also Centre for Orang Asli Concerns
Nong Pai (magazine), 308
Noone, H. D., 1, 14, 24–30, 77, 97, 113–116, 143, 157, 162, 182, 185–186, 204, 214–215, 259, 348, 359, 364, 368, 382, 385–389, 391, 393–395, 397, 400

O'Connor, Stanley, 329
Orang Asli, 1–3, 5, 9, 11, 13, 20, 23–25, 33, 55, 97, 160, 173, 178, 180, 184–185, 210, 259–261, 266, 272, 274–276, 295, 304, 307, 315, 319–322, 324–328, 335–336, 342–343, 345–351, 353–356, 358–362, 364, 380–381, 388, 397
    see also Aborigines, Malayan
Orang Suku Laut (ethnic group), 368, 370
ownability and unownability, 73–75, 92, 96–98, 189–190, 217, 221

Paad (demon), 109–110, 126, 191
panɔh (tiger-medium's hut), 173, 403
panɔɔh, *see panɔh*
parenthood, 129–130, 280, 282, 285, 287–288, 290, 295, 299
Parsons, Claudia, 27, 30, 204
PAS (Islamist party), 311, 381
Pawun (song genre), 403
peasantisation, 23, 275–276, 301, 325, 335, 342

Perolak valley, 36, 38, 41, 46, 58,
    61–62, 67, 89, 94, 100, 117, 134,
    155, 163, 176–177, 184, 186,
    250, 255, 321, 325, 350, 394,
    396–397
Pərɛŋgan (song genre), 404
pərɛnlʉb, see *pɛrlʉb*
pəsoor (to leave grave offerings),
    405, 412
pətərii² (peak-soul of mountain), 35,
    120–122, 126–127, 201, 264
pɛhnɔɔh (séance), *see pɔɔh*
    see also séance
Pɛnhəəy (song genre), 398
pɛnsoor, see *pəsoor*
pɛrlʉb (to instill a spirit-guide), 40,
    165–166, 170, 176, 199, 254–
    255, 396, 399
picəə² (dance type), 395
plants in Temiar religion, 76–105
Plus valley, 3, 24, 64, 65, 117, 184,
    187, 253, 255, 303, 400
pocuk (disease), 11, 80, 85–86,
    104–105, 123–124, 126–127,
    190, 290, 292, 294
Podɛɛw (deity), 118, 182
Polanyi, Michael, 7, 14, 336
potərii², *see pətərii²*
pɔɔh (to hold a séance), 102, 173,
    183, 191, 245, 248–255, 313,
    366, 373–375, 377, 382, 396,
    399, 400
    pɛhnɔɔh séances, healing
        benefit of, 248–253
    pɛhnɔɔh ʔalʉj, 373–374, 377
    see also séance
prophet, 308, 314, 318, 327, 347,
    366, 388
    emissary prophet, 12, 302–303,
        327, 334, 337
    exemplary prophet, 12, 302–
        303, 335, 338

Radcliffe-Brown, A. R., 2, 5, 48, 51,
    204
Radio Malaysia, 208, 333, 343, 376,
    397
radio broadcasts, 25, 214, 333, 376,
    381, 386, 389, 397, 399, 400
ramage (cognatic descent-group),
    22, 46–47, 73
Rank, Otto, 27
rationality, 12, 40, 277, 301–307,
    310, 314, 318, 324, 326, 327–
    328, 337–339, 342, 388
    see also disenchantment, re-
        enchantment
re-enchantment, 12, 301, 303–304,
    314, 328–338, 339, 346, 388
    see also disenchantment,
        rationality
religion (theory of), 5, 7, 11, 14–19,
    47–52
    religions and the Malaysian
        state, 345–349
relocation settlements, 23, 316, 325,
    328, 348
Rening (village), 26, 30, 42, 69, 81,
    83, 118, 134–138, 140, 142–145,
    151, 204, 220, 389, 402
rəwaay (head-soul), 11, 34–37, 40,
    87, 95, 110–114, 116, 118, 120–
    121, 123, 125–126, 130–131,
    135, 144, 159, 168, 191, 245,
    364–365, 283–284, 287–292,
    296–300, 386
rɛywaay (head-soul loss), 112–114,
    125–128, 130, 192, 245, 282,
    288
Rɛm²um (well-known 1960s tiger-
    medium), 177, 255
Rɔŋgɛŋ (song genre), 402–403
rice, 20, 22, 38, 45, 74, 87, 113, 127,
    145, 215, 263, 322, 341, 372
Riɲjoŋ (song genre), 402
ritual, xi–xii, 5, 16, 18, 36–38, 44,

69, 72, 79–80, 88, 93–99, 103–
105, 168–170, 178–179, 190–
192, 198–199, 210–211, 215,
220, 239–240, 278, 280–281,
286–289, 292–297, 305
occasional and ceremonial
rituals, 128–149
thunder rituals, 149–153
see also blowing
river systems, 64–66
Robertson, E. D., 389
Robertson, Peggy, 26, 391
Roseman, Marina, 1, 4–5, 23,
33–34, 37, 40, 79–80, 111, 113,
115–117, 121, 160, 169, 172,
178, 183–184, 187, 199, 242,
245, 248, 281–284, 287, 291,
293, 303, 306, 313, 316, 318,
323, 331–334, 386, 388, 394,
397–398, 400, 402–403

sabat (disease), 11, 80–86, 88, 93,
101, 105, 190, 287, 290–294,
296
Sakai (obsolete term for Orang
Asli), 24, 27, 203–204, 359, 385
Salleh, 36, 38, 152, 172, 248–252
Salɛh, *see* Saleh
sarak (undergound soul of
mountain), 35, 102, 117, 121–
122, 124, 126–127, 173, 176,
201, 254, 257, 264
Schebesta, Paul, 11, 24, 43–44,
59–60, 98–99, 101, 103, 115,
118–119, 125, 149, 152–153,
173, 175–176, 181, 265, 270,
273–274, 326, 398, 405
séance, 38–40, 57, 95, 102, 113,
117, 120, 123, 145, 148, 155,
161–170, 172–173, 175, 181–
184, 189, 198–199, 218, 241,
244–245, 248, 250–257, 259,

270, 324, 332, 357, 366, 382,
386, 397, 400
seasonal fruit trees, 35, 46, 61, 64–
65, 73–75, 95–96, 98, 113–114,
119, 122–123, 127, 172, 189–
190, 195, 242, 270, 399
Second World War, 21, 31, 314,
318, 332, 391
Semai (ethnic group), 5, 9, 24, 31–
33, 42, 44, 59, 64, 87, 103, 111,
119, 125, 143, 152, 160, 163,
174, 180, 185, 199, 208, 276,
278–279, 289, 295–296, 308–
309, 315–317, 320–321, 324,
350, 356, 359, 362–365, 382,
385, 394–395, 401–402, 404
semangat (Malay, 'soul'), 87, 110,
262–264, 266, 278, 288
Semangat 46, Partai Melayu (former
political party), 311, 380–381
Semang (societal tradition), 10, 11,
14, 118, 160, 236,
Semang religion, 11, 176, 261–
262, 264, 265–274, 276
Semnam (ethnic group), 64, 95, 402
Senoi Dreamwork
(psychotherapeutic movement),
see dreams and dreaming
Seri Kelantan (new spirit-guide),
333–335
sexual relations, 97,100, 101, 104,
113, 128, 130, 131–132, 145,
163, 167, 186, 203, 206, 224–
228, 238, 281, 285–286
see also gender relations
səlantab (obligation to offer food),
87, 204–206
Səlumbaŋ (song genre), 38, 58, 99,
183–186, 199, 253, 396, 399–
400, 403
Səribuuʔ (song genre), 403–404
sɛʔnooʔ, *see sooʔ*
sɛʔsooʔ, *see sooʔ*

shadow-soul, *see wɔɔg*

shamanism, 3, 9, 155, 179, 257, 267, 269, 386, 390
    see also halaaʔ, mediumship

Shari'a law, 310, 354

Shi'ite, 310, 314

shrine, 61, 331–333, 335, 338, 344, 346

silaʔ (dance type), 395

Simmel, Georg, 261

sisɛʔ (dance type), 395

Skeat, W. W., 86, 109, 215, 260
    Skeat & Blagden, 149, 236

social control, 46, 158, 195, 202–206

sociocentricity, 264, 271–274, 324, 335

song genres, 397–404

song lyrics, 37, 147, 159, 162, 164, 167, 169–170, 174–175, 185, 195, 199–202, 214–215, 249, 373, 375–377, 399, 401, 403, 404

Soo, Moses, 362–366

sooʔ (to cure by mediumistic means), 199, 321, 349, 362, 376, 405–406

sorcery, 104, 184–185, 270, 402

soul, concept of, *see* animism
    Temiar concepts of soul, 110–125

soul beliefs as nature/culture, 125–128, 262

soul-loss, 39, 95, 114, 268–269, 280, 282–283, 289–290, 295, 388

Sperber, Dan, 7, 15

spirit-guide, 30, 35, 37, 40, 57–58, 63, 66, 80, 84, 102–103, 113–114, 117, 120, 126, 140, 142, 145, 156, 159–177, 180, 182–183, 185, 189, 191–92, 198–202, 214–215, 241–245, 257, 259,

264, 266–268, 270, 284, 300, 306, 371, 375, 388, 390, 414, 416
    see also cənɔɔy, gunig, spirits

spirit-invasion, 39, 268–269, 280, 283, 289

spirits, 17, 18, 34, 35, 40, 102, 109, 130, 133, 137, 152, 155, 164, 165, 168, 169, 176, 183, 184, 186, 191, 199, 220, 243–244, 250, 253, 254, 260–261, 263, 267–273, 277, 278, 282, 283, 288, 294, 332, 333, 386, 387, 390, 391, 398, 403, 404
    see also spirit-guide

spirit-medium, *see* mediumship

spirit-mountain, 201, 242

Stevens, Hrolf Vaughan, 24, 236

Stewart, Kilton, 14, 26–32, 82, 111, 114–115, 119, 143, 157–159, 162, 170–171, 173–174, 176, 184, 186, 239, 386, 388, 394, 396–397, 400, 414, 416

susut (dance type), 395

swidden, xi, 20, 22–23, 42, 45, 46, 47, 59, 62, 68, 71, 73–75, 113, 119, 123, 125, 127, 133, 137, 202, 208, 217, 230, 233, 238, 285, 293, 341, 406, 409, 412

symbolism, 7, 15, 50, 71, 75, 93–94, 97, 106, 108, 131, 141, 270, 273, 284, 293
    see also religion (theory of)

Talɛŋ (song genre), 398–399

Taaʔ ʔamaaw (well-known 1960s tiger-medium), 58, 177, 186, 254–255

talisman, 185, 318

tanig (disease), 109, 114, 176, 191, 216

Taŋgəəy (song genre), 397–398

Taŋgooy (song genre), 398
Taŋgɔɔy (song genre), 398
Telom valley, 41–42, 94, 114, 143,
    160, 166, 395, 397, 404
Temiar language, xviii–xix, 8, 20–
    21, 23, 32, 33, 43, 45, 66, 79, 85,
    87, 115, 133, 152, 160, 199–200,
    221, 223, 282, 289, 291, 298,
    306, 320, 333, 343, 365, 367,
    385, 399
Temiar people and society, 20–24,
    341–345
Temiar religion and theology
    outlined, 24–54, 188–211, 206–
    207, 216–221
Temuan (ethnic group), 324, 362
tənamuuʔ (spirit-guide welcoming
    wreath), 40, 114, 161–162, 164,
    168, 173, 183, 200, 244–247,
    256, 331, 367, 373, 397, 401–
    404
təracɔɔg (disease), 75, 95, 107–108,
    129, 132, 136, 140, 191–192,
    216, 224, 284, 286, 367
təruuʔ (disease), 80–81, 126, 290,
    292–294
tɛmpɔɔʔ (plaited head-crown), 161,
    245, 251–252, 256, 258–259,
    331, 366–367, 377, 398
tɛnruuʔ, see təruuʔ
tohaat (form of address to a healer),
    79, 116, 224–225, 227–228, 288
Tohaat (deity), 116–119, 180, 182,
    224, 317, 366
    see also Tohan
Tengku Razaleigh (Malaysian
    politican), 311, 381
theology, 188–211, 206–207,
    216–221
Thunder (as deity), 60–61, 71, 98,
    128, 143, 195, 221, 270, 281,
    293, 322, 370
    see also Karey

thunder rituals, 149–154
tiger-beliefs, 35, 37, 68, 77, 96, 98,
    102, 115–116, 117, 122–127,
    142, 158–160, 169, 173–182,
    186, 189–190, 192, 195, 199,
    201–202, 205–206, 215, 242,
    245, 263–265, 269, 291–292,
    306–307, 371, 386–387, 398–
    404
tiger-mediumship, 253–258
Tohan (deity), 214, 224, 317, 321–
    322, 324, 351
    see also Tohaat
trance, 30, 33, 40, 61, 64–65, 93,
    113, 114, 120, 139, 145, 148,
    155, 161–168, 170–171, 173,
    174–178, 199, 216, 240–241,
    245, 250–252, 256–257, 288,
    291, 292, 375, 386, 395, 397,
    400, 401, 402, 403, 404
    phenomenology of, 35–37,
    239–243
    see also mediumship
tree burial, see death and burial:
    exposed burial
tree imagery, 282, 297–299

UMNO, Malaysian party, 311, 340,
    381
United Nations Declaration on the
    Rights of Indigenous Peoples,
    354

van Baal, Jan, 7, 336

Wakil ʔabaaɲ, 55, 96, 98, 120, 122,
    167, 176, 181, 254–256, 394,
    397–403, 406, 408
Wavell, Stewart, 26
Weber, Max, 6–7, 12, 48, 54, 170,

301–305, 307, 324, 326–327,
335–337, 339, 347
Wee, Vivienne, xvi, 310, 327, 332
were-tigers, 124, 126, 159–160,
182, 263
Wind (as deity), 61–62
wɔɔg (shadow), 111, 116, 119, 144,
266, 283, 403

Wuuk (death-dealing agent), 142–
143

Yai valley, 183, 214, 255, 316, 318,
321, 382, 396, 398–400
Yang Kee Leong, 316, 321
Yaŋyɔw (river-spirit), 130, 288–289